Jeff Herman's GUIDE TO BOOK PUBLISHERS, EDITORS & LITERARY AGENTS

Also by Jeff Herman

Write the Perfect Book Proposal: 10 That Sold and Why
(with Deborah Levine Herman)

Jeff Herman's GUIDE TO BOOK PUBLISHERS, EDITORS & LITERARY AGENTS

Who They Are, What They Want, How to Win Them Over

Jeff Herman

New World Library
Novato, California

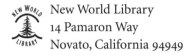 New World Library
14 Pamaron Way
Novato, California 94949

Text design by Tona Pearce Myers
Index by Carol and Nina Roberts

Library of Congress Cataloging-in-Publication Data is available.

First printing, November 2014
ISBN 978-1-60868-309-3
ISSN 1548-1344 (print)
ISSN 2376-5909 (online)

Printed in Canada on 100% postconsumer-waste recycled paper

 New World Library is proud to be a Gold Certified Environmentally Responsible Publisher. Publisher certification awarded by Green Press Initiative. www.greenpressinitiative.org

10   9   8   7   6   5   4   3   2

You can't be lost if searching.
Truth is a writer's deliverance, and freedom the reward.
When a writer leaps, the universe applauds.

CONTENTS

Part 3. Independent Presses (US)

Part 4. University Presses (US)

Part 5. Canadian Book Publishers

Part 6. Literary Agents

Part 7. Independent Editors

INTRODUCTION

Welcome back, or welcome for the first time. This is the latest edition of the book I've been producing since 1990, and I have invested considerable time and resources into revising almost every aspect of it.

Much has changed and much has remained the same since my journey in publishing began in the 1980s. Dozens of long-lasting independent (mom-and-pop) publishers have either disappeared or been absorbed into a numerically tiny oligarchy of multinational, trillion-dollar conglomerates, and relatively few start-ups have emerged. Digital retailing has displaced physical retailing, and most books will soon be bought in digital form. Though aggregate revenues have been enhanced, ever fewer writers are able to support themselves by writing.

However, millions of Americans from all backgrounds and conditions are writing with as much passion and determination as ever, and self-publishing has become a respectable option for countless writers who previously would have been effectively locked out. While the literary agency community has suffered from what has been a harsh economic culling, hundreds of dedicated independent agents still tenaciously continue to help writers make their dreams come true.

In the beginning, my primary motive for doing this book was to give writers valuable information that was cloaked from them by habit, if not volition. It seemed that the screening process was unduly influenced by factors entirely separate from merit. Those who were fortunate enough to be from certain communities, to have attended certain schools, or to have the right connections were more likely to get published. If access to the process wasn't fairly distributed, it followed that the opportunities were rigged. Clearly, cultural constraints are harmful for society, whether imposed by a government or by inbred subcultures. My vision was, and is, to simply give writers crucial information about the industry and its primary players, blended with accessible road maps and advice about overcoming likely obstacles. Over the years thousands of writers and industry insiders have told me the book helped them, which in turn gives me the inspiration and motivation to keep doing it. And it has given me a special sense of accomplishment to see that some of my methods have become generic over time.

Finally, I view myself as both a teacher and a student. Nothing anyone says will be correct every time, nor can anyone predict every result before it happens. You should be directed and inspired by what you don't know, and be curious about anything that feels easy. If something is effortlessly predictable, it is simply waiting to be altered and improved, if not by you then by someone else, which is why new books are often written about old subjects. Someone once asked me to define the measurement of 1, which I failed to do to her satisfaction. In her world, math was an unnatural limitation, the product of human fear of the unknown and its infinite possibilities. In that light, please use what I and others suggest as a place to begin, not the ground upon which to settle. The realities you dare to conjure will prove to be what's most enduring and meaningful.

Jeff Herman
Stockbridge, MA, July 2014

Part 1

ADVICE FOR WRITERS

What You (Might) Need to Know about Publishing, Even If It (Not You) Is Boring and Stupid

PERFECTLY IMPERFECT ADVICE AND RANDOM THOUGHTS

Jeff Herman

Except for a few hiatuses, I have been in the book publishing business since the early 1980s, when I was in my early twenties. I entered the business without any forethought. I wasn't an avid book lover or English major. My primary mission was to be respectfully employed in a Manhattan skyscraper where people wore jackets and ties and performed seemingly important tasks. That was my projection for post-college success, and I imagined it as glamorous and exotic. Reality was a hard, slow grind compared to the glorious images painted by youthful endorphins and innocence, and getting what we wish for tends to be easier than wearing the shoes day in and day out.

I answered countless blind ads in the employment section of the *New York Times* for entry-level office jobs. One day, someone with a harried, high-pitched voice called to schedule an interview. I showered and showed up on time in a decent suit. I said little and tried to smile and nod on cue. The only question I recall was if I could start work the following Monday (it was a Friday) for $200 a week (1981) as a "publicity assistant." It was a small independent book publishing company with a compelling list and history. I was second-in-command of the firm's two-person publicity department, which entitled me to do the filing, phone answering, and typing — none of which I knew how to do before doing it. I knew nothing about publishing or what the job entailed. My most important attributes may have been a calm persona of sanity and an apparent willingness to follow orders. Or maybe it was just my sincere promise to show up. In a nutshell, that explains how I "chose" the business I am in.

I tell this vignette because people often ask how I got into the business. But there's also a larger reason why I share this. I didn't have much of a plan or fixed direction, but yet I arrived somewhere and along the way made decisions (good or otherwise), grew, and helped make constructive things happen for myself and others. Maybe it's okay to not know what we want or where we are going in order to accomplish what we should. When I was young, a wise man told me that "man plans, god laughs," and I have subsequently heard that phrase many times. Frankly, I had to *grow into* understanding what that meant, and I frequently question it all over again. Perhaps writers shouldn't overplan what they write or will write. For sure, they can't fully control what happens to their work after they write it, short of destroying it.

Because it can be useful to consider what others say about what you do and wish to achieve, I have generated this section of the book. Read what you will with absolute discernment. Not all of it is for you, and all of it is imperfect — same as you and me. The only perfection is that you and I are here now together.

LITERARY AGENTS: WHAT THEY ARE AND WHAT THEY DO

Jeff Herman

Think of a venture capitalist: those people who invest their resources in other people's talents and dreams in exchange for a piece of the glory. The capitalist's skill is the ability to choose wisely and help manifest the endeavor. Literary agents are conceptually similar. For an industry-standard 15 percent commission ("ownership"), we invest considerable measures of time, expertise, and faith in the writers we choose to represent. Our professional credibility is on the line with each pitch we make. We don't directly provide the cash; part of our job is to get the publisher to put its money on the line. If you stick with the trajectory of information that follows, the reasons why most writers elect to have an agent will be made clear.

Publishers Overtly Discourage Unagented/Unsolicited Submissions

A typical publisher's in-house functions include product acquisition and management, back-office administrative tasks, editing, production, distribution, sales and marketing, accounting, and numerous other indispensable aspects related to publishing a book and running a business. However, all editorial content is outsourced and managed from the inside — that is, unlike magazines and newspapers, books are rarely written by in-house staff, which means that they are entirely dependent on "freelance" writers, including you.

If people stopped writing new books, publishers wouldn't have anything new to publish. So it might seem counterintuitive and ironic that most traditional publishers make it difficult, if not impossible, for writers to submit their work for consideration. But from the publisher's perspective, it's about being functional. For every book that gets published at a given moment, there are at least 1,000 manuscripts vying for the same opportunity at the same time. Imagine George Clooney or your favorite heartthrob standing in Times Square and announcing that he's looking for a wife. It would be a chaotic situation, and it's possible he and others would be trampled to death. This illustrates why publishers feel the need to barricade themselves against writers even though they can't exist without them. Not only do publishers lack in-house writers; they also lack an infrastructure for screening and filtering unagented/unsolicited works.

How Do Publishers Find Books to Publish?

Solicitation. Proactive editors sometimes have their own book ideas and will seek people to write them. They might read various literary publications in which virgin content is often debuted, and then contact the writers who impress them. Editors might also scan the news for interesting events and discoveries and then reach out to the people involved. Whenever the editor commences the conversation and offers someone the opportunity to be published, it is solicitation (not the illegal kind).

Agency representation. Editors rely on agents to do hardcore screening and to only represent writers and works that merit publication. Editors don't have time to screen hundreds of works in order to discover one they can publish; they don't have to, because the agents do it for them. When an editor receives a submission from a trusted agent, he or she immediately assumes that the work is professionally qualified and merits quality attention.

Having an agent equals access to editors. Not having an agent usually means the opposite, no matter how good the work might be.

Who Do Agents Work For?

The majority of literary agents are self-employed small-business people. They work for neither the publisher nor the writer but are indispensable to both for different reasons. The agent's constant interest is to generate commissions against the client's advance and subsequent royalties. The healthier the agent can make the client, the healthier the agent can make herself. The agent's revenues are tied to the client's revenues, and this mutuality of interests drives the agent to make the client as successful as possible.

Agents have clear lines that they won't/can't cross on behalf of a client. There are a finite number of publishers and an infinite number of potential clients. An agent can replace an unsatisfied client in a minute and perhaps can never replace an aggrieved publisher. Losing a publisher as a possible customer for future submissions is like permanently losing a large percentage of the business. In practice, it's rare for the agent to be forced into making such choices, and the agent will usually manage to preempt destructive conflicts by simply telling the client what is and isn't acceptable or possible.

The client needs to understand that a literary agent isn't the same as a litigator and won't relentlessly fight for issues that often can't be achieved anyway, such as a 20-city media tour. The agent's interests will stray from the client's interests if the agent-publisher relationship becomes threatened due to the client's actions or demands. However, any author who becomes more problematic than profitable will unilaterally burn all his bridges anyway. An author's profitability must always outpace her negatives, or she will be of diminishing value to both the agent and the publisher. However, agents usually confront publishers if they violate or ignore contracts and what's customary. If a publisher disrespects the client, the agent will feel as if he is being similarly abused and will push back. A key distinction is that for the agent you're a "client," whereas for the publisher you're an "author."

How Do Agents Make Money?

In the context of the agency-client relationship, agents make a 15 percent commission from all the advance and royalty revenues the agent's efforts enable the client to earn.

The above percentage pertains to the moneys received from the US publishers, which usually is the lion's share, if not the only source, of all revenue. The percentages assessed against subsidiary rights from deals made by the agent will vary by agency. For translation deals, most of the time US agents team with foreign agents in the respective countries, and the foreign agent wants at least 10 percent off the top, which generally is charged to the author in addition to the US agent's commission. That's the way it's done. If the US publisher controls the foreign rights, which they often do, the same sub-agent deal is also usually involved, except now the US publisher is also taking a cut. This sounds like a lot of dealings absent the author, but few authors can make these arcane deals unilaterally and they are the primary beneficiaries. Think of it as free money.

How Do False Agents Make Money?

Bogus agents make money in countless ways other than by doing what real agents do. Bogus agents tend not to ever sell works to traditional publishers and don't operate on the basis of earning commissions. Instead, they may offer amazing promises and an itemized menu of nonagent services, like simply reading your work for a fee. Sometimes they will offer a range of editorial services that are not necessarily useful or needed. If someone says she will be your agent if you pay her money, then she isn't a bone fide agent.

Legitimate agencies receive hundreds of unsolicited pitches each month. If a modest fraction of these were converted into a $100 "reading (consideration) fee," it would be a substantial monthly windfall without accountability. Eventually, the internet often exposes such scams, but by that time the bogus agent may have changed their company's name and be exploiting fresh pods of unjaded writers. It's like changing a parking spot if your time limit expires. Sometimes law enforcement will step in, but even then individual monetary losses probably won't ever be recouped, though valuable lessons hopefully will have been learned.

What's the Association of Authors' Representatives (AAR)?

The AAR is nothing like the Bar Association, American Medical Association, or any other mandatory-membership professional organization. Agents don't have to belong to or be licensed by any outside entity to be legal. The AAR can loosely be compared to a nonprofit country club minus a physical address, paid staff, and the usual accoutrements. A large percentage of agents choose to join the AAR because it offers a collegial way to network with other agents and find relief from their cloistered offices. To varying degrees, agents are compelled to be competitive with each other for clients, and AAR meetings serve as a refreshing "no-kill" zone where they can presumably be friends with others who understand what they do for a living.

AAR membership is restricted to agents who have made a specific number of actual book deals within a specific time frame and promise to adhere to the AAR's strict codes of conduct. The majority of codes are generic common sense, and a lot of space could be saved if they simply stated "Don't break the law"; but overeducated people prefer to deliberate over everything, and we have all been conditioned to make work for America's bloated legal establishment. However, some of the codes are archaic and prevent many qualified agencies from wanting to join. For instance, the codes seem to proscribe members from establishing separate divisions dedicated to nonagent services, like editing, collaborating, and helping writers self-publish. The fast-changing nature of publishing has made it impossible for an ever-increasing number of boutique agencies to rely only on commission-based services, and agents are exceptionally qualified to provide these kinds of traditionally fee-based services.

What Services and Assets Do Agents Provide in Exchange for Their Commissions?

1. They deliver access to the appropriate editors at traditional publishing companies. Few writers can achieve the same level of access without an agent because editors don't want to do mass screening; they rely upon the agents to do that on their behalf.
2. The agents know who the appropriate editors and publishers are for the works they represent.
3. Agents can accelerate the sales process by going to many publishers simultaneously with the same project, which sometimes creates a competitive bidding war, called "auction."
4. Agents know how to tweak and improve the work in order to maximize its sale to a publisher.

5. Agents understand publisher contracts and how to modify the language to the writer's advantage.
6. Agents know how to assess a work's potential monetary value and are positioned to negotiate the best terms possible.
7. Agents help clients understand how to interact with editors and publishers after the publisher's contract is signed.
8. Agents can provide valuable consultations about what is marketable.

What Won't Agents Do as Part of Their Commission?

I can't speak for all agents, or even for myself in all situations, but in the context of agenting in general, agents shouldn't be counted on as editors — meaning they don't have much time for perfecting or fixing afflicted manuscripts in detail; nor are they publicists or sales reps. The agent may be able to provide excellent referrals for these and other needs or may even have excellent in-house divisions for generally fee-based services. Though there's nothing wrong with an agent offering fee-based services, the agency should make it clear that these services are absolutely separate from commission-based services and that representation isn't contingent on retaining the fee-based services from the agent or from those specifically recommended by the agent.

How Do You Get an Agent?

Getting an agent might not be as difficult as you think. But if you're not thinking about it, don't expect it to be easy. If it were easy, you'd have no reason to buy this book. Some people make it look easy, but what are you seeing? Observing a person's accomplishments absent their likely struggles is rarely a worthy endeavor. Here are some things to consider when trying to land an agent.

- *Expect rejections.* The prima facie percentages are disconcerting. On average, agents reject about 98 percent of what's pitched. There's no rational reason for them to represent something without believing they can sell it to a publisher. Doing so would simply be a waste of everyone's time and not a good way for the agents to leverage their editor relationships. So the odds are that you will receive rejections.

- *Pitch the right agents.* Most agents have areas of editorial specialization and categories they rarely, if ever, deal with. You might have an excellent romance novel, but if you pitch only to agents who never handle romances, your rejection rate will be 100 percent. Conversely, only pitching to appropriate agents might give you a 100 percent "yes" rate. You need to find out who the right agents are for your work, and there are many proven ways to do that. Start by using the agency section in this book (see page 207), but that doesn't need to be the full extent of your research. Each agency's website will probably include a clear statement about what to pitch and what not to bother them with. Visit physical bookstores that have a large shelf of books in your category and read the acknowledgments sections; most of the time the author's agent will be acknowledged. Join local and national organizations that either specialize in your category or seem to have many like-minded members, and make friends. Friends will often share valuable information and experiences with each other and may even make valuable introductions on your behalf. If you enter the community with a sense of generosity you will receive much generosity in turn.

- *Prepare to become a pitcher.* It won't matter how good your content is if you fail to properly pitch it. Writers can greatly compensate for editorial mediocrity by embellishing via their pitch skills. Fear of rejection prevents many talented people from reaching their full potential. Replacing fear with hunger and determination removes all limitations. It's often not the most talented people who rise to the top of their fields but those who want it the most.

- *Good pitching is power.* The publishing business is about editorial content, so your pitch will need to be expressed in the form of a pitch letter, often referred to in "pub-speak" as a query letter. *Query* means you are asking a question or making a request, which in this context means asking the agent to consider representing your work. Agents receive hundreds to thousands of such queries every year, and reading them can be a mind-numbing process. In order to be competitive it's best to avoid asking for anything while offering everything; a pitch should be an offer of something that will benefit the agent — an enticement, a seduction. For advice on writing the best pitch possible, please refer to the essay dedicated to this subject (see page 19).

- *Pitch by email* and *snail mail.* Use both simultaneously. I'm serious. Agency digital submission boxes are overflowing, and not just with legitimate pitches. The internet is a blessing and a curse for all the obvious reasons. In the early years of the current century, emails were still relatively exotic and appreciated, and not everyone had fully "switched" yet. There was the "You've got mail" announcement each time we booted up and maybe a mere dozen emails every 24 hours, mostly spamless. Dealing with inboxes today is like flossing teeth after a corn-eating orgy. Ironically, hardcopy mail has now become exotic and thus might be seen and read much more quickly than the digital version of the same material. So why not hedge your bet by using both conveyance methods? Yes, some agents say they prefer that you use their digital mailboxes. But what they really prefer is what works out best in the long run. Shoot for best-case results, and everyone will be happy in the end. However, you might want to mention at the end of your letter that you've sent it via both hardcopy and email.

An unimportant side note: Many of my veteran colleagues still refer to receiving submissions "over the transom," which is a dated metaphor for anything that's unrequested. Until about 50 years ago, most New York offices had open windows above hallway entrances, which were called "transoms." Most mail and other deliveries were simply tossed into the offices through the transoms.

- *Pitch in batches.* If you're not in a big hurry to get published, meaning you're willing to wait many years, you should only pitch one agent at a time. Frankly, some agents will never respond, period. Others may take a very, very long time. These are understaffed mom-and-pop businesses, and dealing with recent submissions is often a low priority compared to servicing current clients. Do yourself a favor and pitch about 10 agents at a time. Pitching more than that at a time isn't wise, because you may see ways to constantly upgrade your pitch with each cycle. Every four weeks, if you're still in limbo, go out there with a fresh batch of 10 pitches. Most successful authors have a bloody past of rejections and humiliations; amass your bloody past as efficiently as possible so that you can reach your future while still breathing.

There are obvious exceptions. If you make a connection with a particular agent you like and he invites your submission, then play it out on an exclusive basis, but not forever. If he disappears from your radar for more than four to eight weeks, it may be time to play the field.

- *Sell yourself to the agent.* The agent is already 98 percent sure he doesn't need you. Even if he skips reading your work and goes straight to "reject," there's a less than 2 percent chance that he made a mistake. It's incumbent upon you to make the agent think you could be one of the magic 2 percent and avoid giving the impression you are one of the 98 percent.

- *Put yourself in the shoes of an agent.* What does an agent want? Commission-eligible clients, moron. What doesn't an agent want? If you can't answer this question by yourself, then you really are a moron.

What Else Should You Know about Agents?

Literary agents aren't that smart. Nor are they especially stupid. In other words, they're pretty much like everyone else, and that probably includes you. A combination of geography, respective subculture, and opportunities is what brings people to agenting. I might not have become an agent if I were not a New Yorker and had not been conditioned to be a "mind worker" by family, community, and subculture. Joining the military, for instance, would have marked me as an extreme outlier in my community, as opposed to a conformist if I were from Tennessee. Many agents are former in-house book editors; it's a way for them to move on while still using the skills and connections they already possess. Some agents were nurtured from when they were career virgins, meaning they landed an entry-level job in an agency, instead of in a publishing house, out of college.

Do Agents and Editors Have Similar Traits?

The primary difference is that editors get paychecks, whereas most agents are self-employed and get paid only if they generate commissions. Agents can become millionaires if they strike the right deals, whereas in-house editors can become rich only through marriage, through an inheritance, or by becoming an owner/partner instead of an employee where they work. Agents run businesses and are risk takers, whereas editors serve the needs of the companies they work for.

Do Agents and Editors Make "Sweetheart" Deals?

Yes, all the time, but we prefer not to think about it that way. There are fewer than 1,000 full-time acquisitions editors and agents in total, and an even smaller core of those who are the most active. We have to keep working within this tight circle to get our mutual needs met. The system succeeds for writers because agents must push author revenues in order to push their own revenues. Writers are the conduits through which agents eat, and they're the people who generate the raw material that editors can't live without.

Who Can Be an Agent?

Anyone can self-declare him- or herself a literary agent. Of course, succeeding as an agent is a different story. Finding raw product is actually easy, because so much is generated all the time. But knowing how to discern the tiny fraction of the unfiltered mass content that publishers will pay for is mostly an acquired skill. Forming direct relationships with editors is an unrestricted process, but they won't buy what they don't want, no matter how strong the agent-editor relationship is. Knowing what publishers will pay for is tantamount to knowing what the public will pay for.

What If an Agent Offers You Representation?

Bull's-eye. Mazel tov. Before you commit, settle any unfinished business with other agents who are still considering your work. Tell them you have an offer and need to make an immediate decision. Before accepting an agent's offer, you're entitled to ask reasonable questions and do your due diligence:

- Ask for a list of books the agent has sold to publishers, including the publishers' and authors' names. Some or all of this information might already be posted on her website.
- Check the internet for any "bad news." But be discerning about what you read. Disgruntled people often publicly rant in ways that are unfair.
- Have a conversation about why he likes your book, how he plans to sell it, how much he thinks he can get for it, the time frame, and if he believes in sexual monogamy (just checking if you're awake).

How Do You Know If Your Agent Is Doing a Good Job?

If your agent gets you a book deal with a traditional publisher, then she most likely did a good job for you. However, typically agents can sell only about half the works they represent in any given 12-month period. Having representation should mean your work receives quality access to the right editors, but that doesn't guarantee that any of them will make an offer. In fact, most agented works probably never get published, especially in the literary fiction zone. Editorial quality is just one factor determining what does and doesn't get published. If a particular category or concept is overpublished, for instance, many excellent prospects become surplus content. Timing is very important and impossible to deliberately control, though many people wish they could. You can't get a deal without correct access, but access won't guarantee you a deal.

What If the Agent Is Unable to Sell Your Work?

If your work is unsold after a long time (six months to a year), you should determine what the problem is and what the next steps might be. Upon request, the agent should let you know where the work was submitted, each submission's status, and any available details about rejections received. In consultation with your agent, it might be a good idea to consider some revisions or ways to tweak what editors are seeing.

Try to nail down whether the agent is still confident about selling the work. Sometimes an agent might no longer be confident but is reluctant to release a work he has already invested himself in. The bottom line is, does the agent plan to keep actively pitching the work? In the absence of that crucial intent, there's no good reason for the agent to hold you and your work in limbo, and you should arrange for a friendly release. Getting a new agent requires following the same process you used when getting your first agent.

It might not be your agent's fault that your work is unsold. Often it wouldn't have mattered who was representing it. Putting an unsold manuscript on the back burner for a year or so and working on something else might be the best move to make, instead of permanently burning your agent relationship. Many successful fiction writers were unable to sell the first manuscript(s) they wrote until after they became successful. There's no law that says your works have to be published in the order in which you wrote them.

Agent-jumping is tricky. It's not easy to get an agent in the first place, and agents may not see any reason to be enthusiastic about representing a work that your previous agent failed to sell. But if the work wasn't widely circulated or shown to the right editors, a new agent might see fresh opportunities or ways to fix what's broken. You should be clear with yourself about why you want to switch agents, or you are likely to encounter the same grievances all over again.

What Will Happen to Agents as a Category over the Next Several Years?

This question makes most agents uncomfortable, because trends are not favorable. As I see it, literary agents will continue to be as important as ever in the context of traditional publishing. Actually, their standing and purpose have never been at risk. The problem is that traditional publishing will continue to become a less friendly environment for writers and, by extension, their agents. Writers and agents are in the same beleaguered boat. Each year, more agencies will either close or merge to form larger agencies, and a diminishing number of new agents will enter the business. Those at greatest risk will be the boutique agencies that are most reliant on maintaining a fresh flow of new deals, as opposed to having the luxury of resting on their laurels. Publishers are acquiring fewer books and paying less for most of the books they still acquire. In order to survive, many boutique agencies will be forced to offer related fee-based services, such as editing, collaborating, and helping writers self-publish, in addition to commissionable services.

Do Agents Sell Everything They Represent?

Only if they represent very few projects. Agents usually know at the outset which projects are likely slam dunks and which are comparatively marginal. But this business is loaded with surprises; agents plan, and the process laughs at them. They hedge their bets by signing up more projects than they expect to actually get offers for. In fact, the ratio is probably less than 50/50 for the toughest categories, such as literary fiction. However, no bona fide agent will intentionally represent a project that he doesn't feel is viable, unless there are unseen motives or pressures to do so.

What's the Typical Agent's Sales Process and How Long Does It Take?

Velocity is an agent's and writer's friend. You would presumably prefer not to observe your own book-launch party from heaven, which probably happens more than you realize. (I'm assuming that all writers go to heaven, of course.) Usually, the agent will make a multiple submission, which means selecting approximately a dozen appropriate editors from distinct houses or divisions within the same house. Agents know which houses/divisions and which editors might be inclined to like the project in hand. The agent might make calls to prescreen or sell the project or might just go ahead and email it over and then follow up to see what the early response is.

Email has greatly altered the pitch process for agents. Until 1999 or so, almost all submissions were made in hardcopy. Agents had to run up large photocopying and delivery balances and had to allocate a lot of physical space for storing everything. Now everything tends to go by email, which makes it easier and cheaper to deal with.

Agents typically follow up for some kind of response from each of the editors in cycles of one to four weeks, depending on the project and other circumstances. However, editors can't make instant unilateral decisions without going through in-house protocols. An editor may like a project but be prevented from acquiring it by his colleagues for a variety of possible reasons, such as list redundancies or the sales department vetoes it.

The agent keeps the process from stalling by making subsequent submissions as needed. Often, the agent will use the rejections as a learning opportunity and encourage the client to revise the work accordingly. Sometimes it may be as simple as altering the title to something more compelling or clear. If/when a genuine offer is close at hand, the agent will attempt to provoke a competitive bidding process. If at least two publishers are eager to acquire the same work, the agent might hold a formal auction in which the competing houses are forced to blindly bid against one another until only one house remains standing. But don't get too excited; auctions are the exception, not the rule.

Sometimes an agent will have good reasons to give a specific editor an exclusive or preemptive opportunity to consider and make an offer on a particular project before anyone else. The agent will generally set a deadline by which a verbal deal needs to be made.

How long might all of this take before a verbal deal is in hand? For certain kinds of nonfiction, such as basic how-to books, within eight weeks the agent may have a deal or know there probably won't be a deal. Arcane nonfiction or fiction by unpublished writers might require a much longer time. A slow process doesn't necessarily mean the agent isn't doing the job; some projects compile many rejections over time before finding the right editor at the right publisher at the right time.

How Do Agents Find Their Clients?

Agents need clients in order to function. An agent without clients is like a playboy without girlfriends. Yet some agents seem to be elusive to the point of invisibility, at least from the potential client's point of view. Not all agents want or need new/more clients, so, yes, they will make themselves unavailable. Most agents, to varying degrees, are always looking for new product, which means they are looking for new clients. But follow the sequence of the last sentence: the word *product* precedes *client*, because it's the viability of the product that counts. Writers who write salable products will get agents and publishers. Don't forget that the industry and the reader are interested in the product first and the author second, if at all. Over time successful authors become interesting to their readers as people, but it doesn't start out that way. Of course, the author's ability to help promote her books forms a large part of how agents and publishers assess the value of the product.

Agents discover clients by responding to submissions and referrals; by attending conferences; by writing books or appearing in books; by proactively reaching out to experts and writers with ideas and inducements. Most agents are willing to scan and reject thousands of submissions a year in order to find a few dozen projects they feel confident about selling to publishers.

If You Get 20 Agent Rejections, Is It Unlikely You'll Get an Agent?

Don't answer the above question affirmatively or it will be your truth, and it shouldn't be. Of course, there is the little matter of talent or the lack thereof, and that can't be dismissed as unimportant. But let's get real: a lot of highly talented people live below the poverty line, and a lot of mediocre people are self-made millionaires. On average, unsuccessful people are no smarter or dumber than successful people. Simply being gifted is like being an unmined and uncut diamond. If you want to get published, scratch your way to the surface and struggle to the point of refinement. Countless others have and are, and they have the results to prove it. Success is the great equalizer because you don't have to be the best in order to reach the top. Corruption and nepotism are also perpetual factors, but they benefit only a small fraction of us. I assure you that some of the best-written manuscripts are, and will remain, unpublished simply because their authors did a poor job at trying to get them published. Conversely, some of the most mediocre manuscripts are, or will be, successfully published simply because their authors did a stellar job at getting them published. Hunger and determination frequently overcompensate for raw talent.

Agents aren't in lockstep. We tend to be specialized and often make dumb decisions.

Receiving 20 agent rejections might mean many things. Maybe you've been submitting your romance novel to sci-fi agents. Maybe those first 20 are over capacity and not taking new clients. Maybe you need to rewrite your pitch letter. Babe Ruth had many more strikeouts than hits, and two-thirds of the time Ted Williams didn't get past the batter's box.

How Do Agents Like to Work with Their Clients?

How do you like to work with your significant other, neighbors, children, bosses, and subordinates? Exactly — it depends on the people in question. There is no one way for agents to interact with their clients. Some agents are loquacious and some might be on the autism spectrum. However, there are certain universal professional protocols that should be expected and followed. You're entitled to know what your agent's plan and schedule for selling the work are. It's appropriate for you to know who your project has been submitted to and what the results are. If many weeks go by without any word, you should check in for news. If nothing is happening, you should determine if your agent has lost confidence and hasn't gotten around to telling you yet.

Good clients ask good questions and can discern good answers. Like, "What if I tweak the overview — will that change the way editors are seeing the project?" Or "How about I generate a list of 10 prestigious people who are likely to endorse and recommend the book?" These aren't really questions; they are proactive solutions. It may be on the agent to generate the deal, but the agent will move to the next project if a deal doesn't materialize. As a writer you don't have that luxury. You have the most to gain and the most to lose. Obviously, you don't want to be a nuisance and get in your agent's way or your own way, but there are many cooperative and constructive ways you can help overcome the challenge of getting your book published.

Is It Okay to Switch Agents?

Agent-hopping happens a lot, especially for writers who have already been published. Published writers are at an advantage because agents see them as proven commodities. Unpublished writers seeking to switch are often perceived as having been "fired" by their last agent; at any rate, they still haven't earned their first stripe.

When I hear from a published author who wants to change agents, the first thing I ask is, "Why?" Certain answers are reasonable, and others are alarm bells. I think it's okay if the writer expresses that it's simply not a mutually satisfying relationship. Of course, it's probably a bogus and evasive answer, but that's exactly why it's okay. I respect that the author just wants to move on without any annoying whining or backstabbing (we can always save that for later). An alarm bell rings when the author complains about low advances, low book sales, or lack of publisher support. The first thing that enters my mind is: could I have done better? This question is especially meaningful if I happen to respect the agent in question. Even if the author is a decent commodity, agents are wary of authors who are serial jilters or bigmouths.

What Kind of Client Do Agents Dislike?

That's a loaded question because it meshes business with personal. The real question is: what are the agent's priorities as a businessperson? It's theoretically possible that an agent might tend to release the clients she likes the most. Why would that happen? Because all the likability in the world can't compensate for a book that doesn't sell. If a likable client is dead weight, he's an endangered client. If an obnoxious client is sufficiently and reliably profitable, she's safe. If you are a superstar who generates the rent money, you can get away with behaving like Godzilla. No one will like you, but everyone will want a piece of you.

How Come Rejection Letters Are Generic, and Why Are There No Useful Comments?

Reading and evaluating manuscripts is very consuming and requires special expertise. It's impossible for an agent to dedicate any measure of his time to providing that level of service pro bono to the people he is rejecting. Any expectation to the contrary is naive, misguided, and unreasonable.

WRITE THE PERFECT QUERY LETTER

Jeff Herman and Deborah Herman

The query is a short letter of introduction to publishers or agents, encouraging them to request to see your fiction manuscript or nonfiction book proposal. It is a vital tool, often neglected by writers. If done correctly, it can help you avoid endless frustration and wasted effort. The query is the first hurdle of your individual marketing strategy. If you can leap over it successfully, you're well on your way to a sale.

The query letter is your calling card. For every book that makes it to the shelves, thousands of worthy manuscripts, proposals, and ideas are knocked out of the running by poor presentation or inadequate marketing strategies. Don't forget that the book you want to sell is a product that must be packaged correctly to stand above the competition.

A query letter asks the prospective publisher or agent if she would like to see more about the proposed idea. If your book is fiction, you should indicate that a manuscript or sample chapters are available on request. If nonfiction, you should offer to send a proposal and, if you have them, sample chapters.

The query is your first contact with the prospective buyer of your book. To ensure that it's not your last, avoid common mistakes. The letter should be concise and well written. You shouldn't try to impress the reader with your mastery of all words over three syllables. Instead, concentrate on a clear and to-the-point presentation with no fluff.

Think of the letter as an advertisement. You want to make a sale of a product, and you have very limited space and time in which to reach this goal.

The letter should be only one page long, if possible. It will form the basis of a query package that will include supporting materials. Don't waste words in the letter describing material that can be included separately. Your goal is to pique the interest of an editor who has very little time and probably very little patience. You want to entice her to keep reading and ask you for more.

The query package can include a short résumé, media clippings, or other favorable documents. Do not get carried away, or your package will quickly come to resemble junk mail. If you're sending a hardcopy package, include a self-addressed stamped envelope (SASE) with enough postage to return your entire package. This will be particularly appreciated by smaller publishing houses and independent agents.

For fiction writers, a short (one- to five-page), double-spaced synopsis of the manuscript will be helpful and appropriate.

Do not waste money and defeat the purpose of the query by sending an unsolicited manuscript. Agents and editors may be turned off by receiving manuscripts of 1,000-plus pages that were uninvited and that are not even remotely relevant to what they do. Though digital submissions obviously don't consume physical space, nobody enjoys a cluttered, overburdened inbox.

The query follows a simple 4-part format (which can be reworked according to your individual preferences):

- Lead
- Supporting material/persuasion
- Biography
- Conclusion/pitch

Your Lead Is Your Hook

The lead can either catch the editor's attention or turn him off completely. Some writers think getting someone's attention in a short space means having to do something dramatic. Editors appreciate cleverness, but too much contrived writing can work against you. Opt instead for clear conveyance of thoroughly developed ideas and get right to the point.

Of course, you don't want to be boring and stuffy in the interest of factual presentation. You'll need to determine what is most important about the book you're trying to sell, and write your letter accordingly.

You can begin with a lead similar to what you'd use to grab the reader in an article or a book chapter. You can use an anecdote, a statement of facts, a question, a comparison, or whatever you believe will be most powerful.

You may want to rely on the journalistic technique of the inverted pyramid. This means that you begin with the strongest material and save the details for later in the letter. Don't start slowly and expect to pick up momentum as you proceed. It will be too late.

Do not begin a query letter like this: "I have sent this idea to 20 agents/publishers, none of whom think it will work. I just know you'll be different, enlightened, and insightful and will give it full consideration." There is no room for negatives in a sales pitch. Focus only on positives — unless you can turn negatives to your advantage.

Some writers make the mistake of writing about the book's potential in the first paragraph without ever stating its actual idea or theme. Remember, your letter may never be read beyond the lead, so make that first paragraph your hook.

Avoid bad jokes, clichés, unsubstantiated claims, and dictionary definitions. Don't be condescending; editors have egos, too, and have power over your destiny as a writer.

Supporting Material: Be Persuasive

If you are selling a nonfiction book, you may want to include a brief summary of hard evidence, gleaned from research that will support the merit of your idea. This is where you convince the editor that your book should exist. This is more important for nonfiction than it is for fiction, where the style and storytelling ability are paramount. Nonfiction writers must focus on selling their topic and their credentials.

You should include a few lines showing the editor what the publishing house will gain from the project. Publishers are not charitable institutions; they want to know how they can get the greatest return on their investment. If you have brilliant marketing ideas or know of a well-defined market for your book where sales will be guaranteed, include this rather than other descriptive material.

In rereading your letter, make sure you have shown that you understand your own idea thoroughly. If it appears half-baked, the editors won't want to invest time fleshing out your thoughts. Exude confidence so that the editor will have faith in your ability to carry out the job.

In nonfiction queries, you can include a separate table of contents and brief chapter abstracts. Otherwise, that material can wait for the book proposal.

Your Biography: No Place for Modesty

In the biographical portion of your letter, toot your own horn, but in a carefully calculated, persuasive fashion. Your story of winning the third-grade writing competition (it was then that you knew you wanted to be a world-famous writer!) should be saved for the documentary done on your life after you reach your goal.

In the query, all you want to include are the most important and relevant credentials that will support the sale of your book. You can include, as a separate part of the package, a résumé or biography that will elaborate further.

The separate résumé should list all relevant and recent experiences that support your ability to write the book. Unless you're fairly young, your listing of academic accomplishments should start after high school. Don't overlook hobbies or non-job-related activities if they correspond to your book story or topic. Those experiences are often more valuable than academic achievements.

Other information to include: any impressive print clippings about you; a list of your broadcast interviews and speaking appearances; and copies of articles and reviews about any books you may have written. This information can never hurt your chances and could make the difference in your favor.

There is no room for humility or modesty in the query letter and résumé. When corporations sell toothpaste, they list the product's best attributes and create excitement about the product. If you can't find some way to make yourself exciting as an author, you'd better rethink your career.

Here's the Pitch

At the close of your letter, ask for the sale. This requires a positive and confident conclusion with a phrase such as "I look forward to your speedy response." Such phrases as "I hope" and "I think you will like my book" sound too insecure. This is the part of the letter where you go for the kill.

Be sure to thank the reader for his or her attention in your final sentence.

Finishing Touches

When you're finished, reread and edit your query letter. Cut out any extraneous information that dilutes the strength of your arguments. Make the letter as polished as possible so that the editor will be impressed with you, as well as with your idea. Don't ruin your chances by appearing careless; make certain your letter is not peppered with typos and misspellings. If you don't show pride in your work, you'll create a self-fulfilling prophecy: the editor will take you no more seriously than you take yourself.

Aesthetics are important. If you were pitching a business deal to a corporation, you would want to present yourself in conservative dress, with an air of professionalism. In the writing business, you may never have face-to-face contact with the people who will determine your future. Therefore, your query package is your representative.

For hardcopy submissions, you should invest in a state-of-the-art letterhead — with a logo! — to create an impression of pride, confidence, and professionalism. White, cream, and ivory paper are all acceptable, but you should use only black ink for printing the letter. Anything else looks amateurish. If editors receive a query letter on yellowed paper that looks as if it's been lying around for 20 years, they will wonder if the person sending the letter is a has-been or a never-was.

For electronic submissions, keep your email formatting simple and readable, and be sure to include all your contact information. Also, most agents' websites include detailed guidelines for electronic submissions. Be sure to adhere to them, or your work might be rejected solely because you have not followed the rules.

Don't sabotage yourself by letting your need for instant approval get the best of you. Don't call editors. You have invited them to respond, so be patient. Then prepare yourself for possible rejection. It often takes many nos to get a yes.

One more note: This is a tough business for anyone — and it's especially so for green-horns. Hang in there.

Query Letter Tips

If you have spent any time at all in this business, the term *query letter* is probably as familiar to you as the back of your hand. Yet no matter how many courses you've attended and books you've read about this important part of the process, you may still feel inadequate when you try to write one that sizzles. If it's any consolation, you're far from being alone in your uncertainties. The purpose of the query letter is to formally introduce your work and yourself to potential agents and editors. The immediate goal is to motivate them to promptly request a look at your work, or at least a portion of it.

In effect, the letter serves as the writer's first hurdle. It's a relatively painless way for agents and editors to screen out unwanted submissions without the added burden of having to manhandle a deluge of unwanted manuscripts. They are more relaxed if their inboxes are filled with 50 unanswered queries as opposed to 50 uninvited 1,000-page manuscripts. The query is a very effective way to control the quality and quantity of the manuscripts that get into the office. And that's why you have to write good ones.

The term *query letter* is part of the lexicon and jargon of the publishing business. This term isn't used in any other industry. I assume it has ancient origins. I can conjure up the image of an English gentleman with a fluffy quill pen composing a most civilized letter to a prospective publisher for the purpose of asking for his work to be read and, perchance, published. Our environments may change, but the nature of our ambitions remains the same.

Let's get contemporary. Whenever you hear the term *query letter*, you should say to yourself "pitch" or "sales" letter. Because that's what it is. You need the letter to sell.

Here are a few more tips to make your query letter the best it can be.

- *Don't be long-winded.* Agents/editors receive lots of these things, and they want to mow through them as swiftly as possible. Ideally, the letter should be a single page with short paragraphs. (I must admit I've seen good ones that are longer than a page.) If you lose your reader, you've lost your opportunity.

- *Get to the point; don't pontificate.* Too many letters go off on irrelevant detours, which makes it difficult for the agent/editor to determine what's actually for sale — other than the writer's soapbox.

- *If sending your letter on hardcopy, make it attractive.* When making a first impression, the subliminal impact of aesthetics cannot be overestimated. Use high-quality stationery and typeface. The essence of your words is paramount, but cheap paper and poor print quality will only diminish your impact.

- *Don't say anything negative about yourself or your attempts to get published.* Everyone appreciates victims when it's time to make charitable donations, but not when it's time to make a profit. It's better if you can make editors/agents think that you have to fight them off.

Why Not Simply Submit Your Manuscript?

You might be wondering why you can't bypass the query hurdle and simply submit your manuscript. You may do that — and no one can litigate against you. But if you submit an unsolicited manuscript to a publisher, it's more likely to end up in the so-called slush pile and may never get a fair reading. If it's sent to an agent, nothing negative may come of it. However, most agents prefer to receive a query first.

Sending unsolicited nonfiction book proposals is in the gray zone. Proposals are much more manageable than entire manuscripts, so editors/agents may not particularly mind.

But you may want to avoid wasting time — and, in the case of hardcopy submissions, money — sending unwanted proposals. After all, the query is also an opportunity for you to screen out those who clearly have no interest in your subject.

Also, you shouldn't be overly loose with your ideas and concepts. After all, you can't protect ideas in the context of writing and publishing. You don't want to become overly cautious, but neither do you want to be a runaway train. Focus on pitching your ideas to those who are genuinely qualified to help you manifest them.

These pointers, in combination with the other good information in this book and all the other available resources, should at least give you a solid background for creating a query letter that makes a lasting impression.

For Deborah Herman's biography, see page 55.

YOU (MIGHT) BELONG IN THE SLUSH PILE (OR ELSEWHERE)

Jeff Herman

It's not you per se who might belong in the slush pile; it's your written product. Until about 12 years ago slush piles were almost entirely physical, whereas now they probably exist about 80 percent "in the cloud." Perhaps the term should be changed to *slush cloud*, which sounds much more tasty than a *slush pile*. My question is: what are publishers doing with all the extra physical space that was formerly used for slush piles? But let me back up.

Most traditional publishers have a written policy that they won't accept or consider unagented/unsolicited submissions. If not submitted by a literary agent, the work is un-agented. If no one at the company invited you to submit your work, it is unsolicited. If your work falls into either category, you're an "Un." In the context of publishing, a Un is a noncitizen or an untouchable. That sounds harsh, but it's the most accurate way to paint it, and it's virtually every writer's starting point. No one is born with or inherits a book deal. The good news is that it's entirely within every writer's power to self-mutate from being a Un to becoming an agented or solicited writer. You most likely already believe that, or you wouldn't be reading this book.

So what happens to Uns' submissions? They get returned, thrown out, or placed in the slush pile with countless other Uns' submissions.

Why does this policy exist? Because for every book traditionally published there are more than 1,000 manuscripts trying to be published at the same point in time. Publishers don't have the in-house staff to screen what's submitted to find the fraction of a percent-age they can publish. Instead, they make direct solicitations for writers and experts they might want, or they rely on the several-hundred-strong literary agency community to do the screening and essentially nominate what's publishable.

What happens to the slush pile? That's an interesting question for which I have no scientifically proven answers, but I do have true anecdotes. Every once in a while, a low-level person in the editorial hierarchy will volunteer without prodding to wander through the slush pile and randomly select something to read, and occasionally they find a gem. Excellent books have been discovered in the slush pile and successfully published, and it will keep on happening. But trying to get published through the slush is like trying to pay for college with lottery scratch-offs.

A Random Prediction

Thousands of years from now, a new species or civilization will discover ancient man-uscripts and digital archives within the ruins of a once-great metropolis that had been abruptly destroyed by a surging sea. They will have no context for any of it and will pon-der and debate its significance at the highest levels. Unknown to them, they will have unsealed a massive slush pile, the unpublished manuscripts written with love and passion by thousands of ordinary people from a lost and little-understood society.

A museum will be constructed for the purpose of housing and displaying the wit, wisdom, and dysfunctions of this period from Earth's beleaguered past. In one fell swoop, an entire slush pile will finally be published.

A True Story

Approximately 20 years ago, there lived a man in Florida who was unable to get an agent or a publisher for his fiction manuscript. Then he had an idea. He was an admirer of a Pulitzer Prize–winning novel named *The Yearling*. The work had been published more than 50 years earlier, sold millions of copies, and was made into a feature film starring a young Gregory Peck. Though no longer a popular book, it still sold tens of thousands of copies each year as a classic reprint.

Our hero repurposed the book into a raw manuscript and changed its title and the author's name. Only someone familiar with the classic book would have recognized the manuscript as blatant plagiarism. He then proceeded to make unagented and unsolicited submissions of "his" work to all the usual publishing prospects. What happened next was easily predictable. In some cases, he never received any response, ever. Some publish-ers at least returned the manuscript, clearly unread, with an unsigned letter stating that unagented/unsolicited submissions would not be considered, ever.

Refreshingly, he actually received some genuine rejection letters seemingly written by entry-level editors and interns. The letters were brief and dismissive and expressed no appreciation for the work's merits or encouragement for it prospects. One of these rejec-tion letters was from the same publisher that was still profitably publishing *The Yearling*.

What Does the Above Story Tell Us?

Each of my rejection letters includes a job application for my favorite fast-food establish-ment (if you're not sure whether I'm kidding, try me: submissions@jeffherman.com). Frankly, considering the lack of respect and encouragement that struggling authors tend to experience, such an attachment wouldn't be out of place.

Even though this story is 20 years old, it's no less telling today. At first blush, we see that a bestselling, Pulitzer Prize–winning novel that was made into a major motion picture couldn't even get itself arrested. What's unseen is what's most crucial, which is that the work's merits were worthless in the absence of genuine *access*. Without access, you don't really exist and the game can't begin. The dude didn't have an agent, was unsolicited, and didn't do anything to get quality access. The negative outcome is unsurprising for those who have been to the rodeo.

Publishers have surrounded themselves with firewalls to avoid being trampled by the relentless surge of eager writers. Having an agent is tantamount to a VIP bypass. For editors it's a safe assumption that if agented it merits *access*.

What If You Can't Get an Agent? Join the Battle of the Uns!

If you bang your head against a publisher's firewall, the wall won't move but your head will. Though it makes no sense to throw yourself against the wall, it's wise to remember that all walls have inherent limitations that can be exploited.

What if you can't get an agent? You are far from alone and are in excellent company; many superb writers don't connect with agents when first starting out. Fortunately, there are ways to get access to editors and get published even if you don't have an agent. Here's a big secret: publishers actually will consider unagented/unsolicited submissions, but they don't want you to know that. In fact, they may not even know it. Remember this: the rule exists for their convenience, not yours. If you rigidly follow their rules, you're only serving them, not yourself. It's reasonable for you to consider ways to bypass the rule. Ironically, your success will also be the publisher's success; it's a win-win.

Guess what? Being published isn't only for the best writers, though it's invariably for those who are the best at getting published. Writing and getting your writing published are distinct endeavors. No one can keep you from writing, but you can be prevented from traditionally publishing your work. Guess what? Mediocre writers are frequently published while countless überwriters are left stranded at the gate. How does that happen? Keep reading.

1. No agent? No problem. Appoint yourself as your agent, and be your only client. You can even sign a contract with yourself and assign a 15 percent commission to your doppelgänger agent. What does this mean? Learn what an agent needs to know by finding out who publishes books like yours and who the appropriate editors are at each of those houses. You can do that by using this book, researching on Amazon and bookstore shelves, and reading the acknowledgments sections of similar books for editor names.

2. Cold-call. Another trick is to cold-call publishers asking to be routed to the editorial departments of the divisions/programs in question. Once a live voice says something like "Editorial," you'll have reached your destination. The next step is to cajole this person into giving you the name of an editor for romance titles or for whatever category your manuscript falls into. Accumulating relevant editor names will enable you to bypass the slush pile. Actually submitting your work to a real person who helps make crucial decisions is a tremendous upgrade from sending it to "Editorial Department" or "Submissions." Your work needs to be directed to an actual person with the genuine clout to acquire books. If the editor is interested in your work, you will enter the exalted "solicited" zone, which means you have avoided the knee-jerk deportation to the slush graveyard. You will have achieved access…

3. *Know what editors do.* You can't deeply understand what someone else does if you have never done it yourself. But gaining superficial knowledge about their basic functions and needs is immensely better than complete ignorance or misinformation. Obviously, editors edit, but not as much as you might think or as much as they might prefer. An accurate job description for today's editor could easily be Product Acquisition and Management. Notice that the word *editor* doesn't even appear? That's because they are not being paid or rewarded for their editing skills. In fact, those secondary tasks are often outsourced (to the chagrin of fussy authors). Book publishers no longer provide the intense fact-checking and word-smashing that urbane publications like the *New Yorker* are still famous for. In fact, some unsatisfied authors use their own funds to hire editors to go beyond what their publishers will do.

An editor's career track is tied to the success of the books that he acquires, not that he edits. Critically acclaimed books that are economic failures are not good for an editor's career unless they also attract commercially successful books to the editor. An editor's career success will match the commercial success of the books he or she acquires, regardless of the books' literary or cultural standing.

What's a successful career for an editor? Frankly, I can't imagine how most of them manage to support a full household in the Northeast unless both spouses are gainfully employed or there's a trust fund. Many years of toil are required before decent six-figure incomes are attained. In 1981 my entry-level publishing job paid $5 per hour, which was okay for a 22-year-old at that time. That same job today probably pays about $15 per hour, but I don't think the 300 percent increase has kept pace with New York's inflation rate. For instance, back then TV was still free and landlines were the only option, at less than $20 per month.

Let's keep our eyes on the ball. Editors need to acquire good product (books) in order to justify their employment. Your job as a writer is to give it to them. If you succeed at giving them what they need, you will get what you want (a deal). It's really that simple, yet too many writers don't seem to get it. They approach editors on their knees asking for mercy and attention, which is also how they confront agents. That's not pitching; that's begging, and it's unappealing. Don't be a beggar; be a giver and a maker. Initiate the process by communicating your intent and power to make everyone else very happy.

You don't have to actually believe it any more than you believed you were really Juliet when you portrayed her in the school play. When you pitch your work, what you feel about yourself doesn't have to match how you want other people to feel about you. In fact, how other people see you might be more accurate than how you see yourself. No one wants losers for clients or authors. Don't ever apologize for being a writer who wants to get published; your apology might be accepted, but your manuscript won't be. When pitching your work, please believe you are offering others a generous opportunity to share your inevitable success. I have been pitched thousands of times by phone, in person, and through written expression. Arrogance, delusions of grandeur, and an unwarranted sense of entitlement are powerful turn-offs. But presenting a negative persona about one's own abilities and prospects can be even worse. Between these extremes there's plenty of space for a compelling blend of humility and confidence.

Editors can't make unilateral decisions about what to acquire or how big an advance to offer. When they discover something they want, they are required to sell and defend it at so-called editorial meetings. Other editors may act like the devil's advocate, testing the editor's resolve and if she has fully considered the risks. Strong editors can usually get what they want, whereas marginal editors often don't. An editor who mostly fails to get green-lighted should be calling the headhunters, because he's already been marked for failure by his peers.

Also at these meetings is the in-house sales staff. If they say, "We can't sell it," it's game-over for that book. If they call their contacts at Barnes & Noble and Amazon and they say, "We won't order it," it's game-over for that book. If someone calls one of the company's boss-people, and she says, "I don't care what anyone else says, I want that book," it's game-on. So what can you do? Hedge your bet by learning how to impersonate the boss's phone voice and make sure she's heard loud and clear. If you can pull off a con like that, there's no reason you can't also generate a bestseller. Seriously, make sure you give editors (and your agent, if you have one) all the ammunition they might need to get the job done in your behalf.

4. Know what publishers do. If you have ever seen a book, then you know what publishers do. More specifically, they curate editorial products that the marketplace will presumably support; they produce them into consumable formats; they make them appealing; they get them into the hands of reviewers, media contacts, and key bloggers; they produce print and digital catalogs for distribution to retail accounts and employ salespeople to generate orders; they maintain inventory, fulfill orders, issue invoices, and manage the accounting; they pay authors varying percentages of revenues received; they sell subsidiary rights; they do what few authors can do by themselves. If I left anything out, *I'm sorry.* You go ahead and spend your spring weekends writing all of this not knowing if anyone will even bother to read it. IS ANYONE ACTUALLY READING THIS? Prove it: jeff@jeffherman.com.

Perhaps the most significant value that traditional publishers provide is credibility. Everyone in the business and throughout the supply chain knows that each traditionally published book is like a lucky sperm, or maybe we should say a "sperm with merit." Forget about sperms. For every book that publishers choose, at least 1,000 have been rejected. And publishing a book isn't cheap. Separate from the advance, the typical book costs at least $25,000 of a publisher's overall resources; much more if large inventories are called for.

By the way, having an agent shouldn't excuse you from learning everything you can about how the business works. The more you know, the better you will be at helping your agent and yourself to get the best results possible.

I am confident that this runaway essay has given everything that was promised and more. The journey continues.

THE KNOCKOUT NONFICTION BOOK PROPOSAL

Jeff Herman

The quality of your nonfiction book proposal will invariably make the difference between success and failure. Before agents and publishers will accept a work of fiction (especially from a newer writer), they require a complete manuscript. But nonfiction projects are different: A proposal alone can do the trick. This is what makes nonfiction writing a much less speculative and often more lucrative endeavor (relatively speaking) than fiction writing.

You may devote five years of long evenings to writing a 1,000-page fiction manuscript, only to receive a thick pile of computer-generated rejections. Clearly, writing nonfiction doesn't entail the same risks, for the simple reason that you don't have to write an entire manuscript before you can begin pitching it. On the other hand, writing fiction is often an emotionally driven endeavor in which rewards are gained though the act of writing and are not necessarily based on rational, practical considerations. Interestingly, many successful nonfiction writers fantasize about being fiction writers.

As you'll learn, the proposal's structure, contents, and size can vary substantially, and it's up to you to decide the best format for your purposes. Still, the guidelines given here serve as excellent general parameters.

Appearance Counts

Much of what follows becomes less relevant, or perhaps not possible, if all your material is conveyed solely through digital transmission. However, even digital items should look as good as possible, and many people greatly prefer to print a hardcopy to read from. In my opinion, physicality is still king (or queen) when it comes to making best impressions.

- Your proposal should be printed in black ink on clean, letter-sized (8½″ x 11″), white paper.
- Letter-quality printing is by far the best. Make sure the toner or ink cartridge is fresh and that all photocopies are dark and clear enough to be read easily. Publishing is an image-driven business, and you will be judged, perhaps unconsciously, on the physical and aesthetic merits of your submission.

- Always double-space, or you can virtually guarantee reader antagonism — eye-strain makes people cranky.
- Make sure your proposal appears fresh and new and hasn't been dog-eared, marked-up, or abused by previous readers. No editor will be favorably disposed if she thinks that everyone else on the block has already sent you packing. You want editors to think you have lots of other places to go, not nowhere else.
- Contrary to common practice in other industries, editors prefer not to receive bound proposals. If an editor likes your proposal, she will want to photocopy it for her colleagues, and your binding will only be in the way. If you want to keep the material together and neat, use a binder clip; if it's a lengthy proposal, clip each section together separately. Of course, email submissions negate the above issues.

Proposal Contents

A nonfiction proposal should include the following elements, each of which is explained below:

- Title page
- Overview
- Biographical section
- Marketing section
- Author platform
- Competition section
- Promotion section
- Chapter outline
- Sample chapters

Title page. The title page should be the easiest part, but it can also be the most important, since, like your face when you meet someone, it's what is seen first.

Try to think of a title that's attractive and effectively communicates your book's concept. A descriptive subtitle, following a catchy title, can help you achieve both goals.

It's very important that your title and subtitle relate to the book's subject, or an editor might make an inaccurate judgment about your book's focus and automatically dismiss it. For instance, if you're proposing a book about gardening, don't title it *The Greening of America*.

Examples of titles that have worked very well are:

How to Win Friends and Influence People by Dale Carnegie
Think and Grow Rich by Napoleon Hill

Baby and Child Care by Dr. Benjamin Spock

How to Swim with the Sharks without Being Eaten Alive by Harvey Mackay

And, yes, there are notable exceptions: An improbable title that went on to become a perennial success is *What Color Is Your Parachute?* by Richard Bolles. Sure, you may gain confidence and a sense of freedom from such exceptional instances. By all means let your imagination graze during the brainstorming stage.

However, don't bet on the success of an arbitrarily conceived title that has nothing at all to do with the book's essential concept or reader appeal.

A title should be stimulating and, when appropriate, upbeat and optimistic. If your subject is an important historic or current event, the title should be dramatic. If a biography, the title should capture something personal (or even controversial) about the subject. Many good books have been handicapped by poorly conceived titles, and many poor books have been catapulted to success by good titles. A good title is good advertising. Procter & Gamble, for instance, spends thousands of worker hours creating seductive names for its endless array of soap-based products.

The title you choose is referred to as the "working title." Most likely, the book will have a different title when published. There are two reasons for this:

1. A more appropriate and/or arresting title may evolve with time.
2. The publisher has final contractual discretion over the title (as well as over a lot of other things).

The title page should contain only the title, plus your name, address, telephone number, and email address — and the name, address, and phone number of your agent, if you have one. The title page should be neatly and attractively spaced. Eye-catching and tasteful computer graphics and display-type fonts can contribute to the overall aesthetic appeal.

Overview. The overview portion of the proposal is a terse statement (one to three pages) of your overall concept and mission. It sets the stage for what's to follow. Short, concise paragraphs are usually best.

Biographical section. This is where you sell yourself. This section tells who you are and why you're the ideal person to write this book. You should highlight all your relevant experience, including media and public-speaking appearances, and list previous books, articles, or both, published by or about you. Self-flattery is appropriate — so long as you're telling the truth. Many writers prefer to slip into the third person here, to avoid the appearance of egomania.

Marketing section. This is where you justify the book's existence from a commercial perspective. Who will buy it? For instance, if you're proposing a book on sales, state the number of people who earn their living through sales; point out that thousands of large and small companies are sales dependent and spend large sums on sales training, and that all sales professionals are perpetually hungry for fresh, innovative sales books.

Don't just say something like "My book is for adult women, and there are more than 50 million adult women in America." You have to be much more demographically sophisticated than that.

Author platform. The platform has become a crucial piece of the proposal in recent years. It's expected that as a minimum the author is sufficiently savvy about social media to have a large digital network of like-minded "friends" who can be tapped to purchase the book. It's all about the number of relevant people ("communities") you can access, and the expectation that they will either buy your book or at least tell others about it ("viral marketing"). Mention the number of contacts you have through social media, as well as subscribers to your newsletter or professional services, and be as specific as possible about the numbers who visit your website.

Competition section. To the uninitiated, this section may appear to be a set-up to self-destruction. However, if handled strategically, and assuming you have a fresh concept, this section wins you points rather than undermining your case.

The competition section is where you describe major published titles with concepts comparable to yours. If you're familiar with your subject, you'll probably know those titles by heart; you may have even read most or all of them. If you're not certain, just check Amazon or Abe's Books, where pretty much anything ever published is listed. If the titles in question are only available through "resellers," and not the original publishers, they are most likely out of print. Don't list everything published on your subject — that could require a book in itself. Just describe the leading half dozen titles or so (backlist classics, as well as recent books) and *explain why yours will be different.*

Getting back to the sales-book example, there is no shortage of good sales books. There's a reason for that — a big market exists for sales books. You can turn that to your advantage by emphasizing the public's substantial, insatiable demand for sales books. Your book will feed that demand with its unique and innovative sales-success program. Salespeople and companies dependent on sales are always looking for new ways to enhance sales skills (it's okay to reiterate key points).

Promotion section. Here you suggest possible ways to promote and market the book. Sometimes this section is unnecessary. It depends on your subject and on what, if any, realistic promotional prospects exist.

If you're proposing a specialized academic book such as *The Mating Habits of Octopi,* the market is a relatively limited one, and elaborate promotions would be wasteful. But if you're proposing a popularly oriented relationship book along the lines of *The Endless Orgasm in One Easy Lesson*, the promotional possibilities are also endless. They would include most major electronic broadcast and print media outlets, advertising, maybe even some weird contests.

You want to guide the publisher toward seeing realistic ways to publicize the book.

Chapter outline. This is the meat of the proposal. Here's where you finally tell what's going to be in the book. Each chapter should be tentatively titled and clearly abstracted.

Some successful proposals have fewer than 100 words per abstracted chapter; others have several hundred words per chapter. Sometimes the length varies from chapter to chapter. There are no hard-and-fast rules here; it's the dealer's choice. Sometimes less is more; at other times a too-brief outline inadequately represents the project.

At their best, the chapter abstracts read like mini-chapters — as opposed to stating "I will do…and I will show…" Visualize the trailer for a forthcoming movie; that's the tantalizing effect you want to create.

Also, it's a good idea to preface the outline with a table of contents. This way, the editor can see your entire road map at the outset.

Sample chapters. Sample chapters are optional. A strong, well-developed proposal will often be enough. However, especially if you're a first-time writer, one or more sample chapters will give you an opportunity to show your stuff and will help dissolve an editor's concerns about your ability to actually write the book, thereby increasing the odds that you'll receive an offer — and you'll probably increase the size of the advance, too.

Nonfiction writers are often wary of investing time to write sample chapters since they view the proposal as a way of avoiding speculative writing. But this can be a short-sighted view; a single sample chapter can make the difference between selling and not selling a marginal proposal. Occasionally, a publisher will request that one or two sample chapters be written before he makes a decision about a particular project. If the publisher seems to have a real interest, writing the sample material is definitely worth the author's time, and the full package can then be shown to additional prospects, too.

Many editors say that they look for reasons to reject books and that being on the fence is a valid reason for rejecting a project. To be sure, there are cases where sample chapters have tilted a proposal on the verge of rejection right back onto the playing field!

Keep in mind that the publisher is speculating that you can and will write the book upon contract. A sample chapter will go far to reduce the publisher's concerns about your ability to deliver a quality work beyond the proposal stage.

What Else?

There are a variety of materials you may wish to attach to the proposal to further bolster your cause. These include:

- Laudatory letters and comments about you
- Laudatory publicity about you
- A headshot (but not if you look like the Fly, unless you're proposing a humor book or a nature book)
- Copies of published articles you've written
- Videos of TV or speaking appearances
- Any and all information that builds you up in a relevant way, but be organized about it — don't create a disheveled, unruly package

Length

The average proposal is probably between 15 and 30 double-spaced pages, and the typical sample chapter an additional 10 to 20 double-spaced pages. But sometimes proposals reach 100 pages, and other times they're 5 pages in total. Extensive proposals are not a handicap.

Whatever it takes!

DUMB-ASS RANDOM QUESTIONS & ANSWERS

Jeff Herman

By being snarky, I bet I got your attention. And now that I have it, hold on to your hat, because there's more to know. By the way, did your grade-school teachers ever say, "There's no such thing as a stupid question," before asking if there were any questions? Well, they were wrong. I've attended a lot of writers' conferences and have entertained many stupid questions. However, I tended to hear the same stupid questions over and over again. It finally dawned on me that a large percentage of writers had the same stupid questions. Besides, where do we draw the line between a stupid and a smart question, and who gets to decide? I came to the decision that stupid isn't bad, but choosing to remain stupid might be. And I concede it's kind of stupid for me to think about stuff like this with such intensity.

What Is an Advance?

The advance is the money that a traditional publisher gives you in exchange for granting them the exclusive right to publish your book. Unless you breach the terms of the publisher's contract, you never have to return the advance, even if your book sells only 3 copies. However, all royalty income will be charged against the advance, so you won't see any more money until your royalties (see below) surpass the advance.

How Are Advances Determined?

The amount of the advance is roughly determined by the publisher's best estimation of how many copies and subsidiary rights they can sell within the first year of publication. Presidential aspirant Hillary Clinton can easily command many millions of dollars as a single advance, because the publisher can count on making a lot of money by publishing her book. At the other extreme, your obscure neighbor Jim James will probably be ecstatic to receive a more typical $5,000 advance for his recipe book about ways to boil water.

What Are Royalties?

Traditional publishers pay their authors a percentage of the book's revenues. Many variables determine the royalty percentage, and publishers don't all offer the same structure. However, the following structure is accurate more than half the time: Hardcovers start at 10 percent of the listed retail price and escalate to 15 percent after 15,000 copies are sold. Paperbacks are usually fixed at 7.5 percent of the list price. However, many retailers are able to force publishers into granting them better than 50 percent discounts. These are known as "high-discount" sales, and every book contract contains fine print allowing the publisher to pay a significantly reduced royalty against copies sold at high discount. Refusing to grant the high discount often means losing the sale and the royalty altogether. The lower royalty is "justified" because the publisher's profit margin is supposedly also reduced. You or your agent can negotiate these kinds of contingencies to a point but won't be able to entirely negate them.

Most independent presses pay royalties on the basis of "net" receipts, which means what the publisher receives from the bookstore. Most of the time, wholesalers, bookstores, and other retailers pay publishers around 50 percent of the list price for print books. However, the independent presses usually manage to equalize the royalty situation for their authors by simply doubling the royalty percentages. For instance, whereas a list royalty might be 7.5 percent, a net royalty might be 15 percent.

Paperback originals are much more common now than they were in the past. Publishers will only issue a hardcover edition if confident about selling a requisite number of units. Library sales were much more robust in the past, and libraries greatly preferred hardcovers because they were more durable. Hardcover profit margins are much higher than those for paperbacks, but only some books can command a $30+ list price, and no one wants to end up losing more revenues than were generated. For obvious reasons, paperbacks sell many more copies, and most hardcovers are converted to paperback after the first year anyway, unless they do not have good sales, in which case they may simply disappear from print without ever migrating to paperback.

Digital sales have surged over the past few years and represent a large percentage of overall sales. However, the rapid growth seems to be leveling off lately, though I'm not sure anyone knows why. It may simply be that most readers who prefer digital jumped on the bandwagon all at once. In any case, authors tend to receive 25 percent of the publisher's net earnings from each digital sale.

Why Have Ebooks Changed the Business?

Obviously, it's expensive to print, store, and ship physical books. Because most retail sales are based on consignment, which means that the stores can return unsold books instead of paying the publisher for them, all books are printed at significant risk. Ebooks bypass all of the above, which means publishers potentially save tens of thousands of dollars in speculative overhead. If everyone simply decided to buy only ebooks, it's hard to say how many jobs and functions would disappear. But once the dust settled, stability would eventually return, and many of the same players would still be standing. Digital publishing has made self-publishing much more viable and is a great opportunity for entrepreneurial independent publishers. The real wild card is that no one knows if/when physical books will disappear or how rapidly readers will continue to convert to ereading.

Physical bookstores might be facing a potential disaster, because if enough sales shift to digital there simply won't be enough reason for them to continue existing, especially if Amazon continues to gobble up market share of all print sales. Barnes & Noble might be at the greatest risk of sudden collapse due to its huge inventory of stores, warehouses, staff, and other capital-draining infrastructure. A sudden steep and permanent drop in revenue could push them into default. In contrast, mom-and-pop stores require little capital investment and tend to be embedded in their communities as preferred destinations for recreational book shopping, even if their prices are a bit higher. For many people, selecting and reading books isn't a function; it's a passion. For them, boutique venues and the "book experience" are inviolable. If their love is passed on to future generations, then technology's dictates will be slightly thwarted.

What Happens after You Deliver Your Finished Manuscript to Your Publisher?

First, congratulations for having a traditional publishing deal and for meeting your deadline. Your publisher will take 30 to 60 days to have someone read the manuscript and make all kinds of suggestions and demands about what to revise or add. You get to decide if you want to make the suggested changes or if you want to protest them. It's okay to disagree, but unless you convince your publisher to see it your way, by contract it's their way or the highway and you may have to return the advance. The work isn't considered to be accepted until the publisher says so, at which point you'll get another advance payment. In my long experience, serious editorial grievances between authors and publishers are rare.

Next, the manuscript goes into production (including line editing/copyediting, typesetting, and proofreading), which takes several months and is like what happens to a cow that's repurposed into a sirloin steak, except nothing gets killed and rendered. Your publisher will consult with you about cover and title ideas. They get final say, though a consensus is greatly preferred. Then the book is posted in the frontlist of the publisher's catalog (print or digital), which goes to all booksellers.

Will the Publisher Promote Your Book?

If you mean will they pay to send you on a multicity or even a uni-city media tour, the answer is usually no. Every traditional publisher has in-house publicity and marketing departments that will, to varying degrees, try to get you interviewed by relevant media outlets and send the book to prospective reviewers and bloggers. But here's a sobering fact: Fortune 500 companies like Procter & Gamble pay their in-house sales and marketing professionals healthy six-figure incomes, and many of them have MBAs from the top programs. This isn't a model that publishers can even remotely afford to follow. Though talented people work for the publishers, the in-house staffs are small and most titles are neglected. The small number of books that received the biggest advances will consume the most attention, because the publisher needs to recover its relatively huge investments in those titles. In fact, the publisher might even pay to outsource some of the marketing to help maximize sales.

It's wise for most authors to learn how to be a self-marketing machine. One of the attributes that probably made you attractive to your publisher in the first place was the fact that you wouldn't be dependent upon them to drive sales.

There are significant differences between the ways corporate houses and smaller houses market their books. Large publishers can afford to lose money a lot of the time, thanks to their huge backlist catalogs. Smaller presses lack that kind of cash cushion and must be doubly certain that every dollar spent is likely to generate more than $1 in return. They need to make every book as successful as possible, but they can't afford placing big bets.

What's an "Author Platform"?

Platform is one of the more recent terms to enter the publishing world's collective conversation, and, for better or worse, it has become something of an obsession. If misunderstood, a platform can become more like a gallows.

A platform is everything you already possess or can quickly manifest to almost guarantee that your book will be commercially successful. This is where your editorial ability could become secondary to other qualities. Specifically, publishers want to be convinced that you have mature and vibrant social media and professional networks, which need to exist largely in cyberspace for optimal speed, volume, and value. You're expected to receive high-volume, quality traffic to your website, and to appear often and early whenever you or your subject is searched for. Basically, they want you to be able to enter a few clicks and sell 10,000 copies minimum. There are authors who can do that and much more. The good news is that you don't have to spend a lot of money or be a techno-geek to learn how to become an internet player. Furthermore, there are few rules and truly no limitations to what can be done. New marketing paradigms emerge all the time from humble home-based jockeys. When people say, "that won't work," you should assume they might be 100 percent wrong.

When it comes to internet marketing, nothing succeeds until it does. It's simply a matrix of infinite problems and challenges waiting to be manipulated. Human psychology is the ultimate arbiter for what does and doesn't work. For instance, Facebook succeeds because it gives people the feeling of instant connection to friends and family, which is a primal instinct. What people have always wanted the most is what they will always want the most, and technology has not changed that fact.

If you don't have much of a platform, some agents and editors will automatically dismiss you for that reason alone. But please don't throw in the towel, because there are countless ways to compensate for whatever is lacking in your overall package. For obvious reasons, I want my clients to have vibrant platforms. But guess what? I have signed up and sold projects by authors who totally lacked conventional platforms, and their books did well. I'm sure the same is true for most of my colleagues. Caveat: There are many expensive services and products promising to make you a platform avatar. There are also many good books devoted to the subject for less than $25 each.

Fiction writers don't get a break in this regard, though they need to have a different kind of platform than authors who write self-help books. Fiction writers greatly benefit from popular fan pages, for instance.

Why Are Publishers Always Fighting with Amazon?

During the first decade of this century, publishers were frequently in public contention with Barnes & Noble, and no one had any issues with Amazon. But over the past several years Amazon has become the strongest single force in publishing, while B&N has been struggling to redefine itself.

Publishers squabble with Amazon for reasons similar to those for which European countries squabble with Russia. It's about who will dominate the present and the future. The irony is that Amazon decisively won the fight when they introduced the Kindle ereader several years ago, but some publishers still don't realize that they have already lost the war and that it's time to sue for peace.

Amazon is the only player with an innovative spirit, and that's the essence of the conflict. Oh, Amazon also happens to be rather selfish, greedy, and imperialistic, but that's the nature of corporate competition and combat. Any of the Big 5 publishing houses could have accessed their parent company's deep pockets to internally capitalize the creation of digital readers in advance of the Kindle, or could have partnered with Sony or one of the other early ereader producers. This would have given them unilateral control over the editorial product and a competitive digital delivery system. It's no accident that the early radio and TV set manufacturers were also the first content producers. In fact, self-retailing their own digital products through their own readers might have been a brilliant strategy for the major publishers. But instead they all sat on their hands and conducted business as usual while Amazon created the future, and therefore Amazon now owns it.

The area of major dispute at the time of this writing is about Amazon's intention to keep more digital revenues for itself. Naturally, publishers don't want to see their margins diminished. But when a publisher refuses to comply with Amazon's dictates, Amazon simply stops selling that company's products, and that hurts the publisher much more than it hurts Amazon. True, consumers can easily buy the embargoed products elsewhere, and many do. However, several million consumers pay $99 a year to be Amazon Prime members, which entitles them to free shipping and easy ordering. Most of these consumers won't shop elsewhere unless they *really* want the embargoed product.

Publishers can't exist without Amazon, nor can they defend themselves against Amazon, which is why they also hate Amazon. The largest houses attempted to take a unified stand against Amazon's domination in 2012 by forming an alliance with Apple, and were subsequently sued by the federal government for their troubles. Ultimately, they were collectively fined many millions of dollars as part of a settlement for allegedly acting in concert with one another in violation of antitrust codes. Amazon emerged unscathed and more confident than ever.

When publishers lose money, their authors lose money. So it's no surprise that the largest author organizations are having anti-Amazon tantrums in unison with agents and publishers. But as I said before, Amazon won the war before it was actually fought. Now it's time to move on and refigure the pie. Amazon can't afford to kill off publishers. It needs the publishers to generate the products that it sells the most of. In that light, a settlement will eventually be reached between all parties, and publishers will be forced to accept reduced per-unit revenues from Amazon but perhaps will sell more volume in return.

By the way, Amazon has been a godsend for self-publishers because it provides the only comprehensive, full-service retail platform with massive traffic.

What about Self-Publishing?

I've heard self-publishing causes blindness and hair to grow on your palms. This book is about traditional publishing, which will remain the preferred method for the vast majority of writers into the foreseeable future. That said, self-publishing is a viable alternative, but you'd better understand what it is and isn't before choosing it.

I read somewhere that more than 500,000 "books" will be self-published in 2014. Most of them are digital or print-on-demand (POD). But what this staggering figure doesn't reveal is that at least 95 percent of self-published books sell fewer than 10 copies a year. As a self-publisher, are you prepared to invest enough resources to not be one of the 95 percent? Do you even know what that investment means? Sadly, many self-publishers retain an array of expensive services that promise them the moon but end up delivering credit-card debt. Yes, a fraction of self-publishers are exceedingly successful or at least self-satisfied with the results. But most of them have probably leveraged their preexisting business skills and connections to make it work. They probably had a realistic business plan and budget in place before pulling the trigger, the same as they would with any other self-financed venture.

Today, anyone can self-publish anything at any time. That's the easy part, but self-selling/marketing and self-distributing are where most self-publishers fall down the stairs. Brick-and-mortar retailers aren't interested in stocking self-published books. Amazon will give you a webpage, but that will mean nothing if you don't drive sales to the page.

If you know who your customers are likely to be, how many there are, and how to reach them, then self-publishing might make more sense than traditional publishing. And it's better to self-publish than no-publish if you can't get a traditional deal. But don't get bamboozled by expensive self-publishing packages. You can make it happen for less than $1,000 — or even less than $100 if you don't need a professional copyedit and cover design — and take it one frugal step at a time from there. Many excellent books (mostly self-published) are devoted to the subject.

Here's the flip side: self-publishers are filling important editorial niches that traditional publishers neglect. For instance, some of the bestselling craft, hobby, and specialized how-to books are self-published. So are many of the bestselling "fan fiction" titles in such categories as vampires and zombies. Most of these successful self-publishers have figured out online selling and don't want to do business through traditional retailers because they would make much less money going the traditional route. It's likely that the importance of self-publishers as niche micropublishers will explode over the next few years. Maybe you can get a piece of the action.

Will Traditional Publishing Become Extinct Anytime Soon?

That's very unlikely. However, midsize independent publishers are endangered because many of them lack the cash flow to survive a fast-changing environment and can't jettison fixed costs fast enough. Every year, they become fewer and fewer. Small presses will manage to survive simply because they are small and can more easily manage their overhead and shift to digital publishing and POD as needed. The Big 5 can't fail because of their billion-dollar backlist catalogs. In a worst-case scenario, all they have to do is stop acquiring expensive frontlist titles and just rely on midlist acquisitions and backlist sales. Their revenues would plummet, but ironically their profit margins would soar.

ONLINE MARKETING FROM SOMEONE WHO DOESN'T UNDERSTAND IT

Jeff Herman

If you're like me, you don't know much about digital marketing, except that it's important and getting more important all the time.

When I first began visiting Facebook, my question was: how can I send emails to all one billion members? I figured that FB must have a way to do it, so it was just a question of piggybacking on their system. I couldn't find any information on how to pay them for that, and I didn't want to pay a king's ransom to post something on FB's landing page.

I figured the only way to get access to all or any members was to hack into the system. But that would be not only illegal but probably also close to impossible, or else people would be doing it already. On the other hand, maybe people do manage to hack FB, and FB deliberately makes a deal in which the culprits promise to shut up about it. After all, it wouldn't reflect well on FB if it became publicly known that it was hackable.

I didn't have nasty intentions. I hoped to simply send a concise email telling people about the book in your hands and how they could buy a copy. Would that have been so wrong? Who would I have been harming? I figured that if only 1/100th of 1 percent of the billion FB members bought a copy, I'd sell 100,000 copies. So how could I make it happen?

I decided to manually compile every FB member from A to Z and organize them into the following categories.

1. Those who could be emailed via their FB accounts.
2. Those who had posted other email or website addresses.
3. Those whose email addresses had to be researched via search engines.

I estimated that the endeavor would require countless thousands of hours. I would need interns — a lot of them. But I'd probably have to pay them something, so to help finance the labor, I decided to initially focus on only those FB members who could be easily contacted via their Facebook accounts. And if I converted merely 1 percent of those contacts into a book sale, I would have enough cash flow to keep the process humming into the next decade. Admit it, it's a darn good plan, and it defines what online marketing should be: researching and clicking forever and ever... for money.

I broke down the process into these basic steps:

1. Write the perfect pitch letter.
2. Hire the right interns.
3. Set up some cubicles with necessary hardware and bandwidth.
4. Generate dummy-proof written directions for the interns.
5. Turn them loose to compile the addresses and email the pitch each time an address was collected.
6. Set up a functioning website to route the orders to online booksellers.

Here are what I saw as the possible obstacles:

1. My pitches would end up in spam catchers and never be read.
2. People wouldn't bother reading them because we've all been conditioned to ignore emails from strangers.
3. By breaking some kind of etiquette, I would become a pariah for the rest of my life and even beyond.
4. That it's all just a stupid idea and waste of time.

As I said above, I'm the furthest thing from a tech geek. But conceptually, my idea seems like the way to go. It's why Willy Sutton robbed banks: "it's where the money is."

As of this writing I have not yet gone beyond the thinking stage with any of this. But by the time you're reading this I may be deep into it.

Fortunately for you, the very next essay in this book is by someone who knows infinitely more than me about online marketing. So all you have to do is turn the page.

HOW TO OPTIMIZE YOUR BLOGGING TO MAXIMIZE YOUR PLATFORM

Arielle Ford

People often ask me how they can increase their platform when seeking a publisher for their books. Any aspiring writer would benefit from starting a blog before writing a book or book proposal and before creating an overall promotion plan for their online marketing. This gives you access to a built-in audience and helps you develop material that you know will be of interest to your audience.

Blogging is not difficult. Intuitively I understood the importance of blogging for increasing traffic to my site, growing my email list, search-engine optimization, earning expert status, and the list goes on. On a practical level I initially saw blogging as one more platform on which I needed to create value-added content. Don't get me wrong — I love providing support to people on the topics I feel very passionate about, but I was not sure I could stay on top of it or smoothly integrate social networking into my marketing plan. I was happy to learn that I was wrong on both points, and if I could find a process that works for me and make heads or tails of it all, so can you! I would like to share my strategies and some of the results I have seen so far.

Creating Your Blogging Strategy

Stay on topic. Brand expansion through blogging requires that you, well, blog about your brand! Remain consistent with your messaging, your tone, and your reason for sharing with your audience. If you feel strongly about a topic or event outside your industry, always tie it back in with appropriate relevance and provide insight related to how it may impact your reader. Use self-promotion blogs sparingly, as your visitors will get bored and annoyed by this and they will not return.

Plan ahead. Although it may at first seem difficult to brainstorm multiple blog topics in advance, it is important to plan out what and when you will blog so that you stay on track and hold yourself accountable. Look at some of the comments people have been making on your social networking sites for inspiration. Of course there will be times that a particular current event may spur your interest for blogging, and that's great. On your editorial calendar, remember to always plan a blog before a book signing, speaking engagement, or teleclass to create a buzz. Also, post a blog within 48 hours after an event so that you can share a great audience question and provide your answer for those who did not attend.

Create a community. Whenever appropriate, elicit comments to your blog post. If your blog is a "How to" or "10 Steps to…" ask your readers what has worked best for them. By doing this you create a discussion and community from which you and others can learn. Who knows, you may even come up with another blog idea, or even your next book!

Make your blog page effective. Make it easy for any visitor to connect with you once they are on your blogging page. If you are program-savvy do it yourself, or have someone else add Twitter, Facebook, Pinterest, LinkedIn, and Google+ buttons to your blog page. Also, your subscriber form should be very visible on this page, because once the visitor likes what you have to share and how you share it, he or she will want to learn more from you.

Create social media infrastructure. If you are taking the time and mental energy to create great content on your blogs, it would be a shame if no one knew about it or read it.

- Use your Facebook personal profile, Facebook Fan Page, and Twitter accounts to announce a new post and drive traffic to the blog.
- Craft interesting status updates (at least five per blog post) and use a shortened URL account such as Bit.ly to track how many people are going to your blog (known as "click-through rates").
- Have your blogs automatically posted to your Facebook account through the networked blog feature and the auto blog import via the Notes feature.

Use a scheduling account. SocialOomph and similar programs allow you to preplan the posting of your updates for time efficiency and Retweet effectiveness. (Hint: there are certain times of the day and week that are the best for getting great click-through rates and Retweets, as I mentioned in a blog post on the *Huffington Post*.)

Results

Within only six weeks of consistent blogging, I saw my click-through rates grow from 150 to as high as 863. My Facebook fans increased by 60 percent, and my enewsletter consistently obtained new subscribers. I have also seen colleagues earn solid teleclass and webinar participation as a result of regularly posting value-added content.

Strong results will not happen overnight. You will gain traction if you continue to be present and add value to your online community. Over time they will become loyal fans and engaged consumers. There is no need to start from scratch trying to figure out all this on your own. Find a blogging buddy who can help with brainstorming, accountability, and collaboration, or seek out the support of a professional.

Arielle Ford (www.arielleford.com) is a leading pioneer and personality in the personal growth and contemporary spirituality movement. For the past 25 years she has been living, teaching, and promoting consciousness through all forms of media. Her stellar career includes years as a prominent book publicist, author, literary agent, TV lifestyle reporter, television producer, Sirius radio host, publishing consultant, relationship expert, speaker, columnist, and blogger for the *Huffington Post*.

Arielle was instrumental in launching the careers of many *New York Times* bestselling self-help authors, including Deepak Chopra, Jack Canfield, Mark Victor Hansen, Neale Donald Walsch, and Debbie Ford. She was the publicist for dozens of other top-selling authors, such as Wayne Dyer, Gary Zukav, Dean Ornish, Joan Borysenko, Louise Hay, Jorge Cruise, and don Miguel Ruiz.

She is a gifted writer and the author of seven books, including *The Soulmate Secret*, now in 21 languages. Arielle is also the creator of the at-home publishing study course *Everything You Should Know about Publishing, Publicity, and Building a Platform* (www.everything youshouldknow.com).

WHEN NOTHING HAPPENS TO GOOD (OR BAD) WRITERS

a.k.a. Ignored Writer Syndrome (IWS)

Jeff Herman

"I will not be ignored!" screams Alex Forrest, the book editor played by Glenn Close, to her philandering lover, played by Michael Douglas, in the classic film *Fatal Attraction*.

What perfect karma: a book editor being ignored, even though her job was not relevant to the conflict. Too bad about the rabbit, though.

It's an inalienable truth that any writer who aggressively pitches his or her work will encounter abundant rejections along the way. You know that. But what you may not have been prepared for was the big-loud-deafening nothing at all. You followed the given protocols; have been gracious, humble, and appreciative; and have done nothing egregious. And you would never boil a rabbit. So what's your reward? Absolutely nothing; you have been ignored.

A document stating that your work has been rejected, even if clearly generic, may be a much more welcome outcome than the silence of an empty universe. At least that formal rejection letter reflects that you are part of a genuine process. True, you have been turned away at the gate, but it still seems that you belong to a fraternity of sorts. It's like you're an understudy, or simply wait-listed. Your existence is acknowledged even if unwelcome, whereas to be ignored is proof of nothing. Nature abhors a vacuum, and any writer with nerve endings will understand why soon enough, if not already.

I write this essay because of the frequent feedback I receive from readers complaining about the nonresponsiveness of editors and agents. I have carefully considered this phenomenon and how it must negatively affect the morale and stamina of those who are endeavoring in good faith to be published. I have decided that to be ignored deserves its own category in the travails of writing, and that it inflicts even more pain and frustration than the proverbial rejection. I shall designate it with a logical term: ignored.

Why are so many writers ignored by editors and agents? I will respond to that with questions of my own. Why are so many children ignored? Why are so many of the poor and needy ignored? Why are so many social problems ignored? I could ask this question in countless ways, and the primary universal answer would essentially remain the same: it's far easier to do nothing.

Let's get back to our specific context. As I mention elsewhere, agents and editors have demanding, often tedious, workloads that overwhelm the typical 40-hour workweek (they tend to put in way more hours than that, even though they can rarely bill by the hour or receive extra pay). They are rewarded for generating tangible results, which is most often measured in the form of monetary revenues. Taking the time to respond to writers, even in a purely perfunctory manner, might be the courteous thing to do, but neither their businesses nor their bosses will reward their kindness. You may feel that such inaction is a misguided and shortsighted "policy," and you might be right, but it doesn't change the facts as they are.

Does being ignored mean that you have actually been read and rejected? This question can't be answered, because you're being ignored. It's possible that someone did read your work and rejected it, and then simply neglected to reply to your email or threw out your proposal even if an SASE was attached. Why would someone do that? Because it's much easier to, and they can't justify the time it would take to answer as many as 150 submissions per week. It's also possible that your submission has not been read and may never be read, because nobody is available to screen the "incoming" in any organized fashion. It's not out of the question that submissions will accumulate in numerous piles, boxes, and email inboxes for several years before they are simply discarded, never to be opened. Does this strike you as harsh or ridiculous? Whatever; it is the way it is.

What is certain is that if your work is read and accepted, you will hear about it. In closing, my message to you is that you not allow being ignored to diminish your dreams and goals. It's simply a part of the process and part of the emotional overhead you might encounter on your road to success. It's also a crucial reason why you should not put all your manuscripts in "one basket." To do so may be tantamount to placing your entire career in a bottomless pit. Making multiple submissions is reasonable and wise if you consider the possible consequences of granting an exclusive without any deadline or two-way communications. Please refer to the other essays and words of advice in this book to keep yourself from becoming a victim of Ignored Writer Syndrome (IWS).

THE WRITER'S JOURNEY
The Path of the Spiritual Messenger

Deborah Herman

If you have decided to pursue writing as a career instead of as a longing or a dream, you might find yourself focusing on the goal instead of the process. When you have a great book idea, you may envision yourself on a book-signing tour or as a guest on a talk show before you've written a single word.

It's human nature to look into your own future, but too much projection can get in the way of what the writing experience is all about. The process of writing is like a wondrous journey that can help you cross a bridge to the treasures hidden within your own soul. It is a way for you to link with God and the collective storehouse of all wisdom and truth, as it has existed since the beginning of time.

Many methods of writing bring their own rewards. Some people can produce exceptional prose by using their intellect and their mastery of the writing craft. They use research and analytical skills to help them produce works of great importance and merit.

Then there are those who have learned to tap into the wellspring from which all genius flows. They are the inspired ones who write with the intensity of an impassioned lover. I refer to them as "spiritual writers," and they write because they have to. They may not want to, they may not know how to, but something inside them is begging to be let out. It gnaws away at them until they find a way to set it free. Although they may not realize it, spiritual writers are engaged in a larger spiritual journey toward ultimate self-mastery and unification with God.

Spiritual writers often feel as if they're taking dictation. Spiritual writing — in any genre: nonfiction, sci-fi, women's fiction, whatever — has an otherworldly feeling and can teach writers things they would otherwise not have known. It is not uncommon for a spiritual writer to read something after a session in "the zone" and question if indeed she wrote it.

Writing opens you up to new perspectives, much like self-induced psychotherapy. Although journals are the most direct route for self-evaluation, fiction and nonfiction also serve as vehicles for a writer's growth. Writing helps the mind expand to the limits of the imagination.

Anyone can become a spiritual writer, and there are many benefits to doing so, not the least of which is the development of the soul. On a more practical level, it is much less difficult to write with flow and fervor than it is to be bound by the limitations of logic and analysis. If you tap into the universal source, there is no end to your potential creativity.

The greatest barrier to becoming a spiritual writer is the human ego. We treat our words as if they were our children — only we tend to be neurotic parents. Children are not owned by parents, but rather must be loved, guided, and nurtured until they can carry on, on their own.

The same is true for our words. If we try to own and control them like property, they will be limited by our vision for them. We will overprotect them and will not be able to see when we may be taking them in the wrong direction for their ultimate well-being. Another ego problem that creates a barrier to creativity is our need for constant approval and our tendency toward perfectionism. We may feel the tug toward free expression but will erect blockades to ensure appropriate style and structure. We write with a "schoolmarm" hanging over our shoulders, waiting to tell us what we are doing wrong.

Style and structure are important to ultimate presentation, but that is what editing is for. Ideas and concepts need to flow like water in a running stream. The best way to become a spiritual writer is to relax and have fun. If you are relaxed and pray for guidance, you'll be open to intuition and higher truth. However, writers tend to take themselves too seriously, which causes anxiety, which exacerbates fear, which causes insecurity, which diminishes their self-confidence and leads ultimately to mounds of crumpled papers and lost inspiration. You are worthy. Do not let insecurity prevent you from getting started and following through.

If you have faith in a Supreme Being, the best way to begin a spiritual writing session is with the following writer's prayer:

Almighty God [Jesus, Allah, Great Spirit, etc.], Creator of the Universe, help me to become a vehicle for your wisdom so that what I write is of the highest purpose and will serve the greatest good. I humbly place my [pen/keyboard/recording device] in your hands so that you may guide me.

Prayer helps to connect you to the universal source. It empties the mind of trash, noise, and potential writer's blocks. If you are not comfortable with formal prayer, a few minutes of meditation will serve the same purpose.

Spiritual writing as a process does not necessarily lead to a sale. The fact is that some people and concepts have more commercial potential than others. Knowledge of the business of writing will help you make a career of it. If you combine this with the spiritual process, it can also bring you gratification and inner peace. If you trust the process of writing and make room for the journey, you will grow and achieve far beyond your expectations.

Keep in mind that you are not merely a conduit. You are to be commended and should take pride in the fact that you allow yourself to be used as a vessel for the Divine. You are the one who is taking the difficult steps in a world full of obstacles and challenges. You are the one who is sometimes so pushed to the edge that you have no idea how you go on. But you do. You maintain your faith and you know that there is a reason for everything. You may not have a clue what it is…but you have an innate sense that all your experiences are part of some bigger plan. At minimum they create good material for your book.

In order to be a messenger of the Divine you have to be a vessel willing to get out of the way. You need to be courageous and steadfast in your beliefs because God's truth is your truth. When you find that your inner truth does not match that of other people, you need to be strong enough to stay true to yourself. Your soul, that inner spark that connects you to all creation, is your only reliable guide. You will receive pressure from everywhere. But your relationship with your creator is as personal as your DNA. You will be a house divided if you try to please other people by accepting things they tell you that do not resonate with your spirit.

When you do find your inner truth, your next challenge is to make sure that you do not become the person who tries to tell everyone else what to believe. When a spiritual writer touches that moment of epiphany it is easy to become God-intoxicated. There is no greater bliss than to be transformed by a connection to the source of all creation. It is not something that can be described. It is individual. This is why it is important for a spiritual writer to protect this experience for another seeker. The role of a spiritual messenger who manifests his or her mission through the written word is to guide the readers to the threshold of awakening. Bring them to the gate but allow God to take them the rest of the way. Your job is to make the introduction. From there the relationship is no longer your responsibility. Your task is to shine the light brightly for some other seeker to find it.

It is difficult to believe so strongly in something while feeling unable to find anyone to listen to you. If you try too hard you might find that there are others who will drain your energy and life force while giving nothing in return. They may ridicule you and cause you to step away from your path. You do not have to change the world by yourself. You need to do your part. Whether it is visible or as simple as letting someone know you care, you are participating in elevating the world for the better. Some people like it exactly as it is. There are those who thrive on chaos and the diseases of the soul. Your job as a spiritual writer is to protect your spirit as you would your own child. Do not give away your energy; make it available for those who truly want it and will appreciate it. When you write, expect nothing in return. While following the protocols of the business world, do not set your goal too high, such as transforming people's souls. If you do, you will elevate your responsibility beyond the capability of simple humans. If you do the groundwork, God will do the rest.

The world of the spiritual writer can be a very lonely place. It is easier to love God, creation, and humanity than it is to feel worthy of receiving love in return. Those of us who devote our energy to trying to make a difference through our writing forget that God has given us this gift as a reward for our goodness, faith, and love. It is a two-way street. What we give we can also receive. It maintains the balance. It replenishes our energy so we can continue to grow and fulfill our individual destiny. We are all loved unconditionally. God knows everything we have ever thought, done, or even thought about doing. We judge ourselves far more harshly than God ever would. We come into this world to learn and to fix our "miss"-takes. We only learn through object lessons. We have free will. Sometimes we have to burn our hands on the stove several times before we learn that it is too hot to touch. I personally have lived my life with the two-by-four-to-the-head method. While not recommended, it is the only way I have been able to learn some of my more difficult lessons. I have often considered wearing a helmet.

When we connect with our inner truth we can become intoxicated with our own greatness. Writing is a very heady thing, especially if we are able to see our name in print. If we have people listening to what we have to say, we can believe that we are the message and forget that we are merely the messenger. Spiritual writers need to start every day by praying for humility. If we don't, and there is danger that we are going to put ourselves before the purity of Divine truth, we will not be able to be the pure vessel that we had hoped to become. The universe has methods of protecting itself. We will experience humiliation to knock us down a few pegs, to give us the opportunity to get over ourselves. I have experienced many instances of humorous humiliation, such as feeling amazed with myself only to literally fall splat on my face by tripping over air. No injury except to my inflated pride. God has a sense of humor.

On a more serious note, spiritual messengers who are taken in by their own egos are vulnerable to negativity. The information they convey becomes deceiving and can help take people off their paths. This is why spiritual writers should always begin each session with a prayer to be a vessel for the highest of the high and for the greater good. While readers have the choice to discern the wheat from the chaff, in this time of rapid spiritual growth, it is important to help seekers stay as close to their paths as possible. There is no time for major detours. We all have a lot of work to do.

We are all here to improve the lives of one another. We are blessed to live in an information age, in which we can communicate quickly and clearly with one another. However, technology also serves to make us separate. We all cling to our ideas without respecting the paths of others. We are all headed to the same place, the center of the maze, where there is nothing and everything all at once. We are all headed for the place of pure love that binds all of us to one another. We don't want to get caught up with trivial arguments about who is right and who is wrong. Our goal right now needs to be to foster everyone's path to his or her own higher truth. We share what we have so others can find it, without wasting time arguing the point to win them to our side. Too many battles have been fought over who is the most right. We all come from the same source.

When it comes down to it, spiritual writers are the prophets of today. You are here to express the voice of God in our world in ways that we as human beings can understand. We need to listen to the essence of the message rather than focusing on who is the greater prophet. In the business of writing, there is no sin in profit. But in the mission of writing, we must not forget that we all answer to the same boss and serve the same master.

You are also a messenger. When you agree to be a spiritual writer, you are also agreeing to bring light into the world. This is no small commitment. Remember to keep your ego out of it. While it is important to learn to promote and support your work, you must not forget that you are the messenger and not the message. If you keep this at the center of your heart and remember that you serve the greater good, you are a true spiritual writer who is honoring the call. May God bless you and guide you always.

Deborah Herman, wife and business partner of Jeff Herman, considers herself a mystic literary agent. She is the author of *Spiritual Writing from Inspiration to Publication* (Atria, 2001), which is currently being updated to reflect the digital age. Herman will be self-publishing in her own imprint, Soul-Odyssey Media, a division of www.offthebookshelf .com, the full-service micropublishing platform of which she is CEO and through which she offers book coaching, editing, and marketing consultation. Herman received certification from the Rutgers mini-MBA program in digital marketing, social media, and entrepreneurship, which she uses to help spiritual writers become writer-entrepreneurs. Her Twitter handles are @spiritualagent and @digitaldeborah.

TRIBULATIONS OF THE UNKNOWN WRITER (AND POSSIBLE REMEDIES)

Jeff Herman

Many nations have memorials that pay homage to the remains of their soldiers who died in battle and cannot be identified. In a way, it seems that the legions of unpublished writers are the Unknown Writers. As has been expressed elsewhere in this book, it cannot be assumed that the works of the unknown writer are of any lesser quality than those works that achieve public exposure and consumption, any more than those soldiers who died were less adept than those who got to go home. To the contrary, perhaps they were *more* adept, or at least more daring, and therefore paid the ultimate price.

No warrior aspires to become an unknown soldier, let alone a dead soldier. Every soldier prefers to believe that her remains will be known, that they will perhaps even explain what happened toward the end and will be presented to her loved ones for final and proper farewells. It is much the same for the writer. No writer worth her ink wants to believe that her legacy of expression will be forever unknown. Even if her other accomplishments in life are magnificent, it is still those words on the pages that she wants revealed, preferably while she's still around to experience and enjoy it.

Obviously, in life and beyond, there are many unknown writers. That's just the way it is.

It may just be that the fear of living and dying as an unknown writer is the extra push you need to bring your work to the first step on the road to publication — getting your work noticed by a publishing professional, be it agent or editor. If you are still reading this essay, then it is absolutely true that you are willing to try harder to reach that goal. In recognition and respect for your aspirations and determination, I will provide additional insights and strategies to help you help yourself avoid the fate of the unknown writer.

But let's make sure that your goals, at least in the early stages of your publishing life, are reasonably measured. It is suitable to imagine yourself one day at the top of the publishing food chain. Why not? Genuine humans have to be there at any given moment, so why not you? However, it is improbable that you will arrive there in one step. Your odds will be enhanced through your dedication to learning, calculating, and paying the necessary dues. For the purposes of the lesson at hand, I will encourage you to focus on the more humble goal of simply transitioning to the realm of being a published writer. For sure, there is more to do after that, but we will leave those lessons for other places in this book, and for other books.

Ways to Be Seen in a Crowd

Established literary agencies, including yours truly's, are inundated with unsolicited query letters (both hardcopy and digital), proposals, pieces of manuscripts, and entire manuscripts. This stream of relentless *intake* easily runs from 50 to 150 uninvited submissions per week, depending on how visible the agency in question is to the world of writers at large. These numbers do not account for the many works that the agency has requested or was expecting from existing clients. Frankly, many successful agents are simply not hungry for more than what they already have and make efforts to be as invisible and unavailable as possible.

The above scenario only tells of the agencies. It's likely that the publishers, both big and small, are receiving the same in even greater volumes, which is of dubious value since many publishers prefer not to consider anything that is unsolicited or unrepresented, period.

How can your work go from being an unseen face in the crowd to a jack-in-the-box whose presence cannot be denied? Here are some suggested steps.

1. ***Don't merely do what everyone else is already doing.*** That doesn't mean that you should entirely refrain from doing what's conventional or recommended. After all, the beaten track is beaten for a reason: it has worked before and it will work again. But be open to the possibility of pursuing specific detours along the way. Look upon these excursions as a form of calculated wildcatting. If nothing happens, or if you end up puncturing the equivalent of someone's septic tank, then just take it as a lesson learned.

2. ***Make yourself be seen.*** A pile of no. 10 envelopes is simply that, and none of the component envelopes that form the pile are seen. Someone once sent me a letter shaped like a circle. It could not be grouped with that day's quota of query letters; it demanded to be seen and touched and dealt with, immediately. Another time I received a box designed as a treasure chest, which contained an unsolicited proposal. I did not appreciate receiving a bag of white powder with a certain proposal. The powder was flushed down the toilet and the manuscript returned without being read. Digital queries are even more prone to disappear into a sea of sameness. But maybe that's why the email gods created the subject line: so that you can say something that can't be ignored.

3. ***Be generous.*** Most submissions are actually a demand for time, attention, and energy. During a long day in the middle of a stressful week in the throes of a month in hell, an agent will see none of those submissions as good-faith opportunities from honorable people. To the contrary, they will feel like innumerable nuisances springing forth from the armpits of manic brain-eating zombies, with drool and odor. I can recall opening a package to find a handwritten card from a stranger telling me how much he appreciated my contributions to the business and how much I have helped him and others, etc., etc. I always remember those kinds of things; wouldn't you?

4. ***Don't be a nag, be a gift.*** Everyone likes gifts, and nobody likes nags. So why do so many aspiring writers (and others) act like nags? It's counterintuitive. Of course, nature teaches us from the moment we are born that the noisy baby gets the tit. Passivity invites neglect. Noise attracts attention. What an interesting conundrum. Nagging is bad. Passivity leads to death. Noise can't be ignored. Well, all of that is equally valid, and none of it disqualifies the original point that you are a gift, so act like one.

5. ***Keep knocking, even after the door is opened.*** That does not make sense, and it might not be appreciated. But if someone were to keep knocking on my door even after I opened it, I would simply have to ask that person why he or she is doing that, and therein is the beginning of a conversation. Of course, it may all go downhill from there, but then it may not. What happens next depends on the nature of the conversation that has just been launched, regardless of its weird genesis.

6. ***Don't ask for anything, but offer whatever you can.*** If that is the energy projected throughout your communications, you will attract due wealth. However, the word *due* is rather crucial in this context. A well-intentioned worm may end up on the end of a fishhook, and a nasty frog may be well fed all summer. Too often people stop at just being nice, and then they become prey. Is it fair that they are eaten for doing nothing at all? Actually, that's exactly what they asked for, to end up nourishing the needs of others. We must all serve a purpose, and we must all consume to survive. If you don't wish to be consumed, then don't present yourself for that. The universe is a layered place of lessons and challenges, and being a writer is just one of many ways to play the game. Don't just give yourself away, any more than you would throw yourself away. If you value the gems you wish to share, you will discern to whom to grant them, and simply refuse to participate with others.

7.   ***Know your gifts and appreciate them.*** I can tell right away when I am reading a query letter from a writer who believes in herself and the quality of her product, and I can see those who are not so sure that they should even be trying. Sometimes the writer is apologetic, or even goes as far as asking me if he should be trying. Ironically, the writer's quality as a writer cannot be predicted by his native sense of self-worth. In fact, great literature has emerged from the hearts of those who are seemingly committed to a life of losing. But there is a logical explanation for that: To each writer is assigned a muse. Some writers may hate themselves while loving their muse, and it shows.

FIND YOUR PASSION AND PISS IT AWAY

Jeff Herman

Headlines mean a lot; sometimes everything. Either they attract immediate attention or they fail. Of course, a high level of preexisting interest in the subject matter can compensate for a feeble headline.

The first rule when trying to get attention is to get attention. Guess what? Getting attention is easy. Just watch a bored kid or ornery dog. But getting positive or appropriate attention is challenging. Return to the above headline. It's magnetically provocative because it's countercultural to the point of deviant. It's not what Deepak would say, or at least not without a smile; though he's always smiling.

The second rule is to understand that further rules won't matter until you accomplish the first rule. Assuming you will, proceed to the third rule.

The third rule is to understand that no rules apply to you unless you choose to follow them, regardless of who makes them. Rules have power if they can be enforced, and many nonsensical rules prevail because defiance is costly. Tax evasion is an example. Many rules are perpetual for the simple reason that enough people mindlessly follow them. Society intrinsically attempts to impose conformity. However, at least 10 percent of any given community will be inherently unable to comply with rules, and many of those people are antisocial criminals. Other serial nonconformists will be condemned to a life of quiet desperation. But a crucial remnant will succeed at creating original realities and innovative possibilities that will potentially deliver progress, destruction, or a combination of both.

The fourth rule is to manage the consequences of the attention you will hopefully attract. For instance, using the above headline requires me to quickly explain the method to my apparent madness and attempt to bring readers to my real purpose. However, I'm not trying to sell anything and may never know if anyone even reads this essay, whereas you will be pitching for, and will be mindful of, specific results. Obviously, you want to begin your sales letters and documents in ways that will maximize attention. But if you take risks by opening your material in absurd ways, then you had better have an immediate conversion process built into the text, or the initial attention you capture may devolve into the equivalent of an errant missile to nowhere, or an unintended destination.

The fifth rule is to remember that beauty without attention equals beauty without attention, whereas mediocrity with attention can be rewarding. If Sophia Loren had ago-raphobia and never left her house, countless generations of men (okay, not all men and some women) wouldn't have been able to include her in their fantasies. It's plausible that women even more beautiful and talented than Ms. Loren were simply unable to tolerate or negotiate what it takes to get attention and will therefore be forever unknown. Conversely, Mae West wasn't a classic beauty but yet was one of the most famous and sexualized women in the world for decades.

The sixth rule is to devise as many other rules as you wish, and then you may destroy or morph them, because that's the process that helps keep us vibrant and connected to the lives we live.

POST-PUBLICATION DEPRESSION SYNDROME (PPDS)

Jeff Herman

If you're struggling to get published, then this essay isn't for you, yet. If you're currently under contract, now is a good time to read this. If you have already been published and experienced what the above title indicates, then hopefully this essay will help you heal and realize you are far from alone.

You don't need to be reminded how much passion, fortitude, and raw energy goes into crafting your work, followed by the grueling process of getting it published. What you're probably not prepared for is the possibility of post-publication blues.

No one directly discusses or recognizes this genuine condition because newly published authors are expected to be overjoyed and grateful for the achievement of being published. After all, each published author is among the fortunate "one out of a thousand" struggling writers who make it to the Big Show. In reality, people who reach the pinnacle of success in any field of endeavor will often feel an emotional letdown in the wake of their accomplishment. The feeling can be comparable to a state of mourning, as the thrill of chasing the goal instantly evaporates and is replaced by nothing. Writers are especially prone to wallowing alone, as theirs is a solitary process by design, and only other writers who have been through the same cavern can be truly empathetic.

Emotional letdowns happen when results don't fulfill expectations. Everything preceding the point of publication involves drama, excitement, and anticipation. Butterflies flutter in the belly and endorphins soar through the brain. One day the writer's goal will be manifested in the body of a published book, and the self-constructed dreams will be displaced by a reality that seems to lack sizzle. What follows might feel sad and unnourishing. No matter how much is achieved, it might feel as if something crucial were left behind.

Achieving awesome goals is a reward unto itself, but it may not be enough to satisfy what's needed. The writer's imagination may have drawn fantastic pictures of glamorous celebrity parties, profound talk-show appearances, instantaneous fame, and goblets of money. But just as the explosive passions and idealized assumptions of first love might be followed by an anticlimactic consummation, finally receiving the bound book in hand might prove to be surprisingly uneventful.

Sometimes the publication is everything the writer hoped for, which of course is a wonderful outcome. But for many it feels like nothing much happened at all. The media aren't calling; few people show up for signings/readings; and, perhaps most upsetting of all, friends and relatives report that the book can't be found. Meanwhile, no one from the publisher is calling anymore and they act like their job is done. In truth, most of the publishing team is probably absorbed with publishing the endless flow of new books, whereas what's already been published is quickly relegated to "yesterday's list." A chirpy in-house publicist may be available, but she may not appear to be doing or accomplishing much while adeptly saying imprecise things in a glib, patronizing manner.

There's abundant information available about how to be a proactive author and successfully compensate for the universal marketing deficits endemic to the book publishing business. But that's not the purpose of this essay. For sure, it's constructive to take practical steps for mitigating disappointments and solving existential problems, but such activities may also distract the troubled writer from the tender places crying somewhere inside. These feelings must be recognized and soothed. Even bestselling writers get the blues.

Seeking or initiating communities of "published writers in pain" should be what the doctor ordered. If done right, such personal connections will help level the loneliness and despair that defines post-publication depression. However, the community must consciously dedicate itself to a positive process. Nothing useful will be accomplished by reinforcing anger, resentment, or a sense of victimhood. Even worse is unsupportive competitiveness or negativity that pushes people down. And — as can happen in any inbred community — distortions, misinformation, and poor advice might circulate with a bogus badge of credibility.

Life is rarely a clear trail. If it looks to be, then unexpected destinations are likely to prevail. Writers will eat dirt and wear thorns in exchange for self-compassion and self-discovery. Pain isn't punishment but a consequence that expands the writer's integrity, authenticity, and relevance. Post-publication depression is an item on a menu in a script written by the writer for the writer. Never fear the pain; just be prepared to live through it and learn from it, and to help others do the same.

GREAT INVENTIONS THAT WILL CHANGE WRITING AND PUBLISHING IN DAYS TO COME (OR NOT)

Jeff Herman

Disclaimer: To my knowledge, none of the products and services described below exist in our current time loop, nor can I guarantee that any of them are even possible within the parameters of human abilities. Nor do I encourage you to attempt to build or use any of these items, at least not without a young person's or extraterrestrial's supervision. Nor do I bear any moral or practical responsibility for the consequences of your choices in combination with these items.

The Thought Smasher

Projected availability: 2019

Initial price (in current dollars): $9,999.99

Inventor and patent owner: Jeffrey H. Herman with his three dogs

Primary function: Your conscious thoughts are immediately printed, no fingers required. You can write anything as fast as you can think it, and because thoughts are faster than the speed of sound, you can potentially write several books a day. All you need to do is keep thinking. Edits are easy: with your mind you simply scroll and mentally dictate your revisions.

Possible defects: Early models might have trouble discerning conscious from unconscious thoughts, which means that the user's deepest sentiments could potentially be memorialized in writing if not deleted. This might be good for self-discovery, but the incidence of divorces, unintentional confessions, and transgender procedures might spike. Not recommended for schizophrenics or people with multiple personalities.

The Goditor

Projected availability: 2020

Initial price (in current dollars): $9,999.99

Inventor/owner: Jeffrey H. Herman with his whippet and miniature dachshund

Primary function: A hard drive and monitor combined into a nonphysical holographic omnipotent PC that can follow the user anywhere and only be visible to her on the basis of perpetually scanning her eyes. Any data can be loaded, saved, and recalled on the basis of thought-command protocols known only to the user. Everyone will have immediate and constant access to everything. It can also be used as an unlimited broadcaster/receiver.

Possible early defects: Users will be inclined to use the product while driving, which isn't recommended. Unwanted visuals might be accidentally sent to billions of other users. Early models might yield "confusion" with unknown consequences if two or more users are too physically close to each other. Activation isn't recommended during sexual intercourse or in subway stations at busy times.

The Icon-Author Replicator

Projected availability: 2021

Initial price (in current dollars): $9,999.99

Inventor/owner: Jeffrey H. Herman with Febe (canine of unknown ethnic lineage)

Primary function: Will rapidly convert any phrase, sentence, paragraph, speech, or entire manuscript into phrasing that a classic writer would have used to say the same thing. Users will be able to choose any of the 500 greatest English-language writers who ever lived, including Shakespeare, Twain, Melville, and Wharton.

Possible defects: Early users might be surprised to discover that their writing isn't actually improved; it's simply converted into the way the selected icon would have expressed it.

The Biblio-Cerebral-Compression Bypasser

Projected availability: 2022

Initial price (in current dollars): $9,999.99

Inventor/owner: Jeffrey H. Herman with his large orange feline that frequently threatens to kill and consume everyone in his immediate vicinity

Primary function: Immediate consumption of any intellectual content through microscopic frontal lobe–implanted port, received via coded broadband-type submission. Everyone laments that they don't have enough time to read. That problem will be solved by this painless implant and the low-cost transmissions of everything that's ever been published. Every page of *Moby Dick* could be "read" and retained in less than 10 seconds.

Possible defect: Shiftless hackers might devise ways to infect the manuscript broadcasts with unknown viruses or random data, causing unsuspecting readers to become irretrievably insane.

The Biblio-Temporal-Quantum Amalgamator

Projected availability: 2023

Initial price (in current dollars): $9,999.99

Owner/inventor: Jeffrey H. Herman with Caruso, a very smelly and snotty black-haired feline of unknown origin

Primary function: The alteration of current circumstances into other desired conditions through the deliberate manipulation of perceptions and intentions. Doesn't everyone have regrets? Lovers who got away; roads not taken; bridges that have been burned; weight that was gained. The megaspeed quantum cerebrum molecular dispersion and recombination technology will enable people to readjust their karma at will without actually affecting anyone else's experiences. In fact, the user will remain in place to follow the same trajectory without knowledge of the shift, but now an entirely original consciousness will be manifested in accordance with the user's self-written script in a distinct loop, and he will have no recall of his other ongoing experience. Eventually, the program will include rapid time and place adjustments within the limits of the user's organic cell parameters. A later version will include the obsolescence of any physical form outside the user's perceptions thereof. A kind of immortality through endless do-overs is close at hand.

Possible defects: Biological and spiritual existence might be incompatible with what is essentially a repurposing of human consciousness without any reversion protocols. Perceptions of existence might be an eternally looping illusion of living, but in reality life will be completely absent. A lot of testing will be required before the process can be licensed for human consumption. Scientists are still debating if distinct loops can collide if inorganically provoked, which could destroy all matter. Warning: It has been theorized that this particular technology is already in use and has been adapted by many of us without our remembering it. If true, Dr. Deepak Chopra is correct when he says that "nothing actually exists."

Part 2
PUBLISHING CONGLOMERATES

THE BIG 5

Jeff Herman

The term "Big 5" has become the vernacular for referring to the largest book publishers in the US. It was the Big 6 until two of them, Penguin and Random House, got married in 2013. It isn't just size that qualifies for membership in this dubious collective. In fact, a handful of independent publishers are large enough (10-figure revenues) to be included, but several unique characteristics in addition to size separate the Big 5 from the independents.

1. Foreign Ownership

Most of the Big 5 are foreign owned, which is fully legal and transparent. In fact, more than half of America's book-publishing infrastructure is foreign owned. The foreign acquisitions commenced in the 1980s, surged, and then peaked in the early 2000s without much noise or pushback, and publishing wasn't the only industry affected. However, the Big 5 domestic operations have remained staffed by Americans, and the books are still mostly written by Americans.

Is massive foreign ownership something to be concerned about? I suggest we should be watchful without succumbing to prejudice or paranoia. Any country's culture is greatly influenced by the books its people read and write, so it should be disconcerting that foreigners have so much control over important aspects of our society. However, inordinate corporate control in general, regardless of address, should also be carefully observed.

If it's of any relief, pretty much all the attractive American fish have already been gobbled up. For sure, there will still be meaningful acquisitions and mergers over the next few years, but they will occur at a more modest pace and magnitude.

2. Books Are a Small Fraction of the Parent Company's Matrix

Most of the Big 5 are owned by companies for which books are a tiny fraction of overall revenues and profits. Massive and burgeoning commercial enterprises, such as cable TV, computer games, websites, pop-culture magazines, sports teams, music, movies, and much more, are where most of these companies live. Book revenues can't come close to these other income streams, and the imbalance will only become more pronounced in the future.

Most of the corporations are publicly traded, even if there's a "celebrity human face" at the helm. This means that important decisions must ultimately satisfy the board of directors and the major shareholders. Losing money, or failing to make enough of it, in the name of "art" or on the basis of editors' aesthetic tastes and hunches is unacceptable in corporate culture.

A natural question is: why do these multinational corporations want to own retro book companies? The answer: money follows power. Correct, few books make big money; but money isn't the only way to measure power. The top 20 percent of any country's population, in terms of education and income, are culturally and politically dominant. Even the most authoritarian governments must appease, manipulate, or intimidate this decisive strata in order to maintain power. The same 20 percent tend to be the most avid consumers of books. Therefore, book publishing delivers levels of influence, prestige, and credibility way beyond what its paltry revenues suggest.

3. Frequent Reorganization and (Too) Many Imprints/Divisions

It's the nature of multinational conglomerates to keep on eating, which is frequently followed by indigestion. As a result, each of the Big 5 is an obese amalgamation of programs with distinct traditions. Integrating the diversity of formerly rogue asteroids into cooperative orbits is never a simple task. To the contrary, it's messy and contentious. Competitive overlapping programs often end up in the same corporate "family," and because corporations abhor redundancies, perfectly viable programs are often suffocated. Many legacy brands within the Big 5 exist in name only and have ceased reflecting their storied histories apart from their inherited backlists.

What Does the Conglomeration of Publishing Mean?

1. *Less risk taking.* Editors are not encouraged to stray from the corporate mission, which is to make money or face the consequences.
2. *More "sameness."* What worked before becomes the model to follow until it fails, which causes less originality or anything else that doesn't fit proven methods.
3. *Steady irrelevance concealed by apparent success.* The lack of forward motion negates innovation, and banality is rewarded. Lack of competition enables domination of the bestseller lists and therefore compounds in-house complacency.

Suddenly, something fresh and better is born and must be killed, acquired, or copied, or else the game changes and power is shifted.

4. *You belong, or you don't.* In China, it helps a lot to be a member of the Communist Party. In America, it helps to be published by the Big 5. However, this being America, opportunities aren't monopolized. The independents, and self-publishers, will always raise their flags high.

THE LISTINGS

HACHETTE BOOK GROUP ❖ www.hachettebookgroup.com

237 Park Avenue, New York, NY 10017, 212-364-1200

Perhaps the French couldn't bear to be left behind. Hachette is a subsidiary of Lagardère, which is a huge France-based media conglomerate that bought the Time Warner Book Group (not Time Warner) in 2006. If you can't properly pronounce these French names, you shall be viewed with utter disdain. But it probably doesn't matter because they have left the US operations to the usual crew of American barbarians. The acquisition didn't allow the continued use of the Warner name, which initially confused people in the book business. HBG is much less fragmented than the other Big 5, because it doesn't have a long history of eating up other companies that were in turn eaten by even bigger companies. But it retains a handful of imprints and legacy brands with distinct missions and catalogs. The real question is the quality of food in the company cafeteria and executive dining room, which is beyond the scope of this book.

GRAND CENTRAL PUBLISHING ❖ www.grandcentralpublishing.com

GCP is the flagship imprint and the inheritor of the Warner catalog and tradition. Its name is presumably derived from the fact that the company offices are located on top of Grand Central Station. GCP publishes a large and varied list of hardcover and paperback originals.

Deb Futter, Editor in Chief. Major books.

Ben Greenberg, Executive Editor. Commercial fiction; pop culture, humor, music, narrative nonfiction, politics.

Mitch Hoffman, Executive Editor. Commercial fiction; narrative nonfiction, politics, current events, pop culture.

Amy Pierpont, Editor in Chief. Forever Romance line.

Helen Atsma, Senior Editor. Commercial fiction.

Michele Bidelspach, Editor. Forever Romance line.

Emily Griffin, Editor. Fiction; narrative nonfiction.

(Ms.) Alex Logan, Editor. Romance, thriller, art history.

Lauren Plude, Associate Editor. Forever Romance line.

Latoya Smith, Associate Editor. Romance, erotica, African American–themed fiction and nonfiction.

Sara Weiss, Associate Editor. Women's fiction; pop culture, food, current events.

Dianne Choie, Assistant Editor. Mystery.

Meredith Haggerty, Assistant Editor. Pop culture, popular science, investigative journalism/narrative.

(Ms.) Megha Parekh, Assistant Editor. Historical and contemporary romance, erotica, paranormal.

Allyson Rudolph, Assistant Editor. "Oddball" fiction and nonfiction.

Libby Burton, Editorial Assistant. "Edgy" fiction; pop culture, music.

Lindsey Rose, Editorial Assistant. Psychological thriller, suspense, crime fiction, women's fiction; popular science, pop culture.

Scott Rosenfeld, Editorial Assistant. LGBT fiction and nonfiction.

Grand Central Life & Style ❖ www.grandcentrallifeandstyle.com

This imprint includes books about wellness, cooking, diet, food, beauty, fashion, inspiration, and relationships.

Karen Murgolo, Editorial Director.

Sarah Peltz, Executive Editor.

Twelve ❖ www.twelvebooks.com

This boutique imprint publishes twelve (or possibly more) new books a year that are presumably extremely/especially/uncommonly special.

Deb Futter, Publisher.

Sean Desmond, Editorial Director.

Brian McLendon, Associate Publisher.

Libby Burton, Editorial Assistant.

Faith Words ❖ www.faithwords.com

10 Cadillac Drive, Brentwood, TN 37027, 615-221-0996

Like its corporate competitors, GCP recognizes the wisdom of keeping a dedicated Christian footprint far from NYC. Faith Words publishes an impressive list of well-known Christian celebrities and writers in fiction and nonfiction.

Christina Boys, Editor.

LITTLE, BROWN AND COMPANY ❖ www.littlebrown.com

LB's storied legacy can be traced to 1847 with the publication of *The Letters of John Adams*. I have not read that book and cannot comment on who the letters were for or about. Today it's a division within a division of a French-owned media conglomerate. Catering to the tastes of American readers, LB and its sister imprints don't typically publish dark narratives about the banality of humanity's existential temporal breakdowns, which explains why you would never know that the imprints are French owned. LB continues to be a prestigious publisher of excellent books.

Tracy Behar, Executive Editor. Health, psychology/self-help, parenting, reference, science.

Judy Clain, Editor in Chief. Literary and suspense fiction; narrative nonfiction.

(Ms.) Asya Muchnick, Executive Editor. Literary and crime fiction; history, culture, popular science.

Michael L. Sand, Executive Editor. American history, pop culture, food and wine.

Laura Tisdel, Senior Editor. Fiction; narrative nonfiction.

Mullholland Books ❖ www.mullhollandbooks.com

A boutique LB imprint dedicated to publishing "top" (meaning, expected to sell a lot of copies) suspense fiction.

Josh Kendall, Editor.
Wes Miller, Editor.

Little, Brown Books for Young Readers ❖ www.hachettebookgroup.com/kids

This imprint boasts a strong back- and frontlist of children's books through young adult, fiction and nonfiction, and most formats.

Andrea Spooner, Editor. Middle grade.

Alvina Ling, Editor. Middle grade.
Bethany Strout, Editor. Picture books, young adult.
Liza Baker, Editor. Picture books.
Connie Hsu, Editor. Picture books, middle grade.
Pam Gruber, Editor. Young adult.

HARPER COLLINS PUBLISHERS ❖ www.harpercollins.com

10 East 53rd Street, New York, NY 10022, 212-207-7000

Harper Collins is owned by News Corporation, which is technically Australian owned, but its founder and dominant shareholder, Australian Rupert Murdoch, became a naturalized US citizen in 1985. News Corp. is a huge international media conglomerate within which book publishing reflects a tiny fraction of revenues and an even smaller fraction of profits. News Corp.'s monetary heart and other primary organs are tied to its 10-figure Fox TV and film properties.

Rupert Murdoch purchased Harper about 20 years ago and has done a good job at making it into a commercially rational enterprise while still leaving room for important books that don't necessarily make any money. The firm is an amalgam of many legacy brands from the good old days of mom-and-pop publishing. As is often the case in corporate publishing, these brands are mostly maintained to give credibility and gravitas to the firm, even though the respective frontlists often have nothing in common with the brands' precorporate histories.

AMISTAD ❖ www.amistadbooks.com

Amistad publishes works by and about people of African descent.

Tracy Sherrod, Editor.

AVON ❖ www.avonromance.com

Avon has been one of the strongest brand names in mass-market romance and women's fiction for many decades and continues to claim a large piece of market share in these thriving categories.

Erika Tsang, Editorial Director. Romantic suspense, "dark, angsty" historical romance.
Lucia Macro, Executive Editor. Contemporary and historical romance.
May Chen, Senior Editor. Contemporary and historical romance, paranormal fiction.
Tessa Woodward, Editor. Books with "sexy, dark, dirty heroes."
Amanda Bergeron, Editor. Contemporary romance with angst and drama.
Nicole Fisher, Editorial Assistant. Sexy and contemporary romance.

BROADSIDE BOOKS ❖ www.broadsidebooks.com

Specializes in conservative political and public-policy books.

Adam Bellow, Editor.

ECCO BOOKS ❖ www.eccobooks.com

Formerly a small independent press, which was acquired by Harper in 1999; currently a "boutique-ish" publisher of wide-ranging quality fiction and nonfiction.

Daniel Halpern, Founder and Publisher.

Hilary Redmon, Editor.

(Ms.) Lee Boudreaux, Editor.

HARPER

The Harper imprint is the heartland of Harper Collins and has existed since the early part of the 19th century. Whether independent or corporate owned, it has always maintained a full range of quality fiction and nonfiction books and carries a deep backlist.

(Ms.) Terry Karten, Editor. General fiction and nonfiction.

Claire Wachtel, Editor. General fiction.

Jennifer Barth, Editor. General fiction.

David Hirshey, Editor. General nonfiction.

Tim Duggan, Editor. General fiction and nonfiction.

Michael Signorelli, Editor. General fiction; pop culture/celebrity stories.

HARPER BUSINESS ❖ www.harperbusiness.com

This boutique imprint specializes in hardcover business biography, memoir, narrative, trends, history, and cutting-edge ideas.

Hollis Heimbouch, Editor.

Colleen Lawrie, Editor.

HARPER ONE ❖ www.harperonebooks.com

353 Sacramento Street, San Francisco, CA 94111, 415-477-4400

Formerly named Harper San Francisco, this cherished imprint has deliberately been maintained on the "other coast" for more than 30 years. It publishes a deep list of serious books about religion, science, alternative health, and new ideas in business and life.

Genoveva Llosa, Editor.

Nancy Hancock, Editor. Health and wellness.

Roger Freet, Editor.

HARPER PERENNIAL

This imprint exists mostly for the purpose of reprinting Harper's successful hardcover books into evergreen backlist paperbacks. But it also publishes many quality fiction and nonfiction paperback originals.

Cal Morgan, Editor.
Eric Meyers, Editor.

HARPER VOYAGER ❖ www.harpervoyagerbooks.com

Voyager specializes in science fiction, fantasy, supernatural, and horror.

Diana Gill, Executive Editor.

HARPER WAVE ❖ www.harperwave.com

Wave is a relatively new imprint specializing in health, wellness, lifestyle, and inspiration.

Karen Rinaldi, Executive Editor.
Julie Will, Executive Editor.
Jake Zebede, Editorial Assistant.
(Ms.) Sydney Pierce, Editorial Assistant.

WILLIAM MORROW

Founded in 1926, Morrow is one of the major legacy names in American publishing. It continues to publish a vibrant and large list of quality fiction and nonfiction titles.

Cassie Jones, Editor. Cooking, practical nonfiction.
Rachel Kahan, Editor. Fiction.
David Highfill, Editor. Mystery, crime, thriller.
Kate Nintzel, Editor. Fiction.
Emily Krump, Editor. Fiction.

Dey Street Books

Dey Street Books is a new imprint formed in 2014 to envelop and displace the It Books imprint, which was launched in 2009 as a home for super-cool books. One of It's limitations was surely the unfortunate name. My first impression was that it was a special home for books by Cousin It and It's freakish cousins.

Harper's new headquarters (currently under construction) will be on Dey Street in lower Manhattan, hence the moniker for their newborn division. Dey Street is expected to follow It's footprints in publishing irreverent pop-culture narratives and edgy celebrity memoirs.

Carrie Thornton, Executive Editor.
Mark Chait, Executive Editor.
Denise Oswald, Senior Editor.
Brittany Hamblin, Editor.
Bethany Larson, Assistant Editor.

HARPER COLLINS CHRISTIAN PUBLISHING ❖ www.harpercollinschristian.com

About 10 years ago, Harper saw "the light," but not in the same way you might. They saw where the money was. The American Christian community is huge and loves books about faith. Harper knew better than to try to start a religion program from scratch and instead opted to purchase two of the most successful and long-standing firms in the Christian community: Thomas Nelson and Zondervan.

Thomas Nelson ❖ www.thomasnelson.com

PO Box 141000, Nashville, TN 37214, 800-251-4000

With roots going back to Scotland more than 200 years ago, Nelson may be the oldest Christian publisher in the world and probably has the biggest catalog. Originally known for its Protestant Bibles and church/Sunday school–related products, it publishes a large range of faith-based books for adults and children.

Brian Hampton, Editor.
Ami McConnell, Editor. Inspirational fiction.
Molly Kempf Hodgin, Editor. Children's books.

Zondervan ❖ www.zondervan.com

5300 Patterson Avenue SE, Grand Rapids, MI 49530, 616-698-6900

For more than 80 years Zondervan has been a powerhouse publisher of Bibles and Christian-themed books for adults and children.

Becky Philpott, Editor. Inspirational fiction; nonfiction.

Zondervan Children's ❖ www.zondervan.com/children.html

Kim Childress, Editor.

As would be expected, Harper has a deep children's program consisting of many legacy and relatively recent imprints.

Balzer + Bray

Balzer is best known for its beautifully illustrated and packaged children's books, middle grade, and young adult novels.

Alessandra Balzer, Publisher.
Donna Bray, Publisher.

Greenwillow Books

A well-respected boutique imprint since 1974, Greenwillow publishes quality books for children of all ages.

Virginia Duncan, Editor.

Harper Collins

Harper is the flagship within the flagship and the heartbeat of the entire children's program in terms of volume and depth.

Nancy Inteli, Editor. Picture books.
Kristen Petit, Editor. Young adult.

Harper Teen ❖ www.harperteen.com

This imprint was recently created to publish exactly what its name implies.

Sarah Landis, Editor.

Katherine Tegen Books

This is a boutique home for books that tell "meaningful stories with memorable characters."

Jill Davis, Editor. Picture books, middle grade through young adult.
Anica Rissi, Editor. Middle grade, young adult.
Sarah Shumway, Editor. Middle grade, young adult.

MACMILLAN PUBLISHERS ❖ us.macmillan.com

175 Fifth Avenue, New York, NY 10010, 212-674-5151

Macmillan is owned by the large German conglomerate Verlagsgruppe Georg von Holtzbrinck, whose name can't be memorized or said fast by Americans. The firm doesn't have any evident history in the chemical, plumbing fixtures, propagation, or armaments industries. Macmillan serves as the umbrella brand encompassing many other legacy US publishing brands that have been amalgamated and sorted in recent years as part of the corporate creative-destruction of America's publishing assets into foreign-owned vassals. Macmillan is a celebrity brand for book people, but its current incarnation is several generations removed from its origins as a powerful UK book publisher. Like a bouncing ball, rights to the Macmillan name have been bought and sold several times in recent years, and it has been permanently severed from its valuable catalogs. For several years the brand was simply missing and presumably forgotten. Suddenly, it reappeared as the name of the Holtzbrinck folks' US- and UK-based operations, probably because Americans couldn't pronounce its German name unless seriously intoxicated or while lifting a piano.

FABER AND FABER ❖ us.macmillan.com/faberandfaber.aspx

Faber specializes in books about the arts, pop culture, entertainment, film, music, and theater.

Mitzi Angel, Editor.

FARRAR, STRAUS AND GIROUX ❖ www.fsoriginals.com

This one is a jackpot brand universally recognized for discovering and nurturing excellent works by new writers. In 1946 the firm was partly founded by refugee Euro-Semites who dedicated themselves to publishing edgy new voices whose works may not have been welcomed elsewhere at the time. Its current program hasn't strayed, but it's no longer a particularly unique venue.

(Ms.) Alex Star, Editor. History, politics, current events.
Amanda Moon, Editor. Popular science.
Eric Chinski, Editor. Fiction; current events.
Emily Bell, Editor. Fiction.

FLATIRON BOOKS ❖ www.flatironbooks.com

Flatiron is a spanking-new editorially autonomous boutique imprint that will endeavor to justify its ongoing existence by publishing a full range of fiction and nonfiction books that enough people will buy.

Bob Miller, Editor.
Colin Dickerman, Editor.

HENRY HOLT AND COMPANY ❖ www.henryholtbooks.com

Holt has been a premier publishing brand since 1866. It still carries a strong reputation as a general fiction and nonfiction publisher with genres including mystery, thriller, social sciences, and current events.

Serena Jones, Editor. Science.
Caroline Zancan, Editor. Fiction; nonfiction.

METROPOLITAN BOOKS ❖ us.macmillan.com/metropolitan.aspx

This imprint was established in 1995 for the purpose of publishing fiction and nonfiction books with a slightly fringe or quirky orientation — just a little outside the mainstream but often perfectly conventional nonetheless.

Sara Bershtel, Editor.
Riva Hocherman, Editor.

TIMES BOOKS ❖ us.macmillan.com/times.aspx

This imprint is owned, or at least substantially controlled, by the New York Times. In fact, approximately half its books are authored by current or former NYT reporters. The imprint is entirely nonfiction and publishes the kinds of subjects you're likely to read about in the NYT, even if not authored by an NYT reporter, though politics and government seem to be dominant.

Paul Golob, Editor.

ST. MARTIN'S PRESS ❖ us.macmillan.com/smp.aspx

Here's another one of the well-respected publishing giants that's been conglomerated in recent years. SMP has managed to maintain itself as it was before the plague and tends to have much less editorial turnover/attrition than other publishing programs. In other words, it has been a reliably stable planet in an unpredictable solar system.

George Witte, Editor in Chief. Literary fiction; current affairs, investigative journalism.

Nichole Argyres, Editor. Literary and commercial fiction, mystery; narrative nonfiction, paradigm-changing ideas, women's interest, medicine, science, parenting, food, politics.

Elizabeth Beier, Executive Editor. Commercial fiction; problem-solving nonfiction, pop culture, cookbooks.

(Ms.) BJ Berti, Senior Editor. Craft, lifestyle, home, style, fashion, food.

Holly Blanck, Associate Editor. Young adult novels, romance, urban fiction, fantasy, women's fiction.

Brenda Copeland, Executive Editor. Commercial fiction.

Hope Dellon, Executive Editor. Contemporary, historical, and crime fiction.

Jennifer Enderlin, Executive Editor. Commercial fiction, including paperback originals.

Michael Flamini, Executive Editor. History, politics, nature, performing arts, food.

Katie Gilligan, Senior Editor. Commercial fiction.

Sara Goodman, Associate Editor. Young adult novels.

Rose Hilliard, Editor. Romance, women's and paranormal fiction.

Michael Homler, Editor. Crime fiction, thriller; biography, quirky narrative, popular science.

Kathryn Huck, Executive Editor. Commercial nonfiction, including current events, politics, lifestyle, health, pop culture.

Keith Kahla, Executive Editor. Commercial fiction.

Vicki Lame, Associate Editor. Women's, literary, and historical fiction.

Matt Martz, Associate Editor. Crime fiction; business, history, science, current affairs.

Monique Patterson, Executive Editor. Mystery, romance, horror.

Daniela Rapp, Editor. Narrative nonfiction, pets, history, popular science, travel stories.

Marc Resnick, Executive Editor. Military narrative, sports, adventure, pop culture.

(Mr.) Yaniv Soha, Associate Editor. Men's fiction; narrative nonfiction, pop culture, humor.

Charles Spicer, Executive Editor. Men's and women's commercial fiction, crime fiction; true crime, history.

Hilary Teeman, Editor. Wide-ranging fiction with strong female characters; popular self-help.

Jennifer Weis, Executive Editor. General and young adult fiction; health/medicine, women's interest.

THOMAS DUNNE BOOKS ❖ us.macmillan.com/thomasdunne.aspx

Dunne is a close sibling to St. Martin's, and they seem to frequently share each other's editors. Perhaps the single distinguishing aspect is that Mr. Dunne still exists and has been laboring as a hands-on editor since before being given his own imprint in 1986.

Tom Dunne, Publisher. British fiction; politics, history, science, current events.

Anne Brewer, Associate Editor. Commercial fiction; fashion, cooking, popular science, psychology, animals, unusual nonfiction.

Kat Brzozowski, Associate Editor. Mystery.

Peter Joseph, Editor. Literary, crime, and historical fiction; science, history, general nonfiction.

Rob Kirkpatrick, Senior Editor. Sports, pop culture, history.

Marcia Markland, Senior Editor. Commercial and literary fiction; animals, psychology, social/current events, women's interest, science.

(Ms.) Toni Kirkpatrick, Editor. Crime, women's, historical, and multicultural fiction.

Peter J. Wolverton, Executive Editor. Commerical and fantasy fiction; sports, outdoors, adventure.

Minotaur ❖ us.macmillan.com/minotaur.aspx

This imprint publishes many of St. Martin's and Dunne's crime fiction titles.

Keith Kahla, Editor.
(Ms.) Kelley Ragland, Editor.
Charles Spicer, Editor.

PICADOR ❖ www.picador.com

Picador was established in 1995 as an imprint for literary fiction and nonfiction. That doesn't sound overly innovative, but hatching imprints is how large houses try to refresh themselves and reward veteran editors who will never earn the salaries they would be worth in other businesses. Picador is also where all the Macmillan divisions repurpose many of their successful titles as paperback cash cows.

Stephen Morrison, Editor. Commercial fiction; eclectic nonfiction.
Anna deVries, Editor. History, science.
Elizabeth Bruce, Editor. Thriller.

TOR/FORGE ❖ www.tor.com

Tor publishes a premier line of science fiction and fantasy. Forge publishes fiction, including historical, thriller, mystery, women's, modern Westerns, military, and young adult novels, as well as some nonfiction.

Kristin Sevick, Editor.
Robert Gleason, Editor.
Paul Stevens, Editor.
Marco Palmieri, Editor.
Liz Gorinsky, Editor.
Susan Chang, Editor. Young adult novels.
David Hartwell, Editor.

PALGRAVE ❖ www.palgrave.com

Palgrave has English roots and is best known for publishing academic titles for educational and professional purposes. The firm was recently rebooted in the US as a base for titles about business, psychology, economics, and politics that can cross over from trade to academia.

Laurie Harting, Editor. Self-help business, economics.
Emily Carleton, Editor. Business, politics, government.
Elisabeth Dyssegaard, Editor. Science, history, current affairs.

MACMILLAN CHILDREN'S ❖ www.mackidsbooks.com

Encompasses many vibrant and deeply rooted imprints.

Feiwel & Friends ❖ us.macmillan.com/feiwelandfriends.aspx

Publishes across the board from prereaders to age 16.

Liz Szabla, Editor. Picture books and young adult.
Jean Feiwel, Editor. Picture books, middle reader, and young adult.

Farrar, Straus and Giroux Books for Young Readers ❖ us.macmillan.com/fsgyoungreaders.aspx

This program boasts a huge catalog of children's classics going back to the 1950s. Its frontlist program includes everything from preschool to young adult.

Janine O'Malley, Editor.
Wesley Adams, Editor.
Joy Peskin, Editor.

Henry Holt Books for Young Readers ❖ us.macmillan.com/holtyoungreaders.aspx

Holt's program is noted for its high-quality picture books, chapter books for young readers, and novels for young adults.

(Ms.) Noa Wheeler, Editor.
Sally Doherty, Editor.

Roaring Brook Press ❖ www.roaringbrookpress.com

This imprint was founded in 2002 and publishes for all ages. (Like me, you may be wondering how all these imprints manage to live with one another. The answer is, they just do, and the editors are glad to have their jobs.)

Katherine Jacobs, Editor.
Simon Boughton, Editor.
Emily Feinberg, Editor.

PENGUIN RANDOM HOUSE ❖ global.penguinrandomhouse.com

December 13, 2013, was perhaps both the most anticlimactic and the most meaningful day in the modern history of American and international publishing. On this day, amid the noise of Christmas consumption, Random House and Penguin legally finalized their friendly merger. It was a gentle event that the Justice Department seemingly ignored. The metaphorical equivalent of an old-growth forest abruptly collapsed in the woods. Everyone knew but no one listened.

In fairness, the handwriting had been on the wall for more than a decade. And there's still plenty of handwriting to be parsed about what might follow. There's still room for more compression both within and between the entities. Though both Penguin and Random House maintain a clear American footprint, don't be fooled. Ownership is primarily German and secondarily British, although a plurality, perhaps even a majority, of revenues are American. More important, book sales are a comparatively small fraction of overall revenues and profits for the corporate parent.

What follows is a breakdown of an especially large and fluid matrix of amalgamated divisions and imprints with ancient legacies and new mandates. However, the merger-digestion process is still in its early stages at the time of this writing, and it's possible that by the time you read this, seemingly safe programs will have been reverted to the dust from which everything derives.

RANDOM HOUSE ❖ www.randomhouse.com

1745 Broadway, New York, NY 10019, 212-782-9000

CROWN PUBLISHING GROUP ❖ www.crownpublishing.com

Until 1988, Crown was a thriving independent, family-owned house, and there was a noticeable measure of protest and concern when Random House announced its consumption of Crown. People understood that it represented an early stage of the Blob War against mom-and-pop publishing. Today, Crown stands as a large, autonomous division encompassing many distinct imprints. However, Crown is now simply a name without a trace of its former face or personality, which is par for the course.

Julian Pavia, Editor. Science fiction, fantasy, thriller, general fiction.
Rachel Klayman, Editor. Science, politics, current events.
Vanessa Mobley, Editor. Economics, current events, politics.
Kevin Doughten, Editor. History, current affairs, science, pop culture, health.
Amanda Cook, Editor. Science, current affairs, business.
Rick Horgan, Editor. Current affairs, business, health/fitness, popular psychology.

Alexis Washam, Editor. General fiction, mystery.

Tina Constable, Editor. Health, celebrity, popular psychology.

Crown Archetype ❖ www.crownpublishing.com/imprint/crown-archetype

This imprint appears to be a boutique pocket for high-profile, mainly nonfiction authors and subjects.

Suzanne O'Neill, Editor. Books by comedians, celebrity memoir.

Mauro DiPreta, Editor. Sports memoir, biography, and narrative; books by comedians, celebrity, current affairs, pop culture.

Stephanie Knapp, Editor. Current affairs, advice, sexuality, health.

Clarkson Potter ❖ www.clarksonpotter.com

This imprint has an impressive pre–Random House history. For many years it was where you'd find a huge array of frontlist and backlist books dedicated to food, cooking, lifestyle, craft/hobbies, decorating, and entertaining.

Rica Allannic, Editor.

Emily Takoudes, Editor.

Jessica Freeman-Slade, Editor.

Crown Business ❖ www.crownbusiness.com

Like it sounds, it's a boutique imprint specializing in high-end business books by authors with large followings.

Roger Scholl, Editor.

Talia Krohn, Editor.

Harmony Books ❖ www.harmonybooks.com

This imprint is a long-lived brand whose standing within RH has ebbed and flowed for years. At one time it was the designated New Age, spirituality, mind-body-spirit program. In recent years it tends to avoid fringe topics while focusing on acceptably alternative books about diet, health, relationships, culture, self-help, and popular psychology.

Leah Miller, Editor.

Heather Jackson, Editor.

Ten Speed Press ❖ www.tenspeedpress.com

6001 Shellmound Street, Emeryville, CA 94608, 510-285-3000

Many publishing professionals were sorry to see this formerly independent publisher fall into the corporate abyss. But that tends to happen when a firm's founder/owner retires, dies, or simply wants to cash out while he/she can. TSP was famous for its quirky and innovative list of books about food, careers, test prep, humor, health, and perhaps anything else you might think of. Lately, the frontlist seems to be mostly about food and cooking.

Julie Bennett, Editor.

Lisa Westmoreland, Editor.

KNOPF DOUBLEDAY PUBLISHING GROUP ❖ www.knopfdoubleday.com

Both Knopf and Doubleday are distinct legacy brands that ended up as part of Random House for different reasons at different times. RH never really figured out what to do with all its brands. After all, they pretty much do the same things, and it's difficult to keep them from creating fiscally wasteful redundancies, which is the kiss of death in corporate culture. RH may have solved the problem by crashing these two brands together without having to stop using either of them.

Alfred A. Knopf ❖ www.knopfdoubleday.com/imprint/knopf

The firm was founded by Alfred Knopf in 1915 and is still one of the few "Rolls Royce/Cartier"–level brand names in American publishing. Louis CK probably wouldn't get published here. People you have never heard of or stayed awake reading might be found here. "Smart people" have always been enthusiastic book buyers. In fact, they used to be the only book buyers. It's fitting that programs exist essentially for them.

Jennifer Jackson, Editor. Fiction.

Lexy Bloom, Editor. Fiction; culture, sociology.

Robin Desser, Editor. Fiction; memoir/narrative.

Victoria Wilson, Editor. Current affairs.

Doubleday ❖ www.knopfdoubleday.com/imprint/doubleday

Doubleday is one of the great publishing brands. Now it's just one of many brands that were long ago decapitated from their foundational souls. The brand has had a rocky tenure as part of the RH "family." But what is a publisher worth if it can't maintain brand value? The ironic answer is that few readers care who the publisher is when they buy a book; but it still means a lot to the people who work in the book business, especially authors and booksellers.

Melissa Danaczko, Editor. General fiction; science.
Bill Thomas, Editor. General fiction; current affairs, history, narrative.

Pantheon ❖ www.knopfdoubleday.com/imprint/pantheon

Pantheon was founded in 1941 by a German refugee and specialized in translating important books by an all-star international roster. The firm was acquired in 1961 by Random House for all the right reasons and was permitted to maintain its special vision for several decades. Though its frontlist has been significantly reduced in recent years, it's still an impressive destination for books.

Deborah Garrison, Editor. General fiction.
Erroll McDonald, Editor. Culture, science, politics.
Dan Frank, Editor. Current affairs, American history, science.

RANDOM HOUSE PUBLISHING GROUP ❖ www.atrandom.com

This isn't a doppelgänger. Situated within RH is RHPG. Within RHPG are several distinct editorial imprints, one of which is named Random House.

Random House ❖ random-house.atrandom.com

The RH imprint carries the glory and burden of the Random House history, which has been one of America's premier publishing brands since 1925. RH was a large independent firm until about a generation ago, when it was acquired by the Newhouse family. A few years later it was acquired by the German-owned media goliath Bertelsmann, which made a lot of money during the middle of the 20th century as the Nazi Party's exclusive designated publisher. This assignment was especially lucrative because buying the books was compulsory for millions of people. Not even Donald Trump can make people buy his books. Today's Random House has one of the biggest and most lucrative backlist catalogs in the world, and its frontlist always consists of a highly respected and diverse assortment of good books.

Andy Ward, Editor. Nonfiction, science, sports, business.
David Ebershoff, Editor. General fiction; current affairs.
Susan Kamil, Editor. General fiction; relationships.
Kate Miciak, Editor. Commercial mystery, thriller, suspense.

Samuel Nicholson, Editor. Fiction.
Will Murphy, Editor. History, current events.
Noah Eaker, Editor. Fiction; pop culture.

Ballantine Books ❖ www.ballantine.atrandom.com

BB was conceived as an innovative unattached firm in 1952 with what at the time was an unusual vision: specializing in mass-market paperback originals, which the old guard disrespected. There was a time not that long ago when paperbacks were the exception. Following WWII, publisher-entrepreneurs broke the cultural glass ceiling by placing paperbacks in unthinkable venues like grocery stores. Somewhere along the line, Random House gobbled up BB, and their destinies have been entwined ever since. BB continues to perform its primary purpose as a publisher of a wide assortment of popular fiction categories and some nonfiction, mostly in paperback. Several recognizable brand names prevail within BB, each with its own rich history.

Susanna Porter, Editor. Psychology, pop culture, narrative.
Kara Cesare, Editor. General fiction, romance, crime fiction.
Pamela Cannon, Editor. Cooking, food.
Linda Marrow, Editor. Mystery, thriller.

Bantam Dell ❖ www.bantam-dell.atrandom.com

If you're a little confused, just be glad not to be part of the management team that has to keep figuring out how to align, or keep alive, its wealth of Brahmin brands that have been amalgamated many times over. Both Bantam and Dell were formerly independent firms specializing in paperback mass-market fiction. That orientation prevails today, with a sizable assortment of nonfiction hardcover refugees that perhaps got lost in the hallway.

Shauna Summer, Editor. Women's fiction, romance.

Del Rey ❖ sf-fantasy.suvudu.com

Part of the Bantam Dell–RHPG–BB thing.

Michael Braff, Editor. Science fiction, fantasy.

Loveswept ❖ www.readloveswept.com

You won't find how-to books about death or taxes here, unless they include cleavage and abs. Women's fiction/romance, duh.

Sue Grimshaw, Editor.

Junessa Viloria, Editor.

Spiegel & Grau ❖ www.randomhouse.com/spiegelandgrau

The S&G home page declares, "We need books more than ever." Some years ago two smart veteran editors were given the space and budget to create and manage their own dedicated list. Large houses often do that as way to maybe shake up internal motivation and creativity, and it's possible something special will bloom. If it doesn't work they just shut it down and move any successful titles into an existing backlist program. Their site also states, "We aim to enhance each author's vision," which I'm sure doesn't mean to imply that no one else wants to do that.

Julie Grau, Publisher. Literary fiction; celebrity books, narrative nonfiction, prescriptive nonfiction.

Cindy Spiegel, Publisher. Groundbreaking nonfiction.

Christopher Jackson, Executive Editor. Literary fiction; narrative nonfiction, ideas, politics, pop culture.

Jessica Sindler, Editor. Big-idea concepts, inspiration, style.

Laura Van der Veer, Associate Editor. Humor, pop culture, food.

Annie Chagnot, Assistant Editor. Fiction; humor, self-help, inspiration.

RANDOM HOUSE CHILDREN'S BOOKS ❖ www.randomhousekids.com

RHCB is arguably the largest and busiest children's publisher in the known universe. Its list includes Dr. Seuss books (game-over), and there are several imprints.

Alfred A. Knopf Books for Young Readers

Full spectrum of children's book. The list and the brand were part of the original Knopf–Random House merger.

Melanie Cecka, Editor.

Nancy Siscoe, Editor.

Nancy Hinkel, Editor.

Allison Worthe, Editor.

Delacorte Press

Publishes a wide range of middle grade and young adult novels and nonfiction.

Wendy Loggia, Editor.

Beverly Horowitz, Editor.

Krista Marino, Editor.

Random House Books for Young Readers

The flagship imprint within the flagship program, this is where Dr. Seuss and Babar live. The program covers every category and age group.

Maria Modugno, Editor.

Michelle Nagler, Editor.

Mallory Loehr, Editor.

Schwartz and Wade

Established in 2005 as a boutique imprint specializing in highly designed illustrated books. Middle grade through young adult; fiction and nonfiction.

Anne Schwartz, Publisher.

(Mr.) Lee Wade, Publisher.

PENGUIN GROUP ❖ www.penguingroup.com

375 Hudson Street, New York, NY 10014, 212-266-2000

PG is the other half of the huge conglomeration of a plurality percentage of America's traditional publishing assets. Ironically, it's not American owned, even though most revenues are generated in America. Needless to say, every kind of book you can imagine is probably published by one or more of the numerous brands, imprints, and divisions found herein. Because there are many inefficient editorial redundancies, an abrupt downsizing and human-resource bloodletting should be expected in the near future, and will probably be announced on the Friday before a three-day holiday weekend.

AVERY ❖ www.penguin.com/meet/publishers/avery

Avery was acquired by Penguin in 1999. It had been a successful independent publisher specializing in alternative health and lifestyle books, and that orientation has been maintained.

Megan Newman, Editorial Director.

Lucia Watson, Senior Editor.

BERKLEY BOOKS ❖ www.penguin.com/meet/publishers/berkley

Berkley was launched as an independent press in 1955 to take advantage of the rapid swing to mass-market paperback publishing. As a consequence of its profitability, it was purchased and sold several times by corporate players. Its current mission appears to be consistent with its traditional strengths, though stand-alone hardcover and trade paper titles seem to randomly pepper each frontlist.

Cindy Hwang, Editor. Romance.

Kate Seaver, Editor. Romance.

Denise Silvestro, Editor. Alternative health, diet, food, relationships, popular psychology.

(Ms.) Leis Pedersen, Editor. Romance, mystery.

Wendy McCurdy, Editor. Romance.

Faith Black, Editor. Mystery.

Michelle Vega, Editor. Mystery.

Shannon Jamieson Vazquez, Editor. True crime.

Ace Books ❖ www.penguin.com/meet/publishers/ace

Ace was founded in 1953 as a science fiction publisher. Many of the classics that you have and haven't heard of still prevail on its backlist. The program has been eaten several times by corporations but continues to survive with minimal alterations to its mission.

(Ms.) Leis Pedersen, Editor.

Anne Sowards, Editor.

Rebecca Brewer, Editor.

Berkley Prime Crime ❖ www.berkleysignetmysteries.com

As the name implies, this is where Berkley places many of its mystery and crime fiction titles.

Michelle Vega, Editor.

(Ms.) Andie Avila, Editor.

Faith Black, Editor.

Robin Barletta, Editor.

(Ms.) Leis Pedersen, Editor.

NEW AMERICAN LIBRARY ❖ www.penguin.com/meet/publishers/nal

NAL was founded in 1948 as New American Library for the purpose of publishing new American voices and cool stuff from Europe. It went on to launch famous imprints such as Signet, which published paperback reprints of popular hardcovers. Like all good independents, the corporations couldn't keep their hands off it. Today it's simply called NAL and publishes a large list of mass-market and some selective fiction and nonfiction originals. In addition to Caliber and Roc (the specialized imprints listed below), its imprints include Signet, Accent, Obsidian, Signet Select, Signet Eclipse, Signet Classics, and NAL Trade Paperbacks and Hardcovers.

Claire Zion, Editor. Romance.

Kerry Donovan, Editor. Romance.

Danielle Perez, Editor. Romance, thriller.

Jennifer Schuster, Editor. Self-help, popular psychology, health.

Tracy Bernstein, Editor. Romance; parenting.

Laura Fazio, Editor. Romance, mystery.

Brent Howard, Editor. Science fiction; military history.

Caliber

Caliber is a small imprint dedicated to military history.

Natalee Rosenstein, Editor.

Roc

Roc is a small imprint dedicated to science fiction and fantasy.

Susan Allison, Editor.

Anne Sowards, Editor.

Jessica Wade, Editor.

BLUE RIDER PRESS ❖ www.penguin.com/meet/publishers/blueriderpress

Blue Rider was created in 2011 for the purpose of generating a special "high-rent" space for some of the veteran editors and their highly esteemed authors, fiction and nonfiction. Beavis and Butt-head memoirs wouldn't be appreciated here.

David Rosenthal, Publisher.

Aileen Boyle, Associate Publisher.

Sara Hochman, Editor.

Vanessa Kehren, Editor.

CURRENT ❖ www.penguin.com/meet/publishers/current

Current was recently created as a home for books about cutting-edge scientific, sociological, and philosophical ideas and discoveries.

Niki Papadopoulos, Editor.
Maria Gagliano, Editor.

DAW ❖ www.penguin.com/meet/publishers/daw

There must be a discernible difference between DAW and Roc, since DAW also specializes in science fiction and fantasy.

Sheila Gilbert, Editor.

DUTTON ❖ www.penguin.com/meet/publishers/dutton

Dutton's history as a major American publisher can be traced to 1852, when Edward Payson Dutton heard the calling to publish Christian books. Over the generations the firm has been resurrected and reincarnated many times. Today it is a premium imprint specializing in top-selling (that's always the plan) fiction and nonfiction hardcover books.

Ben Sevier, Editor in Chief.
Stephen Morrow, Executive Editor. Science, economics, psychology, investigative journalism.
Jill Schwartzman, Executive Editor. Pop culture, music, narrative.
Denise Roy, Senior Editor. Historical and contemporary fiction.
Jessica Renheim, Associate Editor. Mystery, thriller, crime fiction.

GOTHAM BOOKS ❖ www.penguin.com/meet/publishers/gotham

Gotham was launched in 2001 as, per routine, a way to carve out a special style and voice for original books. It must have succeeded at least to some degree because it still exists. Here you'll discover handsomely packaged nonfiction books on a range of commercial subjects, including business, reference, self-help/how-to, spirituality, sports, personal finance, fitness, and pop culture.

Lauren Marino, Executive Editor.
Charlie Conrad, Executive Editor. Investigative narrative, history, pop culture, sports.
Brooke Carey, Editor. Pop culture/entertainment, career advice, science, women's interest, relationships.

HUDSON STREET PRESS ❖

www.penguin.com/meet/publishers/hudsonstreetpress

Hudson was launched in 2003 as a boutique, high-end destination for commercial books about science, psychology, education, health, spirituality, and business.

Caroline Sutton, Editor in Chief.

THE PENGUIN PRESS ❖ www.penguin.com

This is the one that gets to use the flagship brand name, which has a distinguished history originating in London. Today's Penguin (US) was rebooted in 2004 as a home for distinguished nonfiction and a small number of fiction titles.

Ann Godoff, Editor in Chief. Fiction and nonfiction.
Scott Moyers, Editor. Current affairs/politics.
Ginny Smith, Editor. Fiction; health, culture.
Colin Dickerson, Editor. Historical memoir/narrative, culture, health, science.

PERIGEE ❖ www.perigeebooks.com

Perigee is like a melting pot for almost every kind of practical, or simply amusing, nonfiction.

John Duff, Editor in Chief.
Marian Lizzi, Editor.
Meg Leder, Editor.
Jeanette Shaw, Editor.

PLUME ❖ www.penguin.com/meet/publishers/plume

Plume was created in 1970 to serve as the paperback reprint division for New American Library. Its backlist boasts numerous classics. Today its frontlist serves a wide range of commercial nonfiction trade paperbacks and some fiction.

Becky Cole, Editor. Popular reference, humor.
Kate Napolitano, Editor. Business, current affairs, pop culture.

PORTFOLIO

Portfolio was established several years ago as a boutique destination for commercial books about business and investing.

(Mr.) Adrian Zackhein, Editor.
Niki Papadopoulos, Editor.
Maria Gagliano, Editor.

G. P. PUTNAM'S SONS ❖ www.penguin.com/meet/publishers/gpputnamssons

Now here's a big brand that was its own domain for more than a century and even had its own skyscraper. Now it's a brand with a marvelous backlist and a frontlist that competes for relevancy and uniqueness.

Kerri Kolen, Editor. Wide range of popular nonfiction.
Nita Taublib, Editor. General fiction and thriller.
Christine Pepe, Editor. Mystery.
Sara Minnich, Editor.

RIVERHEAD BOOKS ❖ www.riverheadbooks.com

Riverhead was created in 1994 as an editorially autonomous imprint for cutting-edge commercial fiction and high-end nonfiction hardcover originals. It has generated a healthy backlist and is a reliable producer of successful frontlist titles.

Rebecca Saletan, Editorial Director.
Sarah McGrath, Executive Editor.
Jake Morrissey, Executive Editor. Thriller; science, history, culture, religion.
Megan Lynch, Senior Editor.
Laura Perciasepe, Editor.

TARCHER ❖ www.tarcherbooks.net

Jeremy P. Tarcher founded his firm more than a generation ago in Los Angeles, where it thrived as a hero in the independent press community until he sold it and his services to Putnam in 1991. Then and now, the brand is a special place for new ideas about old issues, and old ideas that have been forgotten or neglected, including metaphysics and spirituality.

Joanna Ng, Editor.

VIKING PRESS ❖ www.penguin.com/meet/publishers/vikingbooks

Viking is also part of the 150-year-old legacy of great American publishing that is today a brand within a company within a corporation.

Patrick Nolan, Editor. Serious nonfiction.

PENGUIN YOUNG READERS

There are many vibrant historic imprints meshed here from both Penguin and Random House, and each of their antecedents. Significant consolidation is likely in store.

Dial Books for Young Readers ❖ www.penguin.com/meet/publishers/dialbooksforyoungreaders

Dial is a busy hardcover program of books for preschool through young adult.

Nancy Conescu, Editor.
Jessica Garrison, Editor.
Liz Waniewski, Editor.

Dutton Children's Books ❖ www.penguin.com/meet/publishers/duttonchildrensbooks

Dutton is the oldest continuously operating children's publisher in America. That may explain why Winnie the Pooh and his friends live here. Today, Dutton is a boutique middle grade / young adult imprint and publishes a relatively small list of new fiction titles.

Julie Strauss-Gabel, Publisher.

Grosset & Dunlap ❖ www.penguin.com/meet/publishers/grossetdunlap

GD tends to publish nonfiction paperback series for all ages.

Francesco Sedita, Publisher.

Philomel Books ❖ www.penguin.com/meet/publishers/philomel

Specializes in picture books for preschoolers, and fiction for middle grade through young adult.

Michael Green, Publisher.
Jill Santopolo, Editor.
Liza Kaplan, Editor.

G. P. Putnam's Sons Books for Young Readers ❖
www.penguin.com/meet/publishers/gpputnamssonsbooksforyoungread

This is one of the imprints blessed and/or burdened with a flagship moniker, in this case dating back to 1838. Today Putnam publishes about 50 new titles a year, all of which are hardcover fiction, from picture books to young adult.

Jennifer Besser, Publisher.
(Ms.) Stacey Barney, Editor.
Arianne Lewin, Editor.

Razorbill ❖ www.penguin.com/meet/publishers/razorbill

Publishes about 50 middle grade to young adult titles a year, both fiction and nonfiction. How many kids (or adults) know what a razorbill is?

Ben Schrank, Publisher.
Jessica Almon, Editor.
Rebecca Kilman, Editor.

Viking Children's Books ❖
www.penguin.com/meet/publishers/vikingchildrensbooks

Needless to say, there's a proud and rich history here. Today, Viking publishes about 50 books a year for prereaders to teenagers, fiction and nonfiction.

Ken Wright, Editor.
Kendra Levin, Editor.
Leila Sales, Editor.
Tracy Gates, Editor.

SIMON & SCHUSTER ❖ www.simonandschuster.com

1230 Avenue of the Americas, New York, NY 10020, 212-698-7000

Simon & Schuster was founded in 1924 by Richard L. Simon and Lincoln Schuster. The firm was sold to Marshall Field (the man, not the store, though he also owned the store) in 1944 and was repurchased by its founders following Field's death in 1957. It was sold to Gulf+Western in 1975, which morphed into Paramount Communications in 1989. In 1994 Paramount was acquired by Viacom. In 2006, CBS was split off with Simon & Schuster from Viacom and made into a separate corporation, though it is still part and parcel of Viacom (it confuses me too). The corporate situation has been uneventful since then. As revealed below, S&S is both an imprint and an umbrella for several distinct programs with varying levels of independence, and there are semiautonomous imprints within the divisions.

ATRIA PUBLISHING ❖ imprints.simonandschuster.biz/atria

Atria publishes a large and varied frontlist of commercial fiction and nonfiction categories and includes several specialized imprints.

Peter Borland, Vice President and Editorial Director. Commercial fiction; narrative nonfiction, memoir, biography, pop culture.

Johanna Castillo, Vice President and Senior Editor. Fiction, including women's, thriller, historical; nonfiction, including inspirational, self-help, Spanish translation.

Leslie Meredith, Vice President and Senior Editor. Science, nature, history, spirituality, religion, food/cooking, health/nutrition.

(Ms.) Greer Hendricks, Vice President and Senior Editor. Fiction; nonfiction, including memoir, parenting, health, beauty.

Sarah Branham, Senior Editor. Fiction, including mystery, crime, historical; memoir, cookbooks.

Sarah Cantin, Editor. Fiction, including historical, suspense; nonfiction, including travel stories, pop culture, narrative.

Donna Loffredo, Associate Editor. Nonfiction, including popular history, philosophy, psychology, health, food.

Todd Hunter, Associate Editor. Fiction, including political, suspense, mystery, thriller; African American topics.

Daniel Loedel, Assistant Editor. Fiction; nonfiction, including popular history, current events.

Daniella Wexler, Assistant Editor. Fiction; nonfiction, including humor, pop culture.

Emily Bestler Books

Wide range of commercial fiction and nonfiction categories.

Emily Bestler, Senior Vice President, Editor in Chief.
Kate Cetrulo, Associate Editor.
Megan Reid, Assistant Editor. Focuses on food, travel, fashions, arts.

37 Ink

Fiction and nonfiction titles with African American themes.

Dawn Davis, Vice President and Publisher.

SIMON & SCHUSTER ❖ imprints.simonandschuster.biz/simonandschuster

In addition to being the iconic name of the entire house (mansion), Simon & Schuster is also the name of one of its distinct divisions. Due to the rash of mergers, contractions, and nervous breakdowns endemic to the book business, there are numerous editorial overlaps and shared facilities, and even some healthy competition, between the divisions within each of the corporate entities. The S&S imprint's specialness is marked by the fact that it is the carrier of the nearly century-old name and possesses an immense backlist with many of the best books ever published in the US. In fairness, the same can be said of most of the legacy book brands. S&S's vibrant frontlist program can best be summed up as a wide spectrum of commercial fiction and nonfiction.

Alice Mayhew, Vice President and Editorial Director. History, politics, biography, philosophy, entertainment, pop culture.
Mary Sue Rucci, Vice President and Editor in Chief. Commercial fiction.
Priscilla Painton, Vice President and Executive Editor. Political biography, memoir, narrative, history, politics, science, religion, economics, US current events.
Trish Todd, Vice President and Executive Editor. Popular and literary fiction; practical nonfiction.
Robert Bender, Vice President and Senior Editor. Biography, autobiography, history, current events, popular science, film, music, business narrative, investing, baseball.
Thomas LeBien, Vice President and Senior Editor. History, "new idea/cutting-edge" subjects, science, business.
(Ms.) Jofie Ferrari-Adler, Senior Editor. Politics, current affairs, recent history, military history, sports, narrative/investigative journalism.
Sarah Knight, Senior Editor. Literary and commercial fiction, including thriller, crime, suspense; nonfiction, including memoir, travel and food stories, pop culture, satire.
Ben Loehnen, Senior Editor. Business, psychology, science, nature, religion, narrative style.

Millicent Bennett, Senior Editor. Commercial fiction; social and cultural history, science, women's interest.

Johanna Li, Associate Editor. Literary fiction; art and cultural history.

(Ms.) Sydney Tanigawa, Associate Editor. Literary fiction; science, history, pop culture.

Nick Greene, Associate Editor. Technology, business, culture.

Emily Graff, Associate Editor. Commercial and literary fiction; US history, current affairs.

Jonathan Cox, Assistant Editor. Commercial and literary fiction, including thriller, science fiction, fantasy; psychology, technology, business, economics, science, professional sports.

(Ms.) Brit Hvide, Editorial Assistant. Speculative fiction; pop culture.

Ed Winstead, Editorial Assistant. Literary fiction; Southern US culture and history.

Elizabeth Breeden, Editorial Assistant. Historical fiction.

Simon451 ❖ pages.simonandschuster.com/simon451

This new division commenced publishing in fall 2014. The program focuses on works of "speculative" (their word, not mine) fiction, especially fantasy, apocalyptic, horror, supernatural, and science fiction. The program's curious name must have "insider" meaning (maybe someone there is a devout Ray Bradbury fan?), or perhaps it was randomly selected by a nonsentient being, which is often how the best decisions get made.

Acquisition editors had not been hired as of press time, but unsolicited submissions were actually welcome, per www.simon451.submittable.com/submit.

Threshold Editions ❖ imprints.simonandschuster.biz/threshold

This relatively small imprint specializes in political, historical, and current-affairs subjects targeted specifically for so-called Conservatives. Glenn Beck: no-brainer. Joe Biden: not abided. The S&S editorial team acquires for the list; no editors are exclusively dedicated to it.

Touchstone Books ❖ imprints.simonandschuster.biz/touchstone

Touchstone can best be described as a fusion program combining frontlist original (fiction and nonfiction) titles and evergreen backlist cash cows. It's common for huge publishers to keep legacy brands alive, even if there's no unique purpose and substantial overlap with other imprints. You can never predict if new divisions will live or die, so bets are hedged through a process of cluttering clusters. Sometimes the new brands fail, and then the old brands become a welcome refuge for the surviving titles and editors, and vice versa.

Sally Kim, Editorial Director. Fiction and nonfiction.

Michelle Howry, Senior Editor. Practical nonfiction, self-help/how-to, personal finance, popular psychology, relationships, cooking, health, parenting.

Matthew Benjamin, Senior Editor. Narrative and prescriptive nonfiction, investigative journalism, diet/fitness, sports, men's interest, celebrity, pop culture, some illustrated titles.

Lauren Spiegel, Senior Editor. Women's fiction; pop culture, celebrity.

Elaine Wilson, Editorial Assistant. Historical fiction; food memoir, cookbooks.

GALLERY BOOKS ❖ imprints.simonandschuster.biz/gallery-books

This division was established from scratch about 10 years ago. Its purpose is to be a distinct platform for publishing "fresh voices" (picture a gallery with pictures) in both fiction and nonfiction, with a clear focus on pop culture, entertainment, celebrities, and multimedia tie-ins, which makes sense considering that Viacom is a sister company.

Louise Burke, President and Publisher. Major projects.

Jennifer Bergstrom, Publisher and Vice President. Major projects.

Karen Kosztolnyik, Executive Editor. Fiction and nonfiction.

Lauren McKenna, Executive Editor. Women's fiction, historical and contemporary romance; pop culture.

Alison Callahan, Executive Editor. "Ambitious" fiction; narrative nonfiction, memoir.

Mitchell Ivers, Vice President and Senior Editor. Commercial fiction; memoir, popular history, true crime, politics.

Jeremie Ruby-Strauss, Senior Editor. "Blockbuster nonfiction," celebrity, pop culture, diet/fitness, multimedia tie-ins.

(Ms.) Micki Nuding, Senior Editor. Women's, romance, and historical fiction; nondiet health subjects.

Abby Zidle, Senior Editor. Romance, suspense, thriller, women's and historical fiction; pop culture.

Ed Schlesinger, Senior Editor. "Dark" fiction, horror, science fiction, fantasy, crime fiction; media tie-ins.

Adam Wilson, Editor. Supernatural, thriller, romance, urban fiction, fantasy; pop culture.

Emilia Pisani, Assistant Editor. Women's and historical fiction; pop culture.

(Ms.) Kiele Raymond, Assistant Editor. Women's and historical fiction, fantasy; narrative, humor, pop culture.

Alexandra Lewis, Assistant Editor. "Upmarket" women's fiction, suspense, historical fiction; humor, pop culture.

Marla Daniels, Editorial Assistant. Romance, women's fiction.

Natasha Simons, Editorial Assistant. Commercial fiction; politics, current events.
(Mr.) Trey Bidinger, Editorial Assistant. "Dark" fiction, fantasy, science fiction, horror.

Pocket Books

Pocket has mostly reverted to its origins as a mass-market reprint program. Books that succeed in hardcover or quality paperback formats are often repurposed into less expensive mass-market editions where they prosper as backlist legacies, sometimes for eternity.

HOWARD BOOKS ❖ imprints.simonandschuster.biz/howard

216 Centerview Drive, Suite 303, Brentwood, TN 37027

S&S acquired this independent press in 2006 to gain a footprint in the vibrant Christian/faith-based publishing world and achieve membership in the Evangelical Christian Publishers Association. It's not by accident that the firm has been maintained in Tennessee, as opposed to being relocated to S&S's Manhattan headquarters. The program publishes a large list of theological, inspirational, and pop-culture titles in both fiction and nonfiction. Chelsea Handler's books wouldn't be found here. But *Duck Dynasty* titles thrive due to the Robertson family's frequent Christian-friendly references.

Jonathan Merkh, Vice President and Publisher.
Becky Nesbitt, Vice President and Editor in Chief.
Philis Boultinghouse, Senior Editor.
Beth Adams, Senior Editor.
Jessica Wong, Editor.
Amanda Demastus, Associate Editor.

SCRIBNER ❖ imprints.simonandschuster.biz/scribner

Scribner is one of the extra-holy names in American publishing. When it was founded in 1846 by Charles Scribner and Isaac Baker, the company had a religious orientation. Scribner's sons saw greener, secular pastures, and within a few decades the firm was arguably the number one publisher of nonreligious American literature, which explains why the name became Charles Scribner's Sons as opposed to "& Sons," I assume. The house also launched and managed its own bookstore chain, as New Yorkers over the age of 50 will fondly recall. The forensics for how Scribner became an S&S satellite is a little like tracing the mammalian food chain. In 1984 Macmillan ate Scribner. Several years later Paramount ate Macmillan. Gulf+Western ate Paramount, which then became Viacom, which ate CBS. The sons are long dead, so now it's simply Scribner, and it seemingly struggles to support its autonomy. Without notice, the corporate overlords might decide that Scribner is an unprofitable redundancy, and it will disappear; that's what happened to the Free Press several years ago. However, the Scribner name will always be repurposed somewhere in the realm of publishing, because it's essentially immortal.

Colin Harrison, Vice President and Editor in Chief. Current events, culture, politics, history, sports, science, true crime.

Brant Rumble, Senior Editor. Literary fiction; pop culture, music, sports.

Paul Whitlatch, Editor. Literary fiction, thriller; politics, business, technology, popular science, sports.

Shannon Welch, Senior Editor. Health, wellness, lifestyle, psychology, spirituality, environment, education, sports, inspirational memoir.

John Glynn, Editorial Assistant. Literary fiction. Sports, pop culture, health and wellness.

Katrina Diaz, Editorial Assistant. Literary and women's fiction; history, culture.

(Ms.) Liese Mayer, Editor. Literary and commercial fiction; social and cultural history, investigative journalism.

SIMON & SCHUSTER CHILDREN'S

S&S is especially noted for its large and wide-ranging children's program, which includes several distinct divisions/imprints.

Atheneum Books for Young Readers ❖ imprints.simonandschuster.biz/atheneum

Publishes a full range of picture books, middle grade books, and teen titles.

Caitlyn Dlouhy, Vice President and Editorial Director.

Richard Jackson, Editorial Director.

(Ms.) Reka Simonsen, Executive Editor.

Emma Ledbetter, Associate Editor.

(Ms.) Dani Young, Associate Editor.

Jessica Sit, Editorial Assistant.

Little Simon ❖ imprints.simonandschuster.biz/little-simon

Noted for innovative and attractive books for young children.

Mara Anastas, Vice President and Deputy Publisher. Media tie-ins and novelty titles.

(Ms.) Sonali Fry, Editorial Director.

Hannah Buschbaum, Associate Editor.

Lauren Bisom, Editorial Assistant.

Margaret K. McElderry Books ❖
imprints.simonandschuster.biz/margaret-k-mcelderry-books

A boutique imprint formed in 1972 by its legendary namesake. Well respected for a full range of author- and character-driven works for all ages in all formats.

Karen Wojtyla, Vice President and Editorial Director.
Annie Nybo, Editorial Assistant.

Simon & Schuster Books for Young Readers ❖
imprints.simonandschuster.biz/bfyr

That's correct, Simon & Schuster is also the name of one of its distinct children's divisions. Its large program covers all ages and formats. As mentioned elsewhere, it's common for large houses to maintain multiple overlapping divisions. In most cases, the divisions pre-existed corporate mergers, and allowing them to prevail makes the most sense. Also, it's a way for houses to hedge their bets in case any of the new divisions falter.

David Gale, Vice President and Editorial Director. Contemporary middle grade and teen fiction.
(Ms.) Zareerm Jaffery, Executive Editor. Commercial and literary fiction for teens and middle grade; teen nonfiction.
(Mr.) Christian Trimmer, Senior Editor. Picture books, middle grade and young adult fiction.
Kristin Ostby, Editor. Picture books, middle grade fiction and nonfiction.
Julia Maguire, Associate Editor. Picture books, novels.
Catherine Laudone, Editorial Assistant. Literary and fantasy young adult, adventurous middle grade fiction.

Simon Spotlight ❖ imprints.simonandschuster.biz/simon-spotlight

Focuses on licensed properties, brands, and original series in varied formats for all non-adult ages.

Mara Anastas, Vice President and Deputy Publisher.
Kara Sargent, Editorial Director.
(Ms.) Siobhan Ciminera, Executive Editor.
Lisa Rao, Editor.
Beth Barton, Associate Editor.
Christina Pulles, Assistant Editor.
Chloe Perkins, Editorial Assistant.

Part 3

INDEPENDENT PRESSES (US)

PLANET INDEPENDENT

Jeff Herman

Here's the other half of publishing. Any publisher, no matter how large, that's not owned by one of the Big 5 corporate houses is by default an independent publisher. Some of them are micropublishers with revenues in the four figures, and some are huge, with revenues well into the 10 figures. See my introduction to the Big 5 section (page 69) for a fuller discussion about what separates the two categories.

The number of seven-figure independent houses has greatly declined since I produced the first edition of this book in 1990. Most of those entities were merged into one of the Big 5, and some simply went out of business as their owners retired or couldn't make payroll. Losing those houses has had serious consequences for readers and writers. A huge portion of an invaluable subspecies of book curators has abruptly disappeared and not been replaced — and perhaps it can't be adequately replaced in the current environment. As a direct result, writers have significantly fewer traditional opportunities for publishing their work. However, there's always an upside: the partial extinction, combined with digital technology, has made self-publishing indispensable and inevitable.

Which Publishers Are and Aren't Listed Here?

I have made my best effort to include all the many independent publishers I'm sufficiently familiar with. I'm confident these houses represent a strong cross section of regions, specialties, and subcultures. I welcome your suggestions for additional publishers to include in future editions (jeff@jeffherman.com).

What Advantages Do Independent Houses Offer Compared to the Big 5?

Let's begin by saying that most independent houses are able to do everything the corporate houses do in terms of marketing, quality production, editing, sales, and distribution. It's unusual for the bestseller lists not to include a decent number of independently published books.

The primary advantage is that the vast majority of independent publishers are actually owned and operated by a select group of human beings, not 20,000 shareholders.

INDEPENDENT PRESSES (US)

111

Decisions are made on the basis of people's hearts and guts, not technical modalities. There are far fewer obstacles to editors' taking calculated risks and innovating, and authors are less likely to get lost in bureaucracy. Most successful ideas are generated and germinated by independent operators.

Independent houses are more likely to consider unagented/unsolicited submissions, for the simple reason that they don't receive as many agented submissions as the Big 5.

What Are the Disadvantages?

Frankly, I feel they are minimal. The primary disadvantage is that the Big 5 can and do pay large advances. The irony is that in practice this rarely happens. In fact, most Big 5 advances are on par with what the independents pay for comparable titles. More important, I'm not aware of any evidence showing a difference in total earnings (advance plus royalties) over a book's lifetime between corporate and independent houses for comparable titles. Nor am I aware of any evidence that the Big 5 sell more copies on average over a book's lifetime than the independents do for comparable titles.

Agents definitely prefer selling books to the Big 5 because the potential for a larger advance is always there, and each of the Big 5 acquires many, many more books than most of the independents can afford to.

Keep in mind that typical John Grisham, Stephen King, Danielle Steel, etc., fans neither know nor care who the publishers are. Readers are only focused on the author, not his/her publisher. They also care about price and perhaps what store they give their business to. Only industry insiders pay attention to who someone's publisher is. No writer should ever feel second-class because they are with a relatively obscure publisher. It's not a step down and might even be a step up considering the extra attention indy books often receive. As I said above, it's common for the bestseller lists to be populated by more than a few independently published titles. You probably don't know that because, like most people, you don't care, which further proves the point.

Independent publishing is one of the crucial safety nets against the industry's possible intellectual and creative suffocation. Current economic realities mandate the existence of multinational corporate empires. Naturally, these entities are no more or less enlightened than governments. Collateral damage only matters when it interferes with profits and market share. Destruction is laudable for the purposes of conquest and control. Innovations are driven by fear and greed, not generosity. One of Abraham Lincoln's greatest quotes was that people are more likely to be ruined by power than by adversity.

It's plausible that 10 years from now 90 percent of the book business will be controlled by three entities. In that case, the remaining 10 percent, and those who they publish, will be on the front lines in a war against conformity. Approach this section with the wisdom that independent publishing is both a practical option and a philosophical mission.

THE LISTINGS

ABBEVILLE PRESS ❖ www.abbeville.com

137 Varick Street, New York, NY 10013, 212-366-5585

Founded in 1977, Abbeville publishes fine-art and illustrated books. Subjects include design and decorative arts, fashion, jewelry, food, nature and gardening, design, film, culture, music, sports, and travel. Their website states that they won't be acquiring new projects for the "next several seasons." However, never say "never."

Susan Costello, Editorial Director.

ABC-CLIO ❖ www.abc-clio.com

130 Cremona Drive, Santa Barbara, CA 93117, 805-968-1911

This company is over 50 years old, and I don't know what all the letters actually stand for, which probably doesn't matter anyway. However, they publish an impressive list of reference and academic books for educators and students in all age ranges, covering many subjects. Their products are organized within several imprints and subsidiaries, some of which were formerly independent presses before being acquired by ABC.

ABC-CLIO/GREENWOOD

This imprint publishes a large list of books primarily for the educational and professional markets in such areas as history, humanities, military, and religion.

Cathleen Casey, Editor; ccasey@abc-clio.com.

PRAEGER

Praeger focuses on academic books about psychology, education, health, politics, current events, history, military issues, business, and religion.

Catherine Lafuente, Editor; clafuente@abc-clio.com.

ABINGDON PRESS ❖ www.abingdonpress.com

201 Eighth Avenue South, Nashville, TN 37202

Founded in 1789, Abingdon is the official publisher of the United Methodist Church. As would be expected, it publishes a wide range of faith- and curriculum-based books, including fiction. Its fiction program includes contemporary and historical romances, suspense, mystery, and Amish themes.

Joey Crowe, Editor. Nonfiction.
Ramona Richards, Editor. Fiction.

AMACOM BOOKS ❖ www.amacombooks.org

1601 Broadway, New York, NY 10019

Amacom is the publishing division of the American Management Association, which if taken literally sounds like its purpose is to manage America. It publishes an excellent list of books for business professionals about management, leadership, motivation, training, marketing, public relations, sales, customer service, and finance.

Ellen Kadin, Executive Editor. Marketing, career development, communications, personal development.
Robert Nirkind, Senior Editor. Sales, customer service, finance, project management.
Stephen S. Power, Senior Editor. Management, leadership, human resources.
William R. Helms III, Editor. Training.

ANDREWS MCMEEL PUBLISHING ❖ www.andrewsmcmeel.com

1130 Walnut Street, Kansas City, MO 64106, 800-851-9839

AM was founded in 1970 and originally named Universal Press Syndicate. The firm became extremely successful at syndicating a huge roster of illustrators, cartoonists, and columnists to an archaic physical-content delivery vehicle referred to as "newspapers." The book program was founded as an organic way to repurpose its talented clients. The firm is also famous for its calendar and gift book programs. In recent years, the frontlist program has been downsized to a tight list of mostly cookbooks and gift books, with some humor titles.

Patty Rice, Editor. Humor, gift, and illustrated gift.
Jean Lucas, Editor. Illustrated cookbooks.

BAEN BOOKS ❖ www.baen.com

PO Box 1188, Wake Forest, NC 27588

Baen is a veteran independent publisher of quality science fiction and fantasy books. The good news is that they actually welcome unsolicited manuscripts for acquisition consideration. However, they don't want it to be a particularly personal process where authors get to interact with real people — not a unique preference. The best method is to visit their website and follow the stated submission protocol.

BAKER PUBLISHING GROUP ❖ www.bakerpublishinggroup.com

6030 East Fulton Road, Ada, MI 49301, 616-676-9185

Baker claims to publish books that represent historic Christianity and the diverse interests of evangelical readers. The firm was founded in 1924 by a recent Dutch immigrant, Herman Baker, and became a thriving enterprise. Today's Baker comprises several imprints, most of which have their own storied histories.

Bethany House ❖ www.bakerpublishinggroup.com/bethanyhouse

11400 Hampshire Avenue South, Bloomington, MN 55438

Bethany began more than 50 years ago and is a leader in inspirational fiction, including romance and suspense. Its nonfiction program includes Christian living, theology, and "eternity."

(Ms.) Raela Schoenherr, Editor. Fiction.
Tim Peterson, Editor. Nonfiction.

Revell ❖ www.bakerpublishinggroup.com/revell

PO Box 6287, Grand Rapids, MI 49516

Revell has been publishing Christian books for more than 125 years. Subjects include inspirational and educational fiction, self-help, marriage/family issues, and youth books.

(Ms.) Lonnie Hull Dupont, Editor. Fiction.
Vicki Crumpton, Editor. Nonfiction.

BEACON PRESS ❖ www.beacon.org

25 Beacon Street, Boston, MA 02108, 617-742-2110

Beacon has been a breath of independent air since 1854. It currently publishes books that seem to be about causes, social conditions, theories, and events that have affected, or are affecting, our lives. Women's and environmental subjects are welcome. Health-care issues receive a lot of attention. Although it would be unfair to say that the firm has any political or social agendas, it's clear that many of their books wouldn't be welcome by the Far Right or fundamental-religious communities.

Helen Atwan, Editorial Director. Public health and legal issues.

Amy Caldwell, Executive Editor. Religion from a cultural and historical perspective, science and society, women's studies.

(Ms.) Gayatri Patnaik, Executive Editor. African American issues and history, LGBT issues.

Alexis Rizzuto, Editor. Environmental and educational issues.

Joanna Green, Associate Editor. Social justice, environmental, economic, and judicial issues.

BENBELLA BOOKS ❖ www.benbellabooks.com

10300 North Central Expressway, Suite 530, Dallas, TX 75231, 214-750-3600

BenBella is a successful, independent, outside-the-NYC-box boutique publisher. They tend to publish commercial self-help nonfiction books on timely subjects or by writers with self-marketing skill sets.

Glenn Yeffeth, Publisher.

Debbie Harmsen, Editor in Chief.

Heather Butterfield, Editor.

Erin Kelley, Editor.

Leah Wilson, Executive Editor.

BERRETT-KOEHLER PUBLISHERS ❖ www.bkpub.com

235 Montgomery Street, Suite 650, San Francisco, CA 94104, 415-288-0260

This successful West Coast independent press publishes an eclectic and interesting list of business-oriented books that large publishers might pass over for the wrong reasons. Their books are practical and traditional, and author "platforms" are of course critical.

However, if the late Abby Hoffman had written a real self-help business book, this is one of the venues he might have seriously considered.

Neal Maillet, Editorial Director.

BEYOND WORDS PUBLISHING ❖ www.beyondword.com

20827 NW Cornell Road, Suite 55, Hillsboro, OR 97124, 503-531-8700

Beyond Words has actually been a division of Simon & Schuster for many years and is referenced in the Big 5 section of this book under S&S. However, their origins are independent, and their current editorial process appears to be largely independent from that of their corporate overlord, so I've made an executive decision to also list them as independent. If you've heard of *The Secret*, you'll understand what this boutique player is capable of accomplishing; it's plausible that the New York publishing matrix would have reflexively rejected that book with comments like "trite" or "too down-market." BW tends to publish books that are generally designated as mind-body-spirit.

Emily Han, Editor.

BIBLIOMOTION ❖ www.bibliomotion.com

617-934-2427

Bibliomotion is a recent start-up by two industry veterans. They promise to provide a crucial competitive advantage by integrating the author into every aspect of the publishing process, whereas almost all publishers prefer the opposite approach. They also promise to help their authors understand and use digital marketing. Their list appears to be 90 percent high-quality self-help business books and 10 percent general parenting books.

Erika Heilman, Cofounder and Publisher.
Jill Friedlander, Cofounder and President.

BLOOMSBURY PUBLISHING ❖ www.bloomsbury.com/us

1385 Broadway, New York, NY 10018, 212-419-5300

Bloomsbury qualifies as a multinational independent press with active English-language programs in England, Australia, and India. They publish a varied list of mostly narrative nonfiction books that most sentient beings would be impressed by, even if not inclined to read. It's possible that many Bloomsbury books would be rejected by corporate houses as "noncommercial." Fortunately, the big players are often wrong about what books readers will indeed buy when given the chance.

George Gibson, Editor.
Nancy Miller, Editor.

CAREER PRESS / NEW PAGE BOOKS ❖

www.careerpress.com www.newpagebooks.com

220 West Parkway, Unit 12, Pompton Plains, NJ 07444, 201-848-0310

Career Press publishes the kind of business and personal-development books that real people (as opposed to MBA zombies) buy and read. Its hopping New Page division ranges from pedestrian self-help books about how to organize a traditional wedding to titles on how to organize Wiccan ceremonies. Anything you want to know about selling, extraterrestrials, and much more can be found here.

Michael Pye, Editor.
Adam Schwartz, Editor.

CENTRAL RECOVERY PRESS ❖ www.centralrecoverypress.com

321 North Buffalo Drive, Suite 275, Las Vegas, NV 89129, 702-868-5830

This publisher specializes in books about addiction recovery, behavioral therapies, and general wellness. I'm surprised the casinos don't run them out of town. But then again, it makes sense to have a place to refer "clients" to after they lose their shirts.

Nancy Schenck, Executive Editor.

CHELSEA GREEN PUBLISHING ❖ www.chelseagreen.com

85 North Main Street, Suite 120, White River Junction, VT 05001, 802-295-6300

Founded in 1984 (which, prior to 1984, seemed like it would be an important year), Chelsea is a top-notch publisher of books about sustainable/green living, which can be summarized as "consumption minus destruction."

Joni Praded, Senior Editor.
(Ms.) Makenna Goodman, Senior Editor.
Ben Watson, Senior Editor.
Michael Metivier, Senior Editor.

CHICAGO REVIEW PRESS ❖ www.chicagoreviewpress.com

814 North Franklin Street, Chicago, IL 60610, 312-337-0747

The press was founded in 1973, has nearly 1,000 titles in print, and owns five distinct imprints. Subjects include crafts, film, food, history, music, parenting, pop culture, popular science, sports, travel, women's interest, and children's books.

Cynthia Sherry, Publisher. Nonfiction children's books, travel, popular science.

Jerome Pohlen, Senior Editor. History, gardening, education, popular science, young adult nonfiction.

(Mr.) Yuval Taylor, Senior Editor. Music, film, history.

Lisa Reardon, Senior Editor. Children's and young adult nonfiction, parenting.

Lawrence Hill Books

This imprint was acquired by CRP in 1993. It was founded in 1973 in Brooklyn, NY, and is noted for its books about African American issues, urban subjects, civil rights, progressive politics, and history.

Cynthia Sherry, Publisher.

CHRONICLE BOOKS ❖ www.chroniclebooks.com

680 Second Street, San Francisco, CA 94107, 415-537-4200

Chronicle claims to have been born on the day that paper was invented in the year 105 CE, even though there's no record of the firm's existence prior to 1967 CE. The nature of their claim accurately reflects Chronicle's irreverent publishing personality. Though some of their books are arguably absurd, profits are a reasonable justification after the fact, especially if you're one of the company's owners. Here you will find a delightful array of cleverly packaged and designed theme-oriented books/products for children, adults, and anyone who likes things that are silly and/or useful.

Tamra Tuller, Editor. Children's.

Lisa Tauber, Editor. Adult.

Laura Lee Mattingly, Editor. Adult.

Steve Mockus, Editor. Adult.

Sarah Malarkey, Editor. Adult.

CLEIS PRESS ❖ www.cleispress.com

2246 Sixth Street, Berkeley, CA 94710, 510-845-8000

This publisher could also be named Over-the-Top or On Top Press. Cleis self-outs itself as "the largest queer publisher in America." But their catalog seems to have something for everyone and even offers a lot of books that aren't about orgasms.

Brenda Knight, Editor in Chief.

COFFEE HOUSE PRESS ❖ www.coffeehousepress.org

79 Thirteenth Avenue NE, #110, Minneapolis, MN 55413, 612-338-0125

I'm very happy that there's a publisher with this perky name. Coffee House is a nonprofit company, something many publishers would never admit to. They publish books, poetry included, that their editors deem to be genuine works of art. Guess what? There's a market for that.

(Mr.) Chris Fischbach, Publisher.
Allan Kornblum, Founder and Senior Editor.

DeVORSS & COMPANY ❖ www.devorss.com

PO Box 1389, Camarillo, CA 93011

Since 1929, DeVorss has been publishing books about metaphysics, spirituality, and New Thought concepts, which can also be captioned as mind-body-spirit. The company also distributes and markets titles published by others that are in harmony with its own catalog.

Sonia Dominguez, Editor.

EERDMANS PUBLISHING CO. ❖ www.eerdmans.com

2140 Oak Industrial Drive NE, Grand Rapids, MI 49505, 616-459-4591

Founded in 1911, Eerdmans is an independent publisher of Christian books ranging from academics to theology, Bible studies, and religious history and reference. The firm prides itself on publishing objective viewpoints throughout the "Christian spectrum" without favoring any Christian perspective. They also have a Young Readers program.

Jon Pott, Editor in Chief. Adult program.
Gayle Brown, Editor and Art Director. Young Readers program.

JEFF HERMAN'S GUIDE

120

ENTREPRENEUR PRESS ❖ www.entrepreneur.com/entrepreneurpress

2445 McCabe Way, Suite 400, Irvine, CA 92614, 949-622-3324

Entrepreneur Press is a division of the popular magazine named *Entrepreneur*. As would be expected, they publish books about zoology and proctology. That was a test to see if anyone actually reads what I break my finger bones writing. Per their website, their books "aim to provide actionable solutions to help entrepreneurs excel in all ventures they take on." In fact, they generate a rich assortment of cutting-edge how-to/self-help and reference books for anyone in business, even if not self-employed.

Jillian McTigue, Editor in Chief.

EUROPA EDITIONS ❖ www.europaeditions.com

214 West 29th Street, Suite 1003, New York, NY 10001, 212-868-6844

Europa is an independent publisher of literary fiction, nonfiction, and "high-end crime" fiction. Founded in 2005, the firm specializes in bringing some of Europe's best books to American readers, and vice versa. Authors from several dozen nations, including the US, are published by Europa. It's safe to assume that the firm favors books by Americans that will have international appeal and relevance.

Kent Carroll, Publisher.
Michael Reynolds, Editor in Chief.

F+W MEDIA ❖ www.fwmedia.com

F+W Media is essentially the holding company for a large collection of craft- and hobby-specific book, seminar, and magazine divisions.

Adams Media ❖ www.adamsmedia.com

57 Littlefield Street, Avon, MA 02311, 508-427-7100

Adams was acquired by F+W in 2003 and has continued its successful tradition of generating commercial self-help titles in most areas that typical Americans do or will encounter.

Brendan O'Neill, Editor.
Tom Hardey, Editor.
Christine Dore, Editor.

Writer's Digest Books ❖ www.writersdigest.com

10151 Carver Road, Blue Ash, OH 45242, 513-531-2690

For many decades WD has published a huge list of reference, self-help, and inspiration titles for writers about writing and publishing. Most writers are familiar with the magazine of the same name.

Phillip Sexton, Publisher.

GLOBE PEQUOT PRESS ❖ www.globepequot.com

246 Goose Lane, Guilford, CT 06437, 203-458-4656

Globe is one of the longest-standing and most vibrant independent presses. They were recently acquired by another independent publisher, Rowman & Littlefield, which is also listed in this section (page 136). As of press time, it wasn't yet clear how this acquisition would affect Globe's operations; the effects could range from substantial to marginal. So for the time being I decided to let the Globe listing stand as is, which includes not merging it with Rowman's listing. But be advised that the firm's structure will soon be in play. Currently, Globe's trade book program actually operates under the name Lyons Press and is best known for commercial books about history, pop culture, sports, nature, and general reference. The Skirt! imprint publishes books for the so-called contemporary American woman on such subjects as health, sex, psychology, relationships, family, cooking, and fitness.

Janice Goldklang, Editorial Director.
Mary Norris, Executive Editor. Health, wellness, diet, nature, pets.
Keith Wallman, Editor. Current events, sports, true crime, American history, military history, pop culture.
James Jayo, Editor. History, true crime, entertainment, adventure.
Lara Asher, Editor. Health, fitness, style/design, food/wine/cooking.
Jon Sternfeld, Editor. History, current events, sports narrative, true crime, cultural history, nature/adventure narrative.

GRAYWOLF PRESS ❖ www.graywolfpress.org

250 Third Avenue North, Suite 600, Minneapolis, MN 55401, 651-641-0077

Graywolf is committed to "discovering and energetically publishing" contemporary American and international literature (fiction and nonfiction). They "champion writers in all stages of their careers" and look for "diverse voices." In other words, this is a not-for-profit publisher that won't let potential lack of sales dissuade them from publishing what they deem to be great books. However, in practice, because their catalog is known to be carefully curated by exceptionally astute people, anything they publish is immediately considered to be wonderful by a core community of devoted readers; which is a little like running for mayor of New York City once you get the Democratic nomination. Of course, it's a subjective process, but like-minded communities are by definition homogenously subjective.

Jeff Shotts, Editor.
Ethan Nosowsky, Editor.
Fiona McCrae, Editor.

GROVE ATLANTIC ❖ www.groveatlantic.com

154 West 14th Street, New York, NY 10011, 212-614-7850

"An independent literary publisher since 1917." Several imprints coexist under this revered umbrella, though they appear to share the same editorial team.

Morgan Entreken, Publisher.
Otto Penzler, Editor.
Amy Hundley, Editor.
Peter Blackstock, Editor.
Joan Bingham, Editor.

Grove Press ❖ www.groveatlantic.com/#page=infogrove

Grove was founded in 1947 in America's bohemian heartland (at that time), Greenwich Village, and quickly made a name for itself by publishing numerous bad boys who used foul language, practiced unorthodox sexual methodologies, liked to induce hallucinations, and even tended to compulsively "typewrite" (meant as a cutting criticism at the time). Much ground has been covered along the road since then. In 1993 Grove and Atlantic Monthly Press merged their DNA to become a perfectly respectful and self-supporting publisher of wide-ranging fiction and nonfiction works that tend to have intriguing titles by authors with exotic or sensuous names, which you'll definitely want to read in the absence of noise or other enticements for nimble brains and bodies.

Atlantic Monthly Press ❖ www.groveatlantic.com/#page=infoatlantic

The only obvious distinction (in these times) between the Atlantic and Grove imprints is that Atlantic publishes only hardcover books, whereas Grove also publishes paperback originals and reprints.

Here you will find hard-core noir and adrenaline stimulation, both the old-time classics and new titles by those who dare to attempt following in their footsteps.

HARLEQUIN ❖ www.harlequin.com

223 Broadway, Suite 1001, New York, NY 10279, 212-553-4200

Harlequin is by far the largest publisher of category/genre romance novels on Earth (which is the limit of their authorized distribution). They also publish a modest list of self-help and reference books oriented toward women. They appear to have a dedicated imprint for every romance subcategory you can think of, from African American to "wholesome," though there doesn't seem to be anything for the fast-growing Hasidic community. They genuinely welcome manuscript submissions from complete strangers, and the best process might be to read and follow the submission guidelines posted on their website. I suggest this conservative approach because there are dozens of distinct theme-based imprints and perhaps several dozen editors; that's a tough maze to navigate if you're going rogue without an agent. And unlike most publishers, they seem to actually screen the proverbial slush pile for prospects, probably due to the huge volume of new titles they keep churning out.

THE HARVARD COMMON PRESS ❖ www.harvardcommonpress.com

535 Albany Street, Boston, MA 02118, 617-423-5803

This company has nothing to do with Harvard University, and it probably took early search engines a while to figure that out. Its first location in 1976 was on the town square in Harvard, Massachusetts (located, incidentally, about 30 miles from Harvard University, in Cambridge), which explains the name. Over the years they have earned a well-deserved reputation for high-quality cookbooks. They also publish excellent childbirth and parenting titles.

Bruce Shaw, Publisher.

HARVEST HOUSE ❖ www.harvesthousepublishers.com

990 Owen Loop North, Eugene, OR 97402, 800-547-8979

From the publisher's Mission Statement: "To glorify God by providing high-quality books and products that affirm biblical values…and proclaim Jesus Christ as the answer to every human need." This nondenominational Christian press publishes a large list of practical and accessible self-help books for adults and children about how to confront life's challenges in Christian ways. They also publish inspirational fiction.

Kathleen Kerr, Editor. Parenting.
Kim Moore, Editor. Inspirational.
Terry Glaspy, Editor. Inspirational fiction.

HAY HOUSE ❖ www.hayhouse.com

PO Box 5100, Carlsbad, CA 92018, 760-431-7695

Hay House is a pacesetter in the mind-body-spirit book categories. Many of the most financially successful self-help gurus are published by Hay House (not to be confused with their subsidy/vanity division, Balboa Press).

Michelle Pilley, Editor.
Patty Gift, Editor.

HAZELDEN PUBLISHING ❖

www.hazelden.org/web/public/publishing.page

PO Box 176, Center City, MN 55012, 651-213-4213

Hazelden's stated mission is to help people recognize, understand, and overcome addiction and related problems and challenges. This is the in-house publishing arm of one of the most respected and pioneering recovery facilities in the world. Their books are consistent with the proverbial 12-step approach.

Sid Farrar, Editor.

HEALTH COMMUNICATIONS, INC. ❖ www.hcibooks.com

3201 SW 15th Street, Deerfield Beach, FL 33442, 945-360-0909

"Changing lives one book at a time" (from publisher's website), HCI claims to select books that help readers achieve abundance, consolation, and healing through a huge range of self-help subjects for adults and teens. HCI enjoyed many years in the sun publishing the *Chicken Soup for the Soul* series.

Allison Janse, Editor.

HIPPOCRENE BOOKS ❖ www.hippocrenebooks.com

171 Madison Avenue, New York, NY 10016, 212-685-4373

For more than 40 years, Hippocrene has been a leading publisher of ethnic-food cookbooks, foreign-language dictionaries, and translations.

Anne McBride, Editor in Chief.

HOUGHTON MIFFLIN HARCOURT ❖ www.houghtonmifflinbooks.com

222 Berkeley Street, Boston, MA 02116, 617-351-5000
215 Park Avenue South, New York, NY 10003, 212-420-5800

HMH is an amalgamation of several revered houses. It qualifies as one of the largest independent firms, as opposed to a corporate firm, because its owners only publish books; there are no other, more lucrative priorities. They publish a wide commercial list of fiction and nonfiction for adults and children.

Justin Schwartz, Editor. Cookbooks.
Susan Canavan, Editor. Fiction; narrative sports, history.
Jenna Johnson, Editor. Fiction.
Bruce Nichols, Editor. Political history, current events.
Lisa White, Editor. Nature.
Lauren Wein, Editor. Fiction.
(Ms.) Courtney Young, Editor. Popular psychology and science, economics.
Deanne Urmy, Editor. Politics, current affairs.
Andrea Schulz, Editor. Fiction; politics.

HOUGHTON MIFFLIN CHILDREN'S

Margaret Raymo, Editor. Picture books, young adult.
Ann Rider, Editor. Picture books, middle grade.
Kate O'Sullivan, Editor. Picture books, young adult.

Clarion

Dinah Stevenson, Editor. Picture books.
Lynne Polvino, Editor. Middle grade.
Anne Hoppe, Editor. Picture books, young adult.
Jennifer Green, Editor. Picture books.

HUMAN KINETICS PUBLISHERS, INC. ❖ www.humankinetics.com

PO Box 5076, Champaign, IL 61825

HK is a well-established publisher of books, journals, and educational content relevant to health, physical education, sport sciences, recreation, and dance.

acquisitions@hkusa.com

INNER TRADITIONS / BEAR & COMPANY ❖ www.innertraditions.com

PO Box 388, 1 Park Street, Rochester, VT 05767, 802-767-3174

For more than 30 years, these two recently merged firms have published a rich list of books about ancient mysteries, Celtic studies, Eastern religions, healing arts, martial arts, Tantra, tarot, and many related subjects.

Jon Graham, Editor.

KENSINGTON PUBLISHING ❖ www.kensingtonbooks.com

119 West 40th Street, New York, NY 10018, 800-221-2647

Founded in 1974, Kensington is one of the largest independent publishing houses in the US today, best known for its dense lists of category/genre fiction and some nonfiction, all divided into several imprints.

Dafina

African American–themed romance titles.

Selena James, Editor.

Kensington

Kensington covers the whole waterfront of category commercial fiction.

John Scognamiglio, Editor. Mystery, romance.
Alicia Condon, Editor. Romance.
(Ms.) Esi Sogah, Editor. Romance.
Michaela Hamilton, Editor. Mystery, thriller; true crime.
Martin Biro, Editor. Romance.
Peter Senftleben, Editor. Romance, horror.
Gary Goldstein, Editor. Thriller, mystery.

LLEWELLYN WORLDWIDE ❖ www.llewellyn.com

2143 Wooddale Drive, Woodbury, MN 55125, 651-291-1970

Founded in 1901, Llewellyn is one of the largest independent mind-body-spirit publishers. Specific topics include Wiccan, New Age, metaphysics, and wellness.

Amy Glazer, Editor.
Elysia Gallo, Editor.
Angela Wix, Editor.

MCGRAW-HILL PROFESSIONAL ❖ www.mhprofessional.com

2 Penn Plaza, New York, NY 10121, 212-512-2000

McGraw-Hill is a huge corporation comprising many nonbook divisions. However, everything the firm does is dedicated to generating and distributing content for educators and professionals about many subjects, and their trade book program continues to be an important piece of the corporate matrix. They publish a wide list of titles relevant to all areas of business, personal finance, investing, and entrepreneurship.

Mary Glenn, Publisher. Management and finance.
Donya Dickerson, Senior Editor. Marketing and sales.
Knox Huston, Senior Editor. Leadership, management, investment.
Tom Miller, Senior Editor. Technology, social media.
(Ms.) Casey Ebro, Editor. Popular business, how-to, reference.

MILKWEED EDITIONS ❖ www.milkweed.org

1011 Washington Avenue South, Suite 300, Minneapolis, MN 55415, 612-332-3192

Founded in 1980, Milkweed calls itself an independent publisher of literature and proclaims that its purpose is to "identify, nurture and publish transformative literature [poetry, fiction and nonfiction, and young adult], and build an engaged community around it." The company depends on donations in addition to revenues for its survival. Having that safety net obviously enables its editors to be extra-risky and not entirely beholden to traditional profit-and-loss protocols.

Daniel Slager, Publisher.

MOODY PUBLISHERS ❖ www.moodypublishers.com

820 North LaSalle Boulevard, Chicago, IL 60610, 800-678-8812

According to its website, Moody's purpose is "to proclaim the gospel of Jesus Christ in such powerful ways that people worldwide will live in increasing measure as His fully devoted followers, and to evangelize non-Christians by ethically publishing conservative, evangelical Christian literature for all ages." The Moody umbrella includes several special imprints that focus on specific fiction and nonfiction themes, communities, and categories.

For best results, writers should consult the submission guidelines on the publisher's website.

NAVAL INSTITUTE PRESS ❖ www.usni.org

291 Wood Road, Annapolis, MD 21402, 410-268-6110

From the website: "to advance the professional, literary and scientific understanding of sea power and issues critical to national defense and its historic traditions." Though the press is entirely independent of the Defense Department, its primary markets are the Navy, merchant marines, and relevant communities. Their biggest commercial success was as Tom Clancy's original fiction publisher (he was a Navy alumnus).

Richard Latture, Editor in Chief.

NEW HARBINGER PUBLICATIONS ❖ www.newharbinger.com

5674 Shattuck Avenue, Oakland, CA 94609, 800-748-6273

New Harbinger prides itself on generating a primo catalog of scientifically sound yet cutting-edge self-help books in many areas of physical and mental health and personal growth.

Wendy Millstine, Editor.
Melissa Kirk, Editor.
Angela Autry Gordon, Editor.

NEW HORIZON PRESS ❖ www.newhorizonpressbooks.com

PO Box 669, Far Hills, NJ 07931, 908-604-6311

NHP focuses on true crime, "battles for justice," medical drama, incredible true stories, women's and men's interest, and parenting. Many of its books are optioned for TV movies.

Joan Dunphy, Publisher.

NEW WORLD LIBRARY ❖ www.newworldlibrary.com

14 Pamaron Way, Novato, CA 94949, 415-884-2100

In 1977, on a kitchen table, Whatever Publishing was born. Today it's an eight-figure enterprise. The firm publishes about three dozen new titles each year in the areas of personal consciousness, personal growth, creativity, prosperity, philosophy, spirituality, wellness, nature/environment, and many related subjects — even book publishing.

Georgia Hughes, Editorial Director.
Jason Gardner, Senior Editor.

W. W. NORTON & COMPANY, INC. ❖ www.wwnorton.com

500 Fifth Avenue, New York, NY 10110, 212-354-5500

What began in someone's living room more than 90 years ago has become the largest publishing company entirely owned by its employees. That sounds like a kibbutz, though I'm sure there's an economic/political hierarchy. The firm strives to publish books about influential issues and events that cross into all conceivable areas of human endeavor and discovery. If the Public Broadcasting System had a book division, Norton might be it. They also publish a respected fiction list.

Matt Weiland, Editor. History, literary biography.
John Glusman, Editor. Military and political history.
Brendan Curry, Editor. Current events, political history.
Maria Guarnaschelli, Editor. Unusual food and cookbooks, cultural history.
Jill Bialosky, Editor. Fiction; science.
Jeff Shreve, Editor. Science.
Tom Mayer, Editor. Fiction.
Alane Mason, Executive Editor. Cultural and political history.

THE OVERLOOK PRESS ❖ www.overlookpress.com

141 Wooster Street, New York, NY 10012, 212-673-2526

Overlook successfully publishes a large, eclectic list of fiction and nonfiction titles in such areas as history and culture.

Dan Crissman, Editor. Historical/political biography, current events.
Mark Krotov, Editor. Fiction; history.

PAULIST PRESS ❖ www.paulistpress.com

997 Macarthur Boulevard, Mahwah, NJ 07430, 800-218-1903

According to its website, Paulist "publishes the best in Catholic thought since 1972." The company is part of the Paulist Fathers and strives to bring Catholic-based education, wisdom, healing, growth, and inspiration to all peoples.

Rev. Mark-David Janus, CSP, Editorial Director.
Donna Crilly, Managing Editor.

PEACHTREE PUBLISHERS ❖ www.peachtree-online.com

1700 Chattahoochee Avenue, Atlanta, GA 30318, 404-876-8761

Peachtree publishes quality children's books, from picture books to young adult fiction and nonfiction. In adult categories they publish titles about parenting, health, and anything about the American South.

Helen Harris, Acquisitions Editor.

PELICAN PUBLISHING COMPANY ❖ www.pelicanpub.com

1000 Burmaster Street, Gretna, LA 70053, 504-368-1175

Pelican is best known for travel guides, architectural reviews, holiday-themed books, specialized cookbooks, some fiction, and children's books. As might be expected, many of its titles are relevant to the Gulf Coast. In fact, surviving natural disasters, not to mention the economy, has often been the company's greatest challenge.

Nicola Martinez, Editor.

THE PERMANENT PRESS ❖ www.thepermanentpress.com

4170 Noyac Road, Sag Harbor, NY 11963, 631-725-1101

Since 1978, this micropublisher sustains itself by publishing literary fiction, and some nonfiction, that serious readers can't ignore. Near zero capitalization has never been a worthy excuse for failure in the book business, for the simple reason that quality will outlast all the hype that money can buy. The key has always been patience and the ability to resist making risky expenditures. During times of easy credit it's only too easy to overspend and overborrow, which is why so many worthy independent presses ultimately disappear. We should all pay attention to why some small presses, like this one, prevail.

Judith Shepard, Publisher.

THE PERSEUS BOOKS GROUP ❖ www.perseusbooksgroup.com
212-340-8100

Perseus is a large constellation defined by its many destinations, otherwise known as imprints. Perseus is owned by an ambitious investment group that has successfully acquired and reorganized a litany of independent presses while allowing its conquests to maintain their basic identity and autonomy. You can think of Perseus as being like the Brady Bunch.

Basic Books ❖ www.basicbooks.com
250 West 57th Street, New York, NY 10107, 212-340-8136

Since 1952, Basic has helped shape and inform many conversations and debates in the areas of history, science, sociology, psychology, politics, and current affairs. Basic Civitas is an imprint within the imprint specializing in African and African American studies.

Lara Heimert, Publisher. General history, culinary history, politics.
(Mr.) TJ Kelleher, Senior Executive Editor. Science, natural history, computer science, economics.
(Mr.) Alex Littlefield, Senior Editor. Politics, economics, current affairs, history, gardening.
Alison MacKeen, Senior Editor. Social sciences, health, media, technology, parenting, urbanism, education.
Dan Gerstle, Associate Editor. History, culture, ideas, current events, and sports.
Katy O'Donnell, Associate Editor. Social, cultural, and sports history.

Da Capo Press ❖ www.perseusbooksgroup.com/dacapo
250 West 57th Street, 15th Floor, New York, NY 10107, 212-340-8100

Da Capo continues its long history of publishing books about general history, pop culture, music, sports, and popular business. Da Capo Lifelong Books — again, an imprint within an imprint — specializes in pregnancy, parenting, health, fitness, and relationships.

Renee Sedliar, Editor. Health, fitness, cooking, spiritual wellness.
Robert Pigeon, Editor. History, politics, current affairs.
Ben Schafer, Editor. Culture, entertainment, music, media.
Dan Ambrosio, Editor. Popular business, advice, self-improvement.

Public Affairs (includes Nation Books) ❖ www.publicaffairsbooks.com

250 West 57th Street, 15th Floor, New York, NY 10107, 212-340-8100

As implied by its distinctive name, Public Affairs publishes books about current events, government, economics, politics, foreign affairs, and investigative journalism/narrative. The Nation Books division has an even stronger focus on journalistic exposés about important issues and is associated with *The Nation* magazine.

Susan Weinberg, Group Publisher.
Clive Priddle, Publisher.
Peter Osnos, Founder and Editor-at-Large.
Lisa Kaufman, Senior Editor.

Running Press ❖ www.perseusbooksgroup.com/runningpress

2300 Chestnut Street, Suite 200, Philadelphia, PA 19103, 215-567-5080

Since 1972, Running Press has been an innovative book packager and merchandiser, meaning that many of their books are unconventionally designed and often show up where other books don't. "Impulse" or "gift" describes their distinctive formula, though conventional is also welcome. They generate a varied list of adult and children's titles in such areas as pop culture, humor, food and cooking, crafts, and lifestyle.

Kristen Green Wiewora, Editor. Cooking, crafts.
Jordana Tusman, Editor. Humor, parenting, pop culture.
Cindy De La Hoz, Editor. Relationships, parenting, women's self-help.

Seal Press ❖ www.sealpress.com

1700 Fourth Street, Berkeley, CA 94710, 510-595-3664

According to Seal's website, "A book can change a woman's life." I bet people already know that, and I also bet that men are equally susceptible. But the real point is that Seal's books aim to support "women of all ages and backgrounds." They publish self-help and narrative books for and about women. My understanding is that male writers should not apply, regardless of content, which strikes me as an archaic, if not illegal, restriction. But they will work with male agents, and I've never held back from pitching them appropriate projects or shaking hands with their editors at conferences; nor should you.

Laura Mazer, Editor.

POMEGRANATE COMMUNICATIONS, INC. ❖ www.pomegranate.com
19018 NE Portal Way, Portland, OR 97230, 503-328-6500

Pomegranate isn't an ordinary book publisher. In fact, it seems that most of their products can't be defined as books even though they are made out of paper, like posters, prints, and puzzles. Museum and general gift shops seem to be their primary venues. But there are a lot of interesting and unusual book products here that are bookstore-friendly.

Katherine Burke, Editor.

PROMETHEUS BOOKS ❖ www.prometheusbooks.com
59 John Glenn Drive, Amherst, NY 14228, 716-691-0133

Prometheus defines itself as a leading publisher of popular science, philosophy, humanism, psychology, and perhaps any other topic you can think of. In actuality, this is a somewhat controversial publisher that tends to publish deliberately confrontational and provocative content. For instance, if you want to challenge organized religion, New Age concepts, or unproven alternative-health protocols, this might be your home. The house can't be nailed down as politically left-wing or right-wing. They simply seem to like material that's supported by logic and hard science, as opposed to emotions, sentimentality, or wishful thinking.

Steven L. Mitchell, Editor in Chief.

QUEST BOOKS ❖ www.questbooks.net
PO Box 270, Wheaton, IL 60187, 630-665-0130

Quest Books is the publishing division of the Theosophical Society in America. They publish books that support the society's stated mission to "promote fellowship among all peoples and to encourage the study of religion, philosophy and science, so that people may better understand themselves and their place in the universe." They publish books about transpersonal psychology, alternative health, ecology, spiritual growth, and creativity. Importantly, their authors do not need to belong to the parent organization.

Sharron Dorr, Publishing Manager.

QUIRK BOOKS ❖ www.quirkbooks.com

215 Church Street, Philadelphia, PA 19106

In view of their name, it would be appalling for any of their books to be ordinary, not to mention dull. Quirk's website welcomes "off-the-wall" novels, "playful" cooking and craft books, and "cool photography or crazy illustrations."

Jason Rekulak, Publisher. Adult and children's fiction; humor, pop culture, sports, sex, monsters, "guy stuff."
Tiffany Hill, Editor. Food, drink, parenting, pets, creative reference, making stuff, "girl stuff."
(Ms.) Blair Thornburgh, Editor. Adult and young adult fiction about falling in love or avoiding love; "unconventional narratives," word play.

RED WHEEL / WEISER / CONARI ❖ www.redwheelweiser.com

665 Third Street, Suite 400, San Francisco, CA 94107

What we have here is a synergistic consolidation of several legacy metaphysical/esoteric/spiritual/New Age publishing brands. These forced communities generally work out well enough, the only potential downside being that the resulting amoeba might disrespect the various colonies within its realm. Red Wheel and its imprints publish books in a wide range of mind-body-spirit categories, including metaphysics, alternative health, yoga, relationships, and New Age. The Weiser imprint seems to have a tighter focus on the occult, esoteric philosophies, and the "old" religions. Conari Press has a strong footprint in women's interest.

Amber Guetebier, Editor.
Caroline Pincus, Editor.

REGNERY PUBLISHING, INC. ❖ www.regnery.com

300 New Jersey Avenue NW, Washington, DC 20001, 202-216-0600

Fidel Castro will never be a Regnery author. Neither will Hillary Clinton. But their names are frequently referenced in unflattering ways in many of Regnery's books. Without going to the blatant extremes of fascism, this is where right-wingers are at home, and more than a few of them have landed on the *New York Times* bestseller list. Regnery likes publishing toothy exposés about public figures and issues that tend to liberally draw from hearsay, gossip, and anonymous sources.

(Mr.) Alex Novak, Editor.

Marji Ross, Editor.

RODALE BOOKS ❖ www.rodaleinc.com

733 Third Avenue, New York, NY 10017, 212-697-2040

Rodale Books is the book-publishing division of Rodale, which is internationally respected as a multimedia content generator in the areas of healthy living. Naturally and organically, the book program reflects and supports the company's mission.

(Ms.) Dervla Kelly, Editor.

Jennifer Levesque, Editor.

Ursula Cary, Editor.

Marisa Vigilante, Editor.

ROWMAN & LITTLEFIELD ❖ www.rowman.com

4501 Forbes Boulevard, Lanham, MD 20706, 301-459-3366
5360 Manhattan Circle, Boulder, CO 80303, 303-543-7835
200 Park Avenue South, Suite 1109, New York, NY 10003, 212-529-3888

In recent years, Rowman has accumulated an impressive portfolio of independent presses with strong positions in their respective professional and academic communities (including Globe Pequot Press; see page 122). Under its own name, Rowman publishes a huge list of nonfiction titles for scholars and consumers in the humanities and social sciences.

Jonathan Sisk, Senior Executive Editor (MD). US government, US history, philosophy, public policy, political theory.

Susan McEachern, Editorial Director (CO). International studies, geography, history, regional studies.

Suzanne Staszak-Silva, Executive Editor (NY). Health, psychology, sexuality, food studies, military life studies, criminal justice, crime studies.

Marie-Claire Antoine, Senior Acquisitions Editor (NY). Security, terrorism, intelligence, diplomacy, Middle Eastern and African politics.

Sarah Stanton, Senior Acquisitions Editor (CO). Sociology, religion.

Leanne Silverman, Acquisitions Editor (CO). Anthropology, archaeology, communications.

Susanne Canavan, Acquisitions Editor (NY). Education.

Jason Aronson ❖ www.rowman.com/jasonaronson

Aronson is world famous for books about psychotherapy and Judaica.

Julie E. Kirsch, Publisher (MD). Psychotherapy.

(Ms.) Lindsey Porambo, Assistant Acquisitions Editor (MD). Judaica.

Taylor Trade Publishing ❖ www.rowman.com/taylortrade

Taylor publishes many subjects, including gardening, health, history, family issues, sports, entertainment, nature, and children's titles.

Rick Rinehart, Editorial Director (CO).

Karie Simpson, Assistant Editor (CO).

SASQUATCH BOOKS ❖ www.sasquatchbooks.com

1904 Third Avenue, Suite 710, Seattle, WA 98101, 206-467-4300

Sasquatch is known for its innovative and eclectic list of nonfiction books about food and wine, travel, lifestyle, gardening, and nature. Many of its books are relevant to the Pacific Northwest region.

Gary Luke, Editor.

SCHOLASTIC INC. ❖ www.scholastic.com

557 Broadway, New York, NY 10012, 212-343-6100

Scholastic is the largest publisher of children's and young adult editorial products in the world. They publish for both consumer distribution and classroom adoption.

David Levithan, Editor.

Jody Corbett, Editor.

Lisa Sandell, Editor.

Tracy Mack, Editor.

Arthur Levine, Editor.

Cheryl Klein, Editor.

SEVEN STORIES PRESS ❖ www.sevenstories.com

140 Watts Street, New York, NY 10013, 212-226-8760

Founded in 1995, Seven Stories was named for the seven original authors who took a leap of faith to be published by this untested start-up. In the nonfiction zone, SS is proud of its large list of political and social-advocacy books. In fiction, the house has been a champion for new voices.

Dan Simon, Publisher.

SHAMBHALA PUBLICATIONS ❖ www.shambhala.com

300 Massachusetts Avenue, Boston, MA 02115, 617-424-0030

This house was conceived during the hippie sixties in San Francisco by a group of devout Mormons who ingested LSD that had been inserted into a batch of Big Macs as part of a CIA experiment. Well, the San Francisco part is true, anyway. To sum it up, this is a successful publisher of books that are compatible with Eastern philosophies and religions. Specific subjects include Yoga, martial arts, natural health, crafts, creativity, and green living.

Jonathan Green, Editor.
Dave O'Neal, Editor.
Beth Frankl, Editor.

SKYHORSE PUBLISHING ❖ www.skyhorsepublishing.com

307 West 36th Street, 11th Floor, New York, NY 10018, 212-643-6816

Skyhorse is a gutsy horse, in that they entered when many others were leaving the industry (that is, in 2006). Their founder had the requisite experience and connections to survive, expand, and thrive as an independent publisher. Their eclectic list includes history, politics, rural living, sports, health, humor, self-help, and even some fiction.

Jenny Pierson, Editor. Health and fitness.
Marianna Dworak, Editor. Spirituality.
Jason Katzman, Editor. Science fiction/fantasy.
Joe Svercheck, Editor. Food.
Juli Matysik, Editor. Humor.
(Ms.) Lindsey Breuer, Editor. Cooking, popular science.
Julie Ganz, Editor. Fiction.

SOHO PRESS ❖ www.sohopress.com

853 Broadway, New York, NY 10003, 212-260-1900

Soho endeavors to publish bold new literary voices, international crime fiction, and young adult fiction. Most of their books are fiction with the occasional memoir or narrative.

Mark Doten, Senior Editor.
Daniel Ehrenshaft, Editorial Director. Soho Teen.

SOUNDS TRUE, INC. ❖ www.soundstrue.com

413 S. Arthur Avenue, Louisville, CO 80027, 800-333-9185

ST was founded in 1985. "Disseminate spiritual wisdom" was its business plan. Audio was its only format for many years, which explains the firm's name. The company grew and thrived, and successfully entered the traditional print fray in 2005. Its most popular categories include health, meditation, music, self-empowerment, spirituality, and yoga.

Jennifer Brown, Editor.
Haven Iversen, Editor.

SOURCEBOOKS ❖ www.sourcebooks.com

1935 Brookdale Road, Naperville, IL 60563, 630-961-3900
232 Madison Avenue, Suite 1100, New York, NY 10018, 212-414-1701
18 Cherry Street, Milford, CT 06460, 203-876-9790

Launched in 1987, Sourcebooks has managed to become one of the most dynamic and fastest-growing independent presses in the country. They have been a little ahead of the curve by acquiring even smaller presses with proven niches and by discovering authors with preexisting marketing and sales connections and corporate tie-ins. Sourcebooks has not been coy about helping to discover the digital future. They are especially strong in children's and romance categories and have a large footprint in all areas of nonfiction, including gift books and calendars. Basically, this is a risk-tolerant publisher that knows how to see and follow the money.

Deb Werksman, Editorial Manager (CT). Romance (all categories), women's fiction.
Mary Altman, Editor (NY). Romance (all categories).
Cat Clyne, Assistant Editor (NY). Romance, especially erotica.
Shana Drehs, Editorial Manager (IL). Women's and historical fiction; women's interest, parenting, relationships, self-help, pop culture, gift items, inspiration.

Stephanie Bowen, Editor (IL). Historical and contemporary women's fiction; history, current affairs, women's interest, popular science, psychology, prescriptive.

Anna Klenke, Associate Editor (IL). Commercial fiction.

Steve Geck, Editorial Manager (NY). Children's books through age 14.

(Ms.) Aubrey Poole, Associate Editor (NY). Ages 7 through young adult.

Todd Stocke, Editorial Director (IL). Books that include impressive multimedia applications.

SQUARE ONE PUBLISHERS INC. ❖ www.squareonepublishers.com

115 Herricks Road, Garden City Park, NY 11040, 516-535-2010

SQ1 was founded in 2000 by veteran publishing innovator Rudy Shur. Most of his titles are self-help/how-to oriented by experts in their respective fields. But there's also an assortment of general fiction and nonfiction titles, including cookbooks. As with most independent publishers, acquisitions often depend upon the editor's heart and intuition, as opposed to mere statistics. Actually, statistics would suggest that most small presses shouldn't even exist.

Rudy Shur, Founder and Publisher.

Joanne Abrams, Executive Editor.

Marie Caratozzolo, Senior Editor.

Michael Weatherhead, Editor.

TIN HOUSE BOOKS ❖ www.tinhouse.com/books

2617 NW Thurman Street, Portland, OR 97210, 503-473-8663

Tin House Books follows the same tradition as the company's much-loved magazine of the same name, which is to carefully curate an eclectic list of fiction and nonfiction, as well as some poetry. The firm isn't averse to introducing new voices. It seems that their primary criterion is the depth and uniqueness of the writing. This isn't where you'll find a how-to book about salesmanship, but you might discover the next Kerouac.

Meg Storey, Editor.

Tony Perez, Editor.

Masie Cochran, Associate Editor.

TURNER PUBLISHING COMPANY ❖ www.turnerpublishing.com

424 Church Street, Suite 2240, Nashville, TN 37219, 615-255-2665
445 Park Avenue, 9th Floor, New York, NY 10022, 646-291-8961

It may sound like a cliché, but Turner (no relation to Ted) is one to watch. While many large and small presses are standing still or withering away, Turner is quickly expanding. Though fast growth is often the kiss of death in any business, digital technology has become publishing's great equalizer, because content doesn't have to be solely printed and physically managed, and the content generators (authors) provide outsourced, low-cost labor. Turner recently grabbed a lot of attention by purchasing the rights to several thousand general nonfiction titles that Wiley (see page 142) no longer wanted to carry. With a single signature, Turner became a midsize publisher that few insiders were familiar with, yet. They appear to be on the prowl for all kinds of nonfiction and fiction titles, though specific subject preferences may become clearer in the near future.

Stephanie Beard, Editor (TN).

TYNDALE HOUSE PUBLISHERS, INC. ❖ www.tyndale.com

351 Executive Drive, Carol Stream, IL 60188, 800-323-9400

Stated purpose: "Minister to the needs of people through literature consistent with biblical principles." They publish a wide list of Christian-based fiction, nonfiction, and children's books. Many of the top names in Christian publishing are Tyndale authors. Their most famous (some might say infamous) and successful program was the *Left Behind* fiction series.

Stephanie Broene, Editor.
Carol Traver, Editor.

ULYSSES PRESS ❖ www.ulyssespress.com

PO Box 3440, Berkeley, CA 94703, 510-601-8301

According to *Publishers Weekly*, Ulysses is one of America's "fastest-growing small presses." The firm seems to be publishing something for every category you can think of, so it's difficult, if not impossible, to clearly define what they won't consider. One overriding attribute is made evident by viewing their catalog: every book seems to have a clear title and is for a focused market.

Kelly Reed, Acquisitions Editor.
Keith Riegert, Acquisitions Editor.
Katherine Furman, Acquisitions Editor.

WILEY ❖ www.wiley.com
111 River Street, Hoboken, NJ 07030, 201-748-6000

Though Wiley isn't one of the corporate houses, it is an international, billion-dollar content generator. In recent years, the firm seems to have been selling off its consumer trade book assets and putting more focus on the high-ticket professional and academic markets. Many of its $100+ books have such arcane titles and content that I could never accurately paraphrase what they are about. However, Wiley is still publishing a large list of trade books in the areas of finance, banking, marketing, investing, and general business.

Tiffany Charbonier, Editor. Finance, banking, venture capital.
David Pugh, Editor. Accounting.
Laura Gachko, Editor. Investing, management, leadership.
Brian Neill, Editor. Training.
Richard Narramore, Editor. Sales, marketing, general business.
Matthew Holt, Editor. General business.
Shannon Vargo, Executive Editor. General business, entrepreneurship.

Jossey-Bass

JB used to be a serious independent publisher in the areas of business, education, psychology, and nonprofit management. But many of its programs were probably deemed redundant or simply not profitable enough. Currently its excellent program for educators appears to have a promising future, but its other categories might be on the chopping block.

Kate Bradford, Editor. Books for educators and students.
Karen Murphy, Editor. Leadership/management, nonprofits.

WORKMAN PUBLISHING COMPANY ❖ www.workman.com
225 Varick Street, New York, NY 10014, 212-254-5900

Workman has been a bold independent innovator since 1968. Its clever calendars, humor titles, and gift/illustrated products have always profitably complemented its traditional books. The company has frequently excelled at capturing an inordinate measure of market share in cluttered categories. This is especially true for its *What to Expect* pregnancy and parenting series. Workman's books run the full gamut of nonfiction categories and children's books; for them the key seems to be how to differentiate what they publish in the eyes of the consumer, even if the content is conservative. Ordinary isn't their model.

Bruce Tracy, Editor.
Heather Schwedel, Editor.
Megan Nicolay, Editor.
Suzie Bolotin, Editor.
Justin Krasner, Editor. Children's.
Maisie Tivnan, Editor.

Artisan ❖ www.workman.com/artisanbooks

Artisan specializes in publishing nicely packaged and illustrated books about fashion, decorating, food, dining, and cooking.

Lia Ronnen, Editor.
Bridget Heiking, Editor.
Judy Pray, Editor.

Storey Publishing ❖ www.storey.com

210 Mass MoCA Way, North Adams, MA 01247, 413-346-2100

Storey's stated mission is to publish "practical information that encourages personal independence in harmony with the environment." This publisher may have been ahead of its time and is now clearly on time, since many of its books are dedicated to all aspects of sustainable/green living. They also publish an excellent assortment of books about small farming, pet care, crafts, gardening, and nature.

Deborah Balmuth, Editor. Mind-body-spirit.
Deborah Burns, Editor. Equine, pets, nature.
Gwen Steege, Editor. Crafts.
Carleen Madigan, Editor. Gardening.
Margaret Sutherland, Editor. Cooking, wine, beer.

Algonquin Books ❖ www.algonquin.com

PO Box 2225, Chapel Hill, NC 27515

This formerly independent publisher has been allowed to maintain its special fingerprints since being acquired by Workman many years ago. And they still hold to their stated mission to "publish quality fiction and nonfiction by undiscovered writers." Many of their books have a distinct Southern feel and flavor. They also publish children's books.

Sarah Davies, Editor. Young adult.

Elise Howard, Editor. Middle grade.

Amy Gash, Editor. Nonfiction.

Andra Miller, Editor. Fiction and nonfiction.

Krestyna Lypen, Editor. Children's.

Part 4

UNIVERSITY PRESSES (US)

INTRODUCTION
THE UNIVERSITY AS PUBLISHER
From Academic Press to Commercial Presence

William Hamilton

University presses publish much more than scholarly monographs and academic tomes. Although the monograph is — and will always be — the bread and butter of the university press, several factors over the past quarter century have compelled university presses to look beyond their primary publishing mission of disseminating scholarship. The reductions in financial support from parent institutions, library-budget cutbacks by federal and local governments, and the increasing scarcity of grants to underwrite the costs of publishing monographs have put these presses under severe financial pressure. The watchword for university presses is always *survive*.

While university presses were fighting for their lives, their commercial counterparts also experienced difficult changes. The commercial sector responded by selling off unprofitable and incompatible lists or merging with other publishers; many houses were bought out by larger concerns. Publishers began to concentrate their editorial and marketing resources on a few new titles that would generate larger revenues. Books that commercial publishers now categorized as financial risks, the university presses saw as means of entry into new markets and opportunities to revive sagging publishing programs.

Take a look through one of the really good bookstores in your area. You'll find university press imprints on regional cookbooks, popular fiction, serious nonfiction, calendars, literature in translation, reference works, finely produced art books, and a considerable number of upper-division textbooks. Books and other items normally associated with commercial publishers are now a regular and important part of university press publishing.

There are approximately 100 university presses in North America, including US branches of the venerable Oxford University Press and Cambridge University Press. Of the largest American university presses — California, Chicago, Columbia, Harvard, MIT, Princeton, Texas, and Yale — each publishes well over 100 books per year. Many of these titles are trade books that are sold in retail outlets throughout the world.

The medium-sized university presses — approximately 20 fit this category — publish between 50 and 100 books a year. Presses such as Washington, Indiana, Cornell, North Carolina, Johns Hopkins, and Stanford are well established as publishers of important works worthy of broad circulation.

UNIVERSITY PRESSES (US)

147

All but the smallest university presses have developed extensive channels of distribution, which ensure that their books will be widely available in bookstores and wherever serious books are sold. Small university presses usually retain larger university presses or commissioned sales firms to represent them.

University Press Trade Publishing

The two most common trade areas in which university presses publish are (1) regional titles and (2) nonfiction titles that reflect the research interests of their parent universities.

For example, University of Hawai'i Press publishes approximately 30 new books a year with Asian or Pacific Rim themes. Typically, 8 to 10 of these books are trade titles. Recent titles have included Japanese literature in translation, a lavishly illustrated book on Thai textiles, books on forms of Chinese architecture, and a historical guide to ancient Burmese temples. This is a typical university press trade list — a diverse, intellectually stimulating selection of books that will be read by a variety of well-informed, responsive general readers.

For projects with special trade potential, some of the major university presses enter into copublishing arrangements with commercial publishers — notably in the fields of art books and serious nonfiction with a current-issues slant — and there seem to be more of these high-profile projects lately.

Certain of the larger and medium-sized university presses have in the past few years hired editors with experience in commercial publishing to add extra dimensions and impact to the portion of their program with a trade orientation.

University Press Authors

Where do university press authors come from? The majority of them are involved in one way or another with a university, research center, or public agency or are experts in a particular academic field. Very few would list their primary occupation as author. Most of the books they write are the result of years of research or reflect years of experience in their fields.

The university press is not overly concerned about the number of academic degrees following its trade book authors' names. What matters is the author's thoroughness in addressing the topic, regardless of his or her residence, age, or amount of formal education. A rigorous evaluation of content and style determines whether the manuscript meets the university press's standards.

The University Press Acquisition Process

Several of the other essays in this volume provide specific strategies for you to follow to ensure that your book idea receives consideration from your publisher of choice — but let me interject a cautionary note: the major commercial publishers are extremely difficult to approach unless you have an agent, and obtaining an agent can be more difficult than finding a publisher!

The commercial publishers are so overwhelmed by unsolicited manuscripts that you would be among the fortunate few if your proposal or manuscript even received a thorough reading. Your unagented proposal or manuscript will most likely be read by an editorial assistant, returned unread, or thrown on the slush pile unread and unreturned.

An alternative to the commercial publisher is the university press. Not only will the university press respond, but the response will also generally come from the decision maker — the acquisitions editor.

Before approaching any publisher, however, you must perform a personal assessment of your expectations for your book. If you are writing because you want your book to be on the bestseller list, go to a medium to large commercial press. If you are writing to make a financial killing, go to a large commercial publisher. If you are writing in the hope that your book will be a literary success, contribute to knowledge, be widely distributed, provide a modest royalty, and be in print for several years, you should consider a university press.

Should a University Press Be Your First Choice?

That depends on the subject matter. It is very difficult to sell a commercial publisher on what appears on the surface to be a book with a limited market. For example, the late Tom Clancy was unable to sell *The Hunt for Red October* to a commercial publisher because the content was considered too technical for the average reader of action-adventure books. Clancy sent the manuscript to a university press that specialized in military-related topics. As they say, the rest is history. Tom Clancy created the present-day technothriller genre and has accumulated royalties well into the millions of dollars. Once Clancy became a known commodity, the commercial publishers began courting him. All his subsequent books have been published by commercial houses.

How do you find the university press that is suitable for you? You must research the university press industry. Start by finding out something about university presses. In addition to the listings appearing in this book, a more complete source is *The Association of American University Presses Directory*. The AAUP directory offers a detailed description of each AAUP member press, with a summary of its publishing program. The directory lists the names and responsibilities of each press's key staff, including the acquisitions editors. Each press states its editorial program — what it will consider for publication. A section on submitting manuscripts provides a detailed description of what the university press expects a proposal to contain. Another useful feature is the comprehensive subject grid, which identifies more than 125 subject areas and lists the university presses that publish in each of them.

An updated edition of *The Association of American University Presses Directory* is published every fall and is available for a nominal charge from the AAUP central offices in New York City or through its distributor, University of Chicago Press.

Most university presses are also regional publishers. They publish titles that reflect local interests and tastes and are intended for sale primarily in the university press's local region. For example, University of Hawai'i Press has more than 250 titles on Hawai'i. The books — both trade and scholarly — cover practically every topic one can think of. Books on native birds, trees, marine life, local history, native culture, and an endless variety of other topics can be found in local stores, including chain bookstores.

Almost all university presses publish important regional nonfiction. If your book naturally fits a particular region, you should do everything possible to get a university press located in that region to evaluate your manuscript.

Do not mistake the regional nature of the university press for an inability to sell books nationally — or globally. As mentioned earlier, most university presses have established channels of distribution and use the same resources that commercial publishers use for book distribution. The major difference is that the primary retail outlets for university press books tend to be bookstores associated with universities, smaller academic bookstores, specialized literary bookstores, and independent bookstores that carry a large number of titles.

What to Expect at a University Press

You should expect a personal reply from the acquisitions editor. If the acquisitions editor expresses interest, you can expect the evaluation process to take as long as six to eight months. For reasons known only to editorial staffs — commercial, as well as those of university presses — manuscripts sit and sit and sit. Then they go out for review, come back, and go out for review again!

Once a favorable evaluation is received, the editor must submit the book to the press's editorial board. It is not until the editorial board approves the manuscript for publication that a university press is authorized to publish the book under its imprint.

A word about editorial boards: The imprint of a university press is typically controlled by an editorial board appointed from the faculty. Each project presented to the editorial board is accompanied by a set of peer reviews, the acquisitions editor's summary of the reviews, and the author's replies to the reviews. The project is discussed with the press's management and voted upon.

Decisions from the editorial board range from approval, through conditional approval, to flat rejection. Most university presses present to the editorial board only those projects they feel stand a strong chance of acceptance — approximately 10 to 15 percent of the projects submitted annually. So if you have been told that your book is being submitted to the editorial board, there's a good chance that the book will be accepted.

Once a book has been accepted by the editorial board, the acquisitions editor is authorized to offer the author a publishing contract. The publishing contract of a university press is quite similar to a commercial publisher's contract. The majority of the paragraphs read the same. The difference is most apparent in two areas — submission of the manuscript and financial terms.

University presses view publishing schedules as very flexible. If the author needs an extra six to twelve months to polish the manuscript, the market is not going to be affected too much. If the author needs additional time to proofread the galleys or page proofs, the press is willing to go along. Why? Because a university press is publishing for the long term. The book is going to be in print for several years. It is not unusual for a first printing of a university press title to be available for 10 or more years. Under normal circumstances the topic will be timeless, enduring, and therefore of lasting interest.

University presses go to great lengths to ensure that a book is as close to error-free as possible. The academic and stylistic integrity of the work is foremost in the editor's mind. Not only the body of the book, but the notes, references, bibliography, and index should be flawless — and all charts, graphs, maps, and other illustrations perfectly keyed.

It does not matter whether the book is a limited-market monograph or serious nonfiction for a popular trade. The university press devotes the same amount of care to the editorial and production processes to ensure that the book is as accurate and complete as possible. Which leads us to the second difference — the financial terms.

Commercial publishers follow the maxim that time is money. The goal of the organization is to maximize shareholder wealth. Often the decision to publish a book is based solely on financial considerations. If a book must be available for a specific season in order to meet its financial goals, pressure may be applied to editorial by marketing, and editorial in turn puts pressure on the author to meet the agreed-upon schedule. This pressure may result in mistakes, typos, and inaccuracies — but will also assure timely publication and provide the publisher with the opportunity to earn its expected profit. At the commercial publishing house, senior management is measured by its ability to meet annual financial goals.

University presses are not-for-profit organizations. Their basic mission is to publish books of high merit that contribute to universal knowledge. Financial considerations are secondary to what the author has to say. Producing a thoroughly researched, meticulously documented, and clearly written book is more important than meeting a specific publication date. The university press market will accept the book when it appears.

Do not get the impression that university presses are entirely insensitive to schedules or market conditions. University presses are aware that certain books — primarily textbooks and topical trade titles — must be published at specific times of the year if sales are to be maximized. But less than 20 percent of any year's list would fall into such a category.

University Presses and Author Remuneration

What about advances? Royalties? Surely, university presses offer these amenities — which is not to suggest they must be commensurate with the rates paid by commercial houses.

No and yes. No royalties are paid on a predetermined number of copies of scholarly monographs — usually 1,000 to 2,000.

A royalty is usually paid on textbooks and trade books. The royalty will be based on the title's sales revenue (net sales) and will usually be a sliding-scale royalty, ranging from as low as 5 percent to as high as 15 percent.

As with commercial publishers, royalties are entirely negotiable. Do not be afraid or embarrassed to discuss them with your publisher. Just remember that university presses rarely have surplus funds to apply to generous advances or high royalty rates. However, the larger the university press, the more likely you are to get an advance for a trade book.

Never expect an advance for a monograph or supplemental textbook.

When Considering a University Press

When you're deciding where to submit your manuscript, keep the following in mind. University presses produce approximately 10 percent of the books published in the United States each year. University presses win approximately 20 percent of the annual major book awards. Yet university presses generate just 2 percent of the annual sales revenue.

So if you want your book to be taken seriously and reviewed and edited carefully; if you want to be treated as an important part of the publishing process and want your book to have a good chance to win an award; and if you are not too concerned about the financial rewards — then a university press may very well be the publisher for you.

William Hamilton was the director and publisher of the University of Hawai'i Press for 25 years. He retired in December 2012.

THE LISTINGS

CAMBRIDGE UNIVERSITY PRESS ❖ www.cambridge.org/us

32 Avenue of the Americas, New York, NY 10013-2473, 212-337-5000, newyork@cambridge.org

Dating back to 1534, Cambridge University Press publishes books in many areas of the humanities and social sciences, with particular focus on subjects including law, history, political science, and economics; it is also active across a broad spectrum of scientific and medical publishing. It administers some of the prestigious journals issued by the press, and it also publishes an extremely successful list of books aimed at those learning American English as a foreign or second language.

Adina Berk; aberk@cambridge.org. Psychology, education.

Robert Dreesen; rdreesen@cambridge.org. Political science, sociology, political philosophy and theory.

Ray Ryan; rryan@cambridge.org. Literature.

Vince Higgs; vhiggs@cambridge.org. Astronomy and physics.

Matt Lloyd; mlloyd@cambridge.org. Earth and environmental science.

Ada Brunstein; abrunstein@cambridge.org. Computer science.

Ben Harris; bharris@cambridge.org. Latin, Greek.

Daniele Gibney; dgibney@cambridge.org. Sciences, ICT.

Sheryl Borg; sborg@cambridge.org. Grammar.

Jeff Krum; jkrum@cambridge.org. Adult courses.

Beatrice Rehl; brehl@cambridge.org. Philosophy, classical art and archaeology.

Eric Crahan; ecrahan@cambridge.org. History and political science.

Scott Parris; sparris@cambridge.org. Economics and finance.

John Berger; jberger@cambridge.org. Law.

Marigold Acland; macland@cambridge.org. The Middle East, Asia, Islamic studies.

Lewis Bateman; lbateman@cambridge.org. Political science, history.

Lauren Cowles; lcowles@cambridge.org. Academic computer science, statistics.

Peter Gordon; pgordon@cambridge.org. Mechanical, chemical, and aerospace engineering.

Richard Westood; rwestwood@cambridge.org. Education: literacy/English, mathematics/numeracy, cross-curricular studies.

Claudia Bickford-Smith; cbickford-smith@cambridge.org. International, IEB and other.

Debbie Goldblatt; dgoldblatt@cambridge.org. English for language teaching: adult courses.

Bruce Myint; bamyint@cambridge.org. English for language teaching: adult education.

Kathleen Corley; kcorley@cambridge.org. English for language teaching: applied linguistics and professional books for teachers.

Bernard Seal; bseal@cambridge.org. English for academic purposes and pre-academic ESL reading and writing.

Lesley Koustaff; lkoustaff@cambridge.org. Primary and secondary courses.

Paul Heacock; pheacock@cambridge.org. Reference and vocabulary.

Karen Brock; kbrock@cambridge.org. Short courses and general EFL listening, speaking, reading, and writing.

COLUMBIA UNIVERSITY PRESS ❖ www.cup.columbia.edu

61 West 62nd Street, New York, NY 10023, 212-459-0600

Columbia University Press publishes in the areas of Asian studies, literature, biology, business, culinary history, current affairs, economics, environmental sciences, film and media studies, finance, history, international affairs, literary studies, Middle Eastern studies, New York City history, philosophy, neuroscience, paleontology, political theory, religion, and social work.

Jennifer Crewe, President and Editorial Director; jc373@columbia.edu. Asian humanities, film, food history, New York City.

Patrick Fitzgerald, Publisher for the Life Sciences; pf2134@columbia.edu. Conservation biology, environmental sciences, ecology, neuroscience, paleobiology, public health, biomedical sciences.

Bridget Flannery-McCoy, Editor; bmf2119@columbia.edu. Health economics, sustainability economics, labor economics.

Philip Leventhal, Editor; pl2164@columbia.edu. Literary studies, cultural studies, US history, journalism, media, New York City history and culture.

Wendy Lochner, Publisher for Philosophy and Religion; wl2003@columbia.edu. Animal studies, religion, philosophy.

Jennifer Perillo, Senior Executive Editor; jp3187@columbia.edu. Criminology, gerontology, psychology, social work.

Anne Routon, Editor; akr36@columbia.edu. Asian history, international relations, Middle East studies.

Myles Thompson, Publisher, Finance and Economics; mt2312@columbia.edu. Finance, economics.

CORNELL UNIVERSITY PRESS ❖ www.cornellpress.cornell.edu

Sage House, 512 East State Street, Ithaca, NY 14850, 607-277-2338

Cornell University Press was established in 1869, giving it the distinction of being the first university press to be established in America. The house offers 150 new titles a year in many disciplines, including anthropology, Asian studies, biological sciences, classics, cultural studies, history, industrial relations, literary criticism and theory, medieval studies, philosophy, politics and international relations, psychology and psychiatry, veterinary subjects, and women's studies. Submissions are not invited in poetry or fiction.

Peter J. Potter, Editor in Chief; pjp33@cornell.edu. Literature, medieval studies, classics, ancient history.

Roger Haydon, Executive Editor; rmh11@cornell.edu. Political science, international relations, Asian studies, philosophy.

Michael J. McGandy, Acquisitions Editor; mjm475@cornell.edu. American history, American politics, law, New York State, regional books.

Emily Powers, Acquisitions Assistant.

Max Richman, Acquisitions Assistant.

Comstock Publishing Associates

CUP's many books in the life sciences and natural history are published under the Comstock Publishing Associates imprint.

Kitty Liu, Associate Editor. Biology and natural history, ornithology, herpetology and ichthyology, mammology, entomology, botany and plant sciences, environmental studies.

ILR Press

A list of books in industrial and labor relations is offered under the ILR Press imprint.

Frances Benson, Editorial Director; fgb2@cornell.edu. Workplace issues, labor, business, health care, sociology, anthropology.

DUKE UNIVERSITY PRESS ❖ www.dukeupress.edu

905 West Main Street, Suite 18B, Durham, NC 27701, 919-687-3600

Duke University Press publishes primarily in the humanities and social sciences and issues a few publications for primarily professional audiences (e.g., in law or medicine). It is best known for its publications in the broad and interdisciplinary area of theory and history of cultural production, and it is known in general as a publisher willing to take chances with nontraditional and interdisciplinary publications, both books and journals.

Ken Wissoker, Editorial Director; kwiss@duke.edu. Anthropology; cultural studies; postcolonial theory; lesbian and gay studies; construction of race, gender, and national identity; social studies of science; new media; literary criticism; film and television; popular music; visual studies.

Courtney Berger, Editor; cberger@dukeupress.edu. Political theory, social theory, film and television, geography, gender studies, American studies, Asian American studies, cultural studies of food.

Miriam Angress, Associate Editor; mangress@dukeupress.edu. Religion, women's studies, world history, humanities, cultural studies.

THE FEMINIST PRESS AT THE CITY UNIVERSITY OF NEW YORK ❖ www.feministpress.org

365 Fifth Avenue, Suite 5406, New York, NY 10016, 212-817-7915

The mission of the Feminist Press is to publish and promote the most potent voices of women from all eras and all regions of the globe. Founded in 1970, the press has brought more than 300 critically acclaimed works by and about women into print, enriching the literary canon, expanding the historical record, and influencing public discourse about issues fundamental to women.

To submit, send an email of no more than 200 words describing your book project with the word *submission* in the subject line. Send email query to: editor@feministpress.org.

FORDHAM UNIVERSITY PRESS ❖ www.fordhampress.com

2546 Belmont Avenue, University Box L, Bronx, NY 10458, 718-817-4795

Fordham University Press publishes primarily in the humanities and the social sciences, with an emphasis on the fields of philosophy, theology, history, classics, communications, economics, sociology, business, political science, and law, as well as literature and the fine arts. Additionally, the press publishes books focusing on the metropolitan New York region and books of interest to the general public.

Fredric Nachbaur, Director; fnachbaur@fordham.edu.

Tom Lay, Editor; tlay@fordham.edu. Humanities.

GEORGETOWN UNIVERSITY PRESS ❖ www.press.georgetown.edu

3240 Prospect Street NW, Washington, DC 20007, 202-687-5889

Georgetown University Press publishes in the areas of bioethics; international affairs and human rights; languages and linguistics; political science, public policy, and public management; and religion and ethics.

Richard Brown, PhD, Director; reb7@georgetown.edu. Bioethics, international affairs and human rights, religion and politics, and religion and ethics.

Hope J. Smith LeGro, Assistant Director; hjs6@georgetown.edu. Languages, linguistics. Director, Georgetown Languages.

Donald Jacobs, Acquisitions Editor; dpj5@georgetown.edu. International affairs, human rights, public policy, public management.

David G. Nicholls, PhD, Acquisitions Editor; dgn5@georgetown.edu. Languages.

HARVARD UNIVERSITY PRESS ❖ www.hup.harvard.edu

79 Garden Street, Cambridge, MA 02138, 617-495-2600

HUP publishes scholarly books and thoughtful books for the educated general reader in history, philosophy, American literature, law, economics, public policy, natural science, history of science, psychology, and education, and reference books in all the above fields. The HUP website offers photographs of the editors that you may or may not wish to peruse prior to submitting, as well as detailed submission guidelines that you will not want to miss.

Susan Wallace Boehmer, Editor in Chief.

Michael Aronson, Executive Editor for Social Sciences. Economics, business, law, political science, sociology, especially the problems of capitalism such as distribution and inequality.

Michael Fisher, Assistant Director for University Relations and Executive Editor for Science and Medicine. Evolutionary theory, evolutionary developmental biology, biological and evolutionary anthropology, neuroscience, systems biology and bioinformatives, human genetics, science and society, animal cognition and behavior, history of technology; also books for general readers in physics, astronomy, earth science, chemistry, engineering, and mathematics.

Andrew Kinney, Editor. Human behavior, education, humanities.

John Kulka, Executive Editor-at-Large — American, English, and world literature; modernism; history of criticism; theory; the American publishing industry; political journalism; globalization; democracy; and human dignity.

Ian Malcolm, Executive Editor-at-Large. International economics.

Kathleen McDermott, Executive Editor for History. American history, Atlantic history, European history from late medieval to modern, Russian and Central European history, Asian history, international relations, global history, military history, US western history, Native American history, legal history.

Joyce Seltzer, Senior Executive Editor for History and Contemporary Affairs. Serious and scholarly nonfiction that appeals to a general intellectual audience as well as to students and scholars in a variety of disciplines, especially history across a broad spectrum, American studies, contemporary politics, social problems, and biography.

Shamila Sen, Executive Editor-at-Large. World religions, classics, ancient history, religion.

(Mr.) Lindsay Waters, Executive Editor for the Humanities. Philosophy, literary studies, cultural studies, film, Asian cultural studies, pop culture, conflicting relations among the races in the United States and around the world.

Belknap Press

HUP's Belknap Press imprint strives to publish books of long-lasting importance and superior scholarship and production, chosen whether or not they might be profitable, thanks to the bequest of Waldron Phoenix Belknap, Jr.

INDIANA UNIVERSITY PRESS ❖ www.iupress.indiana.edu

1320 E. 10th Street, Bloomington, IN 47405, 812-855-8817

IU Press is a leading academic publisher specializing in the humanities and social sciences. It produces more than 140 new books annually. Major subject areas include African, African American, Asian, cultural, Jewish and Holocaust, Middle East, Russian and

East European, and gender studies; anthropology, film, history, bioethics, music, paleontology, philanthropy, philosophy, and religion.

Robert Sloan, Editor in Chief; rjsloan@indiana.edu. US history, African American studies, bioethics, philanthropy, military history, paleontology, natural history, Holocaust studies.

Dee Mortensen, Senior Sponsoring Editor; mortense@indiana.edu. African studies, religion, philosophy, Judaism.

Rebecca Tolen, Sponsoring Editor; retolen@indiana.edu. Anthropology, Asian studies, political science/international relations, folklore.

Raina Polivka, Sponsoring Editor; rpolivka@indiana.edu. Digital media, film studies, Latin American studies, gender and sexuality studies, cultural studies.

Linda Oblack, Assistant Sponsoring Editor; loblack@indiana.edu. Regional trade, regional natural history, railroads past and present.

Quarry Books

Quarry Books focuses on everything about Indiana and the Midwest, exploring subjects such as photography, history, gardening, cooking, sports, leisure, people, and places.

JOHNS HOPKINS UNIVERSITY PRESS ❖ www.press.jhu.edu

2715 North Charles Street, Baltimore, MD 21218-4363, 410-516-6900

JHU Press is one of the world's largest and most diverse university presses.

Gregory M. Britton, Editorial Director; gb@press.jhu.edu. Higher education.

Jacqueline C. Wehmueller, Executive Editor; jcw@press.jhu.edu. Consumer health, psychology and psychiatry, history of medicine.

Vincent J. Burke, Executive Editor; vjb@press.jhu.edu. Life sciences, mathematics, physics.

Robert J. Brugger, Senior Acquisitions Editor; rjb@press.jhu.edu. American history, American studies, history of technology, regional books.

Matthew McAdam, Editor; mxm@press.jhu.edu. Humanities, literary studies.

Kelley Squazzo, Editor; kas@press.jhu.edu. Public health.

Suzanne Flinchbaugh, Associate Editor. Political science, health policy, Copublishing Liaison.

Sara Cleary, Assistant Editor; sjc@press.jhu.edu. Anababtist and Pietist studies.

KENT STATE UNIVERSITY PRESS ❖

www.kentstateuniversitypress.com

1118 University Library, 1125 Risman Drive, PO Box 5190, Kent, OH 44242-0001, 330-672-7913

Kent State University Press is interested in scholarly works about history, including military, Civil War, US diplomatic, American cultural, women's, and art history; literary studies; titles of regional interest for Ohio; scholarly biographies; archaeological research; the arts; and general nonfiction.

Will Underwood, Director.
Joyce Harrison, Acquiring Editor.
Mary D. Young, Managing Editor.

LOUISIANA STATE UNIVERSITY PRESS ❖ www.lsupress.org

Johnston Hall, 3rd Floor, LSU, Baton Rouge, LA 70803, 225-578-6294

LSU Press is dedicated to publishing scholarly, general-interest, and regional books. It's one of the oldest and largest university presses in the South and the only university press to have won Pulitzer Prizes in both fiction and poetry.

Rand Dotson, Executive Editor. Slavery, Civil War, Reconstruction, nineteenth- and twentieth-century South, Louisiana roots music.
Alisa Plant, Senior Editor. Media studies, environmental studies.
Margaret Lovecraft, Acquisitions Editor. Regional books, literary studies, landscape architecture.

MASSACHUSETTS INSTITUTE OF TECHNOLOGY / THE MIT PRESS ❖

www.mitpress.mit.edu

1 Rogers Street, Cambridge, MA 02142, 617-253-5646

Science and technology is MIT's strong suit, but its list is broader than the college's name might imply.

Philip Laughlin, Senior Acquisitions Editor; laughlin@mit.edu. Cognitive science, philosophy.
John S. Covell, Senior Acquisitions Editor; jcovell@mit.edu. Economics, finance, business.

Jane Macdonald, Acquisitions Editor; janem@mit.edu. Economics, finance, business.

Robert Prior, Executive Editor; prior@mit.edu. Life sciences, neuroscience, biology.

Doug Sery, Senior Acquisitions Editor; dsery@mit.edu. Design, new media, game studies.

Marguerite Avery, Acquisitions Editor; mavery@mit.edu. Science, technology and society, information science.

Roger Conover, Executive Editor. Art, architecture, visual and cultural studies.

Miranda Martin, Assistant Acquisitions Editor. Environmental studies.

Katie Persons, Assistant Acquisitions Editor. Technology and society, information science.

Christopher Eyer, Acquisitions Assistant. Life sciences, neuroscience, engineering, cognitive science, philosophy.

Emily Taber, Assistant Acquisitions Editor. Economics, finance, business.

Susan Buckley, Associate Acquisitions Editor. Digital media and learning.

Marc Lowenthaul, Associate Acquisitions Editor. Computer science, linguistics, Semiotex.

Justin Kehoe, Assistant Acquisitions Editor. Art, architecture, visual and cultural studies.

Beth Clevenger, Acquisitions Editor. Environmental studies.

NEW YORK UNIVERSITY PRESS ❖ www.nyupress.org

838 Broadway, 3rd Floor, New York, NY 10003-4812, 212-998-2575

NYU Press is interested in titles that explore issues of race and ethnicity. They are also interested in media studies and American studies.

Eric Zinner, Editor in Chief; eric.zinner@nyu.edu. Literary criticism and cultural studies, media studies, American history.

Ilene Kalish, Executive Editor; ilene.kalish@nyu.edu. Sociology, criminology, politics.

Jennifer Hammer, Editor; jennifer.hammer@nyu.edu. Religion, psychology, anthropology.

Clara Platter, Editor; clara.platter@nyu.edu. Law.

Chip Rossetti, Managing Editor; chip.rossetti@nyu.edu. Arabic literature.

Caelyn Cobb, Assistant Editor; caelyn.cobb@nyu.edu. Sociology, criminology, politics, women's studies.

Constance Grady, Editorial Assistant; constance.grady@nyu.edu. Religion, psychology, anthropology, history, law.

OHIO STATE UNIVERSITY PRESS ❖ www.ohiostatepress.org

180 Pressey Hall, 1070 Carmack Road, Columbus, OH 43210-1002, 614-292-6930

Ohio State University Press's areas of specialization include literary studies, including narrative theory; history, including business history, medieval history, and history of crime; political science, including legislative studies; and Victorian studies, urban studies, and women's health. They also publish annual winners of short fiction and poetry prizes, the details of which are available at www.ohiostatepress.org.

Lindsay Martin, Acquisitions Editor; Lindsay@osupress.org. Literary studies.

Eugene O'Connor, PhD, Acquisitions Editor; eugene@osupress.org. Classics, medieval studies, language and linguistics.

OXFORD UNIVERSITY PRESS ❖ www.oup.com/us

198 Madison Avenue, New York, NY 10016, 212-726-6000

Oxford University Press, Inc. (OUP USA), is by far the largest American university press and perhaps the most diverse publisher of its type. The press had its origins in the information technology revolution of the late fifteenth century, which began with the invention of printing from movable type. Oxford's New York office is editorially independent of the British home office and handles distribution of its own list, as well as titles originating from Oxford's branches worldwide. OUP USA publishes at a variety of levels, for a wide range of audiences in almost every academic discipline.

Niko Pfund, Academic Publisher.

Joan Bossert, Associate Publisher; joan.bossert@oup.com. Neuroscience, consumer health, psychological and behavioral sciences.

Catharine Carlin, Associate Publisher; catharine.carlin@oup.com. Cognitive neuroscience, ophthalmology, cognitive psychology.

Brendan O'Neill, Editor; david.oneill@oup.com. American Studies, film, literature.

Scott Parris, Editor; scott.parris@oup.com. Business/management, economics, finance.

Norm Hirschy, Editor; norm.hirschy@oup.com. Dance, music.

Stefan Vranka, Editor; stefan.vranka@oup.com. Classical studies.

James Cook, Editor; james.cook@oup.com. Criminology.

David McBride, Editor; david.mcbride@oup.com. Current affairs, political science, law (trade), sociology (trade).

Sarah Harrington, Editor; sarah.harrington@oup.com. Developmental psychology.

Susan Ferber, Editor; susan.ferber@oup.com. American and world history, art history, academic art and architecture.

Larry Selby, Editor; larry.selby@oup.com. Law (practitioner).

Chris Collins, Editor; chris.collins@oup.com. Law (academic).

Tisse Takagi, Editor; tisse.takagi@oup.com. Life sciences.

Jeremy Lewis, Editor; jeremy.lewis@oup.com. Earth sciences, life sciences, physics.

Peter Ohlin, Editor; peter.ohlin@oup.com. Bioethics, linguistics, philosophy.

Phyllis Cohen, Editor; phyllis.cohen@oup.com. Mathematics, physics.

Cynthia Read, Senior Editor; cynthia.read@oup.com. Religion (trade).

Donald Kraus, Executive Editor; donald.kraus@oup.com. Bibles.

Andrea Seils, Editor; andrea.seils@oup.com. Anesthesiology.

Shannon McLachlan, Editor; shannon.mclachlan@oup.com. American studies, classical studies, English language and literature, literary studies, film.

Terry Vaughn, Editor; terry.vaughn@oup.com. Business management, economics, finance and financial economics.

Mariclaire Cloutier, Editor; mariclaire.cloutier@oup.com. Forensic psychology, clinical psychology.

Craig Panner, Editor; craig.panner@oup.com. Neurology.

Shelley Reinhardt, Editor; shelley.reinhardt@oup.com. Neuropsychology.

Lori Handelman, Editor; lori.handelman@oup.com. Social psychology.

Maura Roessner, Editor; maura.roessner@oup.com. Social work.

Theo Calderara, Editor; theo.calderera@oup.com. Religion (academic).

William Lamsback, Editor; william.lamsback@oup.com. Medicine, neurology, public health.

Suzanne Ryan, Editor; suzanne.ryan@oup.com. Music (books).

Todd Waldman, Editor; todd.waldman@oup.com. Music (sheet music).

Sonke Adlung, Editor; sonke.adlung@oup.com. Physics.

PENN STATE UNIVERSITY PRESS ❖ www.psupress.org

820 North University Drive, University Support Building 1, Suite C, University Park, PA 16802-1003, 814-865-1327

Penn State University Press's strengths include core areas such as art history and literary criticism as well as fields such as philosophy, religion, history (mainly US and European), and some of the social sciences (especially political science and sociology).

Patrick H. Alexander, Director; pha3@psu.edu. American studies, European history and culture, history, medieval and early modern studies, philosophy, regional studies, religion, religious studies, romance studies, and Slavic studies.

Eleanor Goodman, PhD, Executive Editor for the Arts & Humanities; ehg11@psu.edu. Art and art history, architectural history, European history and culture (Spanish, French), literature, medieval and early modern studies, visual culture.

PRINCETON UNIVERSITY PRESS ❖ www.press.princeton.edu

41 William Street, Princeton, NJ 08540-5237, 609-258-4900

Princeton University Press, which celebrated its 100th anniversary in 2005, is one of the country's largest and oldest university presses. With a goal to disseminate scholarship both within academia and to society at large, the press produces publications that range across more than 40 disciplines, from art history to ornithology and political science to philosophy.

Fred Appel, Executive Editor. Anthropology, religion.
Al Bertrand, Editor. Humanities.
Eric Crahan, Senior Editor. Political science, American history.
Seth Ditchik, Executive Editor. Economics, finance.
Alison Kalett, Senior Editor. Biology, earth sciences.
Vickie Kearn, Executive Editor. Mathematics.
Robert Kirk, Executive Editor. Natural history, biology, ornithology, field guides.
Michelle Komie, Executive Editor. Art, architecture.
Anne Savarese, Executive Editor. Literature.
Eric Schwartz, Senior Editor. Sociology, cognitive sciences.
Robert Tempio, Executive Editor. Philosophy, classics, ancient world, political theory.

RUTGERS UNIVERSITY PRESS ❖ www.rutgerspress.rutgers.edu

106 Somerset Street, New Brunswick, NJ 08901, 848-445-7762

Rutgers University Press publishes books in a broad array of disciplines across the humanities, social sciences, and sciences. Fulfilling a mandate to serve the people of New Jersey, it also publishes books of scholarly and popular interest on the state and surrounding region. Strengths include history, sociology, anthropology, religion, media, film studies, women's studies, African American studies, Asian American studies, public health, history of medicine, evolutionary biology, the environment, and books about the mid-Atlantic region.

Leslie Mitchner, Associate Director and Editor in Chief; lmitch@rutgers.edu. Humanities, literature, film, communications.

Peter Mickulas, Editor; mickulas@rutgers.edu.

Katie Keeran, Editor; ckeeran@rutgers.edu.

Lisa Boyajian, Assistant Editor; lmb333@rutgers.edu.

Rivergate Books

Rivergate Books is a recent imprint devoted to New Jersey and surrounding states.

STANFORD UNIVERSITY PRESS ❖ www.sup.org

425 Broadway Street, Redwood City, CA 94063, 650-723-9434

Stanford University Press publishes about 130 books per year. Roughly two-thirds of these books are scholarly monographs and textbooks in the humanities and the social sciences, with strong concentrations in history, literature, philosophy, and Asian studies, and growing lists in politics, sociology, anthropology, and religion. The remaining one-third are textbooks, professional reference works, and monographs in law, business, economics, public policy, and education.

Geoffrey Burn, Executive Editor; grhburn@stanford.edu. Business strategy and security studies.

Eric Brandt, Executive Editor. Jewish studies, Asian American studies, American history, science history.

Kate Wahl, Publishing Director and Editor in Chief; kwahl@stanford.edu. Sociology, law, Middle East studies.

Margo Beth Fleming, Senior Editor; mbcrouppen@stanford.edu. Business, economics, organizational studies.

Emily-Jane Cohen, Senior Editor; beatrice@stanford.edu. Literature, philosophy, religion.

Jenny Gavacs, Acquisitions Editor. Sociology, Asian studies.

Michelle Lipinski, Acquisitions Editor. Anthropology, law.

STATE UNIVERSITY OF NEW YORK PRESS ❖ www.sunypress.edu

22 Corporate Woods Boulevard, 3rd Floor, Albany, NY 12210-2504, 866-430-7869

SUNY Press is one of the largest public university presses in the United States, with an annual output of some 170 books and a backlist of more than 4,000 titles. The press publishes chiefly in the humanities and social sciences and has attained national recognition in the areas of education, philosophy, religion, Jewish studies, Asian studies, political science, and sociology, with increasing growth in the areas of literature, film studies, communication, women's studies, and environmental studies.

Nancy Ellegate, Senior Acquisitions Editor. Religious studies, Asian studies, transpersonal psychology.

Dr. Michael Rinella, Senior Acquisitions Editor. Political science, African American studies.

Andrew Kenyon, Acquisitions Editor. Philosophy.

Dr. Beth Bouloukos, Senior Acquisitions Editor. Education, Hispanic studies, queer studies, women's studies.

Excelsior Editions

Excelsior Editions showcases the history of New York and surrounding states while at the same time making available noteworthy and essential popular books, both classic and contemporary.

James Peltz, Codirector, Excelsior Editions. Film studies, Italian American studies, Jewish studies.

SYRACUSE UNIVERSITY PRESS ❖

www.syracuseuniversitypress.syr.edu

621 Skytop Road, Suite 110, Syracuse, NY 13244-5290, 315-443-5534

Syracuse University Press publishes new books in specialized areas including New York State, Middle East studies, Judaica, geography, Irish studies, Native American studies, religion, television, and popular culture.

Suzanne Guiod, Editor in Chief; seguiod@syr.edu. Disability studies, peace studies, politics, religion, Middle East studies.

Deanna McCay, Acquisitions Editor; dhmccay@syr.edu. Geography, NY State history, American 20th-century history.

Kelly Balenske, Editorial Assistant; klbalens@syr.edu.

TEXAS BOOK CONSORTIUM

The "consortium" of Texas's public and university presses was founded in 1974, and each program is editorially distinct.

Texas A&M University Press

John H. Lindsey Building, Lewis Street, 4354 TAMU, College Station, TX, 77843-4354, 979-845-1436

Texas A&M University Press's primary editorial interests span a range of significant fields, including agriculture, anthropology, nautical archaeology, architecture, borderland studies, Eastern Europe, economics, military history, natural history, presidential studies, veterinary medicine, and works on the history and culture of Texas and the surrounding region.

Mary Lenn Dixon, Editor in Chief; mary-dixon@tamu.edu.
Shannon Davies, Senior Editor, Natural Sciences; sdavies@tamu.edu.
Thom Lemmons, Managing Editor; thom.lemmons@tamu.edu.
Diana L. Vance, Editorial Assistant, Acquisitions; dvance@tamu.edu.

State House Press/McWhiney Foundation Press

PO Box 818, Buffalo Gap, TX 79508, 325-572-3974

State House Press and the McWhiney Foundation Press see their missions as making history approachable, accessible, and interesting, with special emphasis on Texas, West Texas, the Civil War, military, and Southern history.

Texas Christian University Press ❖ www.prs.tcu.edu

3000 Sandage, Fort Worth, TX 76109, 817-257-7822

Texas Christian University Press is among the smallest university publishers in the nation and focuses on the history and literature of the American Southwest.

Texas Review Press

PO Box 2146, SHSU Division of English and Foreign Languages, Evans Building, Room #152, Huntsville, TX 77341-2146, 936-294-1992

Texas Review Press was established in 1979 but published only chapbooks and an occasional anthology until 1992, when it introduced the Southern and Southwestern Writers Breakthrough Series. It now publishes six to eight books a year and has over 40 titles in print in fiction, poetry, and prose nonfiction.

UNIVERSITY OF ALABAMA PRESS ❖ www.uapress.ua.edu

USPS address: Box 870380, Tuscaloosa, AL 35487-0380

Physical/shipping address: 200 Hackberry Lane, 2nd Floor McMillan Bldg., Tuscaloosa, AL 35401, 205-348-5180

The University of Alabama Press publishes in the following areas: American history; Southern history and culture; American religious history; Latin American history; American archaeology; southeastern archaeology; Caribbean archaeology; historical archaeology; ethnohistory; anthropology; American literature and criticism; rhetoric and communication; creative nonfiction; linguistics, especially dialectology; African American studies; Native American studies; Judaic studies; public administration; theater; natural history and environmental studies; American social and cultural history; sports history; military history; and regional studies of Alabama and the southern United States, including trade titles. Submissions are not invited in poetry, fiction, or drama.

Daniel Waterman, Editor in Chief; waterman@uapress.ua.edu. American literature and criticism, rhetoric and communication, creative nonfiction, linguistics, African American studies, public administration, theater, natural history and environmental studies.

Elizabeth Motherwell, Acquisitions Editor for Natural History and the Environment; emother@uapress.ua.edu.

Donna Cox Baker, History Editor.

Wendi Schnaufer, Senior Acquisitions Editor. Archeology, anthropology, food studies, Latin American–Caribbean studies, ethnohistory.

UNIVERSITY OF ARIZONA PRESS ❖ www.uapress.arizona.edu

Main Library Building, 5th Floor, 1510 E. University Boulevard, PO Box 210055, Tuscon, AZ 85721-0055, 520-621-1441

The University of Arizona Press publishes about 55 books annually. These include scholarly titles in American Indian studies, anthropology, archaeology, environmental studies, geography, Chicano studies, history, Latin American studies, and the space sciences. UA Press also publishes general-interest books on Arizona and the Southwest borderlands.

Allyson Carter, Editor in Chief, Social Sciences and Sciences; acarter@uapress@arizona .edu. Anthropology, archaeology, ecology, geography, natural history, environmental science, astronomy and space sciences, related regional titles.

Kristen Buckles, Acquiring Editor; kbuckles@uapress.arizona.edu. Native American literature and studies, Latin American studies, US West history.

UNIVERSITY OF ARKANSAS PRESS ❖ www.uapress.com

McIlroy House, 105 N. McIlroy Avenue, Fayetteville, AR 72701, 479-575-3246

University of Arkansas Press publishes approximately 20 titles a year in the following subjects: history, Southern history, African American history, Civil War studies, poetics and literary criticism, Middle East studies, Arkansas and regional studies, music, and cultural studies. About a third of its titles fall under the general heading of Arkansas and Regional Studies.

Lawrence J. Malley, Director and Acquisitions Editor; lmalley@uark.edu. US history, African American history, civil rights studies, Middle East studies, sports history.

UNIVERSITY OF CALIFORNIA PRESS ❖ www.ucpress.edu

155 Grand Avenue, Suite 400, Oakland, CA 94612–3758, 510-883-8232

Founded in 1893, University of California Press (UC Press) publishes in the areas of art, music, cinema and media studies, classics, literature, anthropology, sociology, archaeology, history, religious studies, Asian studies, biological sciences, food studies, natural history, and public health.

(Mr.) Blake Edgar, Senior Editor. Ecology, biology, archaeology, viticulture.
Mary C. Francis, Executive Editor. Music and cinema studies.
Niels Hooper, Executive Editor. History (except Asia), American studies, Middle East studies.
Reed Malcolm, Senior Editor. Anthropology, Asian studies.
Kim Robinson, Editorial Director. California issues/studies.
Maura Roessner, Senior Editor. Social sciences.
Eric A. Schmidt, Editor. Religion, ancient world.
Naomi Schneider, Executive Editor. Sociology, politics, anthropology, social issues.

UNIVERSITY OF CHICAGO PRESS ❖ www.press.uchicago.edu

1427 East 60th Street, Chicago, IL 60637, 773-702-7700

University of Chicago Press is noted for its large and diverse program of scholarly and occasionally commercial books.

Alan G. Thomas, Editorial Director, Humanities and Sciences; athomas@press.uchicago .edu. Literary criticism and theory, religious studies.
John Tryneski, Editorial Director; jtryneski@press.uchicago.edu. Political science, law and society.

Timothy Mennel, Senior Editor; tmennel@press.uchicago.edu. American history, Chicago history.

Mary E. Laur, Senior Project Editor; mlaur@press.uchicago.edu. Books about writing and general reference.

Joe Jackson, Editor; joejackson@press.uchicago.edu. Economics, business, finance.

Christopher L. Rhodes, Editor; clrhodes@press.uchicago.edu. Law, legal history.

Marta Tonegutti, Editor; mtonegutti@press.uchicago.edu. Music studies.

Susan Bielstein, Executive Editor; sbielstein@press.uchicago.edu. Art, architecture, ancient archaeology, classics, film studies.

T. David Brent, Executive Editor; dbrent@press.uchicago.edu. Anthropology, paleoanthropology, philosophy, psychology.

Karen Merikangas Darling, Senior Editor; kdarling@press.uchicago.edu. Science studies (history, philosophy, social studies of science, medicine, technology).

Elizabeth Branch Dyson, Editor; ebranchdyson@press.uchicago.edu. Ethnomusicology, interdisciplinary philosophy, education.

Christie Henry, Editorial Director; chenry@press.uchicago.edu. Biological science, behavior, conservation, ecology, environment, evolution, natural history, paleobiology, geography, earth sciences.

Douglas Mitchell, Executive Editor; dmitchell@press.uchicago.edu. Sociology, history, sexuality studies, rhetoric.

David Morrow, Senior Editor; dmorrow@press.uchicago.edu. Reference works, including regional reference, intellectual property.

Christopher Chung, Assistant Editor; cdchung@press.uchicago.edu. Life sciences.

Randolph Petilos, Assistant Editor; rpetilos@press.uchicago.edu. Medieval studies, poetry in translation.

UNIVERSITY OF GEORGIA PRESS ❖ www.ugapress.org

320 South Jackson Street, Athens, GA 30602, 706-542-6770

University of Georgia Press publishes 70 to 80 titles each year, in a range of academic disciplines as well as books of interest to the general reader, and is committed to publishing important new scholarship in the following subject areas: American and Southern history and literature, African American studies, civil rights history, legal history, Civil War studies, Native American studies, folklore and material culture, women's studies, and environmental studies. Their regional publishing program includes architectural guides, state histories, field guides to the region's flora and fauna, biographies, editions of diaries and letters, outdoor guides, and the work of some of the state's most accomplished artists, photographers, poets, and fiction writers.

Mick Gusinde-Duffy, Editor in Chief; mickgd@uga.edu.

Walter Biggins, Senior Acquisitions Editor; wbiggins@uga.edu.

Pat Allen, Acquisitions Editor; pallen@uga.edu.

Beth Snead, Assistant Acquisitions Editor; bsnead@uga.edu.

UNIVERSITY OF HAWAIʻI PRESS ❖ www.uhpress.hawaii.edu

2840 Kolowalu Street, Honolulu, HI 96822-1888, 808-956-8255

Areas of University of Hawaiʻi Press (UHP) publishing interest include cultural history, economics, social history, travel, arts and crafts, costumes, marine biology, natural history, botany, ecology, religion, law, political science, anthropology, and general reference; particular UHP emphasis is on regional topics relating to Hawaiʻi, and scholarly and academic books on East Asia, South and Southeast Asia, and Hawaiʻi and the Pacific.

Patricia Crosby, Executive Editor; pcrosby@hawaii.edu. East Asian studies (all disciplines except literature), anthropology, Buddhist studies.

Masako Ikeda, Acquisitions Editor; masakoi@hawaii.edu. Hawaiʻian and Pacific studies (all disciplines), Asian American studies (all disciplines), general-interest books on Hawaiʻi and the Pacific.

Pamela Kelley, Acquisitions Editor; pkelley@hawaii.edu. Southeast Asian studies (all disciplines), East Asian literature.

Nadine Little, Acquisitions Editor; nlittle@hawaii.edu. General interest, Hawaiiana, natural history, natural science.

UNIVERSITY OF ILLINOIS PRESS ❖ www.press.uillinois.edu

1325 South Oak Street, Champaign, IL 61820-6903, 217-333-0950

The University of Illinois Press is one of the founding members of the Association of American University Presses. They publish scholarly books and serious nonfiction, with special interests in Abraham Lincoln studies, African American studies, American history, anthropology, Appalachian studies, archaeology, architecture, Asian American studies, communications, folklore, food studies, immigration and ethnic history, Judaic studies, labor history, literature, military history, Mormon history, music, Native American studies, philosophy, poetry, political science, religious studies, sociology, Southern history, sport history, translations, transnational cultural studies, western history, and women's studies.

Willis G. Regier, Director; wregier@uillinois.edu. Lincoln studies, Nietzsche studies, classics, translations, sports history, food studies, ancient religion, literature.

Laurie Matheson, Editor in Chief; lmatheso@uillinois.edu. History, Appalachian studies, labor studies, music, folklore.

Daniel Nasset, Acquisitions Editor; dnasset@uillinois.edu. Film studies, anthropology, communication studies, military history.

Dawn M. Durante, Acquisitions Editor; durante9@uillinois.edu. African American studies, women's studies, american studies, religion.

Marika Christofides, Assistant Acquisitions Editor; mchristo@uillinois.edu.

UNIVERSITY OF IOWA PRESS ❖ www.uiowapress.org

119 West Park Road, 100 Kuhl House, Iowa City, IA 52242-1000, 319-335-2000

As one of the few book publishers in the state of Iowa, the press considers it a mission to publish excellent books on Iowa and the Midwest. But since the press's role is much broader than that of a regional press, the bulk of its list appeals to a wider audience in the following categories: literary studies, including Whitman studies and poetics; letters and diaries; American studies; literary nonfiction and thematic edited anthologies, particularly poetry anthologies; the craft of writing; literature and medicine; theater studies; archaeology; the natural history of the Upper Midwest; and regional history and culture.

Holly Carver, Director and Editor; holly-carver@uiowa.edu.
Catherine Cocks, Acquisitions Editor; cath-campbell@uiowa.edu.
Elisabeth Chretien, Acquisitions Editor; elisabeth-chretien@uiowa.edu.

UNIVERSITY OF MICHIGAN PRESS ❖ www.press.umich.edu

839 Greene Street, Ann Arbor, MI 48104-3209, 734-764-4388

University of Michigan Press publishes trade nonfiction and works of scholarly and academic interest. Topic areas and categories include African American studies, anthropology, archaeology, Asian studies, classical studies, literary criticism and theory, economics, education, German studies, history, linguistics, law, literary biography, literature, Michigan and the Great Lakes region, music, physical sciences, philosophy and religion, poetry, political science, psychology, sociology, theater and drama, women's studies, disability studies, and gay and lesbian studies.

Aaron McCollough, Director of Editorial; amccollo@umich.edu. Cultural studies, American studies, literary studies, new media, Jewish studies, medicine, history of science/technology.

LeAnn Fields, Senior Executive Editor; lfields@umich.edu. Class studies, disability studies, theater, performance studies.

Ellen Bauerle, Executive Editor; bauerle@umich.edu. Classics, archaeology, German studies, music, fiction, early modern history, African studies.

Kelly Sippell, Executive Editor; ksippell@umich.edu. ESL, applied linguistics.

Christopher J. Hebert, Editor-at-Large; hebertc@umich.edu. Popular music, jazz.

Dr. Melody Herr, Senior Acquisitions Editor; mrherr@umich.edu. Politics, law, American history.

UNIVERSITY OF MINNESOTA PRESS ❖ www.upress.umn.edu

111 Third Avenue South, Suite 290, Minneapolis, MN 55401, 612-627-1970

The University of Minnesota Press's areas of emphasis include American studies, anthropology, art and aesthetics, cultural theory, film and media studies, gay and lesbian studies, geography, literary theory, political and social theory, race and ethnic studies, sociology, and urban studies. The press is among the most active publishers of translations of works of European and Latin American thought and scholarship. The press also maintains a long-standing commitment to publish books that focus on Minnesota and the Upper Midwest, including regional nonfiction, history, and natural science.

Richard Morrison, Editorial Director; morri094@umn.edu. American studies, art and visual culture, literary and cultural studies.

Jason Weidemann, Senior Acquisitions Editor; weide007@umn.edu. Anthropology, Asian culture, cinema and media studies, geography, native studies, sociology.

Pieter Martin, Editor; marti190@umn.edu. Architecture, legal studies, politics and international studies, Scandinavian studies, urban studies.

Erik Anderson, Regional Trade Editor; ando0900@umn.edu. Regional, Scandinavian, music, trade paperback reprints.

Danielle Kasprzak, Associate Editor. Cinema and media studies.

Douglas Armato, Director. Digital culture.

Beverly Kaemmer, Associate Director. Psychology.

UNIVERSITY OF MISSOURI PRESS ❖ www.umsystem.edu/upress

2910 LeMone Boulevard, Columbia, MO 65201, 573-882-7641

The University of Missouri Press publishes more than 70 titles per year in the areas of American and world history, including intellectual history and biography; African American studies; women's studies; American, British, and Latin American literary criticism; journalism; political science, particularly philosophy and ethics; regional studies of the American heartland; short fiction; and creative nonfiction.

Clair Willcox, Editor in Chief; willcoxc@umsystem.edu.
Sara Davis, Managing Editor; davissd@umsystem.edu.
Gary Kass, Acquisitions Editor; kassg@missouri.edu.

UNIVERSITY OF NEBRASKA PRESS ❖ www.nebraskapress.unl.edu

1111 Lincoln Mall, Lincoln, NE 68588-0630, 402-472-3581

UNP publishes in a wide variety of subject areas, including western Americana, Native American history and culture, military history, sports, philosophy, and religion.

Derek Krissoff, Editor; dkrissoff2@unl.edu. Anthropology, geography.
Alicia Christensen, Editor; achristensen6@unl.edu. American studies.
Matt Bokovoy, Editor; mbokovoy2@unl.edu. Native studies.
Kristen Elias Rowley, Editor; keliasrowley2@unl.edu. American studies, cultural criticism.
Bridget Barry, Editor; bbarry2@unl.edu. Military history.

UNIVERSITY OF NEW MEXICO PRESS ❖ www.unmpress.com

1717 Roma Avenue NE, Albuquerque, NM 87106, 505-277-2346

University of New Mexico Press's areas of strong interest are anthropology, archaeology, cultures of the American West, folkways, Latin American studies, literature, art and architecture, photography, crafts, biography, women's studies, travel, and the outdoors. UNM Press offers a robust list of books in subject areas pertinent to the American Southwest, including native Anasazi, Navajo, Hopi, Zuni, and Apache cultures; Nuevomexicano (New Mexican) culture; the pre-Columbian Americas; and Latin American affairs. UNM Press also publishes works of regional fiction and belles lettres, both contemporary and classical.

W. Clark Whitehorn, Editor in Chief; wcwhiteh@unm.edu.

Elise M. McHugh, Senior Acquisitions Editor; elisemc@unm.edu.

UNIVERSITY OF NORTH CAROLINA PRESS ❖ www.uncpress.unc.edu

116 South Boundary Street, Chapel Hill, NC 27514-3808, 919-966-3561

University of North Carolina Press's areas of interest include American studies, African American studies, American history, literature, anthropology, business/economic history, Civil War history, classics, ancient history, European history, folklore, gender studies, Latin American and Caribbean studies, legal history, media studies, Native American studies, political science, public policy, regional books, religious studies, rural studies, social medicine, Southern studies, and urban studies.

Mark Simpson-Vos, Editorial Director. American studies, gender and sexuality, literary studies, Native American studies, Civil War and military history, Southern culture and history.

Charles Grench, Assistant Director and Senior Editor; charles_grench@unc.edu. American history, European history, law and legal studies, classics and ancient history, business and economic history, political science, social science, African American history, craft history.

Elaine Maisner, Senior Executive Editor; elaine_maisner@unc.edu. Religious studies, Latin American studies, Caribbean studies, regional trade.

Joseph Parsons, Senior Editor. Social science, humanities, business and entrepreneurship, health and medicine.

Brandon Proia, Acquisitions Editor. Current affairs, African American studies.

UNIVERSITY OF OKLAHOMA PRESS ❖ www.oupress.com

2800 Venture Drive, Norman, OK 73069, 405-325-2000

OUP is a preeminent publisher of books about the American West and American Indians. Its other scholarly disciplines include classical studies, military history, political science, and natural science.

Charles E. Rankin, Associate Director, Editor in Chief; cerankin@ou.edu. American West, military history.

Alessandra Jacobi-Tamulevich, Editor; jacobi@ou.edu. American Indian, Mesoamerican, and Latin American studies.

Kathleen Kelly, Editor. Women's history.

UNIVERSITY OF SOUTH CAROLINA PRESS ❖ www.sc.edu/uscpress

718 Devine Street, Columbia, SC 29208, 803-777-5245

University of South Carolina Press publishes works of original scholarship in the fields of history (American, African American, Southern, Civil War, culinary, maritime, and women's), regional studies, literature, religious studies, rhetoric, and social work.

Alexander Moore, Acquisitions Editor; alexm@gwm.sc.edu. History, regional studies.

Jim Denton, Acquisitions Editor; dentoja@mailbox.sc.edu. Literature, religious studies, rhetoric, social work.

UNIVERSITY OF TENNESSEE PRESS ❖ www.utpress.org

600 Henley Street, Knoxville, TN 37996-4108, 865-974-3321

University of Tennessee Press is dedicated to publishing high-quality works of original scholarship in regional studies.

Scot Danforth, Acquisitions Director; danforth@utk.edu. American Civil War, American religion, special projects.

Thomas Wells, Editorial Assistant; twells@utk.edu. Archaeology, Native American studies.

UNIVERSITY OF TEXAS PRESS ❖ www.utexas.edu/utpress

PO Box 7819, Austin, TX 78713-7819, 512-471-7233

UTP produces books of general interest about Texas, African and Native Americans, Latinos, and women. Major areas of concentration are anthropology, Old and New World archaeology, architecture, art history, botany, classics and the Ancient World, conservation and the environment, Egyptology, film and media studies, geography, landscape, Latin American and Latino studies, literary modernism, Mexican American studies, marine science, Middle Eastern studies, ornithology, pre-Columbian studies, Texas and western studies, and women's studies.

Jim Burr, Senior Editor. Classics and ancient world, film and media studies, Middle East studies, Jewish studies, Old World archaeology, architecture, applied languages.

Casey Kittrell, Sponsoring Editor; casey@utpress.ppb.utexas.edu. Fiction in translation.

UNIVERSITY OF VIRGINIA PRESS ❖ www.upress.virginia.edu

Box 400318, Charlottesville, VA 22904, 434-924-3468

The UVaP editorial program focuses primarily on the humanities and social sciences with special concentrations in American history, African American studies, Southern studies, literature, and regional books.

Cathie Brettschneider, Humanities Editor; cib8b@virginia.edu.
Richard K. Holway, History and Social Sciences Editor; rkh2a@virginia.edu.
Boyd Zenner, Architecture and Environmental Editor; bz2v@virginia.edu.

UNIVERSITY OF WASHINGTON PRESS ❖

www.washington.edu/uwpress

PO Box 35970, Seattle, WA 98195, 206-543-4050

UW Press publishes titles that cover a wide variety of academic fields, with especially distinguished lists in Asian studies, Middle Eastern studies, environmental history, biography, anthropology, western history, natural history, marine studies, architectural history, and art.

Lorri Hagman, Executive Editor; lhagman@uw.edu. Asian studies, cultural and environmental anthropology.
Tim Zimmermann, Assistant Editor; tjz@uw.edu.
Regan Huff, Senior Acquisitions Editor; rhuff@uw.edu. Environment, art history, Northwest studies.
(Mr.) Ranjit Arab, Senior Acquisitions Editor; rarab@uw.edu. American / Asian American / Native American studies.

UNIVERSITY OF WISCONSIN PRESS ❖ www.uwpress.wisc.edu

1930 Monroe Street, 3rd Floor, Madison, WI 53711-2059, 608-263-1110

University of Wisconsin Press publishes a large range of general-interest books (biography, fiction, natural history, poetry, photography, fishing, food, travel), scholarly books (American studies, anthropology, art, classics, environmental studies, ethnic studies, film, gay and lesbian studies, history, Jewish studies, literary criticism, Slavic studies, etc.), and regional books about Wisconsin and the Upper Midwest.

Raphael Kadushin, Executive Editor; kadushin@wisc.edu. Autobiography/memoir, biography, classical studies, dance, performance, film, food, gender studies, GLBT studies, Jewish studies, Latino/a memoirs, travel.

Gwen Walker, PhD, Editorial Director; gcwalker@wisc.edu. African studies, anthropology, environmental studies, Irish studies, Latin American studies, Slavic studies, Southeast Asian studies, US history.

UNIVERSITY PRESS OF FLORIDA ❖ www.upf.com

15 NW 15th Street, Gainesville, FL 32611, 352-392-1351

University Press of Florida publishes books of regional interest and usefulness to the people of Florida, reflecting its rich historical, cultural, and intellectual heritage and resources. Subjects include African studies, anthropology and archaeology, art, dance, music, law, literature, Middle Eastern studies, natural history, Russian studies, history, Florida, Latin American studies, political science, science and technology, and sociology.

Meredith Morris Babb, Interim Editor in Chief.

UNIVERSITY PRESS OF KANSAS ❖ www.kansaspress.ku.edu

2502 Westbrooke Circle, Lawrence, KS 66045-4444, 785-864-4155

University Press of Kansas publishes regional books that contribute to the understanding of Kansas, the Great Plains, and the Midwest.

Michael Briggs, Editor in Chief; mbriggs@ku.edu. Military history, intelligence studies.

Charles T. Myers, Director; ctmyers@ku.edu. American politics, legal history, presidential studies.

Kim Hogeland, Acquisitions Editor; khogeland@ku.edu. US western history, Native American studies.

UNIVERSITY PRESS OF MISSISSIPPI ❖ www.upress.state.ms.us

3825 Ridgewood Road, Jackson, MS 39211-6492, 601-432-6205

UPM publishes books that interpret the South and its culture to the nation and the world.

Leila W. Salisbury, Director; lsalisbury@ihl.state.ms.us. American studies, film studies, pop culture.

Craig Gill, Assistant Director and Editor in Chief; cgill@ihl.state.ms.us. Art, architecture, folklore and folk art, history, music, natural sciences, photography, Southern studies.

Anne Stascavage, Managing Editor; astascavage@mississippi.edu. Performance studies.

(Mr.) Vijay Shah, Acquiring Editor; vhah@mississippi.edu. American literature, comics studies, Caribbean studies.

UNIVERSITY PRESS OF NEW ENGLAND ❖ www.upne.com

1 Court Street, Suite 250, Lebanon, NH 03766, 603-448-1533

University Press of New England (UPNE) is supported by a consortium of schools — Brandeis University, Dartmouth College, University of New Hampshire, Northeastern University, Tufts University, and University of Vermont — and based at Dartmouth College. The publishing program reflects strengths in the humanities; liberal arts; fine, decorative, and performing arts; literature; New England culture; and interdisciplinary studies.

Michael P. Burton, Director; michael.p.burton@dartmouth.edu. Art, photography, decorative arts, material culture, historic preservation, distribution titles.

Phyllis Deutsch, Editor-in-Chief; phyllis.d.deutsch@dartmouth.edu. Jewish studies, nature and environment, environment and health, sustainability studies, 19th-century studies, American studies, criminology with a gendered component.

Stephen Hull, Acquisitions Editor; stephen.p.hull@dartmouth.edu. New England regional, African American studies, New England sports, sports and society, music and technology, international studies with a civil society component.

Richard Pult, Acquisitions Editor; richard.pult@dartmouth.edu. New England regional/Boston, New England sports, marine biology/ecology, criminology, music/opera, Native American studies, American studies, visual culture, institutional histories.

VANDERBILT UNIVERSITY PRESS ❖

www.vanderbiltuniversitypress.com

2014 Broadway, Nashville, TN 37203, 615-322-3585

The editorial interests of Vanderbilt University Press include most areas of the humanities and social sciences, as well as health care and education. The press seeks intellectually provocative and socially significant works in these areas, as well as works that are interdisciplinary or that blend scholarly and practical concerns.

Eli Bortz, Acquisitions Editor; eli.bortz@vanderbilt.edu.

WAYNE STATE UNIVERSITY PRESS ❖ www.wsupress.wayne.edu

4809 Woodward Avenue, Detroit, MI 48201-1309, 313-577-6120

Wayne State University Press is a distinctive urban publisher with a strong presence in African American studies, Armenian studies, children's studies, classical studies, fairy-tale and folklore studies, film and television studies, German studies, the Great Lakes and Michigan, humor studies, Jewish studies, labor and urban studies, literature, and speech and language pathology.

Kathryn Wildfong, Acquisitions Manager; k.wildfong@wayne.edu. Africana studies, Jewish studies, Great Lakes and Michigan.

Annie Martin, Acquisitions Editor; annie.martin@wayne.edu. Film and TV studies, fairy-tale studies, children's studies, *Made in Michigan Writers Series*, speech and language pathology.

WESLEYAN UNIVERSITY PRESS ❖ www.wesleyan.edu/wespress

215 Long Lane, Middletown, CT 06459, 860-685-7711

Wesleyan University Press publishes in the areas of art and culture.

Suzanna Tamminen, Director and Editor in Chief; stamminen@wesleyan.edu. Dance.

(Mr.) Parker Smathers, Editor; psmathers@wesleyan.edu. Music/culture, film/TV and media studies, science-fiction studies, Connecticut history.

YALE UNIVERSITY PRESS ❖ www.yale.edu/yup

302 Temple Street, New Haven, CT 06511, PO Box 209040, New Haven, CT 06520-9040, 203-432-0960

YUP is one of the largest and most diverse academic publishers in the world.

(Ms.) Jean E. Thomson Black, Executive Editor. Life sciences, physical sciences, environmental sciences, medicine.

Jennifer Banks, Executive Editor. Literature in translation, religion, psychology.

Katherine Boller, Editor. Art and Architecture.

Laura Davulis, Associate Editor, Coordinator of Editorial Internships. History, current events.

Joseph Calamia, Editor. Physical sciences, environmental sciences, geology, applied mathematics, engineering.

Jaya Aninda Chatterjee, Assistant Editor. Politics, international relations, Russian/ Eurasian studies.

Patricia Fidler, Publisher. Art and architecture.

William Frucht, Executive Editor. Political science, international relations, law, economics.

Michael O'Malley, PhD, Executive Editor. Business, economics, law.

Mary Jane Peluso, Publisher. Foreign languages and ESL.

Christopher Rogers, Executive Director. History, current events.

Steve Wasserman, Executive Editor-at-Large. Trade books.

Part 5

CANADIAN BOOK PUBLISHERS

INTRODUCTION
CANADIAN BOOK PUBLISHING AND THE CANADIAN MARKET

Greg Ioannou

There's good and bad news about the Canadian publishing industry for writers. First, the bad: breaking in isn't easy. The good news: most Canadian publishers are interested in new writers. They have to be, because small to midsize Canadian houses operate mainly on government grant money. In order to get that grant money, houses must publish Canadian authors. They also can't afford bidding wars. Instead, they often find new authors, develop them, and hope that they stay — or that their fame will add value to the house's backlist.

The key to getting published is to make sure that you're sending the right manuscript to the right publisher, using an appropriate style for submissions. Publishers are less frustrated by poor writing than they are by poorly executed submissions.

If you've written a nonfiction book about rural Nova Scotia, don't send your manuscript to a children's publisher in Vancouver. Research the publishers first instead of spamming busy editors with manuscripts that don't fit their house's list.

The internet is a fantastic tool for writers. It's easier to research potential publishers online than it is to sit at the library and search through *Quill & Quire's Canadian Publishers Directory* — though that is still a valuable resource.

If you want more information than what's included in the listings that follow, do an online search for Canadian publishers. A few places to start are the Association of Canadian Publishers — which provides a search form by genre and province — and the Canadian Publishers' Council. The Canadian Children's Book Centre is particularly focused and has an annual publication that lists publishers that accept unsolicited manuscripts and artwork. If you see a publisher whose mandate seems to match your book idea, visit their website and locate their submission requirements, or contact a Canadian agent.

Rather than sending your manuscript everywhere, write custom proposals that show the publisher that you know what they publish, you've read their submission guidelines thoroughly, and your manuscript adheres to those requirements. It is okay to show enthusiasm for the press or to suggest where you think your manuscript fits on their list. But don't act as though the publisher would be lucky to get your book. Do not threaten publishers with deadlines; you may bully yourself into an automatic rejection. Take the time to write a brief but informative proposal, including a chapter-by-chapter outline if appropriate, and send a sample of your work. Include in the cover letter the approximate word count, genre, and reading level. Consider contacting the Canadian Authors Association or the Writers' Union of Canada for more information on writing for the Canadian market.

If you're a foreign writer hoping to be published in Canada, offer some form of subject-matter expertise. It's like immigrating to another country: you need to have a skill that a Canadian doesn't have.

American writers should remember that Canada is not part of the United States; Canadian publishers cannot use US stamps to return manuscripts. Use International Reply Coupons (available at any post office) instead, or, if the editor accepts electronic submissions, submit your manuscript via email.

Greg Ioannou is the president of Colborne Communications, which provides a full range of services to the book-publishing industry, taking books from initial conception through writing, editing, design, layout, and print production.

Colborne Communications
Toronto, 416-214-0183, www.colcomm.ca, greg@colcomm.ca

THE LISTINGS

ANNICK PRESS LIMITED ❖ www.annickpress.com

15 Patricia Avenue, Toronto, ON M2M 1H9, Canada, 416-221-4802

Annick Press publishes children's literature, specifically picture books, nonfiction, and juvenile and young adult novels. The company has won many prestigious design and publishing awards, including the Canadian Booksellers Association's Publisher of the Year award. Annick publishes approximately 30 titles annually and seeks titles that speak to issues young people deal with every day, such as bullying, teen sexuality, advertising, and alienation, as well as books on science, fantasy, pop culture, and world conflict.

Colleen MacMillan, Associate Publisher.

ANVIL PRESS ❖ www.anvilpress.com

278 East First Avenue, Vancouver, BC V5T 1A6, Canada, 604-876-8710

Anvil is a literary publisher interested in contemporary, progressive literature in all genres, whose mission is to discover, nurture, and promote new and established Canadian literary talent. It was created in 1988 to publish *subTERRAIN* magazine, which explores alternative literature and art; three years later, the press moved into publishing books as well. It publishes 8 to 10 titles per year and is not interested in publishing genre novels (science fiction, horror, romance, etc.).

Brian Kaufman, Publisher.
Shazia Hafiz Ramji, Publishing Assistant.

ARSENAL PULP PRESS ❖ www.arsenalpulp.com

#101–211 East Georgia Street, Vancouver, BC V6A 1Z6, Canada, 604-687-4233, Twitter: @Arsenalpulp

Arsenal Pulp Press publishes provocative and stimulating books that challenge the status quo in the following genres: cultural studies, political/sociological studies, regional studies and guides (particularly for British Columbia), cookbooks, gay and lesbian literature, visual art, multicultural literature, literary fiction, youth culture, and health. It has been a four-time nominee for Small Press Publisher of the Year, given by the Canadian Booksellers Association (2004, 2008, 2010, 2012). No genre fiction, such as science fiction, thriller, or romance. It has had particular success with cookbooks and publishes 14 to 20 new titles a year.

Brian Lam, Publisher; blam@arsenalpulp.com.
Robert Ballantyne, Associate Publisher.
Susan Safyan, Associate Editor.

BRICK BOOKS ❖ www.brickbooks.ca

431 Boler Road, Box 20081, London, ON N6K 4G6, Canada, 519-657-8579, Twitter: @BrickBooks

Brick Books is a small literary press that seeks to foster interesting, ambitious, and compelling work by Canadian poets. The only press in Canada that specializes in publishing poetry books, Brick was nominated for the prestigious Canadian Booksellers Association Libris Award for Best Small Press Publisher of the Year, 2006. It publishes seven new books and an average of nine reprints every year.

Barry Dempster, Acquisitions Editor.

CORMORANT BOOKS ❖ www.cormorantbooks.com

10 St. Mary Street, Suite 615, Toronto, ON, M4Y 1P9, Canada, 416-925-8887

Established by Jan and Gary Geddes in 1986, Cormorant Books seeks to publish the best new work in the areas of literary fiction and creative nonfiction for the adult market. This award-winning house publishes a select list of literary fiction, trade nonfiction, and works of fiction in translation.

Robyn Sarah, Poetry Editor; r.sarah@cormorantbooks.com.

COTEAU BOOKS ❖ www.coteaubooks.com

2517 Victoria Avenue, Regina, SK S4P 0T2, Canada, 306-777-0170,
Twitter: @CoteauBooks

Coteau publishes novels, juvenile fiction, regional and creative nonfiction, and drama by authors from all parts of Canada. The press seeks to give literary voice to its community and places a special emphasis on Saskatchewan and prairie writers. It also has an active program of presenting and developing new writers. Coteau releases more than a dozen new titles each year. It publishes novels for young readers ages 9 to 12, ages 13 to 15, and 16 and up. It does not publish kids' picture books.

Nik Burton, Managing Editor.

DRAWN AND QUARTERLY ❖ www.drawnandquarterly.com

PO Box 48056, Montréal, QC H2V 4S8, Canada, 514-279-2221, Twitter: @DandQ

Drawn and Quarterly is an award-winning publisher of graphic novels, comic books, and comic book series, with over 20 new titles per year. The publisher acquires new comic books, art books, and graphic novels by renowned cartoonists and newcomers from around the globe.

(Mr.) Chris Oliveros, Publisher; chris@drawnandquarterly.com.
Peggy Burns, Associate Publisher; peggy@drawnandquarterly.com.

DUNDURN PRESS ❖ www.dundurn.com

500-3 Church Street, Toronto, ON M5E 1M2, Canada, 416-214-5544,
Twitter: @dundurnpress

Dundurn was established in 1972 to bring Canadian history and biography to a general readership. Politics, history, and biography were the original mandate, which quickly expanded to include literary and art criticism and large illustrated art books. In the 1990s, Dundurn acquired three other Canadian publishing houses, and since 2007 it has acquired the assets of several more, broadening Dundurn's editorial range to include literary fiction, young adult books, mysteries, and popular nonfiction. It publishes 75 to 80 new titles a year and is now one of the largest publishers of adult and children's fiction and nonfiction in Canada.

Kirk Howard, President and Publisher.
Michael R. Carroll, Editorial Director.

ECW PRESS ❖ www.ecwpress.com

2120 Queen Street East, Suite 200, Toronto, ON M4E 1E2, Canada, 416-694-3348, Twitter: @ecwpress

ECW (Entertainment, Culture, Writing) Press publishes nonfiction and fiction for the adult market. ECW has published close to 1,000 books, which have been distributed throughout the English-speaking world and translated into dozens of languages. Its list includes poetry and fiction, pop culture, political analysis, sports, biography, and travel guides. ECW releases around 50 new titles per year.

Jack David, Copublisher; jack@ecwpress.com.

FIREFLY BOOKS LTD. ❖ www.fireflybooks.com

50 Staples Avenue, Unit 1, Richmond Hill, ON, L4B 0A7, Canada, 416-499-8412, Twitter: @FireflyMike

Firefly Books, established in 1977, publishes and distributes nonfiction and children's books. Firefly's admirable goal is to bring readers beautifully produced books written by experts at reasonable prices. Its particular strengths lie in cookbooks, gardening, astronomy, health, natural history, pictorial books, reference books (especially for children), and sports.

Lionel Koffler, President and Publisher.
Michael Warrick, Associate Publisher.

FITZHENRY & WHITESIDE LTD. ❖ www.fitzhenry.ca

195 Allstate Parkway, Markham, ON L3R 4T8, Canada, 905-477-9700

Fitzhenry & Whiteside Ltd. specializes in trade nonfiction and children's books. The firm also offers a textbook list and a small list of literary fiction. It publishes or reprints 60 to 80 titles per year, specializing in history, natural sciences, forestry, ecology, biography, psychology, reference, Canadiana, antiques, art, photography, and children's and young adult fiction and nonfiction. The children's book list includes early readers, picture books, and middle grade and young adult novels.

Sharon Fitzhenry, President.
Cheryl Chen, Publisher. Children's books.

Fifth House Publishers ❖ www.fifthhousepublishers.ca

FHP publishes children's through adult fiction and nonfiction on subjects that are entirely "Canadian," including books about Native/Aboriginal peoples. The list includes art, culture, history, current events, and the environment.

Sharon Fitzhenry, Publisher.

GASPEREAU PRESS ❖ www.gaspereau.com

47 Church Avenue, Kentville, NS B4N 2M7, Canada, 902-678-6002

Gaspereau Press is a Nova Scotia–owned and –operated trade publisher specializing in short-run editions of both literary and regional interest for the Canadian market. Its list includes poetry, local history, literary essays, novels, and short story collections. Gaspereau was nominated for the prestigious Canadian Booksellers Association's Libris Award for Best Small Press Publisher of the Year, 2006. Gaspereau is one of a handful of Canadian trade publishers that prints and binds books in-house. With only 16 paces between the editor's desk and the printing press, Gaspereau practices a form of "craft" publishing that is influenced more by William Morris and the private press movement of the nineteenth century than by the contemporary publishing culture.

Gary Dunfield, Publisher.
Andrew Steeves, Publisher.

GOOSE LANE EDITIONS ❖ www.gooselane.com

500 Beaverbrook Court, Suite 330, Fredericton, NB E3B 5X4, Canada, 506-450-4251

Canada's oldest independent publisher, Goose Lane Editions is a small publishing house that specializes in literary fiction, poetry, and a select list of nonfiction titles on subjects including history, biography, Canadiana, and fine art. It does not publish commercial fiction, genre fiction, or confessional works of any kind. Nor does it publish for the children's market.

Susanne Alexander, Publisher; s.alexander@gooselane.com.
Angela Williams, Publishing Assistant; awilliams@gooselane.com.
James Duplacey, Managing Editor; jduplacey@gooselane.com.
Ross Leckie, Editor; rleckie@gooselane.com. Poetry.
Bethany Gibson, Editor; bgibson@gooselane.com. Fiction.
Colleen Kitts-Gougen, Editor; ckitts@gooselane.com. Nonfiction.
Brent Wilson, Editor; nbmhp@gooselane.com. Military history.

GREAT PLAINS PUBLICATIONS ❖ www.greatplains.mb.ca

233 Garfield Street South, Winnipeg, MB R3G 2M1, Canada, 204-475-6799

Great Plains Publications is an award-winning prairie-based general trade publisher specializing in regional history and biography. Its mandate is to publish books that are written by Canadian prairie authors. It also publishes books by Canadian authors not living on the prairies that are of specific interest to people living in this region (content, setting).

Gregg Shilliday, Publisher.
(Ms.) Ingeborg Boyens, Executive Editor.

Enfield & Wizenty ❖ www.greatplains.mb.ca/enfield-wizenty

The Enfield & Wizenty imprint publishes "original novels and short story collections by Canadian writers at all career stages."

Maurice Mierau, Consulting Editor.

Great Plains Teen Fiction ❖ www.greatplains.mb.ca/great-plains-teen-fiction

Great Plains Teen Fiction publishes contemporary and historical fiction from authors across the country for readers ages 14 to 18.

Anita Daher, Consulting Editor.

HARBOUR PUBLISHING ❖ www.harbourpublishing.com

PO Box 219, Madeira Park, BC V0N 2H0, 604-883-2730

Harbour focuses on British Columbia's history, culture, fishing, and hunting.

Howard and Mary White, Publishers.

Douglas & McIntyre (2013) Ltd. ❖ www.douglas-mcintyre.com

4437 Rondeview Road, PO Box 219, Madeira Park, BC V0N 2H0, Canada,
800-667-2988

Douglas & McIntyre publishes a broad general program of adult fiction and nonfiction, with an emphasis on art and architecture, First Nations issues, Pacific Northwest history, cookbooks, and current events. It publishes around 35 nonfiction books a year while maintaining a distinguished literary fiction list.

Howard White, Publisher.

HERITAGE HOUSE PUBLISHING CO. LTD. ❖ www.heritagehouse.ca

#103–1075 Pendergast Street, Victoria, BC V8V 0A1, 250-360-0829

Since 1969, Heritage House has striven to be "Canada's storyteller," especially as it relates to the Northwest, also known as the "Cariboo region." Their list covers a wide range of categories, including travel, culture, pioneer history, and young adult.

Rodger Touchie, Publisher.
Lara Kordic, Senior Editor.

Greystone Books Ltd. ❖ www.greystonebooks.com

343 Railway Street, Suite 201, Vancouver, BC V6A 1A4, Canada, 604-875-1550

Greystone Books titles focus on natural history and science, the environment, popular culture, sports, and outdoor recreation. The firm publishes around 30 new books a year.

Rob Sanders, Publisher.
Nancy Flight, Associate Publisher.

HOUSE OF ANANSI PRESS ❖ www.houseofanansi.com

110 Spadina Avenue, Suite 801, Toronto, ON M5V 2K4, Canada, 416-363-4343

House of Anansi Press specializes in finding and developing Canada's new writers and in maintaining a culturally significant backlist that has accumulated since the house was founded in 1967. Anansi publishes Canadian and international writers of literary fiction, poetry, and serious nonfiction, releasing five new fiction titles, eight new nonfiction titles, and four new poetry titles per year. It does not publish genre fiction (mystery, thriller, science fiction, or romance) or self-help nonfiction. The company launched Spiderline, a crime fiction imprint, in 2010. The same year, the imprint Anansi International was started to reflect the company's commitment to publishing voices from around the world.

Sarah MacLachlan, President; sarah@anansi.ca.

Groundwood Books ❖ www.groundwoodbooks.com

Groundwood Books, an independent imprint of House of Anansi Press, publishes children's books for all ages, including fiction, picture books, and nonfiction. It primarily focuses on works by Canadians, though it sometimes also buys manuscripts from international authors. Many of its books tell the stories of people whose voices are not always heard. Books by the First Peoples of this hemisphere have always been a special interest, as well as French-Canadian works in translation. Since 1998, Groundwood has been publishing works by Latino authors, in both English and Spanish, under its Libro Tigrillo imprint. Groundwood is always looking for new authors of novel-length fiction for children in all age areas but does not accept unsolicited manuscripts for picture books. They like character-driven literary fiction and do not publish high-interest/low-vocabulary fiction or stories with anthropomorphic animals or elves/fairies as their main characters.

Patsy Aldana, Vice President and Publisher.

INSOMNIAC PRESS ❖ www.insomniacpress.com

520 Princess Avenue, London, ON N6B 2B8, Canada, 416-504-6270, Twitter: @InsomniacPress

Insomniac Press is a midsize independent press that publishes nonfiction, fiction, and poetry for adults. Insomniac always strives to publish the most exciting new writers it can find. While it publishes a broad range of titles, Insomniac has also developed special niche areas, including black studies books, gay and lesbian books, celebrity musician–authored books, and gay mysteries. Insomniac is actively seeking commercial and creative nonfiction on a wide range of subjects, including business, personal finance, gay and lesbian studies, and black Canadian studies.

Mike O'Connor, Publisher; mike@insomniacpress.com.
Dan Varrette, Managing Editor; dan@insomniacpress.com.

JAMES LORIMER & COMPANY LIMITED ❖ www.lorimer.ca

317 Adelaide Street West, Suite 1002, Toronto, ON M5V 1P9, Canada, 416-362-4762, Twitter: @LorimerBooks

James Lorimer is a publisher of nonfiction, children's books, young adult novels, and illustrated guidebooks. It publishes Canadian authors for a Canadian audience and seeks manuscripts in the following genres: cultural or social history, natural history, cookbooks with a Canadian or regional focus, education, public issues, travel and recreation, and biography. It is especially interested in projects for the southwestern Ontario marketplace.

James Lorimer, Publisher; jlorimer@lorimer.ca.
Christie Harkin, Associate Publisher. Children's and teens'.
Pam Hickman, Acquisitions Editor.

MCGILL-QUEEN'S UNIVERSITY PRESS ❖ www.mqup.mcgill.ca

Montréal office: 1010 Sherbrooke West, Suite 1720, Montréal, QC H3A 2R7, Canada, 514-398-3750

Kingston office: 93 University Avenue, Kingston, ON K7L 3N6, Canada, 613-533-2155

MQUP publishes original scholarly books and well-researched general-interest books in all areas of the social sciences and humanities. While its emphasis is on providing an outlet for Canadian authors and scholarship, some of its authors are from outside Canada. More than half of its sales are international.

Philip J. Cercone, Executive Director and Senior Editor (Montréal); philip.cercone@mcgill.ca. American history, economics, philosophy.

Kyla Madden, Senior Editor (Montréal); kyla.madden@mcgill.ca. World history, religion, history of medicine.

Mark Abley, Editor (Montréal); mark.abley@mcgill.ca. Philosophy, linguistics.

Jonathon Crago, Editor (Montréal); jonathan.crago@mcgill.ca. Art history, architecture, communication studies, film, music, Quebec history.

Jacqueline Mason, Editor (Montréal); Jacqueline.mason@mcgill.ca. Political science, public policy, international studies, law, psychology.

Jill Bryant, Editor (Kingston); jill.bryant@queensu.ca. International development, education, women's studies.

James Macnevin, Editor (Kingston); james.macnevin@queensu@ca. Canadian history, sociology, geography, environment, culture.

MCGRAW-HILL RYERSON LTD. ❖ www.mcgrawhill.ca

300 Water Street, Whitby, ON L1N 9B6, Canada, 905-430-5000, 800-565-5758, Twitter: @McGrawHillCDN

One of the 111 McGraw-Hill Companies around the globe, McGraw-Hill Ryerson is staffed and managed by Canadians but reports to its parent company in New York. Though primarily an educational division, McGraw-Hill Ryerson also has a thriving trade arm, which publishes and distributes reference books on a wide array of subjects, including business, computing, engineering, science, travel, and self-study foreign-language programs. Other areas include outdoor recreation, child care, parenting, health, fine arts, music, sports, fitness, cooking, and crafts.

Claudio Pascucci, President of Professional Division.

NEW SOCIETY PUBLISHERS ❖ www.newsociety.com

PO Box 189, Gabriola Island, BC, V0R 1X0, Canada, 250-247-9737,
Twitter: @NewSocietyPub

New Society Publishers is an activist press focused on social justice and ecological issues. Its mission is to publish books that contribute in fundamental ways to building an ecologically sustainable and just society. It publishes books on food, gardening, health and wellness, energy, sustainable living, urban issues, green building, education, and parenting. All its books are printed on 100 percent post-consumer recycled paper with vegetable-based inks.

Sue Custance, Publishing Director.

NOVALIS ❖ www.novalis.ca

10 Lower Spadina Avenue, Suite 400, Toronto, ON M5V 2Z2, Canada, 416-363-3303

Novalis is a religious publishing house and is a part of Saint Paul University. Novalis publishes and distributes books and other resources touching on all aspects of spiritual life, especially from the Christian and Jewish traditions. While most of its titles are for the general public, Novalis also publishes more specialized works in the area of theology and religious studies. Subjects include personal growth, self-help, spirituality and prayer, children's books, gardening, meditation, Church history, and Celtic spirituality, among others. The largest bilingual religious publisher in Canada, Novalis has equally strong publishing programs in both English and French.

Joseph Sinasac, Publishing Director; joseph.sinasac@novalis.ca.
Grace Deutsch, Editorial Director; grace.deutsch@novalis.ca.
Anne-Louise Mahoney, Managing Editor; anne-louise.mahoney@novalis.ca.

Owlkids Books ❖ www.owlkids.com/books

10 Lower Spadina Avenue, Suite 400, Toronto, ON M5V 2Z2, Canada, 416-340-2700,
owlkids@owlkids.com

Owlkids Books has been publishing children's books for more than 35 years. It specializes in science and nature titles but also looks for nonfiction in a wide range of subjects, including Canadian culture, sports, crafts, activities, history, humor, and picture books.

Karen Boersma, Publisher.
Angela Keenlyside, Associate Publisher.
John Crossingham, Senior Editor.

OOLICHAN BOOKS ❖ www.oolichan.com

PO Box 2278, Fernie, BC V0B 1M0, Canada, 250-423-6113, Twitter: @OolichanBooks

Oolichan Books is a literary press publishing poetry, fiction, and creative nonfiction titles, including literary criticism, memoir, and books on regional history, First Nations, and policy issues. The press is named after the small fish that was once plentiful in West Coast waters and a dietary staple of First Nations people, to whom it was sacred.

Randal Macnair, Publisher.
Carolyn Nikodym, Assistant to the Publisher.
Ron Smith, Editor.
(Ms.) Pat Smith, Consulting Editor.

ORCA BOOK PUBLISHERS ❖ www.orcabook.com

PO Box 5626, Station B, Victoria, BC V8R 6S4, Canada, Twitter: @orcabook

Orca focuses on children's books: picture books and juvenile and young adult fiction. Its limited adult list focuses on general trade nonfiction, including travel and recreational guides, regional history, and biography. The Orca Currents line seeks short novels with contemporary themes written for middle-school students reading below grade level. The Orca Sports line features sports action combined with mystery/suspense. For ages 10 and up, Orca Sports seeks strong plots, credible characters, simple language, and high-interest chapters. The Orca Echoes line features early chapter books for readers ages 7 to 9 at a grade 2 reading level. The Orca Young Readers line has historical and contemporary stories for ages 8 to 11, with age-appropriate plots and storylines.

Andrew Woolridge, Publisher; andrew@orcabook.com.
Bob Tyrrell, Editorial Director.
Sarah Harvey, Editorial Director.
Ruth Linka, Associate Publisher.
Amy Collins, Editor.

PENGUIN CANADA ❖ www.penguin.ca

90 Eglinton Avenue East, Suite 700, Toronto, ON M4P 2Y3, Canada, 416-925-2249, info@ca.penguingroup.com, Twitter: @PenguinCanada

Penguin Canada completed its international merger with Random House in 2013, and the changes were still in play at press time. Initially a distribution arm for Penguin

International, Penguin Books began publishing indigenous Canadian work in 1982 with such notable titles as Peter C. Newman's landmark history of the Hudson's Bay Company, *Company of Adventurers*, and fiction by Robertson Davies, Timothy Findley, Alice Munro, and Mordecai Richler. It also publishes books under other imprints, including Hamish Hamilton Canada, Puffin Canada, and Viking Canada. Penguin Canada's books cover subjects as diverse as Canadian nationalism, homelessness and mental illness, and health care and education.

Nicole Winstanley, Publisher.

Diane Turbide, Editorial Director.

Lynne Missen, Editor.

Hamish Hamilton Canada ❖ www.hamishhamilton.ca

The Canadian counterpart of one of Britain's most distinguished literary lists, Hamish Hamilton Canada has provided a home for an exciting and eclectic group of authors united by the distinctiveness and excellence of their writing. It maintains a deep commitment to literary value, embracing both young and old, the experimental and the new, and continues to be selective with a list of 5 to 10 titles a year.

Nicole Winstanley, Publisher.

PLAYWRIGHTS CANADA PRESS ❖ www.playwrightscanada.com

269 Richmond Street West, Suite 202, Toronto, ON, M5V 1X1, Canada, 416-703-0013, Twitter: @PlayCanPress

Playwrights Canada Press is the largest exclusive publisher of Canadian drama, publishing roughly 30 books of plays, theater history, criticism, biography, and memoir every year. It exists to raise the profile of Canadian playwrights, theater, and theater practitioners. French plays by Canadian authors are published in translation, and the press's mandate includes printing plays for young audiences.

Annie Gibson, Publisher; annie@playwrightscanada.com.

(Mr.) Blake Sproule, Managing Editor; blake@playwrightscanada.com.

RANDOM HOUSE CANADA ❖ www.randomhouse.ca

**One Toronto Street, Suite 300, Toronto, ON M5C 2V6, Canada, 416-364-4449,
Twitter: @RandomHouseCA**

Random House Canada was established in 1944 and in 1986 established its own indigenous Canadian publishing program. The firm completed its international merger with Penguin in 2013, and the fallout wasn't yet clear as of press time.

Random House Canada ❖ www.randomhouse.ca/imprints/random-house-canada

The Random House Canada imprint features a diverse list of literary and commercial fiction, Canadian and international cookbooks, and nonfiction.

Anne Collins, Editor.

Doubleday Canada ❖ www.randomhouse.ca/imprints/doubleday-canada-publishing-group

Doubleday Canada marked its 75th anniversary in 2012. One of Canada's most prominent publishers, it is committed to producing fine fiction from both established and new voices, and developing challenging and entertaining nonfiction. It also maintains a young adult publishing program.

Kristin Cochrane, Editor.
Tim Rostron, Editor.

Knopf Canada ❖ www.randomhouse.ca/imprints/knopf-canada

Knopf Canada was launched in 1991, when Sonny Mehta, president of Alfred A. Knopf, approached prominent editor Louise Denny to create and run a Canadian arm of Knopf in the offices of Random House Canada. It is interested in thoughtful nonfiction and fiction with literary merit and strong commercial potential.

Anne Collins, Editor.

McClelland & Stewart ❖ www.randomhouse.ca/imprints/mcclelland-stewart#

**1 Toronto Street, Toronto, ON M5C 2V6, Canada, 416-364-4449,
Twitter: @McClelland Books**

Established in 1906, M&S is something of a Canadian institution and was an early publisher of Lucy Maud Montgomery's *Anne of Green Gables* and Winston Churchill's *History of the English Speaking Peoples.* Today, it publishes a wide range of poetry, fiction, and nonfiction.

(Mr.) Jordan Fenn, Publisher.
Anita Chong, Editor.
Ellen Seligman, Vice President.
Lara Hinchberger, Editorial Director.

Tundra Books ❖ www.tundrabooks.com

1 Toronto Street, Suite 300, Toronto, Ontario M5C 2V6, 416-364-4449,
Twitter: @TundraBooks

Tundra is a children's book publisher famous for their extremely well-produced and -illustrated books for young readers.

Tara Walker, Editor.

RED DEER PRESS ❖ www.reddeerpress.com

195 Allstate Parkway, Markham, ON L3R 4T8, Canada, 800-387-9776,
Twitter: @RedDeerPress

Red Deer Press is an award-winning publisher of literary fiction, nonfiction, children's illustrated books, juvenile fiction, teen fiction, drama, and poetry. Its mandate is to publish books by, about, or of interest to Canadians, with special emphasis on the Prairie West. The press publishes 18 to 20 new books per year, all written or illustrated by Canadians. Approximately 20 percent of their program is composed of first-time authors and illustrators.

Richard Dionne, Publisher; dionne@reddeerpress.com.
Peter Carver, Children's Editor.

RONSDALE PRESS ❖ www.ronsdalepress.com

3350 West 21st Avenue, Vancouver, BC V6S 1G7, Canada, 604-738-4688,
Twitter: @ronsdalepress

A literary publishing house, Ronsdale Press is dedicated to publishing books from across Canada and books that give Canadians new insights into their country. Ronsdale publishes fiction, poetry, regional history, biography and autobiography, plays, books of ideas about Canada, and children's books. The press looks for thoughtful works by authors who have read deeply in contemporary and earlier literature and whose texts offer genuinely new insights. Ronsdale accepts submissions only from Canadian authors.

Ronald B. Hatch, General Acquisitions Editor.
Veronica Hatch, Children's Acquisitions Editor.

SECOND STORY PRESS ❖ www.secondstorypress.ca

20 Maud Street, Suite 401, Toronto, ON M5V 2M5, Canada, 416-537-7850, Twitter: @_secondstory

The Second Story Press list spans adult fiction and nonfiction; children's fiction, nonfiction, and picture books; and young adult fiction and nonfiction. As a feminist press, it looks for manuscripts dealing with the many diverse and varied aspects of the lives of girls and women. Some of its special-interest areas include Judaica, ability issues, coping with cancer, and queer rights. They publish about 16 new books per year, primarily from Canadian authors.

Margie Wolfe, Publisher.
Carolyn Jackson, Managing Editor.

TALON BOOKS LTD. ❖ www.talonbooks.com

PO Box 2076, Vancouver, BC V6B 3S3, Canada, 604-444-4889, Twitter: @Talonbooks

Talon Books was founded as a poetry magazine at Magee High School in Vancouver in 1963. Since then it has grown into one of Canada's largest independent presses. It publishes drama, fiction, and nonfiction of the political, social, critical, and ethnographic variety.

Kevin Williams, President; kevin@talonbooks.com.

UNIVERSITY OF ALBERTA PRESS ❖ www.uap.ualberta.ca

Ring House 2, University of Alberta, Edmonton, AB T6G 2E1, Canada, 780-492-3662

University of Alberta Press publishes in the areas of biography, history, language, literature, natural history, regional interest, travel narratives, and reference books. The press seeks to contribute to the intellectual and cultural life of Alberta and Canada. Canadian works that are analytical in nature are especially welcome, as are works by scholars who wish to interpret Canada, both past and present.

Linda Cameron, Director; linda.cameron@ualberta.ca.

Peter Midgley, Senior Acquisitions Editor; petem@ualberta.ca.

Fred Bohm, Acquiring Editor; frederic@ualberta.ca.

Mary Lou Roy, Editor; marylou.roy@ualberta.ca.

UNIVERSITY OF BRITISH COLUMBIA PRESS ❖ www.ubcpress.ubc.ca

2029 West Mall, Vancouver, BC V6T 1Z2, Canada, 604-822-5959, Twitter: @UBCPress

UBC Press is the publishing branch of the University of British Columbia. Established in 1971, it is among the largest university presses in Canada, publishing 70 new books annually, with an active backlist of more than 800 titles. UBC Press is widely acknowledged as one of the foremost publishers of political science, Native studies, and forestry books. Other areas of particular strength are Asian studies, Canadian history, environmental studies, planning, and urban studies.

Peter Milroy, Director Emeritus; milroy@ubcpress.ca. Special projects, international rights.

Emily Andrew, Senior Editor; andrew@ubcpress.ca. Asian studies, political science and political philosophy, military history, transnational and multicultural studies, communications.

Randy Schmidt, Senior Editor; schmidt@ubcpress.ca. Forestry, environmental studies, urban studies and planning, sustainable development, geography, law and society.

Darcy Cullen, Acquisitions Editor; cullen@ubcpress.ca. Canadian history, regional, native studies, sexuality studies, northern and Arctic studies, health studies, education.

UNIVERSITY OF MANITOBA PRESS ❖ www.umanitoba.ca/uofmpress

301 St. John's College, University of Manitoba, Winnipeg, MB R3T 2M5, Canada, 204-474-9495

Founded in 1967, University of Manitoba Press publishes innovative and exceptional books of scholarship and serious Canadian nonfiction. Its list includes books on Native studies, Canadian history, women's studies, Icelandic studies, aboriginal languages, film studies, biography, geography, nature, and Canadian literature and culture. It publishes five to eight books a year, meaning each book receives the concentrated focus and attention that are often not possible at a larger press.

David Carr, Director; carr@cc.umanitoba.ca.

Glenn Bergen, Managing Editor; d.bergen@umanitoba.ca.
Jill McConkey, Acquisitions Editor; jill.mcconkey@umanitoba.ca

UNIVERSITY OF OTTAWA PRESS / LES PRESSES DE L'UNIVERSITÉ D'OTTAWA ❖ www.press.uottawa.ca

542 King Edward, Ottawa, ON K1N 6N5, Canada, 613-562-5246,
Twitter: @uOttawaPress

As Canada's only officially bilingual university press, the UOP is both uniquely Canadian and unique in Canada. Since 1936, UOP has supported cultural development through the publication of books in both French and English aimed at a general public interested in serious nonfiction.

Lara Mainville, Director; lara.mainville@uottawa.ca.
Dominike Thomas, Acquisitions Editor; dthomas@uottawa.ca.

UNIVERSITY OF TORONTO PRESS ❖ www.utpress.utoronto.ca

10 Saint Mary Street, Suite 700, Toronto, ON M4Y 2W8, Canada, 416-978-2239,
Twitter: @utpress

University of Toronto Press is Canada's oldest and largest scholarly publisher and is among the 15 largest university presses in North America. Established in 1901, the press publishes scholarly, reference, and general-interest books on Canadian history and literature, medieval studies, and social sciences, among other subjects. Approximately 200 new titles are released each year, and the backlist includes more than 3,500 titles. The house publishes in a range of fields, including history and politics; women's studies; health, family, and society; law and crime; economics; workplace communication; theory/culture; language, literature, semiotics, and drama; medieval studies; Renaissance studies; Erasmus; Italian-language studies; East European studies; classics; and nature. The list includes topical titles in Canadian studies, Native studies, sociology, anthropology, urban studies, modern languages, and music.

Anne Brackenbury, Executive Editor. Anthropology, criminology, geography, native
   studies, Latin/North American studies, sociology.
Natalie Fingerhut, Editor. International relations, Jewish history, Canadian and
   European history, security studies, non-Western history.
Jennifer DiDomenico, Acquisitions Editor. Economics.

Douglas Hildebrand, Acquisitions Editor. Anthropology, criminology, education, GLBTQ studies, geography, Native studies, race and diaspora studies, urban studies.

Len Husband, Acquisitions Editor. Canadian history, natural science, philosophy.

Richard Ratzlaff, Acquisitions Editor. Book history, English literature, modern languages, Victorian studies.

(Ms.) Siobhan McMenemy, Acquisitions Editor. Cultural studies, digital futures, film studies, modern art.

Suzanne Rancourt, Executive Editor. Humanities, classics, medieval and renaissance studies.

Daniel Quinlan, Acquisitions Editor. Political science, law.

Eric Carlson, Associate Acquisitions Editor. Health/medicine studies, social work.

VÉHICULE PRESS ❖ www.vehiculepress.com

PO Box 42094 BP Roy, Montréal, QC, H2W 2T3, Canada, 514-844-6073,
Twitter: @VehiculePress

For more than 35 years, Véhicule Press has been publishing prize-winning poetry, fiction, social history, Quebec studies, Jewish studies, jazz history, and restaurant guides.

Simon Dardick, Editor. Nonfiction.
Dimitri Nasrallah, Editor. Fiction.

WHITECAP BOOKS ❖ www.whitecap.ca

314 West Cordova Street, Suite 210, Vancouver, BC, V6B 1E8, Canada, 604-980-9852,
Twitter: whitecapbooks

Whitecap Books is one of Canada's largest independent publishers. In addition to the cookbooks, gift books, and coffee-table books that it is primarily known for, Whitecap publishes gardening and crafts, photo-scenic, history, arts and entertainment, children's fiction and nonfiction, travel, sports, and transportation books. Its Walrus Books division publishes children's books.

Nick Rundall, Publisher.
Jesse Marchand, Associate Publisher.
Jordie Yow, Editor.

Part 6

LITERARY AGENTS

INTRODUCTION
PLANET LITERARY AGENT

Jeff Herman

Here are the listings for approximately 150 literary agents, most of whom provide the information you need to make intelligent choices about whom to pitch and how to do it.

Who Is and Isn't Listed in This Edition?

To the best of my knowledge, only qualified agents are included. Please let me know if you disagree (jeff@jeffherman.com). I invited more agents than are here and would have gladly included most of them, but to be included, agents must respond to my survey, even if they only list name and website, and many did not. Some agents are at full capacity and don't want to receive unsolicited submissions, and I didn't make adequate contact with everyone I tried to. As you know or soon will, spam filters and unfriendly agency mailboxes can be impenetrable. By the way, I received more than a few boilerplate rejection letters from agents in response to my invitation to include them in this book.

Bottom line: I can confidently say that at least 98 percent of the agents in this section are legitimate. But just because someone isn't here doesn't mean they aren't a real agent.

What's a "Fee-Charging" Agent?

I hope there are no reading-fee agents in this listing. If there are, it's because they conned me, and you need to let me know (jeff@jeffherman.com). A legitimate agent shouldn't charge for the simple purpose of considering your work for representation. Anyone who does is probably not really an agent, which means they never actually sell anything to legitimate publishers.

Think about this: I receive several hundred unsolicited queries each month, as do many of my peers. If I converted a fraction of them into check-stuffed envelopes and PayPal credits, I'd have a nice revenue stream and wouldn't have to rely on commissions. Real agents don't make money from reading your work; they make it from successfully selling your work to a traditional publisher for a 15 percent commission. However, there are a few acceptable exceptions to this rule. A small number of legitimate agents request a modest fee (less than $100) in order to defray the cost of employing people to do first reads. I have included one or two them because their policies are transparent, they have genuine track records, and you can easily bypass them.

THE LISTINGS

AARON PRIEST LITERARY AGENCY ❖ www.aaronpriest.com

708 Third Avenue, 23rd Floor, New York, NY 10017, 212-818-0344

Agent's name and contact info: Aaron Priest, querypriest@aaronpriest.com

Describe what you like to represent and what you won't represent. I represent mainstream fiction, suspense, thriller, biography.

What are the best ways for writers to pitch you? Via email.

Agent's name and contact info: Lucy Childs, querychilds@aaronpriest.com

Describe what you like to represent and what you won't represent. I represent mainstream fiction, women's fiction, literary fiction, some young adult, memoir, narrative nonfiction.

What are the best ways for writers to pitch you? Via email; write an excellent and succinct query letter.

When and where were you born? Chicago, IL.

Describe your education and career history. BFA, University of Minnesota; have been at the Aaron Priest Agency for 19 years.

How would you describe the proverbial "client from hell," and what are the warning signs? Rambling query letters; rambling manuscripts; "entitled" young authors who don't trust me to know what I'm doing.

What do you think about self-publishing? I'm wary.

Do you like Amazon? Like it or not, it's here to stay as a retailer.

What do you want to tell new/unpublished writers? I was an actress for more than 20 years. Get used to being rejected and persevere.

**Agent's name and contact info: Lisa Erbach Vance,
queryvance@aaronpriest.com**

Describe what you like to represent and what you won't represent. Looking for: contemporary fiction, especially women's fiction, with a well-defined narrative voice; observant, thoughtful fiction about families and friends, with fresh perspectives on modern relationships; thriller/suspense with propulsive plots and well-developed characters, especially with a female lead; psychological suspense; contemporary gothic fiction; international fiction (not translation) that takes the reader deep into another culture; a fascinating look into a little-known subculture, in US or abroad; narrative nonfiction, current or historical topics.

Not looking for: horror, science fiction, fantasy, picture books, self-help, screenplays.

What are the best ways for writers to pitch you? Send a straightforward query letter, emailed to queryvance@aaronpriest.com. Give a brief — a paragraph or two — summary of your work that conveys not just what your work is about (including major characters and plot points), but what you want the reader to get out of it. Also tell me a bit about who you are. Paste the first chapter of the book in the body of the email. Do not send attachments — they will not be opened.

When and where were you born? Chicago, IL. (I have a soft spot for books set in the Midwest!)

Do you charge fees? No.

Describe your education and career history. Degree in English literature from Northwestern University. Certificate in Publishing from New York University. First job in publishing: management trainee at Random House, Inc., then foreign rights associate at Crown imprint. Moved to Aaron Priest Literary Agency to become foreign rights director and assistant agent to Aaron Priest; became full agent shortly thereafter.

Why and how did you become an agent? In my trainee job at Random House, I was given the opportunity to rotate through all departments — from editorial to contracts, production, sales and marketing, etc. It was an invaluable experience, and I loved it. But I also came to realize that I wanted more from a career in publishing than working in one department, so I moved to agenting, which requires immersion in all aspects of the publishing process — from book concept through publication and beyond — and I love working directly with authors.

Would you do it over again, or something else? Would absolutely do it over again — no question.

List some representative titles you have placed. Novels from Harlan Coben, Gregg Hurwitz, B. J. Daniels, G. M. Ford, Aaron and Charlotte Elkins, Matt Rees, Gayle Lynds, Amanda Stevens.

Describe yourself as a person. I'm nurturing and dedicated to my clients. I'm also very direct and "bottom line," with a focus on details as well as the big picture. I'm dead serious about my clients' careers, but I love a good laugh and appreciate a smart sense of humor.

Do you miss the way the business "used to be"? Publishing has changed a lot since I got my start in the business in the 1990s, and though there are pros and cons to everything, I can't say I miss the way things used to be in general. Though it can be tougher for a new author to break into "traditional" publishing now, the rise of ebooks and digital media has created opportunities for new authors, established authors, and publishers alike. We're all still figuring out possibilities but generally moving forward into exciting new territory. I think it's much more productive to embrace the future than resist it.

ALLEN O'SHEA LITERARY AGENCY ❖ www.allenoshea.com

615 Westover Road, Stamford, CT 06902, 203-359-9965

Agent's name and contact info: Marilyn Allen, marilyn@allenoshea.com

Describe what you like to represent and what you won't represent. Health, parenting, business, cooking, lifestyle, history.
Not handling fiction, children's, or memoir.

What are the best ways for writers to pitch you? Email.

Do you charge fees? Never.

Describe your education and career history. Trained as an English teacher. I worked for many years on the publishing side in senior sales and marketing positions for Warner, Penguin, Simon & Schuster, and Harper Collins.

Say something about your hobbies and personal interests. Travel, reading, tennis.

Why and how did you become an agent? I became an agent because I like to work with writers. I started my agency after a long publishing career.

List some representative titles you have placed. Please see our website.

Describe yourself as a person. I'm fun and collegial.

How would you describe the proverbial "client from hell," and what are the warning signs? A client who has unreasonable expectations about the industry; expects things like a quick sale to a publisher, a large advance, extensive marketing, and book reviews.

Describe your job and what you like and don't like about it. I help writers shape their book projects, find them a publishing home, and do everything in between.

ANDREA BROWN LITERARY AGENCY ❖ www.andreabrownlit.com

Agent's name and contact info: Lara Perkins, lara@andreabrownlit.com

Describe what you like to represent and what you won't represent. I'm a fan of insightful, page-turning, voice-driven young adult and middle grade fiction, as well as quirky, witty picture books. For middle grade, I'm particularly looking for compelling, unexpected mysteries; stories set in fascinating, unexpected worlds (real or imagined); and stories that hit home in their depiction of ending/changing friendships or family shifts. Humor is always welcome. For young adult, I'm looking for heartbreaking but very funny contemporary (or contemporary with a fantasy or paranormal twist) novels. I love a bittersweet romance between believable, memorable characters when it's solidly grounded in reality. I'm also drawn to character-driven fantasy with striking world-building, and whip-smart, page-turning psychological mysteries. In the picture book realm, I'm drawn to picture books that take a small but universal experience of childhood and draw out something beautiful or hilarious, and an endearingly flawed main character is central for me. I love working with author-illustrators, and I'm drawn to a wide range of illustration styles.

What are the best ways for writers to pitch you? My agency's submission guidelines are posted here: www.andreabrownlit.com/how-to-submit.php.

When and where were you born? I'm a Californian, born and raised.

Describe your education and career history. I have a BA in English and art history from Amherst College and an MA in English literature from Columbia University, where I studied Victorian British literature. In my prepublishing life, I trained to be an architect, before deciding that books, not bricks, are my true passion. I spent over a year at the BJ Robbins Literary Agency in Los Angeles before coming to Andrea Brown Literary.

Say something about your hobbies and personal interests. I love to hike and to travel. My favorite travel story is the time I was bitten by a penguin in Chile. It's the best thing that's ever happened to me.

List some representative titles you have placed. Some of my recent titles include *The Fantastic Family Whipple* by Matthew Ward (Razorbill/Penguin); *A Million Ways Home* by Dianna Dorisi Winget (Scholastic Press); *If Your Monster Won't Go to Bed* by Denise Vega (Knopf/Random House); *The Stepsister's Tale* by Tracy Barrett (Harlequin Teen); and *I'm New Here* by Anne Sibley O'Brien (Charlesbridge).

Agent's name and contact info: Jennifer Rofé, jennifer@andreabrownlit.com

Describe what you like to represent and what you won't represent. Picture book, chapter book, middle grade, young adult — all genres in these categories.

I do not represent adult.

What are the best ways for writers to pitch you? Through an emailed query letter. Carefully follow the submission guidelines at www.andreabrownlit.com.

Do you charge fees? No.

List some representative titles you have placed. The *Mya* middle grade series by Crystal Allen (Balzer + Bray/Harper Collins); *Guardian of the Spear* middle grade adventure series by Christina Diaz Gonzalez (Scholastic); *What Could Possibly Go Wrong?* middle grade nonfiction series by Graeme Stone (Random House); *Cleo Nelson and the Happy Juju Doll* and *Cleo Nelson and the Love Potion* middle grade series by Toni Gallagher (Random House); *Buck's Tooth*, chapter book, by author-illustrator Diane Kredensor (Aladdin/Simon & Schuster); *Finding Paris,* young adult novel, by Joy Preble (Balzer + Bray/Harper Collins); several illustration deals for Eliza Wheeler, Mike Boldt, Renee Kurilla, and Joe Cepeda, to various publishers, including Simon & Schuster, Harper Collins, Random House, Scholastic Canada, Candlewick, Holt, Holiday House, and Little, Brown.

THE ANGELA RINALDI LITERARY AGENCY ❖ www.rinaldiliterary.com

PO Box 7877, Beverly Hills, CA 90212-7877, amr@rinaldiliterary.com, 310-842-7665, fax: 310-837-8143

Agent's name: Angela Rinaldi

Describe what you like to represent and what you won't represent. Fiction: We are passionate about fiction, both commercial and literary, and look for engaging characters, a strong plot, good storytelling, and lovely writing with a distinct voice. We love commercial novels with literary sensibilities. We are actively looking for upmarket contemporary fiction, mainstream women's fiction, and multicultural fiction, as well as mysteries, suspense, literary historical thrillers, gothic suspense, and women's book club fiction — novels where the story leads to discussion. We are also looking for young adult fiction and would like to find the next young adult crossover novel.

We are not the best agents to represent humor, CIA espionage, drug thrillers, technothrillers, category romances, science fiction, fantasy, horror/occult/paranormal, poetry, film scripts, magazine articles, or religion.

Nonfiction: Submissions from nonfiction authors with an original idea who have a national platform will always get our attention, as will authors who have big ideas and can spot trends; authors who can explain the way we live, take the mystery out of every-day occurrences, or have life-transforming messages; authors who have brands and strong media contacts. We are very interested in narrative nonfiction, memoir, women's interest/studies, current issues, biography, love/relationships, psychology, health/medical/

wellness, business, parenting, cookbooks/food narratives/lifestyle/wine, personal finance, and books written by established journalists, academics, doctors, and therapists.

Please do not send us magazine articles, celebrity bios, or tell-alls.

What are the best ways for writers to pitch you? Email submissions should be sent to info@rinaldiliterary.com. Include the word *Query* in the subject line. We will not open attachments or go to your website to read your query. Because of the volume, we can only respond to those queries we are interested in pursuing. We will send an automated reply to your email letting you know if your work is not a right fit for our agency. Please do not query by phone or fax or send CD/DVD or anything with electronic storage. For fiction, please send a brief synopsis and paste the first 10 pages into an email. Nonfiction queries should include a detailed cover letter, your credentials and platform information, and any publishing history. Tell us if you have a completed proposal.

Do you charge fees? Member AAR; no reading fee.

Describe your education and career history. Angela Rinaldi is president of the Angela Rinaldi Literary Agency in Los Angeles. She has been a member of the Literature Panel for the California Arts Council, has served on the board for PEN, and is currently on the membership committee for the Association of Author's Representatives. She established her editorial expertise in New York as executive editor at New American Library and Bantam Books, and senior editor at Pocket Books (Simon & Schuster) and was manager of the *Los Angeles Times* book publishing program for 10 years. Her experience as an editor, publishing liaison, and industry professional, including the time she spent creating books for the *Los Angeles Times*, developed the strong foundation she built her agency on and has given her the contacts and resources to expertly advise authors about all traditional and state-of-the-art publishing options.

Why and how did you become an agent? After working at several publishing houses in New York in editorial positions and publishing books for the *Los Angeles Times* for 10 years, connecting writers with publishers was a natural extension of Angela Rinaldi's long involvement with publishing. The success of the agency is a reflection of our ability to recognize the authors who will capture an editor's attention.

List some representative titles you have placed. We are proud to have represented books like the eight-million-copy bestseller *Who Moved My Cheese?* by Dr. Spencer Johnson; *Zen Golf: Mastering the Mental Game* by Dr. Joseph Parent; *Blood Orange* and *The Good Sister* by Drusilla Campbell; and *From Seed to Skillet* by urban gardener Jimmy Williams and lifestyle journalist Susan Heeger. Our vision is to continue to support distinctive voices.

ANNIE BOMKE LITERARY AGENCY ❖ www.abliterary.com

PO Box 3759, San Diego, CA 92163, 619-634-3415, submissions@abliterary.com

Agent's name: Annie Bomke

Describe what you like to represent and what you won't represent. On the fiction side, I love character-driven fiction, mysteries (cozies, psychological thrillers, and everything in between), historical fiction, women's fiction, literary and upmarket fiction, contemporary and speculative young adult and new adult, and books with multicultural or LGBT characters. So if you have a literary, psychological thriller set in Nazi Germany with a gay protagonist, I'd love to see it. I'm a sucker for books set in the Victorian era, retellings of *Hamlet*, and books about famous historical figures. I also love ridiculously funny novels.

For nonfiction, I'm looking for fresh prescriptive business, self-help, and health/diet books with a great platform. I also love memoir, narrative nonfiction, and big-concept pop-psychology books. I'm fascinated by topics like behavioral economics (for example, *Predictably Irrational* by Dan Ariely) that explore some aspect of why people do the things they do, from either a psychological or biological perspective.

I don't represent romance, poetry, children's picture books and chapter books, middle grade, or screenplays. I'm also not a big fan of genre fiction like science fiction, fantasy, or paranormal, though I like some novels with a slight sci-fi/fantasy/paranormal twist.

What are the best ways for writers to pitch you? While I love an interesting concept, for me it really comes down to the writing, so the best way for authors to pitch to me is to send me a query, a synopsis, and the first two chapters of their book. Then I'll see if I'm pulled in by the writing, and if I want to request more. I take submissions through email and hardcopy.

When and where were you born? I was born in a small town in Ohio in the early 1980s. My parents literally lived on a farm.

Do you charge fees? No.

Describe your education and career history. I have a BA in rhetoric from UC Berkeley. (Don't ask me to define *rhetoric*, because I can't.) During college, I interned at *Zoetrope: All-Story*, a literary magazine founded by Francis Ford Coppola. Then I worked at Margret McBride Literary Agency for 7.5 years, first as an intern, then as the Royalties and Foreign Rights Agent.

Say something about your hobbies and personal interests. I love reading (surprise, surprise), dancing, Sudoku, dogs, pizza, and nature.

Why and how did you become an agent? When I was in high school and college, I wanted to be a writer, but I knew I needed a day job. I had worked briefly as a technical writer, so I figured I'd do that. My last year in college I got an internship at a literary magazine (*Zoetrope: All-Story*), and I absolutely fell in love with publishing. There was just something so thrilling about helping bring writers' voices into the world. I moved back home to San Diego after college, because I had no money, and the only publishing jobs in San Diego were at literary agencies. So I applied to a whole bunch of them and got an internship at Margret McBride Agency. And the rest is history.

Would you do it over again, or something else? I would definitely do it all over again. It's been over 10 years since my internship at *Zoetrope: All-Story*, and I'm still in love with publishing.

Describe yourself as a person. I aspire to be like the woman in the Cake song "Short Skirt / Long Jacket": "With fingernails that shine like justice, and a voice that is dark like tinted glass, she is fast, thorough, and sharp as a tack. She's touring the facilities and picking up slack."

How would you describe the proverbial "client from hell," and what are the warning signs? An author who refuses to take feedback and doesn't listen. Also authors who send angry emails to their editors at 3 AM. I think it's important before an agent signs an author for the agent to be clear about what (if any) major changes he or she expects. You have to make sure you're on the same page with the author, or else you're going to be fighting them the whole way. So a warning sign is if the author hems and haws about what changes they're willing to make and won't give you a straight answer. Or if they make half-assed attempts to address your concerns that don't actually do anything. I once worked with an author who, instead of making changes to address my feedback or telling me why she didn't agree with my feedback, would argue why it was unnecessary to address such concerns in the actual manuscript. For example, if I asked her to expand on an idea, she would write in the manuscript itself something like, "If some want a more thorough explanation of X, they can refer to my earlier chapter where I addressed it." Talk about passive-aggressive!

What do you think about self-publishing? I think self-publishing is a great option for authors who have had trouble finding an agent and want to get their work out there. I just always tell authors to promote the hell out of their self-published books, because if they want a traditional publisher for their future books, their sales figures will make all the difference in the world.

Do you like Amazon? As much as I hate watching brick-and-mortar bookstores disappear, I have to admit I'm a sucker for the prices and convenience of Amazon.

Do you believe in a "higher power"? If by "higher power" you mean unicorns, then yes, yes, I do.

What will agenting be like in 2020? It will be exactly the same as it is now, except instead of cell phones, we'll all have telepathy.

Describe your job and what you like and don't like about it. There are two components to my job: supporting my existing clients and finding new clients. Supporting my existing clients is my number one priority. This entails any number of things, from negotiating contracts to sending them cute panda videos. The finding-new-clients part of my job includes reading queries, participating in Twitter pitch parties, and going to writers' conferences, among other things.

My favorite thing about my job is helping authors' dreams come true. I also love that every day is different. Every day there's something new to do, something new to look at.

My least favorite part of my job is obviously getting rejections on my authors' work and then relating the news to them. I also don't enjoy writing rejections, especially if I've had some back-and-forth with the author already.

Do you miss the way the business "used to be"? Yes, I miss the time when it seemed like a given that we'd sell every book we sent out for a six-figure advance. Who wouldn't miss that?

What does the "Big 5" mean to you? The Big 5 are solid publishers that can offer excellent opportunities to a writer, but they're not the only option. As the Big 5 get more selective about the books they'll publish, independent publishers are continually looking for fresh new books and fresh new ways to promote those books.

What do you want to tell new/unpublished writers? I want to tell them that publishing is probably one of the most subjective businesses there is. When agents and editors say, "This isn't right for me," they really mean it. Their job is not to determine what is objectively good; it's to find books they fall in love with. So my advice to writers is to get as much feedback as you can before you start submitting your book, to make sure it's the best it can be, and then try not to take rejections too personally. Go to writers' conferences and get advance reading appointments with agents so you can get specific feedback about your writing, before you send it out. If you receive the same feedback over and over again, you might want to consider revising your book. But if the feedback you get is all over the place, as it often is, it might just be a matter of finding that right person, which means sending it out to more agents. And do your research before sending it out. If your book is sci-fi, you'll have much better luck with an agent who loves sci-fi than one who has lukewarm feelings about it.

Do you like that everything has become largely digitized? Personally, I love hardcopy books. I love holding books, smelling them, flipping through them, seeing them lined up on a bookcase. Having said that, I like that the advent of ebook rights are letting more authors get published who might not have been published otherwise. I don't have an ebook reader, and I can't imagine a time when I'd want one, but then again, I thought I'd never get rid of my CDs, and now I can't live without my iPod, so who knows.

What do you like reading, watching, and listening to? In my spare time, I read a pretty wide range of books (mostly fiction), from funny, brain-candy novels to psychology books, though mostly I read mysteries. My favorite TV shows are *Parks & Recreation*, *Bates Motel*, *Project Runway*, *It's Always Sunny in Philadelphia*, *Aqua Teen Hunger Force*, *Sherlock*, and *Law & Order* in all its incarnations. I listen to a pretty wide range of music, including crappy dance music and '90s R&B.

Describe a book you would write. I once had a dream that I had written this amazing young adult novel. It was about two sisters who become wards of Edgar Allen Poe. In one scene, they watch Poe perform some kind of dark magical ceremony, spying down on him from a high garden wall. It was all very eerie and mysterious. I might write it someday, if nobody beats me to it.

Joker's wild: My favorite word is *defenestrate*. Any author who works that into their query gets bonus points from me.

ANN RITTENBERG LITERARY AGENCY, INC. ❖ www.rittlit.com

15 Maiden Lane, Suite 206, New York, NY 10038, info@rittlit.com, www.facebook.com/rittlit

Agent's name: (Ms.) Penn Whaling

Describe what you like to represent and what you won't represent. The thing I like about being an agent is that I can represent the kind of books that I personally enjoy reading. My list is very eclectic, ranging from thriller to memoir to young adult, so I wouldn't say there's anything that I would never consider representing, apart from screenplays and poetry. As long as it has a strong voice, great writing, and a compelling story to tell, I'd love to see it.

When and where were you born? North Carolina, 1981.

Do you charge fees? No.

Describe your education and career history. I graduated from the University of Virginia with a BA in poetry writing in 2004. I then moved to New York to pursue a career in publishing. After completing the NYU Summer Publishing Institute, I interned for the

Paris Review, Open City magazine, and a couple of other literary agencies before joining ARLA in 2005.

Say something about your hobbies and personal interests. In addition to reading for pleasure, I enjoy baking elaborate desserts and taking long walks around new neighborhoods in New York City.

Why and how did you become an agent? I basically get paid to read all day, which is what I'd be doing anyway if I were unemployed!

Would you do it over again, or something else? Absolutely!

List some representative titles you have placed. *Behemoth: The History of the Elephant in America* by Ronald B. Tobias (Harper Perennial, 2013); *Generation Roe: Inside the Future of the Pro-choice Movement* by Sarah Erdreich (Seven Stories, 2013); *This Is Not a Writing Manual: Notes for the Young Writer in the Real World* by Kerri Majors (Writers Digest, 2013); *The Red Chameleon* by Erica Wright (Pegasus Crime, 2014); *Helsinki Dead* by James Thompson (Putnam, 2015); *A Matter of Breeding: A Biting History of Pedigree Dogs and How the Quest for Status Has Harmed Man's Best Friend* by Michael Brandow (Beacon Press, 2015).

How would you describe the proverbial "client from hell," and what are the warning signs? Someone who doesn't approach the author-agent relationship with the idea that we're on the same team. A big warning sign is someone who only gets in touch to complain!

What do you think about self-publishing? I think it can be a great way for someone who's written a book that targets a niche audience not currently served by traditional publishers to get their work out there. However, as self-publishing becomes more prevalent, I think there will still be a need for traditional publishers. With so many choices to weed through, I think that readers will continue to rely on the publishers as gatekeepers. Before spending money on a book, I think readers would like to know that it's at least been copyedited first!

Describe your job and what you like and don't like about it. As an agent, my job is basically to find new voices and share them with the world. So, while going through the slush pile can be a chore, it's also fantastically exciting when you find that piece that you love and want to make everyone else in the office read.

What do you want to tell new/unpublished writers? Even if you're not getting paid for your writing yet, treat it like a job. If you don't take it seriously, then agents and publishers won't take you seriously. Do your research and read each agency's submission guidelines!

Do you like that everything has become largely digitized? Yes, it definitely makes submissions easier! And having an ereader when I travel leaves me with a lot more room in my suitcase.

What do you like reading, watching, and listening to? Some favorite authors (besides my own, of course) are Evelyn Waugh, Kent Haruf, Barbara Kingsolver, Margaret Atwood, Roald Dahl, Nancy Mitford, Mary McCarthy, Kazuo Ishiguro, Mary Gaitskill, Fitzgerald, Anthony Burgess, and dozens more I'm no doubt forgetting. Some favorite TV shows are *Monty Python's Flying Circus, Breaking Bad, Absolutely Fabulous, Parenthood, Law & Order*, RuPaul's *Drag Race, Golden Girls, Ren & Stimpy*, and *Call the Midwife*. Some favorite musicians are David Bowie, the Velvet Underground, Janelle Monae, Sleater Kinney, Laura Mvula, Led Zeppelin, and Johnny Cash.

ANN TOBIAS, A LITERARY AGENCY FOR CHILDREN'S BOOKS

520 East 84th Street, New York, NY 10028, atqueries@gmail.com

Agent's Name: Ann Tobias

Describe what you like to represent and what you won't represent. I specialize in work for children — young children, midlevel children, and young adult. In the area of picture books, I prefer to represent work that is both written and illustrated by the same person. Children's book editors do not want to see work written and illustrated by collaborators, so if you are an artist, I hope you will also write your own text, and if you are a writer, make your own art. Whether a picture book or a longer work for older kids, I want to be stunned by writing that is strong and beautiful, whether a light, rollicking story or a dark and serious one.

I avoid vampires, horror, and paranormal, as well as material that aims to educate or improve children — no life lessons, please.

What are the best ways for writers to pitch you? What I want to learn from a query are these simple facts: What have you written that you want me to read — picture book, middle grade novel, or young adult? Fantasy? Realism? A mystery? Historical fiction? Etc. What is the length? What is the age group? What is the age of the protagonist? Give me a sense of the plot in one sentence and the theme in another sentence. If your project is nonfiction, please list your credentials. When sending a query, please include one page of your writing.

When and where were you born? I was born 150 years ago (which has given me the time and opportunity to read 80 gazillion children's books) and grew up in the Midwest and West. I came to NYC after college to work in publishing, starting at Harper (Harper & Row back then) and have lived in NY and Washington, DC, since that time. I am now located in NYC.

Do you charge fees? I do not charge fees.

Describe your education and career history. After college (Northwestern), I worked in children's book publishing — on staff at Harper, William Morrow, and Scholastic. When my children were born, I edited freelance for Dial, Crown, Morrow Jr. Books, Hyperion, and others. Working for so many publishers enabled me to make the jump from editing to agenting, which I did in 1988 when I moved to Washington, DC, and realized that, while it was a lovely city in many ways, there were no publishers, and so Washington held very little opportunity for a displaced children's book editor.

Say something about your hobbies and personal interests. It would be nice to say that I have an intense interest in something unusual and dramatic, but my overwhelming interest is reading. I like to cook something delicious for myself and others. I like movies, mostly frothy, inconsequential ones.

Why and how did you become an agent? I became an agent because of a family move from New York to Washington, DC. I took a deep breath and hung out my shingle. A lot of lawyers and economists in the DC area escape from their boring jobs by writing on the side, so acquiring clients wasn't difficult, and from my years of freelancing as an editor, I had contacts in publishing in place, so it was a benign transition.

Would you do it over again, or something else? Would I change to agenting again, knowing what I know now? Yes, no matter how talented an editor may be, holding on to a job in publishing is uncertain at best these days. I am glad to be my own boss, taking responsibility for my decisions and free to try new ways of doing things, some of which work and some of which don't, so I won't get into examples here.

List some representative titles you have placed. Picture books are hard to place these days, so I am especially pleased to have placed a wonderful collection of short — very short — vignettes of authentically pictured baby animals in an oversized gift book, *Sleepy Time Baby Animals* by Karen B. Winnick (Holt); a debut middle grade fantasy, *The Power of Poppy Pendle*, is being followed by its sequel, *The Courage of Cat Campbell* by Natasha Lowe (Paula Wiseman Books, Simon & Schuster); a third book in the *Red Kayak* series by Priscilla Cummings, *Cheating for the Chicken Man* (Dutton/Penguin).

Describe yourself as a person. As a person, I think I am a great team player, so why am I on my own and why do I enjoy it? A mystery. I definitely miss not reacting to coworkers' manuscripts and hearing them react to those I am interested in. I definitely like earning my agent's fees and keeping all the money!!! (Not that there's that much, considering that I make 15 percent of very little, but it is a good feeling to own it, whatever it is.)

How would you describe the proverbial "client from hell," and what are the warning signs? My clients are hardworking people, and we work closely together to bring their manuscripts to a point where editors find their material irresistible. I worry when clients are too quick to follow my direction and never argue, and I worry when they fight me every inch of the way. Somehow, there is an ideal give-and-take in our editorial discussions that leads to each author or author-artist producing a marvelous manuscript, and for the most part, my clients and I achieve it. When this does not happen, I am seized by a deep desire to move to California and become a surfer.

What do you think about self-publishing? Self-publishing has been a little slower in children's books than in adult books, and while there have been some successes, there has been nothing to match the success of adult self-published books. For the most part, I am unimpressed by the quality of the concepts, the writing, and the appearance of self-published children's books that are submitted to me. When I receive a submission of a self-published book, I regard it as a manuscript, and so far, I have not been even slightly tempted to take on its author as a client.

Do you like Amazon? Amazon is a phenom. It will either implode or pull up its sox and act like a real publisher. I give it 50-50 in either direction.

Do you believe in a "higher power"? No.

What will agenting be like in 2020? Different. I think agents will have an expanded role in actual publishing (we do to some degree now, but, with exceptions, we are not paid for it). There was a recent time when we all pretty much did the same thing. By 2020, I think different agents will have carved out different territories, and so no two agents will be doing the same thing. It will be confusing and lively!

Describe your job and what you like and don't like about it. My primary job, I think, is to see that my clients stay in the business and flourish. It's often difficult to get published for the first time, but it's very much harder to stay published. I love the excitement that accompanies starting out a client's new manuscript — I am full of energy and hope for the project, and it is fun. I don't like the realization that a project is not going to succeed. I don't like having to give a client bad news of any kind — a book is going out of print, sales are falling, a manuscript has been rejected.

Do you miss the way the business "used to be"? Yes, I definitely miss the way business "used to be." Contracts that used to be 15 to 20 pages are now 40, most of it due to ebooks. Wading through them is time-consuming and difficult. I never used to wish I was a lawyer, but now a day does not pass that I don't think a legal degree is necessary — this from a person who craves reading books and manuscripts (not documents).

What does the "Big 5" mean to you? Big 5 means the large publishing houses that are considered most mainstream. They used to be the publishers people most wanted to be published by and still may be, but I think that is changing as self-publishing and ebooks are creating a more fluid atmosphere in the industry.

What do you want to tell new/unpublished writers? I want to shout from the rooftops to new, unpublished writers of children's books that they must read actual published (by mainstream publishers) children's books. They must read at least 200 books in the age group they wish to address in their own manuscripts. They must decide what they think about them and compare them with the classic titles that I am assuming they have already read (and remember), such as *Tom Sawyer, Heidi, Little Women,* the work of E.B. White, *Babar,* the *Angus* books, books by E. Nesbit, *Treasure Island* (oldies but goodies). After reading 200 recently published books in their chosen age group, I strongly suggest they read 100 more published books for children in other age groups, just to get an idea of the scope of publishing for children. I really want people to do this before sending me a manuscript, and here's fair warning: I can always tell when they haven't!

Do you like that everything has become largely digitized? I would prefer that art is not digitized, and I realize I have no choice but to get used to it.

What do you like reading, watching, and listening to? I cannot list the number of writers who are important to me — it would be unwieldy — so instead I will mention that currently I am reading *Cooked* by Michael Pollan, which I think is fascinating. I do not watch much TV, and music is mostly of the chamber variety.

Describe a book you would write. Agents and editors for the most part do not write books. They leave that to authors, and instead have this small talent for finding and helping authors achieve publication. How many of us have been asked whether we write and why not? Countless times. Actually writing my own book is just not in my DNA.

Joker's wild: I assume I can say whatever I want in this last question. So here it is: If you are serious about writing for children, please go back and reread (and act on!) my response to the question "What do you want to tell new/unpublished writers?"

ARCADIA

31 Lake Place North, Danbury, CT 06810, 203-797-0993, arcadialit@sbcglobal.net

Agent's name: Victoria Gould Pryor

Describe what you like to represent and what you won't represent. Nonfiction: science/ medicine, current affairs / pop culture, history, psychology, true crime, true business, investigative journalism, women's interest, biography, classical music.

No fiction (alas), business, memoirs about addiction or abuse, humor, or children's/young adult.

What are the best ways for writers to pitch you? Detailed query letter and SASE. It's fine to send a proposal with the letter, but please take the time to analyze what comparable books are already on the market and how your proposed book fills a niche. Email queries without attachments are fine. If your subject and query letter are enticing, I'll ask you to send the file — either proposal or manuscript — as an attachment.

When and where were you born? New York City.

Do you charge fees? No fees or fee-based services.

Describe your education and career history. BA, Pembroke College / Brown University (modern literature/history); MA, NYU (modern literature). My first job after college was at the John Cushman Agency. Moved to the Sterling Lord Agency and became hooked on agenting. At the Harold Matson Agency I began representing authors and then helped found Literistic, Ltd. Arcadia was launched in 1986.

Say something about your hobbies and personal interests. Classical music and choral singing, gardening, canoeing, current affairs, reading, art, woodworking, science, and medicine.

Why and how did you become an agent? The luck of the draw; I stumbled into the perfect (for me) field that combined a love of reading, people, and business with a smattering of law and social work. And I was fortunate enough to be mentored by some incredibly talented and generous agents.

Would you do it over again, or something else? I'd do it over again, though maybe there'd be a few less stumbles along the way.

List some representative titles you have placed. State of the Unions: How Labor Can Revitalize Itself, Seize the National Debate on Values, and Help Win Elections by Philip Dine (McGraw-Hill); *Every Living Thing: Man's Obsessive Quest to Catalog Life, from Nanobacteria to New Monkeys* (Smithsonian Books), *The Wild Life of Our Bodies: Predators, Parasites, and Partners That Shape Who We Are Today* (Harper), and *The Man Who Touched His Own Heart: True Tales of Science, Surgery, and Mystery* (Little, Brown) by Rob Dunn, PhD; *When Sex Goes to School: Warring Views on Sex since the Sixties* (Norton) and *Salsa Dancing into the Social Sciences* (Harvard University Press) by Kristin Luker, PhD; *The ESP Enigma: The Scientific Case for Psychic Phenomena* (Walker) by Diane Powell, MD; *Unstuck: A Supportive and Practical Guide to Working through Writer's Block* by Jane Anne Staw (St. Martin's); *When the Air Hits Your Brain: Tales of Neurosurgery* (Norton), *Why We Hurt: The Natural History of Pain,* and *The Genius Within: Discovering the Intelligence of Every Living Thing* (Harcourt) by Frank T. Vertosick, Jr., MD; *The Beak of the Finch* and *Time, Love, Memory* (Knopf) by Jonathan Weiner.

How would you describe the proverbial "client from hell," and what are the warning signs? The writer from hell is not respectful of an agent's or editor's time, is unable to hear or apply whatever information or advice is offered, and assumes that business ground rules be set aside for his or her work. Fortunately I don't represent anyone who resembles this.

What do you think about self-publishing? It can be wonderful for the rare author with the needed discipline and skills. But the learning curve is extremely steep, so educate yourself thoroughly and be prepared to put in the necessary time.

What will agenting be like in 2020? The book business will keep chugging along, and creativity and the imagination will still need nurturing. Industry trappings will evolve, but the core will still be the development and spreading of ideas.

Describe your job and what you like and don't like about it. An agent is a combination of talent scout, industrial-strength reader, business manager/career planner/matchmaker, developmental editor, midwife to creativity, and supporter of professional dreams. At its best, my job is about being part of a team of talented, dedicated professionals. It's thrilling to see a book grow from the germ of an idea to a manuscript and then to see the magic that can result when the publisher's expertise and support are added.

Do you miss the way the business "used to be"? Yes, definitely, but there's much that's good about things at the moment. Preserve the best of what we miss and adapt to the way things are at any given time.

What do you want to tell new/unpublished writers? If you're talented, ambitious, hard-working and flexible, that's a very good beginning. A strong stomach and a finely developed sense of humor and irony are also helpful.

What do you like reading, watching, and listening to? I admire nonfiction that helps us understand and/or changes the way we look at the world past and present (*History of the Jews, Embracing Defeat, And the Band Played On, What's the Matter with Kansas, Temperament,* Thomas Cahill's *Hinges of History* series); illuminates areas of science (*Our Kind, How We Die, Love's Executioner, The Man Who Mistook His Wife for a Hat, Anatomy of Love, The Brain That Changes Itself, The Immortal Life of Henrietta Lacks, The Emperor of All Maladies*); or introduces us to people who lived fascinating lives (*Nora*); and quirky or compelling memoirs or narratives (*Year of Reading Proust, A Heartbreaking Work of Staggering Genius, Zookeeper's Wife, Hare with Amber Eyes*).

THE AUGUST AGENCY LLC ❖ www.augustagency.com

Agent's name: Cricket Freeman

Describe what you like to represent and what you won't represent. We are a discreet agency which has worked quietly since 2001, in the US and internationally, offering highly personalized service to an exclusive group of exceptional writers. Primarily we handle mainstream nonfiction, creative nonfiction, narrative nonfiction, memoir, and crime fiction. We favor persuasive and prescriptive nonfiction works, each with a full-bodied narrative command and an undeniable contemporary relevance. We enjoy untangling literary Gordian knots — the intricate story operating on multiple levels — whether historical crime thrillers, narrative memoirs, contemporary creative nonfiction, or anything in between.

We do NOT handle children's, screenplays, poetry, short stories, romance, Western, horror, fantasy, or sci-fi.

What are the best ways for writers to pitch you? More than three-quarters of our clients have come to us through writers' conferences, so it's obvious that's the best way for us to connect. In fact, invite me to your conference to teach a workshop and hear pitches, and during the ride from the airport you can pitch your book and pick my brain mercilessly, and we'll plot your career objectives. Note: We only accept submissions at a conference or by referral. However, occasionally we open up to over-the-transom submissions through our website's online submission form. Unfortunately, we cannot consider queries that come to us any other way. Tip: The best queries are simple, but also slippery and easier said than done. They only have two paragraphs: one about the book and one about you — but those paragraphs have to be golden.

When and where were you born? I'm a baby boomer, a proud fifth-generation Floridian, what locals call a "Skeeter Beater" (someone whose intrepid family was brave enough or wild enough to be here before the advent of mosquito control, when a palm broom hung by each front door to beat the skeeters off your body before you entered). When it comes to my writing and business creativity, I don't grow where bananas don't grow, so my agency is based in South Florida. At the time I founded the August Agency, locating an agency anywhere outside New York City was considered foolhardy, so we maintained a NYC branch for many years. By the time the Recession rolled around and the Internet ruled business, we all opted for sunshine and more fiscal efficiency.

Do you charge fees? We do not charge fees for our services. We earn standard commissions on payments, advances, and royalties.

Say something about your hobbies and personal interests. I write. Other than that, sometimes I can squeeze out time to read, watch movies, design, travel, hike, canoe, or visit with other writers, my favorite people.

Why and how did you become an agent? I didn't go to university to be a literary agent. After all, who does? You wander through the back door from somewhere close at hand — a publishing house, a law office, a media company — and usually because someone opened the door and invited you in. In my case, I was an experienced freelance writer and former magazine editor in chief who knew my way around the publishing world, plus I'd been a real estate broker who boogied through contracts. When I pitched a book at a conference, the agent recognized my value and recruited me. A year later, when I was up to my eyeballs in intriguing work, he wandered out the door; I stayed. Being an entrepreneur, I founded my own agency.

Would you do it over again, or something else? Mmmmmm…of course I would. Being an agent has brought me considerable rare gifts: friendships with delightful, generous, and spellbinding people from all over the globe, many my clients. My life is infinitely richer for it. And the best gift of all: while in Oregon for a writers' conference, I first met my Mr. Freeman on a hilltop under a meteoric sky. Destiny? Methinks so.

List some representative titles you have placed. Not all our clients' projects are books, although that is how they first come to us. We have sold their works for hardcover, trade paper, and mass market paperback editions, but also as digital, film, audio, serial, reprint, gaming, and foreign rights. Outlets have included academic presses, genre presses, regional houses, content providers, and educational testing services, as well as traditional, advance-paying publishers, such as Career Press, John Wiley & Sons, Praeger, Gale, and Amacom Books. A typical title might be *The Office Politics Handbook* by Jack Godwin, PhD.

Describe yourself as a person. Creative, complex, artistic, funny, nurturing, mushy, straightforward, easy, generous, bawdy, Southern, spirited…How long need I fuss about such fripperies?

How would you describe the proverbial "client from hell," and what are the warning signs? Have you heard about the writer whose career got snuffed?

There's this writer. An insecure, desperate writer. But also a skilled, impassioned writer. A writer who's as deft with her pen as a musketeer with his sword, and with as much heart. Fueled by her hopes, this writer pushes forward in her quest till she discovers an agent who believes in her pen. The writer thinks she's finally arrived as a writer. Nothing can stop her now. She dreams of buzzing up the *NY Times* bestseller list, touring the world amid exploding flashbulbs, and laughing it up with Letterman and Kimmel.

But then one day, before the writer finds her place in the sun, she overreacts and goes off on her agent. She jumps to a crooked conclusion, blames her agent for anything and everything, has a bad hair day, gets cursed by an evil witch — take your pick. Whatever triggers it, she acts like a screaming, kicking two-year-old. She shrieks at her agent, she sends flaming emails, she resorts to name calling, ad nauseum. Even if the agent tries to reach out to her, the writer refuses to see it, much less apologize. Somehow, in her convoluted thinking, her bizarre actions and blistering words are justified.

Once the storm is over, all the writer hears is a deafening silence. The agent casts her adrift. The writer's career is over before it truly begins. She doesn't understand why, and her heart is broken. Moreover, the agent cries at such a loss on the rocks of shortsightedness.

The moral of this tragic tale? Throw a temper tantrum and you commit career suicide. Remember, publishing at this level is a relatively small community. It doesn't take too many tantrums, large or small, before word gets around branding you "difficult," "unpredictable," "psychotic."

Why does this single-handedly kill off an otherwise promising career? Trust, from which everything else flows. When a writer throws a conniption fit, the agent immediately asks herself, "Would she throw a tantrum with an editor? Or, oh, my, with a reader at a book signing?" Such embarrassment is something an agent or editor will not accept, despite the writer's talent. Remember: agents are looking not only for good writers, but *professional* writers.

What do you think about self-publishing? Decades ago, before digital publishing, I worked closely with writers wishing to self-publish their books. Prior to founding the August Agency I had Possibilities Press, which provided prepublication preparation for small publishers: ghostwriting, editing, book design, cover design, printing, binding, and market analysis. Even with a professionally produced book, many self-published authors discovered a steep uphill climb. We've come so far since then, from glue pots and typesetting to the click of a mouse, from a social shunning in literary circles to encouragement and acceptance. But some things still remain true for self-published books: Is it ready for prime time? Remember, you only get one shot at your reader with this book, whether an agent, editor, or buyer. At last, from the reader's viewpoint, every book is on equal ground, no matter if it is published by one of the major houses, an academic press, a small regional publisher, or a few-books-a-year micropress, or directly by the author. One thing I have seen is that large publishers today are now viewing self-published books as test-marketed: low sales numbers brand a book as not testing well, but books with high sales are deemed having test-marketed well and worthy of a look.

Do you like Amazon? Amazon is at once a blessing and a curse. It is an amazing research tool, a bargain hunter's paradise, a self-pubbed author's champion, a midlist author's savior, and an industry revolutionizer. But it's also a competition smasher, an industry monopolizer, and a mom-and-pop-hometown-bookstore assassin. When Amazon coughs, the industry holds its breath. So one day I adore it, the next I loathe it — much like spinach.

Do you believe in a "higher power"? I just don't see the relevance of this question to business.

What will agenting be like in 2020? 2020 seems so sci-fi, so far away into the future… But it isn't, is it? Just five years, more or less. But look what's happened in the past 5 or 10. *Egads!* When I became an agent I was one of the few agencies to even have a website. All business was conducted in hardcopy — all queries came by mail (by the bushel basket every day); every manuscript was printed, boxed, and FedExed to publishers; and contracts were faxed back and forth. By contrast, today nothing is handled in hardcopy, everything is digital and handled in the blink of an eye. With distance comes perspective, so I can see trends in my literary crystal ball. I see that opportunities for writers are growing with each year, that having an agent is becoming more necessary in some areas yet less so in others, and that boutique agencies who foster authors' careers, like the August Agency, are becoming scarcer each year.

Describe your job and what you like and don't like about it. I don't see being an agent so much as a job as it is a lifestyle, like being a professional writer, artist, or musician.

Do you miss the way the business "used to be"? Not at all. These are heady times, ripe with possibility, aren't they?

What does the "Big 5" mean to you? The major publishers will always be the gold standard for authors, the definition of having arrived, of being a success at writing — no matter what this freewheeling publishing environment brings to surprise us, how many readers authors have, how many books they sell, or how much money lands in their pockets.

What do you want to tell new/unpublished writers? When a literary agent accepts you as a client you will be in the deep end of the publishing ocean and will be expected to be able to swim on your own. Agents expect to be working with confident professionals who can produce the professional-level materials and information necessary so agents can do their job effectively. Listen to your grandma here: be prepared, do your homework, be kind. And heed Miss Aretha, too: R-E-S-P-E-C-T.

Do you like that everything has become largely digitized? It's an amazing new playground. There's a lot of new and exciting equipment, but be cautious of bullies lurking in the shadows ready to pocket your lunch money.

What do you like reading, watching, and listening to? Of course, books will always be my best friends. I like discovering a ray of light through nonfiction but love getting lost in a novel late at night. And at heart I'm a Rhythm & Blues baby, so anything from Billie

Holiday to Keb Mo to John Mayer will get me rockin'. Then there's streaming media, offering up a bounty of stories with a click. I'm discovering that my favorite TV series and movies are often from outside the US, bringing an out-of-the-ordinary perspective on story construction and delivery.

Describe a book you would write. I am currently researching and writing a creative non-fiction book, neck-deep in the effervescent history of the 1920s.

BALDI AGENCY ❖ www.baldibooks.com

233 West 99th Street, 19c, New York, NY 10025, 212-222-3213, baldibooks@gmail.com

Agent's name: Malaga Baldi

Describe what you like to represent and what you won't represent. I consider the following: general fiction, reference, biography, computers/technology, business/investing/finance, history, mind-body-spirit, travel, lifestyle, cookbooks, science, memoir, cultural history, literary fiction, creative/hybrid nonfiction, gay/lesbian/LGBT/queer fiction.

I do not have experience with category/genre fiction: Western, mystery, thriller, romance, science fiction, fantasy, etc. In general, I do not represent young adult, children's, or middle grade books, poetry, film projects.

What are the best ways for writers to pitch you? Look at www.baldibooks.com for submission information, please. Email baldibooks@gmail.com.

When and where were you born? Philadelphia, Pennsylvania. In the last century.

Do you charge fees? No.

Describe your education and career history. I have been an independent literary agent since 1986, developing and refining my list. In the early eighties I worked for literary agents Candida Donadio and Elaine Markson. I worked as a publicity assistant at Ballantine Books and a clerk at the Gotham Book Mart.

MA, Antioch, March 1980. BA, Hampshire College, January 1977.

Say something about your hobbies and personal interests. I love to go to art galleries. I am a weekend warrior in the spring, summer, and fall — toiling away in a little garden plot. Walking the circumference of NYC in small pieces has been one of my favorite recent activities. Theater, music, dance, and spoken word occupy my free evenings.

Why and how did you become an agent? In 1974 I took a year off from college. I was a mother's helper for Lois Wallace, a powerful and independent agent. She had just left William Morris to start her own agency with a British partner. During the time I worked for her I met Joan Didion, John Gregory Dunne, and Erica Jong. One afternoon there was a knock on her apartment door. We opened the door to Erich Segal. His hard contact lens had popped out. We found ourselves on our knees — six hands gently tapping the marble floor for a hard contact. A lightbulb went off in my head: I can do this.

Would you do it over again, or something else? I would do it all over again.

List some representative titles you have placed. W.W. Norton in 2015 will publish David J. Skal's *Bram Stoker: The Final Curtain*. Norton published his *Hollywood Gothic* and the critically praised *The Monster Show: A Cultural History of Horror*. Beacon will publish *All the Rage* by Obie Award–winning actor/writer Martin Moran in 2016. Open Road Media offers fans of William J. Mann's gay fiction all his novels in a uniform ebook format: *Men from the Boys*, *The Biograph Girl*, *All American Boy*, *Where the Boys Are*. Who isn't in awe of Vanessa Redgrave? Pegasus Books publishes the first-ever biography *Vanessa: The Life of Vanessa Redgrave* by Dan Callahan. Jaded Ibis Productions published two first novels: *An Honest Ghost* by Rick Whitaker and *A Map of Everything* by Elizabeth Earley. FSG publishes *Three Minutes in Poland* by Glenn Kurtz in 2014. *Tinseltown: Murder, Mayhem, Madness at the Birth of Hollywood* by William Mann (IT Books/Harper Collins, Fall 2014).

Describe yourself as a person. Funny, serious, judgmental, introspective, awkward, insecure, loyal, stubborn, proud, and given to bouts of despair. Paralleling my American mongrel multiethnic background — a little bit of everything.

How would you describe the proverbial "client from hell," and what are the warning signs? I have yet to experience a client from hell. It is a big deal to write a book. You have to have high expectations. It is important to be transparent. Being a dreamer and being realistic can work together.

What do you think about self-publishing? This is hard work, and occasionally is very successful. The publicity and distribution that a traditional publisher can offer are hard to replicate.

Do you like Amazon? Amazon is here to stay in some form or another. Of course, I encourage all to buy from their local independent bookstore.

What will agenting be like in 2020? Five years ago I thought I would be driving a UPS truck by now. In six years, who knows?

Describe your job and what you like and don't like about it. I love working with new writers, gaining their confidence, and explaining the industry and the publishing process. I love closing a deal. I also enjoy the downside — talking to an author after a stinging bad review or a rejection on the next book from their home-base publisher. These are the bumps that make for a strong relationship between author and agent. Talking it through, coming up with a plan, and rising from the ashes can be transformative. I have learned more from disappointment than triumph.

What I don't like about it: (1) I wish I controlled the publisher's purse strings. For example, the release of a check on a particular contract payout is taking an excruciatingly long time lately. Why is this taking so long? (2) I do not enjoy being told something is too small or does not have a platform. Small is beautiful. Many of my books are small. I once called an editor at a Big 5 house to follow up on a book I had recently submitted. The assistant asked me what the platform was. Novels do not have platforms. (As far as I know…do they?)

Do you miss the way the business "used to be"? Everything changes, everything stays the same. We wouldn't be here without the past.

What do you want to tell new/unpublished writers? Stick to your guns. NUMBER YOUR PAGES. Never, ever start a book with "The natives were restless." Edit, edit, edit. Tell the truth. Make every word, sentence, paragraph count. Read everything out loud. Write it out in longhand at some point during your process. Read the masters. Be patient. Do not call your novel a fiction novel. Join a writers' group for feedback/encouragement/criticism. Do your research about publishers, agents, contracts. Write every day.

Do you like that everything has become largely digitized? The future is now. Media, communication, sound, environment, food, politics, government, global strategies — everything is changing in our lifetime. It is much easier on your back to have 19 manuscripts loaded on your ereader than to be carrying three manuscripts in your backpack. In many ways digitized publishing has been an advantage.

BARBARA J. ZITWER AGENCY ❖ www.barbarajzitweragency.com

Agent's name: Barbara J. Zitwer

Describe what you like to represent and what you won't represent. International bestselling fiction and some nonfiction. Literary fiction and women's fiction. Writers from around the world who have been published in their home countries. I have a small, focused list.

I do not do health, business, sports, celebrity, young adult, children's, erotic, romance, historical.

What are the best ways for writers to pitch you? Email.

When and where were you born? New York.

Do you charge fees? No.

Describe your education and career history. Owner of my own agency for over 15 years.

Say something about your hobbies and personal interests. Swimming, travel, knitting, dogs.

Why and how did you become an agent? Fell into it.

Would you do it over again, or something else? I have done many other things in my life and when I fell into agenting and working with writers, I found I loved it.

List some representative titles you have placed. *Please Look After Mom*; *I'll Be Right There*; *The Hen Who Dreamed She Could Fly*; *Our Happy Time*; *The Little Old Lady Who Broke All the Rules*; *The Vegetarian*; *The Rising*; *The Friday Night Knitting Club*; *The J. M. Barrie Ladies Swimming Society*; *The Investigation*.

Describe yourself as a person. You should ask my clients and publishers I work with.

What do you think about self-publishing? Opportunities for authors to publish and market themselves.

What will agenting be like in 2020? Maybe to represent the first novel found buried on Mars!

Describe your job and what you like and don't like about it. I love fiction writers with new voices and strong themes that are universal. There is nothing as exciting as reading a new writer who I have never heard of before and then helping them to get published around the world. I love bringing people together from around the world and encouraging communication and global friendship and understanding. I love reading about new cultures and understanding and befriending writers from around the world.

Do you miss the way the business "used to be"? The business is always evolving and changing, and I think it's very exciting to have a global readership at my fingertips. I represent writers in all languages from around the world and sell their world around the world — all from my office in New York City. There are more opportunities around the world than ever before. It is necessary to change and embrace the new and the future if you want stay in business, and it's incredibly exciting, challenging, and fulfilling.

What do you want to tell new/unpublished writers? It takes a village to publish a good book. Great editors and publishers are your partners, and to think that you can do without and that they are not important in today's world of so much self-publishing is a big mistake. No one can edit their own work, and it takes a group effort of experts to publish and sustain an author's long-term career, well. Also, I would say that a reader is your audience and that the act of reading a book is a relationship between writer and reader — think about how you are communicating with your readers. There are no shortcuts to writing a good book; it takes time, and give it the time it takes.

Do you like that everything has become largely digitized? I don't think everything actually is largely digital around the world, but I think digitization is another way to read and get information — the more ways of communication, the better. Ebooks have not killed paper books.

What do you like reading, watching, and listening to? I like literary fiction. I am reading *The Luminaries* and *To Have and Have Not* by Hemingway. Graham Greene is my favorite writer.

Describe a book you would write. Funny, warm, meaningful, happy, universal.

Joker's wild: I am also an author and wrote *The J. M. Barrie Ladies' Swimming Society*, sold in 10 countries and for film, and am working on a new novel. As a writer I have my own agent, Christine Green in London. I think that also being a writer gives me a special understanding of writers and their process and improves my ability to sell their work.

BARER LITERARY LLC ❖ www.barerliterary.com

20 West 20th Street, New York, NY 10011, 212-691-3513

Agent's name and contact info: Julie Barer, submissions@barerliterary.com

Describe what you like to represent and what you won't represent. Literary fiction, historical fiction, women's fiction, international fiction, history, travel.

Not interested in health, fitness, business, investing, children's books, picture books, or screenplays.

Do you charge fees? No.

Describe your education and career history. Vassar College. After working for six years at Sanford J. Greenburger Associates, I left to start my own agency in 2004. Before becoming an agent I worked for Shakespeare & Co. Booksellers in New York City.

Why and how did you become an agent? I became an agent first and foremost because I love to read, and I love the moment of discovering a wonderful novel or story that no one else has read yet and being the person who helps bring that book out into the world. I also love being able to work closely with writers and help shape their work, as well as their careers. Being an agent allows me to be involved with so many aspects of a book's life — from editing and placing a book with the right publisher to helping to conceptualize cover art and promotion and beyond. If I weren't an agent, I'd love to own a bookstore.

List some representative titles you have placed. *Then We Came to the End* by Joshua Ferris (Little, Brown); *Still Life with Husband* by Lauren Fox (Knopf); *What You Have Left* by Will Allison (Free Press); *People I Wanted to Be* by Gina Ochsner (Houghton Mifflin).

BJ ROBBINS LITERARY AGENCY

5130 Bellaire Avenue, North Hollywood, CA 91607, robbinsliterary@gmail.com

Agents' names and contact info: BJ Robbins, robbinsliterary@gmail.com; Angeline Dinh, angie.bjrobbinsliterary@gmail.com

Describe what you like to represent and what you won't represent. I (BJ) represent both fiction and nonfiction. In fiction I prefer voice-driven or character-driven stories that have a strong hook. In nonfiction I love memoir, history, cultural history, popular science, biography, sports, pop culture, travel/adventure, and some self-help if the author has great credentials and a strong platform.

I don't represent romance, science fiction/fantasy, plays, screenplays, poetry, picture books, religious tracts, or technothrillers.

What are the best ways for writers to pitch you? Write a strong query letter. Include in the body of the email why you're querying my agency, a brief description of the project, a short bio, and perhaps the first page or two.

When and where were you born? Manhattan.

Do you charge fees? No.

Describe your education and career history. Graduated from University of Rochester with a BA in English, magna cum laude, Phi Beta Kappa; spent my junior year in England at the University of Sussex. I started in publicity at Simon & Schuster right out of college, and after two years I went to M. Evans as publicist. From there I joined Harcourt Brace Jovanovich as publicity manager. When the general books division moved to San Diego, I moved with them as marketing director. Two years later I persuaded Harcourt to move me back to NY, where I was eventually named senior editor. I moved to Los Angeles in 1991 and started my agency in 1992.

Say something about your hobbies and personal interests. I've been a power forward with the North Weddington Mom's Basketball League for the past 13 years. I see a ton of movies. Oh, and I tap dance.

Why and how did you become an agent? Becoming an agent was the logical next step because it encompassed many of the skills I had learned from working in publicity, marketing, and editorial. Plus, I had just moved to Los Angeles, where publishing jobs were pretty much nonexistent. What really appealed to me was being my own boss, having the freedom to choose projects that reflected my taste, and being able to take on an eclectic group of writers and help nurture their careers.

Would you do it over again, or something else? I can't imagine doing anything else, though knowing how hard it was to launch my agency, I don't know that I'd want to do it over again.

List some representative titles you have placed. *Headhunters on My Doorstep* by J. Maarten Troost (Gotham); *Shake Down the Stars* and *A Pinch of Ooh La La* by Renee Swindle (NAL); *The Blood of Tigers* by J.A. Mills (Beacon Press); *Little Bighorn* by John Hough, Jr. (Arcade); *A Fiction Writer's Guide to Dialogue* by John Hough, Jr. (Skyhorse); *Blood Brothers* by Deanne Stillman (S&S); *The Sinatra Club* by Sal Polisi and Steve Dougherty (Gallery); *The Sweetness of Tears* by Nafisa Haji (Morrow); and *The Blood of Heroes* by James Donovan (Little, Brown).

How would you describe the proverbial "client from hell," and what are the warning signs? The biggest warning sign is someone with unrealistic expectations who doesn't understand anything about publishing, who won't take editorial direction, and who doesn't behave professionally. I'm happy to say that I don't have any "clients from hell."

What do you think about self-publishing? I'm not against it, though I do consider it a "when all else fails" scenario, i.e., if all traditional publishing options have been exhausted. Self-publishing can be effective for those who have a particular niche and know how to market their book to that audience. The truth is that most self-published authors don't understand the difficulties involved in marketing, not to mention the lack of distribution in bookstores. Very few find success, and in my opinion it's not the best way to attract an agent or a traditional publisher.

Do you like Amazon? I find Amazon a bit scary. I don't like that they've put so many wonderful independent bookstores out of business. I do, however, like that they provide a marketplace for so many books.

What will agenting be like in 2020? I imagine that it won't be that different, though at that point there will likely be more consolidation among the big houses and more start-up companies to fill in the gaps.

Describe your job and what you like and don't like about it. What I like: Discovering wonderful writers and helping to shepherd their books to publication, as well as helping to develop their careers. What I don't like: rejections.

Do you miss the way the business "used to be"? I miss the days when editors had more say in what gets published.

What do you want to tell new/unpublished writers? Work hard to develop your craft. Don't send out your work until it's ready. If you're rejected — and you will be! — use that as your impetus to work harder. Learn as much as you can about publishing. Write a great query letter.

Do you like that everything has become largely digitized? Yes! It saves so much time and money from an everyday business point of view. No more lugging manuscripts around! As for ebooks, I see them as another format for delivering content, and I believe that old-fashioned printed books will survive.

What do you like reading, watching, and listening to? I love reading character-driven novels with a strong story as well as historical fiction that transports me to another time and place in a compelling way. I also like suspense and mysteries. In nonfiction I'm drawn to personal narratives, narrative history, anything that tells me a fascinating story and teaches me something I didn't know before. I love most films, especially foreign films, indie films, and the occasional big-budget extravaganza, though I'm not a big fan of action films. As for TV, I am a huge fan of *Mad Men*, *Breaking Bad*, *House of Cards*, *Orange Is the New Black*, the French series *Spiral*, *Downton Abbey*, and some really trashy reality shows that I'm too embarrassed to list here. As for music, I like just about everything except techno and heavy metal. I'm also a big Broadway musical geek.

Describe a book you would write. A *Gone Girl*–ish literary suspense with Machiavellian twists and turns.

BLUE RIDGE LITERARY AGENCY, LLC ❖ www.blueridgeagency.com

query@blueridgeagency.com

Agent's name and contact info: Dawn Dowdle, query@blueridgeagency.com

Describe what you like to represent and what you won't represent. I like to represent cozy mysteries and romances (no erotica). I also like to represent mysteries, women's fiction, middle grade, and young adult.

I do not accept any questions for fantasy/sci-fi.

What are the best ways for writers to pitch you? Go to www.blueridgeagency.com and follow the query instructions

When and where were you born? 1959, Wenatchee, WA.

Do you charge fees? No.

Describe your education and career history. After being a secretary and morphing into working with databases and doing Web development, I took a summer off to spend more time with our daughter. I had been reviewing mysteries for many years and began a freelance editing business, which I thoroughly enjoyed. Because my desire was to help authors, especially newer authors, I opened my literary agency in 2009.

Say something about your hobbies and personal interests. I love reading, watching TV, shopping, spending time with family, and taking vacations.

Why and how did you become an agent? A dear friend was querying agents. One day she said "I wish I could do this myself." She was frustrated with having to have her manuscript pristine to mail it in, and then getting a half-page paper with the wrong manuscript name on it rejecting her manuscript. I began looking into becoming an agent and jumped in feetfirst and never looked back. I set up my agency to work with newer authors.

Would you do it over again, or something else? I would have done it much sooner!

List some representative titles you have placed. *Forget Me Knot* by Mary Marks; *All or Nothing, When I Find You*, and *If Only You Knew* by Dixie Brown (also three more in the series); *Return to Me* by Kelly Moran; *His Game, Her Rules* by Charlene Groome; *Better Homes and Corpses* by Kathleen Greenstein; *The Perfect Gift* and *The Resolution* by Dani-Lyn Alexander; *Santa Wore Leathers* by Vonnie Davis.

Describe yourself as a person. I am a very tenacious and committed person. I am detail oriented and organized to a degree but can usually put my finger on needed data without too much trouble. I am loyal to my friends and like to keep in touch with people, even from the past.

How would you describe the proverbial "client from hell," and what are the warning signs? Someone who is inflexible and wants everything their way. Someone whose writing doesn't grow with assistance or time and who isn't learning new ways to promote their books in this changing publishing climate.

What do you think about self-publishing? I think self-publishing definitely has its place. I don't think every book should be self-published. I do think every self-published book should be well edited and vetted.

Do you like Amazon? Yes. I think that ebooks have revolutionized publishing, and I do a lot of my buying at Amazon.

Do you believe in a "higher power"? I believe in God.

What will agenting be like in 2020? I think it will be similar to what it is now, working closely with our authors. I think ebooks will be an even bigger part of publishing.

Describe your job and what you like and don't like about it. I love working with my authors and getting to know them and what they write. I also enjoy brainstorming with them about fixes or the next book to write. I do a lot of editing of each book I represent and work closely with the author through the editing and querying process. I don't like having to reject manuscripts. I truly enjoy going to conferences and meeting with authors.

Do you miss the way the business "used to be"? I wasn't in business then.

What does the "Big 5" mean to you? Getting contracts with them is validation for my agency and my authors.

What do you want to tell new/unpublished writers? You aren't going to get a six-figure advance on your first book. Learn about your genre. Find out what the accepted word counts are for your genre. Study writing and promoting.

Do you like that everything has become largely digitized? Yes.

What do you like reading, watching, and listening to? Love reading cozy mysteries and romances. Love watching detective shows and cop shows.

Describe a book you would write. If I had time to write, I would write a cozy mystery series. I have started a few, but I prefer to do the editing and agent work involved, rather than the writing.

BONEDGES LITERARY AGENCY

querybonedges001@aol.com

We are a hands-on agency specializing in quality nonfiction and fiction. These turbulent times in the publishing world make it an imperative that we develop relationships with good writers who understand what they must do to promote their work.

Our agency does not charge fees.

Agent's name: John Grassley

Mr. Grassley is interested in well-written thrillers, mysteries, suspense novels, historical fiction, and action-adventure. In nonfiction, well-written memoirs, military strategies, and war stories. Currently handles 60 percent fiction/novels and 40 percent nonfiction.

Email submissions only.

Prior to becoming an agent, John Grassley worked as a film editor at the Sundance Film Festival. During the off season, Mr. Grassley helped launch *Ultra* magazine.

Responds to queries within three to five weeks.

Obtains new clients through recommendations, solicitations, and conferences.

Agent receives 15 percent commission on domestic sales. Agent receives 20 percent commission on foreign sales.

Agent's name: Bonnie James

Represents nonfiction books: biography, business, New Age, women's interest, current affairs, sports; novels: thriller, mystery, suspense, historical.

Prior to becoming an agent, Ms. James worked as an associate editor for the *LA Times* Arts and Entertainment section.

Agent receives 15 percent commission on domestic sales. Agent receives 20 percent on foreign sales.

Agent's name: Mike Macafee

Represents novels: thriller, mystery, suspense, historical, action-adventure; nonfiction: New Age, current affairs, true crime, memoir, biography, history.

Prior to becoming an agent for Bonedges, Mr. Macafee was a magazine editor and freelance writer.

BRADFORD LITERARY AGENCY ❖ www.bradfordlit.com

5694 Mission Center Road, #347, San Diego, CA 92108, 619-521-1201, queries@bradfordlit.com

Agent's name and contact info: Laura Bradford, laura@bradfordlit.com

Describe what you like to represent and what you won't represent. I handle commercial fiction, specifically genre fiction. I love romance (all subgenres), mystery, thriller, women's fiction, urban fantasy / speculative fiction, new adult, and young adult. I do some select nonfiction as well.

I don't handle screenplays, children's books, poetry, Westerns, New Age, religion, horror, epic fantasy.

What are the best ways for writers to pitch you? A simple, professional query letter is very important, one that is specific, articulate, and concise. I don't need an author to be zany to grab my attention — just cut right to the heart of what your manuscript is about and give me a strong hook. Don't be vague. As far as submissions go, please email a query letter along with the first chapter of your manuscript and a synopsis (all pasted into the body of the email) to queries@bradfordlit.com. Please be sure to include the genre and word count in your cover letter. To avoid having your email fall into spam, the subject line should begin as follows: "QUERY:" (the title of the manuscript and any SHORT message you would like us to see should follow).

When and where were you born? February 6th, in the San Francisco Bay Area.

Do you charge fees? No.

Describe your education and career history. I have a BA in English literature from the University of California at San Diego. I came to agenting pretty much straight out of college. I started with my first agency as an intern less than six months after I graduated. I started my own agency in 2001.

Why and how did you become an agent? Once upon a time, I thought I might like to be a novelist, and I joined Romance Writers of America so I could learn what was what. At my first meeting, the speaker was a literary agent, which was something I had never heard of before. I was instantly fascinated. I researched what the job was and how to go about getting started. It seemed like the perfect job for someone who loved books and business, and it would allow me to be around my favorite people: authors. Despite the fact that one of the agents I called about an internship told me that agenting was the worst job on earth and that I shouldn't pursue it, I persevered. Within a couple of months, I landed an internship with Manus and Associates (500 miles away from where I was living), and I quit my job and moved. I worked as a bookstore manager to support myself while I was an unpaid intern. I lived in a relative's house for free until I finally got officially hired at the agency as an assistant. A few years later, after becoming an agent, I struck out on my own so I could focus on genre fiction.

Would you do it over again, or something else? I would do it all over again in a heartbeat. I totally adore my job.

List some representative titles you have placed. *Mercy Mode* by Em Garner (Egmont); *Lay It Down* by Cara McKenna (NAL); *I Want It That Way* by Ann Aguirre (HQN); *Ring in the Holidays* by Katie Lane (Grand Central); *The Best Kind of Trouble* by Lauren Dane (HQN); *Shatter* by Erin McCarthy (Penguin); *Trust Me, I'm Lying* by Mary Elizabeth Summer (Delacorte); *The Sweetness of Honey* by Alison Kent (Montlake); *Lovely Wild* by Megan Hart (Mira); *Top Ten Clues You're Clueless* by Liz Czukas (Harper Teen); *Perfect Couple* by Jennifer Echols (Simon Pulse); *Rough Justice* by Sarah Castille (St. Martin's); *The Night Owls* by Jenn Bennett (Feiwel & Friends).

Describe yourself as a person. I am pretty even-tempered and patient. I am organized (because an agent has to be). I am flexible (because an agent has to be). Kind of bossy. I have a deep appreciation for whimsy. I'm an optimist. I like to think I have a good sense of humor, but I'm probably not the right person to ask about that.

How would you describe the proverbial "client from hell," and what are the warning signs? I think writers come in infinite variety, and I am pleased to work with a lot of different "types." As for some characteristics I don't particularly love…it is hard to work with someone with unrealistic expectations, someone who isn't a team player (and publishing *is* a team sport), someone who does not respect his or her deadlines. My least favorite characteristic of all? Someone who doesn't comport themselves professionally in public. That includes online dealings.

What do you think about self-publishing? I think it is a growing part of the publishing landscape and it can be a wonderful thing. I like that authors have options and access and more agency and control than they ever have before. Some authors are self-publishing in a smart way and finding a lot of success with it. Other authors are not being smart about it but still finding success. Still others are not finding that they enjoy being entrepreneurial or are not happy with the amount of return they are getting for the work they put in. I think it is ideal for some authors and not for others, but it is nice that it is a viable option for all. I have many authors who are publishing traditionally as well as self-publishing. I don't think it has to be an either-or thing. And I do think that agents have a place in that landscape.

Do you like Amazon? Honestly? Yes. As a businessperson, I can admire their success. As a consumer, I can appreciate their convenience. As a former brick-and-mortar-bookstore bookseller, boy, did they annoy me when they were up-and-coming. I do hate that brick-and-mortar bookstores seem to be going the way of the dodo, but I feel like it is really the changing times that I hate, not Amazon. If it hadn't been Amazon changing the retail landscape, it would have been someone else. My authors sell a gazillion books through Amazon, so how can I resent that?

What will agenting be like in 2020? I think that traditional publishing will continue to evolve — it has to — and that agents will still be a part of the picture. As long as an author needs a helpmate, contract advice, career strategizing, a buffer, a designated bad guy, a heavy, agents will still be relevant to them. It really depends on an author's opinion about what they need/want an agent for, whether they choose to have that partner in their publishing life. An agent has their author's back, and there are still a great number of pitfalls in self-publishing that an agent can help steer their author around.

Describe your job and what you like and don't like about it. I love that my days are totally varied. I love the fellowship of being around creative, talented people. I love the satisfaction of being part of something special when I see my author's books on the bookshelves. As far as what I dislike…I don't think anyone really likes to be a part of disappointing people, and agents hand out *a lot* of rejection. I *really* don't like it when I get a nastygram from an author who is angry about me passing on their work. It is surprisingly common and it is unnecessary, unprofessional, and unpleasant.

What do you want to tell new/unpublished writers? Publishing will not be what you expect it to be. Whether you expect it to be awesome or scary, it will defy your expectations and there really isn't a way to prepare yourself for it. Just roll with the punches and remember that everybody on this ride has felt as confused/exhilarated/proud/bewildered/afraid/relieved as you do. Also, be professional.

Do you like that everything has become largely digitized? Sure, it is very convenient. I honestly prefer to read a paperback over an ebook, but I have certainly had a hankering to read something I didn't already own and found the convenience of buying and downloading an ebook on the fly rather wonderful.

What do you like reading, watching, and listening to? I read the kinds of books I represent, actually. Mostly romances. I am actually more likely to listen to an audiobook for fun, though, than to read for fun. Since I read for work all the time, I find I don't as often have an urge to pick up a book for fun anymore. Audiobooks are my work-around. I watch a lot of Discovery and HGTV. And I prefer hour-long dramas to sitcoms.

Agent's name: Natalie Lakosil

Describe what you like to represent and what you won't represent. My specialties are children's literature (from picture book through teen and new adult), romance (contemporary and historical), cozy mystery/crime, upmarket women's/general fiction and select children's nonfiction. Within those genres my interests include historical, multicultural, magical realism, sci-fi/fantasy, gritty, thrilling and darker contemporary novels, middle grade with heart, and short, quirky, or character-driven picture books.

I am not looking for inspirational novels, memoir, adult thriller, poetry, and screenplays.

What are the best ways for writers to pitch you? Please email your query letter, synopsis, and first 10 pages in the body of an email to queries@bradfordlit.com. No attachments are accepted, and the subject line must contain the word *query* to avoid the spam filters. Picture-book authors are welcome to submit the entire picture book in the body of the email.

Do you charge fees? No.

Describe your education and career history. I am an honors graduate of the University of San Diego with a BA in literature/writing. After nearly four years at the Sandra Dijkstra Literary Agency and a brief dabble in writing author profiles and book reviews for the *San Diego Union Tribune*, I joined the Bradford Agency in February of 2011.

Say something about your hobbies and personal interests. My perfect evening would be eating sushi and playing Pictionary with friends. I love curling up with a good book and a hot cup of tea when it rains, and watching *Doctor Who*. My guilty pleasure is bad romantic comedies. I like licorice-flavored jelly beans and am a cat person.

Why and how did you become an agent? I became an agent through an internship with an agency, which led to an office job at that agency, which led to building my own client list. I started out looking to be a writer and realized quickly after my internship that it wasn't the path for me, but being an agent was. Being an agent allowed me the perfect marriage of business, management, and literature I was craving.

Would you do it over again, or something else? I'd do it all over again in a heartbeat.

List some representative titles you have placed. *Renegade* series by Jessica Souders (Tor Teen); *Looming Murder* mystery series by Carol Ann Martin (NAL); *25 Roses* by Stephanie Faris (Aladdin); *Blonde Ops* by Charlotte Bennardo and Natalie Zaman (Thomas Dunn Books); *Noodle Magic* by Roseanne Greenfield Thong (Scholastic); *30 Days of No Gossip* by Stephanie Faris (Aladdin); *Feather Bound* by Sarah Olutola (Strange Chemistry); *'Twas Noche Buena* by Roseanne Greenfiend Thong (Viking); *Unravel Me* by Tori St. Claire (Entangled Publishing); *Trains Don't Sleep* by Andria Rosenbaum (Houghton Mifflin Harcourt); *Gerald the Giant Giant* by Geoff Stevenson (Beach Lane Books); *Vigilante Nights* by Erin Richards (Merit Press).

Describe yourself as a person. Driven, responsive, passionate, organized, and honest.

How would you describe the proverbial "client from hell," and what are the warning signs? A client from hell has unrealistic expectations and gets incredibly upset, even abusive, in correspondence and actions when these expectations aren't met. She or he is unethical and misses deadlines consistently, breaches contract terms, is rude and unprofessional when approached, is entitled, demanding, and manipulative. I'd put up red warning flags if a client started questioning or ignoring my advice, especially legal in nature, or flying off the handle on social media or aggressively emailing with nasty comments several times a day or week.

What do you think about self-publishing? I think it has created a slew of new opportunities for writers, agents, and publishers but is still largely a gamble. It's definitely not an instantaneous moneymaker for all authors; nor is it a sure way for authors to break into traditional publishing.

Do you like Amazon? As a user, yes; it's incredibly convenient and easy. As an agent, I've seen Amazon really push an author to big sales success by taking full advantage of its own website, which is great. I have also loved the opportunities and new genres generated from the self-publishing boom it aided in starting. More objectively speaking, however, I fear the potential consequences if Amazon does monopolize the shopping world, online or otherwise.

Do you believe in a "higher power"? Yes.

What will agenting be like in 2020? A hell of a lot of fun.

Describe your job and what you like and don't like about it. I once heard a colleague describe the agent business as "finding buyers for sellers." I think it's somewhere between that and the magical "making dreams come true." I love selling, contract negotiation, pitching, networking, and reading. I hate rejection and I hate having to share bad news.

What do you want to tell new/unpublished writers? Don't give up.

Do you like that everything has become largely digitized? This is a tough question. I love the convenience of reading submissions on an ereader vs. carting around mail crates, and I love how easy and impulsive it is to purchase ebooks. But nothing beats the smell of a library or the weight of a book in your hands. If I love a book I've read digitally, I will still purchase a hardcopy to add to my library, because it's harder to flip to favorite pages later on an ereader!

What do you like reading, watching, and listening to? Most recently I've enjoyed watching *Bones*, *Once Upon a Time*, *House of Cards*, and *Orange Is the New Black*. I am addicted to romance novels, historical romance in particular, and love to read any published novel getting buzz to simply absorb and enjoy.

CASTIGLIA LITERARY AGENCY ❖ www.castigliaagency.com

1155 Camino del Mar, Del Mar, CA 92014

Agent's name and contact info: Julia Castiglia, castigliaagency-query@yahoo.com

Describe what you like to represent and what you won't represent. Not interested in horror or fantasy.

Do you charge fees? No.

Why and how did you become an agent? It was my destiny.

List some representative titles you have placed. *The Islanders* (Harper Collins); *Freefall* (Berkley); *America Libre* (Grand Central); *Why Did He Cheat on Me?* (Adams Media); *The Leisure Seeker* (Morrow); *Splendor to Revolution* (St. Martin's); *Waiting for the Apocalypse* (Norton); *Barry Dixon Interiors* (Gibbs Smith).

How would you describe the proverbial "client from hell," and what are the warning signs? Not listening to our advice, not trusting our judgment; telling us what to do and how to do it.

Describe your job and what you like and don't like about it. I sell manuscripts from writers unknown and known to publishers who magically turn them into books.

THE CHARLOTTE GUSAY LITERARY AGENCY ❖ www.gusay.com

10532 Blythe Avenue, Los Angeles, CA 90064, 310-559-0831, fax: 310-559-2639, gusay1@ca.rr.com (for queries and general questions)

Agent's name: Charlotte Gusay, owner and founder

Describe what you like to represent and what you won't represent. I enjoy both fiction and nonfiction and books-to-film. Prefer commercial/mainstream but quality material.

Also, like material that is innovative, unusual, eclectic, quirky, literary. Always looking for up-and-coming writers — African American or Hispanic writers, or works in translation. Will consider literary fiction with crossover potential. Our agency often partners with agents who are signatories to the Writers Guild; hence the agency represents screenplays and screenwriters selectively. I especially like to find books to market to film. I'll sometimes look at unusual or unique children's books and illustrators, but mostly limit children's projects to young adult / teen / new adult.

Not too fond of science fiction or horror. (Although I would not turn down the next *Blade Runner*.) And poetry or short stories (with few exceptions) are almost impossible to sell. I do not represent romance genres per se. But don't put it past me to fall in love with a novel that is a corny love story or something outrageous or quirky.

What are the best ways for writers to pitch you? I love to get queries. But please bear in mind, I am very selective. Here's what to do if you wish to query the agency: Please send a one-page query ONLY, either by snail mail (with all your contact info, including a snail mail address and your email). Or you may query about your book project via the agency's general email: gusay1@ca.rr.com. Again, it is helpful if you include your *complete* contact information: complete name, snail mail address, telephone number, and email. If fiction, describe your book (novel, story, collection) and tell us how you think it fits into the current book/publishing market (i.e., is it literary, a thriller, a mainstream novel). Or perhaps it doesn't exactly fit into the current market, and that may be a good thing. We need to know how you see it. It helps for you to tell us a little about yourself — no more than a paragraph or so. If nonfiction, please describe the book in one or two paragraphs and also send one or two paragraphs describing your author credentials for writing this particular nonfiction book. If we are interested, we will *then* request to see your book project, and we'll send you complete instructions for submitting it to us. We usually send such instructions by snail mail. Hence we need your snail mail address. If we have requested your book project and you receive our info in the mail, at that point you will have noted what we ask for: If fiction, we ask for a one-page synopsis and the *first* 50 pages. If nonfiction, we ask for a complete proposal with title, subtitle, overview, table of contents, marketing and promotion and author platform, author bio with publishing history, and one to three sample chapters (one of which should be the first chapter). Even for a memoir or narrative nonfiction, this information is very helpful for me to gain insight into and understand the breadth and depth of you as a writer/author.

When and where were you born? I was born in the Midwest and grew up in California. I love Los Angeles and have lived here for many years.

Do you charge fees? No reading fee. No editorial fees. For our thoughts on the agency's submission process and some notes on my philosophy of business, please see www.gusay .com/contact/default.asp. The information included there helps writers understand the excruciating process I must go through in trying to be as fair as possible to writers/authors while at the same time attempting to maintain my workload and finding a pathway to acquiring quality projects to represent.

Describe your education and career history. Charlotte Gusay holds a BA in English literature/theater and a General Secondary Life Teaching Credential. She had several careers prior to becoming a literary agent. She taught in secondary schools for several years. That was her first career. Soon, interest in filmmaking developed. She founded (with partners) a documentary film company in the early 1970s. Made several documentaries. Soon became interested in the fledgling audio-publishing business. Became the managing editor for the Center for Cassette Studies/Scanfax, producing audio programs, interviews, and documentaries. Soon thereafter she launched headlong into the business of books and publishing and founded George Sand, Books, in West Hollywood, one of the most prestigious and popular bookshops in Los Angeles. It specialized in fiction and poetry, sponsored readings and events and a much-beloved Sunday literary salon. Patronized by the Hollywood community's glitterati and literati, George Sand, Books, was the go-to place for those looking for the "best" literature and quality books and a good chat about books. It was here that the marketing of books was preeminent. After 12 successful years, it closed in late '80s, a year after Charlotte's new little daughter came into her life. Two years later The Charlotte Gusay Literary Agency was opened.

Say something about your hobbies and personal interests. Gardens and gardening, cooking, architecture (especially midcentury modern houses and furniture), fashion, good books (especially juicy novels and delicious memoirs) and reading in general, movies, anything French, anything Greek. But traveling has taken over my interests. In the past few years, I've traveled the globe here and there: Europe (of course), southern Africa (Zambia, Zambezi, Johannesburg, just prior to Mandela's death), Alaska (landed on a glacier in a teeny plane on Denali), the Galápagos, Greece every summer (sailed to Odysseus's home, Ithaca island, and Onassis's island Skorpios), the Czech Republic and Poland (with my countess friend who owns a castle in Opochno and a hunting lodge nearby). Next fall, China, and in May going to Kent, England, for the UK launch of my client Anthony Russell's book *Outrageous Fortune: Growing Up at Leeds Castle* (St. Martin's Press).

Why and how did you become an agent? I started in the book business with a great entrepreneurial spirit, cold calls, seat-of-the-pants daring, 12 years in the retail book business (as founder and owner of a prestigious book shop in Los Angeles called George Sand, Books), and years of business experience, including producing films and editing and producing spoken-word audio programs. However, agenting is the most challenging and rewarding experience I've ever had.

Would you do it over again, or something else? Were I to change my career? Fashion is rather much ingrained in me…I really should have gone into fashion. C'est la vie. La de da.

List some representative titles you have placed. The Charlotte Gusay Literary Agency represents such books-to-film rights as David Shields and Caleb Powell's *I Think You're Totally Wrong: A Quarrel* (Knopf) and Shields's *NYT* bestseller *The Thing about Life Is That One Day You'll Be Dead*. Both books optioned by actor-director-writer James Franco for his production company, Rabbit Bandini Productions. TCGLA also represents the film rights to popular Irish novelist Maeve Binchy's first novel, *Light a Penny Candle* (Viking/NAL/Signet). Other representative titles: *The Burma Spring: Aung San Suu Kyi and the Struggle for the Soul of Burma* by former State Department speechwriter and journalist Rena Pederson, foreword by Laura Bush (Pegasus Books); *The Reputation Economy: How to Become Rich in a World Where Your Digital Footprint Is as Valuable as the Cash in Your Wallet* (forthcoming from Crown Business); *America* by poet Saul Williams (forthcoming from Gallery/Simon & Schuster); *Jacky's Diary* (Yoe Books/IDW); *Outrageous Fortune: Growing Up at Leeds Castle* (St. Martin's Press). Other film options: *What Angels Know: The Story of Elizabeth Barrett and Robert Browning*, screenplay optioned by producer Marta Anderson, also developed as a novel; *Somebody's Child: Stories from the Private Files of an Adoption Attorney* by Randi Barrow (Perigee/Penguin Putnam), optioned by Green/Epstein/Bacino Productions for a television series; *A Place Called Waco: A Survivor's Story* by David Thibodeau and Leon Whiteson (Public Affairs/Perseus Book Group), optioned to Showtime for a television movie; *Love Groucho: Letters from Groucho Marx to His Daughter Miriam*, edited by Miriam Marx Allen (Faber & Faber; Farrar, Straus & Giroux US; and Faber & Faber UK), sold to CBS. And last, please note: TCGLA has many books and several film projects in submission and development at the time of this writing and at any given time. Please check the agency website for more complete descriptions: www.gusay.com.

Describe yourself as a person. People like my intelligence and enthusiasm and my humor. I'm creative, and often if an author's book at first doesn't get a positive reception from an editor, I rethink titles and slants and suggest to the writers to revise proposals. This works often to sell books. On the other hand, in my agent mode, people don't like my selectivity or they don't understand it. If I reject a project, often the writer feels bleak and, well, rejected. Hopefully, writers will come to understand that I accept projects very selectively. I absolutely must have enthusiasm coupled with a conviction that I can sell any given project. That is extremely important for writers to understand.

How would you describe the proverbial "client from hell," and what are the warning signs? The client from hell is the one who does not understand the hard work we do for our clients. Or the one who refuses to build a career in a cumulative manner, but rather goes from one agent to the next, and so on. Or clients who circulate their manuscripts without cooperating with their agents. Or those who think it all happens by magic. Or those who have not done their homework and who do not understand the nuts and bolts of the business or who are overly demanding and thoughtless. Warning signs that this may be a difficult client: demanding telephone calls, rude notes or emails, impoliteness, unprofessional behavior. The perfect client, however, is the one who cooperates. The one who appreciates how hard we work for our clients. The one who submits everything on time, in clean, edited, proofed, professional copies of manuscripts (either hardcopy or digital) and professionally prepared proposals. Clients who understand the crucial necessity of promoting their own books until the last one in the publisher's warehouse is gone. Those who work hard on their bookselling in tandem with the agent. The author-agent relationship, like a marriage, is a cooperative affair built on mutual trust, and it is cumulative. The dream client will happily do absolutely whatever is necessary to reach the goal.

What do you think about self-publishing? Self-publishing is good and not good. The good: I'm so happy as sometimes there comes a time when I can't sell a book I've tried so hard to sell, and my client decides to publish it himself or herself. That is good because the writer often seems very pleased to have his or her book published, no matter who published it. From an agent's perspective, the not-so-good part is that the agent, after working a long time — months, sometimes even years — trying hard to sell such a book to a traditional or even a small or digital publisher, gets no commission whatsoever. The agent loses. Time and money are lost. Of course, a dream client who publishes his or her own books would step up and offer the agent her share of any sales. Also, so many times self-published books are not well edited, full of typos and errors, sloppy formatting, and just amateurish all the way around. As long as self-published books are well developed, well written, and well edited and the final rendering is totally professional, self-publishing is a positive way to go.

Do you like Amazon? Amazon and I have a love/hate relationship. I love, love, love it because I can research titles, get books in an instant on my Kindle/iPad or at my door. (Way too easy for my pocketbook.) But then the downside? Amazon is putting brick-and-mortar bookstores out of business. Bookstores are very important places contributing to our culture. I know because that's how I began in the book business with my beloved bookshop in West Hollywood — George Sand, Books. How sad is it when there is nowhere to go to browse books and talk to people about books?

Describe your job and what you like and don't like about it. An agent's job in the publishing business is essentially that of a bookseller. I sell books. To publishers, producers, and ultimately the retail book trade. Sometimes I develop a book idea. Sometimes I develop someone's story, help the writer get a proposal written. I help to find a coauthor for your story or nonfiction book if such a writer is needed. I've even written proposals myself because I believed strongly in the book, or the person's story, or the salability of an idea. For fiction writers with potential, I sometimes make cursory suggestions. However, I must be clear — I am not an editor and certainly not a fiction editor. Most often I help writers find a professional editor to work on their novel *before* it is submitted to a publishing house. That is key. The manuscript must be pristine. Flawless. I repeat: A manuscript must be complete, polished, and professional.

I love, love, love to get to know writers. I'm excited every day to see what will come in next on my query line. I do not like to "edit." However, I do editing when it's not too big of a job. I do not like to have to "reject" writers. So often books being considered by my agency are borderline ready. If they're not ready, I have to decline to represent them. No matter how good they are.

Do you miss the way the business "used to be"? Yes. I liked it then (whenever and however that was), and I like it now.

What does the "Big 5" mean to you? Here they are exactly: Hachette, Harper Collins, Macmillan, Penguin Random House, Simon & Schuster. These are the first tier of submissions of almost any writer's book project. Good luck.

What do you want to tell new/unpublished writers? Publishers continue to be in great flux and continue to have a difficult time these days. "Conglomeratizing" (see the Big 5 above) and "electrifying" aspects have taken over the book and publishing business. However, publishers are still and always looking for the next great writer, the next great book, and a way to make both successful. (That means selling books in whatever format and making money.) One thing that has evolved as a result of the conglomeratizing of the book business and the digitizing of books is that the major publishers want you to be able to sell a huge number of your books. If you don't have a big, big, big audience, or you're not a celebrity, or you don't have the hot, hot, hot title, you probably are not going to be able to have your book published. But still I keep trying, and very often I succeed. The new writer, unpublished, must, MUST understand this phenomenon.

Also, acquisitions editors are still overworked and underpaid. Therefore, if you wish to have the best chance of having your work accepted, you must do their work for them and don't complain. That is the reality of the editor's milieu. Editors are usually very smart. Most always, if they're any good, they are temperamental, and they know their particular publisher's market. If interested, they know how to make your work fit into their list. Do what your editor (and agent) tells you. No argument.

In my humble opinion, the publishing business continues to overpublish. Too many books are published. Some time ago, I read somewhere that 240,000 books were published within a recent year. Recently, from another source, I read there were 500,000. Whatever the number, be reminded that only 1 percent of manuscripts submitted to publishing houses were actually accepted for publication in a recent year (according to Dee Power and Brian Hill in their book *The Making of a Bestseller*).

Do you like that everything has become largely digitized? Another love/hate relationship. Yes, such a great tool. No more packaging and copying and mailing manuscripts. However, it's very easy for editors to push that Delete button. And — down the line of publishing books — of course, once again, we're putting the bookstores out of business.

What do you like reading, watching, and listening to? Recent and not-so-recent films I liked: *Slam* (my client Saul Williams's film that made him an underground bestselling performance poet/musician/actor), *The Paper Chase*, Bas Luhrman's *Romeo and Juliet*, Monty Python and the Marx Brothers films, forties and fifties films, often for the clothes. A few of my all-time favorite films are *Runaway Train*, *The English Patient*, *Dr. Zhivago*, *Cabaret*, *Rebel without a Cause*, *Woman in the Dunes*, and many more. A few favorite television shows: any *Masterpiece Theatre*; *Homeland*, *Breaking Bad*, *True Detective*, *Girls*, *The Good Wife*. And many, many books — a few all-time favorites: Austen's *Pride and Prejudice*, Hemingway's *The Sun Also Rises*, *The English Patient*, *Dr. Zivago*, *Housekeeping*, *Out of Africa*, Keats's poetry, and many more. I like memoirs if really, really well written. Recently I've read Sterling Lord's memoir, *Lord of Publishing*. And I'm reading Edwidge Danticat's new book, *Claire of the Sea Light*. The one thing these have in common for me: they held my attention, I was moved in some important way, and the writing is always superb and swept me away.

Describe a book you would write. I'm actually writing one: *Pop Culture* — on a well-known woman icon in the world of politics and fashion.

Joker's wild. I like to read books on gambling. Truly, I do (e.g., *Positively Fifth Street*). [Note: This is a bit of my humor. Get it?]

CHASE LITERARY AGENCY ❖ www.chaseliterary.com

236 West 26th Street, Suite 801, New York, NY 10001, 212-477-5100

Agent's name and contact info: Farley Chase, farley@chaseliterary.com

Describe what you like to represent and what you won't represent. I work primarily with narrative nonfiction, from Pulitzer Prize–winning and bestselling history to multiple *New York Times* bestselling memoirs. I have a strong interest in journalism, natural science, military history, sports, pop culture, and humor. I'm also keenly interested in fiction, whether literary or commercial, contemporary or historical — anything with a strong sense of place, voice, and, especially, plot. I also handle visually driven and illustrated books. Whether they involve photography, comics, illustrations, or art, I'm taken by creative storytelling with visual elements.

I don't handle science fiction, supernatural, or young adult.

What are the best ways for writers to pitch you? I prefer a straightforward email query. I respond to all queries that I receive and that address me by name. I'm more attentive to direct queries that reflect a familiarity with the marketplace and my list.

Do you charge fees? No.

Describe your education and career history. I've been an agent since 2002, and I founded Chase Literary Agency in 2012 after working at the Waxman Literary Agency. I've worked at the *New Yorker*, at the New Press, and as an editor at Talk Miramax Books. I'm a graduate of Macalester College.

List some representative titles you have placed. Recent nonfiction titles: *Devil in the Grove: Thurgood Marshall, the Groveland Boys, and the Dawn of a New America* by Gilbert King (Harper Collins); *Heads in Beds: A Reckless Memoir of Hotels, Hustles, and So-Called Hospitality* by Jacob Tomsky (Doubleday); *Pitch Perfect: The Quest for Collegiate A Cappella Glory* by Mickey Rapkin (Gotham); *A Bintel Brief: Love and Longing in Old New York* by Libby Edelson (Ecco); *Ghettoside: The True Story of Murder in America* by Jill Leovy (Spiegel & Grau); *The End of Night: Searching for Natural Darkness in an Age of Artificial Light* by Paul Bogard (Little, Brown). Recent fiction titles: *And Every Day Was Overcast* by Paul Kwiatkowski (Black Balloon); *Bone Dogs* by Roger Alan Skipper (Counterpoint); *The Baptism of Billy Bean* by Roger Alan Skipper (Counterpoint); *The Afrika Reich* by Guy Saville (Henry Holt); *No Shore, a Nick Finn Thriller* by Alex Gilly (Forge); *The Badlands Saloon* by Jonathan Twingley (Scribner).

CORVISIERO LITERARY AGENCY ❖ www.corvisieroagency.com

275 Madison Avenue, 14th Floor, New York, NY 10016, queries@corvisieroagency.com

Agent's name and contact info: Cate Hart, cate@corvisieroagency.com, Twitter: @CateHart

Describe what you like to represent and what you won't represent. Primarily middle grade and young adult. Select new adult, LGBT, and historical romance. I will consider any genre of middle grade and young adult, but I really love fantasy and historical. In historical romance, I will look at any heat level, but I'm not the best fit for BDSM. I will consider select historical nonfiction, but I prefer the quirky, unheard stories of the past as opposed to military history or warfare.

I don't accept women's fiction. It's just not for me.

What are the best ways for writers to pitch you? Email queries to queries@corvisiero agency.com and include *Query for Cate* in the subject line. Include a query letter, the first five pages, and a brief synopsis (with all the spoilers) in the body of the email. I will gladly take pitches at conferences when appropriate.

When and where were you born? Music City, Nashville, TN. New Year's Baby — January 1, 1974.

Do you charge fees? No. Absolutely not.

Describe your education and career history. I graduated from the University of Tennessee with a BFA in theatre. I managed a video store after graduating college and have been working in financial management for the past 10 years.

Say something about your hobbies and personal interests. Reading. I love reading. I also enjoy painting, watercolors and oils. And I still love watching a good movie.

Why and how did you become an agent? After spending several years writing and pursuing publication, I learned so much about the publishing industry. For me, I feel like it's the one place where I belong. It felt natural to shift from writing to helping other authors with perfecting their manuscripts and guiding them through this business. I like to think of myself as a lit-fairy godmother, making dreams come true. I interviewed for an intern position and just loved the work I was doing. I was asked to continue my internship and from there I became an apprentice and now am a junior agent.

Would you do it over again, or something else? I would do it again in a heartbeat.

List some representative titles you have placed. As a new agent, I am still building my list.

Describe yourself as a person. A perfectionist. Kind and always smiling. Optimistic.

How would you describe the proverbial "client from hell," and what are the warning signs? Luckily, I haven't experienced this. I would say that the warning signs would be someone who asks for your professional opinion and guidance and then objects to or refuses your advice. Someone who unprofessionally airs dirty laundry on social media, who publicly rants about the publication process. Talking out frustration in private with others is different from ranting on Twitter or Facebook. Someone who isn't willing to continue to learn their craft, learn about this business. There's so much more than just typing *The end* on a manuscript.

What do you think about self-publishing? For some authors it's right path, and for others, it isn't.

Do you like Amazon? Amazon isn't going to go away. Do I like their methods? Not particularly. Do I use them because it's easier to know something I want is coming in the mail that my local bookstore may or may not carry? Yes, I do. But I support local bookstores, school book fairs, and author book signings, too.

Do you believe in a "higher power"? Of course.

What will agenting be like in 2020? Hybrid. Agents are already becoming flexible to the changing face of publishing. Not only are they helping authors to navigate self-publishing avenues, epublishing, and traditional publishing, but they must help authors to devise marketing plans and promote clients' books with in-agency PR teams. Agents will help authors to establish their brand and become visible in the online community.

Describe your job and what you like and don't like about it. I spend most of my time reading client manuscripts with editorial suggestions. I help make contacts for promoting clients' upcoming releases. The rest is devoted to answering queries and requesting manuscripts that pique my interest.

Do you miss the way the business "used to be"? I'm entering this side of the business at a time of new changes, and I am excited by the possibilities.

What does the "Big 5" mean to you? Traditional publishing. Just one of many avenues available to authors.

What do you want to tell new/unpublished writers? The same advice a *New York Times* bestselling author told me after I wrote my first manuscript: "Find a good critique partner or critique group and have them read your work, because they can see the things that you're too close to the story to see."

Do you like that everything has become largely digitized? I do. I don't like clutter, and everything digital and on the computer makes it clutter-free.

What do you like reading, watching, and listening to? I love reading young adult and fantasy. I want to be transported to some fantastical world. I want to escape the real world for a few hours when I read. Give me the Starks versus the Lannisters any day over someone dying with cancer. It's just not my cup of tea. What I watch is very much a guilty pleasure. I will admit I'm addicted to *Once Upon a Time*. I blame growing up watching the *Wonderful World of Disney* on Sundays with my grandmother. I also love *Sleepy Hollow*, *Downton Abbey*, *Nashville* (of course), *Game of Thrones*, and BBC's *Sherlock*. As for music, I like to unwind with Bob Marley or jazz or Enya. But when I need to get moving, Foo Fighters every time.

Describe a book you would write. Since I do write, something with an element of fantasy and maybe historical. But what I love most is creating unique characters. I love the antihero, the unrepentant vampire, the pirate with a heart of gold (think Han Solo, Captain Jack Sparrow, Damon Salvatore, or Hook). And I love finding queries with these characteristics as well.

Joker's wild: So, not sure what this question is about. Maybe something revealing about me that didn't fit anywhere else? I am distantly related to the first governor of Tennessee.

Agent's name and contact info: Saritza Hernandez, Senior Literary Agent, saritza@corvisieroagency.com

Describe what you like to represent and what you won't represent. Romance, erotica, LGBT fiction.

What are the best ways for writers to pitch you? Check our submission guidelines for details, but make sure your work is ready to go out to editors on the day you submit your query.

When and where were you born? I was one of the last babies delivered at the Ramey Air Force Base Hospital in Aguadilla, Puerto Rico, on June 9, 1973.

Do you charge fees? Nope, never.

Describe your education and career history. I was one of those annoying kids who loved being in school, so when I stopped my college plans to marry the man of my dreams at the ripe young age of 20 with just my associate of arts, my parents likely thought me crazy. A romantic at heart, I knew I would eventually finish my schooling, but three kids, two dogs, and a decade of working for the government later, I yearned for books, learning, and more books. Signed up for online courses at University of Phoenix to finish the 20 credits I needed to obtain my bachelor of science degree.

I have worked in the publishing industry for 12 years doing pretty much every job you can think of, and four years ago I decided to learn the job from the other side of the desk. I fell in love with the learning and the books all over again. As an agent, you're constantly learning about the industry and changing trends. There are books, and, even better, there are authors writing new ones every day! It's the best job in the world, and I've enjoyed every minute of my four years as a literary agent.

Say something about your hobbies and personal interests. Apart from reading, you mean? It is my favorite hobby, after all. I love to read romance and erotica books in every genre, and the dirtier the book, the better.

Why and how did you become an agent? One of my closest friends had written an amazing book and asked me to help her get it published. The more I researched about what literary agents did and what it meant to be on the business side of the desk, the more I wanted to be an agent. I started looking for a mentor in the industry, and one day, on Twitter, Lori Perkins said she was looking for apprentices for her agency. She took me under her wing as the epub agent. I started representing clients whose primary focus was digital publishing and became the first literary agent to represent and sell books in the digital market.

Would you do it over again, or something else? I wish I'd done it earlier! I see some of the new blood in the industry, young men and women who go to school to learn about the publishing industry and go from being interns at publishing houses, literary agencies, and publicity firms to being some of the top literary agents in the field, and I love it!

List some representative titles you have placed. *Guyliner* by J. Leigh Bailey (Spencer Hill Press, gay young adult fiction); *Caught in the Crossfire* by Juliann Rich (Bold Strokes Books, gay young adult fiction); *Playing Knotty* by Elia Winters (Pocket Star, erotica); *Combustion* by Elia Winters (Samhain Publishing, erotic steampunk romance); *Neverwood* series by Diana Copland, Libby Drew, and G. B. Lindsey (Carina Press, male/male new adult romance); *Calling His Bluff* by Amy Jo Cousins (eHarlequin, contemporary romance); *The Vigilante* series by Tere Michaels (Dreamspinner Press, male/male superhero romance).

Describe yourself as a person. Fun-sized, coffee-loving Latina, mother of three amazing kids, wife to the most romantic man on the planet, and lap for the clingiest dog in the universe.

How would you describe the proverbial "client from hell," and what are the warning signs? I'm very blessed to not have experienced a client from hell, but that's why I think "the call" is so important for both the author and the agent. If a client is argumentative, defiant, or unwilling to work, we're not going to mesh well. So I ask a lot of questions to get a feel for how we're going to work together and offer representation if I feel we're a good match.

What do you think about self-publishing? I love it and hate it! I love that it's another opportunity for authors to present their work and expand their repertoire. I hate that it is getting more difficult to find the diamonds in the rough among the ocean of rocks.

Do you like Amazon? Did I mention my ebook hoarding problem? I blame Amazon for my ebook and coffee addiction, as they make it so easy with their one-click shopping for me to spend my money on six new ebooks and two 24-pack boxes of Dark Magic coffee k-cups. I suppose I should prepare to be assimilated soon. As a publishing and distribution opportunity for my clients, I think Amazon is a valuable tool, as many of my clients make a substantial amount of money from their ebook sales monthly.

Do you believe in a "higher power"? Absolutely, I do. I wouldn't be here had I not had some higher power watching over me and keeping me from getting in my own way.

What will agenting be like in 2020? I'm hoping hover boards will be required for something, just because I want to have one, but I don't think it will be too different from what I'm doing now. A lot of our business is being negotiated over the phone, through video conferences in our pajamas with coffee cups in tow and less-high-cost liquid lunches.

Agents are managing more than advance checks and royalty payments. We're now involved in production, distribution, marketing, and publicity opportunities for our clients, and I see that becoming standard practice for agents in the future.

Describe your job and what you like and don't like about it. I love my job! Discovering talent, reading amazing books, and seeing an author's career flourish are almost as fulfilling as seeing my own children succeed. I don't like chasing money owed to my clients.

Do you miss the way the business "used to be"? I'm a futurist so I don't like anything the way it used to be, except maybe '80s music.

What does the "Big 5" mean to you? Wider distribution and exposure for my clients, especially those writing LGBT fiction.

What do you want to tell new/unpublished writers? Don't get discouraged by rejections, learn from those who offer constructive criticism, and strengthen your writing muscle.

Do you like that everything has become largely digitized? Oh, yes! I love my iPad! I can access information at any time from anywhere.

What do you like reading, watching, and listening to? I have eclectic tastes. I read primarily what I represent, so favorites are LGBT fiction (David Levithan, Alex Sanchez, etc.), but I love male/male romance the most and have been a fan of many of the authors who are now my clients writing in the genre. My Kindle app on my iPad is loaded with everything from middle grade titles to heavy erotica. I just love to be transported. I'm rather eclectic when it comes to TV too, as I'm a huge *Downton Abbey* fan but love the futuristic *Almost Human* TV show too. Guilty pleasures include *Doctor Who*, RuPaul's *Drag Race*, and *Diners, Drive-Ins and Dives*. If my Kindle and DVR are eclectic, you can bet my iTunes is a mishmash of everything from Etta James to Disney movie sound tracks. Favorite bands at the moment are OneRepublic and Fun. Favorite solo artist is Pink. Favorite song on repeat is "I Lived" by OneRepublic.

Describe a book you would write. Funny thing is, I've started several and never get around to finishing them, which is why I admire writers who can win NaNoWriMo [National Novel Writing Month]. Maybe one day, I'll finish one of mine.

Joker's wild: I quote movie lines like scripture, especially *Ghostbusters 2*: "Everything you're doing is bad, I want you to know this." — Janosh

Agent's name and contact info: Doreen MacDonald, doreen@corvisieroagency.com

Describe what you like to represent and what you won't represent. I prefer to represent mystery, thriller, fantasy, and paranormal in novel-length projects.

No horror, please — I'm too imaginative!

What are the best ways for writers to pitch you? I'll be open to queries September 2014. Please send to queries@corvisieroagency.com with *Query for Doreen* in the subject line. Email should include (1) the query letter, (2) the first 10 to 15 pages of the manuscript, and (3) a 1–2-page synopsis that tells the full story. Paste it in the body of the email, thank you; no attachments.

When and where were you born? I was born a thousand years ago on the 3rd of June in the great state of New York.

Do you charge fees? No.

Describe your education and career history. My parents helped me circumvent learning disabilities that prevented a traditional degree by designing internships with mentors in PR and marketing, editing, and research. I used this education to run nonprofit organizations for women in crisis and special ed programs for kids who needed nontraditional learning environments, as well as for developmental editing and writing family histories for publication in the private sector.

Say something about your hobbies and personal interests. I'm one of nine children from a very close family, with four generations of people I love to hang out with, including my own son. They're mostly athletes, and I'm not, so I always have a book in hand when the touch football game begins.

Why and how did you become an agent? While I was helping a physician friend edit his first novel, I attended the SEAK Fiction Writing for Physicians Conference to meet agents on his behalf. I was befriended there by the late, great medical thriller author Michael Palmer, who suggested that I submit a manuscript query to Marisa Corvisiero, saying that she was an agent who "was different in a wonderful way." Marisa and I corresponded, and I discovered that Michael was absolutely right! It's an honor to have been invited to join the Corvisiero Agency.

Would you do it over again, or something else? I love people's stories, and I deeply respect their dreams. This is a great profession for helping them to express both successfully.

List some representative titles you have placed. Not yet — exciting projects pending!

Describe yourself as a person. I'm six of one, half dozen of the other: joyful, outgoing, hopeful — and, being Irish, sure the world will end tomorrow. I intend to be reading when that happens.

How would you describe the proverbial "client from hell," and what are the warning signs? No sense of humor. That's hell.

What do you think about self-publishing? I know people who have done it successfully because they knew how to market; I think that is the key. Options make the world work!

Do you like Amazon? I like anything that is simple to deal with and makes my life easier: that's Amazon, and that's a microwave.

Do you believe in a "higher power"? Yes.

What will agenting be like in 2020? Because of digital submissions, I think it will become that much more enjoyable because communication is so straightforward.

Describe your job and what you like and don't like about it. I like the thrill of receiving a synopsis and the first pages of a manuscript. I like the hunt for the right publisher. I like telling a client that the manuscript has been requested for reading. I don't like telling a client that it "didn't fit the list."

Do you miss the way the business "used to be"? I love the Edwardian era, so I'm sure I would have enjoyed the leisured camaraderie of this business then, too.

What does the "Big 5" mean to you? Olympic Gold for author and agent!

What do you want to tell new/unpublished writers? Make your work excellent in substance and presentation for querying agents. Go to writers' conferences and meet other writers and editors and agents. Make friends with these people who are living the dream. Doors will open!

Do you like that everything has become largely digitized? It's tremendous to professionally escape the tidal wave of paper submissions, but I'd never give up the sensory delight of holding and smelling and reading a "real" book.

What do you like reading, watching, and listening to? Rare time to relax, then British mysteries circa 1900–1930, books, TV, and film; and listening to live jazz.

Describe a book you would write. Anyone's family history. To paraphrase Will Rogers, I haven't met a life that's boring.

Joker's wild: I really miss smoking fine cigars. Gave them up with cigarettes when I became a mom. Sigh. I will smoke one more before the world ends. While reading…

Agent's name and contact info: Sarah Negovetich, sarah@corvisieroagency.com (for non-query-related emails), Twitter: @SarahNego

Describe what you like to represent and what you won't represent. I only represent young adult and middle grade novel-length projects. So, no poetry, novellas, or short stories. I'm open to almost every genre in those age groups, but contemporary is not my favorite. I also have an aversion to any story with a large environmental focus. It's a quirk and I own it.

What are the best ways for writers to pitch you? All queries should be sent to Queries @CorvisieroAgency.com with *Query for Sarah* in the subject line. Emails should include (1) the query letter, (2) the first five pages of your manuscript, and (3) a synopsis of the story that includes the end and is full of spoilers. All of this should be pasted in the body of the email. No attachments.

When and where were you born? I was born a full month past my due date, back in the Stone Age of 1979 in Cincinnati, Ohio. It was 3:49 AM, in case you're curious.

Do you charge fees? Nope, no, negative.

Describe your education and career history. I have a bachelor of arts in communication with a focus on PR/marketing. I actually used my degree to work in marketing for many years, first for General Motors and then for St. Jude Children's Research Hospital (a seriously awesome place to work). I have also worked in fast food, at the library, at several gyms, and as a third-shift waitress at the Waffle House. I am a woman of many talents.

Say something about your hobbies and personal interests. I always need to be doing something creative. I play the guitar (poorly) and sing (actually, fairly well). I've been involved in community theater and spent several years singing in an honest-to-goodness barbershop quartet. Now that I have kids, I spend a lot of time playing make-believe.

Why and how did you become an agent? It was actually an accident of sorts. I was brought in as an intern to help out with PR for the agency and fell in love with the beauty of the business side of the literary world. I get to combine my need for creativity with all my marketing knowledge to make people's dreams come true.

Would you do it over again, or something else? Did I mention I get to make people's dreams come true for a living? I love what I get to do. I can only imagine giving it all up if I was offered a starring role in a Broadway musical about barbershop. That would be a hard gig to pass up.

List some representative titles you have placed. Catch Me When I Fall by Vicki Leigh (Curiosity Quills, 2014); *Into the Fire* by Kelly Hashway (Month9Books, 2014); *Perfect for You* by Kelly Hashway writing as Ashelyn Drake (Month9Books, 2014).

Describe yourself as a person. I am an extrovert in the most extreme way. I literally score zero in the introvert column of the MBTI test. I have a clean desk and a dirty kitchen, but friends don't ever need to call ahead. It's a personal belief that there is never a bad time for a dance party.

How would you describe the proverbial "client from hell," and what are the warning signs? Thankfully, I don't have any bad eggs in my client list. I can think of two types of writers that would make me want to run. The first would be the writer who refuses to take any advice. Not that I'm the guru of all things, but if you ignore everything I say I don't think we're a good match. The second would be the writer who stops trying. If you send me a manuscript that's barely been edited expecting me to clean it up because I'm the agent, we have a problem. Editors get paid a lot more than I do.

What do you think about self-publishing? I think it's great. More opportunities for more people to put their work out there mean more chances for readers to find what they're looking for. It's not for everyone and it's not smart for all types of book, but it has its place.

Do you like Amazon? I think as an industry professional I'm not supposed to like them, but I do. I predict we may have a day of reckoning if they reach a mission-critical percentage of the market. But if they do, someone else will come in and challenge them. That's what happens. Until then, I will continue to love their ease of use, free shipping when I buy lots of books, and one-click download to my Kindle.

Do you believe in a "higher power"? Yep. I have personally witnessed the power of God in my life.

What will agenting be like in 2020? I wish I knew. Honestly, it will probably be a lot like it is today. Unless teleportation has been invented by then. That would change everything.

Describe your job and what you like and don't like about it. My job is a lot less reading and a lot more spreadsheets than I would have initially guessed. I love that I get to work with so many talented people and be a small part of their success. I don't like that there never seem to be enough hours in the day and that I have to tell people no.

Do you miss the way the business "used to be"? I haven't been around long enough to miss anything. But if by "used to be" you mean writers had to mail in queries with actual stamps and you needed a drinking problem to be famous, then no, I don't miss it.

What does the "Big 5" mean to you? Exposure. If there's one thing the Big 5 have that can't be duplicated, it's the ability to get your name everywhere. They're the equivalent of a lighted marquee on Broadway.

What do you want to tell new/unpublished writers? There is no shortcut, magic bean, or wish on a star that can get you where you want to go. Hard work mixed with a bit of luck is the only way you will find success in this industry. Anyone who tells you otherwise is likely trying to sell you something, and, trust me, you don't want to buy it.

Do you like that everything has become largely digitized? I love the convenience of my ereader, but I still buy most of my books in print. There's just something about a tangible book that makes the reading experience whole for me.

What do you like reading, watching, and listening to? I read mostly young adult and middle grade. My reading list is pretty much in line with my preferences for representation. I listen to a wide variety of music, because I like to match my mood or activity to different vibes I get from different artists. When it comes to TV, I watch very little. *Dr. Who* is my one vice, though with little ones we tend to have a Disney movie playing most days.

Describe a book you would write. I actually write as one of my creative outlets. I stick with young adult because it's what I know. I'd love to be able to write something that is both hilarious and poignant without being preachy. I would also love to represent that book, so if that describes your manuscript, please query me.

Joker's wild: I'm assuming this is for the odd bits that didn't fit anywhere else? Here goes. I'm short, as in very short. Only 4´10˝. Because of this, from behind, people often assume I'm a kid. Oddly enough, I started going gray at 19, so once I turn around they realize I'm just a fun-sized adult.

Agent's name and contact info: Rebecca "Becca" Simas, Twitter: @BeccaSimas

Describe what you like to represent and what you won't represent. I will represent young adult, new adult, horror, light fantasy, paranormal, and magical realism. I am picky about my romance but not totally opposed to it. I am only interested in novel-length work.

And as much as I love poetry, I do not wish to represent it.

What are the best ways for writers to pitch you? To query me, writers should send their queries to query@corvisieroagency.com. My name should be in the subject line, and I prefer that the one-to-two-page synopsis and first five pages be included in the body of the email. I am not a fan of attachments.

When and where were you born? I was born on June 9, 1988, in Providence, Rhode Island. Wicked.

Do you charge fees? No way!

Describe your education and career history. I have my master's in creative and professional writing with a focus in fiction and public relations. I also have my bachelor of arts in professional writing. I have taught freshman composition and tutored in writing, and have five years' experience working mall jobs, ranging from a toy store to a joke shop to a specialty tea store.

Say something about your hobbies and personal interests. I love to have fun and stay active. I just started taking ballroom dancing lessons. I like running, skiing, camping, and going out dancing. I also like to sing along while my friends play guitar, and I am obsessed with Mexican food. Oh, and my Nintendo 64 is still my primary game system.

Why and how did you become an agent? I sort of stumbled into this position. I heard from one of Marisa Corvisiero's clients that she was looking for a new intern. I had a couple months off before I started a summer job, and since I don't know what to do with myself when I have free time, I decided to apply. I ended up falling in love with the magical world of agenting, and I extended my internship at the end of the three months. I never thought this would turn into a career, but I am so glad and grateful that it did!

Would you do it over again, or something else? This is a job in my field. I know how hard these are to get in the literary world. I wouldn't change a thing! Plus, working remotely gives me so much flexibility.

List some representative titles you have placed. None yet! I opened to queries on April 1, 2014.

Describe yourself as a person. Like a Starburst, I am a walking contradiction. I rock a lot of polka dots and am obsessed with classic Disney, but at the same time I love horror movies and reading stories about serial killers. I am also extremely extroverted and get excited over everything.

How would you describe the proverbial "client from hell," and what are the warning signs? Fortunately I haven't had to deal with this (yet), but I imagine I wouldn't like working with a client who was really argumentative.

What do you think about self-publishing? I think a writer should always try to get published traditionally before they try to self-publish. But if the author knows how to market his or her work, I think it can be successful.

Do you like Amazon? I used to refuse buying books from Amazon because I felt like I would be betraying bookstores, but Amazon Prime was very convenient for me in grad school. I also love that I can peek at book sales on there. It's so helpful if I'm reading a query from an author who has already been published, so I can check out sales rankings.

Do you believe in a "higher power"? I believe in myself, and I believe in angels. That's about all I can say.

What will agenting be like in 2020? Oh, goodness. That's only six years away! I'm not sure what will change by then. Maybe an increase in digital publishers?

Describe your job and what you like and don't like about it. I feel like a talent scout for writers. It's a lot of fun. And I love learning from all the other agents at Corvisiero who know so much more than me. What I don't like is that everyone from the agency is scattered across the country. Sometimes I wish we could all teleport and have our meetings in New York together.

Do you miss the way the business "used to be"? I can't really comment on this much, since I'm brand new to the industry. But I imagine I'd be so overwhelmed by a physical slush pile even more so than I am by the digital slush pile.

What does the "Big 5" mean to you? A dream come true for most writers and their agents.

What do you want to tell new/unpublished writers? Make sure you have someone in your corner, and only send out your manuscript once it's 100 percent ready. And never give up, of course.

Do you like that everything has become largely digitized? I love it because it means an ebook can never go out of print. I will always love my print books, though, and understand fully that it is a dream for most writers to see their names in print.

What do you like reading, watching, and listening to? What I like to read changes often, so I'll go with what I'm currently reading. I'm reading *Night Circus*, *Days of Blood and Starlight*, and *Vampire Academy*. I love female vocalists and keyboards. I watch *The Walking Dead*, *Game of Thrones*, *Parks and Recreation*, and *Breaking Bad*. I'm also not ashamed to admit I've seen every episode of *Glee* and *Grey's Anatomy*.

Describe a book you would write. I already wrote one! For my graduate thesis, I wrote a young adult fantasy novel about a sea monster, a blue moon, a cavernous world, and a girl trying to destroy a curse that includes all three of those things.

Joker's wild: I have an unhealthy obsession with mango and mango-flavored things.

CURTIS BROWN, LTD. ❖ www.curtisbrown.com

10 Astor Place, New York, NY 10003

Agent's name and contact info: Jonathan Lyons, jl@cbltd.com

Describe what you like to represent and what you won't represent. Represent: biography, history, science, health, pop culture, sports, general narrative nonfiction, mystery/crime/thriller, science fiction and fantasy, and young adult fiction.

Does not represent: romance, picture books.

What are the best ways for writers to pitch you? I only accept online submissions via the following link: www.lyonsliterary.com/submissionpage.php.

Do you charge fees? No.

Describe your education and career history. Education: Washington University in St. Louis (BA); Cardozo School of Law (JD). Career: attorney, Law Offices of Mark E. Korn (Aug. 2001–Nov. 2002); agent/foreign rights associate, Curtis Brown, Ltd. (Nov. 2002–May 2005); agent/subsidiary rights manager, McIntosh & Otis, Inc. (May 2005–Jan. 2007); agent/attorney, Lyons Literary LLC (Jan. 2007–Dec. 2012); executive director of subsidiary rights, Folio Literary Management (Jan. 2012–Dec. 2012); attorney, Savur, Threadgold

& Pellecchia LLP (Jan. 2013–Present); agent/director of translation rights, Curtis Brown, Ltd. (Jan. 2013–present).

List some representative titles you have placed. *Jim Henson: The Biography* by Brian Jay Jones; *And We Stay* by Jenny Hubbard; *Babe Ruth's Called Shot* by Ed Sherman; *Half a Kin* by Joe Abercrombie.

DANA NEWMAN LITERARY LLC ❖ www.dananewman.com

9720 Wilshire Boulevard, 5th Floor, Beverly Hills, CA 90212,
dananewmanliterary@gmail.com

Agent's name: Dana Newman

Describe what you like to represent and what you won't represent. I represent nonfiction: narrative and practical nonfiction, memoir, biography, pop culture, lifestyle, health and wellness, business, cultural history, social trends, personal growth, sports; and fiction: literary fiction, upmarket women's fiction (contemporary and historical).

I do not represent science fiction, fantasy, horror, crime, romance, mystery, thriller, religion, children's, young adult, poetry, screenplays.

What are the best ways for writers to pitch you? Please email a well-written, concise query letter — with a great hook that demonstrates you've done your research — to dananewman literary@gmail.com. Identify the category, title, and word count and provide a brief overview of your project, credentials, platform, and previous publishing history, if any. For fiction submissions, please send a query letter and the first five pages of your book in the body of the email (no attachments). If I'm interested in your material, I'll email you a request for a full proposal (for nonfiction) or a synopsis and the first 20 pages (for fiction).

When and where were you born? June 4, Los Angeles, CA.

Describe your education and career history. BA in comparative literature, University of California at Berkeley; JD, University of San Francisco School of Law.

Prior to becoming a literary agent, Dana worked for 14 years as in-house counsel for the Moviola companies in Hollywood, CA, providers of entertainment and communications technologies. Having worked in the entertainment industry during the transition from analog to digital platforms in film editing and audio recording, she's excited about the transition happening in publishing and enthusiastically embraces new technologies and business models for the creation and distribution of books. Dana is also a transactional and intellectual property attorney, advising authors, creators and entrepreneurs on contracts, copyrights, trademarks, and licensing.

Say something about your hobbies and personal interests. Reading (of course), running marathons and half marathons, travel, raising teenage daughters, film, women's interest.

What might you be doing if you weren't agenting? Writing, or working with writers, editors, and publishers in some other capacity.

Do you charge fees? No.

List some representative titles you have placed. *Matchpoint: How Paid Search and Real-Time Bidding Are Transforming Online Advertising and Impacting Our Culture and Commerce* by Michael Smith (Amacom); *Blazed: The Truth about Marijuana Addiction and How to Get Help* by Kevin P. Hill, MD, MHS (Hazelden); *When We Were the Boys: Coming of Age on Rod Stewart's Out of Order Tour* by Stevie Salas with Robert Yehling (Taylor Trade); *Like a Woman* by Debra Busman (Dzanc Books); *Just Add Water* by Clay Marzo and Robert Yehling (Houghton Mifflin Harcourt); *Home Sweet Anywhere: How We Sold Our House, Created a New Life, and Saw the World* by Lynne Martin (Sourcebooks); *Cracked, Not Broken: Surviving and Thriving after a Suicide Attempt* by Kevin Hines (Rowman & Littlefield); *The King of Style: Dressing Michael Jackson* by Michael Bush (Insight Editions); *An Atomic Love Story: The Women in Robert Oppenheimer's Life* by Shirley Streshinsky and Patricia Klaus (Turner Publishing); *How to Read a Client from across the Room: Win More Business with the Proven Character Code System to Decode Verbal and Nonverbal Communication* by Brandy Mychals (McGraw-Hill).

Why and how did you become an agent? I love reading and believe in the power of a compelling narrative to influence culture and impact people's lives. My legal background makes me an excellent advocate for authors and helps in navigating the challenges and complexities of the publishing industry in the digital age. I launched my own literary agency in 2010 and have found that it's the perfect fit for my talents and interests.

How do you feel about writers? I have tremendous respect for writers and their ability to creatively express ideas, tell gripping stories, and share inspiring and/or useful information. Reading a well-written book makes life more interesting and is one of its greatest pleasures.

How do you really feel about editors and publishers? I admire their dedication to bringing deserving books to the market in a very challenging environment. I have found most editors and publishers to be smart, hardworking, talented people. Publishing a book is a collaborative endeavor, and I enjoy working with editors, publishers, and writers in that process.

Describe your job and what you like and don't like about it. My work varies from day to day, which I love. Things I do include assisting writers in polishing their proposals and manuscripts; submitting projects to editors; following up on submissions; negotiating publishing agreements; drafting coauthor agreements; running interference on delivery and production scheduling issues; facilitating cover image discussions; advising on copyright, trademark, and permission issues; working with an author on executing their marketing plan; reading queries, proposals, and manuscripts; attending writers' conferences, where I present workshops on publishing agreements, digital rights, copyright, and trademark issues.

I like discovering a voice that really resonates with me, learning something interesting, and seeing a book project come to life. The only thing I really don't like about agenting is all the rejection — both having to decline to represent writers' projects and dealing with the rejections from editors I've submitted to.

What do you like reading, watching, and listening to? Too many to list, but some of my favorites are *Bel Canto* by Ann Patchett, *One Hundred Years of Solitude* by Gabriel Garcia Marquez, *Crossing to Safety* by Wallace Stegner, *Rosie* by Anne Lamott, *The Anna Papers* by Ellen Gilchrist, *So Big* by Edna Ferber, anything by Jhumpa Lahiri, Joan Didion, or Jeffrey Eugenides — because they're masterfully crafted stories with distinctive voices, characters, and/or worlds you don't want to leave. I'm partial to movies that have a lot of humor mixed with heartfelt personal or emotional stories (*Silver Linings Playbook, Jerry Maguire, American Beauty, Little Miss Sunshine, Juno*), but I'm also drawn to well-crafted darker stories that combine history and entertainment, like *The English Patient* and *Atonement*. I'd rather read than watch TV, but I do like character-driven, edgy dramas and comedies like *Homeland, Nurse Jackie, Girls, Orange Is the New Black*, and *The Newsroom*, and I loved *Six Feet Under*.

How would you describe the proverbial "client from hell," and what are the warning signs? A writer who has unreasonable expectations about the realities of the book business, won't accept any feedback on their work, is unprofessional, is disrespectful of the author-agent and author-editor relationships, and has no sense of humor.

Describe yourself as a person. Endlessly curious, analytical, forthright, a passionate and diligent advocate for people and things I believe in.

Are you optimistic, pessimistic, neutral, or catatonic about the book biz in the future? Optimistic. It is easier than ever before for writers to get their work published and distributed worldwide. There will always be a demand for great, well-told stories, and now there are more ways to experience books and for authors to engage with their readers. The need for curation and readers' preference for professionally edited and published content is where those in the publishing industry who adapt to the changing landscape can provide enormous value.

Describe a book you would write. A narrative nonfiction work that tells a fascinating, little-known true story and reads like a novel, à la *Born to Run, Unbroken*, or *The Orchid Thief*.

DEFIORE AND COMPANY ❖ www.defioreandco.com

47 East 19th Street, Floor 3, New York, NY 10003

Agent's name and contact info: Adam Schear, ajs@defioreandco.com

Describe what you like to represent and what you won't represent. I'm interested in literary fiction and well-crafted commercial fiction, work that captivates the reader with both its prose and its plot, humor, young adult, smart thrillers, short story collections, and quirky debut literary novels. For nonfiction I'm interested in popular science, politics, pop culture, and current events.

What are the best ways for writers to pitch you? Writers can email me at ajs@defioreand co.com with a query letter containing info on the book, their bio, and the first five pages in the body of the email.

Do you charge fees? We do not charge a fee.

DENISE MARCIL LITERARY AGENCY, LLC ❖

www.denisemarcilagency.com

483 Westover Road, Stamford, CT 06902

Agent's name and contact info: Denise Marcil, denise@denisemarcilagency.com

Describe what you like to represent and what you won't represent. I have agented fiction: thriller; suspense; romantic suspense; women's contemporary fiction that reflects the lives, challenges, and love and family issues faced by today's women — from twenty-somethings to retirees; African American fiction; and chick lit. Nonfiction: self-help, business, and popular reference. I represent nonfiction books that help people's lives. I am not currently accepting submissions at this time.

When and where were you born? February 14 — Valentine's Day, Troy, New York.

Describe your education and career history. Skidmore College, BA English with honors. Avon Books, editorial assistant; Simon & Schuster, Inc., assistant editor; Denise Marcil Literary Agency, president.

Say something about your hobbies and personal interests. Ballroom dancing, theater, attending dance performances from contemporary to classic ballet, art history, travel, outdoor adventures, fly fishing.

If you were not an agent, what might you be doing instead? I can't imagine I'd ever find anything else I could feel so passionately about, but if I had to choose another career, I'd be a dancer or art history teacher.

Why and how did you become an agent? A book lover and avid reader since childhood, I majored in English in college and pursued a publishing career. Following a few years working for publishers, a job offer by an agent opened that side of the business to me. I discovered I enjoyed selling, which coincided with my talent for persuasion. Combined with my editorial skills, I discovered a career that became a passion and successful business.

How would you actually describe what you do for a living? I'm the author's business partner who guides, develops, and manages his or her writing career. I'm the advocate and cheerleader for the author and the liaison between the author and the publisher. I balance the author's expectations with the realities of the publishing industry.

What do you think the future holds for writers, publishers, and agents? Like most businesses, publishing constantly changes as new technologies and new means of distribution evolve. The changes offer all stakeholders both opportunities and challenges. Authors have more ways to self-publish their work; publishers will have to address how to protect authors' copyrights with the availability of books on the internet. Agents, authors, and publishers should work together to ensure the longevity of book publishing.

Do you have any particular opinions or impressions of editors and publishers in general? They market and distribute the author's work and play an invaluable role in an author's success. They're on the author's team.

On a personal level, what do you think people like about you and dislike about you? I think people like my generosity of spirit and my direct, honest, straightforward manner. Perhaps some don't like my direct, straightforward manner.

List some representative titles you have placed. *Wind Chime Point* by Sherryl Woods (Mira); *Red Cat* by Peter Spiegelman (Knopf); *Change the Way You See Everything through Asset-Based Thinking* by Kathryn Cramer, PhD, and Hank Wasiak (Running Press); *Diet for a Pain-Free Life* by Harris McIlwain, MD, and Debra Fulgum Bruce (Marlowe); *Big City, Bad Blood* by Sean Chercover (Morrow); *The Baby Book* by William Sears, MD, and Martha Sears, RN (Little, Brown).

D4EO LITERARY AGENCY ❖ www.d4eoliteraryagency.com

7 Indian Valley Road, Weston, CT 06883, 203-544-7180

Agent's name and contact info: Robert DiForio, d4eo@optonline.net

Describe what you like to represent and what you won't represent. I like commercial fiction and nonfiction. Don't pitch me anything I don't like.

When and where were you born? March 19, 1940. Mamaroneck, NY.

Do you charge fees? No.

Describe your education and career history. Williams College, 1964. Harvard Business School, 1978. Kable New Company, chairman and CEO. Founded literary agency in 1989.

Say something about your hobbies and personal interests. Golf.

List some representative titles you have placed. See website.

Describe your job and what you like and don't like about it. I find the right editor/publisher for my client's work.

DH LITERARY, INC.

PO Box 805, Nyack, NY 10960

Agent's name and contact info: David Hendin, dhendin@gmail.com

Describe what you like to represent and what you won't represent. We do NOT ACCEPT NEW PROJECTS/CLIENTS. Our current clients are Judith Martin (Miss Manners), Lincoln Peirce (Big Nate books and comic strips), and Elaine Viets (*Dead End Job* and *Josie Marcus* mysteries).

What are the best ways for writers to pitch you? As mentioned above, no new projects.

When and where were you born? 12/16/1945, St. Louis, MO.

Do you charge fees? No fees, only standard percentage structure.

Describe your education and career history. 23 years with United Feature Syndicate as senior VP syndication and president and publisher of World Almanac Books. BS, biology/education, University of Missouri, Columbia, MO, 1967. MA, medical journalism, University of Missouri School of Journalism, Columbia, MO, 1970.

Say something about your hobbies and personal interests. Reading and writing and doing archaeology.

Why and how did you become an agent? When I was preparing to leave my job as senior VP at United Feature Syndicate and president and publisher of their World Almanac Division, my friend the late Charles M. Schulz (*Peanuts* creator) convinced me it was the right career path.

Would you do it over again, or something else? No complaints.

List some representative titles you have placed. *Big Nate: In the Zone* by Lincoln Peirce (Balzer + Bray/Harper Collins); *Miss Manners Minds Your Business* by Judith Martin and

Nicholas I. Martin (W.W. Norton); *Catnapped* by Elaine Viets (NAL/Penguin); *Weird Life* by David Toomey (W.W. Norton).

DIANA FINCH LITERARY AGENCY ❖

www.dianafinchliteraryagency.blogspot.com

116 West 23rd Street, Suite 500, New York, NY 10011, 917-544-4470, diana.finch@verizon.net

Agent's name and contact info: Diana Finch, diana.finch@verizon.net

Describe what you like to represent and what you won't represent. I love to represent really imaginative, gripping stories written in distinctive and fluent voices. For nonfiction, I am excited about popular science; and I love math; history, particularly of social justice; progressive politics; narrative nonfiction; sports; environmentalism from all angles, including business and lifestyle; smart business advice; health. Because I've always done a lot of work with foreign rights, I love to handle both novels and nonfiction that I know will sell to translation publishers as well as to the US/UK/Canada/Australia/New Zealand English-speaking market.

I don't handle some genre fiction: romance, historical romance, Westerns, horror. I don't handle children's picture books now, although I did handle several wonderful ones early in my career.

What are the best ways for writers to pitch you? Either by email, with the query letter as the text of the email, and the first 10 or so pages of text, either in the email or as an attachment (Word preferred over PDF); or through my site at www.dianafinchliteraryagency .blogspot.com — see instructions on How to Query Me (through the wonderful cloud-based Submittable service).

When and where were you born? I'm a New Hampshire native, born in Hanover, NH, where my father was chair of the English Department and founding chair of the Drama Department at Dartmouth College. It was in some ways the best of both worlds — outdoorsy and athletic, also lots of art and culture.

Do you charge fees? I'm an AAR member, so I don't charge reading fees. I do ask for reimbursement from clients on certain expenses, approved in advance, such as finished books and overseas postage for submissions to foreign publishers.

Describe your education and career history. I graduated from Hanover High School and from Harvard with a cum laude degree in English, where as cocaptain I worked with my field hockey teammates to see the benefits of Title IX come to women's collegiate sports. I earned an MA in American literature from Leeds University, England, because after Harvard, where the reading lists in American lit courses featured authors who were alumni of Harvard, I wanted to study the subject from a bit more of a distance.

Say something about your hobbies and personal interests. My main hobbies are sports — both watching (Yankees, Red Sox, NY Giants, World Cup soccer) and playing (then: field hockey, lacrosse, soccer, skiing; now: running, yoga, swimming).

Why and how did you become an agent? I became an agent when it was time to move up from the assistant editor ranks and the older editors all advised me that if they were my age, they'd become agents because in so many ways the work is so similar to what editors and publishers do, yet as an agent you are wholly on the side of the author. I have found this to be true.

Would you do it over again, or something else? Yes, I would definitely do it over again if I were to relive my life. But if I were starting a career now, in 2014 or 2015, I might possibly find myself in a different field, such as social work or social policy, in part because I think my college experience would be very different now than it was then.

List some representative titles you have placed. *The Zero Footprint Baby* by Keya Chatterjee (Ig Publishing); *The Meat Racket* by Christopher Leonard (Simon & Schuster); *Higher Ed, Greater Debt* by Cryn Johannsen (Seven Stories Press); *Beyond Capitalism* by Loretta Napoleoni (Oneworld, Rizzoli, Paidos); *Banking on Air* by Mark Schapiro (Chelsea Green); *The Other Side of Paradise* by Julia Cooke (Seal Press); *The Secret Lives of Sports Fans* by Eric Simons (Overlook); *Honeymoon in Tehran* by Azadeh Moaveni (Random House); *Black Tide* by Antonia Juhasz (Wiley); *Word of Mouth Marketing* by Andy Sernovitz (foreign editions); *Heidegger's Glasses and Enchantment* by Thaisa Frank (Counterpoint).

Describe yourself as a person. I like to think that I am thoughtful and intelligent, empathetic with a good reserve of energy for the long haul, independent sometimes to a fault, always curious, generally friendly.

How would you describe the proverbial "client from hell," and what are the warning signs? None of mine, I'm glad to say! I think it's important to articulate expectations at the start of an author-agent relationship and to manage communication styles from the very beginning as well.

What do you think about self-publishing? All authors should learn what's involved in self-publishing, the pros and the cons. There's a lot about traditional publishing these days that is more like self-publishing than it is like the traditional publishing of 10 or 15 years ago. My author-agent agreement anticipates that a project might end up self-published rather than sold to a traditional publisher.

Do you like Amazon? I like to be able to look up authors, titles, and book subjects in their amazing database.

Do you believe in a "higher power"? Yes, I do believe in God. I also believe Hamlet: "There are more things in heaven and earth, Horatio, than are dreamt of in your philosophy."

What will agenting be like in 2020? Agents will be working to bring creative work to its audience, globally and in multimedia.

Describe your job and what you like and don't like about it. I both like and am challenged by the fact that there is never a dull moment, and there is always something different, as each book is unique. There is a lot of paperwork and record keeping, which can be satisfying and can be draining. It draws on diametrically opposed skills: keen attention to detail as well as a sense of the big picture, a feel for and interest in overall trends and the zeitgeist, gregarious social skills as well as the ability to be firm and to cut through the fog.

Do you miss the way the business "used to be"? I miss working with a lot of people who have left the business. But missing the way business "used to be" is like missing life in the 1990s. I don't have a desire to go back in time.

What does the "Big 5" mean to you? Consolidation among traditional publishers who are publishing traditional lists in the traditional way and who operate out of a corporate structure.

What do you want to tell new/unpublished writers? Write for the sheer love of writing, and prepare to be an entrepreneur. Approach being an author as if you were a start-up.

Do you like that everything has become largely digitized? I love the ability to search so many things so quickly. The increased speed of communication is of course both a blessing and a curse.

What do you like reading, watching, and listening to? Eclectic taste! Music: Discovering new bands from my yoga instructor's tape, salsa, classics, classic rock. These days I find myself watching as much TV (*The Good Wife*, *Scandal*) as film, and many recent films feel as evanescent as TV series and I find myself watching older movies, everything from *Brokeback Mountain* (based on a story) to *Titanic* (I represented a book about the making of the film) to *The Wizard of Oz* (based on a book by one of my favorite childhood authors) — I think there's a literary connection there!

Describe a book you would write. I'd only write a book if I were absolutely compelled to do so — I see what goes into it and am so familiar with the challenges, all along the way. That said, I could see myself coauthoring a book with an expert whose work I believed in.

DON CONGDON ASSOCIATES, INC. ❖ www.doncongdon.com

110 William Street, Suite 2202, New York, NY 10038, dca@doncongdon.com

Agent's name: Katie Kotchman

Describe what you like to represent and what you won't represent. I'm actively seeking fiction and nonfiction in the following areas: women's fiction (mostly upmarket, but I also handle some genre romance), mystery, thriller, young adult, literary fiction, business (career, leadership, sales, marketing, big idea), narrative nonfiction (true crime, popular science, psychology, adventure, big idea), pop culture. As far as personal taste, I won't shy away from dark or quirky fiction, as long as the writing and characters are compelling. I'm most drawn to novels that successfully combine literary and commercial sensibilities.

I do not represent poetry, screenplays, or children's picture books.

What are the best ways for writers to pitch you? Send me a query letter at dca@don congdon.com. Your letter should describe the concept of the work, your prior publication history (if applicable), and your platform as an author (particularly for nonfiction). Include the first chapter within the body of the email. Be sure to include my full name in the subject line. You can send the same via snail mail, but be sure to include a self-addressed, stamped envelope for my reply.

When and where were you born? I was born and raised in North Dakota.

Do you charge fees? No upfront fees. Some postage and book purchases may be recouped from the author for foreign submissions.

Describe your education and career history. I graduated from Vassar College with a bachelor of arts in English. While at Vassar, I concentrated on late-19th- and early-20th-century American literature, but I wrote my thesis on Shakespeare's *Richard II* tetralogy. Upon graduation, I took an internship with Denise Marcil Literary Agency, which turned into a full-time assistant position. After two years, I became the business and contracts manager, while handling audio and electronic rights. In 2008, I joined Don Congdon Associates as an agent. In addition to my own list, I handle the electronic rights for a substantial portion of the agency's backlist.

List some representative titles you have placed. *Welcome to the Real World* by Lauren Berger (Harper Collins, April 2014); *Any Man I Want* by Michele Grant (Kensington, August 2014); *The Truth Doesn't Have to Hurt* by Deb Bright (Amacom, fall 2014); over 45 historical and contemporary romances by Anita Mills, Jane Bonander, Arnette Lamb, and Anna Eberhardt (Diversion Books); *New York Times* bestselling author Jerry Bledsoe's *Bitter Blood*, *Before He Wakes*, *Blood Games*, and *Death Sentence* (Diversion Books).

DOUG GRAD LITERARY AGENCY, INC. ❖ www.dgliterary.com

68 Jay Street, Suite W11, Brooklyn, NY 11201, query@dgliterary.com

Agents' names and contact info: Doug Grad, doug.grad@dgliterary.com, 718-788-6067; George Bick, george.bick@dgliterary.com, 917-561-2038

Describe what you like to represent and what you won't represent. We like fiction and nonfiction. Fiction: thriller and mystery (including all subgenres of both), science fiction, historical fiction, horror, Westerns, etc. Nonfiction: celebrity, memoir, music, military, history, sports, popular science, business, true crime, humor, health and fitness.

We don't do illustrated children's books, fantasy, romance. Yet…

What are the best ways for writers to pitch you? Fold up a query letter into the shape of a paper airplane and sail it through an open window. Actually, an email query is preferred. We don't accept paper queries/submissions.

When and where were you born? I (Doug) was born in 1962 in Queens, NY, and George was born in 1963, also in Queens. But since there are something like two and a half million people in Queens, no, we didn't know each other growing up.

Do you charge fees? We do not charge fees. However, we will consider bribes. Unmarked bills with nonconsecutive serial numbers are best. JUST KIDDING, PEOPLE! Geez, lighten up…

Describe your education and career history. I went to P.S. 196 in Forest Hills, NY…oh, not that far back? After graduating from Stuyvesant High School (where I studied creative writing with Frank "Angela's Ashes" McCourt when he was still just Mr. McCourt), I studied acting at Northwestern University. After a couple of acting gigs out of college (earning a paycheck of $2.39 one week!), I got a real job at the *Ladies' Home Journal*. I also worked for the Connie Clausen Literary Agency before I got a temp job working for Michael Korda at Simon & Schuster. Six months later, I got a permanent job at Pocket Books as the assistant to the editorial director, Bill Grose. I left Pocket as an associate editor in 1995 and moved to Ballantine (Random House), where I was a full editor. At Ballantine, I published Jeff Shaara's first two novels, *Gods and Generals* and *The Last Full Measure*. I moved to NAL (Penguin) in 1998 as a senior editor, where I edited John Jakes, among others, and had a number of *New York Times* bestsellers. In 2004 I moved to ReganBooks (Harper Collins) — more bestsellers. In 2008, I left to open my own literary agency, just before the bottom fell out of the US economy. But I'm doing okay now.

George has a similar story: after graduating from the Bronx High School of Science, he studied psychology, business, and English at SUNY Albany. He then began a two-year stint in selling commercial refrigeration hardware in LA but moved back to NYC to work in sales at Warner Books and Ballantine (where he and I met and shot rubber bands at each other during sales conferences), then was a publishing manager at Pocket, then a senior VP of sales at Harper Collins, and most recently, an associate publisher at Collins.

Say something about your hobbies and personal interests. I love to play golf and ski, neither of which I have much time (or money) to do anymore. I am also a long-suffering Mets fan (what a dope). I love jazz and played alto sax professionally in a number of rock bands in the 1980s. I love dark beer and single malt scotch. My two kids — a son in middle school and a daughter in high school — keep me plenty busy. My wife is a librarian in the Brooklyn Public Library system and is a member of ALA. We have a pug dog who is the cutest, silliest, stinkiest dog in town. I also love old cars and Chinese food, collect vintage desk accessories, am an amateur genealogist, and coach my son's little league baseball team. I also have a collection of vintage bowties and cuff links. Don't ask.

George is an avid road cyclist, and has a house in upstate NY where he keeps his 1968 Pontiac GTO, which makes me very jealous.

Why and how did you become an agent? I became an agent because when you're an editor in this business and you reach a certain age and salary, you always have to have an exit strategy. I'd also gotten bored doing basically the same job for over 20 years and felt I wasn't being challenged. I became an agent by just doing it. Like a Nike ad.

Would you do it over again, or something else? I would do it over again, but not in 2008! If I'd done it a dozen years earlier, I'd have a uniformed chauffeur driving me around in a Rolls-Royce by now, instead of careening around town in a 12-year-old Dodge. Although George tools about town in a 20-year-old Ford. And he likes it.

List some representative titles you have placed. *EarthEnd Saga* by Gillian Anderson and Jeff Rovin (three books with Simon 451, Simon & Schuster's new science fiction imprint); *Diving the Last U-Boat* by Randall Peffer (Berkley); *Bounty*, a novel by Michael Byrnes (Bantam); the Vietnam memoir *Written Off* by Capt. William Albracht and Marvin Wolf (NAL); *Here by the Bloods*, a Western by Brandon Boyce (three novels with Kensington); *Never Alone*, a mystery by C. J. Carpenter (three novels with Midnight Ink); *Gordie Howe's Son* by Mark Howe and Jay Greenberg (HarperCanada and, in the US, Triumph); an untitled book on the Tehran Conference between Roosevelt, Churchill, and Stalin by L. Douglas Keeney (Turner); *World on a String: A Musical Memoir* by jazz guitarist John Pizzarelli with Joseph Cosgriff.

Describe yourself as a person. If we can't have fun doing this, what's the point? I'm a no-BS kind of guy — a straight shooter who has no patience for idiots. All right, maybe that's too harsh. It's pretty mean to all the idiots out there.

How would you describe the proverbial "client from hell," and what are the warning signs? I drop the client from hell ASAP. Warning signs: they're never satisfied with anything; they call to complain all the time; send emails longer than a few lines — much,

much longer, like the kind that go on for pages; send me interminably long and detailed letters in the mail about every infraction committed against them, real or imagined; and think that I have nothing better to do than work only for them. Screw it — life's too short to bother with that kind of author.

What do you think about self-publishing? I believe in assisted self-publishing (which is not like assisted suicide). In other words, if you want to get your book published without going to a publisher, hire professionals to edit, copyedit, and design the text and cover. Doing it all yourself is like the lawyer who represents himself — he has a fool for a client. Don't be a schmuck — no one can do it all. But beware — good people are not cheap, and they've earned their high prices through years of experience. Don't go into self-publishing lightly! As I like to say, "I'll tell you the secret to making a small fortune in publishing: start with a large fortune." Thank you, I'll be here all week…

Do you like Amazon? I love Amazon as a store. I love Kindle Direct Publishing. I don't love Amazon's "traditional" publishing program. Frankly, I foresee a future where B&N goes belly up, and it's Amazon and the independent bookseller. I don't know how a brick-and-mortar bookstore chain is going to survive. I don't want that to happen, but I wouldn't be surprised if it did.

Do you believe in a "higher power"? Only when I win at poker or break 90 on the golf course.

What will agenting be like in 2020? Pretty much the same as it is now, only I'll (a) have more gray hair, (b) have less hair, and (c) still be looking for that chauffeur-driven Rolls.

Describe your job and what you like and don't like about it. I do everything from soup to nuts (including salad). I read and edit proposals and sometimes edit manuscripts. I submit to publishers, negotiate deals, scrutinize contracts. I'm a clearinghouse for information, a mail center, a marriage broker, and a marriage counselor. I arbitrate disputes, am both the good cop *and* the bad cop. I decipher royalty statements, commiserate with authors when things don't work out. I'm a psychologist, a book doctor, a writer's-block breaker, an ideas man, a bill collector, and a storage facility for these odd products called books. I'm an IT guy, a computer repairman, and a thousand other things you can think of. I don't like being the bad cop, and I hate it when authors aren't happy, when books don't earn royalties, when publishers put lousy art on the covers or drop the ball with sales. I hate butting heads, but I'm an Aries and I can butt heads with the best of them.

Do you miss the way the business "used to be"? Hell yes. Who doesn't? When I got into the business in 1986, you could make a good living from publishing. You could even make a lot of money from publishing. It's so much more difficult now. And it's all because of computers and the internet.

What does the "Big 5" mean to you? That's where the money is.

What do you want to tell new/unpublished writers? There are two things I tell new/unpublished writers: (1.) Don't quit your day job. (2.) *DON'T QUIT YOUR DAY JOB!!!!!!!!*

Do you like that everything has become largely digitized? Yes. If it hadn't, the costs to open my own agency would have been prohibitive, and I would have gone to an established agency.

What do you like reading, watching, and listening to? I recently read *The Complete Annotated Sherlock Holmes* (Norton) and loved it. Three monster volumes the size of the Manhattan White Pages, back when there were still phone books. We listened to Tina Fey's *Bossy Pants* audiobook during a long car ride last summer. A little inappropriate at times for the kids, but laugh-out-loud funny. I've been watching *Mad Men*, *Sherlock* (duh), *Breaking Bad*, and *Foyle's War* on Netflix. Also just watched every *30 Rock* on Netflix. Great comedy writing! Go-to DVDs are the oldies but goodies: Astaire & Rogers, Warner Brothers gangster movies, etc. Listening to everything from Stan Getz's various Bossa Nova albums with Charlie Byrd and Astrud Gilberto from the early 1960s to anything by John Pizzarelli, Zoot Sims, Benny Goodman, and Count Basie, and I love the Ella Fitzgerald/Louis Armstrong albums. I also have a soft spot for the B-52s and Devo.

George likes Kurt Vonnegut, Philip K. Dick, John Kennedy Toole, and Dr. Seuss. He's a fan of *The Walking Dead*, *Sons of Anarchy*, *Top Gear* (UK), *The Simpsons*, *The Daily Show*, *MST3K*, and *An Idiot Abroad*. His favorite music includes the Doors, Pink Floyd, the Kinks, Foo Fighters, and Leonard Cohen.

Describe a book you would write. Years ago, someone asked me why I hadn't written a novel. I told them that I was an editor — that I didn't want to compete with my authors. I didn't want to be one of those frustrated actors who taught acting, etc. I love working with writers to make their work better (sort of like being a director or a producer). I don't know that I'd ever write a novel. But a few years back I did write a screenplay for a horror movie. My wife read it and was aghast because it was so gruesome. I thought it was hilarious — both the screenplay and my wife's reaction to it!

Joker's wild: Jack Barry was a great game show host. I'm not sure why you're asking about *The Joker's Wild*, but whatever happened to game shows? They used to be a staple of morning television. Great hosts, too — Jack Narz (*Concentration*), Tom Kennedy (*Split Second*), Bill Cullen (*Eye Guess*), Allan Ludden (*Password*), Art James (*Who, What or Where?*), Monty Hall (*Let's Make a Deal*), and the best game show host name ever, Wink Martindale (*Gambit*). Oh, wait, you're not talking about game shows? Well, in that case, I'd like to say that everyone should read more books, publishers should pay higher advances and give better royalties, no one should pirate ebooks, and we should all respect the written word more than we do. It seems that writers are the lowest on the payment totem pole, whether in New York or Hollywood. Yet without the stories, there are no books to publish, no movies or TV shows to make. Maybe that's why networks love reality TV — no writers, low production costs. No one can argue that *Here Comes Honey Boo Boo* can touch anything written by any halfway decent writer. Even a halfway lousy writer can do better than that. Even a halfway lousy drunk writer who's missing the letter e on his keyboard can do better. I'll get off my soapbox now. I think I was better off babbling about game shows.

ELDRIDGE-CONNORS LITERARY AGENCY ❖

www.eldridgeconnors.com

info@eldridgeconnors.com

Agent's name and contact info: Lila Matthews, lila@eldridgeconnors.com

Describe what you like to represent and what you won't represent. Fiction that is hopeful, dangerous, and unexpected; nonfiction that is genuine, sharply written, and ultimately fulfilling (for both reader and author).

We do not represent erotica, technical manuals, or screenplays.

What are the best ways for writers to pitch you? Formal queries are always the best way to pitch your manuscript to us. We respect people who follow traditional paths in terms of the way they express themselves as creative writers as well as the mode in which they represent themselves within the marketplace.

When and where were you born? August 15, 1963; Portland, Oregon.

Do you charge fees? We do not charge any fees.

Describe your education and career history. MA, English literature and composition; BA, English literature/creative writing; AA, journalism. Three years of graduate coursework in intellectual property and contract law; 22 years as a professor of literature, composition, technical writing/editing; 7 years as a journalist, primarily specializing in arts and entertainment writing. Many academic essays, journalistic articles, and poems published. Have represented many new writers of fiction and nonfiction.

Say something about your hobbies and personal interests. I love postmodern literature, German opera, and singing, but my first real love is ballet. I was a soloist with the San Francisco Ballet, Ballet West, and Pacific Northwest Ballet Theater in the '80s. And, of course, I write!

Why and how did you become an agent? It all came as a result of teaching composition and creative writing classes at the university level. I saw too many young adults who turned in work that exhibited passion and excellent writing in terms of content, structure, and style, but who lacked confidence in their voices and their talent. I am a motivator by nature, knowing that it takes hard work to accomplish what you want, and that you should never settle for less than you are. I knew I wanted to be a champion for those voices that deserved an audience, especially when these promising writers would walk into their neighborhood mass-market bookstore and feel like their minds and hearts were being swallowed whole in a sea of published mediocrity. I want to act as a conduit for the lover/embracer of words who can succeed and thrive, and who can make the valiant choice to spend their life doing what they love.

Would you do it over again, or something else? I would happily do it all over again! But since working as an agent is relatively new to me (a gutsy move!), I can honestly say I am sure that the best is yet to come!

List some representative titles you have placed. We are presently representing many promising new writers and are actively working with primary and secondary markets for fiction, nonfiction, and academic writing.

Describe yourself as a person. Sensitive, outgoing, outrageous, adventurous, brave.

How would you describe the proverbial "client from hell," and what are the warning signs? Those who feel the world owes them publication; those who only crave fame and money; those whose egos are so frail that they need to bully others and not show respect to those who deserve it after years of hard work and gaining valid traditional education. Warning signs? Not wanting to listen to sound advice, especially in terms of specific ways they could improve their skills as a writer/storyteller.

What do you think about self-publishing? People who feel they have to pay someone to bind their manuscript for them so they can call themselves "published" usually belong to the group described in the question above. Nothing really worth having comes easy. It takes a lot of guts and work to get your manuscript to a point of perfection that a valid, credible publishing house will actually accept.

Do you like Amazon? NO. We are headed in the wrong direction as a society when anyone and everyone can get their "stuff" online and have the marketplace be virtual instead of actual. My conscience is in line with this 100 percent. Our agency believes in traditional paths of persistence and hard work, and we wish to represent only those writers who exhibit these same qualities, which span all tests of time and culture.

Do you believe in a "higher power"? Absolutely. Without it, there is no true passion, no hope, no faith in self or in others. It comes through in the work that we choose to represent.

What will agenting be like in 2020? Hopefully, the same as it is in 2014 — pounding the pavement and picking up the phone, representing writers with diligence, desire, and a genuine voice.

Describe your job and what you like and don't like about it. Reaching out to those who write but do not think of themselves, yet, as writers — motivating them to perfect their ideas and words to make them perfect; this is what I do. Follow-through with contacts at the "Big 5" is probably the biggest daily challenge we face as literary agents. We only have control over our side of the energy and the ongoing conversation to represent our writers, which makes hope such an important part of this business — hope that our hard work, enthusiasm, and stamina will pay off for both our authors and ourselves from the moment our contract to represent is signed to that first advance; taking our writers through the planning, writing/editing, and representation of their subsequent manuscripts as well. Of course, the hardest thing about this business is encouraging writers who *you* believe in but who don't believe in themselves.

Do you miss the way the business "used to be"? Yes. While technology has its obvious benefits, we have become so dependent on it in so many facets of our lives that we forget the joys and benefits of face-to-face interaction. At Eldridge-Connors Literary Agency, we take the old-fashioned approach to maintaining a professional, but still personal, relationship with our clients, because writing *is* personal — it is a deeply emotional thing that we do when we throw our guts, heads, and hearts on a page and want the whole world to share in that nakedness, that truth. Our agency is technologically savvy enough to successfully represent our authors in an up-to-date manner without losing the joy of tradition.

What does the "Big 5" mean to you? Conglomeration — and often a compromise in quality. With growing frequency, it is the secondary- and tertiary-level publishers who work hardest for our writers, investing time and energy that those houses with longer rosters cannot afford. Besides, five years from now, it will probably be "The BIG 1."

What do you want to tell new/unpublished writers? Work hard to write the words of your heart. Realize it is a craft as well as an art that needs daily attention and practice. Gain enough advanced education so that your sentence structure and punctuation are second nature and a source of confidence and ultimate credibility within the publishing marketplace. However, if you are really serious about getting your work ready for publication, be prepared to cultivate a huge amount of patience during the often-grueling process of our dealing with the publisher on your behalf. It can often take years for the process to be complete, but if you have the desire to stick with it, it is well worth the wait!

Do you like that everything has become largely digitized? NO. We need hands-on, real communication with one another if we are to stay human. Some might say we have already lost much of our humanness through our use and overuse of technology. Let's talk to each other, over the phone, over coffee. We need, we desire each other's facial expressions, body language, and physical contact. We need each other.

What do you like reading, watching, and listening to? I read classic fiction possessing elements that exhibit the voyage into human frailty; edgy horror that *does not rely* on sex or gore to sell itself. Things of value. Things that will make me feel great about myself at the end of the experience of it.

Describe a book you would write. Only something that would touch and change the lives of others. Period.

Joker's wild: Message to all writers: Life is too short to not do what you love the most. If you are here on this earth to write, and you know it, then sing your song on the page and let us help you make it your career.

THE ELIZABETH KAPLAN LITERARY AGENCY, INC. ❖

www.elizabethkaplanlit.com

928 Broadway, Suite 901, New York, NY 10010; inquiries to Arielle Datz

Agent's name and contact info: Elizabeth Kaplan, ek@elizabethkaplanlit.com

Describe what you like to represent and what you won't represent. Narrative nonfiction, issue oriented, memoir, literary fiction — everything except genre fiction.

What are the best ways for writers to pitch you? A smart email with author info showing they have done their homework and a short pitch and sample pages.

When and where were you born? Detroit, Michigan.

Do you charge fees? No.

Describe your education and career history. U of Michigan grad, University of Denver Publishing Institute grad. Worked for Jim Silberman at Summit Books, then Sterling Lord at Sterling Lord Literistic.

Say something about your hobbies and personal interests. I am interested in yoga, animals, and children and am pretty much curious about the world I live in.

Why and how did you become an agent? I was an editor and moved to an agency to get a better perspective of the publishing industry and quickly found that it suited my talents and interests.

Would you do it over again, or something else? I feel blessed to have found my calling in my professional life.

List some representative titles you have placed. We Were Liars; Iditarod Calling; The Launch Pad; Childhood Interrupted.

Describe yourself as a person. Optimistic.

Describe your job and what you like and don't like about it. I love developing material and working with thoughtful, creative people. Always wish there was more room for books by these same people.

THE ETHAN ELLENBERG LITERARY AGENCY ❖

www.ethanellenberg.com

150 Broadway, Suite 1803, New York, NY 10038, Attn: Submissions

Electronic Submissions: agent@ethanellenberg.com.
See website for submission guidelines.

Agents' names: Ethan Ellenberg, Evan Gregory

Describe what you like to represent and what you won't represent. We specialize in commercial fiction — fantasy, science fiction, romance, mystery, thriller, suspense, and all women's fiction. We also consider literary fiction with strong narrative. We have a children's list and will consider new adult, middle grade, chapter books, and picture books. In nonfiction we represent health, history, adventure, science.

What are the best ways for writers to pitch you? We love our "agent" account and are very active in looking at electronic submissions. Just please follow our guidelines. We take new clients out of the "agent" account every year.

Do you charge fees? No.

Describe your education and career history. I have a BA in philosophy and worked for Bantam and Penguin before founding my own literary agency.

Why and how did you become an agent? I have always loved fiction and storytelling. I wanted to work in publishing when I was in college, and I was lucky enough to land a job after school. I realized early on that my mix of skills and interests was best suited to agenting.

Would you do it over again, or something else? Very happy with what I do.

List some representative titles you have placed. *Lock In* by John Scalzi, Hugo Award winner (Tor); *Bulldozer's Birthday*, illustrated by Eric Rohmann, Caldecott Medal winner, and written by Candace Fleming, Golden Kite Award winner (Atheneum); *Corsair* by James Cambias (Tor); *Undead and Unwary* by MaryJanice Davidson (Berkley); *Bite Me* by Shelly Laurenston (Kensington); *Dark Matter* by Ian Douglas (Avon); *The Falcon Throne* by Karen Miller (Orbit); *Reign of Ashes* by Gail Martin (Orbit); *The Turning Circle* by Sharon Shinn (Ace); *Love in the Age of Mechanical Reproduction* by Judd Trichter

(Thomas Dunne); *Stone Cold Lover* by Christine Warren (St. Martin's); *12 Harlequin Desires* by Kathie DeNosky (Harlequin).

Describe yourself as a person. I am a person interested in your book.

How would you describe the proverbial "client from hell," and what are the warning signs? This is not an issue for our agency. If we don't work well together, we'll part company. It isn't easy being an author; there's lots of waiting and rejection. We want to support you.

What do you think about self-publishing? It's a viable option for some. It is not for everyone. We still think a sound deal with a Big 5 publisher makes the most sense if it can be had.

What will agenting be like in 2020? I think the expertise agents have — in depth of knowledge of the genres; the ability to coach writers into their best work; expertise in contracts, royalties, subsidiary rights, negotiation, accounting; good, thriving contacts with editors and publishers; and managing important businesses connected to book publication, like the sale of translation rights (we sell about 100 licenses per year), audio rights, and performance rights — means we will have a role in servicing the needs of authors.

Describe your job and what you like and don't like about it. It's a busy whirl of marketing, selling, negotiating, managing, reading, critiquing, collecting monies and remitting same, and doing everything else we do to support our clients.

Do you miss the way the business "used to be"? Editors are way too busy. The business is simply more demanding on all of us.

What does the "Big 5" mean to you? It's very simply the five conglomerates that have the lion's share of American book publishing.

What do you want to tell new/unpublished writers? Follow your muse and your dreams. Your story is still the key element, so write a great book.

Do you like that everything has become largely digitized? It is a boon for managing. It is a vital new source of revenue. It has also hurt the distribution of physical books, and that's bad.

What do you like reading, watching, and listening to? I enjoy fiction still, but because I read so much for work, it is not unusual for me to read history for pleasure.

Joker's wild: It's a cliché, but the more things change, the more they do remain the same. Authors need to be compelling storytellers. Successful ones generate a lot of business, and they need a partner to manage that business. It's really that simple.

FALKIN LITERARY

2605 West 49½ Street, Austin, TX 78731, 512-560-4950, mark.falkin@gmail.com

Agent's name: Mark Falkin

Describe what you like to represent and what you won't represent. I'm looking for fiction that artfully entertains and cannot be easily put down. I am particularly drawn to novels that are not always so easy to categorize, e.g., literary thriller, suburban drama. Would love to see the Next Great Horror Novel, one that truly breaks new ground in the genre. I'd love to see nonfiction by writers/personalities with huge platforms in sports, business, and academics. Cracking narrative nonfiction as well. Short story collections by accomplished writers are always relished.

I am not looking to represent romance, erotica, young adult fantasy, or genre sci-fi.

What are the best ways for writers to pitch you? Query via email, including in the body of the email the first two chapters of a novel, or the first story in a collection.

When and where were you born? 1970, Tulsa, OK, USA.

Do you charge fees? No.

Describe your education and career history. BA, Southern Methodist University, 1993; JD, University of Oklahoma College of Law, 1996. Intellectual property and entertainment attorney, 1997–present. Writer, self-published novel, *Days of Grace* (2006); *Contract City*, a novel, publishing 2014 with Bancroft Press.

Say something about your hobbies and personal interests. Being with my kids, writing, reading, coaching soccer, music, paddling.

Why and how did you become an agent? Since I'm a writer and an entertainment attorney, it was a natural fit. I hung out my shingle and said hello.

Would you do it over again, or something else? Just getting started.

List some representative titles you have placed. *Lesson Plans* by Suzanne Greenberg (Prospect Park Books); *The Gravity between Us* by Kristen Zimmer (Bookouture).

Describe yourself as a person. Empathic, yet strident when necessary. Funny and irreverent. Usually, people who declare they are funny aren't, but I am.

How would you describe the proverbial "client from hell," and what are the warning signs? Haven't had one, but a few queriers I've encountered have been less than ideal. A warning sign that a writer's query may not be something you want to deal with is when the writer doesn't actually query you but instead begins by asking you if you are some kind of jerk and ends with "I'd never query you," as if the writer has some sort of magic bargaining power.

What do you think about self-publishing? I've done it and it's great if you only want to sell to family and friends and maybe a bit beyond. It's just so rare that a self-published book breaks out, e.g, *Wool*. It's very limiting for writers who choose that route.

Do you like Amazon? Like the sun, Amazon is there, the system revolves around it, it giveth life and it taketh away life. If Amazon wasn't there, some other digital seller would be, so what's relevant isn't the existence of Amazon but the technology that brought it into being and maintains it and grows its power.

Do you believe in a "higher power"? I choose to give a nonresponsive answer here, which some will believe speaks volumes and others will take for what it is, which is: it's too personal a question.

What will agenting be like in 2020? Much like it is now. Identifying great work and personal relationships will still drive the business.

Describe your job and what you like and don't like about it. I'm an agent who reviews queries, reads the work that looks promising, seeks publication, and negotiates contracts. There's just not enough time in the day to read all I want to get to. I feel like I pass on work that I may not if I just had more time to assess it.

Do you miss the way the business "used to be"? I'm too new to have a pithy comment.

What does the "Big 5" mean to you? Great distribution and cachet, but maybe writers get lost in the bigness.

What do you want to tell new/unpublished writers? Don't delude yourself about your work and abilities. If you really believe in it, keep pushing it out there. Keep writing. There is no muse. There is only a blinking cursor.

Do you like that everything has become largely digitized? Yes, though I prefer paper books.

What do you like reading, watching, and listening to? Fiction that transports me; films that immerse me; music that moves me or makes me move.

Describe a book you would write. I've written several.

FELICIA ETH LITERARY REPRESENTATION ❖ www.ethliterary.com
555 Bryant Street, Suite 350, Palo Alto, CA 94301

Agent's name and contact info: Felicia Eth, Feliciaeth.literary@gmail.com

Describe what you like to represent and what you won't represent. I handle smart nonfiction of great variety: narrative, journalism, memoir, science, unusual travel, psychological and social concerns, women's insterest, fresh parenting idea, culinary writing. My fiction tends to be literary accessible fiction, historical or suspense novels that transcend genres. I'm open to magical realism or novels set abroad.

No genres, graphic novels, poetry, technical books.

What are the best ways for writers to pitch you? Email or snail mail — query.

When and where were you born? Born in NY, I work as an agent in the Bay Area, after having been an agent in NY.

Do you charge fees? No.

Describe your education and career history. Educated at both Brandeis and McGill, I've worked as an agent on both coasts, with my own agency in the Bay Area and previously at Writers House in NY. Prior to that, I was briefly West Coast editor for St. Martin's Press. Before becoming an agent, I worked in the story departments of both Warner Brothers and Palomar Pictures.

Say something about your hobbies and personal interests. My interests are diverse; as for hobbies, I'm a gardener, a traveler, a horseback rider, a lover and collector of art.

Why and how did you become an agent? I left the movie business because I was more intrigued by books as books rather than as conduits to movies. I also never went to journalism school, which I had deferred admission to since I felt as an agent I could work with journalists and get a far wider array of stories out there.

Would you do it over again, or something else? No regrets, but it's a different business these days than when I started.

List some representative titles you have placed. *The World Is a Carpet* by Anna Backhen (Riverhead Books); *Fastest Things on Wings* by Terry Masear (Houghton/Harcourt); *Tales of Alpine Obsession* by Daniel Arnold (Counterpoint); *Wildfire* by Mary Lowry (Skyhorse Publishing); *Boys at Risk* by Leonard Sax (Basic Books); *The Memory Thief* by Emily Colin (Ballantine Books).

Describe yourself as a person. Oh, come on, what kind of a question is that?

How would you describe the proverbial "client from hell," and what are the warning signs? An ingrate who doesn't listen, thinks he or she knows better, and is relentless — too many emails, too many phone calls, and always pointing out other books (just like his but not as good) that have sold or sold for way more money.

What do you think about self-publishing? I've seen how it can work positively for an author, but I'm not a big proponent.

Do you like Amazon? Yes, I do, but I understand that it's a monolith that can make traditional publishers' life hell, and make independent bookstores quake in their boots.

Do you believe in a "higher power"? The jury's still out, but I don't believe that great writing will be discovered.

What will agenting be like in 2020? Likely to be very different, with more mergers between agencies, and agencies providing many functions for authors that publishers previously did — marketing and publicity, handling online publication, and still fighting the good fight for authors.

Describe your job and what you like and don't like about it. This is a varied job that is full of frustration and work that gets you nowhere, but there's nothing quite like reading something that's incredible, or learning about new ideas every day of the week, becoming a dilettante at everything by virtue of the array of material you're exposed to.

Do you miss the way the business "used to be"? Yes, I do — I miss editors taking risks for little money, I miss the concept of building a writer's career, I miss past small sellers not being held against you, and I miss buying a book because it's a fresh idea worth putting out there, regardless of whether or not the author has a platform. BUT you can't turn back time, so one has to make the most of the way things are at present.

What does the "Big 5" mean to you? Come on — Bertelsmann, Harpers, Macmillan, Simon & Schuster, and Hachette. That is, unless you're referring to the sporting goods store?

What do you want to tell new/unpublished writers? I don't have enough space — so instead, go to some conferences, take some classes, or read about publishing, come in somewhat educated both as to how the world works and how to improve your craft.

Do you like that everything has become largely digitized? It doesn't bother me — after all, I'm writing this on a computer, read on my iPad, and talk on my cell phone.

What do you like reading, watching, and listening to? I read all sorts of things — books, magazines, websites, blogs; not a big TV watcher but like the social aspect of movies and love a wide array of music.

Describe a book you would write. Who knows?

FINEPRINT LITERARY MANAGEMENT ❖ www.fineprintlit.com

115 West 29th Street, Third Floor, New York, NY 10001

Agent's name: Janet Reid

Describe what you like to represent and what you won't represent. I represent narrative nonfiction (history, biography, current events) and commercial fiction (thrillers, crime novels).

What are the best ways for writers to pitch you? A great query letter.

Do you charge fees? No.

List some representative titles you have placed. *Runner* by Patrick Lee; *Wolverine Freight and Storage* by Steve Ulfelder; *Ice Cold Kill* by Dana Haynes; *Man in the Empty Suit* by Sean Ferrell; *Chum* by Jeff Somers; *Into the Teeth of Death* by Jill Farinelli; *Hero of the Crossing: Anwar Sadat and the 1973 War* by Thomas Lippman.

What do you want to tell new/unpublished writers? I keep a blog on how to revise query letters to make them effective at QueryShark.blogspot.com. I also keep a blog of general questions and answers and the occasional rant on publishing in general at JetReidLiterary .blogspot.com

Agent's name and contact info: Peter Rubie, CEO, peter@fineprintlit.com, 212-279-1282

Describe what you like to represent and what you won't represent. Narrative nonfiction such as memoir, biography, books on business, history, popular science and technology, parenting, music, food, health, and self-help; literate fiction, crime, thriller, science fiction and fantasy, a little commercial women's fiction; middle grade and young adult fiction.

No romance, horror, Western, space opera science fiction.

What are the best ways for writers to pitch you? Send me an email query letting me know the gist of the book, relevant things about yourself (bio), and what you've achieved as a writer.

When and where were you born? 1950, England, UK.

Do you charge fees? No.

Describe your education and career history. Peter is a British expatriate and former BBC Radio and Fleet Street journalist. He was a member of the New York University publishing faculty for 10 years, teaching the only university-level course in the country on how to become a literary agent. For several years he was the director of the book publishing section of the NYU Summer Publishing Institute. He is CEO of FinePrint Literary Management, where as a literary agent he represents a broad range of high-quality fiction and nonfiction.

Prior to becoming an agent, for nearly six years Peter was an in-house editor for Walker & Co. whose authors won prizes and critical acclaim. He has also worked independently as a book doctor for Random House, Penguin Putnam, Simon & Schuster, and other mainstream publishing companies. "Back in the day," he was the editor in chief of a Manhattan local newspaper and was once a regular reviewer for the international trade magazine *Publishers Weekly*. He is also a published author of both fiction and nonfiction.

A member of the Association of Authors' Representatives (AAR), he regularly lectures and writes on publishing and the craft of writing. He is also a founding partner of Lincoln Square Books, a publishing consultancy company for independent authors and publishers.

Say something about your hobbies and personal interests. Peter is a published author in his own right, with 2 novels and close to 10 nonfiction books under his belt. What many people do not know about Peter is that he is also an active semiprofessional jazz musician. In any given week, he can be heard playing guitar around jazz venues in New York City — and occasionally in London. He is a keen home cook, plays squash, and dabbles occasionally with woodwork and the Japanese game Go.

Why and how did you become an agent? I was an editor who was among a host of industry people who were cut loose during the late 1980s. I became an agent because I thought my skills as an editor and author's advocate were best suited to agenting.

Would you do it over again, or something else? Well, I'd love to have been a bestselling novelist and/or a more successful jazz musician, but other than that I'm pretty happy with how things are turning out.

List some representative titles you have placed. *Man from Berlin* by Luke McCallin (Berkley); *Sudden Impact* by William P. Wood (Turner); *Benedict Hall* by Cate Campbell (Kensington); *Mozart's Blood* by Louise Marley (Kensington); the *Pulse* trilogy by Patrick Carman (Harper / Katherine Tegan Books); *The Books of Umber* by Paul Catanese (Simon & Schuster); *The Pawnbroker* by David and Aimee Thurlo (St. Martin's Press); *Fiendish Schemes* by K.W. Jeter (Tor); *The Town That Food Saved* by Ben Hewitt (Rodale); *Philip of Spain, King of England* by Harry Kelsey (I.B. Taurus); *Napoleon III, Last Emperor of France* by Alan Schom (Picador); *#Occupy the Bible* by Susan Thistlethwaite (Astor & Blue Editions); *Becoming Something: The Story of Canada Lee* by Mona Z. Smith (Faber & Faber); *The Good Luck Cat* by Lissa Warren (Lyons Press).

Describe yourself as a person. I'm a very good editor, a pretty good agent, fairly easy to get along with, looking for publishing partnerships with writers. I don't give up on things once I commit to them, but I'm also patient, and it can sometimes take a while to get to where I want to be.

How would you describe the proverbial "client from hell," and what are the warning signs? Constantly nagging me to focus on them without thought for the fact that I represent others. Doesn't want to listen to the advice I have to give, has no real understanding or interest in learning how the publishing industry works, and does not understand how and what the industry is morphing into.

What do you think about self-publishing? I think it is a viable option for writers. BUT — there are caveats. Most successful indie published writers are better at marketing and promotion than writing, and once you're self-published you get into a numbers game in terms of going from the minors (indie publishing) to the majors (mainstream publishing).

Do you like Amazon? I think Amazon is clearly a significant presence in the publishing industry, and one we all have to deal with. I continue to reach out and try to build relationships there and feel in large measure I have been successful in that regard. However, I believe that their approach to publishing is arrogant and aloof to many industry professionals (not negotiating contracts readily, not returning communications promptly, if at all), often dictatorial and bullying toward experienced publishers; that they pay lip service to authors' independence while doing little to actually help. And *they* have yet to explain how they can be both a vendor of others' books and a publisher of their own without being involved in a conflict of interest. Bottom line: Amazon is an online retailer who is entirely interested in their own profit line while pretending to care for the writers and others in the publishing industry they are trying to take over and dominate.

What will agenting be like in 2020? I think a variation on what it is now and what it has always been. The evolution of the independent publishing field will clearly change the industry, but not nearly as powerfully as some claim. Ebooks, and digital publishing in general, do a couple of things really well: the first is to replace the failing mass-market paperback format, becoming a way that authors can learn their chops and develop their platforms in terms of writing and sales numbers, just as writers like Elmore Leonard and Richard Matheson did in the heyday of mass-market paperbacks; the second is to break the model of books being a certain length due to the paper/print model that no longer dominates, even though as of this writing (2014), 80 percent of the book market is still print dominated, and it's likely to be still over 50 percent by 2020 for a variety of reasons that have to do with unexpected findings about digital-screen reading and paper reading.

Describe your job and what you like and don't like about it. The paperwork and the juggling of opposing important issues can be stressful, but the ability to work with and help talented writers is a great reward.

Do you miss the way the business "used to be"? It was slower paced and you had more time to focus on a quality product than now, but the "good old days" were only good for some, not all.

What does the "Big 5" mean to you? The remaining major mainstream publishers.

What do you want to tell new/unpublished writers? This is a great time to be a writer, *but* it is harder to break into the mainstream, and the job of writer now encompasses not just writing but self-promotion at the same time. Those into just writing will have a harder time surviving in this environment, though it's certainly possible. Remember, publishing is a business, and the priorities of remaining a viable business are paramount to publishers, not just how well written something is. That's just step one.

Do you like that everything has become largely digitized? I don't think everything has become digitized, though a lot has. It really depends on what you want a digital copy for. There is a certainly a convenience factor, but there is also the whole concept of linear vs. nonlinear reading, which is much too big a concept to go into here but is becoming more and more relevant as we explore the psychology of reading and learning in both digital and paper realms.

Describe a book you would write. A crime novel, likely a historically based one, I think. I have an idea for a new book I've been playing with for ages, as soon as I get some spare time to sit down and start on it…

FOLIO LITERARY MANAGEMENT ❖ www.foliolit.com

Participating agents: Claudia Cross, Erin Harris, Molly Jaffa, Jeff Kleinman, Erin Niumata, Jeff Silberman, Emily van Beek

Agent's name and contact info: Claudia Cross, claudia@foliolitmanagement.com, 212-400-1494

Describe what you like to represent and what you won't represent. What I like to represent: romance, commercial women's fiction, CBA [Christian Booksellers Association] fiction, food/cooking, nonfiction religious, spiritual, and inspirational titles.

What I won't represent: traditional fantasy or science fiction.

What are the best ways for writers to pitch you? I'm looking to get the clear picture of what your book is, based on your query. Authors should be sure that their query letter is detailed yet concise and not more than a page long. Please submit queries to claudia@ foliolitmanagement.com. Please include the query letter and first 10 pages of your manuscript or proposal in the body of the email.

Do you charge fees? No.

Describe your education and career history. When viewed in hindsight, my decision to become a literary agent makes perfect sense: I love discovering books and writers with distinct voices and points of view, and as I wasn't planning on becoming a minister or priest after graduating from Harvard Divinity School, an assistant position in the literary department at the William Morris Agency was a fortuitous choice. One of the first books I ever sold was written by a fellow Divinity School alum. From that auspicious beginning,

I branched out to also represent romance novels, commercial women's fiction, and cooking and food writing, in addition to serious nonfiction on religious and spiritual topics. I appreciate a smart and quirky sense of humor and have represented novels told from the point of view of a dog.

Say something about your hobbies and personal interests. Like my tastes in reading, my interests are wide-ranging. I enjoy spending time with my family, trying out new recipes, and traveling near and far.

Why and how did you become an agent? See above.

Would you do it over again, or something else? Absolutely! Publishing has inherent challenges like any industry, but I thrive on the pace and nature of the job.

List some representative titles you have placed. *Baking with the Brass Sisters: Two Old Friends in the Kitchen* by Marilyn Brass and Sheila Brass (St. Martin's Press, 2015); *Just in Time for a Highlander* by Gwyn Cready (Sourcebooks, 2015); *Make It Happen* by Lara Casey, publisher and editor in chief of *Southern Weddings* magazine (Thomas Nelson, 2015); *Special Heart: A Journey of Faith, Hope, Courage, and Love* by Bret Baier, anchor for Fox News's flagship evening news program (Center Street/Hachette, 2014).

Describe yourself as a person. I am calm, even-keeled, and always inquisitive. I feel unreasonably grateful when books teach me about new things or share beautiful stories that remind me of what matters most in life.

How would you describe the proverbial "client from hell," and what are the warning signs? I don't believe there's a proverbial client from hell, and I try to respond individually to each author I represent. As an agent, my aim is to address my clients' needs promptly and efficiently. That said, phoning to check in on a routine email sent in the same hour might be what I consider a warning sign.

What do you think about self-publishing? I think with the right approach and promotional plan, it can present interesting opportunities for many authors. That said, publishing is an evolving industry, and self-publishing may not be for everyone. It's important to be flexible and aware of all available options.

Do you like Amazon? As a consumer, there are aspects of the Amazon experience that are excellent, such as customer service. From a professional perspective, as with any distributor or publisher, there are a variety of possible outcomes when going into business with Amazon, and for me, it's all about information and assessing the needs of the authors I represent to determine the best choices for each.

What will agenting be like in 2020? Though it's impossible to predict, it's great to embrace the positive aspects of change as we adapt to our ever-evolving world of publishing.

Describe your job and what you like and don't like about it. On a perfect day, my job is all about holding a new book in my hands and reflecting on the journey that brought this dream to fruition — each book represents so many hours of hard work along with the moments of inspiration and joy. On a more difficult day, I spend a lot of time making phone calls, sending emails, and generally trying to advocate for authors when it can feel like an uphill battle.

Do you miss the way the business "used to be"? Since the way business "used to be" feels like an imprecise way of describing events before my time in publishing, I don't find myself pining for the "old days."

What does the "Big 5" mean to you? I believe in the wide world of publishing, and I'm all about making the right connection between author and publisher, whether that happens to include one of the "Big 5" or not.

What do you want to tell new/unpublished writers? Always revise! Please make sure your query is very concise, as short as possible, and to the point. There is so much guidance available online that can be helpful at every step of the publishing process — use these great, informative resources available to you!

Do you like that everything has become largely digitized? I don't agree with this statement, as the publishing market and consumer patterns are constantly evolving.

What do you like reading, watching, and listening to? I belong to a book club and I read many manuscripts for work. I read picture books and chapter books with my children at home and have been known to fall in love with a new voice in a cooking blog that makes me want to rush home and try a recipe. I can be intrigued by the copy on the back of a cereal box or feel unmoved by a novel that has gotten many glowing reviews.

Describe a book you would write. Though books are my passion, I have never felt the call to write a book. I do my best in composing persuasive, effective, and occasionally humorous emails.

Agent's name and contact info: Erin Harris, eharris@foliolitmanagement.com

Describe what you like to represent and what you won't represent. In a nutshell, I represent literary fiction, book club/women's fiction, historical fiction, young adult, and narrative nonfiction.

I don't represent genre novels in the categories of science fiction, fantasy, or romance. I don't represent cookbooks, picture books, or new adult.

A bit more about what I'm looking for:

- Novels set against the backdrop of another time, place, or culture. I'm someone who believes fiction has much to teach us about history, psychology, and anthropology. (I'm a huge fan of Zadie Smith, Orhan Pamuk, Nicole Krauss, Chris Cleave, Sue Monk Kidd, Donald Ray Pollock, and Salman Rushdie.)
- Novels that incorporate some kind of surreal or magical element. (I can't get enough of novels in the vein of Karen Russell's *Swamplandia!*, Téa Obreht's *The Tiger's Wife*, and Karen Thomson Walker's *The Age of Miracles*.)
- Novels with mystery and suspense in their DNA or ones with a noir aesthetic. (Think Gillian Flynn, Tana French, Donna Tartt, Alice Seabold, Cornelia Read, and A.S.A Harrison.)
- Moving contemporary novels about love, family, or friendship, with a strong sense of place. Some recent favorites: Maggie Shipstead's *Seating Arrangements*, Carol Rifka Brunt's *Tell the Wolves I'm Home*, Courtney J. Sullivan's *The Engagements*.

Regarding young adult, I'm interested in:

- Contemporary, voice-driven novels that approach the universal experience of being a teenager from a surprising or an unlikely perspective (some favorite authors: John Green, David Levithan, Laurie Halse Anderson, Jay Asher, and Peter Cameron).
- Though I enjoy some paranormal romances (Laini Taylor's *Daughter of Smoke and Bone*, Josephine Angelini's *Starcrossed*, and Lauren *Oliver's Delirium*), I'm currently shying away from representing anything involving angels, chimera, Greek gods, and dystopias. I am, however, open to young adult books with highly original supernatural concepts or undertones.
- I love a good young adult thriller or mystery, e.g., anything by Kat Rosenfield, Adele Griffin, and Nova Ren Suma.

Regarding nonfiction:

- I'm drawn to adventure narratives, particularly those in which physical and spiritual journeys become intertwined (Jon Krakauer's *Into Thin Air*, Cheryl Strayed's *Wild*).
- I also enjoy memoirs that illuminate another culture or explore cross-cultural conflict (Alexandra Fuller's *Don't Let's Go to the Dogs Tonight*, Ayaan Hirsi Ali's *Infidel*).
- I'm fascinated by "big idea" books that reveal underlying yet unexpected truths about our society (Barbara Ehrenreich's *Nickel and Dimed*, Susan Cain's *Quiet*).

Regardless of genre, I gravitate toward books that have both compelling concepts and impeccable, stop-you-in-your-tracks writing. Give me a topic or an idea that I can't wait to tell editors about — and that I can explain clearly and succinctly. Give me prose that leaps off the page. I'm a real sucker for sentences that demand to be read aloud.

Also, I should mention that I love bad-ass female protagonists across the board.

What are the best ways for writers to pitch you? The best way to pitch me is to fill out my query form on Folio's website: www.foliolit.com/erin-harris. I'd be delighted to hear from you. I also list the conferences I will be attending on this webpage.

When and where were you born? I was born in Southampton, New York (yes, the Hamptons), in the '80s.

Do you charge fees? No. At Folio we observe the standards set by the AAR.

Describe your education and career history. My life in publishing began in 2007, when I interned for the literary agent William Clark of WM Clark Associates. In 2008, I joined the Irene Skolnick Literary Agency, where I first experienced the thrill of advocating for books I believed in and writers I admired. I worked there for four and a half years, representing my own projects and selling subsidiary rights on behalf of the agency.

Early on, it became apparent to me that there was a need for agents who could think like writers. I'd majored in English at Trinity College (Hartford, CT), studying literature from a critical/academic perspective, but I was eager to hone my creative and editorial skills. This desire led me to pursue an MFA in creative writing at The New School. There I studied fiction and nonfiction with Susan Cheever, Sigrid Nunez, Ann Hood, and James Lasdun. I now see myself as a kind of interpreter, an agent conversant in both the language of the writer and the language of the industry, whose job it is to help you navigate publishing's shifting landscape.

Outside the office, I'm an active participant in New York's literary community. I'm a member of PEN American Center and Women's Media Group, as well as a founder and host of H.I.P. Lit, a reading series.

Say something about your hobbies and personal interests. I love art of all kinds — and have a background in the performing arts. On the weekends, when I'm not reading or editing manuscripts or planning the reading series I cocurate, I like to pretend that I'm on vacation in New York and go to museums, plays, concerts, improv, and dance performances with friends and family. I grew up at the beach, so I love to swim.

Why and how did you become an agent? Growing up, I knew I wanted to be an advocate of some kind, and I knew I wanted to be involved with books. I thought about being a professor, an actor, a writer, and a therapist. (A family member recently reminded me that "anthropologist" was on the short list for a while.) In my present position, I feel like I get to dabble in all of these areas. The funny thing is, when I first started interning at a literary agency, I barely knew what a literary agent did! But I found out soon enough, and then I was hooked.

Would you do it over again, or something else? Of course I would do it over again. Absolutely.

List some representative titles you have placed. Daniel Levine's *Hyde*, a reimagining of Robert Louis Stevenson's *The Strange Case of Dr. Jekyll and Mr. Hyde* told from the villain's perspective, transporting the reader into the dark backstreets of Hyde's 19th-century London; Jennifer Laam's *The Fifth Daughter of the Tsar*, in which the lives of three charismatic women from different time periods converge, revealing an alternate history for the Romanov family — one in which a secret fifth daughter, smuggled out of Russia before the revolution, continues the royal lineage to dramatic and unexpected consequences; *Time* magazine contributor and former *Newsweek* correspondent Carla Power's *If the Oceans Were Ink*, built around the year she spent studying the Koran with the renowned Islamic scholar Mohammad Akram Nadwi, providing an exploration of a text that is shaping our world yet remains mysterious to most Westerners and chronicling a friendship between a conservative sheikh and a secular woman; *Huffington Post* contributor and stay-at-home dad Brian Gresko's *When I First Held You*, an anthology of approximately twenty essays written by acclaimed male writers (including eight *New York Times* bestselling authors), offering meditations on fatherhood and modern parenting, as male and female roles continue to shift and blur; Stefanie Lyons's *Dating Down*, a young adult novel in verse chronicling a girl's toxic relationship with "X," an unnamed bad boy, whose negative influence threatens to destroy her friendships and the small-town political ambitions of her father.

Describe yourself as a person. I'm hardworking and dedicated, but I also like to have a good laugh and kick up my heels from time to time. I enjoy working collaboratively with others, even as I have strong opinions and creative vision. I'm equal parts introvert and extrovert. I believe in fighting the good fight and in being kind but firm. I'm an excellent guest at a dinner party, because though I don't enjoy cooking, I love to do the dishes.

How would you describe the proverbial "client from hell," and what are the warning signs? I only work with people with whom I think a productive professional partnership is possible. (Wow, I didn't mean for that to be so alliterative…) So, fortunately, I've never had a "client from hell." But my advice to aspiring authors is to treat the client/agent relationship as you would any other business relationship. Be respectful, be professional, be on time, be pleasant.

What do you think about self-publishing? I think self-publishing can be a wonderful option for some writers, and at Folio we have a self-publishing division, Folio Unbound, designed to help authors self-publish their books, if they so choose.

Do you like Amazon? I've got nothing against Amazon. Amazon has become a vital retailer in our market. I also love brick-and-mortar bookstores. I buy books (even though I can get most books gratis) online, on my Kindle, at indie bookstores, and at Barnes & Noble. I buy books everywhere. The act of buying books is the important thing.

Do you believe in a "higher power"? Yes, provided there's time for me to have coffee in the morning.

What will agenting be like in 2020? 2020 sounds like light-years in the future to me, but it's really just around the corner, isn't it? I think agenting will look much as it does today; however, I think the role of the agent will be slightly more expansive. I think there will be even more synergy between the book business and Hollywood; I think a greater emphasis will be placed on publicity and marketing; I also think agents will continue to do more editorial work with their clients, especially with debut authors of fiction.

Describe your job and what you like and don't like about it. What I like: There are few greater joys than helping to make writers' dreams come true; working every day with narratives and the written word; discovering fresh voices; pitching and selling (which feels a bit like being onstage and helps keep me connected to my theatrical roots); travel; attending literary events. It's my job to stay connected — to attend readings, to network, to know who is who and who is interested in what. If I weren't an agent, I'd want to attend readings and other publishing-related events, anyway. The book industry is filled with smart, talented, and interesting people. It's a pleasure to do business with them and get to know them over the years. Doing book deals is more than mildly addicting.

What I don't like: email — but it's a necessary evil; delivering disappointing news; that there are only 24 hours in one day; that I sometimes feel guilty about reading published books (there's a little voice in my head that tells me I should be reading manuscripts for work instead — I have to remind myself that it's important to read both!).

Do you miss the way the business "used to be"? Well, I've heard there used to be such a thing as a three-martini lunch. Now we have to wait until five o'clock.

What does the "Big 5" mean to you? In no specific order (other than alphabetical) the "Big 5" simply means: Hachette, Harper Collins, Macmillan, Random House / Penguin, Simon & Schuster. There are many wonderful imprints within these houses, and there are also terrific independent publishers and small presses out there. It's all about finding the right fit for your book(s).

What do you want to tell new/unpublished writers? Can I quote Faulkner? I'm going to quote Faulkner: "Read, read, read. Read everything — trash, classics, good and bad, and see how they do it. Just like a carpenter who works as an apprentice and studies the master. Read! You'll absorb it. Then write. If it's good, you'll find out. If it's not, throw it out of the window."

Do you like that everything has become largely digitized? As with everything, there are two sides to this coin. Social media, ebooks, email, the internet — all of it has given us more options than ever before. We're, arguably, more connected now, and communication can take place at breakneck speed. Of course, with more options there's more to sift through, more to be done. Sometimes it's nice to just turn everything off. The good news is, you can turn it back on again when you're ready.

But I do miss letters. I'm a big fan of the handwritten, heartfelt letter. Whenever a client or colleague sends me a thank-you note, I save it in my thank-you-note drawer. I have a whole drawer dedicated to this. It keeps me going. It's just not the same over Insta-Twitter-book.

What do you like reading, watching, and listening to? For the past 10 years, I've been reading a lot of contemporary literature and staying abreast of what's being published in the categories of books I represent. (I've already mentioned some of the writers I admire.) Some friends and I were recently talking about *Lolita*, and that led to a conversation about how we really ought to read and reread the great Russian novelists. (Once again, I'm wishing there were more than 24 hours in a day.) What do I watch? Well, I just discovered TV, like, two years ago (guess I had my nose stuck in a book before then…) and it's absolutely *wonderful*. Some of the best storytelling is happening on the small screen, and aspiring writers can learn a lot about plot, structure, and even character development from watching long-form narrative television. Presently I'm engrossed in *True Detective* on HBO. The writing is brilliant; the acting is phenomenal; it's spooky and gothic (in the Southern sense), philosophically interesting, and visually arresting. I'm all over the map when it comes to music. A true omnivore. Depending on my mood, I could be listening to anything from Renée Fleming to Elliott Smith.

Describe a book you would write. I love Akashic's *Noir* anthology series (e.g., *Brooklyn Noir*, *Lone Star Noir*, *Haiti Noir*). I think I'd want to write an upmarket commercial novel in a "Hamptons Noir" vein, centered around the mysterious murder of a young local girl who washes up on Main Beach in the first scene. As I mentioned, I grew up in the Hamptons, and I think it's a fascinating, schizophrenic sort of place that has many more personalities than its reputation suggests. It would be a novel told from several points of view that deals with issues of race, social class, love, infidelity, and the beauty and cruelty of the natural world.

Joker's wild: An industry friend has given me the nickname "Khaleesi." I'll take it!

Agent's name and contact info: Molly Jaffa, molly@foliolit.com

Describe what you like to represent and what you won't represent. I represent middle grade and young adult fiction.

What are the best ways for writers to pitch you? Please send a query letter and the first 10 pages of your manuscript pasted in the body of the email.

Do you charge fees? No.

Describe your education and career history. I have a BA from Sarah Lawrence College and have worked at Folio since 2010.

List some representative titles you have placed. *Side Effects May Vary* by Julie Murphy (Harper Collins / Balzer+Bray); *True Son* by Lana Krumwiede (Candlewick Press); *Tabula Rasa* by Kristen Lippert-Martin (Egmont); and an untitled middle grade novel by Mahtab Narsimhan (Scholastic).

Agent's name and contact info: Jeff Kleinman

Describe what you like to represent and what you won't represent. Very well-written, character-driven novels; some suspense, thriller, historical; otherwise mainstream commercial and literary fiction; prescriptive nonfiction: health, parenting, aging, nature, pets, how-to, etc; narrative nonfiction, especially books with a historical bent, but also art, nature, ecology, politics, military, espionage, cooking, equestrian, pets, memoir, biography.

Categories/subjects writers shouldn't bother pitching to me: no mystery, romance, Westerns, science fiction and fantasy, children's or young adult, poetry, plays, screenplays.

When and where were you born? Cleveland, Ohio.

Describe your education and career history. BA with high distinction, University of Virginia (English / modern studies); MA, University of Chicago (Italian language / literature); JD, Case Western Reserve University. After graduating from the University of Virginia, I studied Renaissance history in Italy for several years, went to law school, and then joined an art and literary law firm. A few years later, I joined the Graybill and English Literary Agency before becoming one of the founders of Folio in 2006.

Say something about your hobbies and personal interests. Art, history, animals, especially horses (train dressage and event horses).

If you were not an agent, what might you be doing instead? Practicing intellectual property law or training horses, or both.

What are the best ways for writers to pitch you? Preferably to use the form on our website. If that's not an option, then email only (no attachments, please). For fiction, include a cover letter and the first few pages of the novel. For nonfiction, include a cover letter and perhaps a few pages of a sample chapter, and/or an overview/summary.

Do you charge fees? No charges; AAR member.

What are the most common mistakes writers make when pitching to you? Groveling — just pretend this is a job application and act like a professional; providing too much information — telling too much about the project, rather than being able to succinctly summarize it; sending a poorly formatted, difficult-to-read manuscript; sending material that I wouldn't handle (mystery, romance, etc.).

How would you describe the proverbial "client from hell," and what are the warning signs? Someone who doesn't listen, doesn't incorporate suggestions, and believes that the world "owes" him (or her) a bestseller.

What's your definition of a great client? Someone who writes beautifully, who has marketing savvy and ability, who is friendly, accessible, easy to work with, fun to talk to, and can follow directions and guidance without taking offense.

What can a writer do to increase the odds of your becoming his or her agent? For fiction, write a fabulous book with a fresh voice and compelling, unique perspective, and be able to sum up that book in a single, smart, intriguing sentence or two. For nonfiction, *enhance your credentials*. Get published or have some kind of platform or fresh perspective that really stands out above the crowd. Show me (so I can show a publisher) that you're a good risk for publication.

Why and how did you become an agent? My law firm shared offices with an agency, and I did several book contracts. Gradually, I started reading manuscripts, talking to writers, and before long, there I was — a literary agent.

How do you feel about editors and publishers? I think that too often they're overworked and underpaid and don't have the time to really "connect the dots" in a manuscript or a proposal — so it's crucial that we (the writer and I) connect the dots for them.

How do you feel about writers? It depends on the writer. I really love working with a talented writer who has a terrific premise, though I love wading in and taking a solid manuscript and thinking that I can help make it even stronger.

What do you see in the near future for book publishing? A new publisher will figure out the world of indie publishing, really incorporating all the tools that the internet provides to be able to exceptionally and impressively market their books. Enhanced ebooks will grow in popularity and become a serious contender.

In your opinion, what do editors think of you? That I am honest and ethical and have a solid list of clients.

List some representative titles you have placed. *The Art of Racing in the Rain* and *A Sudden Light* by Garth Stein (Harper and Simon & Schuster); Pulitzer finalist *The Snow Child* by Eowyn Ivey (Little, Brown); *The 80 Dollar Champion* by Elizabeth Letts (Ballantine); *The Widow of the South* and *A Separate Country* by Robert Hicks (Grand Central); *And So It Goes* and *Mockingbird* by Charles Shields (Holt); *Unsaid* by Neil Abramson (Center Street); *Sacco & Vanzetti* and several other titles by Bruce Watson (Viking); *Freezing Point* and *Boiling Point* by Karen Dionne (Berkley); *The Patron Saint of Lost Dogs* and *Dog Gone, Back Soon* by Nick Trout (Hyperion); *Finn* by Jon Clinch (Random House).

Agent's name: Erin Niumata

Describe what you like to represent and what you won't represent. Fiction: commercial women's fiction, historical fiction, psychological thriller, suspense, humor — I love sassy Southern and/or British heroines; nonfiction: cookbooks, biography, pets, parenting, self-help, pop culture, humor, women's interest.

Absolutely no Westerns, cozy mysteries, poetry, short story collections, business, travel memoir, fantasy, or picture books.

When and where were you born? Scranton, PA.

Describe your education and career history. BA, University of Delaware.

Erin has been in publishing for over 23 years. She was an editorial assistant at Simon & Schuster in the Touchstone/Fireside paperback division for several years; moved over to Harper Collins as an editor; and then went to Avalon Books as the editorial director, working on romance, mysteries, and Westerns. Erin has edited many authors, including Leon Uris, Stuart Woods, Phyllis Richman, Senator Fred Harris, Dean Ornish, Michael Lee West, Debbie Fields, Erica Jong, Brenda Maddox, Lawrence Otis Graham, and Joan Rivers.

Say something about your hobbies and personal interests. Dogs, reading, running, knitting, sewing, kids' crafts.

If you were not an agent, what might you be doing instead? I would be an editor or a teacher.

What are the best ways for writers to pitch you? For fiction, I prefer a brief synopsis with the first 50 pages. For nonfiction, a cover-letter pitch explaining the book and the author's platform along with sample chapters and an outline.

Do you charge fees? No charges; AAR member.

What are the most common mistakes writers make when pitching to you? Not following the submission guidelines and sending me something I don't represent; telling me that random people have read the book and think it's fantastic.

How would you describe the proverbial "client from hell," and what are the warning signs? Someone who fights every piece of advice and calls/emails incessantly wanting updates or just to "chat."

What's your definition of a great client? Someone who is talented, has a great project, has an open-minded attitude, is eager to learn, is ready to promote the book, and is happy to hear suggestions.

Why and how did you become an agent? I was an editor for 16 years and decided to try my hand at agenting. So far, so good.

How do you feel about editors and publishers? Editors are overworked, attend entirely too many meetings, have piles of manuscripts that are all urgent, have very little time for anything — which is why agents are crucial for authors.

How do you feel about writers? Most are fantastic.

List some representative titles you have placed. *The Cake Boss* and *Baking with the Cake Boss* by Buddy Valastro; *Unthink* by Erik Wahl; *River Monsters* by Jeremy Wade; *Discovery's Cash Cab* by Ben Bailey; *TLC's Extreme Couponing* by Joni Meyer Crothers; the *Too Cute* series and *Puppy Bowl* from Animal Planet; *The Teen Guide to World Domination* and *Jump Shipp* by Josh Shipp; *How to Honey Boo Boo* from TLC; *Sacrifice Fly*, *Crooked Numbers*, and *Dead Red* by Tim O'Mara.

Agent's name and contact info: Jeff Silberman, jsilberman@foliolitmanagement.com

Describe what you like to represent and what you won't represent. My interests are vast, and I am always eager to represent authors who have something to say and projects that inform, inspire, entertain, expose, educate, move, or are just plain fun. Deep down, I think every agent, every publisher, and every reader seeks the same thing. With every book there is a promise. The promise of greatness. And that can take so many forms. It might be in a unique or powerful premise, milieu, character, or chapter in history. It somehow always seems to bring a refreshing, distinctive, compelling, or entertaining voice and perspective. And with that, insights, observations, truths and doorways. Engaging characters. Beautiful (or searing) prose. Something that moves us, or opens us, or entertains us. Wisdom. Insights. Imagination. Discovery. Expansion. Inspiration. Transformation. Education. Empowerment, Laughter. Lessons. We all love to be transported in some way. Or to be reintroduced to the world we thought we knew. Or to simply laugh. I am up for any and all of that. So I love literary, historical, and commercial fiction, narrative and prescriptive nonfiction, memoir, sports, humor, politics, history, the arts, pop culture, science, technology, espionage, religion. And being opened up to new worlds.

I'm not looking for horror, sci-fi, or fantasy.

Describe your education and career history. I began my career as an entertainment attorney representing clients in the motion picture and television industries as well as Pulitzer-nominated and bestselling authors. I grew up in a literary home. Books lined the walls of pretty much every room and spanned pretty much every topic under the sun. My father was on the board of editors of *Fortune* and wrote some highly impactful bestsellers on matters such as race and education, and my mother was a freelance writer who published with any number of national magazines. So I guess you could say publishing is in my blood. I represent a wide range of authors, from celebrities and athletes to novelists and neuroscientists, executives and comedians, journalists and professors, chefs and special forces operatives. I have even expanded my list to include clients of the four-legged variety.

What are the best ways for writers to pitch you? Please submit queries to jsilberman @foliolitmanagement.com. Please write *Query* and the title of your book in the subject line of your email and include enough material for you to feel the book is being well represented.

Agent's name and contact info: Emily van Beek, SVP & Literary Agent, Folio Jr., emily@foliolit.com

Describe what you like to represent and what you won't represent. I represent children's book authors and illustrators exclusively, which is to say, picture books, middle grade, and young adult. I love original, character-driven, brandable, and unique books. I am a great admirer of art and love to represent original illustrators with spectacular vision. For middle grade, I'm looking for commercial adventure, mystery, comedy, books with series potential that have a lively pace and unforgettable characters. Young adult manuscripts must have a voice I cannot put aside. I will give just about anything a try but find I'm most drawn to edgy, contemporary realistic, magical realism, and well-written chick lit with a literary edge. I'd love to find more humorous middle grade and young adult novels, too!

What are the best ways for writers to pitch you? Please send me a concise query letter via our website's online query form. I'd love it if you'd include some background, a short paragraph about the manuscript, and why you are specifically interested in having me as your agent. Also please include your first chapter or picture book manuscript in its entirety, and never apologize for being a debut author or for not having publishing credits.

When and where were you born? Stamford, CT.

Do you charge fees? No.

Describe your education and career history. McGill University and University of Toronto honors major in English with a minor in philosophy. Soon after arriving in New York City I was hired as an editor at Disney Hyperion. I joined Pippin Properties as an agent and rights director in 2003 and then moved to Folio Jr. in 2010, where I am currently an agent and senior vice president.

Would you do it over again, or something else? Building a career in the field of children's publishing was my "Plan A" and I never, ever spent a moment thinking about a "Plan B." I'm living my dream and I hope never to retire.

List some representative titles you have placed. *Samson in the Snow* by Philip C. Stead, the author of the Caldecott Award–winning *A Sick Day for Amos McGee*; *Ideas Are All Around*, also by *New York Times* bestselling author Philip C. Stead; *New York Times* bestselling and beloved young adult novelist Jenny Han's *To All the Boys I've Loved Before*; Michelle Cuevas's exquisite middle grade novel *Confessions of an Imaginary Friend*; Margo Rabb's young adult *Kissing in America*; Katie Finn's *Broken Hearts, Fences, and Other Things to Mend*; and Crystal Chan's inspired middle grade debut, *Bird*.

Describe yourself as a person. Driven, professional, adventurous, passionate, tireless, dedicated, and determined.

How would you describe the proverbial "client from hell," and what are the warning signs? Someone who is unwilling to revise and who believes their work to be perfect and publisher-ready at the outset. We all have to approach this process with humility as we are dealing with the intersection of art and commerce, which is an extremely delicate thing. There's nothing I admire so much as a good work ethic, and a sense of entitlement in a person usually makes itself known fairly quickly.

FOREWORD LITERARY, INC. ❖ www.forewordliterary.com

PO Box 258, La Honda, CA 94020

Agent's name and contact info: Laurie McLean, partner, querylaurie@forewordliterary.com, Twitter: @agentsavant, www.agentsavant.com (blog), facebook.com/laurie.mclean

If you rely on mail or fax, we are not the right agency for you.

Describe what you like to represent and what you won't represent. I represent adult genre fiction (romance, science fiction, fantasy, horror, mystery, thriller, suspense) as well as middle grade and young adult kid lit.

What are the best ways for writers to pitch you? I only accept queries from professional referrals and from writers I've met at conferences and online events. Luckily, I go to a lot of conferences and know a lot of industry professionals.

When and where were you born? I was born in upstate New York in the wonderful month of April, but I've lived in the San Francisco Bay Area for the past 30 years.

Do you charge fees? Nope.

Describe your education and career history. I have a master's degree in journalism from the prestigious Newhouse School of Journalism at Syracuse University. I ran a multimillion-dollar eponymous public relations agency for more than 20 years before becoming a literary agent. I was an agent at Larsen Pomada Literary Agents, the oldest agency in Northern California, for eight years before forming Foreword with Gordon and Pam. I also founded the San Francisco Writers University (SFWritersU.com) and was on the management team for the nonprofit San Francisco Writers Conference (SFWriters.org).

Say something about your hobbies and personal interests. I'm married to a musician I fell in love with while we were in a bluegrass band together, so I am deeply involved in roots music. It's great to have live acoustic music in the house every day. I also like cooking, gardening, reading, writing, and being out in nature.

Why and how did you become an agent? I became an agent because I love using both sides of my brain: the shark-like analytical side and the wonderful creative side.

Would you do it over again, or something else? Representing authors is the perfect job for me.

List some representative titles you have placed. *Hollow World* by Michael J. Sullivan; the *Talon* series by Julie Kagawa; the *Ministry of Peculiar Occurrences* series by Pip Ballantine and Tee Morris; *Edenbrooke* and *Blackmoore* by Julianne Donaldson; the *Immortal Circus* series by A. R. Kahler; the *Moonlight* series by Lisa Kessler; *Lock & Mori* by Heather Petty; *The Book of Kindly Deaths* by Eldritch Black; *Badlands* and *Wild* by Jill Sorenson; *Summoning* and *Binding* by Carol Wolf.

Describe yourself as a person. I am an intellectually curious workaholic who loves the adventures I find in books.

How would you describe the proverbial "client from hell," and what are the warning signs? Since I rep horror, I like hell. ^__^ Every client is different, strong and weak in different areas. Haven't met a client I can't work with yet.

What do you think about self-publishing? I love the options available to authors right now. We specialize, as an agency, in hybrid authors, and I believe that a few years from now every author will have self-, indie-, and traditional-publishing pieces in their bibliography.

Do you like Amazon? I love and fear Amazon. I have sold books to their imprints. I buy books from them as much as I buy books from Barnes & Noble and indie bookstores. Without Amazon, the revolution going on in publishing would not have happened…or it would not have happened the way it is happening now. And that is the most exciting development in publishing at present. It's what made us form Foreword Lit — *be the change!*

Do you believe in a "higher power"? Nope.

What will agenting be like in 2020? Some agents will have quit because by holding on to the way agenting used to be done, they will not make enough money to make a living. Other, more forward-thinking agents will have morphed into career managers for authors, using their unique blend of business and creative talents to help their clients be successful writers for life.

Describe your job and what you like and don't like about it. I love the daily variety and challenges of agenting in today's chaotic digital age. I love the technology that allows me to be a super-agent while working from home as part of a nationwide virtual agency. The only thing I don't like about it is when I look up as it's getting dark and realize I've been working at my computer for 10 straight hours and my neck is killing me!

Do you miss the way the business "used to be"? Not. One. Bit! I came from high tech, and publishing the way it used to be always felt antiquated and slow.

What does the "Big 5" mean to you? It's the Big 1 Plus 4, really. Penguin Random House is larger than Macmillan, Hachette, Harper Collins, and Simon & Schuster's book divisions put together.

What do you want to tell new/unpublished writers? With skill, luck, and perseverance, you will succeed. It's a marathon, not a sprint, so dig in, learn a lot, and have fun along the way. Remember why you decided to write in the first place and never let that idea go.

Do you like that everything has become largely digitized? I couldn't do what I do, and have the success I've achieved, if publishing hadn't become digital. It's pretty amazing what an agent-author team can accomplish together.

What do you like reading, watching, and listening to? Everything I represent, I love to watch and listen to.

Describe a book you would write. An urban fantasy that takes place in near-future San Francisco and features a string-theory experiment gone bad that lets demons into our world — and they stay! In fact, I'm halfway through writing it.

Joker's wild: Does anyone read a book on literary agents when there are websites with all this information? ☺

Agent's name and contact info: Pam van Hylckama Vlieg, partner, querypam@forewordliterary.com, Twitter: @BookaliciousPam

Describe what you like to represent and what you won't represent. I represent middle grade across all genres, young adult across all genres, romance in select genres, select adult genre fiction categories, and select nonfiction pop culture.

What are the best ways for writers to pitch you? You can pitch me via email or at conferences. You can find my submission guidelines on www.forewordliterary.com.

When and where were you born? 1980 in a small town in Virginia on the Tennessee border.

Do you charge fees? No. But I do take cookies.

Describe your education and career history. I never finished my degree because I left school to manage boy bands in Finland. I've lived all over the world doing interesting (and boring) jobs.

Say something about your hobbies and personal interests. I love pop culture and video games like *Assassin's Creed*. Their *Ezio Trilogy* is my absolute favorite video game. I enjoy some television, always on the science fiction and fantasy side. I love travel and will go just about anywhere if given the chance.

Why and how did you become an agent? I became an agent to advocate for books. Plus, it's really cool and heady to know you're a part of a process that influences how people read. I interned at local agencies and became an agent when Laurie offered me a position.

Would you do it over again, or something else? I wouldn't do anything else.

List some representative titles you have placed. *A Better Kind of Truth* by Dan Gemeinhart; *Free Agent* by J. C. Nelson; *The Mark of the Tala* by Jeffe Kennedy; *Three Hearts* by J. C. Nelson; *Riding the Wave* by Lorelie Brown.

Describe yourself as a person. I think I'm fun and snarky. I don't cook. I have a quick wit. I'm really good at tech and HTML. I joke a lot and sometimes am mildly inappropriate. I love books.

How would you describe the proverbial "client from hell," and what are the warning signs? Someone who doesn't trust me to do my job and micromanages every aspect of what I'm doing.

What do you think about self-publishing? I think self-publishing is amazing. I think people who do it well are awesome. I think those who just blurt out a book and throw it up on Amazon with no edits, no cover, and no marketing plan are doing it wrong.

Do you like Amazon? I'm mostly in the fear camp of Amazon. Right now they give good royalties and advances and whatnot, but if they manage to edge everyone else out of business, I don't think the numbers will stay so favorable.

Do you believe in a "higher power"? No. I believe in the power of hard work and getting stuff done.

What will agenting be like in 2020? I don't know, but I hope we have flying cars.

Describe your job and what you like and don't like about it. I love contracts and deals and new clients. I even love going on submission with a book. I don't love the amount of time I put into my job, but that's my own fault.

Do you miss the way the business "used to be"? I wasn't around when it "used to be" different. I love all the change. It's better for authors.

What do you want to tell new/unpublished writers? Work hard and learn your craft.

Do you like that everything has become largely digitized? I still love to sell and hold print, but I'm happy there are so many options.

What do you like reading, watching, and listening to? I read a book a week outside of work. Sometimes two. I mostly listen to sound tracks and scores. I don't watch a lot of movies, but *Supernatural* is one of my favorite TV shows.

Describe a book you would write. A picture book about my bulldog and his antics.

Joker's wild: I don't gamble. :P

Agent's name and contact info: Gordon Warnock, partner, querygordon@forewordliterary.com, Twitter: @gordonwarnock, facebook.com/gordon.warnock

Describe what you like to represent and what you won't represent. About three-quarters of my list is adult nonfiction (in most areas of the general trade market; see www.forewordliterary.com for more info), and the rest is split between graphic novels and select contemporary literary fiction for adults, new adult, and young adult.

What are the best ways for writers to pitch you? Use my submission guidelines. I love it when folks follow directions. The most current info can be found at www.forewordliterary.com.

When and where were you born? I was born in Chicago in 1982, but I've been in California for most of my life.

Do you charge fees? Nope, and all unsolicited cookies will first be referred to Pam.

Describe your education and career history. I am an honors graduate of CSUS with a degree in creative and professional writing. I've been working for agencies since I was an undergrad, and I've had numerous other ventures in the industry, including editing and running marketing for independent publishers, freelance publishing consulting, speaking and teaching for MFA programs and *Writer's Digest*, and, my current favorite, heading the Fast Foreword digital publishing program.

Say something about your hobbies and personal interests. I'm usually happy if you feed me and give me a puppy.

Why and how did you become an agent? I started interning at an agency for my own personal use as a writer, and I fell in love with it. I found success fairly early, and they fast-tracked me to becoming a senior agent. I love the mix of science and creativity involved, especially at Foreword. And I love helping promising authors find the success they deserve.

Would you do it over again, or something else? Anyone who answers "no" to this question shouldn't be in the industry. It's as simple as that.

List some representative titles you have placed. *Turning Japanese* by MariNaomi; *Jacob Wrestling* by Kelly Davio; *A New Way to Be Human* by Robert V. Taylor; *The Measure of a Nation* by Howard Steven Friedman; *The French Quarter Drinking Companion* by Allison Alsup, Elizabeth Pearce, and Richard Read; *You've Got to Be Kidding!* by Nan DeMars; *Scandinavian Classic Desserts* by Pat Sinclair; *A Real Emotional Girl* by Tanya Chernov.

Describe yourself as a person. I'm taller in person.

How would you describe the proverbial "client from hell," and what are the warning signs? Someone who repeatedly promises and doesn't deliver. As with any other job, that's a quick way to get let go.

What do you think about self-publishing? It can do wonderful things for you if you treat it as a tool, a valid option for certain markets, and an integrated part of a larger whole. Those still stuck in the mind-set of self-publishing vs. traditional publishing are doing it wrong.

Do you like Amazon? I like that they're shaking up the industry and actively innovating. That's long overdue, it's what I try to do as an agent, and I hope it continues. I'm not a fan of their more predatory practices that are smart for business but a grave mistake for culture.

Do you believe in a "higher power"? Gordon[2]

What will agenting be like in 2020? The agents who survive will be the ones who celebrate change, not lament it. They'll be the ones who take an involved, long-term focus with their authors instead of just flipping contracts for a paycheck.

Describe your job and what you like and don't like about it. I love that no two workdays, just like no two clients, are exactly alike. Each one presents its own unique opportunity for success. I love how we've embraced technology to be able to get work done wherever and whenever, which, of course, is a double-edged sword. I tend to be that a-hole who is always looking at his phone.

Do you miss the way the business "used to be"? Miss it? I can't get away from it quickly enough.

What does the "Big 5" mean to you? Just one of many facets of the grand ecosystem of publishing.

What do you want to tell new/unpublished writers? Read everything in your genre, and read it well. Know what's been done before, know what the audience expects, and notice how others have delivered it.

Do you like that everything has become largely digitized? Everything hasn't, though. A lot of things have gone digital, but there's still a lot that could benefit from embracing the format.

What do you like reading, watching, and listening to? In addition to the genres I represent, I have a weak spot for groundbreaking small-press fiction. I watch a lot of Food Network and listen to punk rock.

Describe a book you would write. I'm working on the next ebook in our Foreword Literary Guide series, in which our agents demystify different facets of the industry.

Joker's wild: This is where I ask if you're finally going to make this available as an ebook. It's a wonderful resource, but there's a lot of untapped potential. Emoticon.

Agent's name and contact info: Emily Keyes, agent, queryemily@forewordliterary.com, Twitter: @esc_key

Describe what you like to represent and what you won't represent. Most of what I represent is young adult and middle grade, across all genres. I have a very select list of adult genre fiction, including fantasy, women's fiction, new adult, historical, science fiction, and pop culture.

What are the best ways for writers to pitch you? Query me at queryemily@foreword literary.com with your query and the first 10 pages pasted into the body of your email. I take pitches at conferences, which are listed on our company's website.

When and where were you born? I was born and raised in New Haven, CT.

Do you charge fees? No.

Describe your education and career history. I graduated from the University of Connecticut with a degree in English, then got a master's degree in publishing at New York

University. I worked in the Simon & Schuster contracts department for five years before becoming an agent.

Say something about your hobbies and personal interests. I'm a big nerd who enjoys comic books, film, and TV. I like to swim and be near water.

Why and how did you become an agent? I've wanted to be an agent since I found out it was a job. I like that you get to be involved with all parts of the publishing industry this way, and not just one department. It makes my degree feel less worthless.

Would you do it over again, or something else? I'd do it again.

List some representative titles you have placed. *Falling into Place* by Amy Zhang; *Hello, I Love You* by Katie M. Stout; *Girl and the Clockwork Cat* by Nikki McCormack; *My Life as a Lumberjack* by Sara V. Olds.

Describe yourself as a person. My mother used to say I was "always thinking." I like that description. Physically, I am very short, so people have always thought I am younger than I am, which used to be much more annoying.

How would you describe the proverbial "client from hell," and what are the warning signs? Someone who can't write worth a damn.

What do you think about self-publishing? Authors who self-publish need to approach it like they are starting a small business (publishing company), and not on a whim. But when it's done well, it's an excellent thing. I love how much sales data you have at your fingertips then!

Do you like Amazon? I worry about how they treat their workers, squeeze small publishers, and are creating a monopoly. But the Kindle has been a good thing, and people being able to get access to so many books has been a good thing. There needs to be a balance.

Do you believe in a "higher power"? Maybe.

What will agenting be like in 2020? There will be new trends and new devices, but people will always want stories. I think good agents will find a way to get their clients' books read. It will be more about standing out from the crowd. The amount of content in the world is not going to decrease.

Describe your job and what you like and don't like about it. I still like finding really good projects that make me remember the power of a good story. I don't like that I can't seem to stop. I was without internet for two hours and thought I was going to die.

Do you miss the way the business "used to be"? Not really.

What does the "Big 5" mean to you? It still makes me think of basketball; I haven't adjusted to there not being six.

What do you want to tell new/unpublished writers? Hi.

Do you like that everything has become largely digitized? I don't think all these screens are good for my vision. But I don't miss lugging around paper submissions.

What do you like reading, watching, and listening to? Besides books, I read comics. I watch movies. I listen to podcasts.

Describe a book you would write. I wanted to write a cookbook for Hobbits.

Joker's wild: Mark Hamill was my favorite Joker.

Agent's name and contact info: Connor Goldsmith, associate agent, queryconnor@forewordliterary.com, Twitter: @dreamoforgonon

Describe what you like to represent and what you won't represent. I represent adult commercial fiction, primarily sci-fi/fantasy, thriller, horror, and suspense. I'm particularly looking for books by and about marginalized people, like LGBT and/or racial minorities. I am interested in certain nonfiction subjects but only open to proposals for nonfiction by recognized experts. You can see specifics on the Foreword website.

What are the best ways for writers to pitch you? I take pitches at conferences sometimes, but the easiest and most reliable way to query me is by email. You can see my submission guidelines at www.forewordliterary.com.

When and where were you born? I am a lifelong New Yorker: born in the city, raised just outside it, scuttled back in the moment I could.

Do you charge fees? No.

Describe your education and career history. I graduated from Oberlin College with a degree in English and the classics and then went on to get a master's degree in media studies at The New School. Before I changed course and entered publishing in 2012, I was working toward a career in television agenting.

Say something about your hobbies and personal interests. I love great conversation and often can't stop trying to create it. I'm a bit of a social butterfly — I feel as at home in a nightclub downtown as I do working on a great book. I try to strike a balance. (Sometimes I succeed!)

Why and how did you become an agent? I'm a creative person, but the idea of life as an artist, where oneself is the brand, never quite appealed to me. I knew I wanted to work *with* artists and help facilitate art, and I've found agenting to be the most satisfying way to do that. I love being involved in the entire process, like I'm the book's doting godfather or fun uncle.

Would you do it over again, or something else? This is it.

Describe yourself as a person. I'm a Dorothy Zbornak in a clever Blanche Devereaux disguise.

What do you think about self-publishing? I love the way self-publishing has broadened access. It's much easier for a wide variety of people to get their points of view out there now, and that can only be a good thing. That said, I do worry that every big success story in that arena compels a lot of people to go for it when they're unprepared to actually manage an entire publishing business by themselves.

How would you describe the proverbial "client from hell," and what are the warning signs? I'm a very editorial agent, as I think most agents are — and have to be — in the current marketplace. If you're not open to major structural edits and unwilling to make changes to get your vision out there, we might have a problem.

Do you like Amazon? I think the Kindle is marvelous. I worry about the consolidation of power going on at Amazon from a potential monopoly perspective. We'll have to see.

Do you believe in a "higher power"? If they'll help me sell books, I'll make offerings at the altar of whichever deity is open for business.

What will agenting be like in 2020? More and more, an agent's job is going to be acting as an adviser, marketer, and manager rather than as a salesperson. I think it'll become more like agenting for actors and other artists, actually, in that the job will become less about the individual deals and more about consolidating and promoting a long-lasting and specific brand. If you look around, that shift is already happening.

Describe your job and what you like and don't like about it. It still blows my mind that I get to read, edit, and pitch great books for a living. The only downside is when I have to deliver bad news.

Do you miss the way the business "used to be"? I'm pretty new! Someday this moment right now will be what we all call "how it used to be," and we can revisit this question.

What does the "Big 5" mean to you? I still think there was a great missed opportunity to have a major publishing powerhouse called "Random Penguin." Imagine the logo.

What do you want to tell new/unpublished writers? If this is what you really want to do, don't give up.

Do you like that everything has become largely digitized? I prefer reading print books to ebooks, but when it comes to contracts and submissions, it is a godsend to have everything digitized.

What do you like reading, watching, and listening to? I love to read in the genres I represent, of course. I'm also a big comic book guy, and there are a number of blogs I read pretty religiously. I watch more television than is probably good for me, especially given how much of it is reality TV. Scripted television is better than it's ever been, though, and

I think there's a lot to be learned about narrative and characterization from TV at the moment.

Describe a book you would write. There is a big postapocalyptic epic in my head that has been brewing there for many years, but that I never can seem to get down onto paper. That's why I do this, instead of that!

Joker's wild: I'm with Gordon! It'd be great to see this guide available in a digital format.

Agent's name and contact info: Jen Karsbaek, associate agent, queryjen@forewordliterary.com, Twitter: @DevourerOfBooks

Agent's name and contact info: Michelle Richter, associate agent, querymichelle@forewordliterary.com, Twitter: @MichRichter1

Describe what you like to represent and what you won't represent. I represent women's commercial fiction, book club fiction, mystery, thriller, and select historical fiction. I also represent nonfiction: pop culture and science, medicine, economics, and sociology from recognized experts in their fields. See www.forewordliterary.com for more information.

What are the best ways for writers to pitch you? Pitch me at conferences or query me at querymichelle@forewordliterary.com. Please follow my submission guidelines as posted on www.forewordliterary.com.

When and where were you born? I was born in Massachusetts in 1970.

Do you charge fees? No.

Describe your education and career history. I graduated from the University of Massachusetts at Boston with a degree in economics and a minor in Russian. I spent a number of years working in banking and finance in Boston and Baltimore before moving to New York City to attend Pace University's publishing program, where I obtained a master's degree. I then joined St. Martin's Press and worked there eight years.

Say something about your hobbies and personal interests. I love pop culture and will happily dissect a TV show or talk about my favorite character actor or Real Housewife of Wherever. I will never turn down karaoke. I love to travel in the US and abroad. Favorite spots visited include Boise, Asheville (NC), Edinborough, Barcelona, and St. Petersburg (Russia).

Why and how did you become an agent? I enjoyed being an editor but wanted to try being on the other side of the negotiating table, so to speak. I love the idea of being an author's advocate and doing a bit of matchmaking to find them the perfect home. I liked and respected the Foreword team after meeting them at conferences and interacting via social media, so I reached out and was thrilled to be welcomed aboard.

Would you do it over again, or something else? I absolutely would do it again.

How would you describe the proverbial "client from hell," and what are the warning signs? Someone who's less committed to their project than I am.

Describe yourself as a person. I'm very forthright and will always tell it like it is. I also think I'm fun and snarky.

What do you think about self-publishing? Self-publishing is a great opportunity for writers to reach an audience on their own terms, but it's also an obligation for them to wear many hats to get a good copyedit, the right cover, and the right interior design, and come up with great plans for publicity, marketing, and distribution. Or to hire people who'll help them achieve their goals.

Do you like Amazon? As a consumer, I love them for their huge inventory and the innovations they've made. But I'm a bit wary of their sheer size and power in the marketplace, too.

Do you believe in a "higher power"? Maybe.

Describe your job and what you like and don't like about it. I love working with authors and helping them reach their potential and attending conferences to meet new authors and agents and editors. It's tough when I love a project and others don't see how great it is.

Do you miss the way the business "used to be"? I've seen so much evolution in the industry and think so many things just keep getting better. Maybe it's my econ degree talking, but I always think "innovate or die."

What does the "Big 5" mean to you? Connor is so right (see his response above).

What do you want to tell new/unpublished writers? Be passionate and work hard. Know which writers you'll be compared to, and think about what you can learn from those who succeed — and fail.

Do you like that everything has become largely digitized? I think gaining the ability to read manuscripts electronically without being tied to a desktop computer is the best thing to happen to the industry. And loading up a reader (instead of a suitcase) with books is amazing and brilliant. But I think the technology can be utilized even more than it is already.

What do you like reading, watching, and listening to? I love reading mysteries, book club reads, memoir, some literary fiction, and lifestyle titles. Also, tons of magazines, from *Vogue* to *Entertainment Weekly* and *New York*. I love watching TV and movies, especially with smart writing that challenges me, but with some guilty-pleasure reality TV sprinkled in. And all kinds of music, from danceable pop to country and classic rock. Cee-Lo, Katy Perry, Bruce Springsteen, and Keith Urban all are on my iPod.

Describe a book you would write. A funny travel memoir about the highs and lows of trips with my husband. I already have a title, and it's awesome.

Joker's wild: Did you know Jack Nicholson made $50 million playing the Joker, thanks to a back-end percentage in his contract?

Agent's name and contact info: Sara Sciuto, associate agent, querysara@forewordliterary.com, Twitter: @sarasciuto

Describe what you like to represent and what you won't represent. I represent middle grade and young adult fiction — contemporary, historical, gothic/thriller/horror, sci-fi, mystery/suspense, fantasy, and other speculative fiction. I also represent picture books and welcome author illustrators. I have a select list of adult nonfiction (lifestyle, pop culture, how-to).

I am not considering any adult fiction (all genres), and no memoir, please.

What are the best ways for writers to pitch you? I accept only electronic queries (see our website for my complete submission guidelines). I also love to connect with writers in person at conferences.

When and where were you born? I was born and raised in Southern California.

Do you charge fees? No.

Describe your education and career history. I'm a graduate of the University of California, San Diego, and also completed literature coursework at NYU. My first industry experience was working on film and foreign rights with Taryn Fagerness Agency. From there I joined Full Circle Literary, where I specialized in children's literature, and was there for over three years before joining Foreword Literary.

Say something about your hobbies and personal interests. I love new experiences and am always cultivating new obsessions. My latest are photography and sailing — and reading, always. My great passions are books, travel, and good food. My perfect moment is reading a good book while nibbling something delicious at a quaint café in a foreign land.

Why and how did you become an agent? I became an agent because I love to read, especially children's books — what other job would let me do that professionally? I also get a lot of joy from working with debut authors and helping them develop their work and getting it out into the world.

Would you do it over again, or something else? I'm pretty sure this is the best job out there.

List some representative titles you have placed. Aliens Get the Sniffles, Too by Katy Duffield; *Loud Lula* by Katy Duffield; *I Don't Want to Be a Frog* by Dev Petty; *Two Chefs, One Catch* by Bernard Guillas and Ron Oliver.

Describe yourself as a person. I'm a voracious consumer of life.

How would you describe the proverbial "client from hell," and what are the warning signs? An author I wouldn't want to work with is someone who isn't willing to get his or her hands dirty. I'm a very hands-on editorial agent, and I only take on clients who are ready and willing to put in that work with me.

What do you think about self-publishing? It's a nice option, but it's only right for certain people. If you have a very specific vision for your project and don't wish to revise alongside a publishing professional — and you're incredibly savvy with self-promotion — then self-publishing could be right for you.

Do you like Amazon? With regards to publishing, they've definitely shaken things up. But their publishing program is fairly new, so I think it's a wait-and-see moment.

Do you believe in a "higher power"? Yes.

What will agenting be like in 2020? Agents are going to be wearing even more hats and acquire new and stronger skills to help clients navigate an increasingly dynamic and complex marketplace.

Describe your job and what you like and don't like about it. I love the variety in each day and working with authors to help develop their work. The toughest part is when that amazing project doesn't find a publishing home for one reason or another.

Do you miss the way the business "used to be"? I can say I'm very glad I wasn't around for the times of hardcopy submissions and a physical slush pile. Eek!

What does the "Big 5" mean to you? I still think "Big 6" in my head; it's going to take some time…

What do you want to tell new/unpublished writers? You're likely not going to sell the first book you write. It might be book number 2, 5, or 10 that's going to be the one. Keep writing, reading, and honing your craft, and keep faith in yourself.

Do you like that everything has become largely digitized? While I appreciate the convenience of digital books, in the end I love the feel of a print book in my hands. For work, though, I almost always read submissions on my iPad — it makes the sheer volume much more manageable.

What do you like reading, watching, and listening to? As my submission guidelines suggest, I have really broad tastes and read almost all genres in adult, young adult, and middle grade. I watch too much HGTV and Food Network and am also an HBO and Showtime series junkie. When I drive, I listen to alternative, classical, or NPR.

Describe a book you would write. I'll take representing writers over being one.

Joker's wild: I'm better at board games.

FRANCES COLLIN LITERARY AGENCY ❖ www.francescollin.com

Agent's name and contact info: Sarah Yake, queries@francescollin.com

Describe what you like to represent and what you won't represent. My first love is literary fiction, and I definitely gravitate toward quirky material and rich, playful language. I love the arts in general, so work that is set in the worlds of dance or the visual arts, or has characters involved with those worlds, catches my fancy immediately. I also like work with settings that are as interesting as characters, like England or the American West.

What are the best ways for writers to pitch you? Via an email sent to queries@frances collin.com.

When and where were you born? Pennsylvania. I'm old enough to have plenty of experience in the publishing world but young enough to be enthusiastic about all the changes taking place in that world.

Do you charge fees? Nope, never.

Describe your education and career history. MA, English literature, West Chester University.

I started out as a bookseller with a now-defunct midsize bookstore chain and worked my way up to manager. From there I worked for Random House in sales for a number of years. I have been with the agency for almost 10 years.

Say something about your hobbies and personal interests. The perfect work-free day for me includes a stop at an art museum and a stroll through a garden. I find photography relaxing and would take a couple hundred pictures throughout the day — not for Instagram or for a higher purpose but because I find it's the only thing that pushes words to the periphery for a while.

Why and how did you become an agent? I became an agent partly through sheer luck — the story involves a want ad and a neighbor who locked herself out of her house. That said, it was also a case of "luck is what happens when preparation meets opportunity." In many ways, this is the career that all my other jobs were leading to. I just didn't realize it until it was staring me in the face!

Would you do it over again, or something else? I would absolutely do it all over again (after telling my younger self to chill and that everything would work out just fine in the end).

List some representative titles you have placed. Sleight by Kirsten Kaschock; foreign rights for Stoner by John Williams.

Describe yourself as a person. Curious.

What do you think about self-publishing? It's a fine path for those who want to choose it.

Do you miss the way the business "used to be"? Nope. I think there are more amazing authors right now than we could ever read in five lifetimes, aided by new technology and changes in the business, and that's exciting (albeit a bit overwhelming).

What do you want to tell new/unpublished writers? Never give up in the face of rejection.

What do you like reading, watching, and listening to? Favorite authors include Virginia Woolf, Gretel Ehrlich, Connie Willis, Emily Carr (the Canadian painter), and a whole slew of poets too numerous to mention.

GLOBAL LION INTELLECTUAL PROPERTY MANAGEMENT, INC. ❖

www.globallionmanagement.com

PO Box 669238, Pompano Beach, FL 33066

Agent's name and contact info: Alfred Peter Miller III, president and CEO, peter@globallionmgt.com

Describe what you like to represent and what you won't represent. I am an eclectic literary manager who represents all kinds of professional authors.

I do not represent poetry, pornography, or short story collections.

What are the best ways for writers to pitch you? Our submission guidelines are on our website, www.globallionmanagement.com. We prefer an emailed query that includes a synopsis, sample of the manuscript, and detailed description of the social media used by the author in promoting their work.

When and where were you born? August 15, 1948, in Atlantic City, NJ.

Do you charge fees? No. We charge a 15 percent US and Canadian commission and a 25 percent foreign commission, and we frequently package movie and television deals.

Describe your education and career history. I have a BA in fine arts, majoring in speech and theater at Monmouth University. I have been working as an independent literary agent for over 40 years.

Say something about your hobbies and personal interests. I am an avid collector of lions and have been collecting regal and majestic images of lions as celebrated by man for the duration of my career. I have an estimated 2,000 lions in total. I am very health conscious and enjoy cooking delicious, well-balanced meals. I am also an avid world traveler.

Why and how did you become an agent? I became an agent in 1973 as I was producing an off-Broadway musical. I met a man producing a Broadway musical, and we decided to form a literary agency, which became one of the largest independent literary agencies in the world.

Would you do it over again, or something else? I love the life that I have created, but managing hundreds of people for decades and playing caretaker to authors is perhaps not the career I would choose in my next life.

List some representative titles you have recently placed. *A Travel Guide to Life* by Anthony DeStefano; Rhodi Hawk's third novel; *Me School* and *Finding Your Element* by Sir Ken Robinson; *Who's Who in the Bible* by Jean Pierre Isbouts; *The Five Essentials* by Bob Deutch; and numerous others.

Describe yourself as a person. I would describe myself as a hardworking, gregarious lover of books and movies who always tries to make my clients more money.

How would you describe the proverbial "client from hell," and what are the warning signs? The "client from hell" usually submits handwritten, typo-riddled queries, has an arrogant attitude, and dislikes following their agents' advice. I've dealt with my share of these kinds of lunatics already — it's not something I deal with anymore.

What do you think about self-publishing? I think that self-publishing is rapidly becoming overpopulated. Unfortunately, at least 90 percent of all self-published authors have no social media or branded marketing designs for their career. Consequently, there will be hundreds of thousands of books published that will only sell a few hundred copies — not an author's goal, most certainly.

Do you like Amazon? I only like Amazon when they sell a lot of copies of my books (and keep them in stock), but they have become a force of nature in publishing and, as a result of their success, have rendered book clubs all but extinct.

Do you believe in a higher power? Absolutely.

What will agenting be like in 2020? The digital revolution in the modern world is definitely affecting all the aspects of publishing that I have been schooled in over the past 40 years. Everything is being streamlined for digital delivery, and I fully expect physical publishing to decline in favor of digital distribution.

Describe your job and what you like and don't like about it. My greatest passion in life has been successfully representing authors. I have sold approximately 1,300 books, 150 film and television deals, and 21 films in my career, so it could almost be classified as an obsession. What I don't like about the business today is that it is becoming harder to sell a new author than it has ever been in my career.

Do you miss the way the business "used to be"? Yes. I love physical books. I embrace technology and change, but I will always miss that aspect of the business.

What does the "Big 5" mean to you? To me, the Big 5 means Penguin Random House, Simon & Schuster, Hachette, Harper Collins, and Harlequin, although the numerous mergers and other agreements ensure that this list changes fairly frequently.

What do you want to tell new/unpublished writers? Keep your eye on the future! You need to be aware of how things are and how things will be if you are going to survive and thrive in the publishing world.

Do you like that everything has become largely digitized? I don't mind it, but I do miss some of the physical aspects of literature.

What do you like reading, watching, and listening to? I love escaping into any good book, generally narrative nonfiction or fiction. There's also nothing better than a really good audiobook, and I love movies of all kinds. We've had some beautiful films as of late — Hollywood is still making some great movies.

Describe a book you would write. I am presently rewriting my book on the motion-picture, television, and literary industries based on my extensive experience in representing my clients and the difficulties and triumphs therein.

Joker's wild: I have designed my life to embrace the constant opportunities that we have as a result of the ever-changing technology. Utilizing technology as a tool is a key to any literary representative's success in the modern world.

HANNIGAN SALKY GETZLER AGENCY ❖ www.hsgagency.com

37 West 28th Street, New York, NY 10001, 646-442-5770

Agent's name and contact info: Josh Getzler, jgetzler@hsgagency.com

Describe what you like to represent and what you won't represent. Procedural mysteries (particularly, though by no means exclusively, period and foreign), thriller, literary and commercial fiction, religion (not spiritual guidance — books about religious history or philosophy), sports, music.

Not interested in romance, picture books, religious fiction.

What are the best ways for writers to pitch you? Query letter by email.

When and where were you born? May 4, 1968, New York City.

Do you charge fees? No.

Describe your education and career history. BA, University of Pennsylvania; Radcliffe Publishing Course; MBA, Columbia Business School.

I started in editorial at Harcourt in 1991 and left to go to business school, expecting to get back into publishing. Instead I ended up owning and operating a minor league baseball team for 12 years, the Staten Island Yankees, before selling in 2006 and returning to the world of books as an agent. I worked at Writer's House and Russell & Volkening before starting my own agency.

Why and how did you become an agent? When I was selling the baseball team, I was having a conversation with my wife, who told me it was clear I had to work in books again. Having 13 years of experience making deals and looking at contracts, I realized I could be suited to agenting. I decided to target existing agencies rather than start a new one, and got lucky with timing as a position with Writer's House opened up.

List some representative titles you have placed. *Devil's Trill* by Gerald Elias (St. Martin's Press); *The Crown* by Nancy Bilyeau (Touchstone); *The Chronicles of Egg* by Geoff Rodkey (Putnam).

HARTLINE LITERARY AGENCY ❖ www.hartlineliterary.com

123 Queenston Drive, Pittsburgh, PA 15235, 412-829-2483

Agent's name and contact info: (Mr.) Terry Burns, terry@hartlineliterary.com

Describe what you like to represent and what you won't represent. A variety of genres in the Christian and mainstream market.

I don't handle children's books younger than middle readers, curriculum or devotionals, adult science fiction or fantasy. And I don't represent profanity or books with graphic sexual situations.

What are the best ways for writers to pitch you? Send me a proposal at my Hartline email address containing the materials requested in the submission guidelines at www .hartlineliterary.com.

When and where were you born? 1942 in Pampa, Texas.

Do you charge fees? No. Our contract does have a provision for charging for copy and postage on submissions, but I don't even charge that.

Describe your education and career history. BBA from West Texas State (now West Texas A&M), graduate work at Southern Methodist University. I spent 35 years as a chamber of commerce manager, and I discovered that representing businesses in that capacity is very similar to functioning as a literary agent.

Say something about your hobbies and personal interests. Family and camping.

Why and how did you become an agent? Joyce Hart was my agent, and I gradually migrated to working as an agent for her.

Would you do it over again, or something else? If I had it to do over again, I might do it sooner.

List some representative titles you have placed. *Lost in Dreams* by Roger Bruner (Barbour); *Cooking the Books* by Bonnie Calhoun (Abingdon); *The Secret of Lodestone* by Tim Champlin (Berkley); *Bash and the Pirate Pig* series by Burton Cole (B&H Kids); *Hero Tribute* by Graham Garrison (Kregel); two series by Linda Glaz (Heartsong Presents); *A Cry from the Dust* by Carrie Stuart Parks (Thomas Nelson); *The Keystone Kid* (large print) by Frank Roderus (Five Star); *Resurrect* by Dave Stevens (Lion-Hudson); *Rhapsody in Red* by Donn Taylor (Moody); *Highland* series and *MacGregor Legacy* series by Jennifer Hudson Taylor (Abingdon); *Murder at the Painted Lady* by Barbara Warren (Avalon).

Describe yourself as a person. Generally quiet and committed — strong communicator.

How would you describe the proverbial "client from hell," and what are the warning signs? One who refuses advice, constantly changes things so I am never dealing with a known product, and emails constantly.

What do you think about self-publishing? I have no problem with self-publishing if it is a business decision and not a knee-jerk reaction to rejections. The person must know what is required to do it, the skill set they must have to be successful, what they will be giving up, and what they will gain by going that route.

Do you like Amazon? It's hard to not like the number one bookseller in the world.

Do you believe in a "higher power"? I am a Christian and a very strong believer. Although I do not ask my clients about religious beliefs, most if not all of my clients are Christians as well.

What will agenting be like in 2020? I wish I felt like I knew that for sure. I do know we have to make more and more moves to adapt to emerging technology. I do know that whatever the technology, authors will still be needed to provide the content, and I feel that the more convoluted things become, the more those authors need help in navigating the maze.

Describe your job and what you like and don't like about it. I know I handle too many debut authors, but I like helping writers get started. I best describe my role as that of a matchmaker introducing people with product to acquiring editors needing product. If I do it right, everybody wins. I don't like having to give authors bad news about their submissions.

Do you miss the way the business "used to be"? It was much easier.

What does the "Big 5" mean to you? The primary publishers.

What do you want to tell new/unpublished writers? Be patient. Chances are your book will fit at only one place in the industry at any given time, and making that connection can be difficult. Later it will only fit at one place, but now the place is different. I spend most of my time trying to match books with windows of opportunity that will be open only a short time.

Do you like that everything has become largely digitized? I like that most submissions both incoming and outgoing can be handled electronically now. It makes them easier to handle, submit, track, and file. Very few holdouts these days insist on hardcopy submissions, and I find myself not submitting to them often.

What do you like reading, watching, and listening to? I like old movies, particularly Westerns, as an escape. I love gospel quartets to listen to. I spend so much time reading submissions and clients' work that I don't get to read nearly as much as I would like for pleasure.

Describe a book you would write. How about if I plug my *A Writer's Survival Guide to Publication* and the companion book, *Writing in Obedience*, written specifically to assist Christian writers, particularly new Christian writers? The second book was cowritten by editor Linda W. Yezak, who was also the editor of the first book.

Agent's name and contact info: Jim Hart, 412-829-2483, jim@hartlineliterary.com

Describe what you like to represent and what you won't represent. I'm looking for fictional suspense/thriller, romance, women's fiction, young adult, select sci-fi/fantasy. While the book doesn't have to have an overt Christian message, I do look for stories that have strong Christian characters.

I'm also interested in nonfiction regarding church growth, practical Christian living, the arts (especially as they relate to the church), and biography. *Keep in mind that nonfiction topics require a certain level of credentials, experience, and expertise.*

I am not looking at Amish, children/middle reader, picture books, poetry, devotionals, and I don't represent books with graphic sex and profanity.

What are the best ways for writers to pitch you? Queries and proposals can be sent to jim@hartlineliterary.com. Please refer to www.hartlineliterary.com/guidelines.html before sending.

When and where were you born? 1959, Sierra Madre, CA.

Do you charge fees? No.

Describe your education and career history. AS degree in production journalism; ministerial credentials with the Assemblies of God through Global University. 20 years as prepress manager for large direct-mail advertiser. 12 years as supervisor for the hunger program in a large urban ministry. 20 years worship leader. 10 years youth minister.

Say something about your hobbies and personal interests. I love traveling with my wife. Hobbies (obsessions) would be music, songwriting, and home studio recording.

Why and how did you become an agent? The time was right! I've always been on the lookout for "meaningful" work, and this fits.

Would you do it over again, or something else? Should have done this sooner!

List some representative titles you have placed. *What Women Want* by Dr. Gina Loudon, Ann-Marie Murrell, and Morgan Brittany (WND). (As of this writing, I've only been agenting for a number of months.)

Describe yourself as a person. My top five Strengths Finder characteristics are Connectedness, Responsibility, Belief, Empathy, Developer. And I love to laugh and make others laugh!

How would you describe the proverbial "client from hell," and what are the warning signs? Someone who won't take direction or advice, is too impatient, and is not willing to take on the needed responsibility for preparing a great proposal and marketing.

What do you think about self-publishing? It's not for everyone. The author must be able to expend resources for marketing, publicity, and distribution. I've read very few self-published books.

Do you like Amazon? Amazon has made the world smaller but yet has greatly expanded the reach of an author. But for discovering and purchasing books, I still like a trip to the bookstore.

Do you believe in a "higher power"? Yes, I'm a Christian so my belief is in the Christian/Judeo God.

What will agenting be like in 2020? It's hard to imagine where technology will be by then, but it seems like content will continue to be readily available across numerous platforms. Authors will continually be required to be a substantial part of the marketing strategy for their own books, as well as being cognitive of evolving media. As an agent I will be able to access a great amount of content and will be looking for authors who have a firm grasp of marketing/publicity/platform. By 2020 I expect the number of proposals we receive to be even greater than it is now, so I will have to be even more selective in signing client authors.

Describe your job and what you like and don't like about it. I connect great words and writers with an appropriate publisher. I like the relationships that are formed and maintained with all the participants in the industry. I really love discovering a writer who catches me by surprise. However, I'm not fond of looking at a computer screen for hours at a time.

Do you miss the way the business "used to be"? I don't miss doing business by snail mail.

What does the "Big 5" mean to you? The major publishers.

What do you want to tell new/unpublished writers? (1) Do whatever you can to improve your writing skills. Write as much content as you can for a variety of platforms and delivery systems — both print and online. (2) Start building your author platform now and don't stop. (3) Befriend and be a friend to other authors — be an active part of the writing community. (4) Be patient.

Do you like that everything has become largely digitized? Yes, although it can be a challenge because it has increased the volume of work to consider. But not dealing with piles of paper is liberating.

What do you like reading, watching, and listening to? Sci-fi, Westerns, biographies. Almost any style of music, especially Americana and jazz (I've just discovered that 1959 was great year for jazz).

Describe a book you would write. It would be borderline tongue-in-cheek but would give readers something to think about.

Joker's wild: I was never a fan of that game show...

Agent's name and contact info: Joyce A. Hart, owner and principal agent, joyce@hartlineliterary.com

Describe what you like to represent and what you won't represent. All genres of fiction: romance, suspense, mystery, girlfriend, women's, historical, etc. Nonfiction, all genres.
   I do not look at young adult or children's. No profanity or graphic sex.

What are the best ways for writers to pitch you? Send proposals to my Hartline email. Please look at our guidelines on our website and send according to those guidelines.

When and where were you born? I was born in Iowa City, Iowa.

Do you charge fees? No.

Describe your education and career history. Graduate of Open Bible College. Worked at Whitaker House Publishing for 11 years. Did a variety of jobs and became vice president of marketing. Started Hartline Marketing in 1990 and Hartline Literary Agency in 1992.

Say something about your hobbies and personal interests. Reading has always been my favorite hobby. Travel and spending time with friends and family.

Why and how did you become an agent? People kept sending me their manuscripts to read, so I decided to turn it into a business. I love working with authors to help them get published.

Would you do it over again, or something else? I love what I do and would do it all over again.

List some representative titles you have placed. *A Light in the Wilderness* by Jane Kirkpatrick; *The Color of Justice* by Ace Collins; *Man's Best Hero* by Ace Collins; *Smuggler's Cove* by Christy Barritt; *Pursued* by Christy Barritt; *Deceived* by Christy Barritt; *The Butterfly and the Violin* by Kristy Cambron; *Missing Persons Task Force*, three-book series by Lisa Harris; *The Painted Prairie* by Lorraine Beatty; *The Top Ten Most Outrageous Couples in the Bible* by David Clarke.

Describe yourself as a person. Hardworking, loyal to my clients, a people person.

How would you describe the proverbial "client from hell," and what are the warning signs? One who doesn't want to prepare a proposal in the beginning, is not flexible, and is not willing to take suggestions or make changes that editors require. One who does not want to do their own marketing.

What do you think about self-publishing? Self-publishing is here to stay. It is different than it used to be. The successful self-publisher has to be a marketer, and it helps if they speak. They have to be able to sell the books themselves.

Do you like Amazon? Amazon sells books. What else can I say?

Do you believe in a "higher power"? I am a committed Christian, so the answer is yes.

What will agenting be like in 2020? Agents will have to find creative ways to sell books and be of service to their clients. Who knows where technology will go by then. We will have to find ways to stay in business.

Describe your job and what you like and don't like about it. My job is to match authors with editors and help them find a place to publish their books. Also to guide their careers. Also to be an encourager to my clients. To know the business well and to give them the best service possible.

Do you miss the way the business "used to be"? I do. It was much easier a few years back; e-publishing has made our jobs challenging.

What does the "Big 5" mean to you? The primary publishers.

What do you want to tell new/unpublished writers? I tell them that the business is tougher than it used to be but that we are still selling manuscripts regularly. I also tell them not to become discouraged — that it takes patience and hard work, but it is possible to get published.

Do you like that everything has become largely digitized? I like sending and receiving proposals via email and I like being able to put manuscripts on my iPad. I read some books on ereaders but really prefer reading a print book.

What do you like reading, watching, and listening to? I read fiction (romance and suspense) and some nonfiction. On TV I watch mostly old shows, reruns like *Matlock*. I read and watch religious books and programs. Music — I like Southern gospel and classical.

Describe a book you would write. I would write women's fiction.

HARVEY KLINGER, INC. ❖ www.harveyklinger.com

300 West 55th Street, Suite 11V, New York, NY 10019, 212-581-7068

Agent's name and contact info: David Dunton, david@harveyklinger.com

Describe what you like to represent and what you won't represent. I represent young adult fiction (contemporary and sci-fi/fantasy), middle grade fiction (sci-fi/fantasy and contemporary), mostly nongenre adult fiction, cookbooks, memoir, pop culture; and I specialize in music-related nonfiction.

What are the best ways for writers to pitch you? The best way to reach me is to send a query letter along with the opening five pages of your manuscript in the body of an email to david@harveyklinger.com.

When and where were you born? Cincinnati, Ohio.

Do you charge fees? No.

Describe your education and career history. I graduated from Wesleyan University in 1988, worked in editorial jobs at Prentice Hall Press & Fireside/Touchstone for seven years, left to tour with a band, and then started at Harvey Klinger, Inc. in 1996. I've been here ever since.

Say something about your hobbies and personal interests. Hanging out with my wife and kids, playing and listening to music, reading, watching television, hiking, and going to the beach.

Why and how did you become an agent? I loved working on people's ideas and writing but didn't love the many, and seemingly endless, meetings publishers have on a weekly basis. There was never any time for reading or editing during work hours, and that's an absurd fact. After getting out of publishing briefly, I found out that Harvey needed an assistant, and that gave me the opportunity to learn about this side of the equation. When I saw how much attention could be, and was, given to editorial matters, I was sold.

Would you do it over again, or something else? I can't think of any other job I'd rather be doing.

List some representative titles you have placed. *The Last Dragon Charmer* trilogy by Laurie McKay (Harper Collins); *Dead Boy* by Laurel Gale (Crown); *The Battle of Darcy Lane* by Tara Altebrando (Running Press); *I'll Take You There* by Greg Kot (Scribner); untitled George Jones biography by Rich Kienzle (Harper Collins); *Even When You Lie to Me* by Jessica Alcott (Crown); *One Way Out* (*New York Times* bestseller) by Alan Paul (St. Martin's); *Light and Shade* by Brad Tolinski (Crown); untitled Michael Jackson biography by Steve Knopper (Scribner).

Describe yourself as a person. I love what I do and consider myself lucky that I get to do it.

How would you describe the proverbial "client from hell," and what are the warning signs? I'm too wary of being sued to answer this honestly! Suffice it to say, the act of finding an agent, and then a publisher, and then being published, can drive almost anyone to irrational behavior.

What do you think about self-publishing? I can't state it better than Andrea did (see next questionnaire): "I think that it can be a really great thing for a certain type of author and a certain type of book. I try to stay current on all the self-publishing options available so that I can better advise my clients who are thinking of going this route."

Do you like Amazon? I've had limited dealings — for a Kindle single by Michael Lydon, and for a sci-fi novel and then a serial by Jason Sheehan — and both experiences were positive.

Describe your job and what you like and don't like about it. I work with a great crew of people, so it's a joy to go to work each day. Plus, you never know what great project might be lurking in your inbox. I love falling in love with a manuscript — it's all too rare, and it's such a great feeling. I don't, however, like the instances of not being able to find a good home for that beloved manuscript.

Do you miss the way the business "used to be"? We still have a carton of manuscript boxes in our closet, though it's unlikely they'll ever be used for anything — no, I don't miss the way projects used to be disseminated. And I never was a part of the three-martini lunch world, so I don't know whether I miss that.

What does the "Big 5" mean to you? I've had great dealings with all five. I've also had great publishing experiences with much smaller houses. I only hope that the Big 5 doesn't become the Big 3 in my lifetime. Or even worse, the dreaded, mythical UniPub.

What do you want to tell new/unpublished writers? Keep trying. Find other writers who both understand what you're going through and can help you with your projects. Query multiply and simultaneously.

Do you like that everything has become largely digitized? Yes — a story's a story, no matter the form. That said, I prefer printed books and hope that they, like vinyl, are usually an option for me. In which case, digitize away!

Agent's name and contact info: Andrea Somberg, andrea@harveyklinger.com, www.andreasomberg.com

Describe what you like to represent and what you won't represent. I represent a wide range of fiction and nonfiction, including projects aimed at a young adult and middle grade audience. I'm always actively looking to take on new authors who write in the following categories: fiction: literary, commercial, women's, romance, thriller, mystery, paranormal, fantasy, science fiction, young adult, new adult, middle grade. Nonfiction: memoir, narrative, popular science, pop culture, humor, how-to, parenting, self-help, lifestyle, travel, interior design, crafts, cookbooks, business, sports, health and fitness.

What are the best ways for writers to pitch you? The best way to reach me is to send a query letter along with the opening five pages of your manuscript in the body of an email to andrea@harveyklinger.com.

When and where were you born? New York.

Do you charge fees? No.

Describe your education and career history. After graduating from Princeton I joined the Donald Maass agency, and then, a few years later, Vigliano Associates. In the summer of 2005 I joined Harvey Klinger, Inc., where I represent a wide range of fiction and nonfiction, as well as young adult and middle grade. I also teach classes on writing non-fiction and memoir book proposals through Mediabistro.

Say something about your hobbies and personal interests. I love to read. I also like running and drinking really good beers.

Why and how did you become an agent? I thought I wanted to be a social worker until I actually interned for one and realized what a tough job that is. Agenting seemed like a natural fit, in that I love to read and I love people. In college I started interning for the Donald Maass agency, and I never looked back.

Would you do it over again, or something else? Yes, I wouldn't change a thing. I love my job, and I feel really lucky that I found a career that is such a good fit.

List some representative titles you have placed. *The Lost*, *The Missing*, and *The Found*, fantasy series by Sarah Beth Durst (Harlequin); *Oblivion*, young adult thriller by Sasha Dawn (Egmont); *The Hip Pressure Cooker Cookbook* by Laura Pazzaglia (St. Martin's); *The MacGregors: Highland Heirs* (*New York Times* bestseller) by Paula Quinn (Warner Forever / Grand Central / Hachette); *A Field Guide to Lucid Dreaming* by Dylan Tuccillo, Jared Zeizel, and Thomas Peisel (Workman); *Learning to Stay* by Erin Celello (NAL/Penguin); *Quiet, Please*, memoir by McSweeney's writer Scott Douglas (Da Capo); *The Last Good Day of the Year*, young adult novel by Jessica Warman (Walker); *The Metabolism Miracle* (*New York Times* bestseller) by Diane Kress (Da Capo); *Wretched Writing* by best-selling humor authors Kathy and Ross Petras (Perigee/Penguin); *Rules of Protection* by Alison Bliss (Entangled); *Sew Fun* by Deborah Fisher (F&W).

Describe yourself as a person. I'm very passionate about my job and about books in general.

How would you describe the proverbial "client from hell," and what are the warning signs? Fortunately, I haven't had one of these yet, so I'm not qualified to answer! All of my clients have been great.

What do you think about self-publishing? I think that it can be a really great thing for a certain type of author and a certain type of book. I try to stay current on all the self-publishing options available so that I can better advise my clients who are thinking of going this route.

Do you like Amazon? As a consumer, yes, I love them. As someone in the publishing industry, I'm wary.

What will agenting be like in 2020? I'm not sure, but I'm excited to find out! I think that it's a really exciting time to be in this industry, with a lot of interesting innovations and changes.

Describe your job and what you like and don't like about it. I love finding an author whose writing I'm excited about and helping them with their career. What I don't like is how integral rejection is to my job — I hate having to tell authors that I'm not the best fit for their book.

Do you miss the way the business "used to be"? No — it's different but still exciting! And I certainly don't miss hauling around hardcopies of manuscripts.

What does the "Big 5" mean to you? I love working with the Big 5, but I also love working with smaller publishers. All publishers have their unique strengths and weaknesses — the trick is finding the house that is the best fit for the individual project.

What do you want to tell new/unpublished writers? Don't get too discouraged if a few agents pass on your project. There are a lot of great agencies out there — just keep on querying!

Do you like that everything has become largely digitized? I like the convenience of digital. If I want to read something immediately, I can. On the other hand, I do prefer the actual experience of reading hardcopies of books. I think that books, as objects, will never disappear completely.

HORNFISCHER LITERARY MANAGEMENT, LP ❖

www.hornfischerlit.com

Agent's name: Jim Hornfischer

Describe what you like to represent and what you won't represent. Hornfischer Literary Management is actively seeking the best work of talented, ambitious writers. The agency handles most categories of general nonfiction (with a particular interest in narrative nonfiction, US and world history, military history, biography, and memoir), as well as select quality fiction.

What are the best ways for writers to pitch you? Email your query or proposal package (overview, chapter summaries, and two sample chapters) to queries@hornfischerlit.com. Multiple submissions accepted (just tell us). Commission: 15 percent on domestic sales; 25 percent on foreign.

Describe your education and career history. One of the few agents in the country who is both a licensed attorney and a former New York trade book editor, Jim Hornfischer has been a literary agent since 1993, having begun his publishing career in 1987 in New York, where he held editorial positions at Harper Collins and McGraw-Hill. Hornfischer is the author of four well-received nonfiction books of his own. This combination of experience makes him a perceptive editorial adviser as well as an effective advocate for his clients. He has a law degree from the University of Texas at Austin and a bachelor's degree from Colgate.

List some representative titles you have placed. *What Stands in a Storm: A True Story of Life and Death in the South's Tornado Alley* by Kim Cross (Atria); *Operation Paperclip: The Secret Intelligence Program That Brought Nazi Scientists to America* by Annie Jacobsen (Little, Brown); *Money: How the Destruction of the Dollar Threatens the Global Economy — and What We Can Do about It* by Steve Forbes with Elizabeth Ames (McGraw-Hill); *Liberty Is Sweet: The Epic of the American Revolution* by Woody Holton (S&S); *Casablanca: An Epic Story of World War II* by Meredith Hindley (Public Affairs); *Under Fire: The Untold Story of the Attack in Benghazi* by Fred Burton and Samuel M. Katz (St. Martin's); *Avenue of Spies: The Story of an American Family in Nazi-Occupied Paris* by Alex Kershaw (Crown); *The Trident: The Forging and Reforging of a Navy SEAL Leader* by Jason Redman and John R. Bruning (Morrow); *A Curious Madness: An American Combat Psychiatrist, a Japanese War Crimes Suspect, and an Unsolved Mystery from World War II* by Eric Jaffe (Scribner); *Harvey Penick: The Life and Wisdom of the Man Who Wrote the Book on Golf* by Kevin Robbins (Houghton Mifflin Harcourt); *Ashes under Water: The* SS East-land *and the Shipwreck That Shook America* by Michael McCarthy (Lyons Press); *Devil on the Plains: The Epic True Story of Jack Hays, an American Warrior on the Western Frontier* by Paul Knight (NAL); *The Lion's Mouth: A Novel* by James L. Haley (Putnam).

Describe your job and what you like and don't like about it. I run on the rush of making creative, exciting, and important things happen.

What do you want to tell new/unpublished writers? Go big.

Describe a book you would write. Having written four books of my own — of narrative World War II history — I've learned at least as much from my own struggles in the craft of writing as I have from 20 years as an operative in the business of publishing. The synergy is powerful.

INTERNATIONAL PROPERTY GROUP

10585 Santa Monica Boulevard, Suite 140, Los Angeles, CA 90025

Agent's name and contact info: Joel Gotler, joel@ipglm.com

Describe what you like to represent and what you won't represent. Commercial fiction.

What are the best ways for writers to pitch you? Email.

When and where were you born? Brooklyn, NY.

Do you charge fees? No.

Describe your education and career history. BA. Literary agent for 35 years.

Say something about your hobbies and personal interests. Love reading. Harmonica. Yoga.

Why and how did you become an agent? By accident. Human resources at WNEW radio suggested I'd be a good agent, whatever that meant.

Would you do it over again, or something else? Over again.

List some representative titles you have placed. *Life Itself* by Roger Ebert. *The Wolf of Wall Street.*

Describe yourself as a person. Very cool, well rounded, and funny.

How would you describe the proverbial "client from hell," and what are the warning signs? Five phone calls first morning of representation.

What do you think about self-publishing? Nyet.

Do you like Amazon? Yes. They can sell a ton of books and are getting into TV.

Do you believe in a "higher power"? Yup.

What will agenting be like in 2020? Slower.

Describe your job and what you like and don't like about it. I read, I create, I market, I go to the bank. I don't like difficult people.

Do you miss the way the business "used to be"? Nah.

What does the "Big 5" mean to you? Five big publishers. Five major studios. Or Big 5 sporting goods stores.

What do you want to tell new/unpublished writers? Ransom notes would be easier.

Do you like that everything has become largely digitized? I don't mind.

What do you like reading, watching, and listening to? I read anything. I watch sports, news, and documentaries. I listen to blues, country, and classic.

Describe a book you would write. *David Copperfield.*

Joker's wild: Life is good!

IRENE GOODMAN LITERARY AGENCY ❖ www.irenegoodman.com

Agent's name and contact info: Irene Goodman, irene.queries@irenegoodman.com

Describe what you like to represent and what you won't represent. I like upmarket women's fiction, domestic suspense, mysteries, young adult and middle grade, historical fiction, and one or two offbeat novels that are very commercial.

I shy away from fantasy and paranormal, science fiction, new adult, and Fifty Shades of Anything.

What are the best ways for writers to pitch you? If they send a query to my queries email, it will get seen by someone: irene.queries@irenegoodman.com. Most everything else gets deleted.

When and where were you born? In Detroit, Michigan, and it's not nice to ask when.

Do you charge fees? No.

Describe your education and career history. BA and master's from the University of Michigan. I began in publishing as an editorial assistant and established my own agency when I realized I was good at cutting through red tape, getting myself heard, and breaking all the rules. Since then I have built a number of bestselling careers and had one hell of a good time doing it.

Say something about your hobbies and personal interests. I love the Berkshires above all places on Earth. I also like to bake, go to operas, read *Doonesbury*, watch figure skating, and walk barefoot through the grass.

Why and how did you become an agent? I became an agent because I could see that I would be good at it. My second job in publishing was working for an agent. That was such a good fit that I never looked back. I've been doing it for my entire adult life and I wouldn't do anything else.

Would you do it over again, or something else? I don't know what else I would do. Maybe work at the Metropolitan Opera, but there is only one, and if they didn't hire me, I would be out on the street. Or maybe be a political campaign manager, but those people tend to burn out young. I'll be doing this until people colonize Saturn.

List some representative titles you have placed. Go look at my website and you'll see everything we represent.

Describe yourself as a person. I am awesome.

How would you describe the proverbial "client from hell," and what are the warning signs? You think you want the answer to this, but trust me, you don't. Because even if I tell you, you will never think it applies to you.

What do you think about self-publishing? It's not the same as "real" publishing. Except for a handful of internet wizards, there are very few self-published authors who don't want the validation and backing of a print publisher.

Do you like Amazon? Well, they want to take over the world, but it would be a very different world without them.

Do you believe in a "higher power"? I believe that we are here, and that is a miracle. Everything that is here is a miracle. Air is a miracle. Dirt is a miracle. There doesn't have to be anything, but instead there is all this stuff.

What will agenting be like in 2020? Even more digitized than now.

Describe your job and what you like and don't like about it. I like making deals. I don't like not making deals.

Do you miss the way the business "used to be"? I do, because there used to be about 40 places where we could send something, and now there are maybe 15. There used to be a midlist, and now if you don't make it on the first book, you get thrown out the window.

What does the "Big 5" mean to you? It means the state of publishing today, for better or worse. See above question.

What do you want to tell new/unpublished writers? That despite changing technology, a great story never gets old.

Do you like that everything has become largely digitized? Yes. I can remember submitting multiple complete manuscripts, with a messenger lugging twenty hardcopies all over town.

What do you like reading, watching, and listening to? Lots of things.

Describe a book you would write. A shark terrorizes a beach town. Oh, wait, that's been done.

Joker's wild: There was once a Picasso that was auctioned at Sotheby's. It was expected to sell for around $20 million. Instead, it went to a Japanese businessman for $32 million. When asked if it was really worth that much, he replied, "It is now."

JAKE BARTOK LITERARY ASSOCIATES, INC. ❖

www.virgointacta.com

211 East 42nd Street, Suite 1109, New York, NY 10017, 929-241-9057 ext. 1241, fax: 929-241-9063

Agent's name and contact info: Jake Bartok, jbartok@virgointacta.com

Describe what you like to represent and what you won't represent. I represent fiction and nonfiction. I generally won't represent novels that are thinly veiled autobiographies or autobiographies that are thinly veiled novels.

What are the best ways for writers to pitch you? Contact me with a brief email message describing the project. I'll read it and reply. If I'd like to see more I'll ask for it.

When and where were you born? I was born in New York City. I try not to remember when.

Do you charge fees? No fees charged.

Describe your education and career history. I was educated in London and Paris on full academic scholarships and received a bachelor of commerce (magna cum laude) from Oxford University. I went on to earn a master of business administration from Baruch College in New York. Building on my successful career as a business entrepreneur I began devoting a growing portion of my time and energies to agenting.

Say something about your hobbies and personal interests. My hobby is repairing things, which have ranged from cars to electric coffee percolators. I have several personal interests, but literature ranks at the top.

Why and how did you become an agent? I got into agenting in order to nurture talent and balance the scales. By this I mean that my aim is to ensure that writing worthy of publication sees publication and is not summarily cast off.

Would you do it over again, or something else? I haven't finished doing it yet, actually.

List some representative titles you have placed. I try to keep my client list between myself and my direct professional contacts, so please forgive my not listing titles here.

Describe yourself as a person. I find myself amazingly reasonable and rational, at least when compared to many another I've encountered lately.

How would you describe the proverbial "client from hell," and what are the warning signs? I couldn't. I've never actually represented one. Probably this is because if there are signs of someone being that sort of individual they're obvious early and an astute person can spot them and take the necessary actions. I know I have, before such persons have had a chance to become clients.

What do you think about self-publishing? Self-publishing has always been around and has always been an option for even authors of renown. I would need to consider the subject on a case-by-case basis. I have no overarching opinion on the subject, one way or the other.

Do you like Amazon? For 21st-century authors, if Amazon didn't exist it would have to be invented. Does this mean I like it? Possibly.

Do you believe in a "higher power"? I'll have to think that one over.

What will agenting be like in 2020? That depends on several variables. It's possible that most of the profession will have by then or somewhat later become appendages of corporate publishing, which will itself be dominated by a few megapublishers who've gobbled up the rest.

Describe your job and what you like and don't like about it. I like living much of the time in Europe and being able to interact directly with both US and EU publishers. I dislike professional situations in which I'm subject to vacillation from the editorial side.

Do you miss the way the business "used to be"? Somewhat, because it's not just the way the business used to be, but the way society, and its reading habits and tastes, used to be.

What does the "Big 5" mean to you? Maybe tomorrow's Big 2?

What do you want to tell new/unpublished writers? Nothing, since nobody will listen.

Do you like that everything has become largely digitized? Maybe not, but in another twenty years, when we'll all have digital implants in our bodies and brains, I'll probably love it unreservedly.

What do you like reading, watching, and listening to? I'm a billy goat when it comes to reading, watching, and listening, and this includes dietary information on bags of potato chips and VCR tapes other people have the sense to throw away.

Describe a book you would write. If I told you, I couldn't be an agent anymore.

JEANNE FREDERICKS LITERARY AGENCY, INC. ❖

www.jeannefredericks.com

221 Benedict Hill Road, New Canaan, CT 06840, 203-972-9011

Agent's name and contact info: Jeanne Fredericks, jeanne.fredericks@gmail.com

Describe what you like to represent and what you won't represent. I like to represent practical, popular reference books by authorities, especially in health, science, fitness, gardening, and women's interest. I'm also interested in cooking, elite sports, parenting, environment, lifestyle, and antiques / decorative arts.

I do not represent genre fiction (e.g., horror, occult fiction, true crime, romance, Westerns, and sci-fi), juvenile, textbooks, poetry, essays, plays, short stories, pop culture, guides to computers and software, politics, pornography, overly depressing or violent topics, memoirs that are more suitable for one's family or that are not compelling enough for the trade market, manuals for teachers, or workbooks. I rarely represent fiction, and only for existing clients whose novels are a normal outgrowth of their nonfiction writing.

What are the best ways for writers to pitch you? Please query by email without attachments to jeanne.fredericks@gmail.com or by mail with an SASE. No phone calls, faxes, or deliveries that require signatures, please.

When and where were you born? April 19, 1950, Mineola, New York.

Do you charge fees? I do not charge any fees.

Describe your education and career history. BA, Mount Holyoke College, 1972, major in English; Radcliffe Publishing Procedures Course, 1972; MBA, New York University Graduate School of Business (now called Stern), major in marketing, 1979. Career history: Established own agency in 1997 after being an agent and acting director for Susan P. Urstadt, Inc. (1990–1996); prior to that, I was an editorial director for Ziff-Davis Books (1980–1981); acquiring editor, the first female managing editor of Macmillan's trade division, and assistant managing editor (1974–1980); assistant to the editorial director and foreign/subsidiary rights director of Basic Books (1972–1974). Member of AAR and Authors Guild.

Say something about your hobbies and personal interests. I enjoy swimming, yoga, hiking, walking with friends and my Lab, reading, traveling, casual entertaining, gardening, photography, family activities, volunteering at church, and good conversation with friends. I am hoping to return to crew, which was my key outside interest for 10 years.

Why and how did you become an agent? I reentered publishing as an agent because the flexible hours and home-based office were compatible with raising young children. I enjoy working with creative authors who need my talents to find the right publishers for their worthy manuscripts and to negotiate fair contracts on their behalf. I am still thrilled when I open a box of newly published books by one of my authors, knowing I had a small role in making it happen. I'm also ever hopeful that the books I represent will make a positive difference in the lives of many people.

Would you do it over again, or something else? Yes, I would do it again. I enjoy the long-term relationships I have with my authors, the daily challenges of learning something new such as ebook publishing, reviewing promising proposals, pitching proposals I love to publishers, and managing auctions.

List some representative titles you have placed. *Yoga Therapy: The Ultimate Guide to Yoga for Health and Wellness* by Larry Payne, PhD, Eden Goldman, DC, and Terra Gold, DOM (Basic Health); *The Creativity Cure: A Do-It-Yourself Prescription to Happiness* by Carrie Barron, MD, and Alton Barron, MD (Scribner); *My Scarlett: Margaret Mitchell and the Motion Picture "Gone with the Wind"* by John Wiley, Jr. (Taylor Trade); *Jumping the Fence: A Legacy of Race and Family Secrets in Antebellum New Orleans through the Era of Jim Crow and Beyond* by Maureen Gilmer (Cedar Fort); *Dreams and Schemes: How Florida Became America's Fantasyland* by Willie Dyre (Globe Pequot); *The American Quilt* by Robert Shaw (Sterling); *Waking the Warrior Goddess: Dr. Christine Horner's Program to Protect against and Fight Breast Cancer* by Christine Horner, MD (Basic Health); *Lilias! Yoga: Your Guide to Enhancing Body, Mind, and Spirit in Midlife and Beyond* by Lilias Folan

(Skyhorse); *Treasure Ship: The Legend and the Legacy of the* S.S. Brother Jonathan by Dennis M. Powers (Sea Ventures Press); *Artful Watercolor* by Carolyn Janik and Lou Bonamarte (Sterling); *Smart Guide to Single Malt Whisky* by Elizabeth Riley Bell (Smart Guides); *A Woman's Guide to Pelvic Health: Expert Advice for Women of All Ages* by Elizabeth E. Houser, MD, and Stephanie Riley Hahn, PT (Johns Hopkins University Press).

Describe yourself as a person. I love to learn about many subjects, so I continue to be thrilled to work with authors who want to share their expertise with others. I favor building and nurturing long-term relationships with authors but remain open to new talent. I'm an optimist who likes to work with people who see problems as challenges to overcome and know that good results stem from insight, monitoring trends, hard work, and attention to detail, as well as keeping up with new technologies and ways of doing things. My background makes me think on many levels when representing clients — as an MBA, editor, agent, and enthusiastic reader. Though I can be firm and persistent in negotiations, I believe in old-fashioned courtesy and respect among colleagues and love working as a team with them in creating and marketing a book that will have lasting value.

How would you describe the proverbial "client from hell," and what are the warning signs? An arrogant, pushy, self-centered, unreliable writer who does not understand publishing or respect my time and who vents anger in an unprofessional way. Fortunately I've rarely encountered such a person in this business. When I sense an overly inflated ego in the initial correspondence and communication, I steer clear of the person.

What do you think about self-publishing? Self-publishing opens up opportunities for many aspiring writers and levels the playing field to a certain extent since self-published authors can sometimes publish successfully and earn more money than with traditional publishers. They can also have more control over the key decisions in publishing. The problem is discoverability in a world where there are far too many books being published. Unless the self-published author has written a high-quality book and is willing to put in the time to build a marketing platform and fine-tune the metadata for discoverability, the book may sell so few copies that all the effort put into writing and publishing it will seem worthless. Also, if authors aspire to publish POD (print-on-demand) paperbacks, they may be surprised by what they need to know and do to prepare a book for publication, performing time-consuming functions that are taken care of by traditional publishers if they choose instead to have one represent them.

Do you like Amazon? I used to feel that Amazon was the hated behemoth that used its clout to drive out independent publishers who couldn't compete with their discounted pricing and speedy fulfillment of orders. I still think that there is some truth to that view, but over time I realized that I liked the convenience and low prices of buying on their site, and I also found it an excellent tool for research. I admire how Amazon staff continually learn and improve their ways of doing business and take the time to meet with agents and authors to educate them about Amazon's approach to publishing. Now that I am involved with publishing some ebooks and POD books with them, I have huge respect for their quick sizing up of opportunities, their making the steps to publishing seem understandable and doable, and their high level of support to agents who are publishing books in their White Glove program. To remain competitive, publishers and other book retailers are going to have to be proactive in keeping pace and finding ways to offer more, or something better or different than Amazon, or they may find that they will go the way of so many independent bookstores.

Do you believe in a "higher power"? Yes, I believe in God, but I also believe that a person needs to work to make opportunities and achieve success in life. I have been active in my church for decades and am the trustee of a new foundation that fosters small-group ministries and Bible study for people from any denomination.

What will agenting be like in 2020? I imagine that it will be even faster paced and less personal in terms of face-to-face interaction. I think that video will become increasingly important in selling books and that agents who are not tech-savvy will find themselves with fewer clients, especially the younger ones.

Describe your job and what you like and don't like about it. I select authors to represent, help them fine-tune their proposals, find them the right publishers, negotiate the best deals for them, act as their advocate and diplomat through the publishing process, handle the money side of the business so they can focus on what they do best, and help them self-publish once their books have gone out of print. What I don't like doing is rejecting queries and proposals, especially from people who have worthwhile books. I have to do this to too many writers simply because they don't have the necessary marketing platforms to be acceptable to publishers.

Do you miss the way the business "used to be"? When I first started in publishing, publishers would take a risk on a talented author with no marketing platform if they thought he or she had the potential to be promotable. Nowadays I'd be wasting my time representing someone who hasn't already worked on a platform, and I find this a little sad because I think publishers are ruling out authors who could be successful if given guidance in marketing themselves and their books. In the past there was room on publishers' lists for books that deserved to be published but were unlikely to earn much money, so there was more diversity in what was being published by trade houses. I suppose that these kinds of books can be self-published now, so that's a blessing, but I don't like the way publishers' lists seem to be chosen now with more of an eye to how many followers an author has or whether the book is on top of a proven trend, rather than on the basis of an experienced editor's judgment that someone can write well about something worth reading.

What does the "Big 5" mean to you? A necessary concentration of power and economies of scale in back-office, selling, and inventory functions due to the competition of Amazon. From the perspective of an agent, though, it means fewer publishers to pitch, fewer auctions, and less leverage for securing higher advances, better royalties, and improved contractual language.

What do you want to tell new/unpublished writers? Show me that you have thoroughly researched the competition and can convincingly explain why your proposed book is different, better, and needed by large, defined audiences. Be polite and patient and willing to work hard to make your proposal ready for submission. Build your media experience and social media platform even before you submit your proposal.

Do you like that everything has become largely digitized? For the most part, I like the efficiency and find that I can accomplish more in less time and from any location. That said, the daily grind of dealing with hundreds of emails makes me savor phone calls with favorite authors and editors and treasure handwritten notes. I also prefer reading books printed on paper as a break from all my time in front of a computer screen.

What do you like reading, watching, and listening to? I am an eclectic reader who enjoys literary fiction, groundbreaking research-based nonfiction that makes me think in new ways, inspirational books, tempting cookbooks, gardening books, and ones with breathtaking photos. I enjoy classical music as a background to reading and editing (Beethoven, Mozart, Chopin, Brahms, Bach), but I love to dance to classic rock, ethnic music, jazz — anything with a good beat that makes me want to move to the music. I'm a big fan of *Downton Abbey*, *Foyle's War*, *Doc Martin*, *The Midwives*, *Poirot*, movies of Jane Austen's classics, and other Masterpiece productions. I lived in England for a while and my mother was raised there, so I am quite an Anglophile.

Describe a book you would write. Hmm…no idea! My head is too full of the books that others have written or aspire to write. Maybe I will write my own sometime in the future when I have more time to reflect on the life I've lived and what I want to pass on to the next generation.

JEAN V. NAGGAR LITERARY AGENCY, INC. ❖ www.jvnla.com

216 East 75th Street, Suite 1E, New York, NY 10021

Agent's name and contact info: Laura Biagi, lbiagi@jvnla.com, Twitter: @LauraJBiagi

Describe what you like to represent and what you won't represent. In adult fiction, I am especially interested in literary fiction, magical realism, cultural themes, social issues, and debut authors. I'm drawn to strong voices, complex narrative arcs, dynamic and well-developed characters, psychological twists, and apocalyptic literary fiction.

In the young readers' realm, I look for young adult novels, middle grade novels, and picture books. I love young readers' books that have a magical tinge to them and vivid writing.

In both adult and young readers' books, I'm also looking for titles that incorporate high-concept, dark/edgy, and quirky elements, as well as titles that challenge the way we typically view the world.

I occasionally do memoir, but it has to be the right project, as I typically don't go for it. Our primary nonfiction agent is Elizabeth Evans.

I'm probably not the right person for high fantasy or sci-fi or hard-boiled detective mysteries. I just don't love them as much as other types of fiction.

What are the best ways for writers to pitch you? I prefer to receive submissions via our website, at www.jvnla.com/submissions, but I also accept submissions sent directly to my email address, LBiagi@jvnla.com. If you're submitting via the website or by email, please always include the first page of your manuscript, as this is extremely helpful for me when I'm considering your project.

When and where were you born? I was born in Louisville, Kentucky, but I grew up in a smaller town 30 minutes away, Shelbyville.

Do you charge fees? No, our agency does not charge reading fees.

Describe your education and career history. I attended college at Northwestern University, where I studied creative writing (fiction) and anthropology (cultural; I did an eight-week research study in Guatemala for my thesis). My start in publishing was with the Jean Naggar Agency, where I began as an intern. From there, I got hired on as an assistant and now work as an agent! I've also had a brief stint at Barnes & Noble.

Say something about your hobbies and personal interests. I personally like to write adult literary fiction on all topics, especially involving magical realism, absurdism, and/or social issues. This also means that adult literary fiction involving these elements is right up my alley, so I'm always looking for submissions involving them!

Why and how did you become an agent? The roots of how I came to become an agent could probably be traced back to my college studies in creative writing. I loved critiquing manuscripts in writing workshops so much that I chose to enter an industry in which I could read and critique manuscripts for a living! I was also attracted to how collaborative and creative the industry is, and how everyone involved in publishing is driven by a passion for good writing and good stories.

My official start in the book-publishing industry began with my internship at the Jean Naggar Agency. Soon after, I was hired on full-time. As an assistant, I worked closely with Jean Naggar and Jennifer Weltz on their titles. I also worked a great deal on our international rights; I created rights lists for international book fairs and sent materials and reviews to our coagents. I am still involved in our international rights and, in that vein, now sell Australia–New Zealand rights for our published books.

In 2012 I began taking on my own clients. I am very excited to be building up a list of adult literary fiction authors and kids' book authors (young adult, middle grade, and picture books).

THE JEFF HERMAN AGENCY LLC ❖ www.jeffherman.com

PO Box 1522, Stockbridge, MA 01262, 413-298-0077

Agent's name and contact info: Jeff Herman, jeff@jeffherman.com

Describe what you like to represent and what you won't represent. All kinds of nonfiction, especially self-help, how-to, practical/solution driven, spirituality, health, recovery, history, business, psychology.

What are the best ways for writers to pitch you? Whatever works for them.

When and where were you born? 1958, Long Island.

Do you charge fees? Not for agenting.

Describe your education and career history. I graduated from Syracuse University with a bachelor of science degree and entered the public relations business, first for a publishing house and then for a firm that specialized in corporate communications. I spent a little time on a kibbutz and then opened my own public relations office, which morphed into a literary agency when I was 28, and that's what I've been doing ever since.

Say something about your hobbies and personal interests. I enjoy doing nothing at all without any preformed purpose whenever I can.

Why and how did you become an agent? I was doing it without knowing it before I decided I wanted to do it. It's a longer story than that.

Would you do it over again, or something else? I suspect I would make the same choices.

List some representative titles you have placed. More than many, give or take a hundred. A lot of good ones and some excellent ones.

Describe yourself as a person. Critical thinker. Respectful. Low-key but quietly intense. Few things surprise me anymore.

How would you describe the proverbial "client from hell," and what are the warning signs? Manipulative. Exploitative. Mean. Uncaring. Dishonest.

What do you think about self-publishing? It can be great. Don't get ripped off.

Do you like Amazon? What's not to like?

Do you believe in a "higher power"? It rains even when I don't want it to and when no one else wants it to. Something causes that to happen, and it has more power than anyone I know.

What will agenting be like in 2020? Fewer boutique agencies.

Describe your job and what you like and don't like about it. I curate commercially viable books and help manifest their publication. Constant consolidation of publishing at all levels restricts creativity and rewards conformity.

Do you miss the way the business "used to be"? There was more risk taking and individuality.

What does the "Big 5" mean to you? Reality.

What do you want to tell new/unpublished writers? Learn.

Do you like that everything has become largely digitized? I was never a neat person. Digitization has helped me to be a little more neat on the physical plane and has given me more physical space.

What do you like reading, watching, and listening to? I listen to dogs and cats, because they have little to say and a lot to emote. I read newspapers and magazines a lot, because they help me feel connected. I like watching trees because they wave to me in the summer and look scary in the winter.

Describe a book you would write. A how-to book for making time machines.

Joker's wild: You're reading this.

THE JENNIFER DECHIARA LITERARY AGENCY ❖ www.jdlit.com

31 East 32nd Street, Suite 300, New York, NY 10016, 212-481-8484 ext. 362

Agent's name and contact info: Jennifer DeChiara, jenndec@aol.com

Describe what you like to represent and what you won't represent. I'm passionate about representing children's literature (picture books, middle grade, and young adult) in every genre, and I also represent illustrators, adult literary fiction (writers with something special to say and a special way of saying it), commercial fiction, mystery, thriller, horror. In nonfiction, I love to represent celebrity bios and anything and everything about Holly-wood/entertainment/theater/dance/behind-the-scenes, memoir, biography, pop culture, true crime, self-help, parenting, humor. In general, I'm open to any well-written book, either fiction or nonfiction, in any genre.

I don't represent poetry, Westerns, romance, or erotica.

What are the best ways for writers to pitch you? Email a query to me at jenndec@aol.com.

When and where were you born? New York City.

Do you charge fees? No.

Describe your education and career history. Brooklyn College, New York University. Was a dancer and actress, writing consultant, freelance editor for Random House and Simon & Schuster, and literary agent for two established New York City literary agencies. Started my own literary agency in 2001.

Say something about your hobbies and personal interests. It's a struggle for me to do any of the following because I have so little free time these days, but I'm passionate about reading (everything), writing (working on a screenplay at the moment), ballet (someday I vow to get back to it and take classes just for the fun of it), skiing (love shushing down the slopes, but equally love sipping hot cocoa by a roaring fire), travel (I'm in love with Italy and spent several months there recently), movies/theater (what I could have done with that role — oy!), piano (been taking lessons for the past 15 years and will keep at it until I croak).

Why and how did you become an agent? How I became an agent is too long a story to tell, but I started my own agency because I wanted to make a difference: I wanted to help put great books out into the world, and I wanted to help make writers' dreams come true. It was an accidental career for me, but it's what I believe I was put on this planet to do.

Would you do it over again, or something else? I'd do it all over again.

List some representative titles you have placed. *Elf on the Shelf* by Carol Aebersold and Chanda Bell; *A Moose That Says Moo* by Jennifer Hamburg (Scholastic); *Bizz and Buzz Make Honeybuns* by Dee Leone (Grosset & Dunlap); *The Summer Experiment* by Cathie Pelletier; *Geography Club* by Brent Hartinger; *The One-Way Bridge* by Cathie Pelletier (Sourcebooks); *Omega Days* by John Campbell (Berkley); *The Write-Brain Workbook*, 10th Anniversary Edition, by Bonnie Neubauer (F&W Media); *A Memoir* by Danny Aiello (Simon & Schuster); *Not Young, Still Restless* by Jeanne Cooper (Harper Collins); *Psychic* by Sylvia Browne (Harper Collins); *The 30-Day Heartbreak Cure* by Catherine Hickland (Simon & Schuster).

Describe yourself as a person. Compassionate. I care about helping people and making the world a better place.

How would you describe the proverbial "client from hell," and what are the warning signs? Someone who calls or emails constantly for news; expects a phone call from me when there's nothing to discuss; expects me to perform according to their timetable; has no knowledge of the publishing business and wants to call the shots; can't accept rejection or criticism; has a lack of appreciation for my efforts; fails to work as part of a team. Every once in a while a client from hell slips into the agency, but once they show us their horns, we send them back to the inferno.

What do you think about self-publishing? A good option in some cases, a bad one in others.

Do you like Amazon? Yes — it's a great resource for me as an agent, and it makes it easier to buy books, which is always a good thing, especially for writers.

What will agenting be like in 2020? Who knows? But however book formats change, writers will always need agents to help navigate their careers.

What do you want to tell new/unpublished writers? Write for yourself. Don't chase fame or fortune. Chase excellence.

Do you like that everything has become largely digitized? Yes — it's made my job, and my life, a million times easier.

Describe a book you would write. Literary fiction, definitely, and probably an underdog story.

Agent's name and contact info: Linda Epstein, querylindaepstein@gmail.com and linda.p.epstein@gmail.com

Describe what you like to represent and what you won't represent. I represent picture books, middle grade and young adult literature, and adult fiction.

I don't represent romance, any kind of thriller, mystery, horror, Western, or Christian literature. I'm not currently looking for new memoir, narrative nonfiction, or other nonfiction projects.

What are the best ways for writers to pitch you? I take email queries only. I frequently attend conferences.

When and where were you born? I'm a New Yorker, through and through.

Do you charge fees? No.

Describe your education and career history. I was an English major as an undergraduate and did some graduate work in creative writing. I've always been a writer. I took a circuitous route to being a literary agent but ended up exactly where I belong.

Say something about your hobbies and personal interests. My biggest "hobby" is reading. I also like to travel. I'm a foodie. I like talking to people. I'm interested in making the world a better place.

Why and how did you become an agent? Being an agent, for me, is a natural expression of who I am. I love making a difference for people, using my creativity, working with books and people, bringing stories into the world. I began working toward becoming an agent when I looked at my life and said, "Hold on! If I don't do this now, I'm never going to do it!" And then I did the things one needs to do to get into the field.

Would you do it over again, or something else? If I could do it over again, I'd just start when I was a bit younger.

List some representative titles you have placed. *Openly Straight* by Bill Konigsberg (Scholastic / Arthur A. Levine Books); *The Porcupine of Truth* by Bill Konigsberg (Scholastic / Arthur A. Levine Books), *Peanut Butter and Brains* by Joe McGee (Abrams), *Bees in the Trees* by Ruth Horowitz (Scholastic).

Describe yourself as a person. I'm a glass-half-full kind of person. I'm very loyal and a great friend. I can be a bit of a scatterbrain, although I'm also quite dependable.

How would you describe the proverbial "client from hell," and what are the warning signs? The "client from hell" is somebody who doesn't know how to revise, doesn't have patience, doesn't communicate well, and doesn't trust their agent.

What do you think about self-publishing? I think self-publishing can be a good option for people who can put the time, energy, and money into promotion and publicity, which is not everyone. The kink in the self-publishing model, though, is that because there's nobody vetting what gets published, there's quite a lot of self-published work that's just not that good.

Do you like Amazon? I think Amazon has done a lot to change the landscape of publishing. Some of that is good, and some of that has been very challenging. I don't think it's a simple "like" or "don't like" answer.

Do you believe in a "higher power"? Yes.

What will agenting be like in 2020? I have no idea, but I know I'll be part of it, and I'm pretty excited to see how it all pans out!

Describe your job and what you like and don't like about it. My job is to help midwife books into the world, working with some extremely talented and creative people. I edit, sell, and negotiate. I like most things about my job, except for when I can't sell a project that I love.

Do you miss the way the business "used to be"? I miss the way a lot of things "used to be." I also feel extremely lucky to be in this business at this particular time. It's an exciting time to be in publishing.

What does the "Big 5" mean to you? The "Big 5" are just one aspect of publishing. There are many publishing houses besides the "Big 5" that are excellent places for an author to find a home.

What do you want to tell new/unpublished writers? Don't send your work out until it's really ready. When querying, do your research. Be professional. Keep a positive outlook. Don't take anything personally.

Do you like that everything has become largely digitized? In terms of submissions, I very much like that everything is digital. I'm very concerned about the environment, and I love that manuscripts are mostly read on a computer or tablet and we're not using up all that paper.

What do you like reading, watching, and listening to? I just love reading, period. I hardly ever read nonfiction, though. My tastes vary widely, but mostly I stay away from things that are too dark. The same thing applies to my television and movie watching. Regarding music, my taste is eclectic, too, but for the most part I'd say I'm a rock-and-roll girl with alt/indie tendencies.

Describe a book you would write. A cozy mystery that somehow incorporates yarn bombing and good food.

Agent's name and contact info: Stephen Fraser, stephenafraser@verizon.net

Describe what you like to represent and what you won't represent. Generally, books for children and teens, board books, picture books, chapter books, middle grade, young adult. Some adult books.

Not interested in military history, crime.

What are the best ways for writers to pitch you? Email query is best.

When and where were you born? The Boston area.

Do you charge fees? No.

Describe your education and career history. Middlebury College, BA in English; Simmons College, Center for the Study of Children's Literature, MA in children's literature. Editor at Scholastic, Simon & Schuster, Harper Collins.

Say something about your hobbies and personal interests. I see a minimum of two movies per week; reading; travel.

Why and how did you become an agent? After I left Harper Collins, I was offered an agency job, and the rest is history. Prior to that, I had edited a children's magazine, run two children's book clubs, and edited paperback and hardcover books for children and teens.

Would you do it over again, or something else? I'd do it all over again.

List some representative titles you have placed. *Icefall* by Matthew J. Kirby (Scholastic); *Glimpse* by Carol Lynch Williams (Simon & Schuster); *Heart of a Samurai* by Margi Preus (Abrams); *The Hole Story of the Doughnut* by Pat Miller (Houghton Mifflin Harcourt); *The Nora Notebooks* by Claudia Mills (Random House); *Pure Grit* by Mary Cronk Farrell (Abrams).

Describe yourself as a person. Patient, soft-spoken.

How would you describe the proverbial "client from hell," and what are the warning signs? A bad client is someone whose professional behavior is detrimental to the agency, lacking in both respect and appreciation.

What do you think about self-publishing? Rarely a success. Often, this means "impatient."

Do you like Amazon? I am obsessed with buying books from Amazon. Great resource and service.

Do you believe in a "higher power"? Yes.

What will agenting be like in 2020? Essentially the same, though formats may differ from today's. A writer always needs professional guidance for contracts and career.

Describe your job and what you like and don't like about it. A lot of variety daily: pitching books to editors, negotiating deals, guiding writers through revisions, maintaining contact with editors and publishers, speaking at writers' conferences. Chasing down checks and contracts can be tedious; talking writers off cliffs is sometimes tiring. The job is mostly a joy.

Do you miss the way the business "used to be"? Yes, I miss the way it used to be, the way I miss some of "old" New York's stores and restaurants. Publishing used to have less focus on the bottom line and more focus on quality. And there were more "editors' editors" and more author loyalty. But one needs to live in the present.

What does the "Big 5" mean to you? There is value in both small publishers and large ones (the "Big 5"). For instance, some smaller publishers are currently being riskier than some large publishers, who are more corporate driven and fiscally restricted.

What do you want to tell new/unpublished writers? Writing is a craft, and creating a work of art takes time, for both the writer and the editor. Don't be tempted by expediency. You want only your best work to be out there. The real artist keeps working at the craft. Publishing is a confirmation for the writer, but not the only goal.

Do you like that everything has become largely digitized? It doesn't take away the beauty of the printed book.

What do you like reading, watching, and listening to? Love good biographies, literary fiction, and poetry; *Downton Abbey, Mad Men,* and *Dancing with the Stars* (!); classical music, cast albums, Rufus Wainwright, Barbra Streisand.

Agent's name and contact info: Roseanne Wells, queryroseanne@gmail.com

Describe what you like to represent and what you won't represent. For nonfiction I'm interested in authors who have a unique story to tell and are dedicated to building their platform and reaching their audience. I like narrative nonfiction, select memoir, science (popular or trade, not academic), history, religion (not inspirational), travel, humor, food/cooking, and similar subjects. I'm also interested in fresh, modern self-improvement that not only inspires but energizes readers to strengthen and empower themselves in this rapidly evolving world.

In fiction I'm looking for strong literary fiction that emphasizes craft and style equally and doesn't sacrifice plot and character for beautiful sentences; young adult of all genres; very selectively, middle grade that connects me to a strong main character; science fiction and fantasy; and smart detective novels (more Sherlock Holmes than cozy mysteries).

What are the best ways for writers to pitch you? I only accept queries by email, and my submission guidelines are on our website, www.jdlit.com. I also attend conferences, workshops, and events to connect with writers.

When and where were you born? I was born in the San Francisco Bay Area.

Do you charge fees? No.

Describe your education and career history. I went to Sarah Lawrence College and studied literature and dance. When I was a senior, I interned at W. W. Norton. I had previously worked in magazines, and I enjoyed my work, but I really fell in love with the business and the people of book publishing. I worked as an editorial and special-sales assistant for a small publisher of illustrated books, and I interned at a mostly nonfiction agency, and when the assistant left, I moved into being the assistant. I started building a list of nonfiction and fiction titles, and in May of 2012, I joined JDLA.

Say something about your hobbies and personal interests. I grew up as a dancer — mostly ballet and then modern in college. I love cooking and baking: I think anything made with flour and butter and sugar is a good idea. I also love to travel. I studied abroad in Florence, and I have been very fortunate to travel throughout the world. And obviously, I am also a big reader!

Why and how did you become an agent? I was working as a proofreader at *Dance* magazine, and my boss, who was a wonderful mentor, knew I was looking for a position in editorial. She suggested I look into agenting, as it would utilize multiple skill sets, and I might really enjoy it. I started researching what it means to be an agent, and I agreed with her. I found the opportunity to edit, negotiate, and talk with people about books I love and authors I support.

Describe yourself as a person. Creative, loyal, fair, hardworking, loves cake. And ice cream. And pie.

Do you miss the way the business "used to be"? I think one of the advantages of being a newer agent is that there is no comparison to "the good ol' days." I don't get caught up in the nostalgia; I just focus on the present work and the future ahead.

What do you like reading, watching, and listening to? I read mostly in the categories that I represent, as my list closely reflects my own tastes in books. I love half-hour comedies like *30 Rock* and *The Mindy Project* as well as hour dramas like *Scandal* and *Grimm*. I also like lighter dramas, like *White Collar* and *Burn Notice*, and I try to catch up on *The Daily Show* and *The Colbert Report*. I'm listening to a lot of Janelle Monae and Florence & The Machine and K-pop (Korean pop music) as well as podcasts like *The Splendid Table* and *The Writer's Block*.

JENNIFER LYONS LITERARY AGENCY ❖

www.jenniferlyonsliteraryagency.com

151 West 19th Street, 3rd Floor, New York, New York 10011, 212-368-2812

Agent's name and contact info: Jeff Ourvan,
jeff@jenniferlyonsliteraryagency.com

Describe what you like to represent and what you won't represent. I represent nonfiction (history, biography, science, sports, pop culture, finance, religion, and cookbooks) and fiction (young adult, middle grade, children's, mystery, thriller, and literary).

What are the best ways for writers to pitch you? Query by email only to jeff@jenniferlyons literaryagency.com. A writing sample is useful but not required. Please don't send queries by US mail.

When and where were you born? When JFK was president, in New York City.

Do you charge fees? Standard agency fees upon sales.

Describe your education and career history. I have a JD from New York Law School and a BS in geology. Prior to working as a literary agent, I was employed as a geologist, commercial fisherman, magazine editor, PR consultant, lobbyist, corporate attorney, and Subway sandwich engineer — not necessarily in that order.

Say something about your hobbies and personal interests. I enjoy leading my small writing workshops in New York and discovering exciting new writers. I also like swimming in the Hudson River.

Why and how did you become an agent? I found the perfect partner in Jennifer Lyons.

Would you do it over again, or something else? I love what I do.

List some representative titles you have placed. *Gilded* by Christina Farley; *Some Fine Day* by Kat Ross; *The Infectious Microbe* by Bill Firshein; *No Better Friend* by Elke Gazzara; *Eat Mexico* by Lesley Tellez.

Do you like Amazon? Yes. Disregard them at your peril. They combine very capable publishing divisions with awesome marketing power. It can be a terrific place for new authors to land.

Do you miss the way the business "used to be"? I've been an agent for three years and have no nostalgia for the old days. Rather, I'm excited about publishing's evolving future.

What do you want to tell new/unpublished writers? Live courageous lives and experience victory and defeat. Courage is the most important attribute a writer can possess, more than even talent.

Describe a book you would write. *The Star Spangled Buddhist*, which I wrote and was published in 2013.

JIM DONOVAN LITERARY

5635 SMU Boulevard, Suite 201, Dallas, TX 75206, jdliterary@sbcglobal.net

Agents' names: Jim Donovan, Melissa Shultz

Describe what you like to represent and what you won't represent. American history, military, biography, sports, popular reference, pop culture, mystery/thriller, fiction.

What not to pitch: Romance, sci-fi/fantasy, religious/inspirational, poetry, children's, cookbooks, technical/computer, memoir.

What are the best ways for writers to pitch you? Fiction: First, the novel must be finished. And we can't tell anything from a simple query, which involves a different kind of writing than that required to write good fiction. We do want a query that describes the novel, but we also would like to see the first 3 chapters (between 30 and 50 pages) and a full synopsis (no more than 5 pages). If you send a hardcopy, include an SASE if you want the material back. Please don't send us anything until your material is finished and polished. The majority of the submissions we see are not ready for prime time — the writing is just not good enough, the characters are not fresh and believable, or there is no "voice" that we can hear in the writing.

Nonfiction: An intelligent short letter that gets to the point and demonstrates that the writer knows the subject and has something to contribute — and that it's not just a magazine article stretched to book length. Please describe the book succinctly, define its audience (please be specific — who exactly is going to pay $30 for this book and why?), and tell us why you're the perfect person to write it — credentials, publishing history, etc. Credibility and/or experience within the subject area covered by the book are essential. Unless the writer is nationally known for what they're writing about, it's very difficult to obtain a contract if they haven't published in short form first (magazines in the field). Way too many nonfiction writers attempt a book without any previous publishing credentials.

When and where were you born? Brooklyn, New York.

Do you charge fees? No.

Describe your education and career history. BS, film, University of Texas; assistant manager, Congress Avenue Booksellers, Austin, TX, 1981–1984; buyer, Taylors Bookstores chain, Dallas–Fort Worth, TX, 1984–1988; senior editor, Taylor Publishing, 1988–1993.

List some representative titles you have placed. *Manson* by Jeff Guinn (S&S); *Glorious* by Jeff Guinn (Putnam); *Eliot Ness* by Douglas Perry (Viking); *Shot All to Hell* by Mark Lee Gardner (Morrow); *Below* by Ryan Lockwood (Kensington); *Last Stand at Khe Sanh* by Gregg Jones (Da Capo); *The Last Outlaws* by Thom Hatch (NAL); *Crucible of Command* by William C. Davis (Da Capo); *American Queen* by John Oller (Da Capo); *Drive* by G. Wayne Miller (Public Affairs); *The Lords of Apacheria* by Paul Hutton (Crown); *Frontier* by Susan Salzer (Kensington).

What does the "Big 5" mean to you? Everything. They're who I do business with, primarily.

What do you want to tell new/unpublished writers? If you're writing fiction, finish your novel, wait two to four weeks to gain some objectivity (during which time you should read fiction in your area and also a book or two on editing your novel), and then begin the essential process of editing and polishing. Without revision, you will have little chance of finding an agent to represent you. If you're writing nonfiction, become published in reputable magazines, journals, blogs, etc., before attempting a book. It's very hard to garner a contract for an unpublished writer.

Describe a book you would write. I've written several, so I'd like to think I know what it feels like to be on both sides of the publishing process. My last two were *A Terrible Glory: Custer and the Battle of the Little Bighorn — the Last Great Battle of the American West* (Little, Brown; 2008) and *The Blood of Heroes: The 13-Day Struggle for the Alamo — and the Sacrifice That Forged a Nation* (Little, Brown; 2012).

JOELLE DELBOURGO ASSOCIATES ❖ www.delbourgo.com

101 Park Street, Montclair, NJ 07042, 973-773-0836, submissions@delbourgo.com

Agents' names and contact info: Joelle Delbourgo, 973-773-0836, joelle@delbourgo.com; Jacqueline Flynn, jacqueline@delbourgo.com

Describe what you like to represent and what you won't represent. We are a boutique agency representing a wide range of nonfiction and selective fiction: adult, young adult, and middle grade. In nonfiction, we look for books that make a significant contribution to knowledge and culture, distill important research, and/or tell a great story (narrative). Particular areas of interest include history, science, business, health and wellness, parenting, philosophy, and psychology. We represent literary and mainstream women's fiction, as well as smart mysteries and romantic fiction.

Joelle: I like fiction that pulls me into a powerful story, through plot, nuanced character, and a strong sense of place. Do not send science fiction, religious books, screenplays, or picture books.

Jacquie: I am also interested in smart science fiction and fantasy with a fresh premise. I love a story that I can fall in love with, and I have a soft spot for an underdog story.

What are the best ways for writers to pitch you? Referrals are best, but we do accept unsolicited submissions. Our submission guidelines are clearly stated at www.delbourgo.com. Do not cold-call.

When and where were you born?
Joelle: I'll leave out "when," but the place was Alexandria, Egypt.

Jacquie: I was born in Staten Island, escaped early, and am now a proud Jersey girl.

Do you charge fees?
Joelle: No. I am an AAR member. We also offer, through a consulting arm of our company, à la carte editorial and marketing services for select authors.

Describe your education and career history.
Joelle: BA, Williams College (double major in history and English); MA, Columbia University (English and comparative literature).

Jacquie: BA, Bucknell University (international relations).

Say something about your hobbies and personal interests.
Joelle: Aspiring Latin and ballroom dancer, avid traveler, serious foodie, film buff; music, especially live.

Jacquie: When you don't find me hiding with my nose in a book (or an ereader), my husband and I are with one of our boys (there are two) at an ice rink, soccer field, volleyball court, or band concert. When we get a rare break, we race to the woods for some fresh air and a hike.

Why and how did you become an agent?

Joelle: After more than two decades as an editor and senior editorial executive inside publishing houses (Random House, Harper Collins), I needed to step back and gain perspective on the publishing business. This is hard to do when you're working 16 hours a day like a crazy person. I wanted to find a way to be a player in the business I loved but from a different vantage point. I also wanted to build something that allowed me the possibility of pursuing any book that intrigued me without worrying about whether or not it fit the profile at one particular publishing house. As an agent, I have a lot of choices of where to go with my projects. I draw on all the skills I learned as an editor and publisher and consider that I'm still a publisher in drag.

Jacquie. I was an editor for many years and loved shepherding books to market. The downside (besides meetings) is that you are always dancing between the needs of the publisher and those of your books and authors, and you are usually restricted to signing in certain categories. After many years in-house, I was drawn to the freedom of agenting because it meant I could work on projects of my choosing, and I could focus on my preferred role of author advocate and adviser. And, of course, the other reason is Joelle — the chance to work with her sealed the deal.

Would you do it over again, or something else?

Joelle: When I was a kid, I figured out that someone actually wrote the flap copy on books. I wanted to be that person, and pretty much that's what happened. But I could also imagine being a professor or dean of a university, or working in a start-up.

Jacquie: One of my favorite Christmas memories was getting *Farmer Boy* by Laura Ingalls Wilder and finishing it while sitting under the tree before dinner was ready. I never imagined doing anything other than working with books.

List some representative titles you have placed.

Joelle: *World of Trouble*, book three in the *Last Policeman* trilogy, by Ben H. Winters (Quirk Books); *Searching for Sappho* by Philip Freeman (Norton); *The Friendship Lab* by Rob Garfield (Gotham/Penguin); *Then Came Life* by Geralyn Lucas (Gotham/Penguin); *The Lost Gospel* by Simcha Jacobovichi and Barrie Wilson (Pegasus & Harper Canada); *The Middle Economy* by Robert Sher (Bibliomotion); *Pretty in Ink* by Lindsey J. Palmer (Kensington); *Mothers Who Can't Love* by Susan Forward (Harper); *Be Nobody* by Lama Marut (Beyond Words/Atria); *St. Brigid's Bones* by Philip Freeman (Pegasus); *It's OK*

Not to Share, sequel, by Heather Shumaker (Tarcher/Penguin); *Fighting for Love* by Judith Wright, PhD, and Bob Wright, PhD.

Jacquie: *College Revalued* by Kristin White (The Experiment); *Stress-Free Discipline* by Sara Au and Peter L. Stavinoha, PhD (Amacom); *American Pain* by John Temple (Lyons Press); *Fly a Little Higher* by Laura Sobiech (Thomas Nelson); *Papyrus* by John Gaudet, PhD (Pegasus); *The Guardian Herd: Starfire* by Jennifer Lynn Alvarez (Harper Children's); *Asking for It* by Kate Harding (Da Capo); *Trail of the Dead* by Melissa F. Olson (47North); *Promise Bound* by Anne Greenwood Brown (Delacorte); *Mobile Influence* by Chuck Martin (Palgrave Macmillan); *The Gamification Revolution* by Gabe Zichermann and Joselin Linder (McGraw-Hill); *Angels of the Underground: Resistance in the Philippines during WWII* by Theresa Kaminski, PhD (Oxford University Press).

Describe yourself as a person.

Joelle: Passionate, opinionated (hopefully in a good way), warm, encouraging, knowledgeable, professional, a straight shooter, honorable.

Jacquie: I work hard and laugh hard. I know my business, but I'm down-to-earth. I will go to the mat for people and causes I believe in, and I defend my people fiercely. If you want to talk about hockey, I'm probably your girl.

How would you describe the proverbial "client from hell," and what are the warning signs? The angry client. The client who doesn't listen. The entitled client. The know-it-all client. The client who has no boundaries.

What do you think about self-publishing? It is a great option for some authors. But what many learn is how darn difficult it is to do it well. It's hard enough to sell books when you have a publisher behind you. We are dabbling with self-publishing with a few authors through an arrangement we have with Perseus Publishing's Argo Navis. But at the end of the day, the value added when everything aligns in a great publishing house is a beautiful thing that is hard to replicate. It may be hard for unpublished authors to appreciate the value added by having an experienced team and powerful publishing house behind you.

Do you like Amazon? It's a brilliant company, but despite origins in the book business, Amazon comes from a nonbook, tech culture. I find it interesting that Jeff Bezos's wife chose to sign with a "Big 5" house.

Do you believe in a "higher power"? You mean the god of publishing?

What will agenting be like in 2020? There will always be great writers to discover and launch. There will always be great stories to be told and bodies of information to share. We will always need professionals to shape that content. How it is delivered to a reader will continue to change. The agent who will be successful in 2020 needs to have the same skills to be successful in 2015, and that includes embracing new ideas, methods, and roles every day.

Describe your job and what you like and don't like about it.
Joelle: It's like gardening. I select and plant seeds, rake, hoe, and water. Some sprout and bloom, while others die. Some grow tall and strong and provide shade for centuries. As in nature, it's unpredictable. The tedium of the administrative side of running an agency can be mind-numbing. That's the weeding, and it needs to be done for the plants to thrive.

Jacquie: There is nothing more wonderful than making that call to an author to tell them that the book they have poured their heart into will be published. The tough part of being an agent is that rejection is a part of the job, and it's not fun. But you move on and focus on the positive.

Do you miss the way the business "used to be"?
Joelle: Of course I do. I grew up in the industry during a period of explosive growth and possibility. Publishing companies actually made money. I loved the team work, and things weren't nearly as bureaucratic as today. But it was also pressured, political, and incredibly stressful at times. We tend to romanticize the past, but that vision is not accurate. There are so many different pathways to publishing today. The pace of change is dizzying, but where there is change, there is also opportunity.

Jacquie: No! Publishing is full of so many smart, dedicated professionals and brilliant, gifted writers who work together to bring great books to readers. The tools we have are just tools. Being mad at computers or digital is like being mad at the phone.

What does the "Big 5" mean to you? This is the heart of mainstream publishing, five publishing empires comprising many individual publishing houses and imprints, each with a distinct identity. Their standards are very high, and they can be tough to sell to. There are also splendid established companies outside the "Big 5," like Norton and Beacon, as well as newcomers, like Pegasus. Let's not forget the many distinguished university presses, and a slew of hybrid and digital-only companies, some of which are very promising. A relevant agent needs to be knowledgeable and connected to this universe of possibilities.

What do you want to tell new/unpublished writers? Be sure you really are a writer. Are you doing this for the right reason? Don't expect to make a living as a writer; if you are lucky, you might be able to, but that's the exception, not the rule. Learn everything you can about how to get published before contacting publishing professionals; there's a wealth of information out there that is so easily accessed through the Web. Social media, writing groups, and conferences can connect you to other authors and industry experts from whom you can learn.

Do you like that everything has become largely digitized?

Joelle: It drives me crazy at times, but it is also amazing. And I can run a global business from my computer so efficiently. How great is that?!

Jacquie: Line-editing manuscripts on paper and contracts with typed-in marginalia are nothing to feel nostalgic about!

What do you like reading, watching, and listening to?

Joelle: I'm currently hooked on *True Detective* and *Game of Thrones*, *The Good Wife*, *Downton Abbey*, *Girls*, and yes, *Nashville*. I'm a huge movie buff. Recent favorites are *Dallas Buyer's Club*, *American Hustle*, *Captain Phillips*, *Blue Jasmine*. Music is always in the background (thank you, Pandora): Rufus Wainwright, Bruce Springsteen, Mavis Staples, Van Morrison, Leonard Cohen, Natalie Merchant, and Lucinda Williams, to name a few. I read everything: serious history and science, popular psychology, and lots of fiction. Currently, I'm discovering the world of gritty Scandinavian mysteries.

Jacquie: My personal reading is eclectic and ranges from the fun to the serious, including mainstream fiction, classics, history, memoir, and more. Must-see TV includes *Good Wife*, *Downton Abbey*, *Grimm*, and *Once Upon a Time*. My favorite band is U2, but in truth I mostly listen to NPR. When I'm editing I listen to my Pandora Station, "Book-Jacquie's Editing Music," which plays sound tracks like *Last of the Mohicans* and instrumental artists like Ludovico Einaudi, 2Cellos, and Helen Jane Long.

Describe a book you would write.

Joelle: I have two ideas for memoir — one called *Unsuitable Men* and the other, *No Time to Pee*. I think it best that I not write them, don't you agree?

Jacquie: I haven't felt the calling yet; I think my role is helping others bring their books to the world. But you never know.

JUDITH EHRLICH LITERARY MANAGEMENT LLC ❖

www.judithehrlichliterary.com

880 Third Avenue, 8th Floor, New York, NY 10022, 212-580-0736/646-505-1570

Agents' names and contact info:
Judith Ehrlich, jehrlich@judithehrlichliterary.com;
Sophia Seidner, sseidner@judithehrlichliterary.com

Describe what you like to represent and what you won't represent. Fiction and nonfiction, literary and commercial.

No poetry or screenplays.

What are the best ways for writers to pitch you? Emailed query with topic/title in the subject heading.

Do you charge fees? No.

Describe your education and career history. (Judith) Vassar College, Poughkeepsie, New York, bachelor of arts, English major. Professional career: 2002 to present — principal of Judith Ehrlich Literary Management LLC, a full-service boutique agency; 1998–2002 — senior associate at the Linda Chester Literary Agency; 1989–1990 — lead author of national bestseller, *The New Crowd: The Changing of the Jewish Guard on Wall Street* (hardcover, Little, Brown; paperback Harper Collins); award-winning freelance writer — articles appeared in *Family Circle*, the *New York Times Magazine, Atlantic Monthly, International Herald Tribune, Ladies Home Journal, Ms.*, and other publications; 1972–1978 — contributing editor to *Family Circle*, then owned by the *New York Times*; 1977: two-hour movie, *The Long Journey Back*, aired on ABC, based on *Family Circle* piece, "The Girl Who Made the Long Journey Back" — film won a Christopher Award; senior editor at *Family Health* magazine — wrote articles on a range of medical topics; senior editor at *Medical World News* (magazine for physicians) — wrote medical pieces of that era, including development of open-heart surgery and heart transplants; scrubbed and observed Dr. Michael DeBakey and Dr. Denton Cooley operate.

Say something about your hobbies and personal interests. 2001–present — cochair of the Financial Services Leadership Forum (FSLF) now in its 14th season, a subscription breakfast series hosted by the New York Public Library and sponsored by McGraw-Hill Financial; help produce four breakfasts for each series that bring top financial, business, and government leaders to the library to hear speakers including Warren Buffett, Hon. William Jefferson Clinton, Stephen Schwarzman, George Soros, Hon. Hillary Rodham Clinton, and Nobel Laureate Joseph Stiglitz. 1970s–present — member of the American Society of Journalists and Authors; helped launch its writer-referral service many years ago; in recent years, contributed to its Agent Roundup Column. 1990–present — member of the Authors Guild. 2001–2005 — board member of the Shakespeare Society, a not-for-profit organization offering five evenings of commentary and performance each season to increase the enjoyment, understanding, and appreciation of William Shakespeare. 1992–2000 — member of the advisory board of *Partisan Review*. In recent years, participated in Round Table Cultural Seminars on poetry, Henry James's novels, opera, *The Odyssey*, and Marcel Proust's *In Search of Lost Time*.

Clubs and affiliations: 2014 — member of the Cosmopolitan Club. 1977–present — spouse privileges at the University Club and Harmonie Club of the City of New York.

2004–present — member of the Harmonie Club's Literary and Media Committee. 1991–2003 — chair of the Harmonie Club's Literary and Media Committee; produced lunch and dinner events featuring such authors as Doris Kearns Goodwin, Ron Chernow, and Jon Meacham; also served for two years on the club's board of governors.

Why and how did you become an agent? In 1998, I made the transition from author to literary agent after collaborating with Linda Chester on a nonfiction book I brought to her agency: West Coast corporate public-relations guru Michael Sitrick's *SPIN: How to Turn the Power of the Press to Your Advantage* (Regnery). Following that successful first sale, I was invited to join her agency. Timing was right. I was eager to shift gears and work with talented authors on a range of projects (fiction and nonfiction, commercial and literary). I wanted to apply my editorial skills to helping authors transform their work into submission-ready manuscripts that could be taken to market. I wanted to help them build their careers as authors. I started building my own list of authors; books sold included Laura Pedersen's novel *Beginner's Luck* (Ballantine); Julie Fenster's *Race of the Century: The Heroic True Story of the 1908 New York to Paris Race* (Doubleday); and *Here Is My Hope: A Book of Healing and Prayer: Inspirational Stories of Johns Hopkins Hospital* by Randi Henderson and Richard Marek (Doubleday).

List some representative titles you have placed. *Ray Bradbury: The Last Interview and Other Conversations* by Sam Weller (Melville House); *You Were Meant for Me* by Yona Zeldis McDonough (NAL/Penguin); *Little Author in the Big Woods: A Biography of Laura Ingalls Wilder* by Yona Zeldis McDonough (Christy Ottaviano Books / Henry Holt); *Power Branding: Leveraging the Success of the World's Best Brands* by Steve McKee (Palgrave, January 2014); *What was the Underground Railroad?* by Yona Zeldis McDonough (Grosset & Dunlap, December 2013); *Two of a Kind* by Yona Zeldis McDonough (NAL, October 2013); *Confessions of a Sociopath: A Life Spent Hiding in Plain Sight* by M. E. Thomas (Crown, May 2013); *The Typewriter Girl* by Alison Atlee (Gallery, January 2013); *Thornhill (Hemlock Series)* by Kathleen Peacock (Harper Collins, September 2013); *Once We Were (The Hybrid Chronicles)* by Kat Zhang (Harper Collins, September 2013); *What's Left of Me (The Hybrid Chronicles)* by Kat Zhang (Harper Collins, September 2012); *A Wedding in Great Neck* by Yona Zeldis McDonough (NAL/Penguin, October 2012); *The Last Kiss: A True Story of Love, Joy and Loss* by Leslie Brody (TitleTown, October 2012); *Shadow Show: All-New Stories in Celebration of Ray Bradbury* edited by Sam Weller and Mort Castle (William Morrow, July 2012); *Luck and Circumstance* by Michael Lindsay-Hogg (Knopf, October 2011); *Incognito: A Novel* by Gregory Murphy (Berkley, July 2011).

JULIA LORD LITERARY MANAGEMENT ❖

www.julialordliterary.com

38 West Ninth Street, #4, New York, NY 10011, 212-995-2333

Agents' names and contact info: Julia Lord, query@julialordliterary.com; Ginger Curwen, query@julialordliterary.com

Describe what you like to represent and what you won't represent. Narrative nonfiction, reference, biography, history, humor, science, adventure, philosophy, military; fiction: general, literary, historical, young adult, suspense, mystery, and thriller.

What are the best ways for writers to pitch you? READ OUR WEBSITE to see what we handle, then email our query address.

Do you charge fees? No fees.

Describe your education and career history. Julia Lord Literary Management is a small, tenacious literary agency working with high-quality writers in adult fiction and nonfiction.

Julia began her agenting career in 1985 working for actors. She opened the talent agency's literary department, representing writers for film, television, and theater. She moved to books eventually, opening Julia Lord Literary Management in 1999. Her mission is very hands-on — to work with writers to develop their careers, work with them from idea through publication and marketing. Her office is known for its steadfast commitment to each and every author and book project.

Ginger Curwen represents thrillers and mysteries. Ginger's previous publishing experience includes positions at Barnesandnoble.com, Harper Collins Publishers, American Booksellers Association, Bantam Books, and Random House.

Julia Lord Literary Management is committed not only to handling all publishing rights — including film/TV, translation, audio, and electronic — but to helping coordinate publicity, special events, off-the-book-page media, and all other publishing needs of the author. JLLM is a full member of the Association of Authors Representatives, the Authors Guild, and PEN.

Say something about your hobbies and personal interests.

Julia: Reading! Travel, hiking, the out-of-doors, classical music, piano, theater.
Ginger: Reading! Travel, tennis, cross-country skiing, drawing, walking my dog.

Would you do it over again, or something else? Of course! It's great work for someone of voracious and eclectic interests.

List some representative titles you have placed. Plato and a Platypus Walk into a Bar: Understanding Philosophy through Jokes by Thomas Cathcart and Daniel Klein (Abrams/

Penguin); *Warrior Soul* by Chuck Pfarrer (Random House); *How Not to Write a Novel* by Sandra Newman and Howard Mittelmark (Harper); *The Knowland Retribution* by Richard Greener (Midnight Ink); *The Dark Side of the Enlightenment* by John Fleming (Norton); *Bikeman* by Thomas F. Flynn (Andrews/McMeel); *Seal Target Geronimo* by Chuck Pfarrer (St. Martin's Press); *The Trolley Problem* by Thomas Cathcart (Workman); *Travels with Epicurus* by Daniel Klein (Penguin); *NYPD Confidential* by Leonard Levitt (Thomas Dunne Books); *Peacekeepers at War* by Col. Timothy J. Geraghty (Potomac Books); *The Last Four Days of Paddy Buckley* by Jeremy Massey (Riverhead/Penguin).

Describe yourself as a person.

Julia: People say I am tenacious, so I suppose I am. I also care deeply about my work, my clients.

Ginger: I would describe myself as an enthusiast, and when I find a book I love, I want everyone to read it and know about it.

Describe your job and what you like and don't like about it. I love finding a new writer — a new voice, new story, new ideas! Writers are creative and talented people who are so often the first to take financial hits in this marketplace. Writers need a team — and that includes a tough agent. I enjoy fighting for their work and their rights.

What do you want to tell new/unpublished writers? You should know why you are writing and who your audience is. Familiarize yourself with other authors in your genre or field.

JULIE A. HILL AND ASSOCIATES, A.K.A. HILL MEDIA

Agent's name and contact info: Julie Hill, hillagent@aol.com

Describe what you like to represent and what you won't represent. I represent nonfiction of all types. Lately I have done some technology work that has been terrific fun, and I'd like to do more. (*Data Crush* by Chris Surdak, a VP at Hewlett Packard).

No sci-fi, kiddie lit, horror, erotica.

What are the best ways for writers to pitch you? Email or snail, query or full proposal.

When and where were you born? 1948, Pasadena, California.

Do you charge fees? Nope.

Describe your education and career history. BA in history, political science, and journalism from U. of Arizona. Grad work, notably the Publishing Program at UC Berkeley but also some work at UCLA in marketing. Was a writer, now am an agent. Of course I blog, but that's the extent of my writing, other than whiz-bang cover letters to editors.

Say something about your hobbies and personal interests. I love to read almost anything. I am enslaved to *New York* magazine. I am also an astrologer and have represented astrologers, psychics, therapists, and healers. My first sale was *Art and Healing* by Barbara Ganim to Three Rivers / Random House. Her book with Susan Fox, *Visual Journaling*, has become a self-help staple. I love to eat and to cook and to entertain. I do astrology of all kinds but have an emphasis on astrology for writers; see my website called "Astrology for Writers (and Editors Too)" on Publishers Marketplace.

Why and how did you become an agent? I was writing food and travel and knew many other writers, two of whom suggested I try agenting because they thought my personality was a fit. I am an incurable helper type, though I have found over the years that sometimes the best help is direct commands and the unvarnished truth. I wish I still had the energy to sort of coddle people along the way, but we both benefit if authors have read this book's advice before submitting and are fully ready for a publisher's eyes. Too much handholding I have found to be counterproductive for all concerned.

Would you do it over again, or something else? Other than marry money, I'd do this over again. I have met some of the most incredible people on the planet through books and writing.

List some representative titles you have placed. *Data Crush*, mentioned above (Amacom); *Hikes on the Pacific Crest Trail* (an offshoot of *Wild* by Cheryl Strayed, actually; Norton); the rebirth of *Art and Healing* with a new publisher.

Describe yourself as a person. Fun. Great cook. Super nature lover. Word addict.

How would you describe the proverbial "client from hell," and what are the warning signs? One who hasn't educated themselves on how the business works, calls with every news bulletin no matter how small, expects me to come to kids' birthday parties.

What do you think about self-publishing? Great for highly energetic and well-connected people.

Do you like Amazon? The efficiency of Amazon cannot be underrated.

Do you believe in a "higher power"? Yes.

What will agenting be like in 2020? I'll bet there will be very few changes. Agenting hasn't really changed all that much. The end product of what we represent may have changed a bit, but my job is pretty much the same structurally.

Describe your job and what you like and don't like about it. I sell content wherever I can with the authors' best interests at heart. I show great material to great editors and media people and hope I can squeeze enough money out to make the author elated. I am *very* good an negotiating contracts — sometimes people come to me with a deal already and ask me to get a better contract out of it. I keep up on the nooks and crannies of the legalities. I often have editors say to me, "I have never had anyone ask for that." A contract is a wondrous thing, and there are many spots where authors can get paid, or paid better, that a lot of agents don't know about, truth be told. Legal language can hang you too…I am suspicious and curious, and it pays off for my authors. I *love* that. Contracts are my strong suit.

Do you miss the way the business "used to be"? Sort of — it used to be more cut-and-dried. And we could always expect a book to be a cultural artifact: nice paper, wonderful covers…real art. Now, not so much. But time marches on and progress does too.

What do you want to tell new/unpublished writers? Read this book. Learn about promotion. Send your agent luxurious gifts.

Do you like that everything has become largely digitized? Yes and no. More readers, more authors, but the take for authors is often slimmer.

What do you like reading, watching, and listening to? *New York* magazine, *House of Cards*, *Lie to Me*, *NBC Evening News*, classical music except for Stravinsky. Oh, I do like watching Ina Garten on the Food Network. She's astounding. I also never miss reading Michael Lutin's website *Daily Fix*. He wrote for *Vanity Fair* for 25 years.

Describe a book you would write. I did write one. It was called *America's Best Psychics*, and it was self-published(!!) in 1986. It was my open door to the world of publishing. It never dawned on me to get an agent or look for a publisher. I just wrote it (took me three years), printed it, and distributed it. And about the time I was running low of copies, I knew I was out of energy for the project, so I moved to writing for periodicals about all kinds of things, beginning with a directory of "alternative practitioners." Then food and travel.

Joker's wild: Thanks, but I think I've said enough for one person! Thank you, everyone at New World Library and Jeff Herman Agency. This book has been such a boon to my agenting life. I am so grateful.

KELLER MEDIA, INC. ❖ www.kellermedia.com

578 Washington Boulevard, Suite 745, Marina del Rey, CA 90292, 800-278-8706, query@kellermedia.com, www.kellermedia.com/query

Established in 1989, 11 New York Times *bestsellers, 6 international bestsellers, more than 1,200 rights deals concluded worldwide.*

Agent's name and contact info: Wendy Keller, senior agent, www.kellermedia.com/query

Describe what you like to represent and what you won't represent. I am a nonfiction agent *only*. If your book is for children, is fiction, is a screenplay, poetry, illustrated, I am not the right agent for you. Don't waste your time querying me on any of those kinds of books because you'll think I've rejected your content when in truth it's that we're just not a match. I am listed as one of the top 10 US agents for true crime. I keep complaining to that website owner because I've never sold a true crime book in my life and don't plan to do so! I *do* represent and am recognized in this industry for business (sales, management, marketing, finance, entrepreneurship), self-help (anything from physical or mental health to dog training to personal finance to parenting, and everything in between), science (please have credentials as a writer or as a scientist), social issues / current affairs (preference given to actual thought leaders, politicians, and journalists). I also handle the occasional exceptional mass-market-appealing inspirational/spiritual book. See the representative sales below and on our website for examples.

Nothing religious, ever. Spiritual, but not "New Age" spiritual. No Wicca, no crystals, no channeled books.

What are the best ways for writers to pitch you? www.kellermedia.com/query; but first, read www.kellermedia.com/submission-guidelines.

When and where were you born? I was born post-Renaissance, unfortunately, because I'd like to have been an Italian countess and worn a lot of brocade and jewels. Instead, I was merely born in a teaching hospital in Chicago, with dozens of medical interns watching my very conservative mother push me into the world.

Do you charge fees? There are no fees charged to our literary clients in conjunction with representing their books, ever. However, clients are allowed to buy me dinner in New York on the day we close the auction.

Describe your education and career history. I won my first district-wide writing award in fourth grade. I went to college for journalism at age 16 and started my first paid job as a cub reporter two weeks later. I worked for several newspapers and magazines; did a stint at PR Newswire; and eventually became the associate publisher of Los Angeles's then-second-largest Spanish-language newspaper, despite the fact that I spoke very little Spanish. I began this agency in 1989.

Say something about your hobbies and personal interests. I am a competitive sweep rower and an avid amateur archaeologist. I worked on an expedition in Pompeii and restored ancient frescoes in Altamura, Italia. I speak passable Italian, okay French, some German (from attending the Buchmesse, a big publishing conference in Frankfurt), California Spanish, and a handful of words in other languages. I read *Science News* and *National Geographic* from cover to cover every month. I'm currently fascinated by neuroscience and the implications of genomics.

Why and how did you become an agent? I became an agent because I discovered there was not a need for Renaissance-era Italian countesses in Southern California. Okay, really because I've been around ideas, writing, books, and sales my whole life, and this seemed a logical blend.

Would you do it over again, or something else? I would probably *not* do it again. It makes me very sad that so many authors run to self-publish, often because agents like me rejected their marginal books or because they don't know any better. And when their books fail, as most self-published books do, they are discouraged permanently from publishing, or they come to me dragging their tails and expect me to fix the problem they created. Sadly, that's rarely possible. Self-publishing is a good choice for a very few writers, but the majority do themselves a permanent disservice by making that choice. Further to that, the glut of bad/unedited/unprofessional books that self-publishing has poured into the market has watered down the ability of the consumer to find quality reading materials that have been properly vetted. I suspect the decline in reading is largely due to the self-publishing dementia.

List some representative titles you have placed. *The Millionaire Masterplan* by Roger James Hamilton (Hachette); *The Leadership Playbook* by Nathan Jamail (Penguin); *Walking Prey* by Holly Austin Smith (Palgrave Macmillan); *How to Be a Power Connector* by Judy Robinett (McGraw-Hill); *Blue Mind* by Wallace J. Nichols, PhD (Little, Brown); *Think Big, Act Bigger* by Jeffrey Hayzlett (McGraw-Hill); *Forgotten Sundays* by Gerry Sandusky (Running Press); *In the Garden of Thoughts* by Dodinsky (Sourcebooks).

These are a few US titles. In the past 12 months, 16 titles have been placed with non-US publishers, and we've booked speaking engagements, sold bulk sales to companies on behalf of our authors, placed media appearances, and gotten one sponsorship deal for authors represented by this agency.

Describe yourself as a person. I am often told I seem much tougher and meaner until someone gets to know me. Not a bad thing, really. I am fiercely protective of my clients; I don't suffer fools gladly; and if someone queries me or is referred to me and they want me to make them famous but don't want to do any work or take my sound advice, I let them know clearly how I feel about their project. But in my personal life, I am a fairly compassionate, humanitarian person. I'm a mom to a wonderful young woman whom I raised myself. I keep fresh flowers in my house, preferably white lilies. I spend a lot of time in nature, do yoga, and meditate. I have wonderful people in my personal and business life, including most of my clients, editors, vendors, and even some other agents.

How would you describe the proverbial "client from hell," and what are the warning signs? The client from hell is usually screened out early, although a few make it through. They are the ones who call or text me on weekends or late at night because they suddenly want to change a word on page 286 after the book has gone to press, or who are frantic that it sometimes takes me as long as 45 days to sell the book from the day I first put it up for sale, or that their psychic told them to change the shade of orange on their book cover. I don't understand extreme neuroses.

Now, the would-be author from hell — not a client — the kind who will never be published (unless they change!), well, that's someone who has not spent one minute considering that I'm running a business here. These are the ones who start their query with "I know you don't handle books like mine, but…" and ask me to make an exception, or who write basically, "You should be so lucky as to handle my book" or, "I am finally prepared to disclose the facts about the PTSD I've suffered since I was abducted by aliens who turned my hair orange, plucked out my teeth, and painted gang signs on my body with Sharpies." There are a lot of crackpots out there, and a lot of narcissists, too!

Anyone trying to get published who fails to understand the crucial importance of a "platform" will be a mismatch for me. A platform is a group of people (whom you are not paying and to whom you are not related) who are actively engaged with you on the subject of your book, through your blog, speeches, Facebook, direct mail, TV or radio shows, etc. Ideally, your public is paying already to get your opinion on this topic. Publishers will not pay for your book unless you have a platform. If you don't have one, it can be built if you know what to do, but don't think you can skip this step!

Do you like Amazon? I am a rabid fan of Amazon. I see what they are doing as the 500-pound gorilla in the publishing industry's living room, but as a consumer, I adore my Kindle Fire; I buy three times as many books as I did before — and I'm a volume buyer! — and I love that I can read 10–20 samples on a topic before I select the best one for the goal I want to achieve with a particular nonfiction book. I also have become a consumer of fiction (which I do not agent) because of Kindle samples and recommendations from Amazon. Impressive algorithm! I like reading the reviews and am thrilled to watch the sales rankings for my clients' books.

What will agenting be like in 2020? As I gaze into my crystal ball, I see that a mere six years from now, things will be similar. Agents perform an important role in screening the content deluge for worthy editors and crafting and honing the proposed message of worthy future authors. I perform a much bigger role for my clients — aiding them in marketing and platform building — than I ever expected to do, but together we are much more successful. What I do will be in even more demand in 2020.

Describe your job and what you like and don't like about it. I don't have a job and wouldn't want one. What I choose to *do* with my days is a different question. I think of myself as the most marketing-oriented literary agent in the US. I think selling a book for top dollar to the best publisher is the easy part, but the *fun* part of what I do is helping the client find all the ways to leverage that book into their dream (speaker, author, consultant, growing their business, becoming a celebrity, whatever).

Do you miss the way the business "used to be"? I subscribe to the theory that "all progress is good progress," but I will say, when I'm in NYC and I see the charming inscription on the side of the old brick Charles Scribner's Sons building, I wish I could have been in this business at that time. And not just for the adorable suits and hats with feathers that women wore back then, either, although that's part of it!

What does the "Big 5" mean to you? Major publishing houses operating in the US.

What do you want to tell new/unpublished writers? (1) Start to BUILD YOUR PLATFORM FIRST if you are writing nonfiction. (2) Make sure you only pitch to agents who have recently sold and who are currently selling books like yours (your genre), or you will be disappointed. (3) Never, Ever, EVER self-publish until you have repeated step 1 above for at least two years and have an active fan base exceeding 5,000 people. Otherwise, you will fail and you'll think it is your fault. It isn't.

Do you like that everything has become largely digitized? Love it! Bring it on! So much easier than the old days when I had two editorial assistants to open mail, make photocopies of proposals, run my mail room, etc. So many fewer trees lose their lives!

What do you like reading, watching, and listening to? I read parts of literally hundreds of books every year, some unpublished. I read lots of Kindle books on history — especially European; science — especially neuroscience; business; self-help; women's interest; health, diet, and fitness; and biographies of noteworthy figures. What a surprise! Those are also the genres I represent! To feed my soul, I read Don Miguel Ruiz, books on Buddhism or by Buddhists, Thoreau, Coelho, Anthony de Mello, and that entire ilk. For fun, I avidly read Lee Child and similar fiction.

Describe a book you would write. I'd like to write like Paulo Coelho.

Joker's wild: It makes me really sad when authors feel like we're keeping them out of the industry or that we're "too dumb" to recognize the brilliance of their projects. The reality is that this is a business and if agents believe your book has economic viability, we will snatch you up as a client quickly. If you keep getting rejected but you're SURE you are sending it to agents who sell books like yours, there's a pretty good chance your project needs some revising and/or you need to create more of a name for yourself in your content area.

KEN SHERMAN & ASSOCIATES ❖

www.kenshermanassociates.com

1275 North Hayworth, #103, Los Angeles, CA 90046

Agent's name and contact info: Ken Sherman, kenshermanassociates@gmail.com

Describe what you like to represent and what you won't represent. All.

What are the best ways for writers to pitch you? Email.

Do you charge fees? No.

Say something about your hobbies and personal interests. Books, film, making art.

Why and how did you become an agent? By accident. Books were always a comfort zone and films a passion; so I was always looking and reading, and it seemed natural to get involved in writers' professional lives.

List some representative titles you have placed. My clients include Anne Perry, John Updike's estate, Starhawk, John Hersey's estate, Louis Begley.

How would you describe the proverbial "client from hell," and what are the warning signs? Someone who lacks respect for the agent-author relationship.

KIMBERLEY CAMERON & ASSOCIATES ❖

www.kimberleycameron.com

1550 Tiburon Boulevard, #704, Tiburon, CA 94920, 415-789-9191

Agent's name and contact info: Kimberley Cameron, kimberley@kimberleycameron.com

Describe what you like to represent and what you won't represent. I love stories that "pull me in" and "touch the heart." I love all kinds of fiction — not in the market for children's books or screenplays. Nonfiction has to be something unique with an individual point of view.

What are the best ways for writers to pitch you? As I've been saying for 20 years…a polite and professional query is the best way to get my attention.

When and where were you born? Hollywood, CA.

Do you charge fees? Absolutely NOT.

Describe your education and career history. Marlborough School for girls, Humboldt State University, Mount St. Mary's College. Cofounded Knightsbridge Publishing and became partners with the legendary Dorris Halsey of the Reece Halsey Agency. Worked together for many years until her passing — then KC&A was born.

Say something about your hobbies and personal interests. Love to read, obviously. Study French and contemplate spirituality.

Why and how did you become an agent? The next best thing to being an author — I love to introduce new voices into the literary world.

Would you do it over again, or something else? All over again.

List some representative titles you have placed. Please see www.kimberleycameron.com.

Describe yourself as a person. What does this mean? I love to be an author's champion!

How would you describe the proverbial "client from hell," and what are the warning signs? This business takes patience and politeness. A client from hell does not understand what it takes to get something published.

What do you think about self-publishing? Publishing is changing — there are all sorts of "right scenarios."

Do you like Amazon? Amazon has its place in the new publishing paradigm.

Do you believe in a "higher power"? That's personal!

What will agenting be like in 2020? No idea — all is changing so quickly, but agents are becoming more, rather than less, important in managing an author's career.

Describe your job and what you like and don't like about it. I love it. I never know what I'm going to read every day, and calling a writer with good news is a wonderful thrill.

Do you miss the way the business "used to be"? I miss some things — mostly the politeness of a returned call or query.

What does the "Big 5" mean to you? It's just the start of publishing opportunities.

What do you want to tell new/unpublished writers? Believe in your work — polish it and keep going!

Do you like that everything has become largely digitized? Not particularly — I still read and edit manuscripts by hand, but it IS convenient when you want to read several manuscripts and/or books at a time and are traveling.

What do you like reading, watching, and listening to? Great books, great movies, and wonderful music.

Describe a book you would write. Stay tuned.

Joker's wild: What does this mean?

Agent's name and contact info: Amy Cloughley, amyc@kimberleycameron.com, Twitter: @amycloughley

Describe what you like to represent and what you won't represent. I look for unique, clear voices with smart, tightly written prose. I have a soft spot for distinctive, strong, contemporary characters set in small towns and always look for an unexpected story arc, a suitable pace, and a compelling protagonist. I am actively building my client list with both debut and veteran writers. Fiction: literary and upmarket fiction as well as commercial — including well-researched historical (prefer 1800s or later) and well-told women's fiction. Also love a page-turning mystery or suspense with sharp wit and unexpected twists and turns. Nonfiction: narrative when the plot and characters are immersed in a culture, lifestyle, discipline, or industry. Travel or adventure memoir.

I'm not currently looking for military/government thriller, fantasy, sci-fi, or young adult projects.

What are the best ways for writers to pitch you? Please send a query letter in the body of an email to amyc@kimberleycameron.com. Include "Author Submission" in the subject line. For a fiction submission, attach a one-page synopsis and the first 50 pages of your manuscript as separate Word or PDF documents. For nonfiction, attach a full book proposal, as well as sample chapters, as separate Word or PDF documents. Sample chapters should include the first chapter of the book and should not exceed 50 pages.

When and where were you born? I was born and went to school in the Midwest and have been in the San Francisco Bay Area for 15 years.

Do you charge fees? No.

Describe your education and career history. After studying creative writing and earning a BS in magazine journalism, I held positions that straddled the line between editorial and marketing — managing a magazine, advertising campaigns, and marketing projects. I first got into book publishing via an internship at my agency and ultimately started taking on my own clients, coaching writers through classes and conferences, and participating in the myriad of opportunities that agenting has opened up. Certainly my journalism background laid the groundwork for my appreciation of tightly written prose and love of a unique story, whereas my marketing background provided a base for the business side of book publishing. Now I can leverage my background in both words and business to benefit my clients.

Why and how did you become an agent? Working as a literary agent is a lovely balance of all my favorite things: providing editorial feedback, pitching to the editors, negotiating deals, and the thrill of helping writers reach their goals (there really is nothing better than that!). It is truly a business of relationships at every stage. I enjoy the business side of agenting as much as the creative, and I think that all the positions I have held (and the many, many books I have read) have proven to be the perfect base for this career.

List some representative titles you have placed. Since I am a newer agent, I am still in the process of developing my list, but I have placed my first client's book — *The Life We Bury* by Allen Esken (Seventh Street Books, 2014).

Describe yourself as a person. What you see is what you get. I am pretty practical and direct, but true to my midwestern roots, I always try to be nice. I am passionate about my work and want nothing more than to support my clients and help them reach their goals. Professionally, I suppose it is the former project manager in me, but I am all about developing a plan, documenting that plan, and executing that plan so all parties know what is going on.

How would you describe the proverbial "client from hell," and what are the warning signs? As long as clients understand that I have other clients (and a personal life!), we are usually fine. I also treat all my clients as business professionals and partners in this endeavor, and I really need the same courtesy returned.

What do you think about self-publishing? Self-publishing is a good option for the writers who want to control and manage every aspect of their projects — hiring private editors, cover and book design, distribution, promotion, etc. — but it isn't for everyone.

Describe your job and what you like and don't like about it. My job is to be my client's advocate. Through the editorial process, submissions, contract negotiation, publishing, and career development, I am the go-to person for questions and for keeping the momentum moving forward. Whether the author is a debut author or seasoned veteran, each milestone is rewarding, and each stall is disappointing. We are in it together.

What does the "Big 5" mean to you? For many writers, success with the "Big 5" is the ultimate goal. Since my job is to support my clients, that becomes my ultimate goal for them. But for others, independent presses are truly a better fit — whether that is because of the types of books they write or the type of attention that a smaller press can give the clients and their books. Publishing is certainly not a "one size fits all" business.

What do you want to tell new/unpublished writers? It is wonderful to have people in your life that support your writing and love you, but it is also important to have beta readers that you trust to give you honest, helpful feedback on your project — these two groups are often mutually exclusive. It is nearly impossible to create a publishable novel in isolation (especially for first-time authors). Although you may decide to cherry-pick from the advice you receive (it is still your book after all!), it can be amazing what a fresh perspective can sometimes lead to. Take advantage of their feedback to help you tighten and polish your manuscript before you take your next step toward publishing.

What do you like reading, watching, and listening to? With literary/upmarket fiction as well as narrative nonfiction, I want to learn something new and feel like I have been immersed in a life and circumstance that the author has made compelling and engrossing. The characters' interiors need to come through in a way that I can understand their points of view — I don't have to agree with them, but it has to be completely believable and interesting. For commercial projects, I look for a well-paced page turner that has layers and keeps me guessing — a commercial manuscript that has too much backstory up front rarely works for me. When it comes to TV, I like shows that make me laugh or (am I really admitting this?) reality shows. I can't help myself.

Agent's name and contact info: Elizabeth K. Kracht, liz@kimberleycameron.com

Describe what you like to represent and what you won't represent. I'm interested in seeing both fiction and nonfiction projects. I would like to see more nonfiction projects cross my desk, such as narrative, humor, self-help, prescriptive, memoir, true crime, high-concept, or projects on spirituality or sexuality. In fiction, I'd like to see more women's fiction. I'm also drawn to new adult, mysteries, thriller, and historical. In general, my interests drive what I represent, so I'm broad in terms of what I'll look at.

In fiction, I rarely represent fantasy or science fiction. I also do not represent children's (with the exception of young adult), screenplays, or Christian fiction. In nonfiction, I do not represent business or finance.

What are the best ways for writers to pitch you? The best way for writers to pitch me is with a straightforward query, under 250 words, with no gimmicks. I also encourage writers to attend conferences to pitch me. Making a personal connection with an author is important to me.

When and where were you born? I'm a Leo, born on August 1, in San Jose, California.

Do you charge fees? No, our agency does not charge fees.

Describe your education and career history. I have a BA in technical writing. I started my career in publishing as a writer first, with the same ambitions as you: to get published. I made a decision to move to the Caribbean with my then boyfriend because I had the counterintuitive idea that the move would help my writing. I dreamed of writing on the beach in San Juan like Hunter S. Thompson. While in Puerto Rico, I worked for an English-language newspaper and found I liked working with others' writing as much as my own. I found if I was close to words, I was happy. When I moved back to the mainland US, I discovered that the only way into the publishing industry was through internships. I interned with a smart nonfiction publisher in California and was eventually hired. As I learned more, I wanted to see "how the other half lived" (agents) and, concurrently, began an internship with Kimberley Cameron & Associates. Kimberley opened her doors to me in 2010, and I've been agenting since. My education and experience in journalism, publicity, marketing, acquisitions, business, and law make this job a perfect fit for me. I have a lot to offer my authors.

Say something about your hobbies and personal interests. I'm very career focused right now, and reading and editing take up so much of my free time that hobbies have fallen by the wayside, sadly. For exercise, I run, and while I do, I like to geek out on the birds in Richardson Bay. I'm also a compulsive amateur sunset photographer. Nature and wildlife are of huge interest to me, as are spiritual topics. And I'm most comfortable on the planet when in water, underwater, diving.

Why and how did you become an agent? I became an agent because working in publishing is the perfect fit for me. I love working with authors and in a creative field. Working as an agent fulfills me on so many levels. I became an agent through an internship with Kimberley Cameron & Associates.

Would you do it over again, or something else? I would do it over again without doubt or hesitation.

List some representative titles you have placed. As of March 2014, my most recent sale has been *Lamentation* by Joe Clifford (Oceanview Publishing).

Describe yourself as a person. I'm a nice person. I'm very open and accessible to people. I'm a mix of grounded and free spirit. I also have a strong spiritual background, though I'm not affiliated with any church or organization. I like to laugh and am interested in other people and the world around me.

How would you describe the proverbial "client from hell," and what are the warning signs? The first warning sign for me is always an intuitive one, sometimes physical (that gut reaction). I've learned to listen to that part in me that takes pause for a second around a person, whether a potential client or new friend. If I have taken pause, no matter how good the project, I will not sign them. To me the pause signifies trouble down the road. Other warning signs are authors who spend too much time signing the agency agreement or who cross professional boundaries by emailing too frequently or by micromanaging.

What do you think about self-publishing? I think self-publishing is appropriate for some authors. There are many reasons an author chooses to self-publish. I wouldn't recommend self-publishing as a road into the traditional publishing industry if publicity and marketing are not an author's strong suit.

Do you like Amazon? As a person, I like the convenience of Amazon.com. As a professional, our agency is doing business with Amazon, and we consider all avenues when it comes to getting our authors published. Some of our authors do not want to be published by Amazon because many bookstores won't support books published through Amazon. For those authors considering self-publishing, many bookstores will not carry books that use Amazon's print-on-demand (POD) services. Of course, I don't like the gossip I've heard that Amazon wants to take out literary agents and publishers.

Do you believe in a "higher power"? Yes, but not necessarily through a traditional medium. I have a strong background in meditation. I am spiritual in nature, and this spirituality guides my life, though I'd be hard-pressed to put into words what my beliefs are. I take wisdom from many traditions and try to follow my heart. I also pay attention to what my dreams tell me.

What will agenting be like in 2020? I think it will be much the same as it is now, though maybe a little less confused. I can't imagine there will be another big technology jump in six years, but this comes from someone who resists some forms of technology (still don't read on a Kindle, but I'm trying to get there).

Describe your job and what you like and don't like about it. The most difficult thing about agenting, for me, is financial. Agenting is a lot like gambling. It's the perfect fit for me career-wise but not the wisest financial decision I've ever made. In the beginning, there's a bit of a learning curve. Combine this learning curve with an industry experiencing huge flux…Regardless, I'm confident I can make it work. The best thing about my job is working with my authors and colleagues, though I like all aspects of my job, even reading contracts. My authors are an extension of family to me; I get a lot of satisfaction through my interactions with my authors.

Do you miss the way the business "used to be"? I started in the industry during a time of change, so this landscape is what I know. I hear about how things "used to be" through Kimberley, who has a long legacy in publishing. I'm certainly glad I don't have to send hard-copy queries to editors and cart full manuscripts around in the back of my trunk to give to editors. But I do wish publishers had more cushion. Ultimately, I think change is a good thing. I'm sure there are still plenty of things that need to change in the industry, like returns.

What does the "Big 5" mean to you? Opportunity.

What do you want to tell new/unpublished writers? Go to conferences. Always work at improving your writing. Start working on your author platform now (website and social media). Know your genre and its accepted word count. Make sure each chapter is rich, with at least three things happening that drive the story and characters forward.

Do you like that everything has become largely digitized? I like the ease of the digital world for professional communication, but I'm so resistant to it when it comes to reading. I'm sensitive to machines, so I try to take breaks from them whenever possible, though I'm fairly glued to my phone. I want to protect my eyes.

What do you like reading, watching, and listening to? I'm mostly a nonfiction reader. The most recent books I've purchased (two for a friend) are *Your Body's Many Cries* *for Water*; *Tahoe beneath the Surface: The Hidden Stories of America's Largest Mountain Lake*; and *The Lakota Way of Strength and Courage: Lessons in Resilience from the Bow and Arrow*. I don't have a TV, but when I'm desperate, I watch things on my computer. I have recently become addicted to *Homeland* and *House of Cards*. In terms of music, I listen to rock, mostly, but like, and have been influenced by, all kinds of music. My brother recently turned me on to James Blake — good road-trip music.

Describe a book you would write. I'd love to write a humor/gift book. I have a children's picture book I plan to write with my mom. And I've got a memoir to write at some point.

Joker's wild: Weave your backstory in like fine lace. Don't use dialogue tags unless you need them. Avoid adverbs. Is enough happening in each chapter? Is your manuscript starting in the most active and compelling place?

Agent's name and contact info: Pooja Menon, 415-789-9191, pooja@kimberleycameron.com

Describe what you like to represent and what you won't represent. I represent both adult and young adult fiction. In adult fiction, I'm looking for literary fiction, commercial fiction, historical fiction, high-end women's fiction, mystery, thriller, suspense, dark psychological fiction, horror, and multicultural fiction. In young adult, I'm looking for literary fiction, commercial fiction with a big hook, contemporary (both darker and issue driven as well as lighthearted and romantic with a lot of heart), historical fiction (across all genres), mystery, thriller, suspense, horror, fantasy with a fresh premise, magical realism, and multicultural fiction. I also represent nonfiction, mostly narrative and memoir, travel memoir, books on journalism and other human-interest stories, as well as self-help/psychology books that give readers a fresh perspective on an already explored subject matter or an interesting perspective on a different subject matter that is unique and as yet unexplored.

I'm not looking for high sci-fi, high fantasy, chick lit, romance, or military fiction. I'm not overly fond of young adult paranormal romances; however, I'm willing to look at anything as long as the premise is fresh and the voice is strong.

What are the best ways for writers to pitch you? Begin with the category, genre, and word count of your book, then tell me about it. Just plain and simple, tell me the main premise; introduce me to the main characters and the main conflicts, and what's standing in their way; and then round it off by leaving things up in the air — this would encourage me to want to know more. Don't tell me your whole story; don't be abstract when talking about your book; don't tell me what you envision your book to be; and always come with two comparison titles for your book that have been published within the past 5 to 10 years, to give me an idea of the kind of audience and market you see for your book. Do take a deep breath and be calm!

When and where were you born? I was born in Kerala, India, on the 7th of February '87. I grew up in Dubai.

Do you charge fees? I don't charge fees for reading. Aside from the customary 15 percent (agent's commission), we do recoup all reasonable and verifiable expenses directly attributable to the sale of accepted works, including but not limited to postage, with a cap of $100 per work. Fees required for legal contract advice are split 50-50 by the agent and author, with a cap of $500. But we don't use legal services in cases where the advance offered by the publisher is less than $10,000.

Describe your education and career history. I got my BA in English literature and media studies from Nottingham Trent University and my MFA from Otis School of Art and Design; interned with Kimberley Cameron & Associates from 2011 to 2012; and became an agent in the fall of 2012. Currently building my list.

Say something about your hobbies and personal interests. Reading (lots of it!), traveling, watching movies, listening to music, etc.

Why and how did you become an agent? I became an agent in the fall of 2012 after a year-long internship at Kimberley Cameron & Associates.

Would you do it over again, or something else? Yes, over and over. I love my job. If I didn't love books so much, then I would probably be in a people-centric job, such as a social worker or a psychologist. But, fortunately, my job is wonderful, and I have no impulse to find another career path.

List some representative titles you have placed. I'm a fairly new agent, and currently I have projects out on submission, so am looking forward to having a different answer to this question in the near future.

Describe yourself as a person. As an agent, hardworking, optimistic, diplomatic, passionate about the industry I work in and my clients; have an insatiable appetite for good stories; organized; love the editorial part of my job as I'm also a creative person, and I love helping authors polish their diamonds to make them sparkle. I love to multitask and be challenged in whatever I do. Outside of my job, I'm the same, except I channel all the above attributes into whatever I'm doing, maybe on a much more relaxed scale.

How would you describe the proverbial "client from hell," and what are the warning signs? This is a hard one. In any agent-client relationship, it's important for both parties to hear what the other one has to say. It's also important for them to have an open and honest line of communication. Understand that there is a mature way to air disagreements, and then there is the unpleasant way, where feelings are expressed without concern for the way they come out, and that can sour things in a bad way; so this is something to be mindful of. Clients who do not believe in the above qualities, to me, tend to be hard to deal with (thankfully, I've had positive experiences so far).

I appreciate clients who are proactive about their work, who constantly search out ideas and are inspired and positive, who are willing to learn about the industry and understand that the process of publishing is not an overnight process and success takes time and an immense amount of patience and mental strength. There's only so much pushing your agent can do at a certain time. Know that agents are doing their best for their clients, but there is a time for things and a place. Show some trust and faith in your agent; they signed you up because they love your project. But also be mindful that they have other clients as well who require the same amount of attention you do. Constant emails and calls, suggestions on where to submit and whom to submit to (repeatedly), temper tantrums on why things aren't moving at the speed the author wants, and most importantly, fighting the revision process every step of the way — all this makes working together difficult and not the positive experience it's meant to be.

I understand that there are some parts of an author's book he or she won't feel comfortable changing; but give it a chance, hear your agent's suggestions, try it out, find out why the agent has suggested such changes, and then see how you feel once you've tried them out. If something is of utmost importance and you have a valid reason for not wanting to change it, be willing and positive about coming to a middle ground with your agent; they are objective readers who are aware of what the industry wants and doesn't want. Trust their judgment, and know that they will do their job as long as you are willing to be open and positive and respectful while doing yours.

What do you think about self-publishing? I believe these days authors have a variety of choices about how they want to go about publishing their book, so this is a great time to be an author. I'm all for self-publishing if the author decides that's the best outlet for their book. However, if an author does decide that self-publishing is the way to go, then they also need to understand that once they put their book out there, they need to stick it through to the end. They cannot give up (due to lack of sales, etc.) and approach agents in order to help them market their books or take their books out traditionally. That isn't what agents do, and if a book has meager sales, it's going to be hard to take that published book to editors to sell. So before they go down this path, they need to commit to seeing their baby through; they need to strategize and market and promote and go the whole way.

Do you like Amazon? I have neutral views on this.

Do you believe in a "higher power"? Yes, I do.

What will agenting be like in 2020? I think, as agents, we have to keep changing with the technological advancements. By 2020, depending on how much more advanced things get, the need for agents will be equally if not more important, and we will, like we've done today, adapt and change to accommodate the market and the current climate so we can work with our clients to find the best homes and the best outlets for their work.

Describe your job and what you like and don't like about it. I love all aspects of my job, from finding a manuscript out of the slush pile, to helping prep it for submission, to finding out there is strong interest in my project, to everything else that comes after that. Even reading contracts is a fun aspect of this wonderfully varied job. What I don't like: rejections. I don't like having to tell my hardworking, immensely talented clients that their projects are having a hard time finding homes, but I do love reassuring them that the market is a tough place and they have to believe in their writing despite the rejections. I fell in love with their writing; someone else will fall in love with it, too.

Do you miss the way the business "used to be"? I wouldn't be qualified to answer this.

What does the "Big 5" mean to you? The Big 5 is every author's dream. The industry is changing rapidly, and there are a LOT of amazing midlevel houses, as well as small houses, that are doing well, that put out books that are of amazing quality. So there are other options these days, but in a way, the Big 5 will always be the Big 5. Big names, big marketing budgets, big exposure, big distribution (not always, mind you)…but things are changing, and there's room for different kinds of big, even in small sizes, these days!

What do you want to tell new/unpublished writers? Keep at your dream. Do not give up. Rejection is something you'll have to combat every step of the way, even after you're published. So learn to take it with grace and with the intention of learning something from each one. Also, be aware of the market. I don't mean write according to the trends, but do keep track of what has been overdone, and write fresh, write actively, and write uniquely, with a voice that's unique to you.

Do you like that everything has become largely digitized? I think it's convenient that I can have 100 books on my Kindle to read at any time (until the power runs out) and from anywhere; however, I'm a book girl. I love having a book in my hand, feeling the cover, smelling the pages, running my hands under the words, marking words or sentences that strike me in any way…things you can't really do with a digital book.

What do you like reading, watching, and listening to? I love reading everything and anything as long as the plot is interesting and the voice captures me right away. With nonfiction, I love stories that have a personalized point of view, narrative, and memoir. I also love reading psychological self-help books and books about journalism and humanitarian ventures. I don't particularly enjoy chick lit and romances, or military fiction. But everything else I'm open to. With movies, too, I'm open to just about everything. I love quirky movies, commercial films, as well as literary films. I also enjoy foreign films. I find that in my job, since I read so much, I like to watch TV serials more than I watch movies. They're short and fast paced, I get invested in characters on a long-term basis, and I don't have to let them go in the space of three hours. I love that. With music, I love anything with a good beat. Music is mainly to suit the mood, so it depends on what mood I'm in!

Joker's wild: Excusez-moi?

Agent's name and contact info: Mary C. Moore, Twitter: @Mary_C_Moore, mary@kimberleycameron.com (I am NOT open to unsolicited submissions currently.)

Describe what you like to represent and what you won't represent. Literary fiction, fantasy, science fiction, romance.

What are the best ways for writers to pitch you? At a conference, tell me why you wrote the book, how long it is, what genre.

When and where were you born? '82, Oahu, Hawai'i.

Do you charge fees? No.

Describe your education and career history. BS in biology from UCSD; MFA in creative writing from Mills College. Field biologist, veterinarian assistant, SAT instructor, marketing research firm qualitative assistant, technical writer, copyeditor, managing editor, published author, literary agent.

Say something about your hobbies and personal interests. In my prepublishing life, I was a field biologist and zookeeper. Animals of any shape or form delight me. I also dance, ballet primarily.

Why and how did you become an agent? I started my career in publishing as a writer. After freelancing for two years as an editor and writer in nonliterary sectors, I began an internship with Kimberley Cameron & Associates with the desire to learn more about the literary business for my own writing. During the internship, I discovered a passion for helping others develop their manuscripts. Now I balance three jobs — author, editor, and agent — and find that the experience in each helps and supports the others.

Would you do it over again, or something else? Don't have enough experience to know the answer to that. Right now, agenting is still shiny and bright.

List some representative titles you have placed. New agent. Still shopping my first.

Describe yourself as a person. Creative and curious.

How would you describe the proverbial "client from hell," and what are the warning signs? Demanding of your time for small concerns. Egotistical. Unrealistic expectations of the amount of work others will do for them, especially when they are personally lazy.

What do you think about self-publishing? Any new avenue for writers is a good thing. However, it is something to think through carefully and educate yourself about before jumping into it. Also, don't query me with your self-published novel; it's like taking a hot cake out of the oven and asking me to bake it for you.

Do you like Amazon? Honestly, no opinion.

Do you believe in a "higher power"? Maybe.

What will agenting be like in 2020? Very electronic and extremely hands-on. Agents will not only be selling their clients to publishers but also be helping in the publishing process.

Describe your job and what you like and don't like about it. I love finding new manuscripts and developing them. I dislike rejecting queries.

Do you miss the way the business "used to be"? Too new to know the difference.

What does the "Big 5" mean to you? The first place I query my clients, but not the last.

What do you want to tell new/unpublished writers? Find a community. Writing is a lonely business; you need support.

Do you like that everything has become largely digitized? It's easier on the environment, harder on the eyes.

What do you like reading, watching, and listening to? Read: *Cosmic Banditos*, *The Master & Margarita*, anything fantasy with strong female sensibilities (Robin McKinley, Patricia McKillip, Anne McCaffrey). Watch: *Doctor Who*, *The Dick Van Dyke Show*, *Star Wars*, and *Orange Is the New Black*. Listen: Blues, Latin rhythms.

Describe a book you would write. I did write it; a few of them. I'm an author also.

Joker's wild: The ultimate day is the day *Doctor Who* has an episode with smart-ass unicorns in it.

THE KNIGHT AGENCY ❖ www.knightagency.net

570 East Avenue, Madison, GA 30650

Agent's name and contact info: Lucienne Diver, submissions@knightagency.net

Describe what you like to represent and what you won't represent. Fantasy, science fiction, romance, erotica, thriller, mystery/suspense, young adult and middle grade fiction.

What are the best ways for writers to pitch you? Be brilliant. An original concept and a unique voice with unflagging pacing will grip me every time.

When and where were you born? April 27, 1971; Baltimore, Maryland.

Do you charge fees? No, we do not charge any fees.

Describe your education and career history. Lucienne Diver joined TKA in 2008, after spending 15 years at New York City's prestigious Spectrum Literary Agency. With her sharp eye for spotting original new voices, Lucienne is one of the most well-respected agents in the industry. A lifelong book addict, she graduated summa cum laude from the State University of New York at Potsdam with dual majors in English/writing and anthropology. She thus came well equipped for her work as an agent. Over the course of her dynamic career she has sold over 700 titles to every major publisher and has built a client list of more than 40 authors spanning the commercial fiction genres, primarily in the areas of fantasy, science fiction, romance, mystery, and young adult fiction. Her authors have been honored with the RITA, National Readers' Choice Award, Golden Heart, and *Romantic Times* Reader's Choice and have appeared on the *New York Times* and *USA Today* bestseller lists. A publishing veteran, Lucienne has superb industry knowledge, numerous editor relationships, and a keen understanding of the foreign rights market. She is a member of the Association of Authors' Representatives (AAR), Romance Writers of America (RWA), Mystery Writers of America (MWA), and Science Fiction Writers of America (SFWA).

List some representative titles you have placed. The Great Library series by Rachel Caine; *Chicagoland Vampires* series by Chloe Neill; *Jane Yellowrock* series by Faith Hunter; *Cal Leandros* series by Rob Thurman; *The Sinful Scoundrels* series by Vicky Dreiling.

What do you like reading, watching, and listening to? I love anything by Joss Whedon. He's got a talent for perfectly melding dark and light, a well-developed sense of the absurd, an amazing flair for dialogue, and wonderful characters. That's what I look for in the books I represent as well. I'm a huge fan of the BBC series *Sherlock* and of anything involving psychology and suspense, like *Criminal Minds* and *The Following*.

Agent's name and contact info: Pamela Harty, submissions@knightagency.net

Describe what you like to represent and what you won't represent. I love romance, including contemporary, historical, romantic paranormal, and romantic suspense. Women's commercial fiction and young adult. And on the nonfiction side, health, narrative, relationships, memoir, business, parenting, and pop culture.

When and where were you born? July, Atlanta, GA.

Do you charge fees? We do not charge any fees.

Describe your education and career history. I started at the Knight Agency (TKA) after the birth of my second child. I was eager to work with my sister Deidre Knight after leaving a successful sales career. That was almost 14 years ago! I am a runner and occasional cyclist. My favorite place is the beach. I spend lots of time keeping up with my teenagers and, of course, reading.

Agent's name and contact info: Melissa Jeglinski, submissions@knightagency.net

Describe what you like to represent and what you won't represent. I represent romance: contemporary, historical, inspirational, suspense. Middle grade. Young adult. Women's fiction. Mystery: cozies and thrillers.

I do not represent memoir, nonfiction, poetry, or sci-fi/fantasy projects.

What are the best ways for writers to pitch you? Please send a query letter to our submissions email address, to my attention. The query should contain the genre and word count of the finished work, a few short paragraphs about the plot, and a little about the writer. Feel free to paste the first five pages of the manuscript in the body of the email. We do not open attachments. All queries are responded to within a month.

When and where were you born? Pittsburgh, Pennsylvania.

Do you charge fees? No, we do not charge any fees.

Describe your education and career history. After graduating with a BA in English from Clarion University of Pennsylvania, I took a job at Harlequin Enterprises. I worked there for 17 years as an editor. In 2008, I decided it was time for a change and began agenting with the Knight Agency.

Say something about your hobbies and personal interests. I try to read as much as possible to keep up with the current bestsellers, but to unwind I do a lot of different crafts. I also enjoy just hanging out with my family and friends. I'm also addicted to too many television shows.

Would you do it over again, or something else? I wish I'd gone to veterinary school; but I'd probably have 50 pets by now, so maybe the English degree was the perfect choice.

List some representative titles you have placed. *The Paper Gods* series by Amanda Sun; *Camp Fear* by Maggie K. Black; *Agent under Attack* by Lisa Childs; *H.E.A.R.T.* series by Shirlee McCoy.

What do you think about self-publishing? Self-publishing is an excellent avenue for some writers, and I support their choice. If, however, their first choice is to get an agent and sell their work to a traditional publisher, I urge them not to self-publish that work and then try to get an agent. I can't do much with a project that has already been self-published unless its sales are through the roof, and that isn't the norm. A new writer should really have a plan about what they want from their career before they make any commitment.

Do you like Amazon? I think any company that truly has no real competition should always be watched.

KRAAS LITERARY AGENCY

Agent's name and contact info: Irene Kraas, ikraas@yahoo.com

Describe what you like to represent and what you won't represent. I like innovative young adult, and adult thriller.

What are the best ways for writers to pitch you? Make sure you don't send me a generic email starting, "Dear Agent." Just send me a short query and the first five pages embedded in your email. I DO NOT open attachments (unless I request them).

When and where were you born? New York — I plead the fifth.

Do you charge fees? No fees except the standard 15 percent if the manuscript is sold.

Describe your education and career history. Master's degree. I have been in the business 24 years.

Say something about your hobbies and personal interests. I love to read, paint, travel, and eat!!

Why and how did you become an agent? I can't remember why, but I started reading manuscripts for a house in DC and then met a wonderful agent (Ann Tobias) who gave me great help.

Would you do it over again, or something else? I would definitely do it over but would have started when I was younger and actually living in New York.

List some representative titles you have placed. I have recently cut way back (semiretired) but have represented such authors as Janet Lee Carey, Hilari Bell, Chelsea Quinn Yarbro, Paula Paul, Sandra Worth, James Riley, Shirley Raye Redmond, and many others. Except for about 5 percent of my clients, I launched all first-timers. Some who are now on their 14th book.

Describe yourself as a person. I am a strong person with strong beliefs. I am always on the side of the author but try to help the author be realistic. This business is definitely not straightforward.

How would you describe the proverbial "client from hell," and what are the warning signs? One who won't believe me when I tell them what might work. Other than that, I plead the fifth (again).

What do you think about self-publishing? I'm for ebook publishing. But self-publishing a paper version smacks too much of a vanity press.

Do you like Amazon? Yes! It has given good (and bad) writers a vehicle to get their work "out there." New York publishers certainly aren't always right about their decisions.

Do you believe in a "higher power"? What's this question about?

What will agenting be like in 2020? More and more ebook publishing and less and less of hard copies. This has been the publishing trend for years, and unfortunately, the big houses did not work from a realistic business plan.

Describe your job and what you like and don't like about it. Even though I've cut way back, I have always loved agenting. It's a great thrill to sell new writers and see them succeed!

Do you miss the way the business "used to be"? In a way, I do. Mainly because there were more lines, and editors were more willing to take chances on new authors.

What does the "Big 5" mean to you? The big conglomerates who have swallowed the individual publishing houses.

What do you want to tell new/unpublished writers? Don't give up. If it's something you love to do, then do it!

Do you like that everything has become largely digitized? Not really. Sometimes I think I'm stuck back in the 20th century.

What do you like reading, watching, and listening to? I have various tastes in reading, from wonderful literary fiction to thriller (with lots else in between). I watch mostly the great shows on PBS (and there are plenty of them!!!). I love classical music and opera.

Describe a book you would write. Probably sci-fi, thriller, or the "great American novel." I guess that pretty much covers everything.

Joker's wild: I have to be honest and say I really have cut back and let my old clients move on with wonderful new agents. That said, I am still on the lookout (in a small way) for new talent. After 24 years, it's really hard to find something fresh!

THE LA LITERARY AGENCY ❖ www.laliteraryagency.com

PO Box 46370, Los Angeles, CA 90046, 323-654-5288

Agent's name and contact info: Maureen Lasher, maureen@laliteraryagency.com

Describe what you like to represent and what you won't represent. I like to represent the same kinds of books that I buy for myself at a bookstore. At the top of my list is narrative nonfiction, which is storytelling. The subjects are eclectic and difficult to put in one category. A few examples:

- *Light My Fire* by Ray Manzarek (Putnam). With perfect recall, Ray reveals how he founded the Doors with Jim Morrison and takes us on their personal and musical trips, many of them fueled by drugs and alcohol. Reviewers called it "spellbinding," "best rock bio of the year," "striking personal memoir." Ray wrote his first draft in pencil on yellow legal pads.

- *Beyond the Limits* by Stacy Allison (Little, Brown). Stacy was the first American woman to crest Mount Everest. This story became our sample chapter. After years of preparation and several failed attempts, Stacy and her two companion climbers were just hours away from the top of Everest. Without any warning, two of three Sherpa guides suddenly turned around and headed down the mountain because of the escalating dangerous weather. They left the remaining climbers, facing cold and storms, with enough oxygen for only one person to attempt to reach the summit.

- *Where the Money Is* by William Rehder (W.W. Norton). CBS News described FBI special agent Rehder as "America's secret weapon in the war against bank robbers." The review (from *Booklist*) describes what he was able to capture in his book: "unforgettable characters and unbelievable incidents more exciting than any movie or miniseries." And the highest praise came from *Publishers Weekly*: "should become a standard in the genre."

- *Uppity* by Bill White (Grand Central). Bill had three careers in baseball: Major League player, voice of the New York Yankees for eighteen years, and president of the National League for five years (the first African American to reach that level in any sport). In his book, he told many personal stories about the sport and the business, holding nothing back. "Brutally frank…a truly controversial baseball memoir that will not be easily forgotten" (*Publishers Weekly*). "A hard-hitting take-no-prisoners assessment of baseball over the past sixty years…entertains from cover to cover" (*New York Daily News*).

- *Never Too Late* by Bobby DeLaughter (Scribner). DeLaughter, a criminal prosecutor, solved the mystery of Medgar Evers's murder thirty years after the crime. By chance, he found the missing weapon in the closet of a judge — his father-in-law. The judge wasn't hiding the gun; he didn't know that he had the crucial lost piece of evidence in the case.

- *I Am Roe* by Norma McCorvey (Harper Collins). You never know where you will find a wonderful book. When our daughter was in college, she went to a lecture given by Norma McCorvey (a.k.a. Jane Roe of *Roe v. Wade*). Nobody had ever asked Norma to tell her story. A small slice of history: Norma learned about the historic Supreme Court decision in *Roe v. Wade* when she opened up the Dallas daily newspaper lying on her doorstep and read the front-page article about herself.

Fiction is both easier and harder to define. Like everyone in publishing, we long for compelling, beautifully written novels. It can be historical, contemporary, literary, commercial, mystery, suspense, thriller, or unique. It's difficult to sell a first novel, but it happens every day.

Our website will give you a broader overview of the books that the agency has represented.

Describe your education and career history. Following my graduation from Brown University with a concentration in history, I moved to New York and got my first job at Prentice Hall, publisher of college textbooks. I began as an advertising copywriter and eventually was part of a team of three, supervising a staff of twenty-six. The company was based in New Jersey, and for five years I commuted from Manhattan, over the George Washington Bridge, to Fort Lee. When I was offered a position at Random House, which was within walking distance from my apartment, I took it. As associate manager of advertising, I marketed Random House titles to schools, colleges, and libraries. Then I became director of advertising and publicity for Liveright, a small literary publisher with a remarkable history and backlist. They were the first to publish Sigmund Freud, e.e. cummings, Ezra Pound, William Faulkner, and on and on. Today Liveright is an imprint of W. W. Norton — one of the last independent publishers.

Even though I loved New York, I moved to Los Angeles when my husband, Eric, became CEO of Nash Publishing. It was then the largest general publisher west of Chicago but was eventually merged into extinction.

Since Eric and I had extensive publishing experience, from Los Angeles we launched an independent imprint with Houghton Mifflin Company, based in Boston. Our imprint focused on commercial fiction (several were *New York Times* bestsellers) and travel guides, a series which grew to over 20 titles. At the same time, we were reading many excellent manuscripts that we had to pass on because they didn't fit the profile of our imprint. This led to the creation of the LA Literary Agency. (Our first sale was to my alma mater, Random House.)

Say something about your hobbies and personal interests. I've had some interesting side trips from agenting. When I moved to Los Angeles, I started designing and making jewelry — a hobby that requires a blowtorch and a drill. Invited to a party in New York, I wore as much of my jewelry as I could put on — earrings, two silver cuffs, three rings, a necklace, and a belt buckle. A beautiful woman approached me to inquire where I had purchased the pieces. Her name was Vera Wang, then accessories editor at *Vogue*. For the next year, my jewelry was featured every month on the editorial pages of *Vogue* and sold in major department stores such as Bloomingdale's. I enjoyed creating jewelry as a hobby but didn't see it as a career, so I returned to publishing. Today my major hobby is knitting. I've been in love with it since high school. A few years ago, I coauthored a knitting book, *Teen Knitting Club* (Artisan). You can probably find it on a remainder table.

Would you do it over again, or something else? If I could time-travel and graduate from Brown this year (instead of when female graduates were recruited as buyers for department stores), I would pursue an advanced degree in psychology or art history or graphic design. I've always been in love with books, so publishing was a natural direction for me at the time.

When our daughter graduated from college, we wanted her to continue her education. She could become a lawyer, an ophthalmologist, a veterinarian! Instead she became a television writer. During five seasons, she was an executive producer/writer for *Gossip Girl*. One of the episodes she wrote was about publishing, and it featured the president of Simon & Schuster. They cast Jonathan Karp, who really is the president of Simon & Schuster. He was wonderful in the role.

What do you want to tell new/unpublished writers? The internet has opened the floodgates and made it more complicated for writers and agents to find each other. When it's obvious to me that I'm one of scores of agents who have been sent the same email, I'm reluctant to spend any time on it. Nevertheless, I have connected with writers on the internet. A few months ago, I received an email from an academic who remembered me from a writers' conference where we met years ago. Today he lives in Great Britain and is an international expert on Antarctica, and we're beginning to work on his proposal. I'm also representing two novelists who emailed me blind inquiry letters and sample pages. One is a suspense novel set in Amsterdam, where the author lives. The second is in development with a producer whose last movie was nominated for an Academy Award.

Don't give up on the internet, but here's some advice on how to use it: Try to personalize your approach to an agent. Read the acknowledgments in books that are similar to yours and email a note to the agent, referring to the title. Ask everybody you know if they have access to anyone in the publishing world and try to get, at least, an email introduction. Look at your college alumni listings and use that shared experience as an introduction. Don't open your letter with "Dear Sir."

How would you describe the proverbial "client from hell," and what are the warning signs? This is an extreme example, but it happened. Eric and I were scheduled to be on an agent panel in Los Angeles, sponsored by New York–based Volunteer Lawyers for the Arts. The event was widely publicized. Then we and the volunteer lawyers group in New York received anonymous letters explaining why we weren't qualified to be on the panel. The letter was also filled with anti-Semitic rhetoric and physical threats. The authorities, thankfully, took it seriously. They had a plan. Two law enforcement officers went to the conference in plain clothes and when the moderator said that we couldn't be there, a man walked out, clearly angry. The officers followed him and brought him in for questioning. It turned out that we had turned down his novel. If the person is already a client and I want to take a Valium before each phone conversation, I try to end the professional relationship as quickly as possible. Today it's easy for someone who feels ignored or insulted or unhappy to use the internet to vent their anger at you. Hopefully, you can spot that kind of person early and not get involved.

Describe your job and what you like and don't like about it. Most of the time, I work as an editor, and that's what I truly enjoy. For nonfiction, it's essential to have a stellar, best-on-the-editor's-desk proposal. I work editorially with our clients on the proposal, which is harder to write than the book; but when you have it right, you will have a blueprint for your book. In 20 or 30 or 40 pages, the proposal has to do it all. What's the best way to define your book? What will you cover in each chapter? Is the overview effective? What is the best structure? Are the sample chapters good enough? What qualifies you to write this book?

Working with fiction is quite different. Publishers make their decisions based on reading the complete novel. Right now I'm working with two novelists I met through the internet. We had no personal connection, but I was taken by their submission letter. I'm not writing or copyediting (punctuation, spelling, etc.) but am working with them as an editor on plot, characters, dialogue, and pacing.

What do you think about self-publishing? If all you care about is to see your book in print, go for it. If you believe that when your book is in print, the world will find it, please reevaluate your conclusion. If you have a huge success, you've won. Winners are rare.

Do you like Amazon? Answering as a customer: Yes, I like Amazon. I listen to books on my iPhone, buy books on my Kindle and from iBooks, and read them on my iPad. I'm a member of Amazon Prime and joined audible.com six years ago — before Amazon bought the company. But I go to Barnes & Noble at The Grove in Los Angeles about once a week. Their children's section is a playground with books. The display tables highlight books by category, like historical fiction or biography, and it's easy to find some I may have missed. They encourage you to sit in their café with a cappuccino and look through a pile of new titles. Every year, I renew my membership card. If Barnes & Noble closes, I'll be devastated.

Answering as an agent: (1) The publishing business is changing, but I don't have a clue how it will sort itself out. (2) Amazon is a major force. (3) It will be a huge loss to book lovers and the publishing industry if Barnes & Noble doesn't survive because of Amazon. (4) Books aren't going away.

LARSEN POMADA LITERARY AGENTS ❖ www.larsenpomada.com

Agent's name and contact info: Elizabeth Pomada, larsenpoma@aol.com

Describe what you like to represent and what you won't represent. I represent most kinds of fiction, literary and genre, memoir, narrative nonfiction.

Won't handle science fiction and fantasy, young adult, children's books, poetry.

What are the best ways for writers to pitch you? After reading our website, they can send the first 10 pages and a 2-page synopsis of their finished, polished book as an email letter with no attachments.

When and where were you born? I was born in NYC before the earth turned.

Do you charge fees? No.

Describe your education and career history. After graduating from Cornell in 1962, I worked at Holt, Rinehart & Winston, David McKay, and the Dial Press. Moved to San Francisco in 1970 and started our agency in 1972.

Say something about your hobbies and personal interests. We go to Nice every September, and I love to read and shop at flea markets.

Why and how did you become an agent? I became an agent because there was no publisher in San Francisco to hire me and I had to find work. An employment agency who represented writers and artists told me I'd never find a job and then said, "By the way, all these people send me their books, and I have no idea what to do with them." So I went into her office every Tuesday and plowed through the piles and found two novels I wanted to handle. One turned out to be a *New York Times* bestseller, the other was published posthumously — and we were off.

Would you do it over again, or something else? Yes.

List some representative titles you have placed. *Red* by Kate Kinsey; *Raven* by Tim Reiterman (to Octavia Spencer as a movie); *Love on the Run* by Katharine Kerr; *The Forgotten Queen* by D. L. Bogdan; *The Seduction of Lady Phoebe* by Ella Quinn.

Describe yourself as a person. I'm a hardworking romantic, always up for something new. I don't suffer fools gladly.

How would you describe the proverbial "client from hell," and what are the warning signs? The client from hell feels he knows more about publishing than I do and argues. Wants things his way but does not do the work needed to be a success.

What do you think about self-publishing? I think it's a great way to get started and to help build your platform.

Do you like Amazon? Amazon is the evil empire and may be the ruination of the publishing world.

Do you believe in a "higher power"? Absolutely.

What will agenting be like in 2020? We'll be doing more, exploring new ways to do things. It will be more challenging and more rewarding.

Describe your job and what you like and don't like about it. As an agent, I read hundreds of queries to find that one star, and then I read dozens of complete manuscripts to (hopefully) fall in love. I like the fact that I'm my own boss. I don't like the fact that the piles never end.

Do you miss the way the business "used to be"? Yes.

What does the "Big 5" mean to you? The "Big 5" are Penguin Random House, Harper Collins, Simon & Schuster, Hachette, and Macmillan.

What do you want to tell new/unpublished writers? Do your homework. Practice your craft. Don't submit anything before it's ready to be seen.

Do you like that everything has become largely digitized? No.

What do you like reading, watching, and listening to? I like women's books — historical and romance. I watch *Grey's Anatomy* and old movies. I listen to classical music in the morning and jazz in the afternoon — and prefer show music.

Describe a book you would write. A historical novel set in Nice.

Joker's wild: We say no, no, no, all the time — but are delighted to fall in love with something new and different.

LINDA KONNER LITERARY AGENCY

10 West 15th Street, Suite 1918, New York, NY 10011, ldkonner@cs.com

Agent's name and contact info: Linda Konner, ldkonner@cs.com

Describe what you like to represent and what you won't represent. I represent adult nonfiction, especially prescriptive nonfiction (health, self-help, relationships, parenting, personal finance, popular psychology). Also some pop culture, celebrity memoir, popular science, business narrative, cookbooks. All of the above MUST be written by or with a top expert in the field with a substantial author platform.

I do not represent fiction, children's, religion, memoir.

What are the best ways for writers to pitch you? Email, including a brief author bio and a brief book summary. If I'm interested, I will request a full proposal plus one or two sample chapters.

When and where were you born? Brooklyn, NY, in the 1900s.

Do you charge fees? Onetime expenses fee collected only if/when I sell the book to a publisher.

Describe your education and career history. Brooklyn College (BA), Fordham University (MA). Served as a features editor at *Seventeen*, *Redbook*, and *Woman's World*; editor in chief of *Weight Watchers Magazine* and founding editor/editor in chief of *Richard Simmons & Friends* newsletter. Author or coauthor of eight books, including *The Last Ten Pounds* and *Why Can't a Man Be More Like a Cat?*

Say something about your hobbies and personal interests. Theater, travel, poker, *Law & Order* reruns.

Why and how did you become an agent? I was tired of being an author and an editor yet wanted to remain in publishing. I had also negotiated a couple of my own book deals and had many friends who were authors.

Would you do it over again, or something else? Would definitely do it again; it's been my best career of all.

List some representative titles you have placed. *The Calorie Myth* (*New York Times* bestseller) by Jonathan Bailor; *How to Fake Real Beauty* by celebrity makeup artist Ramy Gafni; *Tapping into Wealth* by Margaret M. Lynch with Daylle Deanna Schwartz; *Plant-Powered for Life* by Sharon Palmer, RD; *80/20 Running* by Matt Fitzgerald; *The Fear Reflex* by Joseph Shrand, MD, with Leigh Devine; *Own Your Game* by Yasmin Davidds with Ann Bidou; *A Sweet Taste of History* by Walter Staib.

Describe yourself as a person. Fun-loving but serious about my work.

How would you describe the proverbial "client from hell," and what are the warning signs? Doesn't follow directions; emails incessantly; doesn't meet publisher's deadlines; worries needlessly; has unrealistic expectations about what his or her book is worth.

What do you think about self-publishing? It's proven successful for a small number of writers; but I'm wedded to the traditional model of author-agent-publisher, and most authors are still eager to be a part of that arrangement.

Do you believe in a "higher power"? You mean like Amazon? No.

Describe your job and what you like and don't like about it. I love the independence of making decisions on behalf of my clients and myself. I love most of the authors and editors I work with. I love seeing good books come together. Not very much I don't like.

Do you miss the way the business "used to be"? No, because I came to the agenting business relatively late (in 1996), so I don't know what I've missed! I feel lucky to be doing this now.

What do you want to tell new/unpublished writers? Don't get discouraged in your quest to find an agent. If you haven't tried 50–100 agents, you haven't looked hard enough.

Do you like that everything has become largely digitized? No.

What do you like reading, watching, and listening to? Novels from the turn of the 20th century, but also some more contemporary ones as well as some biographies; watching theater (I attend about 100 times a year with my theater-critic boyfriend); listening to my *Kind of Blue* CD nightly while reading for pleasure.

Describe a book you would write. *Living Apart and Loving It*, based on my successful 36-year relationship.

LINDA ROGHAAR LITERARY AGENCY, LLC ❖

www.lindaroghaar.com

133 High Point Drive, Amherst, MA 01002, 413-256-1921, contact@lindaroghaar.com

Agent's name and contact info: Linda L. Roghaar, AAR member, 413-256-1921, linda@lindaroghaar.com

Describe what you like to represent and what you won't represent. I am most interested in nonfiction that is an extension of the author's life work.

    I seldom handle fiction; never represent science fiction or horror.

What are the best ways for writers to pitch you? A great query letter via email.

When and where were you born? I'm a Massachusetts native, born on September 11.

Do you charge fees? No.

Describe your education and career history. Educated at Arlington (MA) High School, Miami University (OH), and Vanderbilt University. I began my career in the 1970s, when I worked in a library and then a bookstore. I've been in the business ever since, as a bookstore chain field rep (Paperback Booksmith), publisher's sales manager, national accounts sales and marketing manager for independent presses, and head of an independent publishers' rep group. I have been an agent since 1996.

Say something about your hobbies and personal interests. Very interested in genealogy and all things creative.

Why and how did you become an agent? I love making the connection. First it was between the bookstore customer and the book; then between the publisher and the bookstore; now between the author and the publisher. I opened my agency in 1996.

Would you do it over again, or something else? I have always loved books and have loved the business since my first job volunteering in a small library in Hartland, Vermont. Once I began work in a bookstore, I was hooked. Also, I can't do anything else.

List some representative titles you have placed. *The Amazing Thing about the Way It Goes: Stories of Tidiness, Self-Esteem, and Other Things I Gave Up On* by Stephanie Pearl-McPhee (Andrews McMeel); *Adventures in Yarn Farming: Four Seasons on a New England Fiber Farm* by Barbara Parry (Shambhala/Roost); *Crafting a Colorful Home* by Kristin Nicholas (Shambhala/Roost); *JAMerica: The History of the Jam Band and Festival Scene* by Peter Conners (Da Capo/Perseus); *Fierce with Age: Chasing God and Squirrels in Brooklyn* by Carol Orsborn (Turner); *Knit to Flatter: The Only Instructions You'll Ever Need to Knit Sweaters That Make You Look Good and Feel Great* by Amy Herzog (Stewart Tabori and Chang/Melanie Falick); several craft titles on knitting, sewing, etc.

Describe yourself as a person. Friendly, enthusiastic, love to read.

How would you describe the proverbial "client from hell," and what are the warning signs? An author who wants to second-guess my every move and likes to micromanage.

What do you think about self-publishing? It certainly has its place in our world. It can be well or badly done, though.

Do you like Amazon? Yes and no. Can't explain!

What will agenting be like in 2020? Agents will still be making connections and getting quality material into the right hands.

Describe your job and what you like and don't like about it. I love it except for the rejections!

Do you miss the way the business "used to be"? Not really.

What does the "Big 5" mean to you? Random/Penguin, Harper, Hachette, all those headquartered/affiliated at 175 Fifth Avenue, S&S.

What do you want to tell new/unpublished writers? Don't be afraid of criticism. Develop a realistic attitude and a thick skin. Hang in there.

Do you like that everything has become largely digitized? For the most part, yes.

What do you like reading, watching, and listening to? Fiction, PBS, bluegrass, and rock and roll.

Describe a book you would write. Oh, no, not for me. I'm a reader, not a writer.

LIPPINCOTT MASSIE MCQUILKIN ❖ www.lmqlit.com

27 West 20th Street, Suite 305, New York, NY 10011, 212-352-2055

Agent's name and contact info: Laney Katz Becker, laney@lmqlit.com, 212-352-2055

Describe what you like to represent and what you won't represent. Fiction: I gravitate toward anything well suited to book club discussion; and I am a sucker for a fresh voice and well-defined characters. I also enjoy smart, psychological thrillers and novels of suspense. Nonfiction: I'm always on the prowl for narrative, especially from journalists or experts. I am open to practical nonfiction, memoir, and stories about fascinating subjects that teach me something new and/or expose me to different ideas, cultures, and people who make a difference in the world — but only if the author has a strong national platform.

I do NOT represent romance, cozy mysteries, sci-fi, fantasy, paranormal, or dystopian fiction, nor do I handle young adult, children's, middle grade, or poetry.

What are the best ways for writers to pitch you? Email is the best (and only) way that writers should reach out to me. I read all my own queries, and I always reply. (It might take a while, but I get to them all!) I'm proud to say that I've found many of my favorite authors in the slush pile. For fiction, authors are encouraged to include 10 pages or so in the body of their email query. For nonfiction, send the whole proposal.

When and where were you born? Toledo, Ohio.

Do you charge fees? Never.

Describe your education and career history. I graduated from Northwestern University and moved to NYC. My background is as a writer. I started as a copywriter at the ad agency J. Walter Thompson. Over the next two decades, I continued my career as a copywriter (both on-staff at some of New York's best-known agencies and also as a freelancer). I also worked as a freelance journalist; my articles appeared in more than 50 magazines, including *Self*, *Health*, *Seventeen*, and *First for Women*. I am also an award-winning author of both fiction and nonfiction. Somewhere along the way, I decided that spending seven hours a day in my basement writing books was too solitary for me. I wanted to use my marketing, writing, and reading skills in a new and different way. The agenting world allowed me to do just that — and it's never, ever solitary! Prior to joining LMQ, I was an agent at Markson Thoma Literary Agency and Folio Literary Management. My debut authors have made the *New York Times*, national, and international bestsellers lists. They have also been selected as Target Book Club picks and picked for the B&N Discover Great New Writers program.

Say something about your hobbies and personal interests. I'm a tennis fan and a tennis player. I'm a baseball fan and *so* not a player. I like to sew and do almost anything remotely creative — except cook, which people tell me is creative. I don't believe them.

Why and how did you become an agent? Being an agent allows me to do all the things I love to do most: read, edit, talk books, meet interesting people, discover new talent, and help make people's dreams come true. (Cinderella's fairy godmother has nothing on me!)

Would you do it over again, or something else? The reason I've worn so many different hats (all related to writing) is because I've changed and managed my career to coincide with my other priorities, like raising a family. I became an agent because it was the best way to use my skills and indulge in my passions — and it still is!

List some representative titles you have placed. I represent *Obedience* and *Dominance* by *New York Times* and internationally bestselling author Will Lavender; *The Promise of Stardust* by internationally bestselling author Priscille Sibley; *Cemetery Girl*, *The Hiding Place*, *Never Come Back*, and *The Forgotten Girl* by nationally bestselling author David Bell; *The Kings of Colorado* by B&N Discover Great New Writers author David E. Hilton; *The Secrets of Mary Bowser* and *Juliet's Nurse* by Target Book Club–pick author Lois Leveen; *The Crying Tree* by internationally bestselling and B&N Discover Great New Writers author Naseem Rakha; *Life's That Way* by B&N Discover Great New Writers author Jim Beaver; *I Love Mondays* and *Seeking Happily Ever After* by nationally bestselling author and award-winning documentary filmmaker Michelle Cove.

How would you describe the proverbial "client from hell," and what are the warning signs? Defensive writers who don't want to revise, and view agents simply as gatekeepers to editors. I'm also not a fan of writers who fail to say thank you. Writers who, because of my writing background, expect me to do their work for them because "You know how to do this" are also writers I try to avoid. And finally, writers who immediately send back revisions, rather than taking time to let things sit, reread what they've written, and then — only then — once they're certain their work can't be any better, send it back to me for my review.

What do you think about self-publishing? I don't think most writers understand self-publishing. They hear stories of authors "hitting it big" and assume it will happen to them, too. It's like winning the lottery. Yes, it happens, but it's not a business plan. Writers who self-publish should have realistic expectations and a plan for reaching readers.

What will agenting be like in 2020? If you lend me your crystal ball, I'll be happy to answer that.

Describe your job and what you like and don't like about it. The best part of my job is helping people attain their dreams. For some writers, the dream might be to be published for the first time "by a real publisher." For other writers, the dream might be to grow their careers or their readership. Whatever it is, I enjoy being part of it. But what I really love is finding that jewel in the slush pile, and working with the author to polish it up and get it ready for submission. What I don't like about the business? Rejection. I know, I know. I'm supposed to get used to it, but I don't. Every time an editor passes on a project, it's disappointing. It's especially disappointing when the editor loves a project but isn't given the green light in-house. Then we're both miserable! But then, there's that glorious moment when the offers come in, and I find myself thinking, "Who cares about those editors who passed? Their loss!"

What do you want to tell new/unpublished writers? Writing is hard work and involves lots of revisions. If you aren't prepared to revise, I'm not the right agent for you.

What do you like reading, watching, and listening to? Favorite movie: *Apollo 13*. Favorite TV series: *The West Wing*. Favorite book: I don't have one; I have too many. Favorite music: If I tell you I've got the sound track to the Broadway musical *Wicked* on my iPhone but also Rob Thomas and Maroon 5, does that help?

Describe a book you would write. Been there, done that. More than once! Now my time and attention are spent working with authors to make *their* books the best they can be, and then finding a great home for them!

Agent's name and contact info: Shannon O'Neill, shannon@lmqlit.com

Describe what you like to represent and what you won't represent. Nonfiction: narrative, reported memoir, popular science, intellectual history, current affairs, business. Fiction: literary, upmarket commercial.

NO sci-fi, fantasy, horror, children's.

What are the best ways for writers to pitch you? Email.

When and where were you born? Baltimore, 1981.

Do you charge fees? No.

Describe your education and career history. I graduated with honors from Dartmouth College and earned a master's in writing from Johns Hopkins. A native Washingtonian, I still call the capital home. One of my favorite haunts growing up was Politics and Prose, and I later found myself working as a bookseller and marketing manager for the landmark independent bookstore. I spent six years at the Sagalyn Agency as agent and editorial director working with leading thinkers, journalists, and bestselling writers and joined LMQ as an agent in January 2014.

Say something about your hobbies and personal interests. I am an avid long-distance runner, love to travel, and play the piano tolerably.

Why and how did you become an agent? I've always loved the written word. When I realized that publishing was an industry and that one could actually be involved in the genesis of a book and in helping talented writers reach an audience, I knew that was what I wanted to do.

Would you do it over again, or something else? Would absolutely do it again.

Describe yourself as a person. Persistent, creative, love to learn, hardworking, sometimes stubborn, adventurous.

What do you think about self-publishing? Glad that there are more openings for writers to find their readers.

Do you like Amazon? I hate what it has done to book pricing or to authors' livelihoods. I love getting my stuff delivered in two days.

What do you want to tell new/unpublished writers? The business is incredibly tough. Don't let that stop you from creating the work that you feel called to write. Truly distinct voices and truly talented writers carve a path through the jungle of publishing.

LITERARY SERVICES, INC. ❖ www.literaryservicesinc.com

PO Box 888, Barnegat, NJ 08005

Agent's name: John Willig

Describe what you like to represent and what you won't represent. Future bestsellers ☺; fresh, provocative, counterintuitive, well-researched, and well-written presentations. I work primarily in nonfiction categories, with a strong focus in business, finance, personal growth, history, science and technology, psychology, politics, and current events; also interested in historical fiction (mystery/thriller/literary).

What are the best ways for writers to pitch you? Per our website and submissions section, a one-page outline that can be sent via email.

When and where were you born? New York, New York.

Do you charge fees? No.

Describe your education and career history. Graduated from Brown University in 1976 and have worked in publishing for 37 years, starting in academic publishing and then going to professional/trade as an executive editor before founding our agency in 1991.

Say something about your hobbies and personal interests. Spending time with my two sons; enjoy cycling and exploring "new worlds"; collecting antiquarian books, art, and antiques; outdoor festivals of all kinds; quiet time reading "a story well told."

Why and how did you become an agent? To be of better service to writers (hence Literary Services) as their advocate, coach, and counsel. With my "inside" publishing and editorial (which includes legal and financial) experience, I felt I could provide writers and clients expert advice and guidance on all aspects of the publishing process.

Would you do it over again, or something else? Yes.

List some representative titles you have placed. *Leading with Your Legacy in Mind* by Andrew Thorn; *75 Habits for a Happy Marriage* by Ashley Davis Bush; *Speaking Politics* by Chuck McCutcheon and David Marks; *Leadership Conversations* by Alan Berson and Richard Stieglitz; *Joy Inc.* by Richard Sheridan; *Destination Mars* and *Curiosity* by Rod Pyle; *Investing in Energy* by Michael Thomsett; *Creating Your Future the Peter Drucker Way* by Bruce Rosenstein; *Master Negotiation Secrets* by Molly Fletcher; *Restoring Valor* by Doug Sterner; *The Entrepreneurial Equation* by Carol Roth.

Describe yourself as a person. Each day trying to be a good man, father, partner, friend, neighbor, colleague, living a compassionate and honest life.

How would you describe the proverbial "client from hell," and what are the warning signs? Hopefully, they do not become clients. I feel being an agent is also being "of service" to publishers, representing high-quality professionals with integrity and character and (please) a sense of humor and humility…Typically, if you are strident in your views, have unrealistic expectations, do not respect the professional experience of editors, tend to be disorganized and increasingly lack focus and discipline in your writing schedules/obligations, you will become hellish to work with for everyone.

What do you think about self-publishing? Walt Whitman self-published the original version of *Leaves of Grass* and with each new printing added new poems…a lesson in quality which is oftentimes lacking with self-publishers. A few years ago, I established our content coaching services (see website) for writers you do want to self-publish for many valid reasons. Having professionals provide marketing (which begins before a single word is written), editorial, design, and production expertise and experience will significantly improve the overall "product"…which has led agents like myself and others and publishing pros to respect your efforts and propose working together, perhaps for greater worldwide distribution of your work. It's a great country we are blessed to live and work in, so if someone wants to self-publish, all the resources are available to do it well.

Do you like Amazon? Yes…they sell books.

Do you believe in a "higher power"? Besides Jeff Herman? ☺ Yes.

What will agenting be like in 2020? "Predictions are hard, especially when they involve the future." — Yogi Berra

Describe your job and what you like and don't like about it. Agents can wear many hats, working as honest brokers of talent and intellectual property; proposal and content advisers; legal experts; financial deal makers; "sherpas" bringing our clients to their next level of success and sharing in the achievement; cheerleaders, champions for our clients, and sometimes even therapists who need to dispense tough love along with all the pats on the back.

Do you miss the way the business "used to be"? Why? Ever onward.

What does the "Big 5" mean to you? Consolidation and expansion in publishing are like the tides…Since 2008 there have been fewer buyers/imprints for all of us, leading to real supply-and-demand challenges/issues. New opportunities with new indie publishers are always occurring in this industry due to consolidation.

What do you want to tell new/unpublished writers? Be a student…do your homework…research…put your hours in (perhaps less than 10,000 per Macklemore but damn close)…study the craft…subscribe to *Writer's Digest*…respect professionals.

Do you like that everything has become largely digitized? No, but I lose no sleep over it.

What do you like reading, watching, and listening to? Wide range of interests in reading and favorite authors, ranging from mystery/crime to literary fiction; HBO and Showtime; my playlist is fun and eclectic.

Describe a book you would write. *The Sun Also Rises* or something a bit more recent, *Rules of Civility*.

Joker's wild: "Fame is a Vapor, Popularity an Accident, Riches take Wings, only one thing endures and that is Character" (Horace Greeley)…"and a great book" (J.W.).

L. PERKINS AGENCY ❖ www.lperkinsagency.com

Agents' names and contact info:
Lori Perkins, lperkinsagency@yahoo.com;
Sandy Lu, sandy@lperkinsagency.com;
Tish Beaty, tish@lperkinsagency.com

Describe what you like to represent and what you won't represent. Lori Perkins is taking on very few clients, but when she does, she is interested in erotic romance, erotica, and horror. Sandy Lu is most interested in literary fiction, mysteries, thriller, young adult, and urban fantasy. Tish Beaty is the editor who discovered E L James for the Writer's Coffee Shop Publishing House, so she is most interested in erotic romance, romance, erotica, young adult, and new adult fiction.

What are the best ways for writers to pitch you? Brilliant query or meeting me at a conference.

When and where were you born? Lori Perkins was born in New York City in the '60s.

Do you charge fees? No.

Describe your education and career history. I (Lori) went to the Bronx High School of Science and then NYU, where I majored in journalism. At 22, I started a local newspaper in Upper Manhattan. I became a literary agent at Barbara Lowenstein Assoc. and went out on my own in the late '80s. I was an adjunct professor at NYU, teaching journalism and writing for 20 years (while agenting). Have sold more than 3,000 books. Am also the author of 4 books and the editor of 21 anthologies, including *Hungry for Your Love* (St. Martin's Press), the first zombie romance anthology, and *50 Writers on 50 Shades of Grey* (BenBella Books). I believe that epublishing is the future so was the founding editorial director of Ravenous Romance for four years, where I edited 200 novels. In 2012, I became the publisher of Riverdale Avenue Books, where we publish a book a week. I still run the agency.

Say something about your hobbies and personal interests. I also have a BA in art history, but I work 16 hours a day, so there's not a lot of free time right now. I have a 21-year-old son who has an English degree and works in publishing.

Why and how did you become an agent? I love words — reading, writing, editing, and helping people to get published. Also love to mentor, so contact me if you want to learn about publishing.

Would you do it over again, or something else? With the advent of epublishing, I would write. It is now possible to make a good, steady living as a writer if you put in the time, while that was less dependable years ago.

List some representative titles you have placed. *How to Make Love Like a Porn Star* by Jenna Jameson; *The Killer Wore Leather* by Laura Antoniou; *Slow Seduction* by Cecilia Tan; *The Divergent Companion* by Lois Gresh; *Bieber Fever* by Marc Shapiro.

Describe yourself as a person. Passionate, driven, quirky, a typical Aries.

How would you describe the proverbial "client from hell," and what are the warning signs? Someone who doesn't understand my workload and where I am in my career. I don't want a client to micromanage.

What do you think about self-publishing? It has value, especially for niche markets, but it's not for everyone. If you are going to do it, you have to make sure you do it professionally. It is constantly changing, as is publishing right now, which is exciting.

Do you like Amazon? Amazon is the major seller of ebooks, so I better like Amazon.

Do you believe in a "higher power"? Escalated royalties?

What will agenting be like in 2020? Agents will continue to be the gatekeepers and the sifters. We are professional content providers making sure that high-quality material rises to the top.

Describe your job and what you like and don't like about it. Too many books; too little time.

Do you miss the way the business "used to be"? No, it's much more exciting now, and writers can really make a living if they put in the time, which was not the case for the past 30 years. All writers should be traditionally published and epublished. Multiple revenue streams are a beautiful thing for both the writer and the agent.

What does the "Big 5" mean to you? It's the Big 6. I don't know why we don't include Harlequin. I think it's sexist that we don't, especially since 80 percent of the books purchased in America are bought by women and 53 percent of those books are romance.

What do you want to tell new/unpublished writers? Keep writing. Go to conferences. Join a genre organization; read in your genre. There is no excuse for not writing. Get up earlier, stay up later. Now is the time.

Do you like that everything has become largely digitized? Yes.

What do you like reading, watching, and listening to? I read erotic romance and erotica, and horror, which is what I sell. I am a huge *Walking Dead* and *True Blood* fan (surprise?).

Describe a book you would write. I have written so many already. I love *Hungry for Your Love*, my zombie romance anthology. I am working on a historical erotic romance. I just published a femdom novella with Entwined.

Joker's wild: I resent when some people wonder why I am an agent, editor, and writer. I think it's great that I understand all aspects of publishing. You cannot get one over on me (and neither can your editor or your publisher), because I've been there from every angle.

LYNN SELIGMAN, LITERARY AGENT

400 Highland Avenue, Upper Montclair, NJ 07043, 973-783-3631, seliglit@aol.com

Agent's name: Lynn Seligman

Describe what you like to represent and what you won't represent. Represent adult fiction, both commercial and literary, as well as young adult fiction. Nonfiction in many areas, including memoir, narrative, history, biography, entertainment, health and medicine, psychology, and science.

Not representing illustrated children's books or young or middle readers, thriller, mystery.

What are the best ways for writers to pitch you? Send a query snail mail with an SASE or email with no attachments, but I do not respond to email unless I am interested.

When and where were you born? New York City, NY.

Do you charge fees? No fees for reading, but I do charge clients if there are unusual fees, such as sending a package abroad, etc.

Describe your education and career history. My BA is from Goucher College; MA from Columbia; incomplete PhD in French literature. After spending some time in Bogotá, Colombia, working for the French cultural ambassador, I came back to New York, worked for a year as an ESL teacher in an elementary school, decided I did not like teaching, and started my career in publishing. I worked at a small publisher eventually absorbed into Harper, a small book club, Doubleday selling foreign rights, and a group of airline magazines as a book editor, and finally landed at Simon & Schuster, where I eventually became associate rights director. I left S&S to become an agent at Julian Bach Literary Agency, where I stayed for five years, then left to start my own agency, working out of my home in Montclair, NJ, which is where I am now.

Say something about your hobbies and personal interests. I love reading (of course); all kinds of music, but especially opera and voice; ballet and modern dance; art and walking. I can't really say I have hobbies, but I am starting to knit again.

Why and how did you become an agent? I became an agent after falling in love with publishing and especially subsidiary rights. I loved selling but felt somewhat removed from the creative process, which is why I had decided to work in publishing at all. When I examined my options, being an agent seemed to combine perfectly my love of the work and the authors and being able to sell. I found that I could work for Julian, sell foreign rights, and develop a list at the same time, which happened rather quickly, considering I did not work directly with authors at the time. I was lucky to be able to represent two authors of *The Unofficial Preppy Handbook*, a huge bestseller; the first bestselling men's workout book, Charles Hix's *Working Out*; and Bette Midler's *The Saga of Baby Divine* in my first two years as an agent.

Would you do it over again, or something else? Would do it all over again.

List some representative titles you have placed. *To Marry an English Lord* by Carol McD. Wallace and Gail MacColl, audio rights (Tantor Media) and TV rights optioned (Fox); three-book contract for new series by Alexandra Hawkins (St. Martin's Press); *The Dark World* trilogy by Cara Lynn Shultz (Harlequin Teen).

Describe yourself as a person. I am honest, hardworking, love good books and other arts (dance, music, opera, fine art, etc.) as well as most people.

How would you describe the proverbial "client from hell," and what are the warning signs? I generally am good at figuring out how a client will be working with me. I think part of the definition of a "client from hell" is simply that the chemistry is wrong. Someone I can work with may not be the same for another agent. For me, the warning signs are a lack of trust or trying to do my job. I never mind suggestions but am not good with demands.

What do you think about self-publishing? I actually represent a self-published client whose first book I tried to sell, and we have a great relationship. She does some things herself, and I sell others, as well as all the rights on her self-published books. I would be open to other authors like her but have not found anyone as good yet. I think self-publishing is here to stay and agents have to find a way to work with it for their sakes and the authors'.

Do you like Amazon? Hard question right now with everything that's going on with Hachette and will be soon with other publishers. I have had my issues with Amazon Publishing, and they do not seem like any other publisher I have ever worked with in terms of acquiring and editing; but they do a really good job of selling the books in their outlets. As for Amazon as a bookseller, they are essential, but the jury is out on how they will be for books in the future.

Do you believe in a "higher power"? No.

What will agenting be like in 2020? Who knows? It is changing, but I think at least some authors will want an agent in their corner.

Describe your job and what you like and don't like about it. I choose authors I want to represent by reading their work and discussing it with them; I work with the author on the manuscript or proposal; I sell the work to a publisher (hopefully) by developing a list of interested editors and seeing if they want to read the manuscript or proposal; and then I work on selling the subsidiary rights through coagents, such as film, foreign, audio, etc., if we have retained them in the sale to the publisher (which I try to do). I actually enjoy all of these steps for different reasons, but I think I like finding a great book the most. It is so exciting when you know you have something really terrific to sell.

Do you miss the way the business "used to be"? A lot of old-timers, of which I am probably one, say this all the time. However, I think the business has always been evolving, and it is just faster now. It makes no sense to me to mourn what was, but I need to look at what is and work within that. I think learning new things is what keeps my interest fresh.

What does the "Big 5" mean to you? The Big 5 are the bigger publishers, now even bigger: Penguin Random House, Hachette, Simon & Schuster, Macmillan, and Harper Collins.

What do you want to tell new/unpublished writers? Believe in yourself and your book, and find partners, like an agent, editor, and publisher, who also feel the same.

Do you like that everything has become largely digitized? It has positive and negative qualities, like much else nowadays. I still keep a lot on paper for backup.

What do you like reading, watching, and listening to? I read mostly fiction, some memoir and narrative nonfiction on a variety of subjects, and the *New York Times*, the *New Yorker*, and *Vanity Fair* to keep me connected. I also read some online, but not much. I watch some TV and like some good series, like *The Good Wife*, but will admit I watch some junk to escape, especially dance shows.

Describe a book you would write. I do what I do because I never want to write a book.

MANUS MEDIA AND LITERARY AGENCY ❖ www.manuslit.com

425 Sherman Avenue, Suite 200, Palo Alto, CA 94306, 650-470-5151, fax: 650-644-2937, manuslit@manuslit.com

Agent's name and contact info: Jillian Manus, jillian@manuslit.com, 650-470-5151

Describe what you like to represent and what you won't represent. Represent: business, memoir/biography, sports, politics, social trends/issues, current events, diet/well-being, health/medicine, motivation/self-help, religion.

Do not represent: fiction, true crime, young adult, photography, decor, children's books.

What are the best ways for writers to pitch you? Email.

When and where were you born? 1962, New York City.

Do you charge fees? No.

Say something about your hobbies and personal interests. My companies are profit-for-nonprofit models. A large portion of my profits goes to charity to "fund paths of self-sufficiency for women and children." The two biggest areas of investment are in education and health. My commitment to elevate and empower is what fuels my mind and directs my heart. My hobbies include football, baseball, travel, running, Zumba, ballet, theater, swimming, hiking, yoga, golf, and adventure.

Why and how did you become an agent? My mother, Janet Manus, introduced me to this business. She began the agency 40-plus years ago. I expanded the breadth of the work we represent, but she was the original breath that created us.

Would you do it over again, or something else? I would do it all over again…and again!

List some representative titles you have placed. *The Universal Tone* by Carlos Santana; *Wild Tales* by Graham Nash; *40 Changes to Feed* by Howard Buffett; *Success through Stillness* by Russell Simmons; *War to Store Front* by Paul Brinkley; *A Japanese Officer* by

Andrew Pham; *Manopause* by Lisa Friedman Bloch and Kathy Silverman; *The Chaplain of San Quentin* by Reverend Earl Smith; *Speeeeed!* by Stephanie Brown.

Describe yourself as a person. Empathetic, tenacious, dedicated, intuitive, wise, confident, humorous, gregarious, joyful, curious, kind, unstoppable.

How would you describe the proverbial "client from hell," and what are the warning signs? We don't judge clients; we just represent them.

What do you think about self-publishing? Self-publishing is one of the many avenues available to authors in the 21st century. We primarily work with authors who are interested in being published by a traditional publishing house. But the landscape is ever changing, and we want our authors to be aware of all their options.

Do you like Amazon? Yes and no. The world is not black or white; certainly not in business.

Do you believe in a "higher power"? Yes.

What will agenting be like in 2020? I don't think any of us really know the answer. I just take one day at a time, adapting and optimizing with the changes and challenges.

Describe your job and what you like and don't like about it. I see my role as an agent as a composite of the following: to enable my client and their work to reach their highest potential. This is obtained through a process of identification, editing, defining, navigating, advocating, protecting, promoting, admiring, and cheering. What I don't like about my job: passing on projects.

What does the "Big 5" mean to you? Big 5? A sporting goods store and a candy bar. I'd like to believe that publishing has expanded, not retracted. There are so many more options for writers than…five. I don't mourn the past, just use the valuable history of our industry to contribute to the new architecture ahead.

What do you want to tell new/unpublished writers? See writing as a job and never give up. Not finding an agent or a publisher doesn't mean you can't find an audience. There are multiple ways to "deliver" your words. Always keep writing.

Do you like that everything has become largely digitized? As my agency is based in the Silicon Valley, we see the tremendous value to digitization of content to be repurposed on multiple platforms. That said, the bibliophile in me will always prefer turning a crisp page rather than swiping a screen.

What do you like reading, watching, and listening to? Read: memoir, biography, literary fiction, poetry, sports, business, and politics. Watch: Colbert, Stewart, ESPN, CNN, *Dateline*, Bloomberg, Fox, *Modern Family*, and *all* Masterpiece Classics. Listen: '60s rock, classical, selective pop and country, talk radio.

Describe a book you would write. All and none.

Joker's wild: My mind mantra: "Don't Wait!" My heart mantra: "Pass 'It' Forward."

Agent's name and contact info: Penny Nelson, 650-470-5151, penny@manuslit.com

Describe what you like to represent and what you won't represent. I represent primarily nonfiction: narrative, current affairs, politics, social issues and social trends, history, animal and natural sciences, business, work by journalists, international issues, self-help with a strong platform, and, very selectively, travel writing and memoir.

What are the best ways for writers to pitch you? Email or snail mail a query and either an outline or the first couple of chapters of the work.

When and where were you born? Originally, I am from Portland, Oregon.

Do you charge fees? I do not charge fees.

Describe your education and career history. I went to Macalester College, where I studied anthropology and international studies. I spent many years working with wildlife; transitioned to a career in public radio, where I ended up working around many authors… and that very naturally led me to agenting. I find the world and its inhabitants endlessly fascinating. I love to follow politics, current events, science news, sports, and the arts. I am also keenly interested in kids, travel, food, humor, and keeping healthy!

Why and how did you become an agent? I love books and ideas and the life of the mind. After producing plenty of radio shows with authors, I shifted to "producing" books with authors. It has been fantastic!

Would you do it over again, or something else? I would do it over in a heartbeat. There is always something new coming down the road, and I want to be there to spot it.

List some representative titles you have placed. I Dare Me by Lu Ann Cahn (Perigee); *The Message of You* by Judy Carter (St. Martin's Press); *The Introvert's Way* and *Introverts in Love* by Sophia Dembling (Perigee/Penguin); *Generation Rx: A Story of Dope, Death, and Generation Rx* by Erin Marie Daly (Counterpoint Press); *The Forest House: A Year's Journey into the Landscape of Love, Loss, and Starting Over* by Joelle Fraser (Counterpoint); *Among Chimpanzees: Field Notes from the Race to Save Our Endangered Relatives* by Dr. Nancy Merrick (Beacon Press); *The Practicing Mind: Developing Focus and Discipline in Your Life* by Thomas M. Sterner (New World Library); *The Half-Lived Life* by John Lee (Globe Pequot); *The Jesus Machine* by Dan Gilgoff (St. Martin's Press).

Describe yourself as a person. I am persistent and enthusiastic. When I fall in love with a book project, I will leave no stone unturned in order to place it with the right publishing home.

How would you describe the proverbial "client from hell," and what are the warning signs? We don't take on any such clients! We work with authors who are focused on writing the best book possible and treat the publishing end of things as a business. That makes the vast majority of authors we work with "heavenly."

What do you think about self-publishing? Self-publishing is one of the many avenues available to authors in the 21st century. We primarily work with authors who are interested in being published by a traditional publishing house. But the landscape is ever changing, and we want our authors to be aware of all their options.

What do you want to tell new/unpublished writers? I want unpublished writers to know that the caliber of the writing matters. Take the time to write a well-crafted proposal and/ or book. And then, when the time comes to sell it, put on your business hat and understand that this is, indeed, a business.

Do you like that everything has become largely digitized? Much has become digitized, but there is still a lot of book publishing going on in the traditional way. There is room for both.

What do you like reading, watching, and listening to? I like reading smart, sharp, carefully honed writing…if the writing is great, it doesn't even matter what the book is about.

MARCH TENTH, INC. ❖ www.marchtenthinc.com

24 Hillside Terrace, Montvale, NJ 07645, 201-387-6551

Agent's name: Sandra Choron

Describe what you like to represent and what you won't represent. We welcome books on all aspects of pop culture and social science. We have a special fondness for strong biographies in any area, including history.

We do not represent fiction, poetry, or screenplays.

What are the best ways for writers to pitch you? A letter introducing the book is all we need. We will request proposals if interest warrants.

When and where were you born? Bronx, New York, 1950.

Do you charge fees? No.

Describe your education and career history. I graduated from Lehman College in 1967 and worked at Praeger Publishing, Hawthorn Books, and Dell before starting my own agency and book-packaging firm in 1980. I have written more than 10 books of my own and have taught book publishing on the college level.

Say something about your hobbies and personal interests. I'm passionate about reading and about what books have to teach us about relationships and the way in which we make life choices. I love to travel.

Why and how did you become an agent? Working as an editor at three publishing houses gave me a solid education in the plights of authors. Becoming an agent was a natural transition for me. When I left Dell, I had enough contacts to start my own client list. Many of those writers are still faithful clients today!

Would you do it over again, or something else? I would do it again in a heartbeat.

List some representative titles you have placed. *The Answer* by David Niven (St. Martin's Press); *This Is All a Dream We Dreamed: An Oral History of the Grateful Dead* by David Gans and Blair Jackson (Flatiron); *Shakespeare Saved My Life* by Laura Bates (Penguin); *A Connecticut Yankee in King Arthur's Court*, graphic novel, by Seymour Chwast; *Streets of Fire* by Eric Meola (Harper Collins).

Describe yourself as a person. Easy to talk to, open to new ideas, and nurturing where clients are concerned. Make me laugh, and I'll be your friend for life.

How would you describe the proverbial "client from hell," and what are the warning signs? I avoid writers who know little about their competition; those who write on subjects for which they are not qualified; and those who are not willing to roll up their sleeves and get a good job done.

What do you think about self-publishing? It serves a purpose; it's a start. But I don't believe that self-publishers will ever have the bookstore/library presence that traditional publishing affords.

Do you like Amazon? Mixed feelings: I mourn the bookstores that have been overpowered by this giant but must congratulate a company that can command the kind of retail power that Amazon has developed.

Do you believe in a "higher power"? Yes.

What will agenting be like in 2020? Pretty much as it is now. The book-buying public has proved again and again that they will be steady customers for solid information presented in accessible, entertaining ways.

Describe your job and what you like and don't like about it. I love all the excuses I have to pursue whatever subject catches my interest. I am constantly entertained by the variety of people who come my way and learn as much from my clients as I teach them. Being an agent makes my world a vast one. What's not to like?

Do you miss the way the business "used to be"? No.

What does the "Big 5" mean to you? You refer to publishers here, but I'm not sure what the question is.

What do you want to tell new/unpublished writers? Study your competition — not just the books but also websites and other popular sources of information. Know the subject you are writing about inside and out. Become a true expert before you pursue publication. Find a coauthor if your own resources come up short.

Do you like that everything has become largely digitized? Sure. It gives me more time to read books.

What do you like reading, watching, and listening to? Masterful fiction that takes place in cultures I have never experienced (Amy Tan, Jhumpa Lahiri, Khaled Hosseini).

Describe a book you would write. I have written more than 10 books, most of which are anthologies of information: *Planet Dog*, *Planet Cat*, *Planet Wedding*. I love presenting little-known facts and placing them in a modern, useful context.

Joker's wild: So is the book industry! Enter at your own risk.

MARCIL-O'FARRELL LITERARY LLC ❖

www.denisemarcilagency.com

86 Dennis Street, Manhasset, NY 11030

Agent's name and contact info: Anne Marie O'Farrell, annemarie@denisemarcilagency.com

When and where were you born? (Anne Marie) NYC; Pisces.

Describe your education and career history. BA, Queens College. Worked with Denise Marcil Literary Agency from 1986 to 1996. Created Marcil-O'Farrell Literary LLC with Denise Marcil in 2007. I've also owned a successful theatrical company and an adult-education program.

Say something about your hobbies and personal interests. Personal growth, metaphysics, business, basketball, and tennis.

Describe what you like to represent and what you won't represent. Nonfiction: I am open to any book idea that is informative and innovative and interests me. Books on business, creativity, mind-body-spirit, cooking, and basketball especially resonate with me.

If you were not an agent, what might you be doing instead? All the businesses that I've owned have helped to promote life-giving ideas, and I love working with creative people. Perhaps I would be a socially responsible brand marketer or an epublisher.

List some representative titles you have placed. The *Seth* books by Jane Roberts (Amber-Allen Publishing and New World Library); *Lead Positive* by Dr. Kathy Cramer (John Wiley); *Back to Joy* by June Cotner (Andrews McMeel); *Idea Stormers* by Bryan Mattimore

(John Wiley); *The Autobiography of Billy "The Hill" McGill* by Billy McGill and Eric Brach (University of Nebraska Press); *Swingin' 73* by Matt Silverman (Globe Pequot); *The College Bound Organizer* by Anna Costaras and Gail Liss (Sourcebooks); *Discovering Vintage New York* by Mitch Broder (Globe Pequot); *Think Confident, Be Confident for Teens* by Leslie Sokol, PhD, and Marci Fox, PhD (New Harbinger).

THE MARGRET MCBRIDE LITERARY AGENCY ❖

www.mcbrideliterary.com

PO Box 9128, La Jolla, CA 92038, 858-454-1550, staff@mcbridelit.com

Agent's name: Faye Atchison

Describe what you like to represent and what you won't represent. I'm interested in both commercial and niche fiction and nonfiction. My fiction interests include young adult, speculative fiction (especially if it involves alternate history), fantasy, women's fiction, historical fiction, thriller, sci-fi, paranormal, nontraditional Westerns, and anything with unique, well-drawn characters and a dark or offbeat sense of humor. For nonfiction, I prefer pop culture, music, history, health, inspirational (but not spiritual), and extremely well-written narrative.

What are the best ways for writers to pitch you? Via email is best. Direct your pitch to our staff email account, mention my name somewhere in the subject line or salutation, and it will be forwarded to me.

When and where were you born? I was born on the West Coast in the '70s. I'd prefer not to get more specific than that because I'm pretty sure I'd be giving away the answers to the security questions on several of my online accounts. ☺

Do you charge fees? We do not charge fees.

Describe your education and career history. I spent a couple of years at UC Santa Cruz as a philosophy major who was unable to pass symbolic logic, before finally receiving my BA in painting and art history from San Diego State University. I've been at the McBride Agency for many years, first as an intern, then the submissions manager, subrights agent, agent's assistant, projects manager, and now agent.

Say something about your hobbies and personal interests. My hobbies and personal interests include reading, live music, listening to podcasts, starting and quitting fitness programs, quality time with family and friends, traveling, wine and food, and any show on AMC, HBO, BBC, or Bravo.

Why and how did you become an agent? I interned at the agency as a student and fell in love with the process of helping an author find a home for their work. After graduating, I managed to get a part-time position at the agency and have been working here ever since.

Would you do it over again, or something else? I would probably do it all over again.

List some representative titles you have placed. Margret and I generally work as a team. Some of our recent and upcoming titles are *Under the Hood* by Stan Slap (Penguin/Portfolio, 2015); *Opening the Black Box* by John Manfredi, Paul Butler, and Peter Klein (McGraw-Hill, 2015); *Lost Heroes* by Brandon Webb (Simon & Schuster, 2014); *Reading Red Flags* by Wendy Patrick, PhD (St. Martin's Press, 2014); *What Works* by Cal Thomas (Harper Collins/Zondervan, 2014); *Open Your Eyes* by Jake Olson and McKay Christensen (Thomas Nelson, 2013); *Getting to "It"* by Jones Loflin and Todd Musig (Harper Business, 2013); *Adversaries to Allies* by Bob Burg (Penguin/Portfolio, 2013); *The Witness Wore Red* by Rebecca Musser (Hachette/Grand Central, 2013).

How would you describe the proverbial "client from hell," and what are the warning signs? All of our clients are perfect angels! We really try to notice red flags before we sign a new client. Some of those red flags might be a big ego, treating members of our staff disrespectfully, an unwillingness or inability to follow our submission guidelines, being unwilling to take editorial feedback or any advice in general, and my biggest pet peeve: calling to ask general questions about the publishing industry or anything else that could be found with a simple Google search.

What do you think about self-publishing? I have nothing against it. It has been great for a lot of authors and disastrous for others. It all depends on the author, the quality of their work, the amount of research they did beforehand, and the amount of time and energy they put into promoting their work.

Do you like Amazon? I hate how their shady business practices have negatively impacted the publishing industry, but, man, do I love my Amazon Prime account.

Do you believe in a "higher power"? Yes, but I don't believe anyone who claims to understand what that higher power is or what it might want.

What will agenting be like in 2020? I think we'll be more diversified. We'll become more like literary managers. The range of services we provide will probably expand to include contract consultations, ebook production, book packaging, promotion, etc.

What do you want to tell new/unpublished writers? Put in the work. Listen to feedback. Don't give up.

MARSAL LYON LITERARY AGENCY LLC ❖

www.marsallyonliteraryagency.com

PMB 121, 665 San Rodolfo Drive 124, Solana Beach, CA 92075

Agent's name and contact info: Jill Marsal, jill@marsallyonliteraryagency.com

Describe what you like to represent and what you won't represent. I am looking for all types of women's fiction and stories about women, stories of family, interesting relationships, Southern fiction, or multigeneration, and all types of romance, including romantic suspense, historical, contemporary, and category romance. I am also looking for mysteries, cozies, suspense, and thrillers that keep the pages turning and have an original hook. I also like general commercial fiction and welcome a dramatic story line and compelling characters in interesting situations or relationships. If you have a novel that has a highly original concept or voice, I would love to see it. On the nonfiction side, my areas of interest include current events, business, health, self-help, relationships, psychology, parenting, history, science, and narrative. I am particularly drawn to projects that will move readers or leave them thinking, that make provocative arguments or share interesting research, or that offer useful, new advice.

What are the best ways for writers to pitch you? Email a query letter to jill@marsallyon literaryagency.com.

When and where were you born? I was born in Baltimore, Maryland.

Do you charge fees? No.

Describe your education and career history. I am a founding partner of the Marsal Lyon Literary Agency and have been in the publishing industry for over 15 years. Previously, I worked as a literary agent with the Sandra Dijkstra Literary Agency for 8 years and at Dorchester Publications and Tudor Publishing, editing women's fiction and suspense/thrillers. I also have a strong legal background and hold a JD from Harvard Law School and practiced as an attorney with Wilson Sonsini Goodrich & Rosati for 5 years in the Bay Area.

Say something about your hobbies and personal interests. I like reading, hiking, music, the beach, and eating ice cream. Not necessarily in that order.

Why and how did you become an agent? I became an agent because I love reading and editing, and it is so exciting to see a story idea become a book. I love working with authors to help make their stories as strong as possible and hopefully find the perfect publisher for their projects. How did I become an agent? I started as an intern at a literary agency back in high school and then went to work at a publishing house and then eventually moved back into agenting, which is what I really enjoy.

Would you do it over again, or something else? I absolutely would do it over again.

List some representative titles you have placed. Fiction: *The Mango Bride* by Marivi Soliven (NAL); *The Vanishing Thief* by Kate Parker (Berkley); *But Sugar's Twice as Sweet* by Marina Adair (Grand Central); *She Can Hide* by Melinda Leigh (Montlake); *The Red Bikini* by Lauren Christopher (Berkley); *Targeted* by *New York Times* and *USA Today* bestselling author Katie Reus (NAL). Nonfiction: *Put Your Mindset to Work* by *New York Times* bestselling authors James Reed and Paul G. Stoltz (Portfolio/Penguin); *What Makes Your Brain Happy and Why You Should Do the Opposite* by David DiSalvo (Prometheus); *Will My Kid Grow Out Of It?* by Dr. Bonny Forrest (Chicago Review Press); *Mama Koko and the Hundred Gunmen* by Lisa Shannon (Public Affairs); *Unlucky Number: The Murder of Lottery Winner Abraham Shakespeare* by Deborah Mathis (Berkley); *Heart Health* by Dr. Michael Miller (Rodale).

Describe yourself as a person. I'm sure this will come as no surprise, given that I am a literary agent, but I love reading — fiction, nonfiction, all types of books. I start my days early and first thing turn on the computer to go through emails and reading. Also, because I am sitting reading so long, I like to exercise or go outdoors and walk my dog and get some sunshine (when it's nice weather) when I'm not working.

How would you describe the proverbial "client from hell," and what are the warning signs? I think it is really important to have good communication and be responsive so you can build a relationship. Warning signs for me would be a client who doesn't respond to phone calls or emails and doesn't seem excited about their work and taking steps to move forward in the publishing process.

What do you think about self-publishing? I think self-publishing offers many writers another opportunity for getting their work out there. It is important for an author to really identify their goals in publishing when they are evaluating whether to go with a traditional publisher, an epublisher, or self-publishing. We have authors who have chosen each of those paths, and many do a combination. It really depends on what an author is looking for from the publishing experience.

Do you like Amazon? Yes. I think Amazon has really helped the growth of ebooks and opened up new publishing opportunities for many authors.

What will agenting be like in 2020? I think the general goal will be the same as today — to help authors bring their work to readers, help them create the strongest manuscripts possible, and help them figure out the best publishing path to achieve their goals. There are more and more new opportunities developing with epublishers, self-publishing, group publishing, etc., and I think agents will need to stay on top of these and be able to advise about the different options; but at the end of the day, it is all about finding the perfect home for a manuscript.

Describe your job and what you like and don't like about it. I love reading and editing and working with authors to make their manuscripts as strong as possible. It is such an exciting process to be able to work on a manuscript and take it from idea/concept to completed book. And, of course, it is such a great thing to take a manuscript on submission and then get "the call" from an editor and then be able to make "the call" to the author. I like being a part of the process that brings readers books that can impact their lives, offer intriguing stories, take readers to places they would never otherwise experience, and entertain and inspire.

Do you miss the way the business "used to be"? I think it is a glass half-full / glass half-empty. While I do miss the way there used to be more publishers and more spaces for midlist authors and books, and publishers seem more cautious in taking on new projects than they were 5 to 10 years ago, I do think a whole bunch of new opportunities have opened up for authors that have really created some amazing options that did not exist just 10 years ago.

What does the "Big 5" mean to you? The Big 5 makes me think of the larger, traditional New York publishing houses.

What do you want to tell new/unpublished writers? Write. Rewrite. And keep writing. But also read and study books that are successful in the area you want to publish in so you know what is working on the market. If you really want to make this happen, do everything you can to make your work as strong as possible. And then when you believe your manuscript is ready, send it out to agents and try not to get discouraged. It can be a long and trying process, but there are so many stories of writers who received tons of rejections before they found the right agent/editor/publisher, who had the passion for their project and made it happen. It only takes one — you just have to find the right one for your book.

Do you like that everything has become largely digitized? I like that we have a choice between print and digital so that people can pick what they prefer. There is certainly a convenience with things being largely digital, but I still love reading with a book in hand.

What do you like reading, watching, and listening to? I like reading page-turning suspense stories, women's fiction, and nonfiction.

Describe a book you would write. I would write a book with a great voice, original story concept, great hook, fast pacing, interesting characters, and compelling plot.

Agent's name and contact info: Shannon Hassan, shannon@marsallyonliteraryagency.com, www.marsallyonliteraryagency.com/about_shannon.asp, PO Box 6061, Boulder, CO 80306

Describe what you like to represent and what you won't represent. I represent authors of literary and commercial fiction, young adult and middle grade fiction, and select nonfiction. With respect to fiction, I am drawn to fresh voices, compelling characters, and crisp prose and enjoy both contemporary and historical settings. For nonfiction, I am interested in memoirists with a platform and exceptional stories to tell, as well as authors with a strong platform in current affairs, history, education, or law. Based in Boulder, Colorado, I am also eager to hear from authors with a unique perspective on the New West.

I do not generally represent high fantasy or horror.

What are the best ways for writers to pitch you? I look forward to receiving queries at shannon@marsallyonliteraryagency.com. You can read more about my interests at www .publishersmarketplace.com/members/sejohnso. Please include a query, short bio, and 10 sample pages, preferably by email.

When and where were you born? Arlington, Texas, in 1973.

Do you charge fees? No.

Describe your education and career history. I have worked in publishing and law for more than a decade and joined Marsal Lyon in 2013. Prior to becoming an agent, I was acquisitions editor at Fulcrum Publishing and, before that, a corporate attorney at Arnold & Porter in New York. I have a JD from Harvard and a BA from George Washington University, where I studied journalism and economics.

Say something about your hobbies and personal interests. I live in Colorado and love to ski, bike, hike with my husband and 10-year-old twins. We also love to travel, when time permits, and have been all over South America, Europe, and Asia.

Why and how did you become an agent? I started my career as a corporate and licensing attorney and then decided to follow my heart into publishing, where I learned the ropes and then became an acquisitions editor. Becoming an agent was a natural progression for me as it combines my skills and passion.

Would you do it over again, or something else? Yes! I have done other things, and this is exactly what I want to do until I retire. There is nothing better than helping an author achieve his or her publishing dreams.

List some representative titles you have placed. *The Moon in the Palace*, historical fiction based on the life of the famed seventh-century Chinese empress Wu, two-book deal, by Weina Randel (Sourcebooks); *The Summoner's Handbook*, middle grade fiction about a clueless young boy sent from the afterlife on his first "Guardian Agent" mission, by Frank Cole (Delacorte/Random House); *Life and Beth*, young adult fiction about a teenage musician with a deadly gift, by Lisa Amowitz (Spencer Hill Press); *Future Flash*, middle grade fiction about a 12-year-old girl whose touch sparks flashes of the future, by Kita Murdock (Skyhorse Publishing).

Describe yourself as a person. Hardworking, passionate about books and publishing, outdoors lover, mother of twins.

How would you describe the proverbial "client from hell," and what are the warning signs? I have not had any of these! I always call or meet a potential client and get to know them as a person before I commit. I look for authors who are talented, committed to their careers, willing to take criticism, and pleasant to work with.

What do you think about self-publishing? It is often misunderstood by first-time authors as an easy thing to do or a quick fix. Publishing a book, and just as important, reaching your target audience, no matter what route you take, is a long road that requires the help and experience of many.

What will agenting be like in 2020? Formats may change, but I think that the agent's role as advocate, editor, business manager, and champion will stay the same.

Describe your job and what you like and don't like about it. I believe the author-agent relationship should be a true collaboration with open lines of communication. In terms of what to expect after you join our agency, I will first go through the manuscript and offer editorial suggestions and help brainstorm ways to improve any areas that aren't working. Then comes pitching and submitting to editors (and, of course, a waiting period that can feel like an eternity to authors). During that process I always keep authors in the loop with how editors are reacting. After that comes negotiating the deal and the contract terms, offering guidance and advocacy on marketing and publicity, keeping track of the publication process and payments, looking at the big picture, and overall being a strong advocate for the author over the course of his or her career. In terms of what I like, I enjoy editing and contributing to the creative process as much as I do negotiating the deal (and of course announcing good news is always fun!). I still have a difficult time saying no sometimes, especially if it is a good project but just not right for me.

Do you miss the way the business "used to be"? No. I find this an exciting time in publishing.

What does the "Big 5" mean to you? To me, it means the five large publishing conglomerates and all their imprints. I have been fortunate to work with editors at a range of publishing houses, from the "Big 5" to the independents to the smaller presses, and all can be wonderful homes for authors and their work. It's a matter of finding the right fit for each project.

What do you want to tell new/unpublished writers? One piece of advice I like to give new writers is: Read! Read books in your genre to help you gain an understanding of your target audience. And then read books outside your genre to expand your worldview and keep your writing fresh.

Describe a book you would write. I would aspire to write a historical novel with a unique hook and unforgettable characters. If I had the time to write, and maybe a magic wand.

MARTIN LITERARY & MEDIA MANAGEMENT ❖

www.martinliterarymanagement.com

7683 SE 27th Street, Suite 307, Mercer Island, WA 98040, 206-466-1773

NOTE: Our email address is still the same, but we've changed our name from Martin Literary Management to Martin Literary & Media Management, to reflect the agency's increasing involvement in book-to-screen adaptations of our authors' books for feature film, television movies, and reality television.

Agent's name and contact info: Sharlene Martin, president, sharlene@martinliterarymanagement.com

Describe what you like to represent and what you won't represent. As always, we have our long-standing devotion to great narrative nonfiction when it is written with such depth of style and visual clarity that it is naturally adaptable to film. I love to read meaningful memoirs, fun pop-culture subjects, true crime books, and business books (and this even includes how-to books along with self-help or prescriptive books, *provided* that they are original in tone and do not rehash familiar material). And of course, I love doing celebrity bios *if and when* they reach for levels of insight and empathy that readers will not get from the tabloid culture. Clelia Gore (clelia@martinliterarymanagement.com; see page 424), at the helm of our children and young adult division, joined us in September of 2013 and seeks stories with protagonists who have strong voices, characters who are memorable, and plots that show originality.

What are the best ways for writers to pitch you? A standard, businesslike query letter will work, but since we're a "green" agency, we prefer that all queries and submissions be made via email. Please think about the level of competition in the commercial book market, and plan your query accordingly. There is plenty of good information out there about writing effective query letters, and in my own book (duck — plug approaching) *Publish Your Nonfiction Book* (Writer's Digest Books), the importance of the query was stressed. Nothing has changed since then. Consider the contestants on one of my favorite TV shows, *Shark*

Tank, all coming in to make their big pitch. Every one of them has polished their delivery to the line, to the word. They do it like they mean it. I am seeking writers who do it like they mean it, and you would be amazed at how often this is not apparent in their query.

When and where were you born? I was born in Fairfield County, Connecticut. I wasn't born yesterday. I wasn't even born the day before yesterday. And IF I did tell you, then I'd have to kill you, so let's move on!

Do you charge fees? No. An agent who demands any sort of up-front fee is not really an agent, but is more correctly termed a "shmagent," as in "agent-shmagent." It is not especially prestigious to attend a cocktail party with writing peers and announce that you have a new shmagent.

Describe your education and career history. I was a business major in college and upon graduation moved to New York City. I've always been eclectic and entrepreneurial. In fact, I received *Entrepreneur* magazine's Home-Based Entrepreneur of the Year award for a business I started and sold to a competitor in 1989. I moved to Los Angeles and started a production company with a former network journalist/broadcaster and was an independent producer for a number of years, in addition to doing freelance casting for independent and feature films. Because of that experience, I was invited to join a reality television production company and spent time doing acquisitions and talent management. It was there that I realized that my love of show business found its greatest strength in working with passionate and highly skilled writers. I left to start Martin Literary Management in 2002, which has since expanded to become Martin Literary & Media Management, and the lovely success that has followed seems a natural result of the fact that I've never been happier in any line of work.

Say something about your hobbies and personal interests. Film, hiking, cooking, entertaining, visiting my grown kids and their families here in Seattle, occasional travel, provided that it is first-class and four stars! Yes, I am a material girl. You will catch me camping out on the same day that you...oh, forget it. It's not going to happen.

Why and how did you become an agent? Simple: I love the written word. Although I was editor of my high school literary magazine, I never realized my passion for books until later in my career. I want to make a difference in writers' lives by helping them realize their dreams. It's how I realize my own, and this is the path that gets me to that place. I want to protect as many writers as I can from having to attend a cocktail party with their peers and announce that they have a new shmagent.

Would you do it over again, or something else? No regrets. I am happy in this work.

List some representative titles you have placed. *Impossible Odds: The Kidnapping of*

Jessica Buchanan and Her Dramatic Rescue by SEAL Team Six by Anthony Flacco with Jessica Buchanan and Erik Landemalm (Atria/S&S); *Honor Bound: My Journey to Hell and Back with Amanda Knox* by Raffaele Sollecito (Gallery/S&S); *Newtown: An American Tragedy* by Matthew Lysiak (Gallery/S&S); *Picture Perfect: The Jodi Arias Story* by Shanna Hogan (St. Martin's Press); *Walking on Eggshells* by Lyssa Chapman with Lisa Wysocky (Howard Books/S&S); *In the Matter of Nikola Tesla* by Anthony Flacco (Diversion Books); *Hidden Girl: The True Story of a Modern-Day Child Slave* by Shyima Hall with Lisa Wysocky (S&S Young Readers); *Addict Nation* by Jane Velez-Mitchell (HCI); *The Pregnancy Project* by Gaby Rodriguez (S&S Young Readers); *Stealing Rembrandts* by Anthony Amore and Tom Mashberg (Palgrave Macmillan); *It Only Takes One* by Jack Andraka.

Describe yourself as a person. I am a natural advocate and have been all my life. I stand in awe of the abilities displayed by the finest among the writers who send their work to me, people who conjure imaginative tapestries with excellent wordplay and dedicate themselves to their craft. The lengths to which they will to go in order to advance their work can be astonishing. I take inspiration from individuals who so love the written word that they will pour countless hours into their work over many years of time, in the quest to live the writer's life. It's easy for me to work long and hard for such people.

How would you describe the proverbial "client from hell," and what are the warning signs? Self-entitlement is like a bad flu virus moving through our society. It manifests in the writing world in the form of half-baked written work accompanied by explanations for the unfinished condition and a tale of woe about the author's struggles in the task of getting the work to this stage. These people fail to appreciate the truth that everybody struggles if they endeavor to write truly and well, and writers who believe themselves unique in that regard have already revealed a cautionary tale about their lack of insight toward others. Such people seldom deliver meaningful work. They tend to depart amid angry accusations and personal insults, believing that someone else is their problem.

What do you think about self-publishing? Send enough gamblers to Las Vegas, and *somebody* is going to come home a winner. If you catch a wave of public interest in a self-publishing situation, you will make far more money than in a traditional royalty deal — i.e., if you sell 100,000 copies of a self-published book, you can then go out and buy a great house, take a magnificent world tour, or begin planning a comfortable retirement. The vast majority of self-published books will fail because the general public will never be made aware that they exist. Some of them are written well enough to stand beside anything published by a major house, although many are not. A large portion are not very good because the writers become impatient to see the work in print and stop the polishing process in its early stages. These raw efforts not only clog the market; they serve to diminish the potential size of that market by repeatedly burning those intrepid readers who venture into the swamps of self-published books, hoping to find that gem.

So, assuming you have written great stuff and polished it until your readers need dark glasses, then the secret is in the publicity. Specifically, this refers to however well or poorly you can hook your book to some point of public interest. Can you get it up there on the great public billboard and into the general social consciousness? The challenge for you, then, is much like that of the traditional author, in today's world. They probably get more help than you do, but that doesn't have to stop you. The self-published author will rise or fall on the unjust gaze of public awareness, just like the folks with contracts from the Big 5 houses or the gang down at the university press. Find an appropriate way to get awareness of your book in the public eye (operative word, *appropriate*). That means it will not help your writing career to grab for attention by doing something bizarre, like running naked into a major league ball game, unless you are writing about someone who runs naked into major league ball games. In that case, it could be your springboard to the bestseller list. In my entire career, I've taken on two self-published books (*You'll Never Nanny in This Town Again* by Suzanne Hansen and *Notes Left Behind* by the Desseriches), and both became *New York Times* bestsellers. The real gems are few and far between for all the reasons above.

Do you like Amazon? I love the convenience of ordering from Amazon, but most of the hardcover books I buy from our independent bookstore here. When I do buy ebooks, I download to my Kindle. And I haven't had any experience in publishing clients with Amazon yet…so I'll reserve judgment for the time being. Catch up with me in a year, and maybe I'll have more to say.

Do you believe in a "higher power"? I certainly used to, but now that we're all getting green and taking more responsibility about energy consumption, I tend to keep the setting on "Medium Power" while I'm away from home and at "Lower Power" while everyone is asleep.

What will agenting be like in 2020? There is no truth to the rumor that in the year 2020, books will be administered in suppository form. I predict that a fraction of militant bibliophiles will secretly retain actual hardback books, which will then end up being traded as money. Recluses with large personal libraries will suddenly find themselves richer than tech moguls. Thus, more than ever, people will want to write and publish books. I will keep my percentages reasonable.

Describe your job and what you like and don't like about it. I represent wonderful writers and help to make their literary dreams come true. I do lots of reading, plenty of persuasive selling, and creative career counseling. My greatest joy comes from finding effective ways to market my writers and their work. As for things I don't like about it, there aren't many — none worth mentioning here.

Do you miss the way the business "used to be"? I hate to get into missing what used to be. The only approach I've ever found to do any good in that regard is to personally see to it that the positive qualities of the literary world do not have to go under and be lost to declining public civility, as long as there are those who will quietly insist with their behavior that such sensibilities are very much alive and in play. It's funny that for all the grandeur of social planning, the maintaining of civilization turns out to be mostly an individual pastime.

What does the "Big 5" mean to you? The Big 5 are the current top group of traditional publishers, the A-list. There are many other, smaller houses, but they also offer smaller deals. As with the major Hollywood studios, the largest financial arrangements are made with the top-tier publishers.

What do you want to tell new/unpublished writers? Be a voracious reader of the biographies of writers who struggled before they found acceptance. Their stories will make you stronger.

Do you like that everything has become largely digitized? It certainly makes the marketing process faster and more efficient. The amount of office paperwork is vastly reduced also. But I personally still prefer to read a paper book in my hands, since the digital platforms are where I work all day.

What do you like reading, watching, and listening to? TV: Almost anything on the Discovery Channel. Books: *The Glass Castle* by Jeanette Walls; *The Devil in the White City* by Erik Larson; *The Kite Runner* by Khaled Hosseini; *The Road out of Hell* and *Impossible Odds* by Anthony Flacco; *Notes Left Behind* by Keith and Brooke Desserich; *The Last Lecture* by Randy Pausch and Jeffrey Zaslow (RIP to both).

Describe a book you would write. I have done so twice: *Publish Your Nonfiction Book: Strategies for Learning the Industry, Selling Your Book and Building a Successful Career* (Writer's Digest Books) and a humorous book for writers entitled *Literary Fails: Totally (sic)!; 101 Crazy Query Letters Sent by Writers in Their Quest for Fame.* Nothing gets my attention quicker than the opening line of a query letter that says, "Ms. Martin: I read your books…"

Agent's name and contact info: Clelia Gore, clelia@martinliterarymanagement.com, 206-395-6565

Describe what you like to represent and what you won't represent. I represent authors who write books that fit under the "children's book" umbrella. That includes picture books, chapter books, middle grade books, and young adult books. I am very interested in developing my client list for nonfiction young adult memoir. I am looking for exceptional teens who have done exceptional things or have had exceptional experiences.

At this time, I am not representing authors who write in the new adult genre.

What are the best ways for writers to pitch you? The best way to query me is by sending me an email query and following my guidelines listed on the agency website. Because I am a new agent, I look at all email queries.

When and where were you born? I was born in 1983 in New York, New York. I grew up on the Upper East Side and then in Tenafly, New Jersey.

Do you charge fees? No. An agent who demands any sort of up-front fee is not really an agent.

Describe your education and career history. Some may call me overeducated — I have a BA in English from Boston College, a JD from American University, and an MA in publishing and writing from Emerson College. I went to law school straight after college. I then worked as a litigator dealing primarily with contract-based disputes for several years in New York City, in both a large- and small-firm setting, before deciding that I wanted to reroute my career to something I found more fulfilling. I ended up at Emerson, where, in addition to being a graduate student, I taught academic writing to Emerson College freshmen and worked as a full-time intern and freelance copyeditor at Houghton Mifflin Harcourt in their children's book division. I also did a summer stint at Oxford University Press. I moved to Seattle in the summer of 2013 for my husband's job and was fortunate enough to link up with the amazing Sharlene Martin, president of Martin Literary & Media Management, who provided me with the opportunity to helm the children and young adult division of MLM, a position that has proven to be a great combination of my skills and interests.

Say something about your hobbies and personal interests. I guess it is too obvious to say reading. I love to travel — my parents are from different countries and instilled a love of the international in me. My husband and I also like to visit US national parks. Anything that involves planning — vacations, wedding events, elaborately themed birthday parties, etc. I'm a sucker for any media designed for tweens. There is no animated movie I won't get misty eyed watching.

Why and how did you become an agent? I became an agent because I spent several years doing something I was not interested in and where I felt like my skill set was not being utilized in the most optimal way. Being an agent uses all my skills, makes me (and my clients!) happy, and also helps me contribute to art and culture in this country.

Would you do it over again, or something else? I think that this is it for me!

List some representative titles you have placed. At this point in time, I am a brand-new agent and currently out on my first few submissions. I am feeling very optimistic — stay tuned for acquisition news.

Describe yourself as a person. I think I am a kind, genuine person who is smart and loyal. I also think I'm pretty fun…if I do say so myself.

How would you describe the proverbial "client from hell," and what are the warning signs? The client from hell does not understand the way the publishing industry works — and doesn't care to really know. He or she has unreasonable expectations and doesn't fulfill my own expectations by not taking my notes into account, missing deadlines, or not putting the work in.

What do you think about self-publishing? I think it is an excellent resource for authors who may not be able to get published by a traditional publisher. It also offers readers a wider selection of books, often at low cost. There are problems with quality control in self-publishing, but ultimately, I think it's a great way to create a satisfying experience for writers.

Do you like Amazon? I think Amazon is a really innovative company, and I am really grateful that they can deliver my favorite hair product two days after I've run out of it. I have mixed feelings about some of the ways they've influenced the publishing industry in the past few years, but ultimately, I think that when the dust settles, the publishing industry will have benefitted from having its boundaries pushed and being forced to evolve.

Do you believe in a "higher power"? Yes.

What will agenting be like in 2020? The industry is in such a state of transition right now that it is really hard to say — particularly because I am still learning what it is like in 2014! I think there will always be a place for literary agents because people are always going to demand high-quality material, and that is going to keep traditional publishers in business. Editors act as gatekeepers, and we, as agents, are the sweet-talkers who help our writers get past the gate. Whether we will still be expecting to publish a physical book or a digital book at the end of the day — I'm not sure!

Describe your job and what you like and don't like about it. My job consists of a lot of reading and editing. I am very focused on networking right now to help build my business. I also stay on top of everything that is going on in publishing news and in deals being made. My favorite part about being an agent is the fact that there is so much potential in this job — potential to find new, amazing talent; potential to bring beautiful, meaningful books to the marketplace; potential to find fresh viewpoints and stories; and potential to have real successes. All this potential makes this a truly unique job, and I find it very exciting and satisfying. The bad part of the job is that I have to disappoint so many hopeful authors who have queried me along the way.

Do you miss the way the business "used to be"? I'm new to the business, so this is all I know! So far, so good.

What does the "Big 5" mean to you? The Big 5 are publishers with a long, celebrated history and reputation for quality and commercialism — they are the dream publishers of every client.

What do you want to tell new/unpublished writers? It is very, very difficult to break into the book business, and once you do, it's just as hard to become a success. Put your 10,000 hours of work and training in — that may mean writing a few novels that never see the light of day — but it will make you a better, more serious writer, and one who has a higher chance of success. Also, remember to be humble!

Do you like that everything has become largely digitized? I actually think whether I like it or not is irrelevant — it's happening! It's the natural progression based on how influential technology is in our lives. When ereaders first came out, as a book lover, I thought there was no way I would give up physical books — but now I find reading ebooks really convenient, and I read more and more books on my Kindle. But I think there will always be room for physical books in my life — unless the world really becomes like the Jetsons, and then my future self will laugh at this version of myself for saying that.

What do you like reading, watching, and listening to? I obviously read a lot of children's books and young adult. I had to instill some personal reading rules as a way to remember to read adult books every now and then. For every two young adult books I read, I have to read an adult book — and after two cycles of that, I then have to read a classic novel. Strict, but fair. My favorite book of all time is *Charlotte's Web* — I consider my original copy my good-luck charm. I love television — much like my reading selection, I have a wide range. I love critically acclaimed cable shows like *Breaking Bad* and *Veep*, network sitcoms like *The Big Bang Theory* and *The Office*, and shows meant for a much younger audience like *Pretty Little Liars*. I also love going to the movies! I try to go once a week. I'm a sucker for Top 40 pop music…as well as weepy folk or indie music.

Describe a book you would write. I would write a middle grade or young adult book based in reality that had a touch of history. My mother is French, and we spent our summers at my grandparents' beach house in Normandy on what was called Juno Beach during World War II, where Americans, Brits, and Canadians landed on D-day. There was an American WWII tank that served as a memorial right in the dunes! I've always wanted to write something in that setting.

MAX GARTENBERG LITERARY AGENCY ❖

www.maxgartenberg.com

912 North Pennsylvania Avenue, Yardley, PA 19067, 215-295-9230

Agent's name and contact info: Anne G. Devlin, agdevlin@aol.com

Describe what you like to represent and what you won't represent. Nonfiction: current affairs, education, parenting, health, fitness, food, how-to, self-help, business, women's interest, celebrity, true crime, sports, politics, history, music, biography, memoir, environment, pets, narrative; and historical fiction.

No poetry, New Age, or fantasy.

What are the best ways for writers to pitch you? Writers desirous of having their work handled by this agency should first send a one- or two-page query letter. Simply put, the letter should describe the material being offered as well as relevant background information about the writer. If the material is of interest, we will request a proposal and sample chapters. Queries are accepted by both email and post. Please include an SASE for a reply via post.

When and where were you born? Cleveland, OH.

Do you charge fees? No reading fee.

Describe your education and career history. Max Gartenberg Literary Agency has long been recognized as a source for fine fiction and nonfiction. One of the oldest and most prestigious agencies in the US, it was established in 1954 in New York City and has since migrated to the Philadelphia area. After careers in both writing and journalism and the ownership of a large marketing company, I am now managing this agency.

Say something about your hobbies and personal interests. I am interested (of course) in reading, writing, movies, antiquing, traveling, and cooking.

Why and how did you become an agent? I was offered the opportunity to join this firm because of my background in writing, editing, and marketing and have never looked back.

Would you do it over again, or something else? Absolutely. I enjoy the wonderful writing professionals I meet who can be counted on to produce well-made, literate, enlightening, and enjoyable books with a minimum of Sturm und Drang.

List some representative titles you have placed. *Running with Cosmos Flowers* (Pelican Publishing); *Killers in the Family* (Penguin / Berkley Books); *Emote: Using Emotions to Make Your Messages Memorable* (Career Press); *Ogallala Blue* (W.W. Norton); *You Should Be Dancin'* (ECW Press); *Ecology or Catastrophe* (Oxford Univ. Press); *The New Senior Woman* (Rowman & Littlefield); *Everything a New Elementary Teacher Really Needs to Know* (Free Spirit Publishing); *Jack and Lem* (Da Capo Press); *What Patients Taught Me* (Sasquatch Books); *Beethoven for Kids* (Chicago Review Press); *Your Guide to the Jewish Holidays* (Scarecrow Press); *Charles Addams: A Cartoonist's Life* (Random House).

How would you describe the proverbial "client from hell," and what are the warning signs? Client who demands unceasing attention and is never satisfied with the deal the agent brings him (he always has friends who got twice as much) and then delivers his manuscript late and in such disrepair that it is unacceptable. This is not an imaginary character.

What do you think about self-publishing? Self-publishing is a last resort as it lacks the support an author receives from a traditional publishing house's production department, marketing department, sales staff, and distributors. Authors who self-publish need to understand that they will need to promote and publicize themselves in every possible venue and medium.

Describe your job and what you like and don't like about it. I love being an agent because it allows me to learn and discover. As a former newspaper writer and editor as well as a marketing entrepreneur, I enjoy being part of the creation of a great book. I enjoy discovering authors, pitching book ideas, negotiating deals, and being part of an exciting and dynamic industry. I love getting excited about a new book project that I can pitch to the editors. When I work with an author, I help him or her shape proposals and manuscripts to interest editors so that they will make an offer. I submit materials to publishers, negotiate contracts, and generally act as a business manager for the author and intercede whenever necessary throughout the publishing process.

What do you want to tell new/unpublished writers? To be considered, write a brilliant query letter and, when asked, follow it up with a proposal as well, and sample chapters or a manuscript that is even better. Be sure to include your qualifications and experience along with a synopsis of the work.

MIRIAM ALTSHULER LITERARY AGENCY ❖

www.miriamaltshulerliteraryagency.com

53 Old Post Road North, Red Hook, NY 12571, query@maliterary.com

Agent's name and contact info: Miriam Altshuler, query@maliterary.com

Describe what you like to represent and what you won't represent. I love literary/commercial fiction and narrative nonfiction, and also young adult and middle grade fiction. I respond in fiction to stories that are character driven. I love fiction that reflects on a time and place and a part of history or a subject (think *Signature of All Things* and *Life after Life*, both of which I recently read and loved). To me, the writing is the most important thing. For nonfiction, I particularly respond to books which have a social, cultural, or psychological aspect to them. I love narrative and memoir. I love contemporary and historical young adult and middle grade fiction. I also love dystopian and great stories that have some fantasy to them in young adult and middle grade but are not strictly in the genre of fantasy.

I do not represent any kind of genre fiction.

What are the best ways for writers to pitch you? Follow the guidelines on our website (please do not call the office). Send a query via the query email provided, with a short description/synopsis of the book and what it is about. (Think flap copy of a book. I want content and ideas.) And any relevant information about the writer that I should know about in regard to selling or marketing your book. Keep it short and concise, and do not include any attachments. I will not open any attachments, due to virus risks. I like to have the first chapter of a book so I can get a sense of the writing, but include it in the body of the email below the query. Again, follow the guidelines on our website: www.miriam altshulerliteraryagency.com.

When and where were you born? New York, NY, 1961.

Do you charge fees? I am an active member of the AAR and do not charge any reading fees.

Describe your education and career history. I graduated from Middlebury College as an English major with a minor in creative writing and sociology. My first job out of college was as the assistant to Timothy Seldes at Russell & Volkening Literary Agency, which at that time was one of the oldest and most prestigious agencies. I became an agent at Russell two years later and in 1994 left to start my own agency. I have always been a literary agent and always will be.

Say something about your hobbies and personal interests. Like everyone in publishing, I love to read. I am also an avid outdoors person, and I love to horseback ride (my daughter is a competitive horseback rider), ski, and hike. I also love to travel and go to movies and concerts. And most of all, I love spending time with my husband and two children.

Why and how did you become an agent? I love reading, books, and working with people. I am also a great problem solver and love to connect people.

Would you do it over again, or something else? No question, I would do it again. This is the most interesting job with the most interesting and dedicated people.

List some representative titles you have placed. *The Sixteenth of June* by Maya Lang (a modern retelling of *Ulysses* — one of the most wonderful novels I have read in a long time; Scribner); *The Primates of Park Avenue: An Anthropological Memoir of Uptown Motherhood* by Wednesday Martin (Simon & Schuster); *The Box and the Dragonfly* by Ted Sanders (the first book of a middle grade series entitled *The Keepers*; Harper Collins Children's Books); untitled book on narcissism by Dr. Craig Malkin (Harper Wave / Harper Collins); *Living the Secular Life: New Answers to Old Questions* by Phil Zuckerman (Penguin Press); *Good Girl* by Donna Freitas (a romantic young adult novel about grief and love with a compelling mystery; Philomel / Penguin Children's Books); *The Ambassadors* by George Lerner (a wonderful debut novel; Pegasus Books); *Electric City* by Elizabeth Rosner (a new novel by the bestselling author of *The Speed of Light*; Counterpoint Press).

How would you describe the proverbial "client from hell," and what are the warning signs? What I prefer to say here is who is a great client: One who respects the art of writing, who works diligently to make the book the best it can be, and who believes in their craft. A person who respects my time and all the various things I do for everyone. One who respects that I work night and day and weekends, and understands the boundaries of my work, family, and reading time. One who is collaborative in their thinking and promoting of their work, and understands that publishing has changed, so they have to be part of the process from beginning to end. Someone with a sense of humor and who understands I am committed to them and believe in their work.

Agent's name and contact info: Reiko Davis, query@maliterary.com

Describe what you like to represent and what you won't represent. I want to discover books that surprise me and make me feel something. In fiction, I love gorgeous writing, but a book always has to have a compelling story to draw me in. I'm interested in both literary and commercial fiction. I have a weakness for a strong narrative voice; smart, funny heroines; narrowly located settings (towns in the South and Midwest, small communities like one would find in a Kent Haruf novel); and stories that cross borders (in culture, geography, or tradition). For children's books, I love young adult and middle grade fiction — whether contemporary, historical, or fantasy. In terms of nonfiction, I'm looking for memoir and narrative. My areas of interest include arts and culture, history, biography, women's interest, current events, psychology, and narrative science.

What are the best ways for writers to pitch you? Follow the guidelines on our website. Please do not call the office. Send a query via our query email and provide a short description/synopsis of your book, a brief bio, and the first chapter of the book. I prefer to see the first chapter so I can get a sense of the writing. Please paste everything in the body of the email. Do not include any attachments — I will not open them. Again, follow the guidelines on our website: www.miriamaltshulerliteraryagency.com.

When and where were you born? Kansas City, MO, 1987.

Do you charge fees? Our agency does not charge any reading fees. We abide by the AAR's code of ethics.

Describe your education and career history. I went to Brown University, where I concentrated in comparative literature and art history. I then attended the Columbia publishing course, which was a wonderful introduction to the publishing industry. My first job was as an editorial assistant at a poetry publisher. I then started working as a literary assistant to Miriam Altshuler. I have been with the agency for over two years now and am actively taking on my own clients. I also handle much of the subsidiary rights (foreign, audio, ebook, etc). I love my job and couldn't be happier working at Miriam Altshuler Literary Agency.

Say something about your hobbies and personal interests. When I'm not reading manuscripts for work, I love to curl up with a sprawling novel or jaw-dropping book of poems.

I am a rabid tennis player, skier, and crocheter (and by extension, yarn shopper). I love seeing movies at my local arts theater, going to music shows, and enjoying a jazz record in front of a fire with my family. I love dogs (coonhounds in particular). I'm still waiting for the day when I can go backpacking in Greece and the Greek islands.

Why and how did you become an agent? I've loved reading for as long as I can remember. I love thinking about and discussing stories. I love helping writers hone their craft and make their books the best they can be. It means a lot to me to be able to support authors' creative visions, help them find the right publisher, and present their work to the largest possible readership.

Would you do it over again, or something else? Nope. I'm hooked on agenting.

How would you describe the proverbial "client from hell," and what are the warning signs? I'd prefer to describe my ideal client. I love working with people dedicated to the art of writing and to making their books the best they can be. I take my work seriously and spend an enormous amount of time editing and providing feedback, so I love clients who are open to ideas and collaboration, and who respect my efforts to sell and promote their work. When I sign a client, it means I am passionately committed to helping them get their book published.

NEW ENGLAND PUBLISHING ASSOCIATES, INC. ❖ www.nepa.com

PO Box 66066, Lawrence, NJ 08648, 860-973-2439

Agent's name and contact info: Roger S. Williams, roger@nepa.com, 860-973-2439

Describe what you like to represent and what you won't represent. What we like to represent: narrative nonfiction; history and military, with an emphasis on American history; "big think" business concepts; marketing, communications, and consumerism; current events; politics; popular biography; autobiography; memoir (with a proviso: memoirs are like fiction, and the decision to represent memoirs can be very subjective; you may have led a magnificent life or have a remarkable story to tell, but successful memoirs are contingent on two main ingredients — writing style and platform); culture and social policy; medicine and health; mind-body-spirit; psychology and family relationships; the sciences; religion; nature and the environment; language and reference; sports.

What we DO NOT represent: Fiction. I love to read it, but the focus of the agency is nonfiction.

What are the best ways for writers to pitch you? The best process for pitching me is by looking at the "Submissions" tab on www.nepa.com. I like to get a query email; if I like what I read, then I will ask for the proposal and manuscript, but I watch to see if writers have followed the guidelines from www.nepa.com.

When and where were you born? I was born in NYC in 1955; raised in Woodstock, Vermont, and Princeton, New Jersey.

Do you charge fees? No fees. I am a member of AAR, and I subscribe to their code of ethics.

Describe your education and career history. I was an undergrad at Rutgers, graduated from Rider University (NJ) with a BS in marketing. I have been in publishing since I graduated in '78. I spent most of my career in sales, going from sales rep, to sales director at Bantam Doubleday Dell. My wife, author Gina Cascone, opened and operated a bookstore for five years. I moved on to launch a publishing industry website, then to became a VP of sales at Simon & Schuster. In 2009, I purchased New England Publishing Associates.

Say something about your hobbies and personal interests. My occupation is also my avocation. I read a lot of history. I am a docent at a historical park and a member of several historical roundtables, primarily focusing on the American War for Independence. I am also a British motorcar enthusiast and a member of several driving clubs. I'm an avowed Italophile, but most of all, I just love being with my wife, my kids, and my grandchildren.

Why and how did you become an agent? When my wife and I were in college together, she announced she wanted to write books. We jumped into publishing together. I got a job at a bookstore, then started climbing the ranks through corporate publishing. During our short stint as booksellers, I represented a few projects while she published more and more books. After I left Simon & Schuster, I figured that with all the changes happening in the business, there might be an agency whose principals might be interested in transitioning, giving me the opportunity to build author careers from inception and be involved in projects which drive my own creative passions.

Would you do it over again, or something else? I've learned a lot, so if I could do it over again, I would do some things differently; but I love doing what I'm doing.

List some representative titles you have placed. *Terrible Swift Sword*, *Forty Days*, and *Sun Sets on Dixie: The Rebellion's Stirring Finale, January–May 1865* by Joseph Wheelan (Da Capo); *And the Rest Is History*, *Once Again to Zelda*, and *Behind Every Great Man* by Marlene Wagman-Geller (Sourcebooks); *How Safe Is Safe Enough?* by Northwestern engineering professor emeritus E.E. Lewis (Skyhorse Publishing); *Metamorphosis: Eight Technologies That Transformed Humanity* by former professor of anthropology Richard L. Currier (Skyhorse Publishing); *French Lessons* by Julie Barlow and Jean-Benoît Nadeau (St. Martin's Press); *Boston Strong* by Casey Sherman and Dave Wedge (University Press of New England); *Brain Bible* by Dr. John Arden (McGraw-Hill); *History of* *the World in Sixteen Shipwrecks* by Stewart Gordon (University Press of New England); *When Your Adult Child Breaks Your Heart: Coping with Mental Illness, Substance Abuse and Other Issues* by Joel L. Young and Christine Adamec (Lyons Press); *At the Point of a Cutlass* by Gregory Flemming (University Press of New England); *Bears in the Backyard, Coyotes in the Cul-de-Sac: Big Animals, Big Cities and the New Urban Jungle* by Ed Ricciuti (W. W. Norton / Countryman Press); *Talk Like Ted: 9 Public Speaking Secrets of the World's Top Minds* (McGraw-Hill).

Describe yourself as a person. Committed to family and working with my clients to see their careers grow! I love spending time with my bride of 40 years, my kids, and my grandchildren. I love to travel; read; listen to, and talk to, others about history; and I love driving, especially convertibles. Books and publishing are all around me. My family is also in the business. My wife, both of my sisters, my niece, and my brother-in-law are all authors. One thing that I've learned when dealing with authors is that it is important to be forthright and honest.

How would you describe the proverbial "client from hell," and what are the warning signs? The recipe for the most effective agent-client partnership is trust and communication. My job is to represent my clients' interests to the best of my ability. I have found that the yin/yang of this task is to fuel a writer's enthusiasm while keeping them grounded in reality. The agent-client relationship turns into a push-me–pull-you when a client begins second-guessing the agent and operating unilaterally. If that happens, then the client no longer needs me as an agent. Also, while it is true that I earn at the pleasure of the client, I consider myself rather demanding. I thrive on process. Authors are well advised not to react emotionally to business process. If the client thinks their publisher is not performing, or if the publisher is indeed not performing, as agent, it is my responsibility to remedy the situation. Yes, I represent the client, but part of representing the client is to operate within the realistic parameters of the business environment. If the client lashes out at the publisher, they are going to lose. That behavior also reflects on my agency, which may affect my other clients. If that happens, the client will no longer be a part of my agency.

What do you think about self-publishing? There have been a few high-profile success stories in the vast desert called self-publishing. But these oases of success are few and far between. Right now, we are in a Wild West era of false starts, charlatans, and author mills. Anyone can launch an ebook or use print-on-demand (POD). They can even buy paper and print books. If you are considering self-publishing, caveat emptor. There are scores of for-profit businesses that call themselves "independent publishers" that are happy to take your money to post or print your book. A legitimate publisher is one that has an established distribution network into multiple channels to reach more consumers. If I wanted to be a doctor tomorrow, I would not be able to just walk into a hospital and announce that I was ready to do open-heart surgery. Publishing is the same way. You need to learn the business. If you know the business of publishing — editorial, marketing, sales, distribution, and publicity — then maybe self-publishing is an option. But then…if you know everything about the publishing business already, then why are your reading this answer to what I think about self-publishing? ☺

Do you like Amazon? As a research tool, I love Amazon.com. I use it every day. And I understand why Amazon.com is attractive to consumers. But I am always concerned when one corporation changes the publishing business in ways that are not always in the writer's best interests. It affects writers' ability to earn a living as authors.

Do you believe in a "higher power"? Yes. I believe in a higher power.

What will agenting be like in 2020? While I do believe we are in a Wild West era of self-publishing now, agents will transition into a role similar to that of independent publishers today. There are a number of agents currently entering into publishing arrangements with their clients, and by 2020 most agencies will offer those services for certain projects.

Describe your job and what you like and don't like about it. Agenting is a perfect career for a plate spinner — a multitasker's dream. Precariously twirling fragile china on tall rods while Khachaturian's "Sabre Dance" plays at full volume. My job is to find clients who write books I love to read, who I believe have an audience that can be reached with a partner publisher, and who will become an annuity (i.e., whose books will sell for a long time or who will write more books). Important aspects of my job include project management, from proposal preparation to publication; negotiating a fair agreement; outlining the shared expectations; and acting as both consultant and champion for my client throughout the process. What I don't like about my job is small royalty statements with little or no money and all the monotonous back-office paperwork.

Do you miss the way the business "used to be"? As it "used to be" means something different for me than it does for other agents. During the retail real-estate explosion of the '70s through the '90s, corporate publishers were fueling the growth of corporate booksellers; publishers could generally afford a longer earn-out period for their acquisitions. Advances were higher. Now, as online retailing and other factors have changed business models, publishers have scaled back advances and relied more on the authors to bring promotional resources to the partnership. I entered this fray in 2009, well beyond the "good old days" of publisher deep pockets. Since I come from a background of sales and marketing, I leverage my knowledge of the important functions that help gain attention for my clients' projects.

What does the "Big 5" mean to you? The "Big 5" is a bit of a misnomer. To paraphrase Mike Shatzkin of Idea Logical, a more cynical way to look at corporate publishing at this point is not to say the "Big 5," but rather the "Big 1, plus 4 others." The effects of the Penguin–Random House merger are only now beginning to morph into yet more consolidation of resources and fewer imprints. But from my perspective, the landscape is not as bleak as one might think. As of this writing, what we call the "Big 5" still consists of about 55 different adult imprints. I view these imprints the same way I view any of the independent presses. They all have dedicated staff; they all love buying and publishing books; and they all want their authors to succeed. And like the independent presses, they all have to deal with budgets, profit and loss, and office politics. The major difference between the Big 5 and independent presses is that they have to contend with shared resources. Shared resources benefit authors in some ways and detract in others. My job is to know the difference and to help manage those differences to my clients' advantage.

What do you want to tell new/unpublished writers? First of all, be realistic. If you want to get rich quick, buy a lottery ticket. Getting a book published is an exhilarating, confidence-building experience. It can also be fraught with disappointment on many levels. Second, be patient. It may take a long time, and many rejections, before you find the right agent; and then it may take a long time, and many more rejections, for that agent to find an acquisitions editor to commit to your work. Your friends, family, or writing group may like your work, but would they commit tens, perhaps hundreds, of thousands of dollars and the staff hours of dozens of colleagues to publish your work? Successfully launching a book into the market takes the time and cooperation of a lot of people. These days there are two options: self-publishing or partnering with a publisher. Given the technologies, it is easy for anyone to hang up a virtual shingle and claim they are a publisher. The real clout of a legitimate, established publisher is their ability to distribute your work into multiple channels. Hiring an agent is your best option in working with an established publisher. When you hire an agent, you are gaining access to our Rolodex, but also our experience. Once that manuscript is turned in to a publisher, many others need to come on board for the project to reach readers. No matter the subject, a writer puts their heart and soul into their manuscript. Publishing is an emotional business, but it is a business nonetheless. As agent, because I understand the process, I have to manage the business. Publishing in today's marketplace, authors need to also understand their contribution to marketing and self-promotion. Given our experience, we agents can help our writers learn what they need to do to become published authors. But above all, remember, be realistic, be patient, and let your agent be your guide.

Do you like that everything has become largely digitized? Some days yes, some days no. I have a love-hate relationship with email, scanners, MS Word, PDFs, ebooks, iBooks, and the like. But in the end, I love nothing more than to sit down with a real hardcover book and read all day and into the night. That is nirvana.

What do you like reading, watching, and listening to? I like reading books where I can hear the author speaking to me — narrative that can sing or sting — and books that can educate *and* entertain. I represent nonfiction, so I read mostly nonfiction. I have shelves of what I call my "retirement fiction." I walk for exercise and drive a lot, so I listen to a lot of audiobooks. I love musical theater, historical films, or classic films that transport me to different eras. On television, I enjoy political "theater," Britcoms, and miniseries television. I listen to all kinds of music. But when I work, I listen to acoustic guitar, piano, and jazz. My most egregious time waster of late is flash-mob videos.

Describe a book you would write. I will never write a book, but I do love to edit. I mostly edit proposals and title information pages. On rare occasions, I have edited certain client manuscripts. Very proud of that. I have prepared a number of documents for clients on the process of publishing: "Author's Guide to Submissions Materials," "Author's Guide to Marketing and Virtual Self-Promotion," "Process and Publishing Timeline," "Publicity 101," a few others. All together these would constitute a book on how to get happily published, but I reserve these documents for my clients.

Joker's wild: You might have noticed that the agency name and location don't seem to make sense. New England Publishing Associates (NEPA) is in New Jersey? NEPA was launched in 1980 by a dedicated husband-and-wife team, Ed and Elizabeth Frost Knappman. NEPA offices were in Connecticut. I began talking to Ed and Elizabeth about taking over the agency in 2008, and we came to terms in 2009. Throughout the year, Ed and Elizabeth became close personal friends. They taught me so much about agenting, and I strive to maintain their philosophies and traditions. Tragically, Ed died suddenly just six months after we closed on the transfer. It is in their honor that I have kept the NEPA name. And while I now live in the middle colonies, my roots and my heart remain in New England.

PAUL S. LEVINE LITERARY AGENCY ❖ www.paulslevinelit.com

1054 Superba Avenue, Venice, CA 90291, 310-450-6711, fax: 310-450-0181, paul@paulslevinelit.com
Carrier Pigeon: Use street address; train pigeon well.
Strippergram: Must be gorgeous and have a great routine.

Agent's name: Paul S. Levine

Describe what you like to represent and what you won't represent. Commercial fiction and nonfiction for adults, children, and young adults.
We don't represent science fiction, fantasy, and horror.

When and where were you born? March 16, 1954; New York, NY.

Describe your education and career history. BCom, Concordia University, Montréal (1977); MBA, York University, Toronto (1978); JD, University of Southern California, Los Angeles (1981). Attorney for more than 31 years.

If you were not an agent, what might you be doing instead? Practicing entertainment law, reading good books.

What are the best ways for writers to pitch you? Query letter *only* by snail mail, email, fax, carrier pigeon, or strippergram.

Do you charge fees? No.

What are some of the most common mistakes writers make when pitching you? Telling me that they're writing to me because they're looking for a literary agent. Duh!

How would you describe the proverbial "client from hell," and what are the warning signs? One who calls, faxes, emails, or sends carrier pigeons or strippergrams every day. One who constantly needs reassurance that each rejection letter does not mean that the client's project lacks merit and that the client is an awful person.

Why and how did you become an agent? I have loved the book business ever since I started practicing law in 1981. My first client was a major book publisher in Los Angeles.

What, if anything, can writers do to increase the odds that you will become his or her agent? Be referred by an existing client or colleague.

How would you describe to someone (or thing) from another planet what it is you do as an agent? I represent writers — book authors, screenwriters, and writer-producers.

Do you have any particular opinions or impressions of editors and publishers in general? I love them.

PEN & INK LITERARY, LLC ❖ www.penandinklit.com

ab@penandinklit.com, 917-740-9498; to see deal news:
www.facebook.com/PenInkLiterary; Twitter: twitter.com/PENandINKlit

Agent's name: Anne Bohner

Describe what you like to represent and what you won't represent. I'm currently most focused on women's fiction but will accept romance, young adult, memoir, and some popular nonfiction with an outstanding platform.

I generally avoid science fiction.

What are the best ways for writers to pitch you? Email only.

When and where were you born? Would rather not say, considering identity theft. I grew up in Garden City, NY.

Do you charge fees? No.

Describe your education and career history. I graduated from Villanova University, where I was an English major. After college I became an editorial assistant at Bantam Dell

(Random House), where I went on to become an assistant editor. From there I moved to New American Library (Penguin), where I rose in the ranks to senior editor. I've worked with multiple *New York Times* and *USA Today* bestselling authors.

Say something about your hobbies and personal interests. I'm in the trenches with three small children. If I had hobbies before kids, I can't remember.

Why and how did you become an agent? After having a child, I was looking for more work flexibility and stimulation. Creating my own business became a very attractive idea. Considering my wonderful insider contacts as an editor, becoming an agent was a natural next step. I absolutely love it.

Would you do it over again, or something else? Do it over! It's exciting, engaging, creative, and fabulous.

List some representative titles you have placed. *Yes, You Can Get Pregnant: Natural Ways to Improve Your Fertility Now and into Your 40s* by Aimee Raupp (MS Lac); *The Witch of Tivoli Parish* by Suzanne Palmieri; *Empire Girls* by Suzanne Hayes and Loretta Nyhan; *Semi-charmed Life* by Nora Zelevansky; *Left* by Tamar Ossowski.

Describe yourself as a person. Professional, warm, *not* a control freak. I like to surround myself with smart, self-assured authors who communicate clearly but can also take the initiative when it comes to their own writing and promotion. Though I have an editorial background and do like to provide critical feedback, I feel strongly that authors should follow their own instincts regarding their own projects.

How would you describe the proverbial "client from hell," and what are the warning signs? I hope to never use the term *client from hell*, but I do not appreciate overly needy writers or those who don't take it upon themselves to try to understand the publishing world, how to promote themselves, and what is appropriate contact between an author and the publisher. A true "client from hell" would be one who misrepresents him- or herself, lies, or plagiarizes.

What do you think about self-publishing? Self-publishing is another avenue for writers who want options. It has certainly helped to launch several major careers in the past few years, but it's hard to beat the prestige of a major publisher and all their resources, such as packaging, distribution, and promotion. If you don't have knowledge of the ins and outs of the publishing world, it can be difficult to find success. But if you have the verve, vision, and cash, then this is an option. Every author and situation is different.

Do you like Amazon? Amazon is forward thinking and sometimes does unpopular things. But, in terms of the big picture, it keeps the market competitive and forces the publishing world to stay on its toes.

Do you believe in a "higher power"? Yes, though I don't expect everyone else to.

What will agenting be like in 2020? While it's difficult to speculate, I think it may be much the same as it is now. There will always be a market for strong, knowledgeable, honest agents with a good eye for talent.

Describe your job and what you like and don't like about it. I have a small agency and, by design, work with only a handful of clients. This allows me to be totally available to those clients whose work I love. It's not uncommon for me to have a call with an author at 8 AM or on the weekends. Whatever works best for his or her schedule. I often provide editorial feedback, work to sell the projects, and then manage any business issues that may crop up with the publisher after the sale. I make sure the contracts are in order and take seriously my fiduciary responsibility to the client, maintaining and selling rights if possible and maximizing advances. I love the flexibility and sometimes miss the social aspects of being in a large office.

Do you miss the way the business "used to be"? The business has evolved but there's more flexibility and transparency. The same standards hold true: if your work is well done, competitive, fresh, and can find a market, then there's a place for you in the publishing world.

What does the "Big 5" mean to you? The publishers with the most resources. I have many friends at those places.

What do you want to tell new/unpublished writers? Write something that you feel swept up in, that's out of the box with a high concept, that's easily digestible, and that speaks to a certain market. Write every single day.

Do you like that everything has become largely digitized? It makes my life easier and it's probably more efficient and ultimately cost-effective for the publishers.

What do you like reading, watching, and listening to? In my down time I like to read thoughtful women's fiction and some nonfiction about parenting, education, or history such as David McCullough. *Downton Abbey*, *Mad Men*, HGTV, and CNBC are on my television. I'm a fan of Florence and the Machine, the Beatles, the Rolling Stones, and Strauss waltzes.

Describe a book you would write. I would love to write a novel that my book club would read.

Joker's wild: About the agency: Pen & Ink is a boutique literary agency founded by Anne Bohner, who has roughly 10 years of experience in the editorial departments of major trade publishers. Pen & Ink is defined by a love for books, dedication to the author, solid relationships with editors, and insider knowledge of the business. We are friends to many in the industry. Importantly, we know the market and what the publisher wants, which allows us to contour the material to make it more marketable. This gives us a distinct competitive edge.

P.S. LITERARY AGENCY ❖ www.psliterary.com

20033-520 Kerr Street, Oakville, ON, L6K 3C7 Canada,
416-907-8325 (Toronto), 212-655-9276 (New York),
queries: query@psliterary.com, general questions: info@psliterary.com

**Agent's name and contact info: Curtis Russell, principal agent,
query@psliterary.com**

Describe what you like to represent and what you won't represent. For nonfiction, currently seeking memoir, history, politics, current affairs, business (management and leadership, finance, etc.), health (targeting adults and children), wellness, sports, humor, popular science, popular psychology, pop culture, design, and lifestyle. For fiction, currently seeking commercial mainstream, literary (with a commercial angle), world literature, women's fiction, mystery (cozy, private eye, police procedural, etc.), thriller (legal, medical, political, etc.), romance (suspense, contemporary, historical, etc.), new adult (early-twenty-something protagonists), young adult (must be high-concept/commercial), middle grade (must be high-concept/commercial), picture books (must be high-concept/commercial).

I do not represent poetry, screenplays.

What are the best ways for writers to pitch you? I accept submissions via email. Please limit your query to one page and include three paragraphs: (1) introduction — include the title and category of your work (i.e., fiction or nonfiction and topic), an estimated word count, and a brief, general introduction; (2) brief overview — this should read similarly to back cover copy; (3) writer's bio — tell us a little bit about yourself and your background (awards and affiliations, etc.).

Do you charge fees? No.

**Agent's name and contact info: Maria Vicente, 416-907-3025,
maria@psliterary.com, Twitter: @MsMariaVicente, www.mariavicente.com**

Describe what you like to represent and what you won't represent. I represent an eclectic mix of literary/commercial fiction, children's books (young adult, middle grade, and picture books), and select nonfiction titles. For literary and commercial fiction, I am interested in general fiction, magical realism, and genre fiction (science fiction, fantasy, and horror) with mainstream appeal and crossover potential. I look for excellent writing combined with a high-concept plot. I am interested in a variety of young adult and middle grade genres: contemporary, horror, thriller, science fiction, fantasy, and magical realism. I enjoy literary prose, strong voices, and in-depth character development. I am also open to chapter book submissions that are unusual and have series potential. For picture books, submissions should be high-concept and character driven. I like whimsical and eccentric characters with a fun story to tell, and author-illustrators are preferred. For nonfiction, I am mostly interested in the following categories: pop culture, lifestyle, popular psychology, design, and DIY.

I'm not the right agent for romance manuscripts.

What are the best ways for writers to pitch you? Queries should be sent to query@psliterary.com. Address the query to me and include the following: the title, category, genre, and word count of your manuscript or proposal; a brief overview, similar to back cover copy; and an author bio. Do not send attachments unless specifically requested.

When and where were you born? I was born in Saint John, New Brunswick, on a late-summer day in the 1980s. I may live in Ontario now, but I am a Maritimer at heart.

Do you charge fees? No.

Describe your education and career history. I have an English literature degree from Carleton University and an education degree from the University of Western Ontario, and I have taken various post-graduate publishing courses from Ryerson University. Before becoming a literary agent, I was a high school English teacher (and before that, I was a freelance editor, a daycare worker, and a bookstore employee). I have also edited and designed various literary magazines.

Say something about your hobbies and personal interests. Nothing interests me more than books (and, yes, I realize this is a terribly boring answer). I collect anthologies of fairy tales (classics, retellings, and original tales), I love television series way more than I should, and I have 10+ years of graphic and print design experience.

Why and how did you become an agent? I like to think I was always meant to be a literary agent, but it just took some soul-searching to figure it out. I decided to switch careers and took some publishing courses to learn the industry. I completed two internships at agencies during this time and the things I learned were invaluable. My internships were absolute requirements; I never would have known that I wanted to be an agent without the guidance of my mentors.

Would you do it over again, or something else? I would absolutely do it over again. My only regret is that I didn't figure out this path sooner. I could have avoided a lot of student debt in a (somewhat) unrelated field. Alas, we take the paths we take for one reason or another. I'm just glad that I *did* figure things out eventually.

How would you describe the proverbial "client from hell," and what are the warning signs? I am an editorial agent, so I appreciate it when clients are open to feedback. A warning sign for me is when a writer is narrow-minded and unreceptive to constructive criticism. Confidence is necessary, but there is a fine line between that and cockiness. I expect my clients to be dedicated to their work, which includes revising as much as necessary.

What do you think about self-publishing? You do you. Traditional publishing isn't for everyone. Neither is self-publishing.

Do you like Amazon? I have nothing for or against Amazon. That arrow logo seems friendly enough.

What will agenting be like in 2020? Much like it is now, except with more robots — and hopefully time travel so I can get more things done in a single day.

Describe your job and what you like and don't like about it. It is impossible to describe what I do on a regular day, because it always changes. That's what I like most about being a literary agent, being able to wear different hats depending on the client or the task I am dealing with. I love working on new projects with clients and making those books available to readers. I hate the waiting, but I'm learning to accept it.

Do you miss the way the business "used to be"? I'm a newer agent, so I can't comment on the way things "used to be." That being said, I embrace the tumultuous and ever-changing nature of the publishing industry. I wouldn't be doing this if it didn't make me a little bit crazy.

What do you want to tell new/unpublished writers? Work hard and *really* think through decisions that will impact your career as a writer. Dedication and professionalism go a long way in this business. It's easy to get discouraged (there is a lot of waiting involved with being a traditionally published writer), but you need to figure out how to rise above that and make informed decisions to create the writing career you really, truly want.

Do you like that everything has become largely digitized? The digitization of our world certainly makes everyday things easier. I love the internet, I love my computer, and I love being able to read manuscripts on my iPad. When it comes to published books, I still prefer paper copies. I'm not sure I'll ever be able to move away from the collection of books on my shelves and the escapism of holding a physical book in my hands.

What do you like reading, watching, and listening to? I love literary fiction and children's books. I also have quite the graphic novel collection. Daily reads include the hundreds of blogs I have bookmarked on my laptop. I watch *a lot* of television series. Some of my favorite shows are *Fringe*, *Dawson's Creek*, *Buffy the Vampire Slayer*, *Dexter*, and *Glee*. (Musicals are my guilty pleasure.) My music taste varies across every possible genre (quite similar to my reading preferences).

Describe a book you would write. I leave the writing to my clients. ;)

Agent's name and contact info: Carly Watters, Twitter: @carlywatters, www.carlywatters.com, query@psliterary.com

Describe what you like to represent and what you won't represent. I'm looking for women's fiction, commercial fiction, literary mysteries and thrillers, young adult, new adult, health and wellness nonfiction, popular science, popular psychology, business, sports, and memoir. I am not looking for middle grade, serious history, religious texts, poetry, and screenplays. I like projects that make me feel something (yes, make me cry!), entertain me, and make me think about my role in the world at large.

What are the best ways for writers to pitch you? I can be pitched via email at query@ps literary.com with a simple three-paragraph query letter (hook and genre, book blurb, and author bio) and no sample material. I do not accept or open attachments. Please use this subject heading formula: BOOK TITLE for Carly Watters by AUTHOR NAME.

Do you charge fees? The P.S. Literary Agency does not charge reading fees.

Describe your education and career history. I began my publishing career in London, England, at the Darley Anderson Literary, TV and Film Agency and Bloomsbury. I completed my BA in English language and literature at Queen's University and my MA in publishing studies at City University London with a thesis on the social, political, and economic impact of literary prizes on trade publishing. I moved back to Canada in 2010 and after a brief stint in a children's publishing rights department I joined the P.S. Literary Agency.

Why and how did you become an agent? I only ever wanted to work in rights and contracts, so once I learned what a literary agent was, I knew I had found my calling. My first job in publishing was as a literary agency assistant at a successful commercial agency in the UK, and I got a taste for what I liked. Upon moving back to Toronto I joined the P.S. Literary Agency as an associate agent and was promoted to full agent in early 2013. I was lucky enough to have two great mentors and now an amazing roster of clients that make this job the best.

Would you do it over again, or something else? I can't imagine doing anything else. Nothing suits my personality better than the idiosyncrasies of this job: reading, connecting with authors and editors, traveling, negotiating, career management, and brand building.

List some representative titles you have placed. *Forever, Interrupted* by Taylor Jenkins Reid (Atria Books / Simon & Schuster); *After I Do* by Taylor Jenkins Reid (Atria Books / Simon & Schuster); *Maybe in Another Life* by Taylor Jenkins Reid (Atria Books / Simon & Schuster); *The Holders Series* by Julianna Scott (Strange Chemistry Angry Robot); *Not Quite the Classics* by Colin Mochrie (Penguin); *Anchorboy* by Jay Onrait (Harper Collins); *The Wellness Kitchen* by Paulette Lambert (Adams Media); *Ella and the Balloons in the Sky* by Danny Appleby and Lauren Pirie (Tundra Books / Random House).

What will agenting be like in 2020? That's a great question and makes me think about building author brands and selling more subsidiary rights like film and TV rights, video game rights, e-originals, and multimedia rights for devices that haven't even been invented yet. Agenting will be less about physical books and more about managing content creators and securing deals for them in whatever medium suits their work. We'll be called literary brand managers or agents and wear even more hats than we do today.

What do you want to tell new/unpublished writers? You can do it! If you have the skill and tenacity, you can survive the rejection and collaboration that is the publishing industry. Don't give up. Research is your friend. Only circle agents in this book that represent and sell what you write. You don't need an agent who's your friend, but you do need an agent who's going to be vocal about your rights and have your best interest at heart.

THE PURCELL AGENCY, LLC ❖ www.thepurcellagency.com

tpaqueries@gmail.com

Agent's name: Tina P. Schwartz, founder and literary agent

Describe what you like to represent and what you won't represent. I represent middle grade and young adult fiction and nonfiction. I truly enjoy contemporary/slice-of-life/coming-of-age tales.

I do NOT want any more picture books, sci-fi, or fantasy, please.

What are the best ways for writers to pitch you? I love to meet authors at face-to-face pitch sessions at conferences, so check my website for appearances. Otherwise, just email the main company email at TPAqueries@gmail.com and I'll be sure to consider your submission.

When and where were you born? "Back in the summer of '69!" Great song that describes my "when and where." Actually, the "where" is the North Shore suburbs of Chicago, IL, and I was born that June.

Do you charge fees? No, I don't charge fees *ever*.

Describe your education and career history. I have a BA in marketing communication, advertising emphasis, from Columbia College Chicago. (I wanted to write Super Bowl ads for TV!!) For many years I was in advertising as a media buyer, and I also sold radio airtime. At the same time, I began writing and selling 10 books of my own. In 2012, I finally left advertising for good to pursue my true passion of working with authors to develop and help sell their manuscripts.

Say something about your hobbies and personal interests. I absolutely love hanging out with my family. I also truly love babies, dogs, movies, photography, reading, climbing trees (self-proclaimed tomboy), scrapbooking, and knitting.

Why and how did you become an agent? I was an author first. Then, after selling my 10th book (on my own, to traditional publishers) and after helping several others get published, I thought, "Hmm, this might be an interesting full-time career — helping *others* get published! I'm used to negotiating and selling, so why not do it for manuscripts instead of radio time?" Then, while attending a writers' conference (as a speaker), I met four amazing agents who for some reason really took me under their wings. I told them I had decided to become an agent but wasn't sure how to break into it. One amazing agent was going to have me be her assistant but didn't have an opening for nine months. (Plus, she was in LA and I'm in Chicago.) During the waiting period, I had several people asking me about their manuscripts, and I wanted to represent them! I told the woman, who said, "Go for it — hang out your shingle and open your own agency!" So I did.

Would you do it over again, or something else? Absolutely, I'd do it again. I *love* being an agent! While it can get stressful sometimes, there's nothing quite like discovering a new author with a unique voice and a terrific story to tell! It's very exciting to see something go from manuscript to published book.

List some representative titles you have placed. *First Sun* by Tara Tolly; *Heart on a String* by Susan Soares; *Out of the Dragon's Mouth* by Joyce Burns Zeiss; *What Are You Hiding, Tory?* by Melanie Apel; *Shyness: The Ultimate Teen Guide* by Bernardo Carducci and Lisa Kaiser.

Describe yourself as a person. I'm a very friendly, down-to-earth person who always has a smile on her face. I'm a motivated self-starter who thinks that nothing is impossible, and that's been pretty true for me so far. I am a loyal friend, a fiercely protective person of those I am close to, and pretty fun to be around, I hope!

How would you describe the proverbial "client from hell," and what are the warning signs? Someone who tells me what to do (as in, bosses me around: "First, you're going to sign me on as a client. *Then* you're going to market my manuscript to the top publishing houses…"). I've had people tell me I'm wrong about their book and why I *must* love it because x, y, z (fill in the blanks). I don't like people telling me what I will or will not do or think.

What do you think about self-publishing? I feel self-publishing has come a long way, and that there are some great ways for people to get their work out there. But it's a really hard row to hoe. Prospective authors act like it's so easy to do! But to do it properly, a person has to have really had their manuscript critiqued by people they trust, and a good number of people, preferably. Then I still recommend getting a good editor, in addition to critique groups. You've got to get outstanding cover art, and just so many other things to worry about. For me, as a writer, I'd rather leave that to someone else to worry about…editing, copyediting, layout, fonts, artwork, cover art, distribution, advertising, etc. If you *like* all of those different aspects of the business, then self-publishing might be the perfect way to go. It's especially great for those who insist on total and complete creative control! Just go into it knowing that it's a huge responsibility, not to be taken lightly, if you want your book to be a respected book that could get great reviews and win contests or awards.

Do you believe in a "higher power"? Yes.

What will agenting be like in 2020? Authors will be much more thorough about interviewing prospective agents. Since more and more houses are looking for agented authors (having less staff to read through "slush piles" and relying on agents to weed through the countless number of manuscripts available), nearly everyone will have to have an agent, leading to a boom in agents and agencies sprouting up, possibly both good and bad. This will force writers to be more cautious about whom they choose to represent them, but also give the writer back a bit of power. I think agents will have to continue to know the marketplace and continue to impress aspiring writers with big-house contracts and book deals for their clients in order to compete with other agents out there.

Describe your job and what you like and don't like about it. My favorite part of the business is when I *love* a manuscript, get to discuss it with my assistants at length, and then give the author a call personally to offer representation. It is so exciting when they're happy and excited! The part I don't like is falling behind on submissions. I used to have a two-to-three-month response time, now it's more like three to six months. It can be a challenge to respond to every query.

What does the "Big 5" mean to you? Heaven! I admire and respect the books put out by those houses so much. It is the brass ring, in my opinion. I *love* all the houses I've worked with so far, but there's something unique about working with companies that were around decades before I was even born!

What do you want to tell new/unpublished writers? Dream big, and follow your heart. Anything is possible if you try your best and don't give up. Continue to work on your craft. Attend classes and conferences, and take advantage of opportunities online to get better and better at what you do, which is *writing*! Never stop telling stories. Whether you write fiction or nonfiction, for adults or children, you — as a writer — have the most unique thing on earth: voice. It is the thumbprint on your writing. Whether it's your first book or your fiftieth, once people get to know you and your writing, it is your voice that will keep them coming back for more!

Do you like that everything has become largely digitized? Yes. I think it makes reading much more accessible to the general public, especially for those who are homebound, or can't afford to buy hardcover books, or just need that extra convenience of pressing a button and having an affordable book at their fingertips! Libraries have started lending out ebooks, and even ereaders, letting those who may not have been able to read the latest and greatest literature a chance to have the world opened up to them as well. It makes everything that much more global, in my opinion.

What do you like reading, watching, and listening to? I like to read middle grade and young adult books, simply because they always have a ray of hope at the end. Even with dark and edgy books, there seems to be an underlying current of possibility that things *might* get better, that there *is* hope out there. When I read adult literature, I like autobiographies. As for watching, I had to give up TV in 2000 to become a writer. There just aren't enough hours in the day to run a household, be a wife and mother of three, *and* watch TV…plus, no one ever gives me the remote anyway! I do love movies, however. Some women buy shoes, but I buy DVDs. I have over 500 of them! I absolutely love to watch movies when I choose to take a break from my reality. I'm not a huge music fan. I listen to Top 40 stations, and still listen to commercials, since I used to write them — old habits die hard.

Describe a book you would write. I would like to write something that people absolutely can't put down, something that made them read until dawn! I want it to make readers grin to themselves throughout the day when thinking back to it. I want it to come back to the readers again and again.

RED FOX LITERARY, LLC ❖ www.redfoxliterary.com

129 Morro Avenue, Shell Beach, CA 93449

Agent's name and contact info: Karen Grencik, 805-459-3327, karen@redfoxliterary.com

Describe what you like to represent and what you won't represent. Children's books, from picture books through young adult, both fiction and nonfiction.

No adult material.

What are the best ways for writers to pitch you? We are open to submissions via email from attendees of conferences where we present or through industry referrals. We are not accepting unsolicited submissions.

When and where were you born? Orange County, CA. 1955.

Do you charge fees? No.

Describe your education and career history. I have an AA degree and a Certified Shorthand Reporter's License. I was a court reporter for 24 years. People and stories are my passion, and I had the good fortune of being able to transition successfully into the children's book business in 2011.

Say something about your hobbies and personal interests. I love to love and to make the world a brighter place. I hike with my Australian shepherds, do yoga, read voraciously, and pray a lot. I love to make videos of, and for, special occasions, and I try to make every day the very best it can be.

Why and how did you become an agent? I became an agent because of a story I wanted to see published. My friend Lu Chi Fa had been orphaned in China during the Communist revolution and was adopted by a Communist village chief. His story was so remarkable that I spent six weeks taking it down on my stenography machine, then decided that the world should hear it. I started attending writers' conferences in an effort to find an author who would take my verbatim notes and put them into publishable form. I even chased keynote speakers to their cars with my 200 pages of text in hand. I had the good fortune of meeting Becky White, the coauthor who brought Chi Fa's story to life. I then called several literary agencies to see if I could take someone to lunch so that I could learn what to do next. Linda Allen, an agent in San Francisco, laughed at me when she answered and told me to call her the next morning. I told her I would do anything to learn how to sell this story — that I would work for her, pay her, send her on vacations, and buy her presents. She said no one would help her when she had started out in the industry and that she would be happy to help me. Linda taught me how to write a query letter and has been my mentor and dear friend ever since. I then flew to New York to meet with editors, pretending I knew what I was talking about, and I sold *Double Luck, Memoirs of a Chinese Orphan*, to Holiday House less than a year after taking down Chi Fa's first words. Doors opened up in the children's book industry, and Abigail Samoun and I launched Red Fox Literary on June 14, 2011.

Would you do it over again, or something else? I had to do it, and still have to do it. It is my dharma.

List some representative titles you have placed. *The Girls of Gettysburg* by Bobbi Miller; *Water Is Water* by Miranda Paul; *Lost. Found.* by Marsha Diane Arnold; *Lana's Parade* by Erica Silverman; *Sewing Stories: The Life of Harriet Powers* by Barbara Herkert; *Winterfrost* by Michelle Houts; *The Lake Where Loon Lives* by Brenda Reeves Sturgis; *Buster* by Marcia Berneger; *Pug and Pig* by Sue Lowell Gallion; *Biggety Bat* by Ann Ingalls; *Vivien Thomas — the Man Who Saved the Blue Babies* by Gwendolyn Hooks; *Ira's Shakespeare Dream* by Glenda Armand.

Describe yourself as a person. Very considerate, dependable, organized, and earnest. I have to enjoy my working relationships, so my authors' personalities have to be a match for me. I'm more warm and fuzzy than businesslike, so stark, stern, or demanding communication styles don't work for me.

How would you describe the proverbial "client from hell," and what are the warning signs? Someone with an entitlement attitude who is so self-absorbed that they don't care at all about anyone else's feelings. Demanding, disrespectful, childish, and unprofessional in their reactions.

What do you think about self-publishing? I'm thrilled that there is an avenue for people who are not able to get their work traditionally published.

Do you like Amazon? I don't like it or dislike it. I work with what I have, and Amazon is there. I don't spend time wishing that things were different.

Do you believe in a "higher power"? Absolutely.

What will agenting be like in 2020? I have no idea!

Describe your job and what you like and don't like about it. I read, more than anything else —manuscripts, industry news, and what's currently being published. I spend a lot of time communicating with authors, editors, and colleagues. I do a copyedit on all manuscripts before they go out. And I spend a lot of time on record keeping and contract negotiations. I love giving authors good news and hate the daily delivery of bad news. I spend more time disappointing people than making them happy, and that's the hardest part!

Do you miss the way the business "used to be"? No, because I'm relatively new to the business and don't have the "good old days" to reflect back on.

What does the "Big 5" mean to you? The 5 conglomerates that dominate the publishing industry. I'm delighted that they buy my authors' stories!

What do you want to tell new/unpublished writers? There is nothing easy about writing books for children, so please don't do it unless you absolutely have to. Then study the craft.

Do you like that everything has become largely digitized? Love it!

What do you like reading, watching, and listening to? I'm pretty obsessed with learning, so the stories I read must offer more than a good narrative. I want to learn something I would not have known otherwise. I love historical fiction and nonfiction. I love documentaries and romantic comedies. I love listening to music and audiobooks.

Describe a book you would write. I am not a writer or a creator. I'm a matchmaker.

RED SOFA LITERARY, LLC ❖ www.redsofaliterary.com

Agents' names and contact info:
Dawn Frederick, literary agent/owner, dawn@redsofaliterary.com;
Jennie Goloboy, agent, jennie@redsofaliterary.com;
Laura Zats, associate agent, laura@redsofaliterary.com

Describe what you like to represent and what you won't represent.
Dawn Frederick's representative categories: biography — historical, media related, political; creative nonfiction — it needs to be smart, with a noticeable platform, and highly

commercial; graphic novels — no manga, please; history — books that will engage the commercial reader (for example, those by Michael Beschloss); humor — I loved *The Zombie Survival Guide*, *How to Be a Villain*, and *Yiddish with Dick and Jane*; pop culture — especially Americana, and anything quirky; social issues/current affairs, including women's studies, GLBT studies, social sciences; sports — less mainstream, more extreme sport (for example, roller derby); women's narratives, including chick lit nonfiction, Latina, and African American; young adult fiction and nonfiction; middle grade fiction and nonfiction. Absolutely no personal memoirs.

Jennie Goloboy's representative categories: science fiction/fantasy, especially with a literary flair — I would love to see more nontraditional settings and characters, and I'm always open to optimistic, lighthearted fiction but also enjoy a good scare; history — it must have a commercial (nonacademic) focus, and I have a strong interest in American history, especially through 1850; also interested in "history of an idea" books; romance, primarily with sci-fi and fantasy elements; young adult and middle grade, mostly science fiction/fantasy. No paranormal romance, dystopias, or "chosen one" stories, please. Absolutely no personal memoirs.

Laura Zats's representative categories: romance with a feminist bent — no love triangles or damaged, virginal women, please; young adult and middle grade fiction, especially contemporary; contemporary women's fiction, ideally with some comedic flair; science fiction/fantasy — must be character driven; erotica; new adult, particularly coming-of-age tales, romance, and urban fantasy.

PLEASE, NO PERSONAL MEMOIRS or SPIRITUAL/RELIGIOUS QUERIES.

What are the best ways for writers to pitch you? We highly encourage everyone to email a query letter initially, before attempting to send a full book proposal or sample chapters. If there is an interest, we will directly contact the author. Once these materials are received, the response time is usually four to six weeks, sometimes less. Please note that we will not open attachments unless they have been requested in advance. Make sure to clearly explain the project, who you are, and why you are passionately pursuing the idea. We also do take pitches at book conferences and have received referrals from current clients, as well as editors at publishing houses.

If we do request a book proposal, we'd like to see an overview/synopsis, a bio, market (*who* will read your book), competition, promotion (*how* readers will learn about your book), chapter summaries, and any other pertinent info.

When and where were you born?
Dawn: born in Atlanta, GA, and grew up in TN as well.

Jennie: born near Boston, MA.

Laura: born and raised in St. Paul, MN.

Do you charge fees? No.

Describe your education and career history.

Dawn: previously of Sebastian Literary Agency; master's degree, library and information sciences (2000); 10+ years as a bookstore manager/bookseller (independent/chain bookstores); Oliver Press, Ltd.

Jennie: PhD in history of American civilization (2003); master's degree in history (1995); author of *Success to Trade: Charleston's Merchants and the American Middle Class in the Revolutionary Era* (University of Georgia Press, forthcoming, 2015), several essays, short stories under the pen name Nora Fleischer; taught history at Macalester College and Colorado College.

Laura: BA degrees in English and anthropology.

Say something about your hobbies and personal interests.

Dawn: I'm a retired (as of April 2013) roller derby referee; hence there will be more opportunities for new sports (snowshoeing and hopefully cross-country skiing), as well as more time for supporting our local writing community (in Minnesota). I volunteer at the St. Paul Library and am a member of the Twin Cities Advisory Council for Minnesota Public Radio.

Jennie: I enjoy running (slowly), cooking, and embroidering (very slowly). I collect vintage how-to books and often try out old recipes.

Laura: I am a craft beer fanatic, a lindy hop enthusiast, and a habitual cross-stitcher. I also bake more than I could ever hope to eat and have recently begun to collect old vinyl records.

Why and how did you become an agent?

Dawn: I had found myself missing the front lines of the bookstore, being able to engage in conversations with readers (many who were also writers) on a daily basis. I wanted to be more involved with ideas from the early stages of inception and have a bigger role in getting them published. Being an agent was a natural fit, as it is the front lines for new book ideas — a natural fit for my previous years in bookstores and in line with my graduate studies, too.

Jennie: I started interning at Dawn's agency because I'm also a writer and wanted to learn more about the business side of publishing. I decided to become an agent because I became passionate about advocating for other writers. I enjoy cheering them on and pairing them with the right editor.

Laura: I began, like Jennie, as an intern with Dawn. I started working at publishing houses in 2011 and figured that if I was going to make being an editor a permanent thing, I'd better figure out what an agent does. As I learned more about agenting, I fell in love and, luckily for me, Red Sofa wanted to keep me!

Would you do it over again, or something else?

Dawn: Most definitely. I love being an agent, and if anything, it has been a work of love. Being able to work with writers from prepublication through the publication process is extremely satisfying and the main reason I love my job so much.

Jennie: Absolutely, I'd do this again! I love my authors. Plus, it's a great time to be in publishing.

Laura: I love being an agent, and I couldn't imagine doing anything else, as it pairs so well with my editorial experience!

List some representative titles you have placed. Untitled urban fantasy novel by Paul Krueger (Quirk Books, 2015); *Tarot: The Magician* by Tim Kane (Midnight Frost Books, tentatively 2014); *Inked* by Eric Smith (Bloomsbury Spark, 2014); *Renaissance Land* by Carrie Patel (Angry Robot Books, 2015); *The Buried Life* by Carrie Patel (Angry Robot Books, 2014); *One Night in Sixes*, two-book deal, by Tex Thompson (Solaris Books, 2014); *Boxcar Children Guide to Life* by Stacey Graham (Albert Whitman, 2014); *Haunted Stuff: Demonic Dolls, Screaming Skulls, and Other Creepy Collectibles* by Stacey Graham (Llewelyn, 2014); *Wonder Woman Unbound: The Curious History of the World's Most Famous Heroine* by Tim Hanley (Chicago Review Press, 2014); *Severance* by Chris Bucholz (Apex Publishing, 2014); *Wild Cards* by Jamie Wyman (Entangled Publishing, 2013).

Describe yourself as a person.

Dawn: Dedicated, a mother hen to my authors, extremely loyal, obsessively organized, a good multitasker, and very direct. I was once described as a cuddly grizzly bear. Seems an apt description.

Jennie: I'm a hard worker — maybe even a bit of a grind — and a research fiend. To my clients, I'm a coach and cheer squad. An editor once said that I "knew how to mix business with an obvious interest in formulating a friendship."

Laura: I'm a "fixer." To my authors, I aim to be a sounding board for new ideas, solutions to plot holes, and character inconsistencies, and I want to match them with editors who can do that as well. I also pride myself on being an open resource for those who are dedicated to making publishing a part of their life.

How would you describe the proverbial "client from hell," and what are the warning signs?

Dawn: I have a very difficult time working with any client who doesn't allow me to do my job. I make a point to give my authors the room they need to do their jobs, to excel in their creative art. In return I ask that they view us as a team, and that they let me handle the business side of our team; there's no need to hover or tell me how to do my job.

Jennie: I won't stand for unethical behavior — if a client asks me to do something I think is shady, we can't work together.

Laura: For me, an agent-author relationship is all about trust. I am a very editorial agent, so I want authors who are enthusiastic about differing visions of their work and trust that I have their best interests at heart. If you think your work is the best it can be, or that you know what house your book should go to, you're not right for me.

What do you think about self-publishing? We have no problem with self-publishing. In fact, it's a very viable option for some books, especially if timing is essential and/or the book would have a difficult time being placed with a traditional publisher. The important thing is that the same level of professionalism, presentation, and promotion is given to any book that's self-published, so that it has a fighting chance to win over readers in today's marketplace.

Do you like Amazon?

Dawn: In the bigger picture, it's necessary. Many readers use Amazon for their book purchases due to the convenience of how books are made available on their website. However, I'm equally seeing the American Booksellers Association (ABA) make it easier for readers to purchase books through them, and if that means a more balanced marketplace for publishing, I'm totally on board.

Jennie: I've used Amazon to accumulate my unwieldy collection of academic history books — Amazon has grown so big because it executes so well.

Laura: I love Amazon for how effortlessly it brings reader and book together. But in an ideal world, their pricing structure wouldn't affect indie bookstores as negatively as it currently does.

What will agenting be like in 2020?

Dawn: There will be more of a team approach to publishing between agents and editors, from the implementation of the book idea to the actual book-over. (It's starting as we speak, no less). Additionally, print books will be resurging in popularity, much like LPs in 2011 (and up through now). The "book" will be an art form and available in multiple formats, so much that bookstores will be able to "supersize" any book purchase with the option to purchase different versions of any title at minimal cost.

Jennie: The location of the agency, the author, and the publisher will be increasingly irrelevant. But there will still be a role for agents with proven taste in literature.

Laura: I imagine agents will increasingly become more like editors, social media coaches, publicists, and marketing gurus. Our job will focus more on selling the author rather than selling the individual book.

Describe your job and what you like and don't like about it.

Dawn: Because I am the founding owner of Red Sofa Literary, it's a constant juggling act for me. From the administrative responsibilities (which I do enjoy managing) to looking for new projects, as well as working with my current authors, every day is unique. And the work ebbs and flows, which is perfectly fine. Plus, I have a policy of working when the energy is at its best. So if it's best done at odd hours of the day, I make the time. It's all about good time management and keeping a happy real-life balance. My only complaint: I'll never be able to read every single book I want to in this lifetime.

Jennie: I love working with my authors. I love meeting editors and connecting with them. I enjoy the feeling of anticipation when I open a new manuscript — and the excitement when it's really good! I don't like the waiting process, but who does?

Laura: I like to think of myself as my authors' biggest fan. I love being a resource for those who aren't agented or published yet, and I love seeing the potential in a book and helping it get better and finding it the perfect home so that countless other people can become fans too! One thing I don't like, though, is saying no to authors who are interested in working with me.

Do you miss the way the business "used to be"?

Dawn: Not really. There are fewer trips to the post office, more chances to stay in touch with editors and publishers (thanks to social media), and more of a unity between all segments of publishing. Plus, I've met so many great authors in this digital environment that I wouldn't have met pre-internet days. I'm all about the new way of business for agencies.

Jennie: I started in 2011, so not really!

Laura: Well, I can't quite answer this as I'm brand new, but I think this is a very exciting time for publishing, and I couldn't wish for anything more!

What does the "Big 5" mean to you?

Dawn: It means I have my work cut out for me. However, I'm optimistic, as I believe the Big 5 are finally realizing they need to change some of their aged approaches to book publishing in today's social media world. I am hopeful that this means more opportunities for writers, and that midlist books will be given the attention they deserve.

Jennie: I'm delighted to see Simon & Schuster put so much new energy into science fiction and fantasy — I'm hoping this is the start of a trend!

Laura: Opportunity. I think that the big publishers will start allowing their imprints to be more experimental. Hopefully, this will open up some space for amazing, innovative ideas that wouldn't have found a home with a big publisher before.

What do you want to tell new/unpublished writers?

Dawn: Please do your homework and try to avoid rushing the process. It's rare for any writer to be successful overnight. Often the writers we appreciate had to work years upon years to become a household name. Know your book's category, give your book the best experience by making sure it's fully edited, and never take rejection personally.

Jennie: I agree with Dawn — everything will take much longer than you think. Use that time to make sure people are eager to buy your book when it does come out.

Laura: Be nice. Follow the rules. Don't try to do something new and crazy with a query letter. Trust in your book and let your work speak for you. Revise and go through creative processing and beta rounds until your head hurts, and make sure your idea is the best you can make it before you look for agents.

Do you like that everything has become largely digitized?

Dawn: I'm fine with digitization; as long as we don't burn our figurative bridges and remember to keep print books in the marketplace, you'll hear no complaints from me.

Jennie: Yes — it makes my office much neater!

Laura: As long as I can still get my hands on print books, I'm in!

What do you like reading, watching, and listening to?

Dawn: I am a fan of good pop-culture books, as well as smart fiction and graphic novels. I also read quite a few children's and young adult books annually. As for music, I have eclectic tastes, of which my favorite music usually falls in the punk, new wave, '80s, blue-grass, and trance categories. And regarding movies/TV, I'm a card-carrying Joss Whedon fanatic, and there's a good chance you'll find me watching shows like *House of Cards*, *Orange Is the New Black*, *Vampire Diaries*, and any HBO original series.

Jennie: Recently I've enjoyed reading *The Folly of the World* by Jesse Bullington, *Ancillary Justice* by Ann Leckie, and *When London Was Capital of America* by Julie Flavell. Terry Pratchett and Mary Balogh are my comfort reading. Watching: *Sleepy Hollow* (love the characters, angrily tweet about the historical inaccuracies) and *Mad Men*. Really enjoying the Marvel movies. Listening to: Have just formed a record club in an attempt to stay more up-to-date. My most recent favorites are And the Professors' *Our Postmortem* and Fiona Apple's *Idler Wheel*. Really wish Raphael Saadiq would put out a new album.

Laura: Reading: Dark Horse comics, young adult problem novels, and urban fantasy like *The Dresden Files*. Watching: *Archer*, *Dr. Who*, *Buffy* (anything in the Whedonverse, actually), *Psych*, *Breaking Bad*. Listening to: Anything new I've found on vinyl. Usually I gravitate toward jazz, funk, and big-band music. I also am an avid listener to the eclectic Minnesota Public Radio station The Current.

Describe a book you would write.

Dawn: This will never happen. I have no desire to write any book. Ever. But reading good ones? I'm all about it.

Jennie: I'm currently revising a book about merchants in Revolution-era Charleston, South Carolina, and what they show us about the early American middle class — it'll be published by University of Georgia Press in 2015. My next book will probably be about early American humor. I'm also working on a novel that is like *Downton Abbey* with cyborgs.

Laura: I don't think I'll write one, unless it's about tips in the industry, and that's a long way off. I think my authors will write about anything I'd want to see, so I'm happy not being a writer.

Joker's wild: We really enjoy cupcakes and beer at Red Sofa. Sometimes we have meetings where these things are easily accessible ☺

REGAL LITERARY, INC. ❖ www.regal-literary.com

The Capitol Building, 236 West 26th Street, #801, New York, NY 10001, submissions@regal-literary.com, info@regal-literary.com, 212-684-7900, 212-684-7906

Agent's name and contact info: Claire Anderson-Wheeler
We have a handy centralized submissions system, so you can email submissions@regal-literary.com and address it to me.

Describe what you like to represent and what you won't represent. I fall in love with books across a whole range of genres, so it's hard to make clear demarcations there. But in terms of what makes me really fall for a manuscript: I am a plot person, meaning I love a story with some meat on its bones. That doesn't mean it has to be a potboiler — but soft, limpid meditations tend not to work so well for me. I have a pet peeve about literary writers speaking dismissively about plot. Good plotting is *hard*. Character is the other biggie. Authors who are comfortable with their characters, who feel for them but don't overindulge them: that's something you can feel from the first page. There's not too much, genre-wise, that I would discard out of hand, although you're better off trying someone else if you're writing epic fantasy, picture books, erotica, or classic romance (or any combination thereof).

What are the best ways for writers to pitch you? I like to see a simple, straightforward query letter: your manuscript may be full of bells and whistles but a query letter full of them is a headache. Although other agents at Regal typically ask for the first 10 pages, I prefer to see a little more, so I often ask for the first three chapters as an attachment, together with a full synopsis. And by full I mean full — spoilers aren't spoilers in this business! I'm periodically at conferences and always happy to be pitched to in that context. On the other hand, if we meet in a bar and I tell you what I do for a living, please refrain from pulling a bound manuscript out of your satchel.

When and where were you born? Washington, DC, 1985.

Do you charge fees? No, but feel free to enclose some M&Ms.

Describe your education and career history. I grew up in Dublin, Ireland; Geneva, Switzerland; and Brussels, Belgium. I returned to Dublin (Trinity College) to get a law degree, and then moved to the UK (University of East Anglia) for a master's in creative writing. I got my first entrée into agenting with AM Heath in London; I then worked at Christine

Green Authors' Agents (London) and Anderson Literary (New York) before joining Team Regal.

Say something about your hobbies and personal interests. Surprisingly, I still count reading as a favored extracurricular activity. I still write and am part of some wonderful writers' circles, I love food — the cooking and eating of — I love to dance, and I went to circus school for a year. (I still can't juggle, though.)

Why and how did you become an agent? I met all these wonderful agents when doing my master's program in creative writing, and thought, wow — that's really a job. I knew I wanted to work in publishing in some capacity but I loved the idea of working so closely in tandem with authors and their work: being their collaborator and champion, as it were.

Would you do it over again, or something else? Ask me in 10 years, and if I'm solvent, then yes, definitely.

List some representative titles you have placed. *Mindwalker* by A. J. Steiger is the first title I placed here at Regal. It's a young adult title and represents everything I love in a manuscript: a nuanced, sophisticated story with high stakes and serious questions; two protagonists who are flawed, whip-smart, and yearning for something they can't yet place.

Describe yourself as a person. I try to be a sincere person. I think that's perhaps the single most important quality a person can have. I'm half extrovert and half introvert (and thus, occasionally contrarian). I'm an only child, and I'm sure I bear one or two hallmarks.

How would you describe the proverbial "client from hell," and what are the warning signs? Ha! Well I imagine it would be someone who was (a) completely inflexible about their work and resistant to feedback and/or (b) constantly in touch to check that they are still number one on my priority list. And perhaps (c) passive-aggressive and a bit whiney. But to be honest I've never had to work with any authors like that. Writers sensitive enough to write a great book and humble enough to endure the submissions process tend to be pretty great, sane people.

What do you think about self-publishing? I think it works for some people better than others. Partly it depends on what you want to get out of publishing. (Do you want a collaborative process? Do you feel more at home working in a team? Do you want the good old-fashioned cachet of a recognized arbiter putting his or her *yes* stamp on your book?) And I think it depends on what you have to give. (Do you have a lot of free time? Do you have marketing smarts?) Currently its biggest proponents are those who've had enormous success from it, and the reality is that they are outliers. It doesn't mean they're wrong to promote it, but I think it means their truth is subjective.

Do you like Amazon? I like the advances it has initiated in digital reading, cross-platform reading, and tremendous accessibility (in electronic or other form). But I deplore its ongoing strategy to suffocate competition, its insistent representation of publishers as out-of-touch fat cats, and the damage done to author and publisher earnings in its quest for world domination.

Do you believe in a "higher power"? I'm agnostic. I used to be troubled by the fact that I couldn't sign up to a firm yes or no, but I've largely made my peace with it.

What will agenting be like in 2020? Probably tougher and leaner, if that's possible. Probably there will be more hybrid agencies (also acting as freelance editors, speakers' bureaus, self-publishing outfits, etc.). But you know what? I really don't know.

Describe your job and what you like and don't like about it. My absolute favorite thing is when an author turns in a redraft and they've *nailed* it. It's a total fist-pump moment. What are always a drain are the submissions that are sort of beautiful but just don't work. Like a beautiful voice but otherwise a hot mess. Or a fantastic concept but poorly executed. It's that sense of some true potential that's fundamentally unsalvageable. It's frustrating and a bit heartbreaking.

Do you miss the way the business "used to be"? I haven't been around long enough to remember a time of real three-martini lunches. Part of me wishes I had been. But at least I don't have to bear the burden of nostalgia.

What does the "Big 5" mean to you? Clout, competence, and in relative terms, money. On the downside, some unwieldiness.

What do you want to tell new/unpublished writers? Think long-term. Have faith. Always aim for excellence.

Do you like that everything has become largely digitized? I don't mind it being digitized, as long as it's not exclusively digitized.

What do you like reading, watching, and listening to? Reading: all sorts of fiction; biography; *Scientific American* and any of its kin. Watching: nothing beats a good heist flick. Listening: any artist better known for their music than their haircut/celeb spouse.

Describe a book you would write. Really, really good (obviously).

Agent's name and contact info: Markus Hoffmann, markus@regal-literary.com

Describe what you like to represent and what you won't represent. I like strong voices and surprising uses of genre, protagonists who aren't cookie cutter, dialogue that's not an excuse for exposition, and stories that surprise me.

I don't like clichés, mixed metaphors, predictability, plot holes, or writers who try to lecture me.

What are the best ways for writers to pitch you? Please follow the guidelines you'll find on our website.

When and where were you born? December 29, 1970, in Stuttgart, Germany.

Do you charge fees? No.

Describe your education and career history. Master's in English and Russian language and Literature from Ludwig Maximilians University, Munich. I also studied at the Herzen Linguistic University, Moscow, and at Hertford College, Oxford. I've worked in publishing since 1998, starting as a literary scout and then foreign rights agent in the UK. I've been in the US since 2004, working for two years as a senior scout at Maria B. Campbell Associates, and joined Regal Literary in 2006 as a literary agent and foreign rights director. I am currently the agency's managing director.

Say something about your hobbies and personal interests. I still love books, and if I ever don't, it'll be time to look for a job in a different industry. I also play the trumpet and the piano and am a proud member of Brooklyn's Fancy Shapes as well as Half on Signature, publishing's most famous R&B band. I got addicted to surfing a few summers ago so will regularly sacrifice a good night's sleep for the dawn patrol session out in the Rockaways. When the surf isn't up, I practice Ashtanga Yoga.

Why and how did you become an agent? Soon after starting to work in publishing, I realized that I'm not only a good reader but also good at helping others improve on what they've written. Beyond bad teenage poetry, I never had a real ambition to write — my personal artistic outlet is music — but I love being able to assist writers in making their work better. I also, somewhat to my surprise, found out that I love negotiating. So agenting is pretty much the ideal job for me.

Would you do it over again, or something else? I would, unless somehow I figured out how to become an opera director.

List some representative titles you have placed. Novels: *This Is How It Really Sounds!* by Stuart Archer Cohen; *Burning Down George Orwell's House* by Andrew Ervin; *Sand* by Wolfgang Herrndorf. Nonfiction: *The Oldest Start* by Anna Frebel; *Finding West Wind* by John Jacob Kaag; *The Fame Lunches* by Daphne Merkin.

Describe yourself as a person. I look younger than I am, apparently. I have an accent that most can identify as German, although sometimes I manage to be mistaken for being from Scotland or Ireland, which I always consider a personal triumph. I'm a fairly unashamed advocate for high culture but without, I hope, being an elitist. To the disgust of one of my colleagues, I love James Joyce and Thomas Pynchon.

How would you describe the proverbial "client from hell," and what are the warning signs? Somebody who's only interested in money and a movie deal. Somebody who won't listen to professional advice.

What do you think about self-publishing? Can be good if you write genre fiction, but expect to do a lot of work and invest a lot of time and also money if you want to be successful. If you get the chance to work with a publisher, you'll almost always be better off.

Do you like Amazon? Yes and no. The problem isn't Amazon per se but their market power, and the fact that they don't need to make money from selling books.

Do you believe in a "higher power"? No. But I believe in the power of art.

What will agenting be like in 2020? We'll be managers as well as agents. But at Regal Literary, that's been the case for a long time anyway.

Describe your job and what you like and don't like about it. I edit and develop book ideas with really smart people and then help them (and myself) make a living from their writing. That kind of work scores high on my job satisfaction scale. I don't like how easy it is to get distracted from doing real work by email, and how hard it is to find enough time to read.

Do you miss the way the business "used to be"? No. What's the point?

What does the "Big 5" mean to you? Bottlenecks and a lot of money if you get through to them. Some great efforts to publish great books, some lousy efforts to publish great books.

What do you want to tell new/unpublished writers? Read as much as you can.

Do you like that everything has become largely digitized? It hasn't. Ebooks are 25 percent or so of the market. That leaves 75 percent to print. Even if that ratio changes, print books are here to stay.

What do you like reading, watching, and listening to? Too much to list everything here, so instead, some cult classics of mine: novel — *Going Native* by Stephen Wright; TV — *The Kingdom* by Lars von Trier; music: *Brooklyn Babylon* by Darcy James Argue's Secret Society.

Describe a book you would write. A great thriller set in California that combines the cool of Kem Nunn's *Tapping the Source* with the sublime weirdness of Joy Williams.

Joker's wild: Don't go all in on pocket 10s.

REGINA RYAN PUBLISHING ENTERPRISES, INC. ❖

www.reginaryanbooks.com

251 Central Park West, 7D, New York, New York 10024, 212-787-5589

**Agent's name and contact info: Regina Ryan,
reginaryan@reginaryanbooks.com**

Describe what you like to represent and what you won't represent. I like to work on books that have something new and meaningful to say, and that are well written in a fresh, smart, stimulating way. I love a good story, and books about nature of all kinds, but especially birds. Areas I am especially interested in include architecture, history, science (especially the brain), the environment, women's interest, cooking, psychology, health and wellness, diet, pets, lifestyle, sustainability, popular reference, and leisure activities including sports, travel, and gardening.

I won't represent fiction, children's books, screenplays, plays, or poetry.

What are the best ways for writers to pitch you? Please send a one-page query letter to queries@reginaryanbooks.com.

When and where were you born? I was born in New York City.

Do you charge fees? I don't normally charge a fee for any of my services but if I put a lot of work into a project and the author takes my work and goes elsewhere — for instance, he or she decides to self-publish, or go with another agent — then I would consider charging a fee. I warn authors of this in advance.

Describe your education and career history. I was an English major at a small Catholic women's college: Trinity in Washington, DC, now a university. Other alumnae include Nancy Pelosi and Kathleen Sebelius. After a brief stint in advertising, l began my publishing career at Alfred A. Knopf as an assistant. I became an editor and stayed there for 11 years. After that, I became editor in chief of Macmillan Publishing in the Adult Trade Book department, and I was the first woman to hold that position in a major hardcover house. I then went on my own and worked as both a book packager and literary agent. I eventually focused only on being a literary agent for adult nonfiction. I have had my own boutique agency for some 37 years now.

Say something about your hobbies and personal interests. I love nature: I am a bird-watcher and a mushroom hunter, a stargazer and a hiker. I have also been a mad vegetable gardener but now my gardens are all indoors. I love to read and have been a member of a book club that reads only fiction for nearly 20 years. I love music, particularly early and baroque music, and the opera. I am a balletomane as well.

Why and how did you become an agent? I became an agent rather circuitously: When I went on my own after leaving Macmillan, I became a book packager because I loved the process of creating and editing books, from working with the author to helping choose the jacket to working on publicity. I also represented a few authors during that time. However, as the industry changed, and packagers were expected to deliver "branded" books — often on the same old subject but with a different magazine's name appended — I decided to focus entirely on agenting. It gave me a more diverse list of books and authors to work with, which I really like. It's always interesting!

Would you do it over again, or something else? I do think I'm very suited to what I do as an agent, but whether I'd do it over again — given the state of the publishing business now — I'm not sure. Don't know what else I'd be, though, except maybe a park ranger.

List some representative titles you have placed. *So You Think You Know Football?* by Ben Austro (Taylor Publishing); *What's Wrong with My Houseplant?* by David Deardorff and Kathryn Wadsworth (Timber Press); *The Peterson's Guide to Mammal Watching* by Vladimir Dinets (Houghton Mifflin Harcourt); *Jewish Wisdom*, selected and edited by Miriam Chaikin, illustrated by Gabriel Lisowski (Arcade Publishing); *Sexuality and Dementia: Compassionate and Practical Strategies for Dealing with Unexpected or Inappropriate Behaviors* by Douglas Wornell, MD (Demos Publishing); *Dragon Songs: Love and Adventure among Crocodiles, Alligators, and Other Dinosaur Relations* by Vladimir Dinets (Arcade Publishing); *Bountiful Bonsai: Create Beautiful Indoor Container Gardens with Edible Fruits, Herbs and Flowers* by Richard Bender (Tuttle Publishing); *The Sugar Season: A Year in the Life of Maple Syrup, and One Family's Quest for the Sweetest Harvest* by Douglas Whynott (Da Capo Press); *Mingus Speaks: Interviews 1972–1974*, edited by John Goodman (University of California Press); *The Peterson's Guide to Bird Sounds, Eastern and Western Volumes* by Nathan Pieplow (Houghton Mifflin Harcourt); *Cookies for Grown-Ups* by Kelly Cooper (Red Rock Press). *The Thinker's Thesaurus: Sophisticated Alternatives to Common Words* by Peter E. Meltzer (W. W. Norton).

Describe yourself as a person. I'm enthusiastic, curious, friendly, and, I like to think, fair-minded and kind. I'm generally a quiet person, and a good listener. I laugh a lot. I don't get angry often but if I feel my client is being mistreated, watch out!

How would you describe the proverbial "client from hell," and what are the warning signs? The client from hell is one who demands attention — who calls or emails constantly, often for no real reason. The warning sign: when I say I prefer to connect via email, he or she ignores it and keeps on calling.

What do you think about self-publishing? Self-publishing can be a very good alternative in some instances. If a person has a story to tell but not enough of a story or platform to interest a traditional publisher, self-publishing is a very good idea. It's also great for books that are out of print but should be available.

Do you like Amazon? I have very mixed feelings. Amazon is a bully, it seems, and sadly has driven many bookstores out of existence. At the same time it performs a very useful public service by (1) making available many books that bookstores might not carry and (2) making all books available to so many people who would not have access to them any other way. Also, I have put a number of my authors' books up on Amazon as ebooks and the Amazon folks have been wonderful to work with.

Do you believe in a "higher power"? No, I don't.

What will agenting be like in 2020? As the large publishing houses continue to merge and shrink, it will be harder for agents to make a living. Agents will wear more and more hats, as digital producers, business managers, even book packagers, media producers, and publicity advisers (in fact, they are doing much of this right now in search of additional revenue streams!).

Describe your job and what you like and don't like about it. I see myself as a manager and chief cheerleader for my authors' careers and books. Most of my day is spent answering emails, in which I'm putting out firestorms, encouraging and advising my authors, developing proposals, submitting manuscripts, following up on submissions, and sorting out problems. There is an incredible amount of detail work in regard to books that have been published and contracts to be negotiated. What I don't like is the endless small and pesky detail — I'd trade that willingly for more time to read submissions and my authors' manuscripts.

Do you miss the way the business "used to be"? Yes, I do miss the "good old days" when there were many more publishers, and much more money for authors (and agents). The publishing life was easier. It seemed like a less pressure-ridden time as well.

What does the "Big 5" mean to you? The "Big 5" to me means hundreds of imprints crammed under five roofs — many of which will soon disappear.

What do you want to tell new/unpublished writers? Although getting published with some big publisher like one of the "Big 5" has gotten much more difficult, the good news is that there are so many good medium-sized and small publishers popping up. It's also a good time to be an author because authors can take promotion into their own hands, through social media and the Web. It's an empowering time for authors.

Do you like that everything has become largely digitized? Yes. It is much more efficient and makes life easier, especially in the office. I also like reading on my iPad, which I have with me always. I love the fact that I can pull it out and read a book or queries or a newspaper anyplace, anytime, without having lugged, say, a big manuscript with me. It's all there on my magic gadget!

What do you like reading, watching, and listening to? I love reading fiction in my off hours (just read *Billy Lynn's Long Halftime Walk* by Ben Fountain — terrific!), and I enjoy watching TV — especially murder mysteries from England like *Wallander*, *Vera*, *DCI Banks*, or, best of all, *Inspector Morse*. I like to listen to opera while I read. My favorite Pandora radio station is Paul Simon and features Simon, of course, and other great music by the likes of J.J. Cale, James Taylor, Sam Cooke, Sufjan Stevens, Little Feat, and Dan Hicks and the Hot Licks! Love it!

Describe a book you would write. I would like to be good enough as a writer to do something like Annie Dillard — observations and adventures in nature.

Joker's wild: I'm always looking for exciting new projects!

RICHARD CURTIS ASSOCIATES, INC. ❖ www.curtisagency.com

171 East 74th Street, 2nd Floor, New York, NY 10021

Agent's name and contact info: Richard Curtis c/o Pam Valvera, office manager, pv@curtisagency.com

Describe what you like to represent and what you won't represent. Commercial fiction and nonfiction, as well as genre fiction. No screenplays.

What are the best ways for writers to pitch you? One-page letter via US Mail with an SASE. No emails, please.

Do you charge fees? No.

List some representative titles you have placed. Four-title deal with Audible.com for Dan Simmons: *Illium*, *Olympos*, *Song of Kali*, *The Hollow Man*.

THE RICHARD PARKS AGENCY ❖ www.richardparksagency.com

PO Box 693, Salem, NY 12865

Agent's name and contact info: Richard Parks, rp@richardparksagency.com

Describe what you like to represent and what you won't represent. Literary fiction, commercial fiction, including mystery and suspense and upmarket women's fiction, some young adult fiction; narrative nonfiction, memoir, biography, history, pop culture.

Will not represent romance fiction, Westerns, children's books, heavy science or business.

What are the best ways for writers to pitch you? By old-fashioned snail mail with query letter and SASE. I read fiction only by referral.

When and where were you born? I'm a Libra, born in Jacksonville, Florida.

Do you charge fees? No, except to be reimbursed for any unusual expenses incurred at the specific request of the author.

Describe your education and career history. Undergrad BA from Duke University, MA from the University of North Carolina at Chapel Hill. Started in the agency business at Curtis Brown, Ltd. After 10 years, left to work in film and television, first as a studio executive and then as an independent producer. After 9 years of that and 2 movies produced, returned to the agency business and opened my own agency.

Say something about your hobbies and personal interests. I'm an enthusiastic gardener and a passionate reader. I enjoy working with my hands for relaxation — e.g., carpentry. I have three wonderful dogs.

Why and how did you become an agent? Chance and luck. I stumbled into a part-time job at Curtis Brown one summer, and by the end of the summer I was totally hooked on the agency business.

Would you do it over again, or something else? Absolutely! I tried "something else" and ultimately didn't like it.

List some representative titles you have placed. *Lake Utopia* by Holly Robinson (NAL); *The Long and Faraway Gone* by Lou Berney (William Morrow); *Bathing the Lion* by Jonathan Carroll (St. Martin's); *Writing in Pictures: Screenwriting Made (Mostly) Painless* by Joseph McBride (Vintage); *The End of the Point* by Elizabeth Graver (Harper Collins); *The American Sun and Wind Moving Picture Company* by Jay Neugeboren (Texas Tech University Press); *Wingshooters* by Nina Revoyr (Akashic); *Three Weeks in December* by Audrey Schulman (Europa Editions); *Falling to Earth* by Kate Southwood (Europa Editions); *Between Heaven and Here* by Susan Straight (McSweeney's).

Describe yourself as a person. I like people. I'm an even-keeled person. No temper tantrums, no hysteria. I'm very organized. I'm a happy person with an optimistic outlook on life.

How would you describe the proverbial "client from hell," and what are the warning signs? Thank goodness, I've never had one. I've been fortunate enough to work with highly professional, pleasant, and talented people.

What do you think about self-publishing? I think it's valid in certain circumstances, but I think it's far better to have the professional expertise and support of a publisher behind your book.

Do you like Amazon? I haven't worked with them enough to have an opinion.

Do you believe in a "higher power"? Yes.

What will agenting be like in 2020? Who knows? I hope the agent-client relationship at the heart of the business never changes.

Describe your job and what you like and don't like about it. My job, in addition to selling my clients' work, is about keeping their professional lives organized and on track so that they can focus their attention on the creative work at hand. There's almost nothing I don't like about it.

Do you miss the way the business "used to be"? No. I'm happy with it now.

What does the "Big 5" mean to you? Penguin/Random, Hachette, Harper Collins, Simon & Schuster, Macmillan.

What do you want to tell new/unpublished writers? Persevere. Don't let rejection get you down. Always strive to do your best work possible. Good enough won't do.

Do you like that everything has become largely digitized? I'm quite comfortable with digitization. Making submissions electronically is infinitely easier and more efficient, and I like reading on an electronic reader.

What do you like reading, watching, and listening to? Well-written books and magazines, really good movies and the occasional good television program, classical music.

Describe a book you would write. I'm not a writer. I'm an agent.

RITA ROSENKRANZ LITERARY AGENCY

440 West End Avenue, #15D, New York, NY 10024-5358, 212-873-6333

Agent's name and contact info: Rita Rosenkranz, rrosenkranz@mindspring.com

Describe what you like to represent and what you won't represent. All areas of adult nonfiction.

What are the best ways for writers to pitch you? Via email (see address above) or via regular mail.

Do you charge fees? No.

Describe your education and career history. Former editor at major New York publishing houses. Started agency in 1990.

List some representative titles you have placed. *A Mind for Numbers: How to Excel in Math Even If You Flunked Algebra* by Barbara Oakley; *Wrigley Field Year by Year: A*

Century at the Friendly Confines by Sam Pathy; *Back from the Brink: True Stories and Practical Help for Overcoming Depression and Bipolar Disorder* by Graeme Cowan; *Breakthrough Communication: A Powerful 4-Step Process for Overcoming Resistance and Getting Results* by Harrison Monarth; *Discover Magazine's Vital Signs: True Tales of Medical Mysteries, Obscure Diseases, and Life-Saving Diagnoses* by Dr. Robert Norman.

RLR ASSOCIATES, LTD. ❖ www.rlrassociates.net

7 West 51st Street, New York, NY 10019, 212-541-8641

Agent's name and contact info: Scott Gould, sgould@rlrassociates.net

Describe what you like to represent and what you won't represent. We represent literary and commercial fiction (including genre fiction) and all kinds of well-written, narrative nonfiction, with a particular interest in history, pop culture, humor, food and beverage, biography, and sports. We also represent all types of children's literature.

What are the best ways for writers to pitch you? Email me a query letter explaining the book, along with your writing credits. If it's fiction, paste the first chapter in the email.

When and where were you born? Baltimore, MD (Bodymore, Murdaland).

Do you charge fees? No.

Describe your education and career history. As a literary agent for RLR, I oversee all book development within the firm. I began my career in the editorial department of *Playboy* magazine and was later in publicity at Tor/Forge. I am a graduate of New York University, where I received a BA in English and American literature.

Say something about your hobbies and personal interests. I love reading (obviously), and it's probably my number one hobby. And not just books, but all kinds of media (I had at one point, I think, 17 magazine subscriptions). Second to that is trying to live a robust social life — eating, drinking, traveling with friends and family. Is there anything better than hearing a good story at the table after the dessert is cleared away and you're still sipping on the last glass of bourbon?

Why and how did you become an agent? I wanted to be a part of publishing books. I got a taste of agenting while interning for a small agency in SoHo (shout-out to Ethan Ellenberg, great guy!), moved around a bit in the industry, and found my way back.

Would you do it over again, or something else? You're getting rather existential here, my man.

List some representative titles you have placed. *Reckless: The Racehorse Who Became a Marine Corps Hero* by Tom Clavin (NAL/Penguin Random House); *Unbeatable: Notre*

Dame and the Last Great College Football Season by Jerry Barca (St. Martin's Press); *Twerp: A Novel by Mark Goldblatt* (Random House Children's Books); *Kicks* by Slam Magazine (Rizzoli); *Great American Craft Beer* by Andy Crouch (Running Press); *Toots in Solitude* by John Yount (Open Road Media); *Living Loaded: A Memoir with Drinks* by Dan Dunn (Crown / Random House).

Describe yourself as a person. You can ask my mother…

How would you describe the proverbial "client from hell," and what are the warning signs? Crazy is crazy, you can't really put a definition on it, can you?

What do you think about self-publishing? I think it can be fantastic for a very small number of writers.

Do you like Amazon? It's a kind of love like in an abusive relationship. They're incomparable at many things, especially making books available and easy to buy for absolutely everyone, but there seems to be a tendency to treat book culture like a soulless widget.

Do you believe in a "higher power"? Okay, now we're definitely getting pretty existential.

What will agenting be like in 2020? I think a lot like it is now. But with a continually growing focus on every aspect of a writer's career.

Describe your job and what you like and don't like about it. My job is finding and shaping compelling work to shepherd it out into the world. Then putting out countless fires.

Do you miss the way the business "used to be"? "Used to be" is quite the moving target. I'm pretty sure I was in grade school then.

What does the "Big 5" mean to you? The power center of trade publishing. And hopefully now that we're five, even stronger to keep the terms of Amazon in line.

What do you want to tell new/unpublished writers? It's not going to be easy, but the cream does tend to rise to the top.

Do you like that everything has become largely digitized? Yes. I think that paper books will exist for the foreseeable future, but it's great to have digital too. Who wouldn't want to reach more readers?

What do you like reading, watching, and listening to? Slightly unhinged fiction — Sam Lipsyte, Martin Amis, Michael Kimball, et al. Essays — Tim Kreider, Geoff Dyer. Comics — Frank Miller, Alan Moore. History. True crime. The list would go on. TV: I'm a believer we are in the golden age of TV. *The Wire, Sopranos, Eastbound and Down, Louie, Breaking Bad…*

Describe a book you would write. That's your job!

ROBIN STRAUS AGENCY, INC. ❖ www.robinstrausagency.com

229 East 79th Street, Suite 5A, New York, NY 10075, 212-472-3282, fax: 212-472-3833, info@robinstrausagency.com

Agent's name and contact info: (Ms.) Robin Straus, info@robinstrausagency.com

Describe what you like to represent and what you won't represent. High-quality literary fiction and nonfiction. Subject is of less importance than fine writing and research.

What are the best ways for writers to pitch you? Please see our website for submission info. A great query letter and sample material that speaks for itself. Caution: we are a very small agency and are able to take on very few new clients.

When and where were you born? New Jersey.

Do you charge fees? No.

Describe your education and career history. Wellesley College, BA; NY School of Business, MBA.

Say something about your hobbies and personal interests. Reading, traveling, the arts of all kinds.

Why and how did you become an agent? Started at Little, Brown, thinking I'd become an editor but became very interested in the business end so moved to subsidiary rights at Doubleday and then Random House. But missed working with authors, and agenting seemed the best way to combine everything. Joined Wallace & Sheil Agency for four years and started my own agency in 1983.

Would you do it over again, or something else? I love being an advocate for writers, but I also would have been happy being a doctor or raising horses and dogs.

List some representative titles you have placed. Fiction by Alexander McCall Smith and Sheila Kohler, nonfiction by Anthony Beevor, Andrew Hacker, Peter Watson and Sigrid MacRae, photography by Paul Nicklen and David Doubilet.

How would you describe the proverbial "client from hell," and what are the warning signs? Being awakened every morning by a client's phone call.

What do you think about self-publishing? I think authors benefit most from working with skilled editors and publishers.

What will agenting be like in 2020? Even with all the competition for our time, I believe books will always have a critical role in our culture. Publishers will continue to exist as curators and figure out ways to stay central. With the rise of the internet and other electronic media, there is a huge need for content, and authors increasingly will find other venues and audiences for their work. The challenge for agents is to help writers sort through all the opportunities and make sure they are compensated fairly and that their work is protected.

Describe your job and what you like and don't like about it. If you don't like to read, if you aren't organized and detail oriented and a people person who enjoys matchmaking and selling, I wouldn't recommend agenting. When I represent an author, I work with him or her to help shape proposals and manuscripts to entice editors to make an offer. I submit material to publishers, negotiate contracts, vet royalty statements, and sell translation, serial, film, and audio rights on behalf of clients. I generally act as the business manager for the author and intercede whenever necessary through the entire publishing process. I view my relationship with my clients as a continuum that extends over many books. I like helping to shape a writer's career, and I like the fact that I have my hands in all aspects of the publishing process.

Do you miss the way the business "used to be"? Nothing stays the same; one needs to be amenable to change.

What do you want to tell new/unpublished writers? Blow me away with your prose and ideas. Watch your grammar, avoid clichés, and don't overstate claims that a book is revolutionary. Be receptive to suggestions on how to improve your work and understand that publishing works best as a collaborative effort. Be imaginative about how to market yourself and your books.

Do you like that everything has become largely digitized? It hasn't.

What do you like reading, watching, and listening to? I have very eclectic tastes. A good writer can make his or her work captivate me even if I didn't imagine I would be interested in a particular topic. Ditto for movies and music. But no horror, please.

SCHIAVONE LITERARY AGENCY, INC.

236 Trails End, West Palm Beach, FL 22314-2135, phone/fax: 561-966-9294

Agent's name and contact info: James Schiavone, EdD, profschia@aol.com

Describe what you like to represent and what you won't represent. All genres except children's picture books, anthologies, collections, poetry, previously published work in any format (i.e., self-published, POD, online, etc.).

What are the best ways for writers to pitch you? We only accept one-page email query letters; no attachments. No phone calls or faxes. No USPS letters.

When and where were you born? New York City.

Do you charge fees? No.

Describe your education and career history. BS, MA, New York University; EdD, Nova University; professional diploma as reading specialist in secondary school and college, Columbia University; advanced studies, University of Rome, Italy; reading specialist Miami-Dade (FL) public schools; director of reading, K–12 Monroe County (FL) public schools; professor of developmental skills, City University of New York (CUNY).

Why and how did you become an agent? Upon early retirement from CUNY, I made the move from academia to publishing when I established my agency in 1996.

Would you do it over again, or something else? Yes.

List some representative titles you have placed. *Trust Me: A Memoir* by George Kennedy; *The Unofficial Downton Abbey Cookbook* by Larry Edwards; *Beautiful Old Dogs*, edited by David Tabatsky.

What do you think about self-publishing? My position on representation for previously published work in any format may be found at Schiavoneliteraryagencyinc.blogspot.com.

Do you like Amazon? Yes, I have a Prime membership with them and enjoy the numerous benefits they offer. Every book brokered by my agency is available at deep discount via Amazon. Highly recommended.

Do you believe in a "higher power"? Yes.

What will agenting be like in 2020? Publishing is a dynamic industry that keeps up with the latest technology. I envision exciting times for authors, agents, editors, and publishers.

Describe your job and what you like and don't like about it. Selling important books to major publishers is the main thrust of my work. I always look forward to receiving outstanding submissions from prospective clients.

Do you miss the way the business "used to be"? Not at all.

What does the "Big 5" mean to you? The major conglomerates in the Big Apple and their numerous imprints. I keep up with all of them.

What do you want to tell new/unpublished writers? Believe in your abilities and your writing.

Do you like that everything has become largely digitized? Yes. Technology requires this.

What do you like reading, watching, and listening to? Fiction, cable news, classical music.

Describe a book you would write. I have published five trade books and three textbooks.

THE SCHISGAL AGENCY ❖ www.theschisgalagency.com

98 Riverside Drive, 2B, New York, NY 10024, zach@theschisgalagency.com

Agent's name and contact info: Zach Schisgal, zach@theschisgalagency.com

Describe what you like to represent and what you won't represent. My focus is on commercial nonfiction in areas including but not limited to business (leadership, management), self-help, humor, politics, pop culture, health and fitness, media tie-in, cookbooks, narrative, memoir and biography. I am also interested in fiction, mainly series-based genre mystery, thriller, sci-fi. I am interested in anything I think is a good work where I think I can be helpful in the process.

What are the best ways for writers to pitch you? Anyone should feel free to email me by way of introduction.

When and where were you born? I am a native and lifelong New Yorker.

Do you charge fees? I work on a commission basis based on sales and charge no fees above and beyond.

Describe your education and career history. I am a graduate of the Collegiate School in Manhattan and Wesleyan University in Connecticut. I have spent my professional career in publishing, starting as an editorial assistant at William Morrow and working my way up the ladder there to senior editor. I held positions at Harper Collins, Rodale, Random House, and Simon & Schuster. As an editor, I acquired *New York Times* bestsellers by LL Cool J, Bethenny Frankel, Ken Blanchard, Dan Rather, Ivanka Trump, and Heather McDonald.

Say something about your hobbies and personal interests. I devote the bulk of my free time to my family; I have two elementary school age children and draw enormous gratification and enjoyment out of everything I learn from them. I cook and I spend a fair amount of time at the gym. I enjoy running greatly, but I run just so I can eat ice cream.

Why and how did you become an agent? After about 20 years on the corporate editorial side of the business, I wanted to take control of my career; I didn't want people off in meetings in other rooms making decisions about how I'd spend my time. I wanted new challenges. And I also wanted to be a stakeholder in the success of the projects on which I worked.

Would you do it over again, or something else? I'm delighted to have been able to have all the wonderful experiences and meet the incredible people I have along the way. I'd just try to do everything a little better next time around.

List some representative titles you have placed. *The New Vote* by Kristen Soltis Anderson; leading vegan Julieanna Hever; retired Navy SEAL and business consultant Rob Roy; *Mint Juleps with Teddy Roosevelt* by historian Mark Will-Weber.

Describe yourself as a person. One of the most flattering things a boss said about me once was that I took my work seriously, but I didn't take myself too seriously. I run a transparent business, respond to every email and phone call, and am an over-communicator.

How would you describe the proverbial "client from hell," and what are the warning signs? We live in a business where you live and die by your word and I value honesty above all else. It's also a deadline-driven business, and you have to be serious about the work.

What do you think about self-publishing? It's a great opportunity for many authors as long as they realize that simply making the work available as an ebook is about half the work. Publishers bring enormous resources to the process, for which they don't get their share of credit.

Do you like Amazon? I have enormous respect for Amazon, and publishers have allowed them to exploit every weakness built into the traditional publishing construct. That said, their fight against local sales tax gives some insight into what the corporation values.

Do you believe in a "higher power"? Only if it believes in me.

What will agenting be like in 2020? There will be consolidation on all sides of publishing. Retail opportunities will fracture and more agents will also be ebook publishers. The fundamentals will be the same — work hard for each client and collect a commission.

Describe your job and what you like and don't like about it. I love my job. If there weren't headaches, authors wouldn't need agents.

Do you miss the way the business "used to be"? When I started 25 years ago everyone complained about the business just as much as they do now.

What does the "Big 5" mean to you? Hardworking, intelligent people who want to publish good books that do well.

What do you want to tell new/unpublished writers? Follow your passion. Be realistic. Good work gets published. Sometimes it's not a book, it's an app.

Do you like that everything has become largely digitized? Yes. We used to waste so much paper.

What do you like reading, watching, and listening to? I am an odd blend of high and low. I like stupid humor, and Pulitzer Prize–winning writing. Sometimes, you really can have it all.

Describe a book you would write. I am the author of one of the bestselling tailgating cookbooks, *A Man, A Can, A Tailgate Plan*. I would — and did — write that.

Joker's wild: Thanks for reading this far. This book is filled with amazing opportunity, and I wish you the best of luck on your journey. Please be in touch if you'd like to talk more.

SECOND CITY PUBLISHING SERVICES ❖

www.secondcitypublishing.com

Agent's name and contact info: Cynthia Zigmund, cynthia@secondcitypublishing.com

Describe what you like to represent and what you won't represent. We represent both nonfiction and fiction. For nonfiction, we specialize in business, narrative nonfiction, self-help, and current affairs. We will consider fiction by referral only. We do not represent children's books or poetry.

What are the best ways for writers to pitch you? Email us your pitch and/or proposal, following the guidelines posted on our website; if we're interested, we'll get in touch with you.

When and where were you born? New Jersey.

Do you charge fees? We charge fees (in lieu of a commission) if an author is not seeking traditional (commission-based) representation: for example, the author already has a publisher and is interested in a contract review only, or an author is publishing independently and is looking for a manuscript evaluation. For authors we agree to represent, we are paid on commission.

Describe your education and career history. Before founding Second City Publishing Services in 2006, I spent more than 20 years in New York and Chicago publishing, including positions at John Wiley & Sons, Inc., Van Nostrand Reinhold (a technical and reference publisher), and Irwin Professional Publishing (now McGraw-Hill). In 1996, I joined Dearborn Trade Publishing (now Kaplan Publishing) as executive editor. Six months after joining Dearborn I was promoted to editorial director, and I was named vice president and publisher in 2000. During my 10 years with Kaplan, I expanded the organization's program beyond real estate and finance to include management, general business, sales, marketing, and architecture. During my tenure, the organization published a number of business bestsellers and became a leading publisher of business books. I hold a business degree from Monmouth University (West Long Branch, NJ), where I graduated summa cum laude.

Say something about your hobbies and personal interests. I love to hike, bike, and bird-watch, and I'm a big supporter of historic preservation. I love to cook, and I make a mean pie. I also enjoy a good microbrew.

Why and how did you become an agent? Becoming an agent was a natural progression in my career. I was able to take my years of experience working with authors as an editor, and use that experience and insight to help authors who wish to publish either independently or commercially.

Would you do it over again, or something else? I wouldn't change a thing.

List some representative titles you have placed. *Accountability* by Greg Bustin (McGraw-Hill); *Miracle Survivors* by Tami Boehmer (Skyhorse); *In Bed with Wall Street* by Larry Doyle (Palgrave); *Ownership Thinking* by Brad Hams (McGraw-Hill); *Before You Say "I Do"* by Todd Outcalt (Penguin); *This Wasn't Supposed to Happen to Me* by Beverly Smallwood (Thomas Nelson); *Opportunity Knocking* by Lori Ann LaRocco (Agate).

Describe yourself as a person. Patient, persistent, and detail oriented. I work hard and love what I do, but I'm not afraid to unplug.

How would you describe the proverbial "client from hell," and what are the warning signs? If you don't listen, and always try to second-guess me, we won't last.

What do you think about self-publishing? Publishing independently can be the right approach, especially if an author is writing for a niche market. I work with clients who publish commercially and independently; as long as you are willing to make the necessary investment (both personally and financially), it can be a viable option.

Do you like Amazon? Amazon has been good for authors who may have gotten lost otherwise. I also love and support independent booksellers.

What will agenting be like in 2020? I don't waste my time trying to predict the future.

Describe your job and what you like and don't like about it. I spend a lot of time working closely with the clients we accept, to ensure their proposals (and manuscripts) are competitive. I spend a great deal of my day troubleshooting with authors and publishers and pitching projects to publishers. Evenings are often devoted to reviewing proposals and manuscripts. Even after 30-plus years in the business, I still get a rush every time I hold a new book in my hand.

Do you miss the way the business "used to be"? Nothing stays the same forever.

What does the "Big 5" mean to you? Fewer options for authors.

What do you want to tell new/unpublished writers? If you want to be a successful author, take it seriously. Do your homework. Listen to the feedback you get, and remember that some of the most valuable feedback may come from the rejections you get.

Do you like that everything has become largely digitized? As long as authors are compensated fairly, and their rights protected, it's fine. Unfortunately, that's often not the case.

What do you like reading, watching, and listening to? I mostly watch PBS, although I am a closet *House Hunters International* fan (HGTV). Music in the office is almost always classical but my tastes range from Bruce Springsteen (after all, I'm a Jersey girl) and Steely Dan to Celtic, Chicago blues, big band, and indie rock. I read a lot of magazines but enjoy narrative nonfiction or a good mystery.

Describe a book you would write. I'd rather help someone get his or her book published than write one myself.

SEVENTH AVENUE LITERARY AGENCY ❖

www.seventhavenuelit.com

2052 124th Street, South Surrey, BC, V4A 9K3 Canada

Agent's name and contact info: Robert Mackwood, president and principal agent, info@seventhavenuelit.com

Describe what you like to represent and what you won't represent. This is easy — we only represent nonfiction and have for over 30 years. Within nonfiction our primary categories are business, current events, food, cooking, health, politics, history, some self-help, memoir, sports.

What are the best ways for writers to pitch you? Best to email a query *without* attachments.

When and where were you born? 1955, New Westminster, BC, Canada.

Do you charge fees? No.

Describe your education and career history. Diploma of Technology in broadcast journalism from the British Columbia Institute of Technology led to three years in radio before I hosted a public affairs program where authors were interviewed. I became hooked on books and authors in 1983 and haven't left publishing since. Stops along the way: senior publicist at Raincoast Books in Vancouver; VP marketing at Bantam, Doubleday in Toronto; and literary agent back in Vancouver since 1997. Bought out my partner in 2005 and now own Seventh Avenue Literary Agency.

Say something about your hobbies and personal interests. Books, tennis, family, West Coast of Canada.

Why and how did you become an agent? I first met literary agents in Toronto as they pitched projects to Doubleday, and I thought they had both the toughest and most interesting job in book publishing. When we relocated to Vancouver in 1996 I knew what I wanted to do.

Would you do it over again, or something else? On most days it is a great job/profession. It has up and down periods, but I love my clients, and the people in book publishing are great. I left broadcasting because I liked the people in books and still do, more than 30 years later.

List some representative titles you have placed. Most recent three titles: *The Thrive Cookbook* by Brendan Brazier (Penguin Canada); *The Mom Shift* by Reva Seth (Knopf Canada); *Route 66 Still Kicks* by Rick Antonson (Skyhorse Publishing USA). In all, we have placed a couple hundred original projects with book publishers and use a good team of sub-agents to sell translation rights around the world.

How would you describe the proverbial "client from hell," and what are the warning signs? Someone who doesn't listen, believing they know exactly what publishers/editors want and if I only take them on we will be indescribably rich and famous.

What do you think about self-publishing? Love it and always have. Great respect for those who do it right and believe enough in their book that they finance it.

Do you like Amazon? Overall, yes. How can you not like a 24/7 global bookstore that takes all books? But they are becoming increasingly powerful and have forever changed the publishing landscape and not in the best way.

What will agenting be like in 2020? Talented people will always require some sort of representation to act as the go-between. They may come to be described not as literary agents but as managers.

What do you want to tell new/unpublished writers? Be prepared for a marathon, not a sprint. Develop a thick skin and be prepared for work and rejection. Be gracious and kind.

SHEREE BYKOFSKY ASSOCIATES, INC. ❖ www.shereebee.com

PO Box 706, Brigantine, NJ 08203

Agent's name and contact info: Sheree Bykofsky, shereebee@aol.com

Describe what you like to represent and what you won't represent. Very wide-ranging list: health, business, adult nonfiction in all categories (hardcovers and trade paperbacks), quality literary and commercial fiction (highly selective), mysteries.

Please do not query me with horror, occult, poetry, fantasy, or picture books.

What are the best ways for writers to pitch you? Submit an e–query letter, pasted into the body of your email, to submitbee@aol.com or shereebee@aol.com. No attachments will be opened.

When and where were you born? September 1956, New York City.

Do you charge fees? No.

Describe your education and career history. Education: BA with honors, State University of New York, Binghamton; MA in English and comparative literature, Columbia University. Career history: executive editor/book producer, Stonesong Press (1984–1996); freelance editor/writer (1984); general manager/managing editor, Chiron Press (1979–1984); author and coauthor of more than two dozen books, including three poker books with coauthor Lou Krieger and *The Complete Idiot's Guide to Getting Published*, 5th edition, with Jennifer Basye Sander.

Say something about your hobbies and personal interests. Poker, Scrabble, dogs.

Why and how did you become an agent? The career matched my skill set. I love reading books and negotiating contracts, multitasking, reviewing royalty statements, helping authors. I was born to do this.

Would you do it over again, or something else? I lead a charmed life (see Victoria Moran's *Creating a Charmed Life*). Completely blessed and meant to be.

List some representative titles you have placed. *ADHD Does Not Exist* by Dr. Richard Saul (Harper Collins); *Idea to Invention* by Patricia Nolan-Brown (McGraw-Hill); *Be Bold and Win the Sale* by Jeff Shore (Amacom); *Jellyfish Dreams* by M. Thomas Gammarino (Kindle); *The Hour of Lead and Lonesome Animals* by Bruce Holbert (Counterpoint; placed by associate Janet Rosen); *Mimi Malloy at Last* by Julia Chang Macdonnell (Picador; by Janet Rosen); *Sell Your Business for an Outrageous Price* by Kevin Short (Amacom); *Complete Idiot's Guide to Getting Published*, 5th edition, by Sheree Bykofsky and Jennifer Basye Sander (Alpha); *The Book of Strange and Curious Legal Oddities* by Nathan Belofsky (Perigee; by Janet Rosen); *Don't Swallow Your Gum* by Drs. Aaron Carroll and Rachel Vreeman (St. Martin's; by Janet Rosen); *Shell Shocked: My Life with the Turtles, Flo and Eddie and Frank Zappa* by Howard Kaylan (Hal Leonard).

Describe yourself as a person. I love fun and games but enjoy the responsibility and details of owning a business; I am rewarded by helping people (and animals); I am very practical and logical, yet I have had several deep intuitive experiences that I can only describe as psychic. I love brilliant, creative people and people who make me laugh, and I appreciate good grammar and original writing. I love technology and fixing things, and my iPhone! My mom taught me to "think positive," and I live to honor her and my dad's memory.

How would you describe the proverbial "client from hell," and what are the warning signs? I prefer to be positive, but the client from hell would simply be inconsiderate and would look for people to scapegoat.

What do you think about self-publishing? It has become a viable option to date, but most of the time the standard route will still prove more profitable for most authors.

Do you like Amazon? For the most part, I have to say yes.

Do you believe in a "higher power"? I do.

What will agenting be like in 2020? Things are changing, but as long as there are publishers and authors, I do believe there will be agents. I see agents as indispensable advocates for authors.

Describe your job and what you like and don't like about it. I represent authors to publishers; I negotiate contracts; I place authors' books with my contacts; I get authors the best possible terms and advances; I guide my authors through their careers; I handle subrights; I do much reading and assessing, tons of email, bookkeeping and administrative work. It is a business that marries the big and small picture (having a plan and executing it with many details and much organization), and I truly love every bit of it.

Do you miss the way the business "used to be"? I miss Borders and Peter Workman and the frequent six-figure deals, but I don't miss the Selectric typewriter too much.

What does the "Big 5" mean to you? Publishing used to be conducted in "publishing houses" — literally rows of brownstones in midtown Manhattan. With all the consolidations and merging of these houses, there are now about five big conglomerates left that are the publishers, and they understandably don't compete with themselves in book auctions.

What do you want to tell new/unpublished writers? This is not to sell you a book, but reading a book such as *The Complete Idiot's Guide to Getting Published*, 5th edition, will help you understand the industry so that you can get a leg up in securing an agent and a publishing deal. When you are writing a book, the readers' needs have to come first.

Do you like that everything has become largely digitized? That would be a solid yes/no.

What do you like reading, watching, and listening to? The same kinds of books that I represent. My favorite thing to read is a novel that no one else in the world has seen, that keeps me up all night so that I can offer representation in the morning.

Describe a book you would write. I've written over 30 books, including *Secrets the Pros Won't Tell You about Winning Hold 'Em Poker* and *Put Your House on a Diet* (with Ed Morrow and fellow friend and agent Rita Rosenkranz).

Joker's wild: I won $34,000 on *Wheel of Fortune*!

Agent's name and contact info: Thomas V. Hartmann, thomashbee@aol.com

Describe what you like to represent and what you won't represent. My interests include (in no order) Americana/American studies, pop culture, music (especially jazz, R&B, and hip-hop), alternative, art and architecture, photography, cinema and filmmaking, travel narrative, design, how-to, golf, baseball, true crime, health, mystery.

Please do not query me with horror, occult, romance, fantasy, or picture books.

What are the best ways for writers to pitch you? Send an e–query letter, pasted into the body of your email, to submitbee@aol.com or thomashbee@aol.com. No attachments will be opened.

When and where were you born? July 1966, Long Branch, NJ.

Do you charge fees? No.

Describe your education and career history. Education: BA, cum laude, University of Pennsylvania; MA, Columbia University; Writing Center Associates Fellow, Georgetown University. Before joining Sheree Bykofsky, I worked in and around publishing for 17 years, including over a decade spent as an acquisitions editor / senior editor.

Say something about your hobbies and personal interests. My hobbies and personal interests mirror the areas that I seek to represent: Americana/American studies, pop culture, music (especially jazz, R&B, hip-hop, alternative), art and architecture, food/cooking, photography, cinema and filmmaking, travel narrative, golf, baseball, true crime, health, mystery.

Why and how did you become an agent? Working closely with authors was the most satisfying part of my publishing career. This, combined with my extensive knowledge of publishing contracts and overall knowledge of the industry, makes me very well equipped as an agent.

Would you do it over again, or something else? No regrets!

List some representative titles you have placed. I am a new associate at Sheree Bykofsky, so I am working on selling my first books right now.

Describe yourself as a person. I think most people who know me would say that I am broadly and deeply creative; personable and (usually) funny; a "why not?"/green-light thinker; a great listener; a tireless advocate for things in which I believe; a cool head in a crisis. I am a dreamer but, paradoxically, also realistic. I relish the role of mentor, but I doubt I'll ever stop learning or wanting to learn.

How would you describe the proverbial "client from hell," and what are the warning signs? Someone who is unkind.

What do you think about self-publishing? Not so much shame in that game anymore; in short, a viable/reasonable option for some authors.

Do you like Amazon? Yes, but I still buy from indie bookstores, too, and I always will.

Do you believe in a "higher power"? Not in the conventional sense.

What will agenting be like in 2020? I think I'll echo Sheree's comment that "agents are indispensable advocates for authors" and add that we serve an important role for editors as well. How many editors would have missed a great book had it not been for a relationship with an agent?

Describe your job and what you like and don't like about it. I enjoy working closely with authors and helping them reach their goals. I also enjoy the process of negotiation. I don't enjoy having to say no, but, alas, that's inevitable!

Do you miss the way the business "used to be"? No.

What does the "Big 5" mean to you? The implications of consolidation are many; on the positive side of the equation, I think it means opportunities for smaller houses and entrepreneurs to own subjects/spaces that are too small or niche for bigger firms due to revenue requirements.

What do you want to tell new/unpublished writers? Become skilled at marketing and self-promotion; get good at social media; build a platform.

Do you like that everything has become largely digitized? I love digital content and books, about equally.

What do you like reading, watching, and listening to? The same kinds of books that I seek to represent; I read the *New Yorker*, the *New York Times*, the *Atlantic*, *Jacobin*, the *Economist*, the *Guardian*. I'm a big user of Zite/Flipboard. I listen to all sorts of music, also NPR.

Joker's wild: I have been a wine consultant.

**Agent's name and contact info: Janet Rosen,
queries to submitbee@aol.com, janetrosenbee@aol.com**

Describe what you like to represent and what you won't represent. Fiction: character- and plot-driven women's fiction with a sense of place and style (not romance) and crime — would love to find the American Denise Mina or Kate Atkinson! Excellent but unfussy writing. I like modern and historical as long as it keeps me reading and interested.

Nonfiction: pop culture, biography, history, popular and social science, Judaica, African American, language, music, cities, architecture and design, medicine, fashion, military and espionage.

What are the best ways for writers to pitch you? Email a detailed, well-written query that is as good as your book. What is your book, who are you, what are your credentials? NO attachments, please. And NO CALLS. See website for details.

When and where were you born? Brooklyn, but before it was hip.

Do you charge fees? No.

Describe your education and career history. Attended NYU when it was an expensive safety school and probably bumped into the future Mayor DeBlasio (before he changed his name) on my way to the Washington Square News or CBGB. I have been the president of the NYC chapter of the Women's National Book Association and written for *Glamour*, *Publishers Weekly*, *Paper*, and other print and online publications. I worked as an associate book editor at *Glamour*, the senior books and fiction editor at *Woman* (and at a couple of other now-defunct magazines) before turning to agenting at Sheree Bykofsky Associates, where I represent a range of nonfiction and a limited amount of fiction.

Say something about your hobbies and personal interests. Even when I am not working, I still love to read!

Why and how did you become an agent? Serendipity!

Would you do it over again, or something else? Yes, but would also be an interior designer, cartoonist, novelist, stand-up comic, and eccentric recluse. Working on at-home cloning to effect this. I kid, I kid.

List some representative titles you have placed. *Marketplace of the Marvelous: The Strange Origins of Modern Medicine* by Erika Janik; *Pistold and Petticoats: A History of Female Detectives in Literature and in Real Life* (Beacon); *SLIMED! An Oral History of Nickelodeon's Golden Age* by Mathew Klickstein (Plume); *Yes, I Could Care Less: How to be a Language Snob without Being a Jerk* by Bill Walsh (St Martin's); *Mimi Malloy, at Last!* by Julia MacDonnell (Picador); *Dead White Guys: A Father, His Daughter, and the Great Books of the Western World* by Matthew Burriesci (Cleis/Viva); *Soar: The Breakthrough Treatment for the Fear of Flying* by Captain Tom Bunn, LCSW (Lyons/GPP); *Constructive Wallowing: How to Beat Bad Feelings by Letting Yourself Have Them* by Tina Gilbertson (Cleis); *Better Is Not So Far: Decide to Recover from Bingeing, Starving, or Cutting* by Melissa Groman (McGraw-Hill); *Lonesome Animals and the Hour of Lead* by Bruce Holbert (Counterpoint).

Describe yourself as a person. I don't have this much self-awareness — too busy focusing on clients!

How would you describe the proverbial "client from hell," and what are the warning signs? Screaming middle-of-the-night voicemails. Don't do that.

What do you think about self-publishing? If you have the time, energy, and inclination to write your book, plus have it well edited, get it distributed, publicize, approach special-sales outlets, handle all subrights, and so on, feel free! It works well for some kinds of books (writers who have a lot of "back-of-room sales," for example) but not all.

Do you like Amazon? My opinion changes daily.

Do you believe in a "higher power"? My opinion on this changes daily, too.

What will agenting be like in 2020? Ask me in 2021. I don't make projections about that or about the economy.

Describe your job and what you like and don't like about it. I love finding the right match between the projects I love and the right editor.

Do you miss the way the business "used to be"? No. I only miss being a bit younger.

What does the "Big 5" mean to you? Soon to be the big 3 or 4?

What do you want to tell new/unpublished writers? No one piece of advice for all, except "write well." Every writer and project is unique.

Do you like that everything has become largely digitized? I'm adapting!

What do you like reading, watching, and listening to? I'm culturally omnivorous and it is always changing. Besides my clients, this month I have been reading and enjoying Jincy Willett, Edith Wharton, Lore Segal, and mysteries; watching *Inside City Hall* on NY1, *Parks and Rec*, and old episodes of *Naked City*; accidentally found indie movies like *Melvin Goes to Dinner*, *Diggers*, and *Two Family House*. Listening to everything from Prokofiev to old punk like Stiff Little Fingers. This list will be different next month.

Describe a book you would write. I have anonymously written sections of several books. Shhh.

A biography of Louise Fitzhugh (author of *Harriet the Spy*) and her cultural milieu — hey, can someone qualified please send that to me?

Joker's wild: I'm not a game player. (But I have written and performed stand-up comedy. I have said that telling a joke and pitching a book are similar: set up and punch. Only, instead of the laugh from an editor, I want to hear, "Yes, send it!"

SIMENAUER & FRANK LITERARY AGENCY LLC

Formerly Simenauer & Greene (Carole Greene Retired)

PO Box 112735, Naples, FL 34108-0416

Agent's name and contact info: Chris Frank, cfliteraryagent@gmail.com, 239-821-3624

Describe what you like to represent and what you won't represent. Personally I am drawn to intriguing thrillers, especially those that take the reader on a wild roller-coaster ride while offering a satisfying ending. Women's fiction is a given, and if the story contains some historical significance, I always want to take a look. I'm a sucker for mysteries, whether they are serious, cozy, or humorous. Surprise me with any romance — single title, series, contemporary, etc. I am open to all genres if the story is well written and engaging.

What are the best ways for writers to pitch you? Remember that your pitch is usually your first contact with any agent. I want to know not only the title, genre, and word count of your book — I want to know why you feel it will engage readers. Give me a very brief synopsis, but please don't send sample chapters or the entire manuscript unless requested.

When and where were you born? I was born in Baltimore, Maryland, on April 12 and am considered a baby boomer.

Do you charge fees? I am always glad to hear from writers, and I don't shy away from debut authors. There are no fees separate from our commission if we sell your book. Our agency agreement spells out the details.

Describe your education and career history. Surprisingly, my background is in the medical field. I attended Johns Hopkins School of Nursing, which allowed me to take courses at Johns Hopkins University concurrently. Although my heart has always been in the arts, my pocketbook and the thoughts of a regular paycheck led me to medical management. So while I read and wrote for my own pleasure, I spent my career managing a large multispecialty medical practice in the Baltimore/Washington corridor. When I relocated to Naples, Florida, I met my future business partner, Jacqueline Simenauer. Although also a bestselling author, she enjoys using her knowledge to help other writers achieve their publishing goals. She has been the perfect mentor, so when the opportunity arose for us to join forces as the Simenauer & Frank Literary Agency, I knew it was the right move.

Say something about your hobbies and personal interests. Even after reading queries, etc., during the workday, I still love to read for pure pleasure in my free time. If I don't have my nose in a book, I am tending to my orchids (a must for Florida residents!). I have belonged to a wine society for the past 10 years and have probably learned more about wine than I really want to know.

Would you do it over again, or something else? From this vantage point, I know that I should have always been a literary agent or worked in the publishing industry. When you get up each morning and look forward to doing something that you truly love, you realize how lucky you are.

List some representative titles you have placed. Our agency has placed the following titles: *The Caterpillar Way: Lessons in Leadership, Growth, and Shareholder Value* (hit the *New York Times* bestseller list) by Craig T. Bouchard and James V. Koch (McGraw-Hill); *The New Legions: American Strategy and the Responsibility of Power* by Major General Edward B. Atkeson (Rowman & Littlefield); *The Garage Sale Stalker* (sold to Hallmark

Channel for a two-hour movie) by Suzi Weinert; *Passion's Race* by Christine Mazurk (Lachesis Publishing); *Raging Skies* by William Hallstead (Blue Water Press); *River of Madness* by William Hallstead (Blue Water Press); *Jade's Treasure* by Ana Krista Johnson (Crimson Romance / Adam's Media); *The Insulin Resistant Diet*, revised edition, by Dr. Cheryle Hart and Mary Kay Grossman, R.D. (McGraw-Hill) sold over 150,000 copies to date and is still selling.

Describe yourself as a person. I call myself a nurturer. Helping a family member, a friend, or a client brings me joy.

How would you describe the proverbial "client from hell," and what are the warning signs? I haven't met the "client from hell" up to this point, but I've come awfully close. While connecting with an author to follow up on his or her initial query, I try to get a feel for whether we can work well together. If an author makes too many unrealistic demands, I may turn away a potentially great project.

What do you think about self-publishing? All books, whether traditionally published or self-published, need to be marketed to be successful. If you can put together a creative marketing plan and implement it, you are ahead of the game. All of us have a story to tell, but publishers can't take a chance on every project that comes their way. Self-publishing can be a fulfilling way to see your work in print, especially after attempting a more traditional approach.

What will agenting be like in 2020? With all the changes constantly taking place in publishing, I'm not sure how it will affect agenting. I do feel that agents will still play a prominent role, but that role may have a new description.

Describe your job and what you like and don't like about it. There are so many things that I like about my job that it would take up an entire page to list them. Helping writers along their publishing journey ranks at the top. When I am passionate about a project, I will explore every avenue to achieve success. Having to pass on a project is probably one of the most difficult choices to make. In all fairness to the author, I really can't take on a project if I don't feel a connection with the work.

What do you want to tell new/unpublished writers? If I can share one suggestion with new writers it is to write what your head and heart tell you. As we all know, the pendulum continually swings. Perhaps romance novels are all the rage today, but tomorrow it could be mysteries. Don't try to keep up with trends. Let that story inside you come out. It will be judged on its own merit, regardless of genre.

Do you like that everything has become largely digitized? My desire is to see good works available to the reading public. Digitization has made them more available and affordable.

What do you like reading, watching, and listening to? My tastes are rather eclectic, whether in music, books, movies, or television. I listen to classical music back-to-back with New Age or country. The TV gets flipped from *Downton Abbey* to *Pawn Stars*. When a book isn't right at hand, I find myself perusing the cereal box. I'm up for any book as long as it captures my attention within the first few pages. This holds true for both fiction and nonfiction.

Describe a book you would write. My dream is to write a novel based on stories that my husband has shared with me about his family. They traveled from Poland (when under Russian rule) to Cuba, where my husband was born and grew up during the pre-Castro era.

Agent's name and contact info: Jacqueline Simenauer, jsliteraryagent@gmail.com, 239-597-9877

Describe what you like to represent and what you won't represent. I like a wide range of strong nonfiction books that include medical, health, nutrition, popular psychology, how-to, self-help, parenting, women's interest, spirituality, men's interest, relationships, social sciences, beauty, and controversial subjects.

I am not interested in crafts, poetry, or children's books.

What are the best ways for writers to pitch you? My contact of choice is through email. I am open to all well-written nonfiction queries. Please write a really good query letter. This is so important. If you can't get your idea across effectively, then you have lost the agent.

When and where were you born? I was born in New York City on February 23.

Do you charge fees? We do not charge any fees.

Describe your education and career history. After working as an articles editor for a national publication, I decided to start my own literary agency, and as a result of this, I coauthored a number of books with my clients. Some of the six books that I was involved with include *Husbands and Wives* (Times Books); *Singles: The New Americans* (Simon & Schuster), which gained the attention of the White House; the bestselling *Beyond the Male Myth* (Times Books), which was featured on *Oprah*; and *Not Tonight Dear* (Doubleday). They went on to sell over 200,000 copies. My work has also been featured in most of the nation's magazines and newspapers, including *Time*, *Reader's Digest*, *Ladies' Home Journal*, the *New York Times*, and the *Washington Post*. In addition, I have appeared on over 100 radio and TV shows, including *Good Morning America* and *Today*.

Say something about your hobbies and personal interests. I have always worked so hard that I have never found time to even think about a hobby. However, I do love classical concerts. I am a member of a wine society; I love Broadway theater and great fiction.

Why and how did you become an agent? I seem to have always been involved with the publishing world, in one way or another. I have worked for a national publication as an articles editor. I was a freelance writer and coauthor. Agenting seemed the next likely step, so I opened an agency to help guide future writers along the publishing path.

Would you do it over again, or something else? Investment banking was my true calling, but somehow it eluded me, and destiny brought me into the publishing world.

List some representative titles you have placed. See above listing under Chris Frank. Those titles represent our agency.

Describe yourself as a person. Type A, warm, kind, giving.

How would you describe the proverbial "client from hell," and what are the warning signs? I haven't encountered what I would call the "client from hell." Luckily the writers that I have represented over the years have been a joy to work with.

What do you think about self-publishing? Some houses won't even look at a book if it has been previously published in any form. The positive side is that you can still see your work in print using self-publishing. Some self-published books that showed exceptional sales have later been acquired by major publishing houses and on rare occasions have hit the bestseller list.

Do you like Amazon? It has its place.

What will agenting be like in 2020? Books will still be selling in 2020, but the sale of ebooks will be climbing right behind them. Therefore, agents will probably be selling as many digitized works as hard- and softcover books.

Describe your job and what you like and don't like about it. I love the creativity involved, and the fact that a book can influence so many lives. What I don't appreciate is that clients sometimes don't want to accept the fact that we have to part ways. They don't really understand the amount of time and effort that we put into trying to sell their book.

Do you miss the way the business "used to be"? Yes. Why? Because there were no ebooks, and publishers were buying and publishing more hard- and softcover books. Selling was easier then. They weren't afraid to take a chance.

What does the "Big 5" mean to you? The "Big 5" means to me that selling is going to be harder because of the mergers between publishers, and we won't have the choices that we had years ago.

What do you want to tell new/unpublished writers? I couldn't say it better than my partner Chris Frank said in her answer. I agree 100 percent with her.

Do you like that everything has become largely digitized? Yes, in the sense that it can give writers more opportunities to get their works out there.

What do you like reading, watching, and listening to? If it isn't *Shark Tank*, I don't watch it. Instead I enjoy great fiction.

Describe a book you would write. I would love to write the story of my husband's life. He was born in Germany, grew up in China, spent part of his life in Israel, and then went on to a great symphonic career.

THE STEINBERG AGENCY, INC.

98 4th Street, Suite 416, Brooklyn, NY 11231

Agent's name: Peter Steinberg

Describe what you like to represent and what you won't represent. Represent: commercial fiction, literary fiction, short story collections, young adult, middle grade, biography, memoir, humor, sports, style, health/diet.

Will not represent: Screenplays, poetry, picture books.

What are the best ways for writers to pitch you? Concise, informative cover letter that tells us what your project is and why we might be interested in it. See www.steinberg agency.com for more details.

Do you charge fees? No.

Describe your education and career history. NYU Film School, 17 years as an agent, started the Steinberg Agency 7 years ago.

Why and how did you become an agent? I've always loved storytelling, and at first I thought I'd be a filmmaker and I went to NYU Film School. When I graduated I was writing screenplays while temping and by pure chance I ended up temping at Harper Collins. I really loved talking to writers on the phone and seeing how books came about. So when the temp position ended I decided to pursue a publishing position and there was an opening at a great boutique agency called Donadio & Ashworth. Their client list was a who's who of great literary fiction writers (Mario Puzo, Robert Stone, and Edward Gorey to name a few) and after a couple of years as their assistant, I began representing my own writers and selling their books. It was thrilling. My love of storytelling has never waned and I believe it's at the core of what makes me a good agent.

List some representative titles you have placed. *Rivers* by Michael Farris Smith; *Meet Me at the River* by Nina de Gramont; *You Are a Badass* by Jen Sincero; *The Lives of Margaret Fuller* by John Matteson; *Boy on the Wooden Box* by Leon Leyson; *All I Have in This World* by Michael Parker; *Glamorous by George* by George Kotsiopoulos.

What do you want to tell new/unpublished writers? Many things. Here are a few: (1) Make writing routine. Every day if you can. Even five minutes on a day you're busy is better than none at all. Wedge it in between chores. It's not precious. Your environment doesn't have to be "perfect" for you to write. It's your job. (2) Gather a few people in your life who give great, honest, passionate feedback to your work. (3) Read other great writers when you're stuck. (4) Don't show agents your work too soon. Make sure it's ready — with the help of other smart people (see number 2). (5) Don't talk about writing, just write. (6) Don't follow trends, follow your passion. (7) There are many agents out there who are good at recognizing good work, so doors will truly open if your work is good enough (see number 10). (8) Talk to published writers (writers who have already accomplished what you want to accomplish) over coffee or a meal and ask their advice. Pay for their coffee and/or meal. (9) Ignore the naysayers, cynics, people who undermine, people who are just "being realistic." (There will be more of them than you expect if you're doing it right, and it's true — they're just jealous of you.) (10) Never give up.

STERLING LORD LITERISTIC ❖ www.sll.com

Agent's name and contact info: Celeste Fine, celeste@sll.com

Describe what you like to represent and what you won't represent. Serious and commercial nonfiction, select literary fiction.

What are the best ways for writers to pitch you? Email queries.

Do you charge fees? No.

Describe your education and career history. Harvard University. I have been a literary agent for more than 10 years.

Say something about your hobbies and personal interests. My interests are in science, health, wellness, and business.

Why and how did you become an agent? I have always loved books, business, and fast-paced, challenging environments, so it makes sense that I found myself in this world.

Would you do it over again, or something else? I love what I do, but I would like to explore more digital opportunities for my clients and myself. Luckily, now is the time to be doing so.

List some representative titles you have placed. A few recent bestselling authors include: JJ Virgin, Dave Kerpen, Thomas M. Campbell, Jackie Warner, Sara Gottfried, Michelle Bridges, Ciji Ware.

How would you describe the proverbial "client from hell," and what are the warning signs? The best clients are successful in real life, have an interesting idea that works on the bookshelf, have built an engaged following, and know how to sell books without selling.

What do you think about self-publishing? I think self-publishing can be a valuable part of an overall publishing strategy when well executed.

Do you like Amazon? I do. I think Amazon has done much for backlist titles, ebooks, and reader experience. It is also a valuable tool for authors to get a sense of what books are popular in real time.

What will agenting be like in 2020? The spirit of agenting will remain the same: our job is to be experts at publishing books and to help our clients publish books well.

Describe your job and what you like and don't like about it. I like working with people who are great at what they do, have high expectations of what we can do together, over-deliver, and know how to enjoy the accomplishment as a team. I don't like the opposites.

Do you miss the way the business "used to be"? Yes and no.

What does the "Big 5" mean to you? (1) Big advances. (2) Big sales team and distribution. (3) Co-op space. (4) Industry reviews and bestseller lists. (5) Export markets.

What do you want to tell new/unpublished writers? Nonfiction authors: In many cases it is easier to break out in the real world than it is on the bookshelf. Test your idea and build your audience before you approach publishers about the book.

Do you like that everything has become largely digitized? Yes.

What do you like reading, watching, and listening to? The news, podcasts, YouTube, *New England Journal of Medicine*, TED.

Describe a book you would write. I would want to write a research-driven book that changed how we thought about ideas and content.

THE STEVE LAUBE AGENCY ❖ www.stevelaube.com

5025 N. Central Avenue, #635, Phoenix, AZ 85012

**Agents' names and contact info: We have four agents –
Steve Laube, krichards@stevelaube.com;
Tamela Hancock Murray, ewilson@stevelaube.com;
Karen Ball, pwhitson@stevelaube.com; and
Dan Balow, vseem@stevelaube.com**

Describe what you like to represent and what you won't represent. We represent fiction and nonfiction intended for the Christian market.

We do not represent children's picture books.

What are the best ways for writers to pitch you? Please use the guidelines found on our website: www.stevelaube.com/guidelines.

Do you charge fees? No.

Describe your education and career history. Our agents' backgrounds can be found in the "About" section of our website.

List some representative titles you have placed. *For Every Season* by Cindy Woodsmall; *Echoes of Mercy* by Kim Vogel Sawyer; *Take a Chance on Me* by Susan May Warren; *Waterfall* by Lisa Bergren; *Complete Guide to the Bible* by Stephen M. Miller; *On Guard* by William Lane Craig; *Raptor Six* by Ronie Kendig; *Setting Boundaries with Food* by Allison Bottke.

What do you think about self-publishing? Self-publishing is a viable option and always has been, if the author has a vehicle to help sell their books. Current technology has simply made it easier and less expensive to produce.

Do you like Amazon? I celebrate every place that sells books.

Do you believe in a "higher power"? I think "higher power" is a weak description of who I believe is the God of the universe, especially since it suggests that each person can define "higher power" in their own way. Our agency is specifically Christian, and our Statement of Faith is posted prominently on our website.

What will agenting be like in 2020? Similar to what we have today. Finding the great new authors, nurturing their career decisions, and connecting them to the right publishing partners.

STIMOLA LITERARY STUDIO ❖ www.stimolaliterarystudio.com

308 Livingston Court, Edgewater, NJ 07020, 201-945-9353, fax: 201-490-5920

Agent's name and contact info: Rosemary Stimola, info@stimolaliterarystudio.com

Describe what you like to represent and what you won't represent. We represent preschool through young adult fiction and nonfiction.

What are the best ways for writers to pitch you? All queries to be sent to above email with no attachments. We will respond only to those queries we wish to pursue further, within two weeks with a request for material.

When and where were you born? November 6, 1952, Queens, NY.

Do you charge fees? We do not charge any fees and work on a commission-only basis.

Describe your education and career history. BA in elementary education and theoretical linguistics, Queens College; MA in applied linguistics, NYU; PhD in applied linguistics and educational psychology, NYU. Professor of language and literature; children's book-seller; literary agent.

Say something about your hobbies and personal interests. Beachcombing, Latin dance, cockapoos.

Why and how did you become an agent? My years as an academic, combined with my years as a bookseller, laid the perfect foundation for my agenting life. All led me to this profession, which I am proud and pleased to be a part of. I could never see myself doing anything else.

List some representative titles you have placed. *The Conjurers* by Brian Anderson; *Chasing Shadows* by Swati Avashti; *Simon Thorn* by Aimee Carter; *The Hunger Games* by Suzanne Collins; *Hello! Hello!* by Matthew Cordell; *Better Off Friends* by Elizabeth Eulberg; *Scare Scape* by Sam Fisher; *The Secret Hum of a Daisy* by Tracy Holczer; *The Remnant Trilogy* by Mary E. Pearson; *Vasya's Noisy Paintbox* by Barb Rosenstock; *Tea with Grandpa* by Barney Saltzberg; *Courage Has No Color* by Tanya Lee Stone.

Describe yourself as a person. Disciplined, fair-minded, no-nonsense. Prefer collaboration to confrontation but can go to the latter when needed. A firm but reasonable negotiator.

How would you describe the proverbial "client from hell," and what are the warning signs? The "client from hell" has unrealistic expectations and a major ego; is resistant to editor guidance and revision; and always misses deadlines.

What do you think about self-publishing? Self-publishing has a place, but it is overin-flated, creating an illusion of achieving success that is more the exception than the rule, and a vast pool of unedited, unvetted "slush."

Do you like Amazon? Amazon has changed the climate of publishing and business in general; whether it is for the ultimate good remains to be seen.

Do you believe in a "higher power"? I do believe in a higher power. I just don't subscribe to institutional religious beliefs about that power.

What will agenting be like in 2020? I would imagine that changes in technology and busi-ness will demand ever-evolving knowledge of contractual matters so that authors' rights are protected and authors are duly compensated for their creative work, whatever the for-mat or channels of distribution. I do hope, however, that the core personal relationships of agent, author, and editor remain intact.

Describe your job and what you like and don't like about it. My job is fulfilling in many ways. Nothing is more exciting than finding and nurturing new talent. Nothing is more exciting than seeing a book you've helped to shepherd find its wings and fly high. Work hours can sometimes be demanding, but in the end, it's all for a good cause.

Do you miss the way the business "used to be"? I miss the opportunity to "seal a deal" when an editor says, "I love this." The bureaucracy of acquisition can sometimes kill a good book's chances of being published. And I do not appreciate the use of "tracking," looking at an author's past sales, to determine if a new book will be acquired. The past is not always a prediction of the future, and sometimes a few modestly sold novels lead the way to a bestseller.

What does the "Big 5" mean to you? Just that more and more mergers are likely to take place. I fear we may end up with the "Big 1" down the road.

What do you want to tell new/unpublished writers? Not much, except to examine the reasons they write, to write organically, and to not be overly swayed by market trends.

Do you like that everything has become largely digitized? Yes and no. It's great when all works, hell when systems are down.

What do you like reading, watching, and listening to? I am a very eclectic reader, so anything goes. I have become a fan of TV series, watching two to three episodes at a clip on Netflix. Sort of like viewing multiple chapters in a book when my eyes are tired.

Describe a book you would write. I don't really think about writing a book. I leave that to my authors.

STRACHAN LITERARY AGENCY ❖ www.strachanlit.com

PO Box 2091, Annapolis, MD 21404, query@strachanlit.com

Agent's name and contact info: Laura Strachan

Describe what you like to represent and what you won't represent. I like anything that is a compelling story, well told. In general, that means literary fiction and narrative nonfiction. I also handle some young adult fiction. I tend not to take on genre fiction, but that's not hard-and-fast. If it's beautifully written, I am interested.

What are the best ways for writers to pitch you? I am taking on very little new right now. The best way to get my attention is with a referral from a writer I work with.

When and where were you born? I was born in Baltimore, MD, a long time ago(!).

Do you charge fees? I do not charge fees, apart from the standard commission. I used to charge for expenses, but they have by and large disappeared, as the business has become electronic. (And by that I mean we can easily transfer files and paperwork by email.). There are the occasional bank transfer fees.

Describe your education and career history. I studied English lit as an undergrad and then attended law school. I practiced law for a year and decided it was the wrong career path. I hit upon agenting as a way to combine my legal education with what I loved, namely books and good writing. How I got there is a long story, but I was able to make the transition with the help and advice of lots of very smart and talented people in the industry — other agents, writers, and a particular publisher to whom I am indebted for his help and friendship.

Say something about your hobbies and personal interests. My favorite thing to do is read, luckily. But I also enjoy art and the theater. And good food.

Would you do it over again, or something else? That's a tough question. I love what I do, but it's not easy. If I were to do it over again, I might do it differently — start inside the industry rather than coming from outside it — or I might stick with the legal side, focusing on intellectual property.

List some representative titles you have placed. *Misdirected*, young adult, by Ali Berman (Triangle Square/Seven Stories); *Choosing a Good Life: Lessons from People Who Have Found Their Place in the World*, nonfiction, by Ali Berman (Hazelden Publishing); *Wild Edibles*, nonfiction, by Jeffrey Greene (UVA Press); *Painkillers, Heroin, and the Road to Sanity: Real Solutions for Long-Term Recovery from Opiate Addiction*, nonfiction, by Joani Gammill (Hazelden Publishing); *Happy Talk*, fiction, by Richard Melo (Red Lemonade/Cursor); *Chasing Alaska* by C.B. Bernard (Lyons Press/Globe Pequot).

Describe yourself as a person. A recovering perfectionist. It took me a long time to learn that things are what they are. You do what you can, then accept it and move on.

How would you describe the proverbial "client from hell," and what are the warning signs? Bringing a book to market is a collaborative effort. Understandably, the author has a vested interest in the process and should have a say in it, but an author also needs to let the agent and publisher do what they do. The client from hell believes he or she knows best and refuses advice or direction. Likewise, the author who needs constant reassurance and updates. Being an agent does entail a great deal of handholding, and authors should expect reasonable updates, but there is a balance. The wheels of publishing can turn excruciatingly slowly. Patience is a virtue!

What do you think about self-publishing? I am not at all against self-publishing. The sad truth is that many deserving books will never be published, simply because of certain economic realities, so self-publishing provides an avenue for getting that work out into the world. But just because one *can* self-publish doesn't mean that one should. An author should not self-publish something that isn't ready to be published. It's a far different thing to publish a book that has gotten good feedback from industry professionals, who regret that circumstances prevent them from taking it on, than to self-publish 30 seconds after typing "The End." Any author who chooses to self-publish needs to do the homework and research necessary to understand how the business works and to recognize that publishing is only the beginning of the process (something that traditionally published authors need to understand as well).

Do you like Amazon? Yes and no. The detrimental effects of Amazon have been well documented and don't need to be repeated here. But it is also true that Amazon makes my job much easier. It is a great research and reference tool for me to see what else is out there and who is publishing it. And if reduced pricing means someone will purchase one of my authors' books that they may not have purchased at full price, I see it as an opportunity.

Do you believe in a "higher power"? I do. I was raised Protestant, so my "higher power" is the more traditional one, but I am not arrogant enough to think that my beliefs are the only true or right ones. Who's to say that the higher power can't choose to present or reveal itself in multiple ways?

What will agenting be like in 2020? Who knows? I'm not sure it will be terribly different. Authors will always want and need guidance. Agents may need to have a wider range of skills in order to best advise their clients about options, but they will still be useful.

Describe your job and what you like and don't like about it. In a nutshell, I serve as a (hopefully) more informed extension of the author. I give feedback on manuscripts and proposals, help to find the correct publisher for a project, and become both a liaison and a buffer between the publisher and the author. My job is to make the noncreative parts of an author's job easier. The part I hate the most? Rejections. It's just as frustrating and disappointing to me as to the author.

Do you miss the way the business "used to be"? I'm not even sure what "used to be" was. It's always been a tough business.

What does the "Big 5" mean to you? The "Big 5" means tradition and, in most cases, more financial wherewithal. But "Big 5" doesn't necessarily mean the best placement for a project or even the best publication support.

What do you want to tell new/unpublished writers? Learn as much about the business as you can, and don't give up.

Do you like that everything has become largely digitized? I'm definitely a print person. I like holding a book and making notes and comments in the margins. You can't do that — at least the same way — with digitized books. But digitization makes books accessible that might not otherwise be available. That's a good thing.

What do you like reading, watching, and listening to? I like to read what I represent: literary fiction and well-written narrative nonfiction. I watch very little television. Recently I've enjoyed *Downton Abbey* and *True Detective*, and I like the reality competition shows: *Project Runway* and *Top Chef*, etc. I like watching talented people be creative. My musical tastes are wide-ranging, from classical to indie.

Describe a book you would write. I have no desire to write a book. I leave the writing to my authors.

SWAGGER LITERARY AGENCY

601 Shenandoah Valley Drive, Front Royal, VA 22630, 540-636-7076,
swaggerlit@gmail.com

Agent's name: Joseph Brendan Vallely

Describe what you like to represent and what you won't represent. Upmarket nonfiction: current events, biography, history, sports and outdoors, word books, and projects that don't easily fit into those categories

What are the best ways for writers to pitch you? Email only.

Do you charge fees? No.

Describe your education and career history. See website for further info: www.swagger literary.com.

TALCOTT NOTCH LITERARY SERVICES ❖ www.talcottnotch.net

2 Broad Street, Second Floor, Suite 1, Milford, CT 06460,
editorial@talcottnotch.net, 203-876-4959

Agent's name and contact info: Gina Panettieri, president, gpanettieri@talcottnotch.net

Describe what you like to represent and what you won't represent. I like high-concept fiction, and nonfiction that is based on original research and that teaches the reader something they can't learn anywhere else.

I won't represent books that I feel are socially irresponsible, such as young adult books with hypersexualized teens or self-help that I feel has the potential to be damaging or that isn't based in supportable science.

What are the best ways for writers to pitch you? Traditional email queries with a 10-page sample pasted into the letter are always a good way to pitch. I've also found some great clients for the agency at conferences where I have an opportunity to read a sample of the work and have a chance to get to know the writer.

Do you charge fees? No.

Describe your education and career history. I attended Long Island University, Southampton, and then the University of Virginia. I've been in publishing for more than 25 years as an agent, freelance editor, and writer.

Say something about your hobbies and personal interests. I like to get outdoors as much as I can in my free time, so hiking and gardening and finding new parks to explore with my basset, Penny, are always favorite activities. I'm also a political junkie and follow current events obsessively.

Why and how did you become an agent? I started out as a writer, and it was only after having my own agent and helping other writers find publishers and helping them with their contract terms that I realized how much I really love this side of the table. I evolved into an agent very organically.

Would you do it over again, or something else? I'd be doing the same thing, but I would have started years sooner!

List some representative titles you have placed. *Brainscripts* by Drew Eric Whitman (McGraw-Hill); *Big Fat Disaster* by Beth Fehlbaum (Merit Press); *Plastic Jesus* (Salt Publishing, UK); *Firestorm: A Deadtown Novel* by Nancy Holzner (Berkley); *Dead Jed* by Scott Craven (Month9Books); *Tainted* by A. E. Rought (Strange Chemistry); *The Ultimate Book of March Madness* by Tom Hager (MVP Books).

Describe yourself as a person. Fiercely protective, somewhat obsessive, opinionated but practical and reasonable, good sense of humor. I will forget to eat, and I drink way too much tea. Oh, and I pace. All the time. See prior comment re: tea.

How would you describe the proverbial "client from hell," and what are the warning signs? Someone who doesn't respect my time or my boundaries, or doesn't respect his editor and causes unnecessary conflict with his publisher. I'm here to handle the problems, so letting me do my job is to the client's benefit. It's no mystery whether the client is trouble when the client starts to phone incessantly without an appointment or takes advantage of having my cell phone number to call me after hours or on weekends, or I get looped into a confrontational email exchange with the editor.

What do you think about self-publishing? It's an opportunity and a reasonable option for some people, and I've actually suggested it to a few writers who have sent me their work. It's definitely not for everyone, though, and new writers need to be wary of the "easy money for all" stories.

What will agenting be like in 2020? I think agenting has already begun evolving into what it will become, which is a job that involves much more than just selling books, negotiating contracts, etc. As the markets and opportunities available to our clients continue to morph and expand, and the demands for clients to adapt to be successful continue to increase, the job of agent has to continue to adapt as well. We'll be doing even more to help our clients establish their platforms and reach their readers, and we'll be exploring even more ways for them to exploit new rights.

Describe your job and what you like and don't like about it. I love reading and polishing manuscripts, and nothing is better than the day I get to call a client to tell her about an offer, and, of course, the days I talk to a prospective client and we decide to work together. The bulk of my workday involves working with current clients and handling their day-to-day issues, overseeing contracts and subrights, handling any problems they're encountering, reading and commenting on works in progress, reviewing royalty statements, and attending to a host of other details that need my attention. I do most of my reading of new queries and manuscripts after hours and on weekends.

What I don't like about my job is, of course, rejecting any writer's work and passing along rejections I've received to clients. I'm sure that's one of the least favorite things for any agent. I also don't enjoy dealing with anyone who replies unpleasantly to one of our assistants who has forwarded a rejection to a query they're handling for us. I don't understand why anyone would behave unprofessionally this way, and I always make a point of contacting those individuals myself to let them know that this is unacceptable under any circumstances.

Do you miss the way the business "used to be"? I don't miss it. However, I do think it's useful to have a firsthand archival understanding of how publishing has evolved.

What does the "Big 5" mean to you? High quality and great opportunity, but not the be-all and end-all.

What do you want to tell new/unpublished writers? Write what you love, not just what you think will sell. Be an original.

Do you like that everything has become largely digitized? It's certainly made things easier!

What do you like reading, watching, and listening to? I'm an avid pleasure reader and devour everything from young adult to adult dark fantasy and horror to personal investing and Civil War history. I'm the same way with what I watch, though I have a love of classic movies (pre-1960). I also really love old radio shows from the Golden Age of Radio, and NPR or the BBC.

Describe a book you would write. Probably something along the lines of the book I've already written, *The Single Mother's Guide to Raising Remarkable Boys*, something research intensive that I find really challenging and enlightening.

Joker's wild: Take every opportunity you can to polish your craft. Build a network of fellow writers, attend conferences or watch the podcasts online. Surround yourself with writers better than yourself. Never stop learning!

Agent's name and contact info: Rachael Dugas, rdugas@talcottnotch.net

Describe what you like to represent and what you won't represent. I largely focus on two categories: juvenile fiction and romance/women's fiction.

Under juvenile, I am interested in young adult and middle grade of all kinds, though I am slightly more partial to stories that take place in the realistic world. I am not interested in high fantasy, picture books, paranormal, or dystopian. For middle grade, I love contemporary stories in the vein of *Wonder* or historical in the vein of Patricia Reilly Giff's *Lily's Crossing*, though I am also interested in fun and funny and am open to some light fantasy/adventure. For young adult, I love contemporary stories that tug at the heartstrings, stories with an exciting mystery at the core, historical young adult of all kinds, young adult romance, etc.

In romance, I am seeking all sorts of stories that conform well to genre requirements but that, of course, do so in a fresh way. I prefer historical and contemporary, from sweet all the way up to steamy, but I am also open to some urban fantasy/paranormal.

In the miscellaneous category, I am open to a wide range of commercial and literary fiction for adults outside romance. I am an avid foodie and a theater enthusiast, so any nonfiction (or fiction!) related to food, theater, music, or the other branches of the performing arts are always welcome.

I am not particularly interested in fantasy, erotica, or sci-fi.

What are the best ways for writers to pitch you? Email is truly best. Please give some indication as to your genre in your subject line — just the word *Query* will not get you noticed.

When and where were you born? I was born in Connecticut at the tail end of the '80s.

Do you charge fees? We do not charge any fees at Talcott Notch. Our compensation is strictly the standard 15 percent of all author earnings.

Describe your education and career history. I attended Ithaca College, where I received my BA in English and also earned minors in writing and theater. I spent the first few months after college frosting cupcakes at a local bakery but got an internship with Sourcebooks shortly thereafter. I went directly from my long internship with Sourcebooks, where I worked with romance titles, to my position at Talcott Notch. My diverse and numerous side jobs have ranged from administrative assistant to food writer to baker to children's theater performer to camp counselor to SAT tutor — and more!

Say something about your hobbies and personal interests. I often joke that I'm always on the hunt for my next hobby — I do seem to have a habit of collecting them. Other than reading, obviously, I have had a lifelong passion for all things theater. I am an avid patron and act and sing myself — in fact, I am frequently found doing community theater in Connecticut, whenever I can find the time. I am also tremendously passionate about all things food. I watch way too many hours of *Food Network* and have tackled nearly everything from baking chocolate soufflés to making my grill into a smoker for barbequed pulled pork. I am also starting to get into crafting/DIY projects (thank you, Pinterest!) and have made steady progress with my knitting needles over the past few months. I also adore travel, though I don't get to do nearly as much of it as I'd like. I am a huge animal lover, too — I've got a young, poorly behaved Maltese-Yorkie mix and a very old, very sweet cat.

Why and how did you become an agent? My journey to agenting isn't really distinguishable from my career path — I wanted to work in publishing, and when the opportunity came my way to work with Gina Panettieri, our president, I took it. I have always had a passion for reading and, while I like to write, I don't have that compulsion to translate the stories in my head to paper that, to me, is the hallmark of what makes someone a writer. For me, agenting is the perfect opportunity to combine my love of reading and my interest in the craft of writing. I love editing authors' writing and being an author advocate.

Would you do it over again, or something else? Well, I still wouldn't turn down the chance to be a Broadway actress or have my own show on *Food Network*, but as far as realistic jobs go, I'm quite happy with what I'm doing!

List some representative titles you have placed. *The DMS Files* by J. Haight and S. Robinson (Random House/Delacorte); *Summer on the Short Bus* by Bethany Crandell (Perseus/Running Press Teens); *Of Breakable Things* by Amy Rolland (Month9Books); *He's No Prince Charming* by Elle Daniels (Hachette/Grand Central).

Describe yourself as a person. I most often am described as bubbly and creative. Other words I would include are *passionate*, *multifaceted*, and *stubborn*. I am a word nerd and bookworm. My family would tell you I'm sensitive, diplomatic, a daydreamer, and a peacekeeper. Two to three of my friends think I am also funny. Above all else, I would add, I am a study in contrasts. (Though aren't we all?)

How would you describe the proverbial "client from hell," and what are the warning signs? Hmm…I suppose somebody with major trust issues would be challenging for me to work with. I like the agent-client relationship to be collaborative, so anybody who wants to run the show or needs to talk several times a day is probably not a great fit for me.

What do you think about self-publishing? I don't think it's this terrible entity that's going to destroy print/traditional publishing forever (insert lightning bolt here), but I do think it gives writers a lot of opportunities to make major missteps that will ultimately hurt their careers. When you publish a book in any form, it's out there forever. There's much more that goes into making a book successful than most authors think. Without investing significant time and money into editorial assistance, professional cover art, and a solid marketing and publicity plan, it's very hard to sell your book on your own. If you have a poor sales record, it will be forever associated with your name, and that can make it hard to get agents and editors to convince the right people to invest in your book — even if you're a great writer. Is it possible that you might write something so spectacular that it will blow everyone out of the water and sell wildly? Sure. However, it's a one-in-a-million sort of situation. Plus, sometimes there's a difference between a well-written book and a marketable book, and that, above all else, is what I think separates the books that get picked up by traditional publishers from the rest.

Do you like Amazon? I'm sort of neutral on the whole Amazon debate. As a part of the publishing community, I obviously find it a little troubling, but as a consumer, I am definitely a fan. I think we just have to be careful with Amazon, as an industry — I do think we can coexist, however.

Do you believe in a "higher power"? Definitely. However you define it, there are too many unexplained and coincidental things in this world for me to believe it's all totally random.

What will agenting be like in 2020? Probably even more work! As a newer agent, I haven't experienced the shift in the industry myself, but I do know how intensively I work with each title before I begin the submission process. Every day, my colleagues and I are contributing more and more to the process, from title brainstorming to helping tweak back cover copy. I think the line between editor and agent is going to continue to blur as roles keep shifting. Whether the community at large becomes more open or more insular, however, is harder to predict.

Describe your job and what you like and don't like about it. I HATE giving bad news, and I do a lot of it, from rejecting manuscripts to passing on bad news from editors to my clients. For a dreamer, it can be tough to crush other people's hopes daily. Conversely, I love that I can help other big dreamers achieve their goals — telling an author we have an offer (and then seeing the final product!) is, hands down, the best part of my job.

Do you miss the way the business "used to be"? Having never experienced it myself, I can't really comment on this.

What does the "Big 5" mean to you? Literally: Penguin Random House, Hachette, Simon & Schuster, Harper Collins, and Macmillan. Less concretely: tradition, excellence, and prestige. I always refer to them as the Ivy League of publishing — but, as with colleges, that doesn't mean there aren't other equally great options for your book out there. It also doesn't mean they're the best place for everyone to succeed.

What do you want to tell new/unpublished writers? Take risks. Write honestly. Write for *you*. Don't write something because it's trendy — write the story in your heart, whatever that is. Dream big but be realistic. Realize that some stories are just going to be for you, and be okay with it. READ everything and read often. Accept criticism gracefully, but know when to stick to your guns. Most of all, you'll never succeed if you don't try in the first place.

Do you like that everything has become largely digitized? I just bought my first ereader after holding out adamantly for years, and I have to admit I'm really enjoying having instant access to digital materials. However, I still think there's nothing like a physical book. As an agent, I worry about what increased digital availability means for intellectual property. There are pros and cons to a digital world, for sure.

What do you like reading, watching, and listening to? Reading: There's a part of me that will never get over being a 16-year-old girl, so I just LOVE funny or heart-wrenching realistic young adult. It brings me back to that time when we all felt everything so acutely and lived with such passion. However, I do like books written for grown-ups, too. I love everything from fun women's fiction to lushly written literary fiction to classics. I read some nonfiction, especially food memoir. I also read cookbooks cover to cover. Watching: Far too many stupid and embarrassing shows to admit here. (Think 16-year-old girl tastes again.) I'm not embarrassed to admit that I adore *Modern Family* and *The Big Bang Theory* and, in reruns or on DVD, *Gilmore Girls*, *The Office*, and *House*. I also watch Food Network compulsively. I used to go to the moves a lot, too, but I've gotten too busy and cheap these days. I do love to go a few times a year, though, and while I definitely gravitate toward chick flicks, I can be talked into seeing almost anything. (Except horror or disaster movies. Not a fan.) Listening: My iPod is frighteningly eclectic. My all-time favorite artist is Andrew McMahon (formerly of Something Corporate and Jack's Mannequin, now going solo). I have lots of show tunes, some oldies, a bit of pop, and lots of contemporary alternative. I am always on the lookout for new artists to listen to. My favorite recent discoveries have been Passenger, Fitz and the Tantrums, and the *Frozen* soundtrack.

Describe a book you would write. Oh gosh, I don't think I'll ever write a book. If I did, I think it would definitely be young adult and I think it would probably be something along the lines of Sarah Dessen meets Meg Cabot meets Lauren Oliver. Or maybe a really quirky, girly middle grade.

Joker's wild: Five things currently in my unorganized, oversized purse: multiple tubes of lip gloss; Wintergreen Tic Tacs (the only mints I eat); my Nook; leftover Valentine's candy; approximately 688,999,777,373 Dunkin' Donuts receipts. (What can I say? I have a coffee problem.)

Agent's name and contact info: Paula Munier, pmunier@talcottnotch.net

Describe what you like to represent and what you won't represent. Actively looking for strong voices in crime fiction, new adult, young adult, children's, women's fiction, historical fiction, selective sci-fi/fantasy, and most kinds of nonfiction, especially science, cooking, business, and New Age.

No poetry, stories with elves, or misogynist fiction.

What are the best ways for writers to pitch you? Read our query submission guidelines on our website; query me. Or come to one of the many events I attend.

When and where were you born? Seriously?

Do you charge fees? No.

Describe your education and career history. Studied geophysics at Purdue, which only served me so well in the 20 years I spent as a writer, editor, and acquisitions specialist for Gannett, Prima (now part of Crown), Disney, Rockport, F&W Media, and more before I became an agent two years ago.

Say something about your hobbies and personal interests. Reading and writing. The arts. Travel. Teaching, studying, and practicing yoga.

Why and how did you become an agent? I became an agent because my own agent — the wonderful Gina Panettieri, founder of Talcott Notch — asked me to join the agency. I'd just left F&W Media, and after nearly eight years of running acquisitions there, I was ready for a change.

Would you do it over again, or something else? I love this!

List some representative titles you have placed. *The Registry* sci-fi trilogy by Shannon Stoker; two-book deal for the latest in the *Victoria Turnbull* mystery series by Cynthia Riggs; *Sniper* by Vaughn Hardacker; *Hot Dogs & Croissants* by the Saulnier Sisters; *Life's a Bark* by Larry Kay; *Orphan #8* by Kim Van Aldemade; *Dying for Attention* by James Shannon; *The Body language of Liars* by Dr. Lillian Glass; three-book *Algy Temple* mystery series by J. J. Partridge; *Death Dealer* by Kate Flora.

Describe yourself as a person. Hardworking, resourceful, committed to good work and clients doing good work. And fun!

How would you describe the proverbial "client from hell," and what are the warning signs? People who do not honor boundaries, who text me at midnight on Saturday, who balk at rewrites. In short, people who are not professionals and who don't treat me like a professional.

What do you think about self-publishing? It's the right answer for some authors.

Do you like Amazon? Amazon symbolizes the new reality. Adapt or die.

Do you believe in a "higher power"? Namaste.

What will agenting be like in 2020? Who knows? But storytelling will never die — and we'll always need people to help make sure that readers have access to the best stories.

Describe your job and what you like and don't like about it. I love reading great books, discovering new talent, and getting every client a better deal! I'm the midwife privileged to assist in the birthing of new books.

Do you miss the way the business "used to be"? No. That was then, this is now.

What does the "Big 5" mean to you? Sales. But there are other options as well.

What do you want to tell new/unpublished writers? Write. Revise. Repeat.

Do you like that everything has become largely digitized? It makes things easier and harder. Easier: I can read anywhere, anytime, on my iPad. Harder: My inbox is congenitally swamped.

What do you like reading, watching, and listening to? On my bedside table now are books by Pema Chödrön, Craig Johnson, Alice Hoffman, Elizabeth Berg, Joseph Campbell, Mark Nepo, Nik Pizzolatto, George R. R. Martin, and Dashiell Hammett. I'm currently obsessed with *Sherlock*, *Downton Abbey*, *Scott & Bailey*, *True Detective*, *House of Cards*, *Homeland*, *Game of Thrones*, and *Longmire*.

Describe a book you would write. I'll tell you when I finish it.

Joker's wild: "If you're going to have a story, have a big story, or none at all." — Joseph Campbell

TESSLER LITERARY AGENCY, LLC ❖ www.tessleragency.com

27 West 20th Street, Suite 1003, New York, NY 10011

Describe what you like to represent and what you won't represent. Our list is diverse and far-reaching. In nonfiction, it includes narrative, popular science, memoir, history, psychology, business, biography, food, and travel. In many cases, we sign authors who are especially adept at writing books that cross many of these categories at once. In fiction, we represent literary, women's, and commercial.

We do not take on genre fiction or children's books.

What are the best ways for writers to pitch you? Queries are accepted via our web form at www.tessleragency.com.

Do you charge fees? No.

Describe your education and career history. Tessler Literary Agency was formed in 2004 by Michelle Tessler, who previously worked at the prestigious literary agency Carlisle & Company (now Inkwell Management) and at the William Morris Agency. In addition to agenting, Michelle worked as an executive of business development and marketing in the internet industry. In 1994, just as the internet was becoming a mainstream medium, she was hired by bestselling author James Gleick to help launch the Pipeline. She then went on to serve as vice president of new media at Jupiter Communications, and later at ScreamingMedia, before returning to traditional publishing. In light of the digital opportunities that are transforming publishing, Michelle's experience in the internet world is of great benefit to her authors, both as they navigate ebook and app opportunities and as they look for creative and effective ways to market their books to niche communities that can be targeted online via social media. A native New Yorker, Michelle has a master's degree in English literature and is a member of the Association of Authors' Representatives and Women's Media Group.

List some representative titles you have placed. The Drunken Botantist, Wicked Plants, and *Wicked Bugs* (*New York Times* bestsellers) by Amy Stewart (Algonquin); *Underwater Dogs* (*New York Times* bestseller) by Seth Casteel (Little, Brown); *Body Clutter* (*New York Times* bestseller) by Marla Cilley (a.k.a. the Flylady) and Leanne Ely (a.k.a. the Dinner Diva) (Touchstone); *In-n-Out Burger* (*New York Times* bestseller) by Stacy Perman (Harper Collins); *The Bonobo and the Atheist* by Frans de Waal (Norton); *A Slave in the White House* (*New York Times* bestseller) by Elizabeth Dowling Taylor (Palgrave); *The Fruit Hunters* by Adam Leith Gollner (Scribner); *Plastic* by Susan Freinkel (Houghton Mifflin); *The Murder of the Century: The Gilded Age Crime That Scandalized a City & Sparked the Tabloid Wars* by Paul Collins (Crown); *Song of the Vikings* by Nancy Marie Brown (Palgrave); *Visit Sunny Chernobyl* by Andrew Blackwell (Rodale); *Presidential Doodles* from the creators of Cabinet Magazine (Basic); *How to Be Lost* by Amanda Eyre Ward (MacAdam Cage / Ballantine); *Evolution for Everyone* by David Sloan Wilson (Bantam Books); *Emotional First-Aid* by Guy Winch, PhD (Hudson Street Books); *The Chemistry between Us* by Larry Young, PhD, and Brian Alexander (Current / Penguin); *Straphanger: Saving Our Cities and Ourselves from the Automobile* by Taras Grescoe (Times Books); *Saving Dinner* by Leanne Ely (Ballantine); *Mediated* by Thomas de Zengotita (Bloomsbury); *Defining the Wind: The Beaufort Scale and How a 19th-Century Admiral Turned Science into Poetry* by Scott Huler (Crown); *Sink Reflections* by Marla Cilley (a.k.a. the Flylady) (Bantam).

TONI LOPOPOLO LITERARY MANAGEMENT ❖

www.lopopololiterary.com

3463 State Street, #111, Santa Barbara, CA 93105, 215-353-1151

Agent's name and contact info: Toni Lopopolo, lopopolobooks@aol.com

Describe what you like to represent and what you won't represent. Have been successful with business books, books on dogs, women's health, parenting. Fiction: noir, crime, paranormal, speculative, sci-fi, historical, crime, or romance.

Won't agent regular or disguised porn.

What are the best ways for writers to pitch you? A terrific query with short synopsis and the first five pages of the first chapter. Please do not phone.

When and where were you born? I was born on a hot day, July 18th, in Los Angeles, before freeways.

Do you charge fees? Not yet. However, we now offer editorial services. Fees apply.

Describe your education and career history. I have a BA from California State University, San Francisco, plus graduate work. I started at Bantam Books in New York City in the publicity department, worked in marketing at Harcourt Brace, then Houghton Mifflin, became executive editor at Macmillan, then spent 10 years as executive editor at St. Martin's Press. I opened my agency in 1991.

Say something about your hobbies and personal interests. I'm crazy about dogs. I love all critters and work as an animal activist because I'm appalled by the cruelty to animals in the USA; don't get me started on other countries. I look for good writing in film and cable television. Right now, *True Detective*, *Justified*, anything with Jimmy Smits, *Dexter*, *The Americans*, *Homeland*, *Ray Donovan*, *House of Cards*. I collect beautiful books, vintage posters. I look for unusual fabrics for the home. I spend a lot of time in framing shops. Looks like such fun. I enjoy my Saturday fiction intensive workshop called Tea With Toni.

Why and how did you become an agent? Natural segue after working in book publishing. Upon leaving publishing, I worked for an agent, then opened my own literary management business.

Would you do it over again, or something else? I'd do it again. But now I love teaching writing workshops. I love to see the light go on in a budding writer. I'd like to review published books. I'd like to teach full-time. Let's see; maybe I'd start my own writing.

List some representative titles you have placed. See my website, www.lopopololiterary.com.

Describe yourself as a person. I enjoy my own company. My favorite social activity is dinner with super people who talk about interesting (to me) topics. I'm curious about human behavior, so I ask friends a lot of questions about how they were raised, what their parents were like. I enjoy walks on the beach with my dogs. Right now I have one dog left after living with six in the recent past. I can now recognize the behavior of a sociopath. I have yet to meet a sociopathic dog. I haven't had a television for the past four years, not by plan but by circumstances; no cable. I'm afraid if I get mine connected, I won't do my work but will watch HGTV instead.

How would you describe the proverbial "client from hell," and what are the warning signs? Terminally insecure. They use the phone instead of email. I had a client who phoned at midnight to say, "If I can't sleep, nobody sleeps."

What do you think about self-publishing? Easy way to get published without mastering the skills needed to write well, like self-editing. Once in a while someone hits it big-time; fun to see that happen. Take that, publishing editors!

Do you like Amazon? If I had all the money I've paid Amazon, I could buy a Jaguar. Yes, I like Amazon. I like that I can find any book I want from the past or present and read the first chapter before clicking on "Buy." Amazon is good for writers because they can read reviews of their own work from the public.

Do you believe in a "higher power"? I wish.

What will agenting be like in 2020? Fewer.

Describe your job and what you like and don't like about it. I adore reading a new writer who pulls me into the story and I'm not aware of the writing, whether fiction or memoir or any narrative nonfiction subject. I love the moment when I can announce to a client, "We've got a contract." I don't like that publishing has become conglomerated. That every book has to fit a certain set of criteria to please the big guys in the corporate structure, not the reading public. I don't like the poor editing I see in many published novels today.

Do you miss the way the business "used to be"? Like crazy. But I now admit I'm a dinosaur.

What does the "Big 5" mean to you? Trouble. But at least they're still selling to bookstores. Still publishing print books, though now some contracts say the publisher has the option to *not* publish bound books.

What do you want to tell new/unpublished writers? Please master the skills needed. These skills are not taught in school.

Do you like that everything has become largely digitized? Has its benefits.

What do you like reading, watching, and listening to? See my response to the question about my hobbies and personal interests above. I love discovering new writers of crime fiction, like the Scandinavians. The UK writers. American writers with an original character. I listen to NPR on my iPhone.

Describe a book you would write. Crime fiction set in Umbria during the Renaissance about a young woman sent north from Bisceglie on the Adriatic to work in a household in Ferrara. Her name? Immaculata.

Joker's wild: I miss Manhattan and the East Coast like crazy. However, I do enjoy the 95 percent perfect weather here in Santa Barbara, hammock reading, walks on the beach in January, plus flower and fruit growing all year round.

Agent's name and contact info: Susan Setteducato-Donnelly, donnsett@verizon.net

Describe what you like to represent and what you won't represent. Fiction only. A good story well told. I'm not interested in historical romance or romance in general, but a good read would turn my head.

What are the best ways for writers to pitch you? With a brief summary of the main conflict, a sense of the protagonist and what he or she is up against, and a warm introduction to you, the writer. No bragging or comparing yourself to Hemingway. Let the writing speak for itself.

When and where were you born? September 11 (I know, I know), 1953, Newark, NJ.

Do you charge fees? No.

Describe your education and career history. High school, then three years of fine arts training. After that, hard knocks and the school of life. I ran my own sign-painting business for more than a decade, then relocated and worked at various and sundry jobs to support my writing and painting habits. Eleven years under Ms. Lopopolo taught me editing and the craft of fiction writing, which I'm still learning.

Say something about your hobbies and personal interests. I practice yoga so that I can spend longer, more-focused hours writing. I used to have other interests, but writing ate them all.

Why and how did you become an agent? When Toni asked me to read my first query letter, I got hooked.

Would you do it over again, or something else? I'm still here, so that says something. I learn from every submission. Writers amaze me.

List some representative titles you have placed. A title I edited is now on Amazon. Look for *Florentine Gold* by Peter Rucci.

Describe yourself as a person. Driven.

How would you describe the proverbial "client from hell," and what are the warning signs? The client from hell spends more time complaining and less time writing. Warning sign? When the say something like, "I'm the next Hemingway."

What do you think about self-publishing? I think it's an option when all others have been exhausted. When is that? After you've revised and revised and been edited and revised some more, and you are absolutely sure that you've given it your best. Even after that it's hard to know.

Do you like Amazon? Yes and no. Yes, because they are here and in the game and we might as well make friends with that. And no because I'm not sure I like their monopoly-esque tendencies.

Do you believe in a "higher power"? Yup.

What will agenting be like in 2020? Like now, only with more buttons.

Describe your job and what you like and don't like about it. Right now my main job is writing fiction. There's nothing I don't like about it. Even when it's hard.

Do you miss the way the business "used to be"? That would be a waste of time. Even if a lot has changed, the bottom line is still good stories, good writing. That never changes.

What does the "Big 5" mean to you? The place to aim for. Write your book with the big boys and girls in mind. Go for the gold. It can't hurt.

What do you want to tell new/unpublished writers? Read voraciously. Write every day. Write from your heart, and never give up.

Do you like that everything has become largely digitized? No. I like to hold a book in my hand. Especially one bound in leather. You can't digitize that smell…

What do you like reading, watching, and listening to? I love fiction. Urban fantasy (Lev Grossman, Jim Butcher), crime novels (Ian Rankin, Michael Connelly). James Lee Burke is a hero of mine. So is J. K. Rowling. I watch a lot of series TV on Netflix, especially British drama. It's a good place to study storytelling and dialogue. I live on a farm, so I listen to geese a lot.

Describe a book you would write. The tale of a young New Jersey girl who gets tangled up with dragons.

Joker's wild: Not sure what this means, but I'm a writer first, so I'll blab. Storytelling is ancient. And it comes from inside us. We invented it so that we'd have something to navigate by. Something to use as a guidepost going forward. I think writers and those who help midwife their efforts into the world are the coolest people in the universe. Amen.

Agent's name and contact info: Theora Tiffney, 4410 Nueces Drive, Santa Barbara, CA 93110, twtiffney@gmail.com

Describe what you like to represent and what you won't represent. Young adult and new adult, speculative fiction, science fiction and fantasy, particularly steampunk. I'm also interested in historical fiction. Strong female protagonists are a huge plus.

Describe your education and career history. I graduated from the University of California, Santa Barbara, College of Creative Studies, in 2014 with a BA in biology and a minor in history. I've published one novel and have been working with Lopopolo Literary Management since 2013.

Say something about your hobbies and personal interests. I'm passionately interested in science and history; my emphasis in my major is the evolution of disease and the history of medicine. In my free time, I enjoy hiking, cooking, working on "cosplay" for conventions, and building instruments. I'm a writer working on a second novel.

What do you want to tell new/unpublished writers? Editing is your friend. So is persistence. Indulge in copious quantities of both.

Do you like that everything has become largely digitized? Though I'm a member of the generation that's grown up with digital everything, I find that it's a lot easier to work on things when they're on paper in front of me — for one thing, I'm constrained by the size of my desk, not by the size of my monitor. I far prefer physical copies of books, too.

What do you like reading, watching, and listening to? I like reading young adult and speculative fiction, interspersed with nonfiction about biology and history. As for watching, almost anything goes — my tastes run from Disney to *The Intouchables*. I enjoy classical music, movie sound tracks, and some rock.

TRACY BROWN LITERARY AGENCY

PO Box 772, Nyack, NY 10960

Agent's name and contact info: Tracy Brown, president, tracy@brownlit.com

Describe what you like to represent and what you won't represent. Current events, memoir, history, biography, health, psychology, travel, literary fiction.

What are the best ways for writers to pitch you? Email query letter with description before sending any attachments.

Describe your education and career history. I held senior editorial and executive positions in book publishing for close to 30 years before becoming an agent in 2003. My jobs in publishing included editor in chief of Book-of-the-Month Club, executive editor at Holt, editor at Viking, and senior editor at Ballantine.

List some representative titles you have placed. *The State of Affairs: Cheating in the Age of Transparency* by Esther Perel (Harper Collins); *Tap Dancing to Work: Warren Buffett on Practically Everything, 1966–2012*, collected and expanded by Carol J. Loomis (A Fortune Magazine Book/Portfolio); *The Man in the White Sharkskin Suit: My Family's Exodus from Old Cairo to the New World* by Lucette Lagnado (Ecco).

TRIADA US LITERARY AGENCY ❖ www.triadaus.com

PO Box 561, Sewickley, PA 15143

Agent's name and contact info: (Mr.) Uwe Stender, uwe@triadaus.com

Describe what you like to represent and what you won't represent. I am open to pretty much any project that truly excites me the moment I hear the hook or the scope/topic of the project, except for adult sci-fi and adult fantasy.

What are the best ways for writers to pitch you? Send me a well-written and error-free email, or pitch me in person at a conference.

When and where were you born? In Germany during the last millennium.

Do you charge fees? No.

Describe your education and career history. PhD in German literature, literary agent (since 2004), university lecturer (German, film, writing).

Say something about your hobbies and personal interests. I enjoy running and training for marathons. I love big dogs like German shepherds and black Labs, and any kind of music except for heavy metal.

Why and how did you become an agent? I have always loved literature (thus went all the way to a PhD in the academic field), and after years of researching the field from a publishing perspective, I decided to become an agent (with the mentoring and support from several well-connected publishing insiders). I simply love the thrill of discovering a *great* book.

Would you do it over again, or something else? I would do it over again. The only other thing I would consider doing would be to become a music producer.

List some representative titles you have placed. The Land of the 10,000 Madonnas by Kate Hattemer; *The Vigilante Poets of Selwyn Academy* by Kate Hattemer; *The Tragedy Paper* by Elizabeth LaBan; *The Kids' Outdoor Adventure Book* by Stacy Tornio and Ken Keffer; *Wild Connection* by Jennifer Verdolin; *The Reappearing Act* by Kate Fagan; *In Faith and in Doubt* by Dale McGowan; *Love Isn't Supposed to Hurt* by Christi Paul; *Race Baiter* by Eric Deggans; *Hotter than a Match Head: Life on the Run with the Lovin' Spoonful* by Steve Boone with Tony Moss; *Garden Therapy* by Stephanie Rose.

Describe yourself as a person. I am passionate, work hard, and am still *very* European after all these years in the USA.

How would you describe the proverbial "client from hell," and what are the warning signs? I have no clients from hell. I wouldn't sign them. I have a folder in my email entitled "Nutjobs" — that is where a potential client from hell would go.

What do you think about self-publishing? It is a great way to be discovered, if for some reason you have not been discovered yet.

Do you like Amazon? Not really. I don't like entities that thrive to become monopolies. Monopolies are unfair and boring.

Do you believe in a "higher power"? Yes.

What will agenting be like in 2020? Only the higher power I believe in knows.

Describe your job and what you like and don't like about it. It is all about discovering really creative and brilliant people and projects, and I find all of that supremely exciting.

Do you miss the way the business "used to be"? Since I am a relative newcomer, I don't know how it used to be, and looking back in a nostalgic way is a lose-lose proposition in anything in life, anyway.

What does the "Big 5" mean to you? They are dimensions of personality. The Big 5 Factors are openness, conscientiousness, extroversion, agreeableness, and neuroticism. And I know that is not what you implied with your question.

What do you want to tell new/unpublished writers? Follow your dreams!

Do you like that everything has become largely digitized? Yes. It is way more efficient.

What do you like reading, watching, and listening to? Great books, great TV/movies, and great music! For example, in books: *Huckleberry Finn*, *The Big Sleep*, and *Eleanor and Park*. In TV/films: *The Sopranos*, *Cinema Paradiso*, and *Sherlock Holmes* (with Benedict Cumberbatch). In music: anything by Ellie Goulding, the Black Keys, Daft Punk, and Brian Wilson.

Describe a book you would write. It would be a young adult novel about heartbreak, longing, and redemption.

Joker's wild: Buy me a good drink, and I will listen to your pitch no matter what.

VERITAS LITERARY AGENCY ❖ www.veritasliterary.com

601 Van Ness Avenue, Opera Plaza, Suite E, San Francisco, CA 94102, Member AAR & Authors Guild

Agent's name and contact info: Katherine Boyle, katherine@veritasliterary.com

Describe what you like to represent and what you won't represent. I represent literary and commercial fiction including young adult and middle grade (especially series); serious and humorous nonfiction of all stripes, including narrative, memoir, popular science, biography, women's interest, business, and pop culture.

No genre fiction (send to Michael; see next questionnaire), children's picture books, hippie memoirs, sports books, haiku collections, etc.

What are the best ways for writers to pitch you? Email query to submissions@veritas literary.com. No hardcopy submissions, please.

When and where were you born? Stanford, CA, sometime in the last century.

Do you charge fees? No.

Describe your education and career history. BA in English and psychology from Stanford University; publishing program at Berkeley. Established Veritas in 1995.

Say something about your hobbies and personal interests. Art, music, and nature lover; pet fanatic; connoisseur of islands.

Why and how did you become an agent? I studied English and psychology, the perfect mix for what we do.

Would you do it over again, or something else? Happy where I am.

List some representative titles you have placed. *Holy Sh*t: A History of Swearing* (Oxford); *In the After & In the End* (Harper Teen); *The Secret History of Vladimir Nabokov* (Pegasus); *If I Am Missing or Dead* (Simon & Schuster); *So Shelly* (Delacorte).

Describe yourself as a person. Patient, honest, friendly, overly garrulous, and a bit of a pushover at times (except with publishers).

How would you describe the proverbial "client from hell," and what are the warning signs? I know the warning signs, so I don't take them on.

Do you like Amazon? Very mixed feelings here. I've seen authors benefit from increased opportunities, but I don't think Amazon has had an overall positive impact on the industry or on the valuation of books.

What do you like reading, watching, and listening to? Literary fiction, post-punk, foreign movies, British TV.

Describe a book you would write. I might ghostwrite my cat's autobiography one day.

Agent's name and contact info: Michael Carr, michael@veritasliterary.com

Describe what you like to represent and what you won't represent. I represent science fiction and fantasy, historical, contemporary thriller, and science or history nonfiction.

What are the best ways for writers to pitch you? I prefer a straight query with the first five pages included in the body of the email. I tend to skip the outline or synopsis and just get to the pages. I am especially turned off by gimmicky, boastful queries.

Do you charge fees? No. Authors should never pay agents to do their job.

List some representative titles you have placed. *Shadowdance*, six-book series, by David Dalglish (Orbit/Hachette); *The Plum Tree* and *What She Left Behind* by Ellen Marie Wiseman (Kensington); *Killing the Poormaster: A Saga of Poverty, Corruption & Murder in the Great Depression* (Chicago Review).

What do you think about self-publishing? I think it's a great option for people who have been failed by the industry, for whatever reason. It is quite possible to earn money writing excellent but niche books that would not interest traditional publishers.

Describe your job and what you like and don't like about it. I love working with books. That has been a dream of mine since I was a kid. I don't like rejecting manuscripts, especially ones that are pretty good. It can be draining to keep telling people no, which is mostly what reading submissions is about.

What do you want to tell new/unpublished writers? It's a tough business, but if you're happier writing than doing anything else, give it everything you've got.

Do you like that everything has become largely digitized? I read a fair bit on my Kindle, but I'll always prefer a paper book. Having said that, I think the digital revolution is a good thing for writers and for readers in general.

What do you like reading, watching, and listening to? In my spare time, I read more non-fiction these days than fiction, mostly history and popular science. I read plenty of fiction for work, and it's hard to turn off the inner critic. I listen to a variety of music, everything from classical to '80s pop to heavy metal. I don't watch a lot of TV.

Describe a book you would write. Probably something crazy, like a mystery set in a polygamist cult.

WALES LITERARY AGENCY, INC. ❖ www.waleslit.com

PO Box 9426, Seattle, WA 98109-0426, 206-284-7114

Agents' names and contact info: Elizabeth Wales, president; Neal Swain, assistant agent; general email: waleslit@waleslit.com

Describe what you like to represent and what you won't represent. We represent quality mainstream fiction and narrative nonfiction. In fiction and nonfiction, we look for talented storytellers, both new and established, and we're especially interested in projects that could have a progressive cultural or political impact. Clients are from the entire country; we also represent a strong group of Northwest, West Coast, and Alaskan writers.

We don't represent the following: children's books, how-to, self-help, and almost all genre projects (romance, true crime, horror, action/adventure, most science fiction/ fantasy, technothrillers).

What are the best ways for writers to pitch you? Writers should send their email queries without attachments to waleslit@waleslit.com, or by mail to our PO Box, with an SASE. We do not accept queries by phone.

Do you charge fees? We do not charge fees. Our agency works only on commission: 15 percent of domestic sales and 20 percent of foreign sales.

Describe your education and career history. Elizabeth Wales: BA, Smith College; graduate work in English and American literature, Columbia University. Member, Association of Authors' Representatives (AAR). Founded the agency in 1990 with Dan Levant.

List some representative titles you have placed. The United States of Cheddar by Gordon Edgar (Chelsea Green, 2015); *Badluck Way: A Year on the Ragged Edge of the West* by Bryce Andrews (Atria / Simon & Schuster, January 2014); *Growing a Feast: The Chronicle of a Farm-to-Table Meal* by Kurt Timmermeister (W.W. Norton, January 2014); *The Urban Bestiary: Encountering the Everyday Wild* by Lyanda Lynn Haupt (Little, Brown, September 2013); *American Savage: Insights, Slights, and Fights on Faith, Sex, Love, and Politics* by Dan Savage (Dutton/Penguin, May 2013; paperback published by Plume, May 2014); *Unterzakhn: A Tale of the Lower East Side*, graphic novel by Leela Corman (Schocken/Pantheon, 2012); *Happiness Is a Chemical in the Brain*, stories by Lucia Perillo (W.W. Norton, 2012).

WATERSIDE PRODUCTIONS, INC. ❖ www.waterside.com

Agent's name and contact info: Bill Gladstone, president, bgladstone@waterside.com

Other agents at Waterside Productions: Carole Jelen, carole@jelenpub.com; Margot Maley Hutchison, mmaley@waterside.com; David Nelson, davidmthope@aol.com. Their profiles can be found at www.waterside.com.

Describe what you like to represent and what you won't represent. Technology, business, and health are our primary categories. We do not represent fiction or memoir.

What are the best ways for writers to pitch you? Email.

When and where were you born? New York City, many years ago.

Do you charge fees? Not for agenting, but we do charge for our hybrid ebook publishing through Waterfront Digital Press.

Describe your education and career history. Yale and Harvard. Editorial director, ARCO Publishing; senior editor, Harcourt, Brace.

Say something about your hobbies and personal interests. Golf, tennis, and the beach.

Why and how did you become an agent? I had the relationships and could help authors.

Would you do it over again, or something else? I love being an agent. I would not change anything. I also write books and produce films, so I am never bored, even as pure literary agenting is changing. We also represent online courses and do our own ebook publishing.

List some representative titles you have placed.
Bill: *What God Said* by Neale Donald Walsch (Berkley/Penguin); *Soul Healing Miracles* by Master and Dr. Sha (BenBella); *The Crash of 2016* by Thom Hartmann (Twelve/Hachette); *Stickability* by Greg Reid and the Napoleon Hill Foundation (Tarcher/Penguin).

Carole: *Hacking Happiness: Why Your Personal Data Counts and How Tracking It Can Change the World* by John Havens (Penguin, 2014); David Busch's digital-camera guide series (Cengage Learning); *The Entrepreneurial Bible to Venture Capital: Inside Secrets from the Leaders in the Startup Game* by Andrew Romans (McGraw-Hill).

David: *The Emotional Edge* by Crystal Andrus; *Pom Poms Up!: From Puberty to Pythons and Beyond* by Carol Cleveland; *A License to Live: James Bond's Trade Secrets for Living Well with Depression* by Stefanie Glick and Michael Grais.

Describe yourself as a person. Outgoing and fun loving, comfortable with a variety of people, and good with numbers.

How would you describe the proverbial "client from hell," and what are the warning signs? Needs lots of hand-holding; asks questions more than once; does not follow advice given; has unrealistic expectations. Warning signs are any form of self-absorption and self-delusion.

What do you think about self-publishing? It is fine if an author is unable to attract a traditional book publisher.

Do you like Amazon? Amazon generates almost 50 percent of all revenue from print and ebook sales. How can you not like that? Of course, their tactics, unwillingness to speak with publishers, and arrogance are not attractive.

Do you believe in a "higher power"? Absolutely.

What will agenting be like in 2020? A few big agencies will dominate print books. Smaller agencies will still exist but will be handling ebooks, advising on self-publishing, and increasingly acting as publishing consultants and managers.

Describe your job and what you like and don't like about it. Today it is mostly answering emails, reading book proposals, and talking with authors and editors. Except for the fact that I receive too many emails and phone calls, I wouldn't change anything.

Do you miss the way the business "used to be"? Yes. It was more personal and more fun.

What does the "Big 5" mean to you? We all know who they are. We love them. They pay out the big advances. It's harder and harder to sell books to them. We have always depended on the success of independents and actually generate the majority of our royalties from the smaller publishing houses and not the Big 5.

What do you want to tell new/unpublished writers? Be patient. Do not expect to make any significant money directly from your books for three to five years. Only write books if you love to write or have a business that will benefit from your being a published author. The other reason to write books is if you love to write and would write whether anyone was paying you or not.

Do you like that everything has become largely digitized? From a work perspective, yes, as it is much easier to communicate and less paper is used. I still print out all proposals and manuscripts since I do not, despite having an iPad, enjoy reading digital documents except for short ones. I guess I am showing my age.

What do you like reading, watching, and listening to? I love reading newspapers and book reviews. I read cutting-edge manuscripts all the time so rarely read books not written by my clients. I avoid fiction altogether. I like music from the Beatles and almost all the music from the '60s. Films are increasingly disappointing, though *American Hustle*, *Blue Jasmine*, and *Wolf of Wall Street* were worth watching. *Downton Abbey*, *The Good Wife*, *Parenthood*, and *Game of Thrones*, along with tennis, golf, and the Olympics, are my television preferences.

Describe a book you would write. I have written three novels: *The Twelve*, *The Power of Twelve*, and *The Golden Motorcycle Gang*. My nonfiction books are *Be the Deal*, *Tapping the Source*, and *Test Your Own Mental Health*. I am currently writing a new book with Master and Dr. Sha on the science behind unconventional healing.

Joker's wild: Send dark chocolate with your proposal, and I am more likely to read it. No guarantees, though, and the chocolate should be 70 percent cacao or higher.

WENDY SCHMALZ AGENCY ❖ www.schmalzagency.com

402 Union Street, Unit 831, Hudson, NY 12534, 518-672-7697

**Agent's name and contact info: Wendy Schmalz,
wendy@schmalzagency.com**

Describe what you like to represent and what you won't represent. Lately, I've been focusing on young adult fiction. I prefer realistic, edgy young adult and middle grade with an original voice. For adults I like literary fiction and American history.

I don't like high fantasy, sci fi, or romance. I'm not taking on any picture book writers.

What are the best ways for writers to pitch you? I accept email queries, but not snail mail queries. Include a brief synopsis in the body of the email. Please don't send the manuscript unless I've asked to see it. I'll respond to queries within a week after receipt of the query. Please note, I only respond to queries if I want to read the manuscript. If I don't respond, it means it's not for me.

When and where were you born? Abington, PA, 1956.

Do you charge fees? NO.

Describe your education and career history. I graduated from Barnard College in NYC with a BA in American studies. I worked for a year in the film department of Curtis Brown. I went from there to Harold Ober Associates, one of the oldest agencies in the country. Eventually, I became a principal in the agency. I opened my own agency in 2002.

Say something about your hobbies and personal interests. I'm fascinated by mid-20th-century American history, especially the civil rights movement and LBJ. I do a lot of volunteer work at the local library.

Why and how did you become an agent? When I was in high school, I read Tennessee Williams's autobiography. He talked a lot about his agent. That was the first time I knew such a thing existed. It seemed like a really cool way to make a living. When I was in college, I was working for a reporter whose wife was a novelist. She asked what I wanted to do. When I told her I wanted to be an agent, she arranged an interview for me at the agency that represented her, Curtis Brown, Ltd. They hired me a few weeks before I graduated from college.

Would you do it over again, or something else? I can't imagine being anything else. I love doing what I do.

List some representative titles you have placed. *A Point Last Seen* series by April Henry (Holt); *The Thunder of Giants* by Joel Fishbane (St. Martin's); *The Half Life of Molly Pierce* by Katrina Leno (Harper); *Nickel Bay Nick* by Dean Pitchford (Putnam); *Lies My Girlfriend Told Me* by Julie Anne Peters (Little, Brown); *Gracefully Grayson* by Ami Polonsky (Hyperion); *Diamond Boy* by Michael Williams (Little, Brown).

Describe yourself as a person. I have a good sense of humor. I'm loyal. I have a bit of a temper. I can be terse.

How would you describe the proverbial "client from hell," and what are the warning signs? There are two main ingredients in a client from hell — the unwillingness to revise and constant, but disingenuous, self-deprecation.

What do you think about self-publishing? It's great for some authors and some books, and bad for other authors and books. It really depends on the situation.

Describe your job and what you like and don't like about it. The thrill of selling some-one's first book never gets old. On the flip side, telling someone whom you've represented for a while that their manuscript isn't sellable is always difficult.

Do you miss the way the business "used to be"? No.

What do you want to tell new/unpublished writers? Develop a very thick skin and don't give up.

Do you like that everything has become largely digitized? Very much so. I've gotten to the point that I don't read anything on paper.

What do you like reading, watching, and listening to? I read lot of nonfiction. My favorite books of all time are Robert Caro's volumes on LBJ. I was a big *Breaking Bad* fan, and I love *House of Cards*.

Describe a book you would write. If I were a writer, I'd want to be a biographer.

WOLFSON LITERARY AGENCY ❖ www.wolfsonliterary.com

PO Box 266, New York, NY 10276, 646-454-1683, query@wolfsonliterary.com

Agent's name and contact info: Michelle Wolfson, michelle@wolfsonliterary.com
Queries should be directed to query@wolfsonliterary.com.

Describe what you like to represent and what you won't represent. I represent commercial fiction and nonfiction, although the balance is definitely skewing more and more toward fiction as the years pass. I like to represent books that I love, books that I can't shut up about because that's how much I love them and love talking about them. You know, where people move past being annoyed by me and start to think it's cute again how much I love the books I represent. If I don't feel like that about your writing, then I'm probably not the best agent for you, and you should find someone who does feel that way or has a different philosophy.

In terms of what I won't represent, I'd say there's more a vague list of things I'm not that likely to represent. But, hey, if you can convince me otherwise with an incredibly well-written book, then let's move ourselves up into the paragraph above this one and never discuss this again. That said, I don't represent children's picture books or screenplays. Everything else is hit or miss. I challenge you to make me love it!

What are the best ways for writers to pitch you? The best way to pitch me is usually via email at query@wolfsonliterary.com. I have found several clients in the slush, and I continue to actively search there. However, if we happen to be at a conference, or somewhere else where you have a chance to meet me in person, please feel free to come up and chat with me. It's always nice to meet in person.

When and where were you born? I grew up in a suburb just north of New York City, and now I live in Manhattan. I was born toward the end of the Nixon administration but otherwise claim no association with or any other connection to said Nixon administration.

Do you charge fees? Nope.

Describe your education and career history. I have a BA from Dartmouth and an MBA from NYU. I spent several years working in nonprofit and finance before making the switch to become a literary agent. I spent four years working at two different agencies before leaving to start my own agency in December 2007.

Say something about your hobbies and personal interests. I'd love to say I have some secret bird-watching or stamp-collecting hobby that makes me really well rounded and interesting, but the truth is, I don't. I love sports but hate exercise. I still love to read even after 10-plus years of being an agent, and I hope that never changes.

Why and how did you become an agent? Since this was a career switch for me, I really thought through this decision after talking to many people in the industry and doing my best to find out the day-to-day details of what agents really do. I think what appealed to me then (and it still does) was the variety of the work. My biggest fear was always becoming bored at my job, and I can honestly say that I never find this work boring. Difficult and frustrating sometimes? Sure. But never boring!

Would you do it over again, or something else? I would absolutely do it over again, especially since I think I tried everything else.

List some representative titles you have placed. *In the Shadows* by Kiersten White and Jim Di Bartolo (Scholastic); *Illusions of Fate* by Kiersten White (Harper Teen); *The Fill-In Boyfriend* by Kasie West (Harper Teen); *21 Kisses* by Daisy Whitney (Bloomsbury Spark); *The Fire Artist* by Daisy Whitney (Bloomsbury Children's); *Ben Fox: Squirrel Zombie Specialist at Your Service* by Daisy Whitney (Spencer Hill Press); *Becoming the Boss: New Rules for the Next Generation of Leaders* by Lindsey Pollak (Harper Business); *The Big Fix* by Linda Grimes (Tor); *Marine for Hire* by Tawna Fenske (Entangled Brazen); *Sparks Fly* by Lauren Blakely (Entangled Brazen); *Maggie Malone and the Mostly Magical Boots* by Jenna McCarthy and Carolyn Evans (Sourcebooks Jabberwocky); *Game. Set. Match.* by Jennifer Iacopelli (Coliloquy).

Describe yourself as a person. Just do it. Oh crap, is that slogan taken? How about "just did it"?

I feel like my answer to this could change on any given day, depending on my mood. Wait, does that make me moody? I'm definitely not moody. In general, I think I adapt to situations fairly easily, which I think is a good skill for an agent, since we have to be different things to different people.

How would you describe the proverbial "client from hell," and what are the warning signs? I've been very fortunate to have pretty wonderful clients, for the most part. I think the key is good communication, common courtesy, and respect that goes both ways.

What do you think about self-publishing? Self-publishing is a great option for a lot of people. I don't know that people always realize how difficult it is to be discovered — now more than ever, perhaps, with the influx of new books each year due to traditional and self-published books. However, I do think it can be a terrific option for people who are motivated to get out and sell their product on their own. I also think that "hybrid publishing," or mixing traditional and self-publishing, is interesting, and I expect we'll see more of that as time goes on.

Do you like Amazon? I guess I think it's possible that one day we might wake up and find ourselves in a dystopian society called the United States of Amazon. Maybe it's getting to be a little bit of a problem, but I'm not really sure what to do about it. Maybe we should Google the solution? It's also possible I read too much young adult.

Do you believe in a "higher power"? Like "higher royalties"? Then yes.

What will agenting be like in 2020? I think of the biggest part of agenting as managing relationships and managing careers, rather than selling any one individual book. So I like to think that that part will still look very similar. As the industry changes, we all need to stay flexible and be able to adapt to changes, but the time and attention and care that I give to my clients is something that stays the same.

Describe your job and what you like and don't like about it. I feel like I get to deliver awesome news and watch dreams come true right before my eyes. This never gets old. I love strategizing about what should come next, which is handy because in this ever-changing market, we have to be nimble and able to react quickly. Of course, I don't love the disappointments and frustrations that are inevitable when you work in publishing, but I give a damn good pep talk, and I try to approach them as new challenges. And, again, the variety of this job keeps the work fresh and interesting.

Do you miss the way the business "used to be"? I have only just started saying, "It used to be…" now that I've been doing this for more than 10 years. However, for the most part, I don't spend a lot of time worrying about the changes or wishing them away. I embrace the challenges that come with an ever-changing industry. It's one of the things I love most about agenting.

What does the "Big 5" mean to you? Elephant, rhinoceros, lion, cape buffalo, and the ever-elusive leopard.

What do you want to tell new/unpublished writers? Be persistent.

Do you like that everything has become largely digitized? I love that everything has become largely digitized for several reasons aside from the obvious environmental benefits. As a small agency, the overhead costs are greatly reduced with email submissions of manuscripts, both incoming and outgoing. I spend less on paper, postage, foreign rights postage, etc. And my general efficiency is so much higher. I read all manuscripts on my Kindle. Admittedly, I can still get bogged down in digital manuscripts the way we used to get bogged down in paper, and I'm always looking to fine-tune my process, but still, I can "carry" a lot more manuscripts around with me. The downside to digitization is that it can be easier to dash off an email when you know you should really call. It's important not to forget that we are still real people falling in love with real books. A lunch or coffee with an editor may help me when it comes time to decide who might be the best fit for a new manuscript. One email address is very much like another, but two people I've had lunch with stand out in my mind as having very different personalities and different tastes. So, yes, I embrace the efficiencies that digitization has brought. But still I like to think that a robot wouldn't do my job better than I do.

What do you like reading, watching, and listening to? I read a variety of books, although my taste, much like my list, tends to be pretty commercial and mostly fiction, with the occasional nonfiction or literary read. In recent years I've somehow abandoned all my TV drama for sitcoms and reality shows, which of course bring their own brand of drama. I find them entertaining, but I can easily jump in and out, both within a show and a season, which suits my current stage of life.

Describe a book you would write. If there's a book I would write, I haven't thought of it yet.

WORDSERVE LITERARY GROUP ❖ www.wordserveliterary.com

7061 S. University Boulevard, Suite 307, Centennial, CO 80122, 303-471-6675, fax: 303-471-1297

Agent's name and contact info: Greg Johnson, president, greg@wordserveliterary.com

Describe what you like to represent and what you won't represent. Broad range of inspirational and Christian books: fiction in all genres (except sci-fi and fantasy), nonfiction, memoir, biography, self-help. Also, we have carved a nice niche in military nonfiction in the general market.

What are the best ways for writers to pitch you? Go to our website at www.wordserve literary.com and follow the instructions on submissions.

When and where were you born? Oregon boy. Go, Ducks!

Do you charge fees? No.

Describe your education and career history. Twenty years as a literary agent; author of 22 books before then.

Say something about your hobbies and personal interests. Golf, movies, travel.

Why and how did you become an agent? I loved the business end of publishing more than the writing and promoting. Love the creative process. Love making authors happy.

Would you do it over again, or something else? Love what I do.

List some representative titles you have placed. *A Higher Call* (*New York Times* bestseller) by Adam Makos; *Into the Free* (*New York Times* bestseller and CBA Novel of the Year) by Julie Cantrell. Our additional authors include Bob Welch, Marcus Brotherton, Mike Yorkey, Gilbert Morris, Lynn Morris, Jim Burns, Wayne Cordeiro, Doug Fields, and 150 others.

Describe yourself as a person. Father and stepfather of six, grandfather of six; Christ follower, but not a "Fundy."

How would you describe the proverbial "client from hell," and what are the warning signs? Someone who doesn't listen to experienced advice; who listens to friends and family; who wishes they were agenting themselves but doesn't know enough people to do so.

What do you think about self-publishing? Some genre fiction sells well this way; not a bad last resort.

Do you like Amazon? Yes. Good deals and value for books.

Do you believe in a "higher power"? Yes, a very personal and loving one.

Do you miss the way the business "used to be"? Yes, but everything changes. We're changing with it by offering our clients a marketing vehicle through the nationwide website www.faithhappenings.com.

WRITERS HOUSE, LLC ❖ www.writershouse.com

21 West 26th Street, New York, NY 10010, 212-685-2400

Agent's name and contact info: Stephen Barr, 212-685-2663, sbarr@writershouse.com

Describe what you like to represent and what you won't represent. I've got a consistent hankering for unexpected memoirs with itchy voices, narrative nonfiction that tackles hard-to-tackle issues, wry and rarely paranormal young adult, laugh-until-you-squirt-milk-out-of-your-nose middle grade (with heart!), sweet and wacky (but still logical) picture books from innovative author-illustrators, and any fiction that rewards the reader line by line and gets to know at least one character really, really well (recent favorites include *Jeff in Venice*, *The Lazarus Project*, *Diary of a Bad Year*, and *Horns*, which was awesome). I'm also willing to be a sucker for mysteries that bend reality, ghost stories that blow reality to hell, humor that's more than just an infinitely repeated gag in sheep's clothing, and Secret Book X (I don't know what Secret Book X is, but suffice it to say, I'm open to the occasional curveball).

There's very little I'll categorically refuse to represent, but it's hyperunlikely that I'll ever work on any unflinching self-help, or unflinching romance, or unflinching religious fiction. But everyone flinches every now and then!

What are the best ways for writers to pitch you? Far and away the best approach is just to send me an honest, conversational email describing the book, describing the author, describing some hopes and dreams, and then let the first 10 or 15 pages do the talking.

When and where were you born? I was born on September 18, 1985, sometime in the early morning, in Orange County, California. At least, that's what my parents told me! I guess they could be covering up a secret about how I was born on a pirate ship or whatever.

Do you charge fees? Nope! No fees, no how.

Describe your education and career history. In short, I was always obviously going to be an English major, then I was (at UCLA), then I moved to New York 12 seconds after graduating, failed to get about 17 jobs, landed an internship at an awesome, intimate film/literary agency called Hotchkiss & Associates, landed a simultaneous internship at an awesome, intimate literary agency called Writers House, and I'm so fond of my job that I'll probably do it even after I become a skeleton.

Say something about your hobbies and personal interests. I should maintain *some* element of mystery about myself, shouldn't I? I'm interested in…mysteries? My hobby is being a mystery. Also playing the guitar and the drums and the piano and kitchen instruments (this is a stupid way of saying I like to cook).

Why and how did you become an agent? I think I became an agent because my favorite thing in the world is talking to people about things that don't exist (or don't exist yet), and writers' brains are full of things that don't exist (or don't exist yet). I became one (an agent, that is, not a thing that doesn't exist) by thinking that I was supposed to be an editor, and then — while chasing a job as an editorial assistant — discovering that there was a job that could often put me even closer to the germination moment of a book.

Would you do it over again, or something else? I would do it all over again, but with a different haircut.

List some representative titles you have placed. *Honor Girl: A Memoir* by Maggie Thrash (Candlewick); *Fraidyzoo* by Thyra Heder (Abrams Children's); *I'm Trying to Love Spiders* by Bethany Barton (Viking Children's); *The Accidental Savant* by Jason Padgett and Maureen Seaberg (Houghton Mifflin Harcourt); *Fakebook* by Dave Cicirelli (Sourcebooks).

Describe yourself as a person. Excited and excitable, warm and warmable, pretty jokey, sporadically obsessive, creative and happy, and an appreciator of well-timed solitude.

How would you describe the proverbial "client from hell," and what are the warning signs? Pitchfork, horns, tail, hooves, carrying a memoir about how hard it is to date.

What do you think about self-publishing? It's perfect for some, the same way that traditional publishing is perfect for others!

Do you like Amazon? They are obviously very creative and very ambitious and capable of many incredible things. I just think they could be all those things while simultaneously being much, much, much more sensitive to their peers in the bookselling industry — succeeding by being the best when they can be the best, not by preying on others who might be better sometimes.

Do you believe in a "higher power"? Objection: irrelevant!

What will agenting be like in 2020? In the important, fundamental ways, identical to agenting in 2015. But we'll have to know even more about how to truly assist writers with self-promotion, and I'm excited about having to know more!

Describe your job and what you like and don't like about it. I help authors with every single step of their book's birth, creatively, artistically, strategically, financially, you-name-it-ly. I love being a sounding board / brainstorming partner for my clients' ideas, sometimes being present at the very moment their inspiration finally clicks into place. I hate giving bad news.

Do you miss the way the business "used to be"? I don't think I'm old enough yet to have "good old days" nostalgia, though I hope to never have it, I suppose.

What does the "Big 5" mean to you? I know what it's supposed to mean, but it first reminds me of a sporting goods chain, Big 5, and how I got my soccer cleats there every year before the season started. Hopefully they will both be around for many big years to come.

What do you want to tell new/unpublished writers? It's worth every single ounce of hard work.

Do you like that everything has become largely digitized? This question is largely simplified!

What do you like reading, watching, and listening to? Idiosyncratic but still grounded fiction; inventive, gorgeous picture books; TV shows with emotionally weird protagonists; songs with that "everything's sad but that's okay" vibe to them.

Describe a book you would write. Inevitably long-winded but good for a few laughs, I'd hope, with a main character who talks about his feelings too much, probably.

Joker's wild: Nah, didn't you hear? Joker settled down and is married and has two kids and a gazebo.

Agent's name and contact info: Alec Shane, ashane@writershouse.com

Describe what you like to represent and what you won't represent. I'm always looking for great horror (but no zombies, please!!), mystery, thriller, historical fiction, literary fiction, science fiction based in reality and meticulously researched, and young adult/middle grade books geared toward boys. On the nonfiction side, I love to see humor, biography, history (particularly military history), true crime, "guy" reads, and all things sports.

Not looking for romance (paranormal or otherwise), women's fiction, religious fiction or nonfiction, picture books, high fantasy, cookbooks, space opera sci-fi, or anything featuring aliens and intergalactic warfare. I also think I've seen enough angels, werewolves, vampires, selkies, and merpeople to last several lifetimes.

What are the best ways for writers to pitch you? Email is best, as it's easiest to keep track of, but I take snail mail as well. I'm always encouraging authors to pitch and submit to me at any time; all I really ask is that if you're going to pitch me your novel, please do some research first and make sure that my reading interests align with your book — and it's tremendously helpful if you give some indication in your query letter that you're submitting to me for a reason. I can tell you right now: I don't care how good it is, a historical romance set in Victorian England just isn't going to resonate with me. Make sure your submission is for a book I would potentially enjoy.

When and where were you born? 1981, in Toronto, Canada (although my family moved to Bermuda almost immediately after).

Do you charge fees? No fees.

Describe your education and career history. I received both my undergrad and graduate degrees from Brown University (English/education studies with an MAT in secondary education), both of which I put to immediate use by moving to Los Angeles after graduation to become a professional stunt man. I worked in all facets of the entertainment industry for three years, both in front of and behind the camera, before moving to New York to pursue a career in publishing. I was fortunate enough to land an internship at

Writers House in 2008 and simply refused to leave. This is my first and only publishing job, and if all goes well it will stay that way.

Say something about your hobbies and personal interests. I don't have any interesting hobbies, although I have every intention of one day becoming a semicompetent jazz pianist. I'm also way more of a New England Patriots fan than any healthy person should be and get far too emotionally invested in Boston sports. I like to stay relatively active — sitting behind a computer all day warrants it — and sit completely on the fence regarding the existence of ghosts.

Why and how did you become an agent? I honestly had no idea what agents were or what they did when I first moved to New York; all I knew was that I loved books and wanted to be in this world. But after landing my internship at Writers House, I knew that agenting was what I wanted to do with my life. I was lucky enough to get hired by Jodi Reamer just as my program ended, and the rest is history.

Would you do it over again, or something else? Absolutely; there aren't many jobs where you get to read for a living.

List some representative titles you have placed. *American Panic* by Mark Stein, *Chocolate* by HP Newquist, *Seeing America* by Nancy Crocker, *Shark Wars* by EJ Altbacker, *You Might Remember Me: The Life and Times of Phil Hartman* by Mike Thomas, *The Last Weekend* by Nick Mamatas.

Describe yourself as a person. Ugh. I have no idea. I will say that I recently took an online quiz to see what kind of dog I was, and the answer was "pit bull." I should note, however, that I'm really, really not the kind of person to take online quizzes. I just see that as a great cop-out for answering this question.

How would you describe the proverbial "client from hell," and what are the warning signs? The client from hell thinks that (a) he or she is the only author I have on my list, (b) everything that he or she has to say is significantly more important than anything else I have going on in both my professional and personal life, and (c) writes only to make money and wouldn't do it if he or she wasn't getting paid. The biggest red flag I get when talking to an author I'm thinking about taking on is when I sense that the author feels he or she is doing me a huge favor by talking to me. The author-agent relationship is all about meshing and sharing the same vision, and if one party is approaching it from some place of superiority, then it just isn't going to work.

What do you think about self-publishing? There used to be a time when the term *published author* carried some clout; not so much anymore, as all you need to be a published author is a computer. However, self-publishing has exposed us all to significantly more content, and when the amount of content increases, the quality of the stuff that rises to the top increases as well. As long as self-publishing is used properly — i.e., doesn't become just a dumping ground for the unpublishable and extremely impatient — then I think it can actually be a good thing.

Do you like Amazon? I feel like I should hate Amazon…but I don't. It's just one of those things that's out there in the world, and I'm right there with it. I also try not to hate anything; it takes up a lot of energy.

Do you believe in a "higher power"? I do, although I don't really know what that higher power is. But then again, nobody really does.

What will agenting be like in 2020? I think that, at the end of the day, the fundamentals of what an agent does will be the same. The job of the agent is to manage the author's career and make the author's books better — and I don't think that that will change. No matter how much the industry changes over the years (and changing it is), there will always be the business of publishing; any author who only wants to worry about writing and nothing else would do well to find an agent who will keep his or her ear to the ground and keep up with the times.

Describe your job and what you like and don't like about it. My job is basically to manage my authors' careers in every way — not just to sell their manuscripts but to edit them, strengthen them, and promote them. I also make sure authors stay on deadlines, are effectively marketing themselves through social media, and are taking the necessary steps to grow their careers. I'm also in contact with a fair number of production companies and keep my ear to the ground regarding the book-to-film world. Basically, I help the author do absolutely everything except for actually write the books. I love what I do for a living, so there's not a whole lot about it that I don't like. The only real negative about my job is that it isn't the kind of work where you clock out at five or six and then go home for the day to do whatever you want with your free time; I'm pretty much always working (thanks, iPhone!). I also find that I have to be extremely diligent to carve out time to read books for pleasure, as opposed to only reading for work; when I first started my career I went through an extended period of feeling guilty every time I picked up a book I was dying to read, as there were always 10 or so manuscripts awaiting my attention.

Do you miss the way the business "used to be"? I don't really know what "used to be" means, to be honest, as I started my career in 2008 and the industry has been constantly in flux since then.

What does the "Big 5" mean to you? The Big 5 are the places that buy my authors' books. They are businesses, just like anywhere else, and they want to get the best possible products out there, just like anywhere else. We're all in this together — author, agent, and editor alike — and so I see the Big 5 as an important element of getting a great story out into the world.

What do you want to tell new/unpublished writers? You, the unpublished/new/undiscovered author, are hands down the best part of my job. As much as I love pitching and selling books to editors, there is nothing more exciting than finding a new author in the slush pile and being one of the first people to read a book that goes on to sell thousands of copies. As an agent, I really, really want to like your submission, and finding that one manuscript that I'm exceptionally excited about is well worth sifting through the novels that aren't quite right for me. As demoralizing as the submission-and-rejection process can be, never lose sight of that.

Do you like that everything has become largely digitized? Anytime there is a technology in place that allows me to recommend a book to you, and for you to have that book 30 seconds later, that's absolutely a good thing. That said, there is just something about holding a book in your hand, the act of physically turning pages, and leaving your own tangible imprint on the book itself that the digital world can never replace. I still do most of my pleasure reading with print books.

What do you like reading, watching, and listening to? I'm a huge horror fan, both in print and in film, and I'm always willing to give a low-budget scary movie a shot. I haven't been to the movies in years — I'm more than happy to wait a few months and watch it at home — and so I miss out on a lot of the big blockbusters when they first come out, but that's okay. I also love mysteries and thrillers, both book and movie, and I love books that teach me something new about a subject that I thought I had a solid grasp on. Ultimately, though, I'll pretty much read anything. I don't watch all that much non-sports-related TV, to be honest, and tend to avoid shows that require you to watch the entire series in order, or else you won't know what's going on. I'm proud to say I have never "binged" on a TV show and don't plan to anytime soon. Musically, I'm all over the place. I have zero playlists on my iPod, almost always keep my music on shuffle, and my subway ride (when I'm not reading, which is rare) can consist of Sinatra, the Doors, bad '90s pop, an '80s hair band, and an up-and-coming rapper from Brooklyn who gave me his CD for free as I was walking down the street over the weekend.

Describe a book you would write. Getting boys to read again is something I take seriously, so if I had the skill to do so, I would write an adventure or ghost story geared toward younger male readers. I loved the *Goosebumps* series as a kid, as well as the *Choose Your Own Adventure* stories, so I'd love to write something along that vein. That, or a sports memoir about a fan who follows the New England Patriots around for an entire season and interacts with the fans, both at home and away, as a broad-strokes overview of the impact of a consistently positive professional sports milieu on the ever-changing American landscape. But that book would mainly just be a weak excuse to watch a lot of football.

Joker's wild: I don't have Facebook (not as some form of protest but I was simply too lazy to sign up for a profile), but I did just recently get on Twitter. I use it solely for work-related items and to talk about publishing in general as well as the kinds of books I'm both receiving at the moment and looking to acquire. So feel free to follow me and keep up with any new submission guidelines, trends I'm seeing, or books I'm particularly excited about. @alecdshane.

Agent's name and contact info: Rebecca Sherman, rebeccasubmissions@writershouse.com

Describe what you like to represent and what you won't represent. Picture books: I want picture books that can hold up to readings night after night. I'm highly selective in this category, and I accept illustrators and author-illustrators only — if you've just written picture book text, I'm not the best match for you.

Middle grade fiction: I'm looking for timeless stories that could become instant classics. I have a soft spot for fresh retellings and inventive folklore, fairy tales, and mythologies. I'm equally excited by contemporary stories, particularly friendship stories. Occasionally I fall for character-driven historical fiction with a seldom-explored setting.

Young adult: I'm looking for books with something to say — books that make me laugh, and characters that truly remind me of how confounding and wonderful (ridiculous! frightening! glorious!) adolescence can be. I enjoy contemporary stories of young love and growing up. I am not the right person for high fantasy/sci-fi submission. However, I am game for a novel with fantastical elements in the world we know — urban fantasy/magical realism. Super-edgy and/or issue-driven books aren't for me, either.

For all fiction, I'm very much looking for highly illustrated work — not necessarily graphic novels or illustrated diaries, but projects that include inventive uses of artwork to help tell the story.

What are the best ways for writers to pitch you? Emailing is the best route (email submissions should be sent to rebeccasubmissions@writershouse.com). No attachments. All submissions must include a query letter. Middle grade and young adult submissions should include a sample chapter (approx. 10 pages) and a synopsis. Please include one entire text for picture book submissions and sample illustrations or a link to an online portfolio or a dummy. Again, I do not accept picture book texts by authors only. You must be an author-illustrator to submit picture book material. Middle grade, young adult, and adult nonfiction submissions should include a proposal. Snail mail submissions must include an SASE. Please be patient as I consider your work. My response time varies, but my assistant or I will attend to your submission as soon as possible and respond. Please tell me on the query if it is a multiple submission. Please keep me informed via email about other agents' interest or offers for representation. Do not accept representation until you have given me a fair chance to extend an offer as well.

When and where were you born? Chicago, IL.

Do you charge fees? No.

Describe your education and career history. I'm a graduate of Northwestern University and began my career at Writers House over 12 years ago. I've built a list of dynamic and award-winning picture book illustrators and author-illustrators, as well as middle grade and young adult novelists.

Say something about your hobbies and personal interests. I am an avid theatergoer, taking full advantage of New York by seeing both Broadway and off-Broadway musicals and plays. Storytelling — whether on stage, screen, or the page — will always be a personal interest of mine.

Why and how did you become an agent? I became an agent because I love books and want nothing but to help the people who make them — to put my clients in the spotlight and in circumstances that give their books the best chance of succeeding and being read by children who will remember them as their favorites as they grow up. Before taking on clients of my own, I got the very best on-the-job training as an assistant at Writers House for years and then became a senior literary agent.

Would you do it over again, or something else? 100 percent.

List some representative titles you have placed. *The Doldrums*, books 1 and 2, by Nicholas Gannon (Greenwillow Books / Harper); *Bedtime at the Nuthouse*, books 1 and 2, illustrated by Scott Magoon (Little, Brown Books for Young Readers); *The Case for Loving* by Selina Alko and Sean Qualls (Arthur A. Levine Books / Scholastic); *I'm My Own Dog* by David Ezra Stein (Candlewick); *Snow White* by Matt Phelan (Candlewick); *Glory: Honoring Black War Heroes* by Andrea Davis Pinkney, illustrated by Brian Pinkney (Hyperion); *Platypus Police Squad*, books 1 to 4, by Jarrett J. Krosoczka (Walden Pond Press / Harper); *Doug Unplugged on the Farm* and *Billy and Goat* by Dan Yaccarino (Knopf Books for Young Readers); *Pirate, Viking & Scientist* and *Steve Raised by Wolves* by Jared Chapman (Little, Brown Books for Young Readers); *Ling & Ting*, books 1 to 4, by Grace Lin (Little, Brown Books for Young Readers); *Sprout Street Neighbors*, books 1 and 2, by Anna Alter (Knopf Books for Young Readers); *The Dullards* illustrated by Daniel Salmieri (Balzer + Bray).

What do you like reading, watching, and listening to? Favorite childhood picture books: *The Monster at the End of This Book*, *Miss Nelson Is Missing!*, *Where the Wild Things Are*, anything by Richard Scarry. Favorite contemporary picture books: *Olivia*, *Me...Jane*, *The Incredible Book-Eating Boy*, *Orange Pear Apple Bear*, *Balloons over Broadway*, and *Adventures of the Dish and the Spoon*.

Favorite childhood middle grade books: *The Westing Game, Charlotte's Web, The BFG, From the Mixed-Up Files of Mrs. Basil E. Frankweiler*, and *Holes* (actually, I read this last one when I was an adult). Favorite contemporary middle grade books: *The Wednesday Wars, The True Meaning of Smekday, Emma Jean Lazarus Fell out of a Tree, The Strange Case of Origami Yoda, The Real Boy*. Favorite contemporary young adult: *The Absolutely True Diary of a Part-Time Indian, Elsewhere, Stargirl, Blankets, Eleanor & Park, Why We Broke Up, The Disreputable History of Frankie Landau Banks*.

THE ZACK COMPANY, INC. ❖ www.zackcompany.com
Agent's name: Andrew Zack

Describe what you like to represent and what you won't represent. Serious narrative nonfiction: history and oral history, particularly military history and intelligence services history, and also military nonfiction by special operations veterans, e.g., snipers, SEALs, Delta, etc.; politics and current-affairs works by established journalists and political insiders or pundits; science and technology and how they affect society, by established journalists, science writers, or experts in their fields; biography, autobiography, or memoir by or about newsworthy individuals, individuals whose lives have made a contribution to the historical record; personal finance and investing; parenting by established experts in their field; health and medicine by doctors or established medical writers; business by nationally recognized business leaders or established business writers, for example, from the *Wall Street Journal*; relationship books by credentialed experts, that is, psychiatrists, psychologists, and therapists with prior publishing credits.

Commercial fiction: thrillers in every shape and form — international, serial killer, medical, scientific, computer, psychological, military, legal; mysteries and not-so-hard-boiled crime novels; action novels, but not action/adventure; science fiction and fantasy, preferably hard science fiction or military science fiction and big, elaborate fantasies (not coming-of-age fantasies) that take you to a new and established world; urban fantasy that takes our world and twists it in wonderful ways; horror novels that take you on a roller-coaster ride; historical fiction (but not Westerns); women's fiction and romance.

What are the best ways for writers to pitch you? Via the eQuery™ form on our website at www.zackcompany.com.

When and where were you born? In a hospital during the Johnson Administration.

Do you charge fees? We charge back if we have to spend money on behalf of the client, e.g., for copies of their books or shipping their books.

Describe your education and career history. After more than 25 years in the publishing business, this would be a very long paragraph. I will spare you the details, but if you really want them, you can read my full and far-too-long biography on my website at www.zack company.com.

Why and how did you become an agent? After becoming a full, capital-E Editor at the tender age of 24, I found myself unemployed at the less tender age of 26. About a year later, some veteran agents left their agency to start a new one and made me an offer to join them.

Would you do it over again, or something else? I very much enjoy the editorial process and often wished I had stayed in editorial. It's what drove me to become a publisher myself and start a separate publishing company, Endpapers Press (www.endpaperspress.com).

Describe yourself as a person. Find a picture of Brad Pitt. Add 75 pounds. There you go.

How would you describe the proverbial "client from hell," and what are the warning signs? Clients from hell have probably published two or three, or maybe three or four, books. These are likely fiction but might be nonfiction. They have "fired" their previous agent because their career is going nowhere and that is, of course, the agent's fault. They are looking for an agent who can "make things happen." Clients from hell believe that their needs outweigh everyone else's: their agent's, their editor's, their publicist's, and the needs of all the other authors with whom those people may be working.

What do you think about self-publishing? I think when someone who is self-publishing does it the right way, it can really demonstrate the growing ability of the average author to reach an audience. But self-publishing the "right way" is far more costly and time-consuming than most authors realize. If a book published by Random House is a Toyota Camry, then most self-published books are soapbox racers. They are generally not edited, copyedited, or proofread by a professional. The covers are often built on templates or by designers without experience in the book business. Readers need to be astute enough in choosing books to see that an ebook published by Random House should cost more than one self-published by the author, and critical enough to voice their frustrations with poorly published books.

Bottom line: traditional publishers will always offer a greater, more valuable service *for readers*: judgment. There remains an actual editorial process in place at publishing houses, a process that helps filter the good books out from the bad and then takes those books and makes them that much better. Publishers also promote and publicize on a scale that many authors cannot achieve themselves. Thus, while some self-published works will find a readership, most will not, as authors lack the necessary resources to garner distribution and reviews. While self-published ebooks may achieve wider success than self-published print books, they will still lack the market penetration of those published by traditional publishers.

Do you like Amazon? Thanks to Amazon, more books are in print and more available than ever before, which is a great thing. But I think the business has declined drastically over the years *because* of Amazon. The pressure from B&N during the eighties and nineties to increase discounts drove up prices and cut publishers' profits. The pressure and outright hostility by Amazon toward publishers has further driven pricing up and profits down. That's right, it's driven pricing up. By demanding higher discounts off the retail price, Amazon (B&N before it) forces publishers to increase the retail price to protect profits. And profits are not a bad thing. Without profits, there's no reason for publishers to stay in business.

Further, Amazon's loss-leading pricing on ebooks has had a negative impact on the book industry as a whole. Readers now expect the price on the ebook of a $25 hardcover book to be less than $5. That's insane. It completely devalues the content of that book and the blood, sweat, and tears every author puts into his or her work.

Arguably, Amazon has massively increased the market for books, but it has essentially turned books into widgets only slightly more respected than that "avocado keeper" that actually costs more than many books. And when you factor in the thousands of self-published books that Amazon facilitates the publication of every year — books that have never been edited, copyedited, or proofread — it's arguably doing more to lower our literary standards than raise them.

Do you believe in a "higher power"? I believe in what my grandfather always taught me: "Plan your work and work your plan."

What will agenting be like in 2020? The business of representation is overdue for a large consolidation, but what's happening instead is that every agent is, in some way, becoming a publisher. Perhaps in the way that every actor supposedly wants to direct, I guess every agent wants to be a publisher. And we are now at a point in terms of technology and distribution where that is possible. This will continue, and perhaps we'll see more direct publishing by authors facilitated by agents.

But what I think *should* happen is for more agencies to come together and work together to develop greater economies of scale. Just as publishers can afford to publish smaller books thanks to the profits of books by bestselling authors, agencies could afford to do more with greater economies of scale, e.g., by having dedicated subsidiary rights people or royalty accounting people.

Describe your job and what you like and don't like about it. I represent authors in the licensing of their works to publishers, film studios, audio companies, and so on. That means reviewing materials to see if I believe there is a market for them, locating the best markets for them, concluding the license, negotiating the contract on behalf of my client, and continuing to follow up with the licensee to ensure that the process goes well and that the licensee is using the best efforts to make the work a success.

The best part of working with my clients is that they are all passionate about writing and many are genuinely brilliant. In a sense, my job lets me be a perpetual student of literature, history, science, and many other subjects, which is a great thing.

That said, authors, alas, are often a challenge. They often feel they are doing their publishers a favor by letting them bring their books out. Publishers always feel they are doing authors a favor. Nearly 100 percent of the time, authors are disappointed in the job their publisher does with their books. And if a book succeeds, it is not because of anything the publisher did, authors think, and publishers think they did *everything* to make that book a success. And there, in the middle, sits the literary agent. Further, the number of authors with a good day job who are writing for the enjoyment of writing and aren't massively worried about the income from their books is much smaller than the ones who are desperate to get paid immediately, whether or not money is due. This often creates unpleasant situations between authors, publishers, and agents. And, again, in the middle is the agent…

Many industries have clients. Law, accounting, and advertising are a few. And everyone has a joke that "the job would be great if not for clients and _____ [judges, the IRS, buyers]." Being an agent is no different. It's a great job except for the authors and publishers!

Do you miss the way the business "used to be"? Yes. I think the pacing of the business, email, and social media have all contributed to make publishing a less "thoughtful" business and certainly a less considerate one. Do I love that I don't have to kill a tree to send out twenty manuscripts to publishers? Yes. But maybe agents were pickier and more careful about what to represent when they had to spend $400 on photocopying to submit a novel. And certainly there was less competition in the marketplace as there were very, very few self-published books. "Breaking out" a book has always been hard, but now there is that much more static to cut through to get the message out.

What does the "Big 5" mean to you? Random House, Simon & Schuster, Harper Collins, Hachette, Macmillan.

What do you want to tell new/unpublished writers? The author-agent relationship is a business partnership. Agents have their role, and authors have their role. Neither is an employee of the other. Interestingly enough, I never hear about agents or authors *hiring* each other, but I hear about them firing one another all the time. Agents, obviously, are businesspeople. Authors need to be businesspeople, too. Authors should do their best to be as informed as possible about the nature of the publishing business. My best client is an educated client. I find that the hardest thing about the agent-author relationship is communication. Authors should be able to ask their agents all the questions they want, and if an author's agent disagrees with that, it's time to find another agent. But authors also need to recognize that every minute spent on the phone with them is a minute that could be spent selling their projects. As long as authors understand the job they have and the job agents have in the author-agent relationship, the business partnership will flourish and be profitable.

Do you like that everything has become largely digitized? No. I feel that we suffer from a worldwide case of ADHD brought on by the availability of too much media and information in digital form. Our social interactions suffer, and the time available to work quietly on writing or reading or editing seems to have become as rare as any endangered species.

ZIMMERMANN LITERARY ❖ www.zimmermannliterary.com

submit@zimmagency.com

Agent's name and contact info: Helen Zimmermann, submit@zimmagency.com

Describe what you like to represent and what you won't represent. Nonfiction: memoir, relationships, health/wellness/nutrition, pop culture, sports, music, women's interest.

Fiction: *Very* simple criteria — strong characters and a plot that will keep me up at night!

What are the best ways for writers to pitch you? Email queries only, please. For fiction, I like to see a single paragraph summary, a bio, and a bit about the audience/readership/marketing. Please don't attach chapters to the email unless I request them, but you can put the first chapter into the *body* of the email. For nonfiction, again, brief summary and bio, and a bit about the audience/readership/marketing. As it's just me who reads these, please understand that I can't answer every query. Sorry! I do read them with enthusiasm, and if I have interest in seeing more material, you will hear from me within two weeks.

When and where were you born? Bronxville, New York, 1964.

Do you charge fees? No.

Describe your education and career history. After graduating from SUNY Buffalo with a double major in psychology and English literature, I started my publishing career in the marketing department of Random House. I soon became the director of advertising and promotion for one of their divisions, the Crown Publishing Group. After 12 years I moved to New York's Hudson Valley, where I was the author events director at a successful independent bookseller. I founded the agency in 2003 and enjoyed early success with the *New York Times* bestseller *Chosen by a Horse*. My experience working at a large publishing house and an independent bookstore gives me unique and invaluable insight into each project that I work on. I am well aware of the value of in-house buzz, online marketing, store placement, social media, author platform, etc., and I work hard to make sure all these marketing components are in place for each and every project. I have been a member of AAR since 2007.

Say something about your hobbies and personal interests. Probably the "biggest" thing I do outside publishing is my volunteer work with my local fire department as an EMT. I have been doing this for 10 years. It's a strange combination, literary agent and EMT, but there you have it. I am also an avid hiker; I recently completed all 46 of New York's Adirondack High Peaks. Took me 10 years, but I did it! I am a runner, a skier, and an occasional Netflix binge watcher. Oh! And I read. A LOT.

Why and how did you become an agent? As an events director, I spoke with many aspiring writers at the readings. They would always ask me, "How do I get published?" to which I would always reply, "You need an agent." After this conversation took place about a dozen times, I offered to show an author's material to some publishers, since I still had many contacts. I never did sell that first project, but the next one I went out with became a bestseller. Voilà. An agent is born. Even though I became an agent kind of by default, I wouldn't have kept with it all these years unless I truly loved it. Being a part of making writers' dreams come true is pretty darn awesome.

List some representative titles you have placed. *The Learning Habit: A Groundbreaking Approach to Homework and Parenting That Helps Our Children Succeed in School and Life* (Perigee/Penguin); *Pocket Paleo* (Harlequin Nonfiction); *Sound City: Big Hits, Fast Times, and Epic Tales from Inside Rock and Roll's Legendary Studio* (St. Martin's); *The Champion's Mind: How the Best Athletes Think, Train, and Thrive* (Rodale); *Snap Strategies: Lasting Solutions to Common Relationship Pitfalls* (Seal Press).

Describe yourself as a person. I'm affable, smart, compassionate, and athletic. And I go to bat for my clients like a mother at a PTA meeting.

How would you describe the proverbial "client from hell," and what are the warning signs? Someone who doesn't listen to my advice! That's what I'm here for — because I know the industry inside and out!

What do you think about self-publishing? Self-publishing is great as long as you do it right. Which is a *full-time job* on the part of the writer.

Part 7

INDEPENDENT EDITORS

INTRODUCTION
EDITORS VS. SCAMMERS

Jeff Herman

What Is an Independent Book Editor?

Someone who is qualified to make your proposal and/or manuscript better than you could do by yourself.

Why Might You Want to Retain an Editor?

Because even "perfect" writers are imperfect and can greatly benefit from an objective and qualified edit. Selling your work to agents and publishers is extremely competitive, so you want your editorial product to be as strong as possible. Typos, grammatical errors, and missed opportunities to say it better can mean the difference between "yes" and "no." Even if you already have a publishing deal, the reality is that in-house editors are not necessarily going to do a pristine editing job, and what gets published is a reflection on you not them. Self-publishers should be especially vigilant about having their work professionally vetted and edited prior to publication.

What Kind of Editor Should You Retain?

Someone who has a genuine history of editing the kind of work you are writing. It's best if you actually read some of the works they have edited and communicate with some of the people who have used their services.

Where Can You Find Qualified Editors?

This section lists twenty-nine of the most experienced and qualified independent editors in America. Most of them have many years of traditional in-house publishing experience, and they may have even edited one or more of your favorite books. The editors in this section are members of small, informal organizations that enable freelance editors to network, teach, and support each other in mutually beneficial ways. For instance, an editor who specializes in romance novels can refer science fiction writers to an appropriate editor, and vice versa. The editors prefer to keep their groups no larger than the number of people that can comfortably fit in a Manhattan living room, which is why new groups keep forming.

Most affiliated members reside in and around New York City, which is only natural since almost all of them have worked for New York publishers. However, there surely are many excellent editors throughout the country who don't belong to one of these organizations and haven't worked for a New York publisher. They can be found through Google or the Editorial Freelancers Association (www.the-efa.org) and by networking with fellow writers. No editor should be dismissed simply because they aren't listed in this section. I was only able to list the editors I have personal confidence in, and membership in one of these groups gives me that confidence. I welcome your suggestions for additional editors to include in future editions (jeff@jeffherman.com).

What Does It Cost to Hire an Editor?

Frankly, I'm not sure. It obviously depends on what type or level of editing you need, who you use, and when you use them. More experienced editors, and those with some "big hits" on their résumés, will presumably charge more than others. Even stated rates might be negotiable. The best thing to do is ask experienced people and shop around.

What about Scams?

Unfortunately, scams are legion. You need to be careful and discerning. Here are some tips.

- Only retain the actual person who will be working with you, not a company that will randomly assign someone to you.
- Avoid anyone who makes outlandish promises before they have even seen your work. Actually, don't give anyone money before they see your work and give you a proposal for what they will do and what it will cost.
- Check references and the internet for complaints.

An independent editor isn't a literary agent or a publisher. If they are offering to represent and/or publish you for money (you pay them), it's likely a scam. If someone is promising to fulfill your most cherished publishing dreams for a fee, it's probably too good to be true.

AN EDITOR OF ONE'S OWN

Members of Words into Print
(For information about Words into Print, see page 556)

Are book doctors really worth it? What do they do that agents and in-house editors might not? With all the help a writer can get on the journey from manuscript to published book, why hire an editor of one's own?

Before the Age of the Independent Editor, literary agents and publishing staff were the first publishing insiders to read a proposal or manuscript. Today, however, the focus on business interests is so demanding and the volume of submissions so great — agents alone take in hundreds of query letters a month — that a writer's work has to be white-hot before receiving serious consideration. In light of these developments, a writer may turn to an independent editor as the first expert reader in the world of publishing's gatekeepers.

What Else Do Independent Editors Do, and How Much Do They Charge?

Services. Not every writer and project will call for the services of an independent editor. However, if you are looking for the kind of personalized and extensive professional guidance beyond that gained from workshops, fellow writers, online sources, magazines, and books, hiring an editor may well be worth the investment. An editor of your own can provide a professional assessment of whether or not your project is ready to submit, and to whom you should submit it; expert assistance to make your manuscript or book proposal as good as it should be; help with preparing a convincing submissions package; and an advocate's voice and influence to guide you in your efforts toward publication.

Another key role an independent editor plays is to protect writers from querying their prospects before their material is irresistible. Premature submissions cause writers needless disappointment and frustration. Your editor can zero in on the thematic core, central idea, or story line that needs to be conveyed in a way that is most likely to attract an agent and a publisher. In short, an editor of your own can identify the most appealing, salable aspects of you and your work.

Rates. "Good editing is expensive," our venerable colleague Jerry Gross, editor of the book *Editors on Editing*, prudently notes. What kind of editing is good editing and how expensive is it? The internet and other sources quote a wide range of rates from a variety of editors. The numbers are not necessarily accurate or reliable. We've seen hourly rates ranging from about $25 to well above $200. Several factors account for this spread: the type of editing, the editor's level of experience, and the publishing venue. For example, rates for copyediting are lower than those for substantive editing. Moreover, standards in book publishing are particularly rigorous because books are long, expensive to produce, made to last, and vulnerable to the long-term impact of reviewer criticism.

Process. Book editors are specialists. Every book project arrives on the desk of an independent editor at a certain level of readiness, and the first task is to determine what the project needs. A deep book edit is typically a painstaking, time-consuming process that may move at the pace of only three or four manuscript pages per hour — or, when less intensive, eight to twelve pages per hour. Occasionally a manuscript received by an independent is fully developed, needs only a light copyedit, and may well be ready to submit as is. In other cases, the editorial process may require one or more rounds of revisions. If you are hiring an editor to critique your work, you should be aware that reading the material takes considerably more time than writing the critique. Sometimes a flat fee, rather than an hourly rate, may be appropriate to the project. Sometimes an editor will offer a brief initial consultation at no charge. A reputable independent book editor will be able to recommend a course of action that may or may not include one or more types of editorial services, and give you a reliable estimate of the time and fees involved.

But Won't the In-House Editor Fix Your Book?

Sometimes. Maybe. To an extent. Independents and in-house editors are, in many ways, different creatures. For starters, in-house editors spend much of the day preparing for and going to meetings. Marketing meetings. Sales meetings. Editorial meetings. Production meetings. The mandate for most of these in-house editors is to acquire new book projects and to shepherd those that are already in the pipeline. With so many extended activities cutting into the business hours, the time for actually working on a manuscript can be short.

Many in-house editors have incoming manuscripts screened by an already overworked assistant. (The days of staff readers are long gone.) The only quiet time the editor has for reading might be evenings and weekends. We have known editors to take a week off from work just to edit a book and be accessible to their authors. These days, too, the acquiring editor may not do any substantive work on a book project under contract, leaving that task to a junior editor. There is also a distinct possibility the acquiring editor may leave the job before that book is published, and this can occur with the next editor, too, and the next, threatening the continuity of the project. All of which doesn't mean that there aren't a lot of hardworking people at the publishing house; it means that editors have more to do than ever before and must devote at least as much time to crunching numbers as to focusing on the writer and the book.

Independent editors, on the other hand, spend most of their business days working exclusively with authors and their texts. They typically handle only a few manuscripts at a time and are free from marketing and production obligations. An independent editor's primary interest is in helping you to get your book polished and published. An editor of your own will see your project through — and often your next book, too.

What Do Agents Say about Independent Editors?

"As the book market gets tougher for selling both fiction and nonfiction it is imperative that all submissions be polished, edited, almost ready for the printer. Like many other agents I do as much as possible to provide editorial input for the author, but there are time constraints. So independent editors provide a very valuable service these days in getting the manuscript or proposal in the best shape possible to increase the chances of impressing an editor and getting a sale with the best possible terms." — **Bill Contardi**

"Agents work diligently for our clients, but there are situations in which outside help is necessary. Perhaps a manuscript has been worked on so intensively that objectivity is lacking, or perhaps the particular skill required to do a job properly is not one of an agent's strong suits. Maybe more time is required than an agent can offer. Fortunately, agents and authors are able to tap into the talent and experience of an outside editor. The outside editors I've worked with offer invaluable support during the editing process itself and for the duration of a project. Their involvement can make the difference between an author getting a publishing contract or having to put a project aside, or the difference between a less- or more-desirable contract." — **Victoria Gould Pryor**

"The right editor or book doctor can make all the difference in whether a manuscript gets sold. A debut novelist, for example, may have a manuscript that is almost there, but not quite. With the input of a good editor, the novel can reach its full potential and be an attractive prospect to a potential publisher. Similarly, someone writing a memoir may have had a fascinating life but may not really have the god-given writing talent that will turn that life into a compelling and readable book. An editor can take that person's rough-hewn words and thoughts and turn them into a memoir that really sings on the printed page." — **Eric Myers**

"Occasionally a novel will land on my desk that I feel has talent or a good concept behind it but for whatever reason (the writing, the pacing) needs an inordinate amount of work. Instead of just rejecting it flat out I may then refer the author to a freelance editor, someone who has the time and expertise to help the author further shape and perfect their work." — **Nina Collins**

"I have had several occasions to use the help of freelance editors and think they provide incalculable good service to the profession. In these competitive times, a manuscript has to be as polished and clean as possible to garner a good sale to a publisher. If it needs work, it simply provides an editor with a reason to turn it down. My job is to not give them any excuses. I do not have either the time or the ability to do the editorial work that may be required to make the manuscript salable. Paying a freelance professional to help shape a book into its most commercially viable form ultimately more than pays for itself."

— Deborah Schneider

So How Can You Find the Right Editor?

You've searched online. You've looked in directories such as this one. You've asked around. A personal recommendation from a published writer-friend who has used an independent editor for his or her work may or may not do the trick. Every author has different needs, every author-editor dynamic a different chemistry.

Although sometimes an author and editor "click" very quickly, many editors offer free consultations, and it's fine to contact more than one editor at this stage. A gratis consult may involve an editor's short take, by phone or in writing, on sample material the editor asked you to send. But how to distinguish among the many independent editors?

Some editorial groups are huge, and they are open to all who designate themselves as editors; it might take some additional research to identify the members who are most reputable and best suited to your work. The smaller groups consist of editors who have been nominated, vetted, and elected, which ensures the high quality of the individual professionals. They meet with regularity, share referrals, and discuss industry developments. Your consultation, references offered, and the terms of any subsequent agreement can tell the rest.

Another way to find the right editor is to prepare your manuscript to its best advantage — structurally, stylistically, and mechanically. Asking the opinion of one or more impartial readers — that is, not limiting your initial reviewers to friends and relatives — is a great strategy as well. If you have the benefit of a disinterested reader, you may be able to make some significant changes before sending an excerpt to an independent editor. One more element to consider: editors often will take your own personality and initial written inquiry into account as carefully as they do your writing. Seasoned independents do not take on every project that appears on their desk; they can pick and choose — and, working solo, they must.

Tales from the Trenches

We hope we've given you a sense of what an editor of your own can do for you and where we fit into the publishing picture. But next to firsthand experience, perhaps nothing communicates quite as sharply as an anecdote. Here are a few of ours:

"An in-house editor called me with an unusual problem. He had signed up an acclaimed author for a new book project. She had written a number of stories — nonfiction narratives about her life in an exotic land. The problem was this: some of the stories had already been published in book form in England, and that collection had its own integrity in terms of theme and chronology; now she had written another set of stories, plus a diary of her travels. How could the published stories and the new ones be made into one book?

"I decided to disregard the structure of the published book altogether. As I reexamined each story according to theme, emotional quality, geographical location, and people involved, I kept looking for ways in which they might relate to each other. Eventually, I sensed a new and logical way in which to arrange them. I touched not one word of the author's prose. I did the same thing I always try to do when editing — imagine myself inside the skin of the writer. A prominent trade book review had this to say about the result: 'One story flows into the next….'" — **Alice Rosengard**

"A writer had hired me to help with his first book after his agent had sold it to a publisher because he wanted to expedite the revisions and final approval of his manuscript. As a result of our work together, the book came out sooner than anticipated; it also won an award and the author was interviewed on a major TV news program. The same author hired me a year later for his second book, purchased by a larger publisher, and this book, too, entailed some significant developmental editing. At that point we learned the in-house editor had left the publisher and a new one had come aboard. This editor not only objected strongly to one whole section of the book; she also gave the author a choice: revise the section in one week or put the project on hold for at least six more months.

"From halfway across the world, the writer called me on a Friday to explain his publishing crisis, which was also coinciding with a personal crisis, and asked if we could collaborate closely on the fifty pages in question over the weekend. I agreed and cancelled my weekend plans, and we camped out at each end of the telephone and email-boxes almost nonstop for three days. He resubmitted the book on Tuesday, the book received all requisite signatures in-house, and a month later it went into production. This hands-on and sometimes unpredictable kind of collaboration with writers helps illustrate the special nature of independent editing." — **Katharine Turok**

"A writer with a truly astonishing story to tell received only rejections when he sent his query letter to agents. He had an informal proposal and assumed that his extraordinary experiences on the Amazon River would be enough to get him a book deal for his memoir. I could see right away that the query letter was confusing and didn't present him or his story in a powerful-enough light.

INDEPENDENT EDITORS

"I culled the most effective parts of his story and reworked the book proposal so that his enthusiasm and vivid tales dominated. We hammered out a succinct and compelling query letter. I offered the names of several agents I thought might be interested, and this time it worked. He signed with an agent who sold his manuscript to a major publisher."

— **Linda Carbone**

"My work on a book about a near-extinct bird species was greatly enhanced when the author gave me a tour of a California estuary. Guided by his passion and on-site expertise, I was able to spot exquisite birds, hear bird-watching lingo, and see his high-end scope in action. Now I understood the thrill of what he was writing about and was better able to help him communicate it.

"One of my most challenging assignments was to add action scenes to a memoir by an Olympic fencing champion. Here was a subject I knew nothing about. I tried to bone up in advance through reading, but my author had a better idea. Working his way across my living room floor, he sparred with an invisible opponent, demonstrating what he wished to describe in his book. I wrote down what I saw.

"As an independent editor, I have the time and freedom to work 'outside the book,' to literally enter the worlds my authors are writing about."   — **Ruth Greenstein**

"An author seeking help with her debut novel presented a specific challenge: a knockout story to tell along a recently well-trodden road. After several rounds that involved radically restructuring the point of view and making subtle style shifts, we produced an originally crafted, unique result that, to our mutual chagrin, could not be placed with an agent. (This often happens when a hot title kicks off a zeitgeist craze and the niche market is flooded.) Believing in the value of what we had, I encouraged my client — who was on the verge of giving up — to pursue an alternate route to publishing. Using an independent platform, not only did she manage to garner the coveted Kirkus star, but her novel went on to be named one of *Kirkus Reviews*' Best Indie Books of 2012."   — **Michael Wilde**

THE LISTINGS

BOOK DEVELOPMENT GROUP ❖ www.bookdevelopmentgroup.com

Book Development Group (BDG) is an alliance of independent New York City publishing professionals. All the BDG editors have at least 25 years of experience, and they work with first-time and seasoned writers in both fiction and nonfiction. The editors work independently of one another with services that range from developing a strong book concept to completely editing a manuscript and — for authors who wish to self-publish — producing a printed book.

The editors of Book Development Group can help you with:

- idea and concept development
- manuscript evaluation
- in-depth manuscript editing
- query letters and book proposals for agents
- project management for self-publishing books and ebooks
- coaching throughout the writing process
- assistance and advice for related publishing services

Whether you are a writer of fiction or nonfiction, BDG editors can help you transform your manuscript into a polished and professional book.

Janet Spencer King, janet@bookdevelopmentgroup.com

Specialties: Fiction — most genres in commercial/mainstream fiction including, among others, mystery, women's, and young adult. Nonfiction — health/fitness/nutrition, relationships, medical, narrative, self-help/popular psychology, business, spirituality, travel, women's interest.

Janet Spencer King has been an editor and writer for more than 25 years and was previously a literary agent, placing both nonfiction and fiction with key publishing houses. King has been the author or coauthor of five books published by major houses. She started her career in magazine publishing, eventually becoming editor in chief of three national magazines. Today she works one-on-one with writers, providing them with professional guidance throughout the entire book-writing process; she also specializes in managing production of self-published books.

Diane O'Connell, diane@bookdevelopmentgroup.com

Specialties: Fiction — commercial/mainstream, thriller/mystery/suspense, fantasy/science fiction, women's, young adult. Nonfiction — business, biography/memoir, health/fitness/nutrition, narrative, self-help/popular psychology, spirituality/New Age, true crime.

With over 25 years' publishing experience, including as an editor at Random House, and the author of six books, Diane O'Connell specializes in working with first-time authors and has helped numerous authors get deals with major publishers, including some that have become bestsellers. She edits manuscripts, coaches writers, writes and edits book proposals, and is available to work in person with authors. She welcomes authors at any stage of the book-writing process.

Olga Vezeris, olga@bookdevelopmentgroup.com

Specialties: Fiction — commercial/mainstream, general, thriller/mystery/suspense, historical novels and sagas. Nonfiction — narrative, self-help/popular psychology, health/fitness/nutrition, art/architecture, business, food/entertaining, illustrated and gift books on all subjects, lifestyle/decorating, travel, true crime.

Olga Vezeris has extensive experience in the publishing industry, having held senior editorial and subsidiary rights positions at companies including Simon & Schuster, Grand Central Publishing (Warner Books), Workman, Harper Collins, and the Bertelsmann Book Club group, where she has acquired, edited, or licensed many commercial fiction and nonfiction titles and illustrated books. Currently she works with authors, editing proposals and manuscripts and guiding them in all aspects of traditional and ebook publishing.

THE EDITORS CIRCLE ❖ www.theeditorscircle.com

This group of independent book editors has more than 100 years of collective experience on-staff with major New York publishers. They have come together to offer their skills and experience to writers who need help bringing their book projects from ideas or complete manuscripts to well-published books, whether the authors choose to work with traditional publishers or self-publish.

As publishing consultants (or "book doctors"), they offer a variety of editorial services that include:

- defining and positioning manuscripts in the marketplace
- refining book ideas

- evaluating and critiquing complete or partial manuscripts and book proposals
- editing, ghostwriting, or collaborating on proposals, manuscripts, and web content
- offering referrals to agents and publishers
- helping authors develop platforms and query letters
- guiding authors through the publishing process
- consulting on publicity and marketing

If you need help with your book project, the publishing professionals of The Editors Circle can offer you the editorial services you seek, a successful track record of projects placed and published, and the behind-the-scenes, hands-on experience that can help you take your idea or manuscript wherever you want it to go.

Bonny V. Fetterman, 718-739-1057, bonnyfetterman@theeditorscircle.com

As a professional Judaica editor with an MA in Jewish studies from Brandeis University, Bonny edits popular and scholarly books of Jewish interest in the fields of history, religion, biblical studies, biography, memoir, and historical fiction. In addition to editing, she critiques manuscripts, writes book proposals, and serves as a publishing consultant from contract to publication. Her most recent projects are *Exit Berlin* by Charlotte Bonelli (Yale University Press); *Commodore Levy* by Irving Litvag (Texas Tech); and *Forgotten Trials of the Holocaust* by Michael Bazyler and Frank Tuerkheimer (NYU Press). Based in New York City, she was senior editor of Schocken Books for 15 years and held editorial positions at Harper & Row and Basic Books.

Rob Kaplan, 914-736-7182, robkaplan@theeditorscircle.com

As an editor, ghostwriter, and collaborator on nonfiction book proposals, traditionally published and self-published books, and web content, Rob specializes in the areas of business, self-help, popular psychology, parenting, history, and other subjects. Among his recent projects are *Rethinking Public Administration* by Richard Clay Wilson, Jr. (Mill City Press); *The Facts of Business Life* by William McBean (Wiley); and *By the Grace of God: A 9/11 Survivor's Story of Love, Hope, and Healing* by Jean Potter (AuthorHouse). Prior to becoming an independent editor, he held senior editorial positions at Amacom Books (American Management Association), Macmillan, Prentice Hall, and Harper Collins, and he is currently based in Cortlandt Manor, New York.

Beth Lieberman, 310-403-1602, bethlieberman@theeditorscircle.com

Beth has acquired, edited, and published more than 500 books, including a number of *New York Times* bestsellers. She is a skillful writing coach for novelists and memoirists, a dedicated developmental editor of book proposals, and a keen navigator in the world of independent publishing. Her not-so-secret passion is working with Jewish wisdom texts. Beth has worked on-staff at New American Library, Warner Books, Kensington Publishing, Dove Books and Audio, and NewStar Press. She lives and works in both Los Angeles and New York. Her most recent projects include *Enchantress* by Maggie Anton (Penguin/Plume); *The Invitation* by Clifton Taulbert (NewSouth Books); and *Wise Aging* by Rachel Cowan and Linda Thal (Behrman House).

John Paine, 973-783-5082, johnpaine@theeditorscircle.com, www.johnpaine.com

Among the services John offers are developmental editing, line editing, fiction evaluations, and nonfiction proposals. He helps authors both within traditional publishing and with ebooks. Areas of interest in fiction include thriller, mystery, historical, and African American. Trade nonfiction specialties include health, memoir, true crime, and business. Among his recent projects are the bestselling *Calorie Myth* by Jonathan Bailor (Harper); *My Country 'Tis of Thee* by Congressman Keith Ellison (Gallery); and *Japantown* by Barry Lancet (Simon & Schuster). He developed his editing skills at Dutton and New American Library, imprints of Penguin Books USA, and he now works in Montclair, New Jersey.

Susan A. Schwartz, 212-877-3211, susanschwartz@theeditorscircle.com

Susan has developed and edited *New York Times* bestsellers and ghostwritten eight nonfiction books. She specializes in women's fiction and medical, legal, and political thriller, as well as fitness and health books, memoir, business, relationships, and popular reference books (all subjects), and has extensive experience developing book proposals for writers, publishers, and literary agents. Her current focus is on editing and producing corporate reference, conference, and marketing publications (histories, biographies, essays, and website content). Susan is based in Manhattan, where she is a member of Women's Media Group and maintains her contacts with the industry's movers and shakers. Her previous on-staff experience includes Random House (2 years), Doubleday (15 years), Facts On File (4 years), and NTC/Contemporary Books (3 years).

THE INDEPENDENT EDITORS GROUP ❖ www.bookdocs.com

The Independent Editors Group is the longest-running continuous professional affiliation of New York City–based independent editors (sometimes called "outside editors" or "book doctors") who work with writers, editors, publishers, and agents in trade book publishing. Years of distinguished tenure at major publishing houses qualify them to provide the following editorial services on fiction and nonfiction manuscripts and book proposals:

- thorough evaluations and detailed critiques
- plot restructuring
- developmental and line editing
- reorganization, revision, and rewriting
- consultation, conceptual development, and sample chapter writing on book proposals
- ghostwriting and collaboration
- salvaging of endangered or orphaned book projects
- project guidance and assistance on all aspects of self-publishing
- author coaching

If an editor is unavailable, referrals will be made to other appropriate IEG members. Résumés and references can be found at www.bookdocs.com. For fees, consult editors individually.

Sally Arteseros, 212-982-3246, sarteseros@bookdocs.com

Having worked as an editor and then senior editor at Doubleday for more than 25 years, Sally edits all kinds of fiction: literary, commercial, women's, historical, and contemporary, as well as short stories. And in nonfiction: biography, history, science, psychology, anthropology, business, religion, inspiration, essays, academic books.

Harriet Bell, 212-249-5625, harrietbell@verizon.net, www.bellbookandhandle.com

Specializes in nonfiction categories such as memoir, lifestyle, cookbooks, self-help, illustrated books, business, health and fitness, diet, and fashion. Writes proposals and website copy, ghostwrites books, edits manuscripts, and packages books. See her website for more information.

Toni Burbank, 718-499-3993, toniburbank@bookdocs.com

Former vice president and executive editor at Bantam Dell / Random House, with particular interest/expertise in psychology, health, women's interest, spirituality, and self-help. She has edited more than 10 *New York Times* bestsellers; authors include Daniel Goleman, Christiane Northrup, MD, Jack Kornfield, and Brian Wansink. Offers developmental and line editing, manuscript evaluation, and proposal writing.

INDEPENDENT EDITORS

Susan Dalsimer, 212-496-9164, susan.dalsimer@gmail.com

Former vice president and publisher of Miramax Books, specializing in editing literary and commercial fiction and young adult fiction. In nonfiction, areas include memoir, spirituality, biography, psychology, theater, film, and television.

Paul De Angelis, 860-672-6882, pdeangelis@bookdocs.com, www.pauldeangelisbooks.com

Manuscript evaluations, rewriting or ghostwriting, and editing. Thirty-five years' book-publishing experience in significant positions at St. Martin's Press, E.P. Dutton, and Kodansha America. Special expertise in history, current affairs, music, biography, literature, and translations. Authors have included the Delany sisters, Mike Royko, and Jorge Luis Borges.

Michael Denneny, 212-362-3241, mldenneny@aol.com

Thirty years' editorial experience at the University of Chicago Press, Macmillan, Crown, and St. Martin's Press. Edits commercial, literary, and mystery fiction; in nonfiction, works with biography, history, current affairs, memoir, psychology, and almost any narrative nonfiction. Also works with writers on book-proposal packages.

Emily Heckman, 917-837-3817, emilyheckman@aol.com

Editor of adult and young adult fiction and nonfiction. In fiction, areas of interest include women's, suspense, thriller, and horror. Areas of interest in nonfiction include memoir, health, psychology, pop culture, history, and spirituality. Writer of nonfiction books (coauthor, ghostwriter) including bestselling memoirs. Training includes senior editorial positions at major publishing houses (Simon & Schuster, Random House, etc.).

Susan Leon, 914-833-1422, scribe914@gmail.com

Editor specializing in book proposals, collaborations, and heavy rewrites for deadlines. Ghostwrote two *New York Times* bestsellers. Fiction interests: historical novels and contemporary stories with compelling, affirmative themes. Nonfiction: history (special expertise), memoir, biography, women/family, entertainment, design, and lifestyle.

Richard Marek, 203-341-8607, rwmarek@earthlink.net

Former president and publisher of E.P. Dutton. Specializes in editing and ghostwriting, both fiction and nonfiction. Edited Robert Ludlum's first 9 books, James Baldwin's last

5, and Thomas Harris's *The Silence of the Lambs*. Ghostwrote 14 books, including Trisha Meili's *I Am the Central Park Jogger* and James Patterson's *Hide and Seek*.

Sydny Miner, 914-391-8665, sydny.miner@gmail.com

Sydny has extensive experience as an editor at major publishing houses (Crown Publishing Group, Simon & Schuster), working primarily in nonfiction, with a special emphasis on cookbooks, food and nutrition, health and wellness, diet, fitness, exercise, psychology, and self-help. She has worked closely with high-profile authors (including two First Ladies) and edited numerous bestselling and award-winning titles, taking projects from concept to outline to finished book. She sees herself as a midwife, helping authors to put their unique voice and vision on the page, deconstructing their expertise and making it accessible to the layperson.

Beth Rashbaum, 212-228-9573, bethrashbaum@gmail.com

A veteran of over 35 years in publishing, Beth was an editor most recently at Bantam Dell / Random House. She edits all kinds of nonfiction — including memoir, biography, investigative journalism, Judaica, health and wellness, yoga, psychology, and popular science. She also edits and writes proposals, has ghostwritten one *New York Times* bestseller, and was coauthor, with Olga Silverstein, of *The Courage to Raise Good Men*.

Betty Kelly Sargent, 212-486-1531, bsargent@earthlink.net

Founder and CEO of BookWorks.com — The Self-Publishers Association and former editor in chief of William Morrow, specializing in collaborations and developmental editing for both literary and commercial fiction as well as general nonfiction including memoir, health, humor, psychology, and spirituality. Coauthor of seven published books and recent consultant for those who want to self-publish and take advantage of social media for book promotion.

James O'Shea Wade, 914-962-4619, jwade@bookdocs.com

With 30 years' experience as editor in chief and executive editor for major publishers, including Crown / Random House, Macmillan, Dell, and Rawson-Wade, James edits and ghostwrites in all nonfiction areas and specializes in business, science, history, biography, and militaria. Also edits all types of fiction, prepares book proposals, and evaluates manuscripts.

MARVELOUS EDITIONS ❖ www.marvelouseditions.com, www.facebook.com/MarvelousEditors

Marvelous Editions is the partnership of respected independent editorial consultants Marlene Adelstein and Alice Peck. With over two decades of expertise in developmental and line editing as well as ghostwriting, proposal drafting, and screenplays, they provide comprehensive guidance for writers from the first inspiration to the published work — be it through a mainstream publisher, independent press, self-publishing venture, periodical, or website. When appropriate, they also provide referrals to reliable and talented designers, copyeditors, proofreaders, publicists, and agents. Marlene and Alice usually work independently but have joined forces when appropriate, editing authors including Kristen Wolf, Nicole Bokat, and Kim Powers.

Marlene Adelstein, marlene@fixyourbook.com, www.fixyourbook.com

Provides thorough, constructive critiques, developmental and line editing, advice on a book's commercial potential, and agent referrals when appropriate. Over 20 years' experience in publishing and feature-film development. Specializes in commercial and literary fiction: mystery, thriller, women's, romance, historical; young adult; memoir; screenplays. Recent authors include Peter Golden, Antoinette May, Anne Serling, Karan Bajaj, Jeanne Bogino, Peter Hayes, and Amanda McTigue.

Alice Peck, alicepeck@alicepeck.com, www.alicepeckeditorial.com

Evaluates and edits memoir, narrative, spirituality, and fiction (especially first novels); writes and edits proposals; ghostwrites. Acquired books and developed them into scripts for film and television before shifting her focus to editing in 1998. Recent authors include E.A. Aymar, Jon Buchan, Tim Cockey, Lama Surya Das, Alison L. Heller, Susan McBride, Jeri Parker, Dr. Jeffrey B. Rubin, Judith Sanders, Mark Schimmoeller, Joanie Schirm, Hannah Seligson, and Bonnie Myotai Treace.

WORDS INTO PRINT ❖ www.wordsintoprint.org

Words into Print is one of New York's top networks of independent book editors, writers, and publishing consultants. Founded in 1998, WiP is a professional alliance whose members provide editorial services to publishers, literary agents, and book packagers, as well as to individual writers. Members of WiP have extensive industry experience, averaging 20 years as executives and editors with leading trade book publishers. As active independent professionals, members meet individually and as a group with agents and other publishing colleagues; participate in conventions, conferences, panels, and workshops; and maintain affiliations with organizations that include PEN, AWP, the Authors Guild, the Women's National Book Association, the Modern Language Association, and the Academy of American Poets.

The consultants at Words into Print are committed to helping established and new writers develop, revise, and polish their work. They also guide clients through the publishing process by helping them find the most promising route to publication. WiP's editors and writers provide:

- detailed analyses and critiques of proposals and manuscripts
- editing, cowriting, and ghostwriting
- expert advice, ideas, and techniques for making a writer's project the best it can be
- assistance in developing query letters and synopses for literary agents and publishers
- referrals to literary agents, publishers, book packagers, and other publishing services
- guidance in developing publicity and marketing strategies
- project management — from conception through production
- inside information writers need to make their way successfully through the publishing world

Words into Print's editors offer top-tier assistance at competitive rates. Brief profiles appear below. For more information, please visit www.wordsintoprint.org.

Martin Beiser, martin.beiser@gmail.com

Has spent three decades in the book and magazine publishing world. At Free Press, he edited numerous bestselling and award-winning books. He was managing editor at *GQ* magazine for 12 years. Offers thorough critiques, line editing, and developmental editing. Specializes in narrative nonfiction, history, current affairs, politics, sports, business, biography, memoir, travel/adventure, magazine journalism, nonfiction proposals, the extended essay.

Linda Carbone, lindacarbone@optonline.net

Twenty-five years of experience editing all types of nonfiction, particularly memoir, health, and psychology, but including parenting, self-help, and social science. Former senior developmental editor with Basic Books. Has worked with Paul Bloom, Stephen Carter, Lama Surya Das, Seth Godin, and Alice Miller. Offers detailed critique and developmental, substantive, and line editing of manuscripts and proposals. Can assist with finding an agent when appropriate.

Ruth Greenstein, rg@greenlinepublishing.com

Editing debut and multibook authors since 1989. Literary fiction, biography/memoir, social issues, cultural criticism, arts, travel, nature, popular science, health, psychology, religion/spirituality, poetry, photography, media companions. Cofounder of WiP; formerly with Harcourt and Ecco. Has worked with Anita Shreve, Erica Jong, John Ashbery, Gary Paulsen, Alice Walker, Sallie Bingham, and Dennis Lehane. Offers a full range of editorial services, plus synopsis writing, submissions guidance, career strategy, and Web presence development.

Alice Rosengard, arosengard1@gmail.com

Developmental and detailed editing, manuscript and proposal evaluation. Concentrations: literary and mainstream fiction, history, memoir, biography, science, international affairs. Over 35 years of experience guiding new and established writers published by Harper Collins, Palgrave Macmillan, Doubleday, Basic Books, St. Martin's, and Bantam, among others. Authors worked with include Stephen Mitchell, Martha Rose Shulman, Larry Sloman, Bette Bao Lord, John Ehle, Avner Mandelman, Sue L. Hall, MD, Jay R. Tunney, George C. Daughan, and Gilad Sharon.

Katharine Turok, kturok@gmail.com

Manuscript evaluation; developmental, substantive, and line editing; rewriting; condensing. Literary and mainstream fiction; autobiography/memoir, biography, contemporary issues, film, history, nature, poetry, psychology, popular reference, theater, travel, visual arts, women's interest, translations. Over 20 years' international experience acquiring and editing works from new and established writers, published by major houses, including Bloomsbury, Dutton, Folger Shakespeare Library, and Scribner, and independent presses.

Michael Wilde, michaelwildeeditorial@earthlink.net

Provides first-time and experienced authors with all manner of editorial services and help with writing. More than 20 years' experience working with leading authors and publishers in subjects ranging from scholarly and professional books to pop culture, literary and mainstream fiction, children's books, and young adult novels. Can assist in finding an agent when appropriate.

ACKNOWLEDGMENTS

Georgia Hughes, my remarkable editor at New World Library, deserves my eternal gratitude for her confidence in this book and in me. She was one of my very first editors more than 15 years ago. Since then this book has experienced many publishers and editors, so it felt like a homecoming to be embraced by her once again.

I was extremely fortunate to have Kristen Cashman, the managing editor at New World Library, on my side. She is smart and incredibly patient, and got me to do a better job than I would have without her.

For more than 20 years, Deborah Herman, my partner in life and work, has contributed more than she knows to this book throughout its history with her perfectly timed comments and words of encouragement.

Finally, a huge "thank you" to all the people who taught me to be humble and appreciative — even if I'm frequently appointed to learn it all over again.

GLOSSARY

A

abstract A brief sequential profile of chapters in a nonfiction book proposal (also called a synopsis); a point-by-point summary of an article or essay. In academic and technical journals, abstracts often appear with (and may serve to preface) the articles themselves.

adaptation A rewrite or reworking of a piece for another medium, such as the adaptation of a novel for the screen. (*See also* **screenplay.**)

advance Money paid (usually in installments) to an author by a publisher prior to publication. The advance is paid against royalties: if an author is given a $5,000 advance, for instance, the author will collect royalties only after the royalty moneys due exceed $5,000. A good contract protects the advance if it should exceed the royalties ultimately due from sales.

advance orders Orders received before a book's official publication date, and sometimes before actual completion of the book's production and manufacture.

agent The person who acts on behalf of the author to handle the sale of the author's literary properties. Good literary agents are as valuable to publishers as they are to writers; they select and present manuscripts appropriate for particular houses or of interest to particular acquisitions editors. Agents are paid on a percentage basis from the moneys due their author clients.

American Booksellers Association (ABA) The major trade organization for retail booksellers, chain and independent. The annual ABA convention and trade show offers a chance for publishers and distributors to display their wares to the industry at large and provides an incomparable networking forum for booksellers, editors, agents, publicists, and authors.

American Society of Journalists and Authors (ASJA) A membership organization for professional writers. ASJA provides a forum for information exchange among writers and others in the publishing community, as well as networking opportunities. (*See also* **Dial-a-Writer.**)

anthology A collection of stories, poems, essays, and/or selections from larger works (and so forth), usually carrying a unifying theme or concept; these selections may be written by different authors or by a single author. Anthologies are compiled as opposed to written; their editors (as opposed to authors) are responsible for securing the needed reprint rights for the material used, as well as supplying (or providing authors for) pertinent introductory or supplementary material and/or commentary.

attitude   A contemporary colloquialism used to describe a characteristic temperament common among individuals who consider themselves superior. Attitude is rarely an esteemed attribute, whether in publishing or elsewhere.

auction   Manuscripts a literary agent believes to be hot properties (such as possible best-sellers with strong subsidiary rights potential) will be offered for confidential bidding from multiple publishing houses. Likewise, the reprint, film, and other rights to a successful book may be auctioned off by the original publisher's subsidiary rights department or by the author's agent.

audiobooks   Works produced for distribution on audio media, typically MP3, other downloadable electronic formats, or audio compact disc (CD). Audiobooks are usually spoken-word adaptations of works originally created and produced in print; these works sometimes feature the author's own voice; many are given dramatic readings by one or more actors, at times embellished with sound effects.

authorized biography   A history of a person's life written with the authorization, cooperation, and, at times, participation of the subject or the subject's heirs.

author's copies/author's discount   Author's copies are the free copies of their books that the authors receive from the publisher; the exact number is stipulated in the contract, but it is usually at least 10 hardcovers. The author may purchase additional copies of the book (usually at 40 percent discount from the retail price) and resell them at readings, lectures, and other public engagements. In cases where large quantities of books are bought, author discounts can go as high as 70 percent.

author tour   A series of travel and promotional appearances by an author on behalf of the author's book.

autobiography   A history of a person's life written by that same person, or, as is typical, composed conjointly with a collaborative writer ("as told to" or "with"; *see also* **coauthor**; **collaboration**) or ghostwriter. Autobiographies by definition entail the authorization, cooperation, participation, and ultimate approval of the subject.

B

backlist   The backlist comprises books published prior to the current season and still in print. Traditionally, at some publishing houses, such backlist titles represent the publisher's cash flow mainstays. Some backlist books continue to sell briskly; some remain bestsellers over several successive seasons; others sell slowly but surely through the years. Although many backlist titles may be difficult to find in bookstores that stock primarily current lists, they can be ordered either through a local bookseller or internet retailer or directly from the publisher.

backmatter   Elements of a book that follow the text proper. Backmatter may include the appendix, notes, glossary, bibliography and other references, lists of resources, index, author biography, offerings of the author's and/or publisher's additional books and other related merchandise, and colophon.

bestseller   Based on sales or orders by bookstores, wholesalers, and distributors, bestsellers are those titles that move the largest quantities. Lists of bestselling books can be local (as in metropolitan newspapers), regional (typically in geographically keyed trade or consumer periodicals), or national (as in *USA Today*, *Publishers Weekly*, or the *New York Times*), as well as international. Fiction and nonfiction are usually listed separately, as are hardcover and paperback classifications. Depending on the list's purview, additional industry-sector designations are used (such as how-to/self-improvement, religion and spirituality, business and finance); in addition, bestseller lists can be keyed to particular genre or specialty fields (such as bestseller lists for mysteries, science fiction, or romance novels, and for historical works, biography, or popular science titles) — and virtually any other marketing category at the discretion of whoever issues the bestseller list (for instance, African American interests, lesbian and gay topics, youth market).

bibliography   A list of books, articles, and other sources that have been used in the writing of the text in which the bibliography appears. Complex works may break the bibliography down into discrete subject areas or source categories, such as General History, Military History, War in the Twentieth Century, or Unionism and Pacifism.

binding   The materials that hold a book together (including the cover). Bindings are generally denoted as hardcover (featuring heavy cardboard covered with durable cloth and/or paper, and occasionally other materials) or paperback (using a pliable, resilient grade of paper, sometimes infused or laminated with other substances such as plastic). In the days when cloth was used lavishly, hardcover volumes were conventionally known as clothbound; and in the very old days, hardcover bindings sometimes featured tooled leather, silk, precious stones, and gold and silver leaf ornamentation.

biography   A history of a person's life. (*See also* **authorized biography**; **autobiography**; **unauthorized biography**.)

blues   (or bluelines) Once photographic proofs of the printing plates for a book with a telltale blue hue, these are now more likely delivered as PDF format electronically. Plates and bluelines have been rendered archaic by current techniques. Blues are reviewed as a means to inspect the set type, layout, and design of the book's pages before it goes to press.

blurb A piece of written copy or extracted quotation used for publicity and promotional purposes, as on a flyer, in a catalog, or in an advertisement (*see also* **cover blurbs**).

book club A book club is a book-marketing operation that ships selected titles to subscribing members on a regular basis, sometimes at greatly reduced prices. Sales of a work to book clubs are negotiated through the publisher's subsidiary rights department (in the case of a bestseller or other work that has gained acclaim, these rights can be auctioned off). Terms vary, but the split of royalties between author and publisher is often 50 percent/50 percent. Book club sales are seen as blessed events by author, agent, and publisher alike.

book contract A legally binding document between author and publisher that sets the terms for the advance, royalties, subsidiary rights, advertising, promotion, and publicity — plus a host of other contingencies and responsibilities. Writers should therefore be thoroughly familiar with the concepts and terminology of the standard book-publishing contract.

book distribution The method of getting books from the publisher's warehouse into the reader's hands. Distribution is traditionally through bookstores but can include such means as telemarketing and mail-order sales, and of course online via websites, as well as sales through a variety of special-interest outlets such as health-food or New Age venues, sports and fitness emporiums, or sex shops. Publishers use their own sales forces as well as independent salespeople, wholesalers, and distributors. Many large and some small publishers distribute for other publishers, which can be a good source of income. A publisher's distribution network is extremely important, because it not only makes possible the vast sales of a bestseller but also affects the visibility of the publisher's entire list of books.

book jacket *See* **dust jacket**.

book producer or **book packager** An individual or company that can assume many of the roles in the publishing process. A book packager or producer may conceive the idea for a book (most often nonfiction) or series, bring together the professionals (including the writer) needed to produce the book(s), sell the individual manuscript or series project to a publisher, take the project through to manufactured product — or perform any selection of those functions, as commissioned by the publisher or other client (such as a corporation producing a corporate history as a premium or giveaway for employees and customers). The book producer may negotiate separate contracts with the publisher and with the writers, editors, and illustrators who contribute to the book.

book review   A critical appraisal of a book (often reflecting a reviewer's personal opinion or recommendation) that evaluates such aspects as organization and writing style, possible market appeal, and cultural, political, or literary significance. Before the public reads book reviews in the local and national print media, important reviews have been published in such respected book-trade journals as *Publishers Weekly*, *Kirkus Reviews*, *Library Journal*, and *Booklist*. A gushing review from one of these journals will encourage booksellers to order the book; copies of these raves will be used for promotion and publicity purposes by the publisher and will encourage other book reviewers nationwide to review the book.

Books in Print   Listings published by R.R. Bowker, of books currently in print; these were once yearly printed volumes (along with periodic supplements such as *Forthcoming Books in Print*). Now they exist more online than in print; they provide ordering information, including titles, authors, ISBNs, prices, whether the book is available in hardcover or paperback, and publisher names. Intended for use by the book trade, *Books in Print* (www.booksinprint.com) is also of great value to writers who are researching and market-researching their projects. Listings are provided alphabetically by author, title, and subject area. Most libraries subscribe to their service or have access to some form of the metadata.

bound galleys   Copies of uncorrected typesetter's page proofs or printouts of electronically produced mechanicals that are bound together as advance copies of the book (*compare* **galleys**). Bound galleys are sent to trade journals (*see* **book review**) as well as to a limited number of reviewers who work under long lead times.

bulk sales   The sale, at a set discount, of many copies of a single title (the greater the number of books, the larger the discount).

byline   The name of the author of a given piece, indicating credit for having written a book or article. Ghostwriters, by definition, do not receive bylines.

C

casing   Alternate term for binding (*see* **binding**).

category fiction   Also known as genre fiction. Category fiction falls into an established (or newly originated) marketing category (which can then be subdivided for more precise target marketing). Fiction categories include action-adventure (with such further designations as military, paramilitary, law enforcement, romantic, and martial arts); crime novels (with points of view that range from deadpan cool to visionary, including humorous capers as well as gritty urban sagas); mysteries or detective fiction (hard-boiled, soft-boiled, procedurals, cozies); romances (including historical as well as contemporary); horror (supernatural, psychological, or technological); thrillers (tales of espionage, crisis, and the chase); Westerns; science fiction; and fantasy. (*See also* **fantasy**, **horror**, **romance fiction**, **science fiction**, **suspense fiction**, and **thriller**.)

children's books   Books for children. As defined by the book-publishing industry, children are generally readers ages 17 and younger; many houses adhere to a fine but firm editorial distinction between titles intended for younger readers (under 12) and young adults (generally ages 12 to 17). Children's books (also called juveniles) are produced according to a number of categories (often typified by age ranges), each with particular requisites regarding such elements as readability ratings, length, and inclusion of graphic elements. Picture books are often for very young readers, with such designations as toddlers (who do not themselves read) and preschoolers (who may have some reading ability). Other classifications include easy storybooks (for younger schoolchildren), middle grade books (for elementary to junior high school students), and young adult (sometimes abbreviated YA, for readers through age 17).

coauthor   One who shares authorship of a work. Coauthors all have bylines. Coauthors share royalties based on their contributions to the book. (*Compare* **ghostwriter**.)

collaboration   Writers can collaborate with professionals in any number of fields. Often a writer will collaborate in order to produce books outside the writer's own areas of formally credentialed expertise (for example, a writer with an interest in exercise and nutrition may collaborate with a sports doctor on a health book). Though the writer may be billed as a coauthor (*see* **coauthor**), the writer does not necessarily receive a byline (in which case the writer is a ghostwriter). Royalties are shared, based on respective contributions to the book (including expertise or promotional abilities as well as the actual writing).

colophon   Strictly speaking, a colophon is a publisher's logo; in bookmaking, the term may also refer to a listing of the materials used, as well as credits for the design, composition, and production of the book. Such colophons are sometimes included in the backmatter or as part of the copyright page.

commercial fiction   Fiction written to appeal to as broad-based a readership as possible.

concept   A general statement of the idea behind a book.

cool   A modern colloquial expression that indicates satisfaction or approval, or may signify the maintenance of calm within a whirlwind. A fat contract for a new author is definitely cool.

cooperative advertising (co-op)   An agreement between a publisher and a bookstore. The publisher's book is featured in an ad for the bookstore (sometimes in conjunction with an author appearance or other special book promotion); the publisher contributes to the cost of the ad, which is billed at a lower (retail advertising) rate.

copublishing   Joint publishing of a book, usually by a publisher and another corporate entity such as a foundation, a museum, or a smaller publisher. An author can copublish with the publisher by sharing the costs and decision making and, ultimately, the profits.

copyeditor   An editor, responsible for the final polishing of a manuscript, who reads primarily in terms of appropriate word usage and grammatical expression, with an eye toward clarity and coherence of the material as presented, factual errors and inconsistencies, spelling, and punctuation. (*See also* **editor**.)

copyright   The legal proprietary right to reproduce, have reproduced, publish, and sell copies of literary, musical, and other artistic works. The rights to literary properties reside in the author from the time the work is produced — regardless of whether a formal copyright registration is obtained. However, for legal recourse in the event of plagiarism or other infringement, the work must be registered with the US Copyright Office, and all copies of the work must bear the copyright notice. (*See also* **work-for-hire**.)

cover blurbs   Favorable quotes from other writers, celebrities, or experts in a book's subject area, which appear on the dust jacket and are used to enhance the book's point-of-purchase appeal to the potential book-buying public.

crash   Coarse gauze fabric used in bookbinding to strengthen the spine and joints of a book.

curriculum vitae (abbreviated **CV**)   Latin expression meaning "course of life" — in other words, the résumé.

D

deadline   In book publishing, this not-so-subtle synonym is used for the author's due date for delivery of the completed manuscript to the publisher. The deadline can be as much as a full year before the official publication date, unless the book is being produced quickly to coincide with or follow up on a particular event.

delivery   Submission of the completed manuscript to the editor or publisher.

Dial-a-Writer   A project-referral service of the American Society of Journalists and Authors, in which members, accomplished writers in most specialty fields and subjects, list their services.

direct marketing   Advertising that involves a "direct response" (which is an equivalent term) from a consumer — for instance, an order form or coupon in a book-review section or in the back of a book or mailings (direct-mail advertising) to a group presumed to hold a special interest in a particular book.

display titles   Books that are produced to be eye-catching to the casual shopper in a bookstore setting. Often rich with flamboyant cover art, these publications are intended to pique bookbuyer excitement about the store's stock in general. Many display titles are stacked on their own freestanding racks; sometimes broad tables are laden with these items. A book shelved with its front cover showing on racks along with diverse other titles is technically a display title. Promotional or premium titles are likely to be display items, as are mass-market paperbacks and hardbacks with enormous best-seller potential. (Check your local bookstore and find a copy of this *Guide to Book Publishers, Editors, and Literary Agents* — if not already racked in "display" manner, please adjust the bookshelf so that the front cover is displayed poster-like to catch the browser's eye — that's what we do routinely.)

distributor An agent or business that buys or warehouses books from a publisher to resell, at a higher cost, to wholesalers, retailers, or individuals. Distribution houses are often excellent marketing enterprises, with their own roster of sales representatives, publicity and promotion personnel, and house catalogs. Skillful use of distribution networks can give a small publisher considerable national visibility.

dramatic rights Legal permission to adapt a work for the stage. These rights initially belong to the author but can be sold or assigned to another party by the author.

dust jacket (also **dustcover** or **book jacket**) The wrapper that covers the binding of hardcover books, designed especially for the book by either the publisher's art depart-ment or a freelance artist. Dust jackets were originally conceived to protect the book during shipping, but now their function is primarily promotional — to entice the browser to actually reach out and pick up the volume (and maybe even open it up for a taste before buying) by means of attractive graphics and sizzling promotional copy.

dust-jacket copy Descriptions of books printed on the dust-jacket flaps. Dust-jacket copy may be written by the book's editor but is often either recast or written by in-house copywriters or freelance specialists. Editors send advance copies (*see also* **bound galleys**) to other writers, experts, and celebrities to solicit quotable praise that will also appear on the jacket. (*See also* **cover blurb**.)

E

ebook Refers to any book that exists in digital form, regardless of whether or not it also exists in a traditional physical form.

editor Editorial responsibilities and titles vary from house to house (often being less strictly defined in smaller houses). In general, the duties of the editor in chief or exec-utive editor are primarily administrative: managing personnel, scheduling, budget-ing, and defining the editorial personality of the firm or imprint. Senior editors and acquisitions editors acquire manuscripts (and authors), conceive project ideas and find writers to carry them out, and may oversee the writing and rewriting of manu-scripts. Managing editors have editorial and production responsibilities, coordinat-ing and scheduling the book through the various phases of production. Associate and assistant editors edit; they are involved in much of the rewriting and reshaping of the manuscript and may also have acquisitions duties. Copyeditors read the manuscript and style its punctuation, grammar, spelling, headings and subheadings, and so forth. Editorial assistants, laden with extensive clerical duties and general office work, perform some editorial duties as well — often as springboards to senior editorial positions.

Editorial Freelancers Association (EFA)   This organization of independent professionals offers a referral service, through both its annotated membership directory and its job phone line, as a means for authors and publishers to connect with writers, collaborators, researchers, and a wide range of editorial experts covering virtually all general and specialist fields.

el-hi   Books for elementary and/or high schools.

endnotes   Explanatory notes and/or source citations that appear either at the end of individual chapters or at the end of a book's text; used primarily in scholarly or academically oriented works.

epilogue   The final segment of a book, which comes "after the end." In both fiction and nonfiction, an epilogue offers commentary or further information but does not bear directly on the book's central design.

F

fantasy   Fantasy is fiction that features elements of magic, wizardry, supernatural feats, and entities that suspend conventions of realism in the literary arts. Fantasy can resemble prose versions of epics and rhymes or it may be informed by mythic cycles or folkloric material derived from cultures worldwide. Fantasy fiction may be guided primarily by the author's own distinctive imagery and personalized archetypes. Fantasies that involve heroic-erotic roundelays of the death dance are often referred to as the sword-and-sorcery subgenre.

film rights   Like dramatic rights, these belong to the author, who may sell or option them to someone in the film industry — a producer or director, for example (or sometimes a specialist broker of such properties) — who will then try to gather the other professionals and secure the financial backing needed to convert the book into a film. (*See also* **screenplay**.)

footbands   *See* **headbands**.

footnotes   Explanatory notes and/or source citations that appear at the bottom of a page. Footnotes are rare in general-interest books, the preferred style being either to work such information into the text or to list informational sources in the bibliography.

foreign agents   Persons who work with their US counterparts to acquire rights for books from the United States for publication abroad. They can also represent US publishers directly.

foreign market   Any foreign entity — a publisher, broadcast medium, etc. — in a position to buy rights. Authors share royalties with whoever negotiates the deal or keep 100 percent if they do their own negotiating.

foreign rights   Translation or reprint rights that can be sold abroad. Foreign rights belong to the author but can be sold either country by country or en masse as world rights. Often the US publisher will own world rights, and the author will be entitled to anywhere from 50 percent to 85 percent of these revenues.

foreword   An introductory piece written by the author or by an expert in the given field (*see* **introduction**). A foreword by a celebrity or well-respected authority is a strong selling point for a prospective author or, after publication, for the book itself.

Frankfurt Book Fair   The largest international publishing exhibition — with 500 years of tradition behind it. The fair takes place every October in Frankfurt, Germany. Thousands of publishers, agents, and writers from all over the world negotiate, network, and buy and sell rights.

Freedom of Information Act   A federal law that ensures the protection of the public's right to access public records — except in cases violating the right to privacy, national security, or certain other instances. A related law, the Government in the Sunshine Act, stipulates that certain government agencies announce and open their meetings to the public.

freight passthrough   The bookseller's freight cost (the cost of getting the book from the publisher to the bookseller). It is added to the basic invoice price charged the bookseller by the publisher.

frontlist   New titles published in a given season by a publisher. Frontlist titles customarily receive priority exposure in the front of the sales catalog — as opposed to backlist titles (usually found at the back of the catalog), which are previously published titles still in print.

frontmatter   The frontmatter of a book includes the elements that precede the text of the work, such as the title page, copyright page, dedication, epigraph, table of contents, foreword, preface, acknowledgments, and introduction.

fulfillment house   A firm commissioned to fulfill orders for a publisher — services may include warehousing, shipping, receiving returns, and mail-order and direct-marketing functions. Although more common for magazine publishers, fulfillment houses also serve book publishers.

G

galleys   Typeset proofs (or copies of proofs) on sheets of paper, or printouts of the electronically produced setup of the book's interior — the author's last chance to check for typos and make (usually minimal) revisions or additions to the copy (*see also* **bound galleys**).

genre fiction   *See* **category fiction**.

ghostwriter (or **ghost**)   A writer without a byline, often without the remuneration and recognition that credited authors receive. Ghostwriters often get flat fees for their work, but even without royalties, experienced ghosts can receive quite respectable sums.

glossary   An alphabetical listing of special terms as they are used in a particular subject area, often with more in-depth explanations than would customarily be provided by dictionary definitions.

H

hardcover   Books bound in a format that uses thick, sturdy, relatively stiff binding boards and a cover composed (usually) of a cloth spine and finished binding paper. Hardcover books are conventionally wrapped in a dust jacket. (*See also* **binding; dust jacket.**)

headbands   Thin strips of cloth (often colored or patterned) that adorn the top of a book's spine where the signatures are held together. The headbands conceal the glue or other binding materials and are said to offer some protection against accumulation of dust (when properly attached). Such bands placed at the bottom of the spine are known as footbands.

hook   A term denoting the distinctive concept or theme of a work that sets it apart as being fresh, new, or different from others in its field. A hook can be an author's special point of view, often encapsulated in a catchy or provocative phrase intended to attract or pique the interest of a reader, editor, or agent. One specialized function of a hook is to articulate what might otherwise be seen as dry, albeit significant, subject matter (academic or scientific topics; number-crunching drudgery such as home bookkeeping) into an exciting, commercially attractive package.

horror   The horror classification denotes works that traffic in the bizarre, awful, and scary in order to entertain as well as explicate the darkness at the heart of the reader's soul. Horror subgenres may be typified according to the appearance of were-creatures, vampires, human-induced monsters, or naturally occurring life-forms and spirit entities — or absence thereof. Horror fiction traditionally makes imaginative literary use of paranormal phenomena, occult elements, and psychological motifs. (*See* **category fiction; suspense fiction.**)

how-to books   An immensely popular category of books ranging from purely instructional (arts and crafts, for example) to motivational (popular psychology, inspirational, self-awareness, self-improvement) to get-rich-quick (such as in real estate or personal investment).

imprint A separate line of product within a publishing house. Imprints run the gamut of complexity, from those composed of one or two series to those offering full-fledged and diversified lists. Imprints also enjoy different gradations of autonomy from the parent company. An imprint may have its own editorial department (perhaps consisting of only one editor), or the house's acquisitions editors may assign particular titles for release on appropriate specialized imprints. An imprint may publish a certain kind of book (juvenile or paperback or travel books) or have its own personality (such as a literary or contemporary tone). An individual imprint's categories often overlap with other imprints or with the publisher's core list, but some imprints maintain a small-house feel within an otherwise enormous conglomerate. The imprint can offer the distinct advantages of a personalized editorial approach while availing itself of the larger company's production, publicity, marketing, sales, and advertising resources.

index An alphabetical directory at the end of a book that references names and subjects discussed in the book and the pages where such mentions can be found.

instant book A book produced quickly to appear in bookstores as soon as possible after (for instance) a newsworthy event to which it is relevant.

international copyright Rights secured for countries that are members of the International Copyright Convention (*see* **International Copyright Convention**) and that respect the authority of the international copyright symbol, ©.

International Copyright Convention Countries that are signatories to the various international copyright treaties. Some treaties are contingent upon certain conditions being met at the time of publication, so an author should, before publication, inquire into a particular country's laws.

introduction Preliminary remarks pertaining to a piece. Like a foreword, an introduction can be written by the author or an appropriate authority on the subject. If a book has both a foreword and an introduction, the foreword will be written by someone other than the author; the introduction will be more closely tied to the text and will be written by the book's author. (*See also* **foreword**.)

ISBN (International Standard Book Number) A 13-digit number that is linked to and identifies the title and publisher of a book. It is used for ordering and cataloging books and appears on the dust jackets of hardcovers, the back covers of paperbacks, and all copyright pages.

ISSN (International Standard Serial Number) An 8-digit cataloging and ordering number that identifies all US and foreign periodicals.

J

juveniles   *See* **children's books**.

K

kill fee   A fee paid by a magazine when it cancels a commissioned article. The fee is only a certain percentage of the agreed-on payment for the assignment (no more than 50 percent). Not all publishers pay kill fees; a writer should make sure to formalize such an arrangement in advance. Kill fees are sometimes involved in work-for-hire projects in book publishing.

L

lead   The crucial first few sentences, phrases, or words of anything — be it a query letter, book proposal, novel, news release, advertisement, or sales tip sheet. A successful lead immediately hooks the reader, consumer, editor, or agent.

lead title   A frontlist book featured by the publisher during a given season — one the publisher believes should do extremely well commercially. Lead titles are usually those given the publisher's maximum promotional push.

letterhead   Business stationery and envelopes imprinted with the company's (or, in such a case, the writer's) name, address, and logo — a convenience as well as an impressive asset for a freelance writer.

letterpress   A form of printing in which set type is inked, then impressed directly onto the printing surface. Now used primarily for limited-run books-as-fine-art projects. (*See also* **offset**.)

libel   Defamation of an individual or individuals in a published work, with malice aforethought. In litigation, the falsity of the libelous statements or representations, as well as the intention of malice, has to be proved for there to be libel; in addition, financial damages to the parties so libeled must be incurred as a result of the material in question for there to be an assessment of the amount of damages to be awarded to a claimant. This is contrasted to slander, which is defamation through the spoken word.

Library of Congress (LOC)   The largest library in the world, located in Washington, DC. As part of its many services, the LOC will supply a writer with up-to-date sources and bibliographies in all fields, from arts and humanities to science and technology. For details, write to the Library of Congress, Central Services Division, Washington, DC 20540.

Library of Congress Catalog Card Number   An identifying number issued by the Library of Congress to books it has accepted for its collection. The publication of those books, which are submitted by the publisher, is announced by the Library of Congress to libraries, which use Library of Congress numbers for their own ordering and cataloging purposes.

***Literary Market Place* (*LMP*)**   An annual directory of the publishing industry that contains a comprehensive list of publishers, alphabetically and by category, with their addresses, phone numbers, some personnel, and the types of books they publish. Also included are various publishing-allied listings, such as literary agencies, writers' conferences and competitions, and editorial and distribution services. *LMP* is published by Information Today and is available in most public libraries.

literature   Written works of fiction and nonfiction in which compositional excellence and advancement in the art of writing are higher priorities than are considerations of profit or commercial appeal.

logo   A company or product identifier — for example, a representation of a company's initials or a drawing that is the exclusive property of that company. In publishing usage, a virtual equivalent to the trademark.

M

mainstream fiction   Nongenre fiction, excluding literary or avant-garde fiction, that appeals to a general readership.

marketing plan   The entire strategy for selling a book: its publicity, promotion, sales, and advertising.

mass-market paperback   Less expensive smaller-format paperbacks that are sold from racks (in such venues as supermarkets, variety stores, drugstores, and specialty shops) as well as in bookstores. Also referred to as rack (or rack-sized) editions.

mechanicals   Typeset copy and art mounted on boards to be photocopied and printed. Also referred to as pasteups.

middle grade   Just like the name implies, books for fourth to eighth graders.

midlist books   Generally mainstream fiction and nonfiction books that traditionally formed the bulk of a publisher's list (nowadays often by default rather than intent). Midlist books are expected to be commercially viable but not explosive bestsellers — nor are they viewed as distinguished, critically respected books that can be scheduled for small print runs and aimed at select readerships. Agents may view such projects as a poor return for the effort, since they generally garner a low-end advance; editors and publishers (especially the sales force) may decry midlist works as being hard to market; prospective readers often find midlist books hard to buy in bookstores (they have short shelf lives). Hint for writers: Don't present your work as a midlist item.

multimedia   Presentations of sound and light, words in magnetically graven image

— and any known combination thereof as well as nuances yet to come. Technological innovation is the hallmark of the electronic-publishing arena, and new formats will expand the creative and market potential. Multimedia books are publishing events; their advent suggests alternative avenues for authors as well as adaptational tie-ins with the world of print. Meanwhile, please stay tuned for virtual reality, artificial intelligence, and electronic end-user distribution of product.

multiple contract   A book contract that includes a provisional agreement for a future book or books. (*See also* **option clause/right of first refusal**.)

mystery stories or **mysteries**   *See* **suspense fiction**.

N

net receipts   The amount of money a publisher actually receives for sales of a book: the retail price minus the bookseller's discount and/or other discount. The number of returned copies is factored in, bringing down even further the net amount received per book. Royalties are sometimes figured on these lower amounts rather than on the retail price of the book.

New Age   An eclectic category that encompasses health, medicine, philosophy, religion, and the occult — presented from an alternative or multicultural perspective. Although the term has achieved currency relatively recently, some publishers have been producing serious books in these categories for decades.

novella   A work of fiction falling in length between a short story and a novel.

O

offset (offset lithography)   A printing process that involves the transfer of wet ink from a (usually photosensitized) printing plate onto an intermediate surface (such as a rubber-coated cylinder) and then onto the paper. For commercial purposes, this method has replaced letterpress, whereby books were printed via direct impression of inked type on paper.

option clause/right of first refusal   In a book contract, a clause that stipulates that the publisher will have the exclusive right to consider and make an offer for the author's next book. However, the publisher is under no obligation to publish the book, and in most variations of the clause the author may, under certain circumstances, opt for publication elsewhere. (*See also* **multiple contract**.)

outline   Used for both a book proposal and the actual writing and structuring of a book, an outline is a hierarchical listing of topics that provides the writer (and the proposal reader) with an overview of the ideas in a book in the order in which they are to be presented.

out-of-print books   Books no longer available from the publisher; rights usually revert to the author.

P

package   The package is the actual book; the physical product.

packager   *See* **book producer**.

page proof   The final typeset copy of the book, in page-layout form, before printing. Proofs are read and reviewed by the author and the publisher's proofreader for errors.

paperback   Books bound with a flexible, stress-resistant, paper covering material. (*See also* **binding**.)

paperback originals   Books published, generally, in paperback editions only; sometimes the term refers to those books published simultaneously in hardcover and paperback. These books are often mass-market genre fiction (romances, Westerns, Gothics, mysteries, horror, and so forth) as well as contemporary literary fiction, cookbooks, humor, career books, self-improvement, and how-to books — the categories continue to expand.

pasteups   *See* **mechanicals**.

permissions   The right to quote or reprint published material, obtained by the author from the copyright holder.

picture book   A copiously illustrated book, often with very simple, limited text, intended for preschoolers and other very young children.

plagiarism   The false presentation of someone else's writing as one's own. In the case of copyrighted work, plagiarism is illegal.

platform   Refers to the author's professional connections and popularity, measured by internet and media presence, and the extent to which such can be leveraged to sell books.

preface   An element of a book's frontmatter. In the preface, the author may discuss the purpose behind the format of the book, the type of research upon which it is based, its genesis, or an underlying philosophy.

premium   Books sold at a reduced price as part of a special promotion. Premiums can thus be sold to a bookseller, who in turn sells them to the bookbuyer (as with a line of modestly priced art books). Alternatively, such books may be produced as part of a broader marketing package. For instance, an organization may acquire a number of books (such as its own corporate history or the biography of its founder) for use in personnel training and as giveaways to clients; or a nutrition/recipe book may be displayed along with a company's diet foods in nonbookstore outlets. (*See also* **special sales**.)

press agent   *See* **publicist**.

press kit   A promotional package that includes a press release, tip sheet, author biography and photograph, reviews, and other pertinent information. The press kit can be put together by the publisher's publicity department or an independent publicist and sent with a review copy of the book to potential reviewers and to media professionals responsible for booking author appearances.

price There are several prices pertaining to a single book: the invoice price is the amount the publisher charges the bookseller; the retail, cover, or list price is what the consumer pays.

printer's error (PE) A typographical error made by the printer or typesetting facility, not by the publisher's staff. PEs are corrected at the printer's expense.

printing plate A surface that bears a reproduction of the set type and artwork of a book, from which the pages are printed.

producer *See* **book producer**.

proposal A detailed presentation of the book's concept, used to gain the interest and services of an agent and to sell the project to a publisher.

publication date (or **pub date**) A book's official date of publication, customarily set by the publisher to fall six weeks after completed bound books are delivered to the warehouse. The publication date is used to focus the promotional activities on behalf of the title — so that books will have had time to be ordered, shipped, and available in the stores to coincide with the appearance of advertising and publicity.

public domain Material that is uncopyrighted, whose copyright has expired, or that is uncopyrightable. The last category includes government publications, jokes, titles — and, it should be remembered, ideas.

publicist (press agent) The publicity professional who handles the press releases for new books and arranges the author's publicity tours and other promotional venues (such as interviews, speaking engagements, and book signings).

publisher's catalog A seasonal sales catalog that lists and describes a publisher's new books; it is sent and/or emailed to all potential buyers, including individuals who request one. Catalogs range from the basic to the glitzy and often include information on the author, on print quantity, and on the amount of money slated to be spent on publicity and promotion. Now also available online.

publisher's discount The percentage by which a publisher discounts the retail price of a book to a bookseller, often based in part on the number of copies purchased.

Publishers' Trade List Annual A collection of current and backlist catalogs arranged alphabetically by publisher, available in many libraries.

Publishers Weekly (*PW*) The publishing industry's chief trade journal. *PW* carries announcements of upcoming books, respected book reviews, interviews with authors and publishing-industry professionals, special reports on various book categories, and trade news (such as mergers, rights sales, and personnel changes).

quality   In publishing parlance, the word *quality* in reference to a book category (such as quality fiction) or format (quality paperback) is a term of art — individual works or lines so described are presented as outstanding products.

query letter   A brief written presentation to an agent or editor designed to pitch both the writer and the book idea.

remainders   Unsold book stock. Remainders can include titles that have not sold as well as anticipated, in addition to unsold copies of later printings of bestsellers. These volumes are often remaindered — that is, remaining stock is purchased from the publisher by specialty distributors at a huge discount and resold to the public. Both online and physical bookstores have high-discounted sections where these books can be bought for pennies on the dollar.

reprint   A subsequent edition of material that is already in print, especially publication in a different format — the paperback reprint of a hardcover, for example.

résumé   A summary of an individual's career experience and education. When a résumé is sent to prospective agents or publishers, it should contain the author's vital publishing credits, specialty credentials, and pertinent personal experience. Also referred to as the curriculum vitae or, more simply, vita.

returns   Unsold books returned to a publisher by a bookstore, for which the store may receive full or partial credit (depending on the publisher's policy, the age of the book, and so on).

reversion-of-rights clause   In the book contract, a clause that states that if the book goes out of print or the publisher fails to reprint the book within a stipulated length of time, all rights revert to the author.

review copy   A free copy of a (usually) new book sent to electronic and print media that review books for their audiences.

romance fiction or **romance novels**   Modern or period love stories, always with happy endings, which range from the tepid to the torrid. Except for certain erotic specialty lines, romances do not feature graphic sex. Often mistakenly pigeonholed by those who do not read them, romances and romance writers have been influential in the movement away from passive and coddled female fictional characters to the strong, active modern woman in a tale that reflects areas of topical social concern.

royalty   The percentage of the retail cost of a book that is paid to the author for each copy sold after the author's advance has been recouped. Some publishers structure royalties as a percentage payment against net receipts.

sales conference   A meeting of a publisher's editorial and sales departments and senior promotion and publicity staff members. A sales conference covers the upcoming season's new books, and marketing strategies are discussed. Sometimes sales conferences are the basis upon which proposed titles are bought or not.

sales representative (sales rep)   A member of the publisher's sales force or an independent contractor who, armed with a book catalog and order forms, visits bookstores in a certain territory to sell books to retailers.

SASE (self-addressed stamped envelope)   It is customary for an author to enclose SASEs with query letters, proposals, and manuscript submissions sent via snail mail. Many editors and agents do not reply if a writer has neglected to enclose an SASE with correspondence or submitted materials.

satisfactory clause   In book contracts, a publisher will reserve the right to refuse publication of a manuscript that is not deemed satisfactory. Because the author may be forced to pay back the publisher's advance if the complete work is found to be unsatisfactory, the specific criteria for publisher satisfaction should be set forth in the contract to protect the author.

science fiction   Science fiction includes the hardcore, imaginatively embellished technological/scientific novel as well as fiction that is even slightly futuristic (often with an after-the-holocaust milieu — nuclear, environmental, extraterrestrial, genocidal). An element much valued by editors who acquire for the literary expression of this cross-media genre is the ability of the author to introduce elements that transcend and extend conventional insight.

science fiction/fantasy   A category-fiction designation that actually collapses two genres into one (for bookseller-marketing reference, of course — though it drives some devotees of these separate fields of writing nuts). In addition, many editors and publishers specialize in both these genres and thus categorize their interests with catchphrases such as *sci-fi/fantasy*.

screenplay   A film script — either original or based on material published previously in another form, such as a television docudrama based on a nonfiction book or a movie thriller based on a suspense novel. (*Compare with* **teleplay**.)

self-publishing   A publishing project wherein an author pays for the costs of manufacturing and selling his or her own book and retains all money from the book's sale. This is a risky venture but one that can be immensely profitable (especially when combined with an author's speaking engagements or imaginative marketing techniques); in addition, if successful, self-publication can lead to distribution or publication by a commercial publisher. (*Compare with* **subsidy publishing**.)

self-syndication   Management by writers or journalists of functions that are otherwise performed by syndicates specializing in such services. In self-syndication, it is the writer who manages copyrights, negotiates fees, and handles sales, billing, and other tasks involved in circulating journalistic pieces through newspapers, magazines, or other periodicals that pick up the author's column or run a series of articles.

serialization The reprinting of a book or part of a book in a newspaper or magazine. Serialization before (or perhaps simultaneously with) the publication of the book is called *first serial*. The first reprint after publication (either as a book or by another periodical) is called *second serial*.

serial rights Reprint rights sold to periodicals. First serial rights include the right to publish the material before anyone else (generally before the book is released, or coinciding with the book's official publication) — either for the United States, a specific country, or a wider territory. Second serial rights cover material already published, in either a book or another periodical.

series Books published as a group either because of their related subject matter (such as a series on modern artists or on World War II aircraft) and/or single authorship (a set of works by a famous romance writer, a group of books about science and society, or a series of titles geared to a particular diet-and-fitness program). Special series lines can offer a ready-made niche for an industrious author or compiler/editor who is up-to-date on a publisher's program and has a brace of pertinent qualifications and/or contacts. In contemporary fiction, some genre works are published in series form (such as family sagas, detective series, fantasy cycles).

shelf life The amount of time an unsold book remains on the bookstore shelf before the store manager pulls it to make room for newer incoming stock with greater (or at least untested) sales potential.

short story A short work that is more pointed and more economically detailed as to character, situation, and plot than a full novel. Published collections of short stories — whether by one or several authors — often revolve around a single theme, express related outlooks, or comprise variations within a common genre.

signature A group of book pages that have been printed together on one large sheet of paper that is then folded and cut in preparation for being bound, along with the book's other signatures, into the final volume.

simultaneous publication The issuing at the same time of more than one edition of a work, such as in hardcover and trade paperback. Simultaneous releases can be expanded to include (though rarely) deluxe gift editions of a book as well as mass-market paper versions. Audio versions of books are most often timed to coincide with the release of the first print edition.

simultaneous (or **multiple**) **submissions** The submission of the same material to more than one publisher at the same time. Although simultaneous submission is a common practice, publishers should always be made aware that it is being done. Multiple submissions by an author to several agents is, on the other hand, a practice that is sometimes not regarded with great favor by agents.

slush pile   The morass of unsolicited manuscripts at a publishing house or literary agency, which may fester indefinitely awaiting (perhaps perfunctory) review. Some publishers or agencies do not maintain slush piles per se — unsolicited manuscripts are slated for instant or eventual return without review (if an SASE or email address is included) or may otherwise be literally or figuratively pitched to the wind. Querying a targeted publisher or agent before submitting a manuscript is an excellent way of avoiding, or at least minimizing the possibility of, such an ignoble fate.

software   Programs that run on a computer. Word-processing software includes programs that enable writers to compose, edit, store, and print material. Professional-quality software packages incorporate such amenities as databases that can feed the results of research electronically into the final manuscript, alphabetization and indexing functions, and capabilities for constructing tables and charts and adding graphics to the body of the manuscript. Software should be appropriate to both the demands of the work at hand and the requirements of the publisher (which may contract for a manuscript suitable for electronic editing, design, composition, and typesetting).

special sales   Sales of a book to appropriate retailers other than bookstores (for example, wine guides to liquor stores). This classification also includes books sold as premiums (for example, to a convention group or a corporation) or for other promotional purposes. Depending on volume, per-unit costs can be very low, and the book can be custom designed. (*See also* **premium**.)

spine   That portion of the book's casing (or binding) that backs the bound page signatures and is visible when the volume is aligned on a bookshelf among other volumes.

stamping   In book publishing, the stamp is the impression of ornamental type and images (such as a logo or monogram) on the book's binding. The stamping process involves using a die with a raised or intaglioed surface to apply ink stamping or metallic-leaf stamping.

submission guidelines   An agent or publisher's guidelines for approaching them about publication of a work. Usually can be found on the agency or publisher website.

subsidiary rights   The reprint, serial, movie and television, and audiotape and videotape rights deriving from a book. The division of profits between publisher and author from the sales of these rights is determined through negotiation. In more elaborately commercial projects, further details such as syndication of related articles and licensing of characters may ultimately be involved.

subsidy publishing   A mode of publication wherein the author pays a publishing company to produce his or her work, which may thus appear superficially to have been published conventionally. Subsidy publishing (alias vanity publishing) is generally more expensive than self-publishing, because a successful subsidy house makes a profit on all its contracted functions, charging fees well beyond the publisher's basic costs for production and services.

suspense fiction   Fiction within a number of genre categories that emphasize suspense as well as the usual (and sometimes unusual) literary techniques to keep the reader engaged. Suspense fiction encompasses novels of crime and detection (regularly referred to as mysteries). These include English-style cozies, American-style hard-boiled detective stories, dispassionate law-enforcement procedurals, crime stories, action-adventure, espionage novels, technothrillers, tales of psychological suspense, and horror. A celebrated aspect of suspense fiction's popular appeal — one that surely accounts for much of this broad category's sustained market vigor — is the interactive element: the reader may choose to challenge the tale itself by attempting to outwit the author and solve a crime before detectives do, figure out how best to defeat an all-powerful foe before the hero does, or parse out the elements of a conspiracy before the writer reveals the whole story.

syndicated column   Material published simultaneously in a number of newspapers or magazines. The author shares the income from syndication with the syndicate that negotiates the sale. (*See also* **self-syndication**.)

syndication rights   *See* **self-syndication**; **subsidiary rights**.

synopsis   A summary in paragraph form, rather than in outline format. The synopsis is an important part of a book proposal. For fiction, the synopsis portrays the high points of story line and plot, succinctly and dramatically. In a nonfiction book proposal, the synopsis describes the thrust and content of the successive chapters (and/or parts) of the manuscript.

T

table of contents   A listing of a book's chapters and other sections (such as the front matter, appendix, index, and bibliography) or of a magazine's articles and columns, in the order in which they appear; in published versions, the table of contents indicates the respective beginning page numbers.

tabloid   A smaller-than-standard-size newspaper (daily, weekly, or monthly). Traditionally, certain tabloids are distinguished by sensationalism of approach and content rather than by straightforward reportage of newsworthy events. In common parlance, *tabloid* is used to describe works in various media (including books) that cater to immoderate tastes (for example, tabloid exposé, tabloid television, the tabloidization of popular culture).

teleplay   A screenplay geared toward television production. Similar in overall concept to screenplays for the cinema, teleplays are nonetheless inherently concerned with such TV-loaded provisions as the physical dimensions of the smaller screen and formal elements of pacing and structure keyed to stipulated program length and the placement of commercial advertising. Attention to these myriad television-specific demands is fundamental to the viability of a project.

terms   The financial conditions agreed to in a book contract.

theme   A general term for the underlying concept of a book. (*See also* **hook**.)

thriller   A thriller is a novel of suspense with a plot structure that reinforces the elements of gamesmanship and the chase, with a sense of the hunt being paramount. Thrillers can be spy novels, tales of geopolitical crisis, legal thrillers, medical thrillers, technothrillers, domestic thrillers. The common thread is a growing sense of threat and the excitement of pursuit.

tip sheet   An information sheet on a single book that presents general publication information (publication date, editor, ISBN, etc.), a brief synopsis of the book, information on relevant other books (sometimes competing titles), and other pertinent marketing data such as author profile and advance blurbs. The tip sheet is given to the sales and publicity departments; a version of the tip sheet is also included in press kits.

title page   The page at the front of a book that lists the title, subtitle, author (and other contributors, such as translator or illustrator), as well as the publishing house and sometimes its logo.

trade books   Books distributed through the book trade — meaning bookstores and major book clubs — as opposed to, for example, mass-market paperbacks, which are often sold at magazine racks, newsstands, and supermarkets as well.

trade discount   The discount from the cover or list price that a publisher gives the bookseller. It is usually proportional to the number of books ordered (the larger the order, the greater the discount) and typically varies between 40 percent and 50 percent.

trade list   A catalog of all of a publisher's books in print, with ISBNs and order information. The trade list sometimes includes descriptions of the current season's new books.

trade (quality) paperbacks   Reprints or original titles published in paperback format, larger in dimension than mass-market paperbacks, and distributed through regular retail book channels. Trade paperbacks tend to be in the neighborhood of twice the price of an equivalent mass-market paperback version and about half to two-thirds the price of hardcover editions.

trade publishers   Publishers of books for a general readership — that is, nonprofessional, nonacademic books that are distributed primarily through bookstores.

translation rights   Rights sold either to a foreign agent or directly to a foreign publisher, either by the author's agent or by the original publisher.

treatment   In screenwriting, a full narrative description of the story, including sample dialogue.

U

unauthorized biography   A history of a person's life written without the consent or collaboration of the subject or the subject's survivors.

university press   A publishing house affiliated with a sponsoring university. The university press is usually nonprofit and subsidized by the respective university. Generally, university presses publish noncommercial scholarly nonfiction books written by academics, and their lists may include literary fiction, criticism, and poetry. Some university presses also specialize in titles of regional interest, and many acquire projects intended for commercial book-trade distribution.

unsolicited manuscript   A manuscript sent to an editor or agent without being requested by the editor/agent.

V

vanity press   A publisher that publishes books only at an author's expense — and will generally agree to publish virtually anything that is submitted and paid for. (*See also* **subsidy publishing**.)

vita   Latin word for "life." A shortened equivalent term for *curriculum vitae* (*See also* **résumé**).

W

word count   The number of words in a given document. When noted on a manuscript, the word count is usually rounded off to the nearest 100 words.

work-for-hire   Writing done for an employer, or writing commissioned by a publisher or book packager who retains ownership of, and all rights pertaining to, the written material.

Y

young adult books   Books for readers generally between the ages of 12 and 17. Young adult fiction often deals with issues of concern to contemporary teens.

young readers or **younger readers**   Publishing terminology for the range of publications that address the earliest readers. Sometimes a particular house's young-readers program typifies books for those who do not yet read, which means these books have to hook the caregivers and parents who actually buy them. In certain quirky turns of everyday publishing parlance, young readers can mean anyone from embryos through young adults (and *young* means you when you want it to). This part may be confusing (as is often the case with publishing usage): sometimes *younger adult* means only that the readership is allegedly hip, including those who would eschew kids' books as being inherently lame and those who are excruciatingly tapped into the current cultural pulse, regardless of cerebral or life-span quotient.

Z

zombie (or **zombi**)   In idiomatic usage, a zombie is a person whose conduct approximates that of an automaton. Harking back to the term's origins as a figure of speech for the resurrected dead or a reanimated cadaver, such folks are not customarily expected to exhibit an especially snazzy personality or be aware of too many things going on around them; hence some people in book-publishing circles may be characterized as zombies.

INDEX

Agents and Agencies

Independent Editors

Publishers, Imprints, and Agents by Subject

INDEX

JEFF HERMAN'S GUIDE

JEFF HERMAN'S GUIDE

ABOUT THE AUTHOR

Jeff Herman opened his literary agency in the mid-1980s while in his mid-20s. He has made nearly 1,000 book deals, including many bestsellers. His own books include *Jeff Herman's Guide to Publishers, Editors & Literary Agents* (more than 500,000 copies sold) and *Write the Perfect Book Proposal* (coauthored with Deborah Herman). He has presented hundreds of workshops about writing and publishing and has been interviewed for dozens of publications and programs.

In 1981, shortly after graduating from Syracuse University, Herman was riding the subway on a hot summer day when he spotted an ad stating: "I found my job in *The New York Times*." He promptly bought a copy and answered some Help Wanted ads. A few days later he was summoned for an interview with the publicity director at an independent publishing house and was hired on the spot as her assistant for $200 a week. Showering, shaving, wearing a suit, saying little, and promising to show up were the clinchers.

The publicity department comprised Herman and his boss, who took her summer vacation his first week on the job. He was left "in charge," though he knew nothing about publicity, publishing, or how an office functioned. But he was a quick study and soon helped make *When Bad Things Happen to Good People* a massive bestseller.

In time, Herman followed the money into corporate marketing, where he worked on various product-promotion campaigns for Nabisco, AT&T, and many other large and small brands. But books were his passion and calling.

Today, Jeff Herman is an exceptionally successful veteran literary agent, entrepreneur, and author. His areas of editorial expertise include popular business, spirituality, and most other areas of nonfiction. "If I feel I can sell it, I'll represent it," says Herman.

The Jeff Herman Agency, LLC
PO Box 1522 • 29 Park Street • Stockbridge, MA 01262
413-298-0077 • jeff@jeffherman.com • www.jeffherman.com

a